FLEET STREET

Also by Dennis Griffiths

200 Not Out
The Encyclopedia of the British Press (editor)
Plant Here The Standard
300 Years of Fleet Street
A History of the NPA 1906–2006

Fleet Street

Five hundred years of the Press

DENNIS GRIFFITHS

THE BRITISH LIBRARY

2006

First published 2006 by
The British Library
96 Euston Road
London NW1 2DB

British Library
Cataloguing in Publication Data
A CIP record for this volume is
available from The British Library

ISBN 0-7123-0697-8

Typeset in Sabon by
Hope Services (Abingdon) Ltd.
Printed in England by
Cromwell Press Ltd
Trowbridge

Contents

Illustrations

illustrations in text

Foreword

CHARLES PEBODY in *English Journalism and the Men who Made It* (1881) lamented the lack of historical record: 'The history of English journalism has yet to be written. It ought to be one of the most interesting works upon our library shelves . . . . yet there never was an institution better deserved to have its history written than the Newspaper Press.' It is hoped, therefore, that this volume will go some way towards redressing this omission.

From the moment Wynkyn de Worde set up his press near St Bride's Church in 1500 to the twentieth century, Fleet Street *was* the centre of the newspaper world. True, national newspaper offices are now widely dispersed – from Wapping and Canary Wharf in the east to Kensington and Victoria in the west, plus those in the City and at Clerkenwell – but the term 'Fleet Street' lives on to describe our industry.

Much has changed in the past two decades. No longer are newspaper managements beset by excessive union demands and restrictive practices. The move to Wapping by News International in 1986 led the way for other groups to welcome new technology, thereby providing a better product for their readers.

Throughout the five-hundred year history of Fleet Street, there has been one underlying theme – the fight for a free Press. From Richard Baldwin in the seventeenth, to John Wilkes and Junius in the eighteenth, to Richard Carlile in the nineteenth century and to the imprisonment of Reg Foster and Brendan Mulholand in 1963, for not revealing their sources, journalists have fought against any bans. And even today the Press must remain on its guard.

Another threat, in the past few years, has been an encroachment from the internet, hence the involvement of national newspapers in embracing this new medium. But, as Rupert Murdoch declared recently: 'Great journalists will always be needed but the product of their work may not always be on paper – it may ultimately just be electronically. There will always be room for good journalism and good reporting.'

DENNIS GRIFFITHS

March 31, 2006

Erratum

Please note that the two plate sections have inadvertently been transposed. The plates between pages 78 -79 should appear between pages 206-207, and the plates between 206-207 should appear between pages 78-79.

Acknowledgements

MANY PEOPLE have kindly assisted in my research but special mention is due to Professor Donald Trelford, former editor, *The Observer*; Ed King, Head of the British Library Newspaper Library; for reading and commenting on the complete text; and to Eddie Young, Group Legal Adviser, Associated Newspapers, for checking many of the chapters. I must thank also Professor Ray Boston, Vice-Chancellor Aled Jones and Robert Edwards for reading much of the work; and Luke Dodd, Guardian Newsroom; Eamon Dyas, News International; John Entwisle and Professor Donald Read, Reuters; Bill Hagerty, *Daily Mirror*; Brian MacArthur, *Today* and *The Times*; George Newkey-Burden, *The Daily Telegraph*; and Dr Huw Richards, *Daily Herald*; for their comments. I am grateful also to Ian Reeves, editor, and Jon Slatery, deputy editor, *Press Gazette*, for reading the final chapters. Special thanks go to the late Charles Wintour, former editor of the *Evening Standard*, for his advice and comments, and Dr Joseph O. Baylen, Regents' Professor of History Emeritus, Georgia State University.

Newspaper personalities rendering assistance have included the late Lord Burnham, Sir Eric Cheadle, Lord Cudlipp, Michael Davey, Sir Alastair Dunnett, Sir David English, Arthur Firth, Lord Goodman, George Griffiths, Sir Denis Hamilton, Lord Hartwell, Louis Heren, Johnnie Johnson, Sir John Junor, Sir Larry Lamb, David Linton, Lord MacGregor, Lord Matthews, Arthur Montgomery, Sir Edward Pickering, Percy Roberts, Lord Rothermere III, Stewart Steven, George Malcolm Thomson and Joe Wade.

Of the present day, I should like to thank Sir Frank Barlow, Lord Beaverbrook III, Guy Black, Sheila Black, Mark Bolland, Richard Bourne, Tobi Carver, Tony Carver, David Chipp, Ann Chisholm, Lady Jodi Cudlipp, Paul Dacre, Baroness Dean, Lord Deedes, Jeremy Deedes, Professor Anthony Delano, Richard Desmond, Robin Esser, Michael Foot, Sir Harold Evans, Paul Ferris, Vic Giles, Stephen Glover, Geoffrey Goodman, Tony Gray, Felicity Green, Professor Roy Greenslade, Peter Grimsditch, Trevor Grove, Adrian Hamilton, Bert Hardy, Vyvyan Harmsworth, Duff Hart-Davis, Sir Max Hastings, Bevis Hillier, Sir Bernard Ingham, Lord Hussey, John Frost, Eric Jacobs, Derek Jameson, Sir Simon Jenkins, Philippa Kennedy, Philip Knightley, Louis Kirby, Sir Nicholas Lloyd, Iverach McDonald, Murdoch MacLennan, Linda Melvern, Chris Moncrieff, Jean Morgan, Kenneth Morgan, Piers Morgan, Canon David Meara, David Newell, Dugal Nisbet-Smith, Sir Christopher Meyer, Canon John Oates, Steve Oram, John Owen, Bruce Page, Amanda Platell, Eve Pollard, Peter Preston, Jane Read, Alan Rusbridger, Eddy Shah, Leo Simmonds, Bernard Shrimsley, Sarah Sands, Godfrey Smith, Richard Stott, Sir Jocelyn Stevens, S.J. Taylor, Clive Thornton, Tim Toulmin, Lord Wakeham, Alan Watkins, George Westropp, Charles Wilson and Sir Peregrine Worsthorne.

ACKNOWLEDGEMENTS

In the field of academia, my thanks are due to Professor Jeremy Black, Professor Lucy Brown, Dr Mark Bryant, Dr Richard Cockett, Dr Louise Craven, Professor James Curran, the late Professor John Dodge, Dr John Hill, Vice-Chancellor Deian Hopkins, Dr Fred Hunter, Dr Dilwyn Porter, the late Professor Stephen Koss, Professor Colin Seymour-Ure, Professor Hugh Stephenson, Professor Joel Weiner and Professor Keith Wilson.

I am indebted to all the libraries who went to so much trouble to provide information: The British Library, especially Andrew Phillips; the British Library Newspaper Library, Eve Johansson, Geoffrey Hamilton, Geoffrey Smith, John Byford, Jill Allbrooke; Express Newspapers, Peter Aldridge; Associated Newspapers, Steve Torrington; House of Lords Library, Kathleen Bligh; St Bride Printing Library, James Mosley, Nigel Roche; the staffs of the Bodleian Library, Oxford; Guildhall Library, London; City University Library; the London Library; and the London Press Club.

I should like to thank also the Earl Bathurst, the late Earl Halsbury, David Elliot, Victor Gray, the late Admiral Sir Ian, and Lady, Hogg, Anna Purcell and Sir John Vassar-Smith.

At the British Library my gratitude goes to David Way, who commissioned the book, Kathleen Houghton, for picture research, and John Trevitt for his exemplary editing.

Finally, and above all, I must thank my wife Elizabeth who has lived with five centuries of Fleet Street during the past decade.

Readers' notes

Over the years, some newspapers have undergone minor changes of title, for example *The Sunday People* changed its name to become *The People*. Titles used in the text, therefore, are as of the time. Original spellings have been used in quotations throughout.

Chronology

Titles still published are marked * at first mention. Unless otherwise indicated, title only citation is the date of the first isssue

1476 Caxton sets up first English printing press at Westminster

1500 Wynkyn de Worde sets up his press next to St Bride's Church, Fleet Street
1537 First post-Reformation Royal declaration on Press censorship
1557 Grant of Royal Charter to the Stationers' Company
1586 Star Chamber decree on printing

1620 First known English-language coranto, published in Amsterdam
1621 First titled newspaper, *Corante, or Newes from Italy, etc.*, printed in London for 'NB' (Nicholas Bourne and Nathaniel Butter)
1625 Ben Jonson's anti-Press comedy, *Staple of News*
1637 Star Chamber decree requiring deposit of all printed works via the Stationers' Company for the Bodleian Library, Oxford
1638 Bourne and Butter granted Royal Authority to print
1641 Abolition of Star Chamber – although the Press far from liberated
1642 *Perfect Diurnall* (first of the authorized Parliamentary newsbooks)
1643 Board of Licensers set up, as public rivalry grew between Royalist and Parliamentary *Mercuries*. Berkenhead starts the Royalist *Mercurius Aulicus* as a regular weekly; followed by Nedham's *Mercurius Britannicus* in the Parliamentary cause
1644 John Milton's *Areopagitica*
1649 Cromwell suppresses all newsbooks
1651 Milton appointed Official Censor
1657 Nedham's and Newcome's *Publick Adviser* – the first advertisement-only newsbook
1660 Under the Restoration, Muddiman given news monopoly. Williams' *Perfect Diurnall* – daily for nearly a month
1662 Press Licensing Act, widening legal deposit requirements to King's Library, nucleus of British Museum collection, and the University Library at Cambridge, as well as the Bodleian; Act finally lapsed in 1694
1663 Roger L'Estrange, as Surveyor of Printing, given news monopoly
1665 *Oxford Gazette* (later *London Gazette**)
1679 Benjamin Harris's *Domestick Intelligence*
1690 *Athenian Gazette* (from no. 2, *Mercury*)

1693 *Ladies' Mercury*, earliest of all women's journals
1696 *Lloyd's News*, forerunner of original *Lloyd's List*
1698 *Dawks' News-Letter*; *English Spy*

1702 *Daily Courant*, first daily newspaper
1706 First evening newspaper, the tri-weekly *Evening Post*
1709 First Copyright Act; *Tatler* (Sir Richard Steele and Joseph Addison)
1710 *Examiner* with Jonathan Swift briefly as editor followed by Mary de la Riviere Manley, the first woman editor
1711 *Spectator* (Addison and Steele)
1712 First Stamp Act signals period of repression; Advertisement, Paper and Stamp Duties
1719 *Daily Post* with Daniel Defoe as contributor; *London Journal*
1725 Second Stamp Act extended earlier regulations to all newspapers
1726 Henry Woodfall I takes over *Daily Post*, changes title to *London Daily Post & General Advertiser*; *Craftsman*
1727 *London Evening Post*
1730 *Grub-street Journal*; *Daily Advertiser*, initially advertisements only
1731 *Gentleman's Magazine*; parliamentary reports introduced therein five years later
1732 The first *London Magazine*
1738 All parliamentary reporting suppressed
1739 *Champion* (Henry Fielding)
1741 *Gazeteer & London Advertiser*
1750 *Rambler* (Dr Samuel Johnson)
1753 *World* published by Robert Dodsley
1757 *London Chronicle or Universal Evening Post*
1762 John Wilkes's *North Briton*
1763 Prosecution of Wilkes for seditious libel
1769 *Morning Chronicle*
1770 Official inquiry into authorship of 'Junius Letters' in *Public Advertiser*
1771 Press wins right to report parliamentary debates
1772 *Morning Post*
1774 Hansard first report parliamentary debates
1775 Lords permit reporting of debates
1779 Mrs E. Johnson's *British Gazette & Sunday Monitor*, first Sunday newspaper
1780 *Morning Herald* launched by Henry Bate Dudley
1785 John Walter I founds *Daily Universal Register*
1788 *Daily Universal Register* renamed *The Times**; first regular evening newspaper, *Star*
1791 *The Observer**
1792 Fox's Libel Act granted the Press trial by jury; John Bell, *World*, reports in person on war against France in the Low Countries
1794 *Morning Advertiser**

1800 *Porcupine*
1802 Cobbett's *Weekly Political Register*
1803 *Globe* (London evening)

1808 *The Times* sends Henry Crabb Robinson to the Penninsular War
1812 Publication of *Parliamentary Debates*, commenced by William Cobbett in 1804, taken over by Hansard
1814 Koenig steam press introduced by *The Times*
1819 The Six Acts, two of them affecting Radical Press; John Tyas, *Times* reporter, imprisoned following 'Peterloo Massacre'
1821 *Manchester Guardian* (later *theguardian**)
1822 *Sunday Times**; agreement by Stamp Office to pass to British Museum copies of newspapers at end of their legal life
1827 *Standard**
1836 (Provincial) Newspaper Society founded
1843 *News of the World**
1844 First transmission of news by electric telegraph – in *The Times*
1846 *Daily News* (edited by Charles Dickens)
1851 Reuters News Agency opens in London
1853 Advertisement Duty abolished
1855 Stamp Duty abolished; *The Daily Telegraph**
1857 Stereotyping introduced in *The Times*
1861 Paper Duty abolished
1865 *Pall Mall Gazette*
1871 Central Press starts telegraphic operation
1881 *Evening News*, *Tit-Bits*, *People**
1882 Press Club (London) founded
1884 National Association of Journalists (Institute of Journalists, 1890) founded
1885 William Stead imprisoned because of his Maiden Tribute series in *Pall Mall Gazette*
1888 Alfred Harmsworth founds *Answers*; *Star* edited by T.P. O'Connor; *Financial Times**
1890 *Daily Graphic*
1896 *Daily Mail** launched by Harmsworth; *Lloyd's Weekly News* announces circulation of 1,000,000

1900 C.A. Pearson starts *Daily Express**
1903 *Daily Mirror**, edited by Mary Howarth, launched by Harmsworth
1904 *Standard* and *Evening Standard* sold to Pearson
1905 Harmsworth (now Lord Northcliffe) buys *The Observer*
1906 Newspaper Proprietors Association founded
1907 National Union of Journalists founded
1908 *The Times* taken over by Lord Northcliffe
1909 First Imperial Press Conference held in London, basis of Commonwealth Press Union
1911 William Waldorf Astor becomes new owner of *The Observer*
1912 *Daily Herald* launched
1915 *Sunday Pictorial* (later *Sunday Mirror*) launched by Lord Rothermere; *Evening Standard* sold to Edward Hulton II; Berry brothers buy *Sunday Times*
1917 Max Aitken (later Lord Beaverbrook) takes controlling share of *Daily Express The Standard* (morning paper) closes

1918 Beaverbrook launches *Sunday Express*
1919 Berry brothers purchase *Financial Times*
1922 Northcliffe dies; Associated Newspapers and Amalgamated Press pass to Rothermere; John Jacob Astor secures control of *The Times*; Labour Party and TUC take over *Daily Herald*
1923 Hulton chain acquired by Rothermere; Beaverbrook takes over *Evening Standard*
1924 Berry brothers and Edward Iliffe form Allied Newspapers from most of former Hulton chain plus *The Sunday Times*
1925 Press Association takes majority holding in Reuters
1926 General Strike: Government's *British Gazette*; TUC's *The British Worker*
1928 *The Daily Telegraph* purchased by Berry brothers and Iliffe
1930 *Daily Chronicle* merged with *Daily News* to form *News Chronicle*; *Daily Worker* (later *Morning Star*) launched
1932 British Museum Newspaper Library opened at Colindale
1937 *Daily Telegraph* absorbs *Morning Post*
1940 Newsprint rationing
1941 *Daily Worker* suppressed; Press Association and Newspaper Proprietors Association become joint proprietors of Reuters
1942 *Daily Mirror* warned
1947 First Royal Commission on the Press
1950 *News of the World* circulation approaches 8,500,000
1952 Rothermere's Associated Newspapers reacquires *Daily Graphic* (later *Daily Sketch*)
1953 *Daily Mirror* sells 7,161,704 copies on Coronation Day, a record for a British daily; *Scotsman* purchased by Roy Thomson; General Council of the Press established; month-long national newspaper strike
1957 *Financial Times* absorbed by Pearson Group
1959 Thomson acquires Kemsley Group, including *The Sunday Times*
1960 *News Chronicle, The Star, Sunday Graphic, Empire News* cease publication
1961 Second Royal Commission on the Press; *Sunday Dispatch* merged into *Sunday Express*; *The Sunday Telegraph* launched
1964 Beaverbrook dies; General Council of the Press re-formed as Press Council;
1966 *The Times* moves news to front page; paper and its supplements bought by Lord Thomson
1968 Newspaper Proprietors Association renamed Newspaper Publishers Association
1969 *News of the World* and *The Sun* bought by Rupert Murdoch's News International
1970 Reed International formed from Reed Group and IPC
1971 *Daily Mail*, having absorbed *Daily Sketch*, converts to compact
1974 Third Royal Commission on the Press
1975 Two subsidiaries – Mirror Group Newspapers and IPC (periodical) formed by Reed International.
1976 Atlantic Richfield takes majority shareholding in *The Observer*
1977 Beaverbrook Newspapers (later re-titled Express Newspapers) and Morgan-Grampian (magazines) bought by Trafalgar House
1978 *Daily Star* launched from Manchester; publication of *The Times* and *The Sunday Times* suspended for 11 months (1978–79)

1979 *Financial Times* launches international edition in Frankfurt

1980 *Daily Star* printed simultaneously in Manchester and, by facsimile, in London; *Evening News* closed; joint ownership of *Evening Standard* (retitled *New Standard* and then *Standard*)

1981 *The Times* and *The Sunday Times* bought by News International; *The Observer* purchased by Lonrho

1982 Trafalgar House publishing interests, except *Standard*, demerged as Fleet Holdings; *The Mail on Sunday* launched; NGA absorbs SLADE; SOGAT absorbs NATSOPA and becomes SOGAT '82

1984 Robert Maxwell purchases Mirror Group; Reuters floated as public company

1985 Fleet Holdings (Express Newspapers) purchased by United Newspapers; Conrad Black secures controlling interest in *The Daily Telegraph* and *The Sunday Telegraph*; *Standard* fully owned by Associated Newspapers

1986 News International (*The Times*, *Sunday Times*, *Sun*, *News of the World*) moves to Wapping; Eddy Shah launches *Today*; *Independent** initiated by Andreas Whittam Smith

1987 *London Daily News* started by Maxwell; *Evening News* temporarily relaunched; *News on Sunday*

1988 *Daily Mirror* launches colour revolution in nationals

1989 *Sunday Correspondent*

1990 *Independent on Sunday**

1991 Press Complaints Commission replaces Press Council; NGA and SOGAT merge as Graphical, Paper and Media Union (GPMU); death of Maxwell

1993 The Guardian Media Group purchase *The Observer*

1996 Merger between United News and Media (including Express Newspapers) and MAI Group

1998 Dublin-based Independent Newspapers acquire total ownership of Newspaper Publishing, *The Independent* and *Independent on Sunday*

1999 Launch of the *Metro* in London by Associated Newspapers

2000 Richmond Desmond takes over Express Newspapers

2002 Three hundred years of Fleet Street celebrated on March 11

2004 Barclay brothers acquire *The Daily Telegraph* and *The Sunday Telegraph*; *The Independent* followed by *The Times* converts to compact

2005 *theguardian* re-launches in 'Berliner' size

2006 Centenary of the Newspaper Publishers Association

Fleet Street 1985: pre exodus

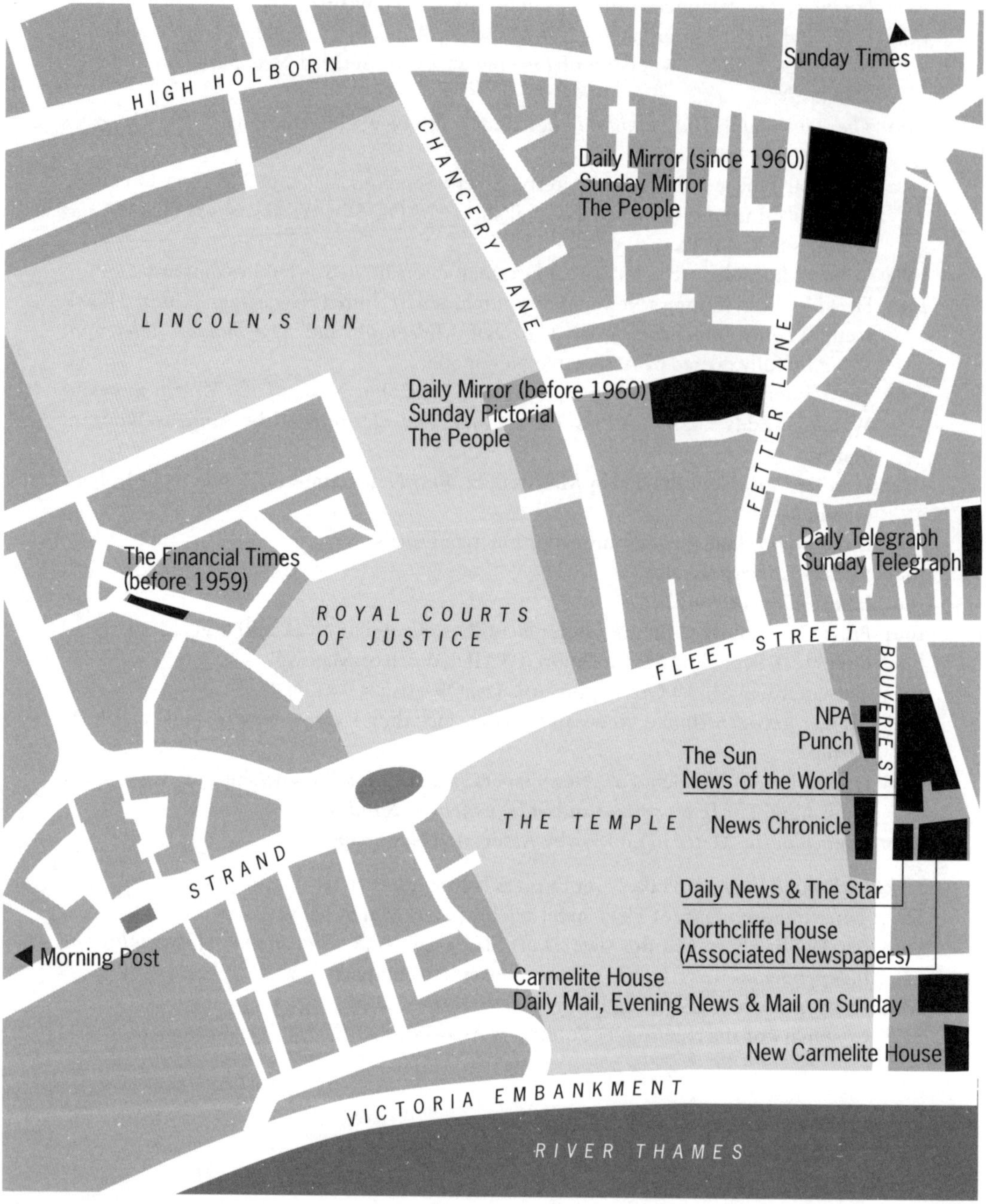

Key

1930 Daily News & Daily Chronicle merge to form News Chronicle
1937 Daily Telegraph absorbs Morning Post
1960 Daily Mail & Evening News take over News Chronicle & The Star
1963 Sunday Pictorial becomes Sunday Mirror
1974 The Times moves to Sunday Times premises
1980 Evening Standard absorbs Evening News

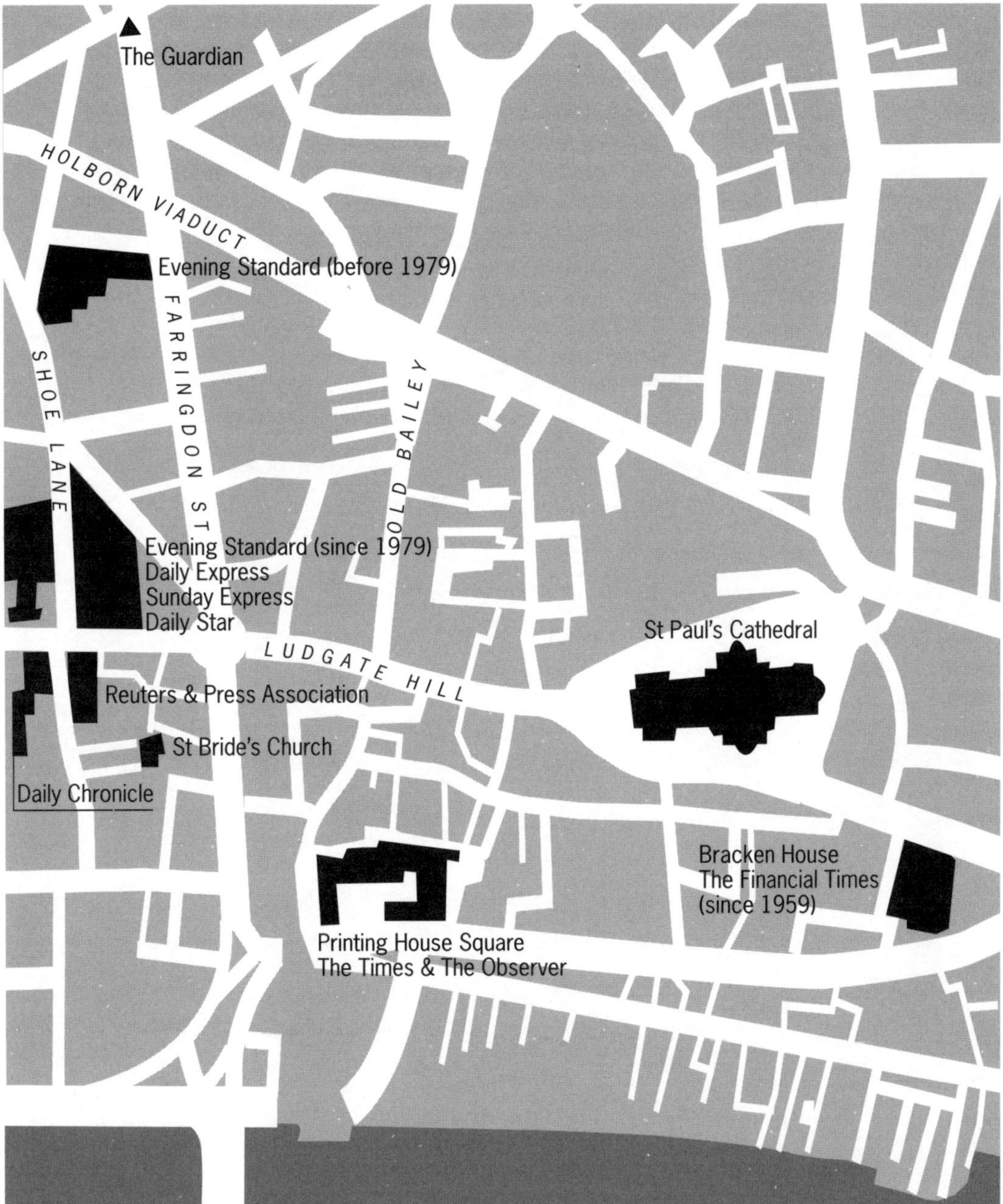
The Guardian
HOLBORN VIADUCT
Evening Standard (before 1979)
FARRINGDON ST
SHOE LANE
OLD BAILEY
Evening Standard (since 1979)
Daily Express
Sunday Express
Daily Star
LUDGATE HILL
St Paul's Cathedral
Reuters & Press Association
St Bride's Church
Daily Chronicle
Bracken House
The Financial Times
(since 1959)
Printing House Square
The Times & The Observer

1

Printing comes to Fleet Street

MORE THAN TWO HUNDRED YEARS before the first daily newspaper, printing came to England when William Caxton set up his business at Westminster in 1476; and less than three decades later, in 1500, Caxton's apprentice, Wynkyn de Worde, established his press at the sign of the *Sun* next to St Bride's Church, Fleet Street. For, as the main artery between the commercial centre in the City of London and the Crown, Court and Church at Westminster, Fleet Street occupied a singularly strategic position.

After the establishment of monastic foundations such as the Blackfriars, Whitefriars and the Knights Templar in the area – followed by the Inns of Court – it was natural that Fleet Street should become the main legal thoroughfare. With lawyers there would always be a need for scriveners to write out copies of legal or official documents; and with the coming of printing it was inherent that printers would set up their presses in this area.

The first of these printers was Wynkyn de Worde; and in the words of Dewi Morgan, a former rector of St Bride's:[1]

> Wynkyn looked at London and saw that around St Bride's had grown a heavy concentration of ecclesiastics who had a monopoly of literacy. The prelates thus congregated were Wynkyn's magnet. It was because the church was there that the press came to Fleet Street .... If Caxton was the father of English printing, Wynkyn was the progenitor of mass communications. He owned and occupied two houses at the sign of the *Sun* in Fleet Street, one as a dwelling and the other as his printing works. St Bride's Church, beside which he set up his press, became the godparent of a cultural and sociological revolution.

Wynkyn published his final book – *The Complaint of the Too-Soon Martyred* – in 1535, dying a few weeks later; and in his will directed that the Guild of St Bride's should attend his funeral in their russet gowns. To the Guild he left 10*s*. 'to ease his soul's passage to peace', and to the poor of St Bride he bequeathed a yearly sum of 20*s*. plus £36 to buy land whose profits 'should maintain an obit for his soul'.

Following his death, his press was confiscated and given to Richard Pynson, and then to Thomas Berthelet, Printer to the King, 'who made it the centrepiece of the first officially recognized state printing works, built into an old monastery at Blackfriars'. And there, according to a Royal Proclamation of 1538, it was concerned with 'expelling and avoiding the occasion of erroneous and seditious opinions'.

¶ Hereafter ensue the trewe encountre or..
Batayle lately don betwene . Englãde and:
Scotlande. In whiche batayle the . Scottis-
he . Kynge was slayne.

¶ The maner of thaduaũcesynge of my lord of
Surrey tresourier and . Marshall of . Englande
and leuetenũte generall of the north ptíes of th
e same with . xxvi . M. men to wardes the kynge of . Scottz and his . Armye vewed and noum/
bred to an/hundred thousande men at/theleest.

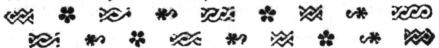

The first ‘newspaper’

In just 40 years, Wynkyn had produced more than eight hundred publications – representing some 15 per cent of all known works printed before 1557: 'Briefly it was to give the public a variety of books on subjects known to have a popular appeal, and to issue these in easily handled volumes likely to attract readers who would recoil from large and expensive volumes.'

However, despite de Worde's vast output of published matter, he was not the first to print a 'newspaper' in England. That honour belongs to Richard Faques, who on 9 September 1513 produced a news-pamphlet giving an eye-witness account of the battle of Flodden, including lists of casualties, headed 'Hereafter ensue the trewe encountre or Batayle lately don betwene Englade and Scotlande'.[2] This is the first account of any such historical event to be printed in England, and as such has been called the foundation stone of English journalism. But, even after the appearance of this first-ever 'newspaper', the ordinary person would still have had to rely upon ballad singers or the town-crier for his news; and, with the government centred in London, immediately adjacent to the Royal Court, only a small number of people would have had intimate knowledge of the full range of state affairs.

Throughout the sixteenth century the Crown had been determined to exercise strict control on all printed matter: in 1503, the Frenchman Guillaume Faques, anglicised to William Fawkes, was appointed King's Printer and given a monopoly of all published works; and this was followed by further strictures in 1520 with the appointment of official licensers – and enhanced by Henry VIII in 1538. Six years later, the Crown declared that 'all printed books should bear the name of the author, the printer and the place of publication'. And in Edward VI's reign, 'spoken news or rumour' was prohibited by proclamations of 1547 and 1549.

Nevertheless, there were some publishers who were determined to print news sheets, evidenced by one such that appeared in 1555:[3]

> The copie of a letter sent into Scotland on the arivall and landyng and most noble marryage of the most Illustre Prince Philippe, Prynce of Spaine, to the most excellent Princess Marye, Quene of England solemnized in the Citie of Winchester, and howe he was receyved and installed at Windsore, and of his triumphing entries in the noble Citie of London.

Two years later, however, as a further step in censorship, the Stationers' Company was granted a Royal Charter, incorporation of which was to bring the craft's regulating body the status and power of a City livery company, but which had also provided the Crown with a channel for the enforcement of Press control. The charter limited the craft to London and required Company members to provide parties for search and seizure of presses and printed materials as necessary:

> It was then that they began a Register in which were recorded all books printed by their members. Such recording gave the printer an exclusive copyright and made 'Entered at Stationers' Hall a mystical phrase'. . . . The Master and members were also empowered to seize and burn all prohibited books and imprison offenders. The actual burning was done by the common executioner.

Elizabeth I inherited this network of legislation, and she added to it with further restrictions; by 1581 the production of seditious literature had become a capital offence. The following year, Christopher Barker, the Queen's Printer, was to write in his *Notes of the State of the Company of Printers* that there were twenty-two printing houses in London, whereas eight or ten, he thought, would have sufficed for the whole of England and Scotland. He then discussed the persons involved in the trade:

> In the tyme of King Henry Eighte there were fewe Printers, and those Were of good credit and compotent wealth; at which tyme and before there was another sort of men that were writers, lymners of bookes and dyverse thinges for the Churche and other uses, called stacioners; which have and partly to this daye do use to buy theire bookes in grosse of the saide Printers to bynde them up, and sell them in their shops, wherby they well mayntayned theire families.

Despite these strictures, during the final years of the sixteenth century, one printer – John Wolfe, an established member of the Stationers' Company – did manage to publish and circulate small newsbooks, measuring just 4 × 2 inches, one such title being *A briefe discourse of the cruell dealings of the Spanyards in the Dukedomes of Gulick and Cleue*.[4] There had also now begun to develop an English-language, news-pamphlet Press on the Continent, and of these the most important was *Mercurius Galli-Belgicus,* published half-yearly from Cologne and Frankfurt. These pamphlets were printed in German because the Crown claimed the right to publication of all English matters; and in order not to arouse too much official restraint the pamphlets dealt exclusively with foreign news. Writing in 1614, Robert Burton could comment: 'If any read nowadays, it is a play, booke or pamphlet of news.'

In addition to news-pamphlets, there were broadsheet ballads, written in rough verse around any great happening, and hawked about the streets. Small quarto pamphlets – called discourses – were also printed to mark important events: many of these were translated from foreign news-pamphlets, and were then usually available for sale at the north door of St Paul's Cathedral.

First English-language Newspapers

Although published irregularly, the first English-language newspapers – folded news-sheets – were being produced in Holland for circulation in England by the early years of the seventeenth century. Chief publisher of these was George Veseler, who, in 1620, from his Amsterdam premises produced such titles as *Corante, or Newes, from Italy.* During this period there was also a number of business periodicals in English arriving from Amsterdam and Cologne:[5]

> They were very expensive, and dangerous to possess. But they were authorative, having been authorised by the Fuggers of Augsburg and the Mandels of Frankfurt, Europe's leading bankers. They also carried human-interest news, sub-titled 'Domestic News'.

This influx of Continental-printed matter was to lead to native publishers becoming involved, and the following year Thomas Archer began selling news-sheets from

The 23. of May.

VVEEKELY Nevves from Italy, GERMANIE, HVNGARIA, BOHEMIA, the PALATINATE, France, and the Low Countries.

Translated out of the Low Dutch Copie.

LONDON,
Printed by *I. D.* for *Nicholas Bourne* and *Thomas Archer*, and are to be ſold at their ſhops at the *Exchange*, and in *Popes-head Pallace*.
1622.

Pope's Head Alley, off Fleet Street. However, in September 1621 he was imprisoned for printing unlicensed comments on the war in the Palatine; and in his absence on 9 October Nicholas Bourne began producing the *Corante Newes from Italy*,

On 23 May 1622 Archer and Bourne became the first Englishmen to produce a numbered newsbook of foreign news: *Weekely Newes from Italy, Germanie, Hungaria, Bohemia, the Palatinate, France and the Low Countries, Translated out of the Low Dutch Copie*. Typical of the aims of these newsbooks can be gathered from the following:

> I can assure you, there is not a line printed nor proposed to your view, but carries the credits of other Originals, and justifies itself from honest and understanding authority; so that if they should faile there in true and exact discoveries, be not you too malignant against this Printer here, that is so far from any invention of his owne, that when he meets with improbability or absurdity, he leaves it quite out rather than startle your patience.

Because of the severe censorship of the Star Chamber, these newsbooks were permitted to deal only with foreign news. Seven years later, in 1629, the Spanish ambassador complained, and on 17 October 1632 they were banned by the Star Chamber.

In 1638, Bourne, now with Nathaniel Butter, was allowed to resume publication; and under Charles I they enjoyed a 21-year monopoly of the printing of foreign news – subject to an annual payment of £10 towards the upkeep of St Paul's.

A Freeman of the Stationers' Company, Butter had in 1605 published an account of two murders in Yorkshire, and was later to produce *Newes From Spain* and *Newes From Most Parts of Christendom*. Having printed a number of ephemeral news-sheets, he decided to start a weekly title, and in August 1622, launched the *Weekeley News*; and he was to declare his intentions in a subsequent issue:[6]

> If any gentleman or other accustomed to buy the weekly relations of newes be desirous to continue the same, let them know that the writer, or transcriber, rather of this newes hath published two former newes, the one dated the 2nd and the other the 13th of August, all of which do carry a like title with the arms of the King of Bohemia on the other side of the title page, and have dependence one upon another; which manner of writing and printing he doth purpose to continue weekly by God's assistance from the best and most certain intelligence; farewell this twenty-third day of August, 1622.

In an intermittent manner, Butter continued to produce the *Weekeley Newes* for the next decade. 'The paper came out with fair regularity when exciting events took place on the Continent during the Thirty Years War; but when a truce took place, or winter put an end to military movements, the publication ceased.'

As a leading publisher, Butter, much to his chagrin, had been celebrated as Cymbal, the manager, in Ben Jonson's *The Staple of News*, printed in 1631, the first play to deal with newspapers:[7]

> O! you are a butter-woman; ask Nathaniel, the
> Clerk, there how like you the news; they are as
> good as butter could make them . . . in a word
> they were beautifully buttered!

> See divers men's opinions; unto some
> The very printing of 'em makes them news;
> That have not the heart to believe any thing,
> But what they see in print.

Regarded as a monopolist and hated by the minor members of his craft, Butter was now being harried by the Press Censor, and despite help, financial and otherwise, from Sir Harry Vane, the Secretary of State, and others he was forced to cease publication of the *Weekeley Newes* in 1641.

During this period, radical Protestants – vociferous in their criticism of Charles I's growing Catholicism – now produced a flood of unlicensed pamphlets, provoking Archbishop Laud, as Censor of the Press, to carry out his duties with extreme cruelty. It was not uncommon for printers to be fined heavily, whipped through the streets and thrown into prison. One of the worst instances concerned John Bastwick, Henry Burton and William Prynne, who in 1638, having printed *Historio-Matrix*, were found guilty by the Star Chamber; and as a consequence were branded and had their ears cut off.

With the abolition of the Star Chamber in July 1641, religious tracts, political sheets and almanacs poured from the presses; and on November 22 there appeared the *Heads of Severall Proceedings in this Present Parliament*, the first official printed report of parliamentary news. Published by John Thomas and edited by Samuel Pecke, it was soon to face another nine weekly newspapers in competition; and by the end of 1642 more than a hundred titles – many of them, true, short-lived – had been launched.

The Civil War had brought about a remarkable advance, for not only did it provide important news that everyone was anxious to read, but both Royalists and Roundheads had an interest in exploiting it. Corantos and Diurnalls gave place to the most famous of all the early newsbooks, the Mercuries.

Among these were John Berkenhead's *Mercurius Aulicus*, which 'Communicated the Intelligence and Affaires of the Court to the Rest of the Kingdom' – the first official royalist newsbook. In the initial issue, published at Oriel College, Oxford in January 1643,[8] Berkenhead, a Fellow of All Souls, with the assistance of Dr Peter Heylin, announced: 'The world hath long enough been abused with falsehoods. And there's a weekly cheat put out to nourish the abuse amongst the people . . . . whereas we shall proceed with truth and candour.' That was not, however, the opinion of John Aubrey, who believed that Berkenhead, although 'exceedingly confident and witty would lye damnably'.

This influx of new titles now led to the Long Parliament empowering the 'Committee for Examinations to search for unlicensed presses', and to re-establishing the licensing system in the spring of 1643. There immediately sprang up a strong opposition, among whom John Milton was to play a leading role; and in 1644 he published his *Areopagitica* which attacked the Order of 1643 that had declared that 'No book shall be henceforth printed unless the same be first approved and licensed by such'. Milton wrote: 'If we think to regulate printing, thereby to rectify manners, we must regulate all recreation and pastimes . . . . As good almost kill a man as kill a good book; who kills a man kills a reasonable creature, God's image, but he who destroys a book kills reason itself.' Despite the pressures of Parliament to restrict the Press, the citizens of London were still able to purchase a dozen different newspapers a week:

Monday	*A Perfect Diurnall; Certaine Informations; Mercurius Aulicus*
Tuesday	*The Kingdomes Weekly Intelligencer*
Wednesday	*The Weekly Account; A Continuation of Certain Speciall and Remarkable Passages*
Thursday	*Mercurius Britannicus; Mercurius Civicus*
Friday	*The Parliament Scout; The Scottish Dove; Occurrences of Certain Remarkable Passages*
Saturday:	*The True Informer*

For the persons who wrote, edited and printed these publications, it was a hard and precarious existence:[9]

> Their hand presses might have been crude, they were easily dismountable. It needed but a few moments to break down and load a press with its founts of type onto a handcart. Any dark, dingy room was adequate for the purpose, and all that was needed, in addition, to put a newspaper into production was a modest supply of paper such as a man could carry himself, and a small quantity of ink . . . In the face of daunting regulations, an almost entirely illicit publishing industry grew up.

Berkenhead, meanwhile, continued to prosper, and in 1645, in a pamphlet *The True Character of Mercurius Aulicus*, he stated: 'The Malignant do pay sometimes as deare for the pamphlet as the psalm book; one of the last was sold for 18 pence a peece. We now say to the Malignants that what Aulicus writteth is true.'

Following the Restoration, Berkenhead became a Member of Parliament. He withdrew from public life, however, after accepting a knighthood and being appointed Master of Requests.

A Scribe with Venom in His Pen

His main rival had been Marchemont Nedham, chief writer, of the *Mercurius Britannicus*, launched in August 1643. Born in Burford, Oxfordshire, he began as an apothecary's assistant, and then turned lawyer's clerk before becoming a publicist. 'A prolific, ingenious rogue with "trapstick" legs and a large stomach', Nedham was a scribe with venom in his pen, who was to attack everyone, including the King:[10]

> Where's King Charles? What's become of him? It were best to send Hue and cry after him. If any man can bring any tale or tiding of a wilful King, which hath gone astray these four yeares from Parliament, with a guilty conscience, bloody hands, a heart full of vowes and protestations . . . . Then give notice to *Britannicus* and you shall be paid for your paines.

For this, Nedham and his editor, Captain Thomas Audley – 'a swarthy chest-nut coloured captaine who lived in Bloomsbury near the great cherry garden' – were committed to the Gatehouse Prison. Released some months later, Nedham, on 21 May 1646, attacked Parliament in print. Arrested, he admitted that he had been responsible for the last 80 issues of *Britannicus*; and found guilty he was committed to Fleet Prison. Within a month, he had secured his release, being ordered to pay bail and being barred from journalism. Nedham, therefore, turned to medicine!

Anthony Wood, the antiquarian and historian, was to comment on Nedham: 'Siding with the scum and rout of the people he made them weekly sport by railing at all that is noble in his Intelligence called *Mercurius Britannicus* wherein the endeavours were to sacrifice the fame of some Lord or person of quality – nay, of the king himself – to the beast with many heads.' The following year, 1647, Nedham, received the royal pardon and now began to attack Cromwell – dubbed 'Copper-nose' – and his followers, publishing *Mercurius Pragmaticus.* The government immediately sought to suppress it, and sent its printer, Richard Lownes, to prison. (Nedham had prudently left London for Oxford.)

On 30 January 1649 King Charles I was executed, an event that was brilliantly and simply reported in *A Perfect Diurnall of Some Passages in Parliament and the Daily Proceedings of the Army under his Excellency the Lord Fairfax* (29 January to 5 February 1649):[11]

> Tuesday, January 30. This day the King was beheaded, over against the Banqueting house by Whitehall. The manner of Execution, and what passed before his death take thus. He was brought from Saint *James* about ten in the morning, walking on foot through the Park, with a Regiment of Foot for his guard, with Colours flying, Drums beating, his private Guard of Partizans, with some of his Gentlemen before, and some behind bare-headed. Doctor *Juxon* late Bishop of *London* next behinde him, and Col. *Thomlinson* (who had the charge of him) to the Gallery in Whitehall, and so into the Cabinet Chamber where he used to lye, where he continued his Devotion refusing to dine (having before taken the Sacrament) onely about 12, at noone, he drank a Glass of Claret Wine, and eat a piece of bread. From there he was accompanyed by Dr. *Juxon*, Col. *Thomlinson*, Col. *Hacker* and the Guards before mentioned through the Banqueting-house adjoyning, to which the Scaffold was erected, between Whitehall Gate, and the Gate leading into the Gallery from Saint *James*: The Scaffold was hung round with black, and the floor covered with black, and the Ax and Block laid in the middle of the Scaffold. There were divers companies of Foot and Horse, on every side of the Scaffold, and the multitudes of people that came to be Spectators, very great.The King making a Passe upon the Scaffold, look'd very earnestly on the Block, and asked Col. *Hacker* if there were no higher; and then spake thus directing his speech to the Gentlemen upon the Scaffold .... Then the King took off his cloak, and his George, giving his George to Dr. *Juxon*, saying, Remember, (it is thought for the Prince,) and some other small ceremonies past; after which the king stooping down laid his neck upon the blocke, and after a little pause stretching forth his hands, the Executioner at one blow severed his head from his Body. Then his Body was put in a coffin covered with black Velvet and removed to his lodging chamber in White hall.

As for Nedham, later that year, in June, he was arrested and committed to Newgate, but discharged after three months – following agreement to write for the

Commonwealth. A pamphlet, *The Case of the Commonwealth*, produced the following year brought him £50 and a pension of £100; and that same year he launched *Mercurius Politicus*, a weekly – notable for its leading article – which he was to edit for the next decade (John Milton, now Censor of the Press, was also associated with the paper). To this title, Nedham added the *Public Intelligencer*, an official journal, but published on Mondays instead of Thursdays.

Not content, on 1 May 1657 he launched the *Publick Advertiser*, the first all-advertisement weekly. Among the announcements for houses to be let or to be sold and persons wanting employment was an advertisement for a new and fashionable drink:[12]

> In Bartholomew Lane on the back side of the Old Exchange, the drink called Coffee (which is a very wholsome and physcal drink, having many excellent virtues, closes the Orifice of the Stomack, fortifies the heat within, helpeth Digestion, quicketh the spirits, makes the head lightsom, is good against Eye-sores, coughs or colds, rhumes, consumptions, head-ach, Dropsie, Gout, Scurvy, King's Evil and many others) is to be sold both in the morning, and at three o'clock in the afternoon.

In that same issue, Nedham also informed his readers of travel arrangements between London and the Midlands:

> All such persons as desire to travell by Coach from Coventry to London, and from London to Coventry, may be supplied every Monday morning at the Star in Coventry, to be in London early every Wednesday; and every Thursday at the Ram in Smithfield to be in Coventry every Saturday night, at the fare of ten shillings the Passenger, and they are desired to give timely notice of their Intentions at the Houses aforesaid. The Stage Coaches for Westchester go from the George near Aldersgate every Monday, Wednesday, and Friday, to carry Passengers for 35 shilling a peece in four days.

And the following year, on 23 September 1658, in issue no. 435 of his *Mercurius Politicus*, he was advertising the efficacy of tea 'That excellent and by all physicians approved China drink, called by the Chineans Tcha, by other nations Tay, alias Tee, is sold at the Sultaner's-head, a Cophee-house in Sweeting's Rents, by the Royal Exchange, London.' In less than two years, though, Nedham's publishing career came to an abrupt end, for in the issue of the *Parliamentary Intelligencer* of 26 March 1660, General Monck's Council of State authorized the following statement:[13]

> Whereas *Marchemont Nedham*, the Author of the Weekly News Books called *Mercurius Politicus* and the *Public Intelligencer*, is by Order of the Council of the State, discharged from Writing or Publishing any Publique Intelligence; The Reader is desired to take notice, that by Order of the said Council *Henry Muddiman* and *Giles Drury*, are authorised henceforth to Write and Publish the said Intelligence

Fleeing from England in May 1660, Nedham found refuge in Holland, but a few months later he obtained his pardon 'for money given to an hungry courier' and was able to return. For the remainder of his days, he practised as a physician, with the occasional incursion into pamphleteering until 'this most seditious, mutable and railing author' died suddenly in Devereux Court, near Temple Bar, in November 1678. An anonymous poet was to write of him:

Here lies *Britannicus*, Hell's cur,
That son of Belial who kept damned stir;
And every Munday spent his stock of spleen
In venomous railing on the King and Queen
Who though they both in goodness may forgive him
Yet, (for his safety) we'll in hell receive him.

A State Monopoly of News

As the number of printers who had been imprisoned could testify, it had been a difficult time to have been involved in publishing, for during the Protectorate of Oliver Cromwell there had been effectively a state monopoly of news under the supervision of a government censor, with the Licensed Press being suppressed from October 1649 to June 1650 and again from September 1655. At the Restoration, five years later, the system was transferred to the Royalists, and under the Comprehensive Printing Act of 1662 the Press was placed formally under tight parliamentary control.[14]

Because of these strictures, publishing was a precarious business, and any titles that offended parliament were immediately suppressed, a great number of the authors and printers being fined and imprisoned. As for the hawkers and mercuries (many of whom were women) who sold the publications in the street, they were often treated as common rogues and whipped or sent to gaol. Despite these risks, however, a great number of newsbooks appeared during this period, some often short-lived, but the desire was there for a free Press.

Samuel Shepherd, a clergyman/publisher, who had himself been imprisoned, wrote at the time: 'What a pannique possesses the souls of the Universe when the hawkers come roaring along the streets like the religious singers of Bartholomew Fayre.' In 1652, Shepherd had published his *Mercurius Matrix* aimed at 'Faithfully Lashing All *Scouts*, *Mercuries*, *Spyes*, and others; who cheat the Commonwealth under the name of Intelligence'. He declared:[15]

> No rest day nor night with these cursed *Caterpillars*, *Perfect Passages*, *Weekly Occurrences*, *Scout*, *Spye*, *Politicus*, *Diurnal*, the devil and his dam . . . . But the cream of the jest is, how they take their times and rises; one upon Munday, t'other on Tuesday, a third on Wednesday; and so come over one another's backs, as if they were playing at Leap-frog. Nay, it's fine to see how authentically and positively these Caytiffs obtrude their parboyl'd Non-sense; with what impudence they'll rout you an Army at five hundred leagues distance, and with one dash of a pen piece it up again, and make it as whole as ever it was . . . . These fellows come flurting in, and style themselves by new names; they flie up and down a week or two, and then in a moment vanish. Seriously I would wish it were enacted, that whosoever did betake himself to this Lying trade, should be bound at least seven years to it.

On 16 March 1660 the Long Parliament was dissolved to be replaced by General Monck's Council of State, prior to the restoration of the monarchy. For some three weeks before this dissolution, Oliver Williams, a former publisher of 'Offices of Intelligence', was to make journalistic history by producing a daily newsbook – a report of the proceedings of the House of Commons from 21 February to 16 March 1660. His next newsbooks to be launched were revivals of Nedham's *Mercurius Politicus* and the *Publick Intelligencer* from his Office of Intelligence, near the Old Exchange. However, both were to be short-lived, for on 25 June 1660 – a few weeks after the return of Charles II – Parliament passed a resolution 'that no person whatever do presume at his peril to print any votes of this House without the special leave and order of this House'.

Surveyor of the Press

With the Press under parliamentary control, there now sprang up a series of licensers, of whom Sir Roger L'Estrange was the foremost. Having served in the Royalist cavalry during the Civil War, he had offered to capture the town of Lynn for Charles I, and raised a regiment in Norfolk for the purpose. But he was seized by the Roundheads, tried at a court-martial as a traitor and ordered to be shot. He was, however, imprisoned, and escaped after four years, fleeing to the Continent. At the Restoration, he made an appeal to Charles II to enforce Press censorship, and as a result in February 1662 was made Surveyor of the Press.[16]

His first deed was to suppress all newspapers that were hostile to the Crown, and in return he received a royal patent granting him 'the sole privilege of writing, printing and publishing all narratives, advertisements, Mercuries, Intelligences, Diurnals, and all other books of public intelligence'. From his base at the King's Printing Office, Blackfriars, L'Estrange could state in his prospectus issued in August 1663 : 'I find it in general, with the printers as with their neighbours, there are too many of the trade to live by one another. But, more particularly, I find them clogged with three kinds of people: foreigners, persons not free of the trade, and separatists.'

L'Estrange's initial venture into publishing was to launch the *Intelligence* on 31 August 1663; and below the masthead he proclaimed that it was :

> Published for the Satisfaction and Information of the PEOPLE
> The *Way* (as to the Vent) that has been found Most *Beneficiall* to the *Master* of the *Book* has been to *Cry*, and *Expose* it about the Streets, by *Mercuries* and Hawkers; but whether that Way be advisable in some *other respects*, may be a *Question*; for under the Countenance of that Imployment, is carried on the *Private Trade* of *Treasonous* and *Seditious Libels*, (nor, effectually, has anything considerable been dispersed, against either Church, or State, without the *Aid*, and *Privity* of this sort of *People*)

Within months, however, it was suspended when the *Oxford Gazette* (later *London Gazette*) was launched on 7 November 1665. The first true newspaper, other than a newsletter, the *Oxford Gazette* arose through Charles II and his Court being forced to leave London during the Great Plague of 1665 for the purer air of Oxford. The *Gazette* was written and edited by Henry Muddiman, under the guidance of Joseph Williamson; and the two-column layout it used was to become the standard for newspapers during the next fifty years. The first issue noted: 'The accounts of the weekly Bill at London runs thus: Total 1,359. Plague 1,050. Deceased 428.' Samuel Pepys could say of the *Gazette*: 'Very pretty, full of news, and no comment in it.' The imprint read: 'Oxon, printed by Leonard Litchfield and re-printed in London, for the use of Merchants and Gentlemen who desired them.' This is the first known occasion in which a newspaper was printed in more than one city in England. Following 23 issues, the *Oxford Gazette* became the *London Gazette*, and, with the return of Charles II to London in January 1666 after the plague had abated, the *Gazette* was then printed solely in the capital.

In his earlier days, after leaving Cambridge, Muddiman had worked as a schoolmaster before becoming publisher of the *Kingdome's Intelligencer* and *Mercurius Publicus*. His editorship was to cause comment, especially from Samuel Pepys, who on 9 January 1660 wrote in his diary: 'I found Muddiman a good scholar, an arch rogue; and owns that though he writes newsbooks for the Parliament, yet he did declare that he did it only to get money; and did talk basely about them.'

A fortnight later, in issue dated Thursday, 24 January–Thursday, 31 January, Muddiman printed the following in the *Mercurius Publicus*:[17]

> Westminster:
> This day (Jan. 26), in pursuance of an Order of Parliament, the carcasses of those two horrid Regicides, Oliver Cromwell and Henry Ireton, were digged up out of their graves, which (with those of John Bradshaw and Thomas Price) are to be hang'd up at Tyburn, and buried under the gallows . . . . after which they were taken down, their heads cut off, and their loathsome Trunks thrown into a deep hole under the Gallows.

A week later the *Mercurius Publicus* reported:

> The Heads of those notorious Regicides, Oliver Cromwell, John Bradshaw and Henry Ireton are set upon poles on the top of Westminster Hall by the common Hangman. Bradshaw is placed in the middle (over that part where that monstrous High Court of Justice sate), Oliver Cromwell and his son-in-law Ireton on both sides of Bradshaw.

Now, after editing the first 25 issues of the *Gazette*, and then resigning, on 4 June 1666 Muddiman launched another official newspaper, the *Current Intelligence*. This was a short-lived affair, though, of only 26 issues, ceasing publication because of the Great Fire of London.

After 1666, Muddiman devoted his time to writing and publishing newsletters;[18] and for these, he charged £5 a year. Muddiman had been fortunate in that although L'Estrange controlled the printed word he had not been given the power over handwritten newsletters. Muddiman, who already had the privilege of free postage for his letters, was quick to seize upon this loophole; and until his death was the principal provider of this material, circulation of which was mainly confined to the coffeehouses and persons of means.

As for L'Estrange, his next venture had been to launch the *City Mercury*, which was a commercial success, and 'the paper of the London citizens'. It ran for six years until in 1681 he started the *Observator*, which continued until the Revolution of 1688.

L'Estrange has been described as the most distinguished writer of the reigns of Charles II and James II, and the journalist of the Restoration. In contrast, for his work as Surveyor of the Press, L'Estrange was paid £200 a year – and he carried out his duties with a conscientiousness bordering on the obsessive. In 1663, he published *Considerations and Proposals in Order to the Regulation of the Press* in which he recognized the connection between the proverty of the printers and the incentive to seditious printing: 'One great evil is the multiplicity of printers who for want of public and warrantable employment are forced to play the knaves in corners, or want for bread.'

He let it be known that informers would be rewarded at his office in Ivy Lane. L'Estrange did not have long to wait, for within months of his publishing *Regulations of the Press,* the premises of John Twyn, of Cloth Fair, were raided in October 1663. Twyn was to be the most unfortunate of the victims, for he was found guilty of printing sheets which expounded that 'If the magistrates prevent judgement, the people are bound by the law of God to execute judgement without them and upon them.' For this, Twyn was hanged, disembowelled and quartered. Passing sentence, the judge declared:[19] 'He be hanged from the neck, cut down before he was dead, shamefully mutilated, and his entrails taken out. With you still living the same to be burnt before your eyes, your head to be cut off, and your head and quarters to be disposed of at the pleasure of the king's majesty.'

The Printers' Chapel

But, despite all the fears of Parliament, the printing industry in London remained small. A survey of 1668 reported that there were 26 masters, 24 apprentices and 148 journeymen, making a total of 198 men employed on sixty-five presses. Of these, the King's Printer had six presses; there were two printers with five; three with four; five with three; eight with two; and six with only one press. The King's Printer employed eighteen workmen, and larger offices from seven to thirteen, but most had less than half a dozen and several only one or two.

Over all this, the Stationers' Company still retained its role as the arbiter of the printing trade, but its power had been steadily declining for more than twenty years; and, when Charles II restored the monarchy in 1660, the master printers were in dispute with the merchants of the Company, and had suggested that they should be given the authority to regulate the trade. L'Estrange, in his role as Surveyor, was quick to dismiss their claim:

> It were a hard matter to pick out twenty master printers who are both free of the trade, of ability to manage it, and of integrity to be trusted with it; most of the honester sort being impoverished by the late times, and the great business of the Press being engrossed by Oliver's creatures .... It seems a little too much to reward the abusers of the Press with the credit of superintending it; upon a confidence that they who destroyed the last King for their benefit will now make it their business to preserve this to their loss.

While the master printers had been able to seek the protection of the Stationers' Company, their workmen had banded together into companionships known as chapels; and as Joseph Moxon was to write in his *Mechanick Exercises* published in 1683:[20]

> Every Printing House is by the Custom of Time out of Mind called a Chappel; and all the Workmen that belong to it are Members of the Chappel; and the Oldest Freeman is Father of the Chappel . . . . Every new workman to pay half-a-Crown; which is called the Benvenue being so constant a Custome is still lookt upon by all Workmen as the undoubted Right of the Chappel; and therefore never disputed.

Moxon then listed the nine rules 'usually and generally accepted' for which members could be punished:

1. Fighting in the Chappel
2. Swearing in the Chappel
3. Abusive Language, or giving the Ly in the Chappel
4. To be drunk in the Chappel
5. For any Workman to leave his Candle burning at Night
6. If the Compositor let fall his composing stick, and another take it up
7. Three Letters and a Space to lye under the Compositor's Case
8. If a Pressman let fall his Ball or Balls, and another take it up
9. If the Pressman leaves his Blankets in the Tympan at Noon or Night.

As for L'Estrange, he was knighted by James II in 1685, but three years later, with the overthrow of his patron, he lost his office, and then suffered two terms of imprisonment before his death in 1704 at the age of 88 – sixty years after having been reprieved by Parliament. Although Samuel Pepys thought him 'a man of fine conversation . . . . most courtly' and John Evelyn considered him 'a person of excellent part', his obituary, at least in the eyes of many of his contemporaries and posterity, may be summed up in the words of a latter-day author, Thomas Babington Macaulay: 'From the malice of L'Estrange the grave was no hiding place, and the house of mourning no sanctuary.'

First American Newspaper

A leading radical publisher during this period was Benjamin Harris, who first came into prominence in 1673 when he published *War With the Devil*, a religious book, quickly followed by others opposing Roman Catholics and Quakers. This led to his being fined £500 for printing Protestant works. Refusing to pay, he was sent to King's Bench Prison, but was illegally released before completing his term. On 7 July 1679 he produced his first newspaper, *The Domestick Intelligence, Or News from Both the City and the Country* (later retitled *The Protestant Domestick Intelligence*), which appeared with several interruptions until it was suppressed on 15 April 1681. Apart from his newspaper, Harris was proprietor of a coffee-shop and also sold patent medicines.[21]

After just 15 issues, on 26 August 1679 Harris had faced an identical rival, when Nathaniel Thompson – known as 'Popish Nat' – published his own *Domestick Intelligence*. Two weeks later, on September 2, Harris announced: 'There has stolen into the World a Nameless Pamphlet under the Title of the *Domestick Intelligence* printed by a person 'who has been Tenant to most of the prisons in and about

London' and that there was 'no Real *Domestick Intelligence* but what is printed by Benjamin Harris, who was the first Contriver and Promoter thereof'.

As Ray Boston has written:[22]

> On September 5, Thompson gave his own impudent version of what had happened: 'There hath lately dropt into the World an Abortive Birth (some fifteen days before the legitimate issue) by a factious, Infamous and Perjured Anti-Christian.' He continued to produce his deliberate copy and Harris was forced to change his title to *The Protestant (Domestick) Intelligence*, which left him dangerously exposed. Harris managed to steer clear of watchful authority until he published an anti-Catholic pamphlet, *An Appeal from the Country to the City*, attacking the Duke of York and advocating the claims of the King's illegitimate son, the Protestant Duke of Monmouth, to the throne.

As a fierce opponent of James II and the 'Popish plot', Harris was arrested for owning and printing seditious literature; and on 6 February 1680 was sentenced to one year's imprisonment, fined £500 and forced to stand in a specially-erected pillory outside his shop. There his wife protected him from the mob. He was then jailed but continued to edit his publication from his cell. His shop was raided again in 1686, and Harris fled to Boston. Within a year of his arrival in America, Harris had opened the London Coffee House and followed this with the launch of the *Boston Almanack* in 1687; and three years later *The New England Primer*. That same year, 1690, he launched *Publick Occurrences, Both Foreign and Domestick*, which was suppressed after one issue – this was the first attempt at producing a newspaper in the American colonies.

The paper had been closed by the authorities 'because he [Harris] did not obtain a licence . . . . and because the issue contained offensive references to the French king and the Indian wars'. Within months, Harris had been named official printer to the governor and council, and in 1692 he printed *The Acts and Laws of Massachusetts*. He returned to England in 1694, and the following year founded the *Intelligence Foreign and Domestick*, but it was a failure and soon folded. In 1699, he started the *London Post*, which was a success and lasted until 1706. His final venture was the *Protestant Tudor*.

The Glorious Revolution

In November 1688 had come the moment that many printers and publishers had long been waiting for: the Glorious Revolution and the landing of William of Orange at Torbay, followed by the flight on December 12 of James II, his wife and baby son to the court of Louis XIV. The Revolution secured the Protestant religion; brought the revenue and expenditure of the State under the control of the House of Commons; and established the Freedom of the Press.

With William and Mary now on the throne, for the many Protestant printers a new era was about to begin – and the most prominent among them was Richard Baldwin, who, until his death ten years later, was to publish almost 250 books, of which 150 had a political slant, and of these, 75 were anti-French in their content. Following the decision by Parliament in 1679 to allow the Printing Act to lapse, there had been an immediate increase in the number of new publications. However, many of these had been suppressed through the use of royal proclamations and the law of seditious libel.

Among the new publishers, Richard Baldwin was to stand out as a champion of English political freedom, and this was to continue until his early death in 1698, when his support of the Protestant cause was then carried on by his widow, Anne, until 1713.[23]

Having recently avoided imprisonment through 'Printing and publishing a Book Intituled *The Protestant Plot*', on Monday 10 October 1681 Richard Baldwin launched *Mercurius Anglicus*, a single folio sheet printed every Monday and Thursday; and begged the indulgence of his readers for any errors and misreports which are 'the common fate of Discurses relating to Publick Affairs'. Unfortunately, the paper was not a success and was discontinued after only three issues. Six months later, in April 1682, Baldwin started the *London Mercury*, printed by Thomas Vine, an equally enthusiastic anti-Bourbon colleague, which was to be another failure, lasting only six months.

Not content with the *Mercury*, on 24 April 1682, Baldwin had also launched *The Protestant Courant, Imparting News Foreign and Domestick*. A two-sided sheet with just four columns, it did, however, carry about 25 per cent of advertising matter, including those for purging and purifying the blood. Also included was a poem, *Upon the death of the late Usurper, Oliver Cromwell*, written by John Dryden. Born in 1631, Dryden was at that time Poet Laureate, with a stipend of £300 a year.

From the first issue, Baldwin was determined that the *Protestant Courant* should live up to its name and prove a worthy competitor to the loyalist papers, the *Observator* and the *Heraclitus Ridens*. However, publication of the *Courant* was not without its difficulties, as he so sublimely declared in the issue of 1–6 May:[24]

> Whereas the paper (according to our Promise) have come out on Thursday last. These are to give Notice that some of the Popish Crew .... despairing of totally suppressing it, were resolved to try an experiment on the Printer, which did and detained him so long in Merry Company, that he wanted time to finish the Paper by the day appointed, so that now we have changed our Printer and our Days, and hereafter these Papers every Wednesday and Saturday.

Unfortunately, the *Protestant Courant* was to be another short-lived venture, and within weeks it had closed, but not before Baldwin, in its fifth issue, had taken the opportunity of attacking Sir Roger L'Estrange. On the front page, he was described as a 'Papist, proved by several Depositions upon Oath, etc., or for Declaring him as an Enemy of Parliament and the Protestant Religion'. Surprisingly, L'Estrange, still Surveyor of the Press, did nothing.

Baldwin's repeated libels of the Stuart regime did not find favour with the officers of the Stationers' Company, and in the spring of 1682 his house was searched and he was 'perfidiously taken in Execution in a Publick Coffee House'. He was subsequently fined £10 6*s*. for his derogatory remarks, and was informed that the writ for his seizure had been issued at the request of the Master of the Company, Thomas Vere. The reply was swift and scathing: in the next issue of the *Protestant Courant*,

Baldwin described Vere as 'one of so High Birth that he is ignorant of the Original of his Family but to be sure he claims Adam for his first Ancestor'.

Despite his short-lived venture into newspapers, Baldwin was now a successful publisher with a succession of anti-Stuart books and pamphlets. His next adversary was the dreaded L'Estrange, who in January 1683 wrote to Sir Leoline Jenkins:[25]

> Had my importunities to have had the sifting of Baldwin prevailed, he should have either delivered up some persons more considerable than himself or not have been in a condition this day to do more mischief. Today is published by him a libel entitled *A Defence of the Charter and Municipal Rights of the City* written by Hunt of venomous malice against the King and the Duke, so far as I can judge by dipping into it.

It was to be six months, however, before the case came to court, when the Attorney General declared that 'the books in Baldwin's hands may be seized by warrant from any judge of the King's Bench and detained till the matter be determined'. Bearing in mind the unfortunate experience of fellow-printer John Twyn in his brush with L'Estrange and the law, Baldwin must be considered a lucky individual.

In March 1688, Baldwin launched yet another newspaper, with the quaint title of *An Account of the Proceedings of the Meetings of the Estates of Scotland*; and within the next three years he sponsored *The Dublin Intelligence*, a newspaper for Irish Protestants living in London; and followed it with *The Scottish Mercury*, which was designed to give 'a true account of the daily proceedings and most remarkable Publick Occurrences in Scotland'.

Among the many rivals to Baldwin's titles was *The True Protestant Mercury*, which in its issue of 8 January 1689 declared: 'News, Rare, New, True News, Delicate, Dreadful, Horrible, Bloody News from France and Ireland, you never heard the like before you were born.'[26] Another newspaper circulating during this period was the *Ladies Mercury*, which stated in its issue of 6 March 1693: 'All questions relating to love, etc, are still to be desired to be sent in to the Latin Coffee House in Ave Mary-Lane, to the Ladies' Society there, and we promise that they shall be weekly answered with all the Zeal and Softness becoming the sex.'

With the increase in his business, Baldwin had in 1691 moved to larger premises 'near the Oxford Arms in Warwick Lane'; and there he was to remain, in the shadow of Wren's masterpiece, the rebuilt St Paul's Cathedral. Three years later, on 11 August 1694, Baldwin's most successful and enduring newspaper, *The Post-Man*, was launched; a publication that was to outlast him by more than thirty years. It began as the oddly-titled *Account of the Publick Transactions in Christendom*, and was called, briefly, *The Holland Paquet Book*.

Opposition newspapers to be launched at this time included the *The Flying Post*, *The English Courant* and *The Weekly Messenger*. To service these titles, there was to emerge a new breed of scribes, among them Jean de Fonvive, a Huguenot exile, who was later to edit *The Post-Man*. As one of the capital's leading newspapers, *The Post-Man* appeared every Tuesday, Thursday and Saturday, and retained correspondents in Italy, Spain, Portugal, Flanders and Holland. Its renown was such that the Duke of Marlborough insisted that it alone should carry his front-line despatches.

Fonvive, reputed to be earning £600 per year as editor of *The Post-Man*, laid out his paper's policy in one of the early issues:

> I shall write to you as often as I shall have any subjects, but you must not always expect from me extraordinary things; so neither must you expect that I should take notice of all little trifles. This is the Province of the most Common News-Writers, with whom I do not deign in the least to interfere.

Coffee-House Readership

One of the chief sources of information for these news-writers was the coffee-house – and it also provided the basis for their newspapers' circulations. Towards the end of the century there were almost five hundred such premises in London, each with its own distinctive clientele. Describing the role of the news-writer, Thomas Macaulay wrote that:[27]

> He rambled from coffee-room to coffee-room collecting reports, squeezed himself into the Sessions Houses at the Old Bailey if there was an interesting trial, nay, perhaps obtained permission to the gallery in Whitehall and noticed how King and Duke looked. In this way he gathered material for weekly epistles destined to enlighten some country town or some bench of rustic magistrates. Such were the sources from which the inhabitants of the largest provincial cities, and the great body of the gentry and clergy learned almost all they knew of the history of their own time.

Among these coffee-houses was one owned by Edward Lloyd, who in 1692 moved to premises in Lombard Street, which soon became known as the centre of shipbroking and marine insurance. Four years later, in September 1696, he launched *Lloyd's News*, a two-page shipping and commercial paper, which appeared three times a week. However, it ceased publication on 26 February 1697, after only 76 issues.[28]

In the final issue, Lloyd had offended the government, leading the *Protestant Mercury* to comment: 'Mr Edward Lloyd was desired that the statement being groundless, and a mistake, he doe rectifie it in his next.' Lloyd refused and suspended publication. The closure of the paper, though, did not prevent Lloyd's coffee-house prospering in the next two decades, and it is mentioned by both Steele in *The Tatler* (no. 268) and Addison in *The Spectator* (no. 46) '. . . . my Papers of Minutes which I had accidentally dropped in Lloyd's Coffee-House, where the Auctions are usually kept'. In 1726, the paper was revived under the title *Lloyd's List* and still continues.

Meanwhile, in the autumn of 1695, Baldwin and his editor, Fonvive, were to commence a war of words with former associate Abel Roper, and in the 16 October issue of *The Post-Man* there appeared the following statement:

> Whereas I have for several months published a News Paper called the *Post Boy*, and the Historical Account I have now for some reasons thought fit to continue my Historical Account by the same Author, with the additional title of *The Post-Man* and to give notice that what advertisements shall be sent to me, shall be incerted in my News Paper as formerly.

Roper's retort, in his *Post Boy* the following week, was to the point:

> Whereas R. Baldwin did on Thursday last publish a Paper called the *Post-Man* where he could insinuate that the same was writ by the author of the *Post Boy*. This is to give notice that the Same is altogether False, for the author of the said *Post-Man* and Historical Account is Monsieur de Fonvive and the the *Post Boy* is, always was, writ by me, and no other. If any has occasion to insert Advertisements therein, they are desired to send them to A. Roper, J. Moxon and R. Beardwell.

A feature of the period was the Postscript, and in the issue of *The Post-Man*, dated 4–6 February 1696, Baldwin announced: 'This paper having found a General acceptance the Publisher has thought fit to add a Postscript on the 3d [third] side of the whole sheet which shall be done upon good Paper and shall contain all the most Remarkable occurences of any Gentleman or News Writer shall think fit to make use of them, etc.' The paper would be printed off a full rather than a half sheet, leaving pages 3 and 4 blank, and any late news could then be written on these blank sides.

Baldwin asserted, with some pride, that:

> They may have them at a very reasonable rate at the Publisher at the Oxford Arms in Warwick Lane, and there will be space left, for business of what other means they shall think proper to incert, they are designed to be publisht at 4 in the afternoon every Post day and will begin next week.

The success of this brought a host of imitations and forgeries; and so concerned were the publishers of *The Post-Man* that they were forced to list the booksellers and news hawkers from whom these newspapers were available.

Apart from two short-lived newspaper ventures – *The Pacquet of Advice from France* which appeared for six issues in April 1691 and *Mercurius Reformatus or The New Observator* which ran from April to November 1691 – Baldwin had maintained a sure touch. A string of publications had issued from his press, and among these were *The Gentleman's Journal; or the Monthly Miscellany*, which numbered contributions from Dryden and songs from Purcell. Another was *Miscellaneous Letters*, a literary journal, which included selections from 'English books printed in London' and a digest of foreign books.

Now a a prosperous businessman, Baldwin had in December 1692 been admitted to the livery of the Stationers' Company, and from his premises he continued to be a guardian of the Press, remaining ever scornful of the Bourbons and Papists. He had, however, been unwell for a number of years, and, after much suffering from consumption, he died at his premises and was buried in his native High Wycombe on 24 March 1698. His long-standing friend and customer, John Dunton, summed up the man in a fulsome and worthy tribute:[29]

> Mr Richard Baldwin. He printed a great deal, but got as little by it as John Dunton. He bound for me and others when he lived in the Old Bailey; but, after removing to Warwick Lane, his fame for publishing spread so fast, he grew too big to handle his small tools.
>
> Mr Baldwin having got acquaintance with Persons of Quality, he was now for taking a shop in Fleet Street; but Dick, soaring out of his element, had the honour of being a Bookseller but few months. However, to do Mr Baldwn justice, his inclinations were to oblige all men and neglect himself. He was a man of generous temper, and would take a

> cherishing glass to oblige a Customer. His Purse and his heart were open to all men that he thought honest; and his conversation was very diverting. He was a true lover of King William; and, after he came on the Livery, always voted on the right side.
>
> His wife, Mrs A Baldwin, in a literal sense was an helpmate, and eased him of all his publishing work; and since she has been a Widow, might vie with all the women in Europe for accuracy and justice in keeping accompts; and the same I heard of her beautiful daughter, Mary Baldwn, of whom her father was very fond. He was, as it were, flattered into his grave by a long consumption; and now lies buried in Wickham parish, his native place.

The death of Richard did not, however, mark the end of the House of Baldwin, for in his widow, Anne, he left a person determined to maintain his standards in an outspoken Protestant Press. Under her guidance, and the editorship of Fonvive, *The Post-Man* grew to become one of the most successful newspapers of the period, with a circulation of between 3800 and 4000. However, the largest-selling title remained *The Gazette,* which, printed on Mondays and Thursdays, sold 6000 copies. Four newspapers – *London Post, English Post, Flying Post* and *Review* – had circulations of less than 400, while the *Observator* sold 1000 and Abel Roper's *Post Boy* 3000.

Production of the newspapers was still basic, for using the hand press the printers could ink and pull only 250 single sheets in an hour. But, by working in relays, 2000 copies could be produced in eight hours; and with a popular newspaper such as *The Post-Man* four presses would be used so as to speed up production. Make-up remained simple, generally consisting of a single folio half-sheet, with two columns front and back, and a decorative masthead and initial drop letter.

Apart from the coffee-houses, the news vendors, or mercuries, were the chief means for the distribution of the newspapers. They controlled a circulation of some thousands in and around London, and, as a consequence, bore the brunt of the prosecution against the newspapers they distributed. John Dunton wrote of them: 'I might also characterize the honest (mercurial) women, Mrs Baldwin, Mrs Nutt, Mrs Curtis: Mrs Mallett, Mrs Croome, Mrs Taylor, and I must not forget Old Bennett, that loud-mouthed promoter of the *Athenian Mercury*.'

More than forty years later the unauthorized news vendors were still providing a problem for the authorities – only by then they were better organized. The Attorney-General could complain:

> By their Mercuries and Hawkers [they] not only dispose of them [unstamped newspapers] in great numbers in the streets of London and Westminster, but in all contiguous counties and have lately taken up a practice and have found means to disperse them 50 to 60 miles from London by their agents and hawkers some travelling on horse and others on foot going from town to town and house to house.

The Liberties of Alsatia

As the century was drawing to a close, so Fleet Street, with its abutting alleys and many small printing offices, was becoming more and more civilized – evidenced by the growing number of coffee-houses. However, there remained one area that still remained lawless – Alsatia. This ran south of Fleet Street and embraced the precincts of the former Whitefriars Monastery, extending from the Temple to Whitefriars Street and from Fleet Street to the Thames.[30]

After the monastery had been dissolved by Henry VIII, the buildings and lands had been given to William Butte, the royal physician. The property, however, soon fell into disrepair; and in 1580, in return for attending St Paul's, the inhabitants were allowed by Elizabeth I to appoint their 'own officers, arrest any rogues found in the precincts and look after their own poor'.

In 1608, these privileges had been confirmed by James I, and as as result Alsatia – named after the disputed territory between France and Germany – soon developed into an area of complete lawlessness, abounding in brothels and crime. Alsatians accepted no liability for taxes; they accepted no responsibility for cleaning their ordure-piled alleys.

Having a myriad of entries and exits from their disorderly boltholes, they mocked any authority which tried to apprehend them. They were a complete community – including their own dissipated parsons who had to be dug out of a bawdy house or brandy shop when wanted. They were a remarkable exercise in human bestiality and fit material for Hogarth who drew them.

As Walter Scott was to write in *The Fortunes of Nigel*:

> The wailing of children, the scolding of their mothers, the miserable exhibitions of ragged linens hung from the windows to dry, spoke the wants and distresses of the wretched inhabitants; while the sounds of complaint were mocked and overwhelmed by the riotous oaths, shouts, profane songs and boisterous laughter that issued from the ale-houses and taverns, which as the signs indicated were equal in number to all the other houses, and, that the full character of the place might be evident, several faded, tinselled and painted females looked boldly at strangers from their open lattices.

One facet of Alsatia was the unlawful 'Fleet Street marriage' performed by 'parsons' who would place advertisements in Fleet Street shops and taverns. One of the most notorious was the *Hand and Hen* public house near Fleet Ditch – and the usual sign was a male and female hand conjoined. For these marriages, a fee between 12*s*. and £1 was charged, with no questions asked. Many unlawful marriages also took place in the nearby Fleet Prison, 'solemnized' by ordained men who had been thrown into prison for debt. Such was the demand that in the four months beginning 19 October 1704 almost three hundred 'weddings' took place. This practice was allowed to continue until Fleet marriages were declared void by Lord Hardwicke's Marriage Act, 1753.

Macaulay was later to write that 'at any attempt to extradite a criminal, bullies with swords and cudgels, termagent hags with spits and broomsticks poured forth by the hundred and the intruder was fortunate if he escaped back into Fleet Street, hustled, stripped and jumped upon'. In 1688, Thomas Shadwell described the area in his play *The Squire of Alsatia*:[31]

> I'll rout this lot of most pernicious knaves, for all the privileges of your place. Was ever such impudence suffered in a Government? Ireland's conquered; Wales subdued; Scotland united; but there are some few spots of ground in London, just in the face of the

> Government unconquered yet, that hold in rebellion still. Methinks 'tis strange that places so near the King's Palace should be no part of his dominions . . . . Should any place be shut against the King's writ?

Daniel Defoe, himself a one-time resident, wrote of Alsatia in *Moll Flanders*. However, it was not until 1697 that King William, strict to his Protestant standards, abolished its privileges.

As for the Press and Fleet Street, since 1695 censorship had been allowed to lapse – and Milton's dream of 'liberty of unlicensed printing' was finally realized. It was to be a short-lived freedom, however, for within a matter of a few years the newly unfettered Press was no more . . . .

2

The first daily newspaper

ON 8 MARCH 1702, King William's death ushered in the reign of Queen Anne, a reign which was to coincide with a period of extraordinary riches in English letters. This was the age of Jonathan Swift, Joseph Addison, Richard Steele, Alexander Pope and Daniel Defoe – and the time of *The Tatler* and *The Spectator.*

Three days later, on 11 March 1702, there occurred a momentous event in English journalism: the first daily newspaper, *The Daily Courant*, was launched by Edward and Elizabeth Mallet, 'next Door to the King's Arms Tavern at Fleet Bridge'. The son of a stationer and printer, Edward Mallet came from a Somerset family; and his wife, Elizabeth, has been described as a 'Mercury woman who had a stall or shop near Fleet Ditch in Fleet Street' and was 'known during the hard times of James the Second's reign as the publisher of the lists of Judge Jeffries' victims in the West'.

Priced one penny, *The Daily Courant* was printed on one side only, and consisted of just two columns, containing six paragraphs translated from the *Haarlem Courant*, three from the *Paris Gazette* and one from the *Amsterdam Courant*; and at the end of the second column there was an 'Advertisement', which set out the Mallets' policy:[1]

> It will be found from the Foreign Prints, which from time to time, as Occasion offers, will be mention'd in this Paper, that the Author has taken Care to be duly furnish'd with all that comes from Abroad in any Language. And for an Assurance that he will not, under Pretence of having Private Intelligence, impose any Additions of feign'd Circumstances to an Action, but give his Extracts fairly and Impartially; at the beginning of each Article he will quote the Foreign Paper from whence 'tis taken, that the Publick, seeing from what Country a piece of News comes with the Allowance of that Government, may be better able to Judge of the Credibility and Fairness of the Relation: Nor will he take upon him to give any Comments or Conjectures of his own, but relate only Matter of Fact; supposing other People to have Sense enough to make Reflections for themselves.
>
> *This Courant (as the Title shews) will be Publish'd Daily; being design'd to give all the Material News as soon as every Post arrives: and is confin'd to half the Compass, to save the Publick at least half the Impertinences of ordinary News-Papers.*

The entire first issue, remarkably, contained not one item of home news and consisted of just 104 lines in ten paragraphs; and, according to Daniel Defoe, 'it prospered mightly', the complete print run being sold out before noon in the City.

The Daily Courant.

Wednesday, March 11. 1702.

From the Harlem Courant, Dated March 18. N. S.

Naples, Feb. 22.

ON Wednesday last, our New Viceroy, the Duke of Escalona, arriv'd here with a Squadron of the Galleys of Sicily. He made his Entrance drest in a French habit; and to give us the greater Hopes of the King's coming hither, went to Lodge in one of the little Palaces, leaving the Royal one for his Majesty. The Marquis of Grigni is also arriv'd here with a Regiment of French.

Rome, Feb. 25. In a Military Congregation of State that was held here, it was Resolv'd to draw a Line from Ascoli to the Borders of the Ecclesiastical State, thereby to hinder the Incursions of the Transalpine Troops. Orders are sent to Civita Vecchia to fit out the Galleys, and to strengthen the Garrison of that Place. Signior Casali is made Governor of Perugia. The Marquis del Vasto, and the Prince de Caserta continue still in the Imperial Embassador's Palace; where his Excellency has a Guard of 50 Men every Night in Arms. The King of Portugal has desir'd the Arch-Bishoprick of Lisbon, vacant by the Death of Cardinal Sousa, for the Infante his second Son, who is about 11 Years old.

Vienna, Mar. 4. Orders are sent to the 4 Regiments of Foot, the 2 of Cuirassiers, and to that of Dragoons, which are broke up from Hungary, and are on their way to Italy, and which consist of about 14 or 15000 Men, to hasten their March thither with all Expedition. The 6 new Regiments of Hussars that are now raising, are in so great a forwardness, that they will be compleat, and in a Condition to march by the middle of May. Prince Lewis of Baden has written to Court, to excuse himself from coming thither, his Presence being so very necessary, and so much desir'd on the Upper-Rhine.

Francfort, Mar. 12. The Marquiss d' Uxelles is come to Strasburg, and is to draw together a Body of some Regiments of Horse and Foot from the Garisons of Alsace; but will not lessen those of Strasburg and Landau, which are already very weak. On the other hand, the Troops of His Imperial Majesty, and his Allies, are going to form a Body near Germesheim in the Palatinate, of which Place, as well as of the Lines at Spires, Prince Lewis of Baden is expected to take a View, in three or four days. The English and Dutch Ministers, the Count of Frise, and the Baron Vander Meer, and likewise the Imperial Envoy Count Lowenstein, are gone to Nordlingen, and it is hop'd that in a short time we shall hear from thence of some favourable Resolutions for the Security of the Empire.

Liege, Mar. 14. The French have taken the Cannon de Longie, who was Secretary to the Dean de Mean, out of our Castle, where he has been for some time a Prisoner, and have deliver'd him to the Provost of Maubeuge, who has carry'd him from hence, but we do not know whither.

Paris, Mar. 13. Our Letters from Italy say, That most of our Reinforcements were Landed there; that the Imperial and Ecclesiastical Troops seem to live very peaceably with one another in the Country of Parma, and that the Duke of Vendome, as he was visiting several Posts, was within 100 Paces of falling into the Hands of the Germans. The Duke of Chartres, the Prince of Conti, and several other Princes of the Blood, are to make the Campaign in Flanders under the Duke of Burgundy; and the Duke of Maine is to Command upon the Rhine.

From the Amsterdam Courant, Dated Mar. 18.

Rome, Feb. 25. We are taking here all possible Precautions for the Security of the Ecclesiastical State in this present Conjuncture, and have desir'd to raise 3000 Men in the Cantons of Switzerland. The Pope has appointed the Duke of Berwick to be his Lieutenant-General, and he is to Command 6000 Men on the Frontiers of Naples: He has also settled upon him a Pension of 6000 Crowns a year during Life.

From the Paris Gazette, Dated Mar. 18. 1702.

Naples, Febr. 17. 600 French Soldiers are arrived here, and are expected to be follow'd by 3400 more. A Courier that came hither on the 14th. has brought Letters by which we are assur'd that the King of Spain designs to be here towards the end of March; and accordingly Orders are given to make the necessary Preparations against his Arrival. The two Troops of Horse that were Commanded to the Abruzzo are posted at Pescara with a Body of Spanish Foot, and others in the Fort of Montorio.

Paris, March. 18. We have Advice from Toulon of the 5th instant, that the Wind having long stood favourable, 22000 Men were already sail'd for Italy, that 2500 more were Embarking, and that by the 15th it was hoped they might all get thither. The Count d' Estrees arriv'd there on the Third instant, and set all hands at work to fit out the Squadron of 9 Men of War and some Fregats, that are appointed to carry the King of Spain to Naples. His Catholick Majesty will go on Board the *Thunderer*, of 110 Guns.

We have Advice by an Express from Rome of the 18th of February, That notwithstanding the pressing Instances of the Imperial Embassadour, the Pope had Condemn'd the Marquis del Vasto to lose his Head and his Estate to be confiscated, for not appearing to Answer the Charge against him of Publickly Scandalizing Cardinal Janson.

ADVERTISEMENT.

IT will be found from the Foreign Prints, which from time to time, as Occasion offers, will be mention'd in this Paper, that the Author has taken Care to be duly furnish'd with all that comes from Abroad in any Language. And for an Assurance that he will not, under Pretence of having Private Intelligence, impose any Additions of feign'd Circumstances to an Action, but give his Extracts fairly and Impartially; at the beginning of each Article he will quote the Foreign Paper from whence 'tis taken, that the Publick, seeing from what Country a piece of News comes with the Allowance of that Government, may be better able to Judge of the Credibility and Fairness of the Relation: Nor will he take upon him to give any Comments or Conjectures of his own, but will relate only Matter of Fact; supposing other People to have Sense enough to make Reflections for themselves.

This Courant (as the Title shews) will be Publish'd Daily: being design'd to give all the Material News as soon as every Post arrives: and is confin'd to half the Compass, to save the Publick at least half the Impertinences, of ordinary News-Papers.

LONDON. Sold by *E. Mallet*, next Door to the *King's-Arms* Tavern at *Fleet-Bridge*.

After just nine issues, *The Daily Courant* was being published by Samuel Buckley 'at the sign of the *Dolphin* in Little Britain' (near St Paul's Cathedral); and within a month was printed on both sides of the sheet. By the end of the first year the paper had a page and half of news translated from French and Dutch newspapers, some shipping items and a half column of advertisements. Buckley himself had excellent connections at the Hague, then the centre of European news, and with a good knowledge of languages was able to do his own translations. However, he did not rely entirely on Dutch newspapers for his information, and gained access to a source that was altogether more privileged: the British Embassy at the Hague.[2]

Apart from being his own news collector, Buckley was also editor, chief writer 'as well as on emergency not only publisher but printer'. One of his main features was a daily letter from the French capital, 'manufactured out of the shapeless paragraphs, though containing all he wanted, in the *Paris Gazette*'. Under his guidance, *The Daily Courant* soon became a four-page paper and, on occasions, rose to six pages with some ten advertisements – and a circulation of more than 800. Although the 'well-educated, gentleman civil servant' Buckley was editor, the real power lay with Lord Godolphin, the Secretary of State – Sir Robert Walpole's predecessor. Writing to Godolphin in 1708, Defoe offered the opinion that 'the excellent *Daily Courant* seemed to be doing very well in the skilful hands of its principal writer, Samuel Buckley' and was run by some twenty booksellers 'whose aim is to gain of it'.

But the copying of material from Continental newspapers was not without its hazards, and, following the publication of an article in the *Courant* of 7 April 1712, Buckley appeared before a specially appointed House of Commons committee.[3] He told the committee that he had copied the offending article from a Dutch newspaper; and upon a divided vote the publisher was taken into custody. Arising from this episode, the committee met five days later to consider licensing the Press, and on April 22 reported to Parliament with a series of twelve resolutions which were to form the basis of the Stamp Act.

As for the *Courant*, it continued to be published daily for more than thirty years, and for much of that time was receiving subsidies and news favours from official sources. For instance, in 1713 the government was paying for 750 copies of the *Courant* to be sent to the Post Office every post day; in 1732 for 850, and in 1733 for 900. *The Daily Courant* survived until June 1735 when it was suddenly terminated. Its primary function of defending the ministry 'was deemed no longer necessary in the present happy calm which is spread over His Majesty's affairs'. *The Daily Courant* was then merged with the *Free Briton* and the *London Journal* to form the *Daily Gazeteer*, which declared that 'to render our paper still more generally entertaining, we shall sometimes make a digression from politics and insert essays on miscellaneous subjects'.

'Father of English Journalism'

During the early years of *The Daily Courant*, one journalist stood out above all others – Danel Defoe, who has been dubbed the 'Father of English Journalism'. Born at Cripplegate, London, in 1660, he was the son of James Defoe, a butcher, and educated at Morton's Academy for Dissenters at Newington Green with a view to entering the ministry. However, after travelling extensively on the Continent, he married Mary Tuffley in 1683 and become a hosiery merchant at Cornhill. He then took part in Monmouth's Rebellion, and in 1688 joined the supporters of William of Orange. Four years later, Defoe was bankrupt, but in 1695 his fortunes changed and he secured a civil service post.

Within two years he was to publish his first important work, *Essay upon Projects*, where he commented on such subjects as schooling, finance and lunatic asylums. This was followed by *The True-Born Englishman* in 1701, a stinging satire in support of William III; and the following year he wrote, anonymously, a savage pamphlet, *The Shortest Way with Dissenters*. So magniloquent were his suggestions putting forward the High Church point of view that the irony was generally missed: found out, a £50 reward was then offered for his arrest. He was, according to the notice posted up in Fleet Street taverns and on city walls, 'a middle-sized, spare man, about forty years old, of a brown complexion, and dark brown-coloured hair, but wears a wig; a hooked nose, a sharp chin, grey eyes and a large mole near his mouth.'[4]

Arrested, he was imprisoned at Newgate pending his trial. Pleading guilty, he was sentenced to stand three times in the pillory, to pay a fine, to remain in prison during the Queen's pleasure and to find sureties for his good conduct during the next seven years. Dreading the ordeal, on 31 July 1703, alongside Temple Bar, Fleet Street, Defoe was locked in the pillory; but he was received not with eggs and abuse but with flowers, and men drank his health. His *Hymn to the Pillory* published that morning 'was earning him money from eager purchasers around his "curious throne"':

> Tell them the men that placed him here
> Are scandals to the times:
> Are at a loss to find his guilt
> And can't commit his crimes.

Through the offices of Robert Harley, a Whig politician – and future Tory Secretary of State – he was pardoned in November 1703 and released from prison. Three months later, in February 1704, Defoe launched *A Weekly Review of the Affairs of France; Purg'd from the Errors and Partiality of News-Writers and Petty Statesmen of All Sides*; and in an early issue commented: 'Governments will not be jested with, nor reflected upon. Learn this and you will prosper.' This publication was to be a milestone in the early history of English journalism. It was not really a newspaper; but it contained better writing and far more constructive criticism than anything that had preceded it, including the 'Scandal Club', which anticipated such magazines as *The Tatler* and *The Spectator*. Beginning as a weekly, it was then produced twice weekly, and from the second year appeared three times a week. The paper lasted nine years and Defoe wrote it single-handed. The title was shortened to *The Review*, and, apart from politics, there were articles on social and commercial topics.[5]

Although stressing that he was completely independent in his writing for *The Review*, he was greatly influenced by Harley, and years later Defoe was to say:

> Let anyone put himself in my stead! and examine upon what principles I could ever act against either such a Queen, or such a Benefactor! . . . Let any man who knows what principles are, what engagements of honour and gratitude are, make this case his own! And say what I could have done less, or more, than I have done.

A condition of Defoe's release had been that he was to act as a secret agent for Harley; and between 1703 and 1714 he travelled around the country, gathering information and checking political opinion. Continuing his pamphleteering, Defoe was not discouraged by possible further spells in prison: in 1713 he published three pamphlets on the Succession Question, and wrote a comment in his *Review*, actions that led to a brief imprisonment for contempt of court – and a warning from one of the judges that he might come to be hanged, drawn and quartered.

He was in trouble again the following year with a letter to *The Flying Post*, held to be a libel on the Earl of Anglesey, one of the Lords Regent. Defoe was released and not tried until 1715, when he was found guilty; but, through the offices of Townshend, the Whig Secretary of State, the prosecution was not pursued. For this, Defoe switched his allegiance to the Whigs, ostensibly writing for Tory periodicals such as *Mist's Weekly Journal*.

His first contribution in the *Journal* was on 3 August 1717, in which he set out a manifesto, which proclaimed that the paper would not be disloyal and would provide the most up-to-date foreign news. For the next few years, Defoe was to be a regular contributor, and his articles, plus Mist's outspokenness, were to lead the proprietor into conflict with the government. It was not, however, until December 1720 that Nathaniel Mist was found guilty at the Guildhall of 'scandalously reflecting the King's interposition in favour of Protestants abroad'. He was sentenced in February 1721 to stand in the pillory at Charing Cross and at the Royal Exchange, to pay a fne of £50, to be imprisoned for three months and to be bound over for seven years. Like Defoe, on a previous occasion, Mist was well treated by the mob while in the pillory; but unable to pay his fine he was kept in prison.[6]

Meanwhile, Defoe in 1719, when aged nearly 60, had published *Robinson Crusoe*; and his career took a new turn as he became a successful author. During the next twelve years Defoe's other titles included *Moll Flanders* and *Journal of the Plague Year*, and throughout his life he was to produce almost six hundred books, pamphlets and journals. He died at his lodgings in Ropemakers' Alley, Moorfields, and was buried at Bunhill Fields, where his grave is marked by an obelisk erected through public subscriptions 150 years later.

Defoe was to sum up his journalistic style in the following: 'If any man was to ask me what I would suppose to be a perfect style of language, I would answer, that in which a man speaking to five hundred people of all common and various capacities, idiots or lunatics excepted, should be understood by them all.'

As for his former colleague, Nathaniel Mist had continued to be a scourge of the authorities. In May 1721 he was brought before the House of Commons for publishing an article criticizing the King and the Duke of Marlborough; and, refusing to reveal the names of his writers, he was committed to Newgate Prison. He remained there until the end of the year, when, with no evidence brought against him, he was released. A further libel on the government in 1724 led to a fine of £100 and 12 months' imprisonment and an order to 'find sureties for good behaviour during life'.

With sales of between 8000 and 12,000 copies per issue, *Mist's Weekly Journal* was one of the most popular periodicals of its day, and a good vehicle for advertisements. In the issue of 22 May 1725 Mist could declaim:[7]

> There is a great deal of useful learning sometime to be met in Advertisements. I look upon mine to be a kind of Index of All Arts and Services, they contain the Advices both from the learned and unlearned World; Fools and Philosophers may there meet with equal Matter to divert and amuse themselves.

Two years later, on 15 September 1727, a warrant was issued for the arrest of Mist for a libel on George I. Mist was fined £100 and once more ordered to give security for his good behaviour, and he was kept in prison until the year's end. In January 1728, Mist fled to Rouen, but with the aid of his friends still managed to publish his paper. However, in the August, yet another libel – this time against George II – led to more than twenty people being arrested, and the following month the printing press was destroyed on the orders of the government. Nevertheless, the government did not always prosecute newspapers automatically for any alleged infringements:

> Prosecutions ought to be avoided as much as possible. For papers of this kind, if not taken notice of, seldom survive the week, and fall into very few hands; but when a prosecution is commenced everybody is enquiring after them, and they are read by thousands . . . . [However] where His Majesty's title is called into question, or there are insinuations in favour of the Pretender, I think that prosecutions are absolutely necessary.

Not beaten, a week later there appeared the first issue of *Fog's Weekly Journal*, and in it Mist, in a signed article, wrote: 'Dear Cousin Fog, The Occasion of my present Address to you, is to acquaint you, that I was lately seiz'd with an Apoplectic Fit, of which I instantly died.' He continued to publish this paper until his death of asthma on 20 September 1737.[8]

As an outspoken critic of the authorities, Mist was to summon up his credo in one of his leaders: 'English men have always looked upon it as part of their right to speak and write upon public affairs.'

A strong rival to Mist's journals during this period was Nicholas Amhurst's *The Craftsman*, launched on 5 December 1726. Under the pseudonym of Caleb D'Anvers, of Grays-Inn Esq., he vigorously opposed the policies of Sir Robert Walpole. At its peak, *The Craftsman* had a circulation of more than 10,000 copies; and with the assistance of William Pulteney and Viscount Bolingbroke – with his scathing 'Remarks on the History of England' under the pseudonym of Humphrey Oldcastle – it became one of the most important political journals of the age.

However, on 2 July 1737 there appeared in the paper an ironical letter purported to have been written by Colley Cibler, the poet laureate, suggesting that the new licensing act for plays should be extended to cover old plays and that he should be appointed the licenser. For this 'suspected libel' the printer was arrested by warrant, but Amhurst took his place, only being released through *habeas corpus*. When

Numb. 59

The TATLER.

By *Isaac Bickerstaff* Esq;

Quicquid agunt Homines nostri Farrago Libelli.

From *Tuesday August* 23. to *Thursday August* 25. 1709.

White's Chocolate-house, August 24.

Æ*SOP* has gain'd to himself an immortal Renown for figuring the Manners, Desires, Passions, and Interests of Men, by Fables of Beasts and Birds: I shall in my future Accounts of our modern Heroes and Wits, vulgarly call'd *Sharpers*, imitate the Method of that delightful Moralist; and think, I cannot represent those Worthies more naturally than under the Shadow of a Pack of Dogs; for this Set of Men are like them, made up of Finders, Lurchers, and Setters. Some search for the Prey, others pursue it, others take it; and if it be worth it, they all come up at the Death, and worry the Carcass. It would require a most exact Knowledge of the Field, and the Harbours where the Deer lie, to recount all the Revolutions in the Chase: But as I intend to write for the Preservation of the Game, rather than the Instruction of the Pursuers, I shall content my self with only giving Notice to all, that the Hounds are out, and letting 'em know their several Faculties. But I am diverted from the Train of my Discourse of the Fraternity about this Town by Letters from *Hampstead*, which give me an Account, there is a late Institution there, under the Name of a *Rattling-Shop*, which is, it seems, secretly supported by a Person who is a deep Practitioner in the Law, and, out of Tenderness of Conscience, has, under the Name of his Maid *Sisly*, set up this easier Way of Conveyancing and Alienating Estates from one Family to another. He is so far from having an Intelligence with the rest of the Fraternity, that all the humbler Cheats who appear there, are fac'd by the Partners in the Bank, and driv'n off by the Reflection of superior Brass. This Notice is giv'n to all the silly Faces that pass that Way, that they may not be decoy'd in by the soft Allurement of a Fine Lady, who is the Sign to the Pageantry. And at the same Time Signior *Hawksly*, who is the Patron of the Houshold, is desir'd to leave off this interloping Trade, or admit, as he ought to do, the Knights of the Industry to their Share in the Spoil. But this little Matter is only by Way of Digression. Therefore to return to our Worthies: The present Race of Terriers and Hounds would starve, were it not for the enchanted *Actæon*, who has kept the whole Pack for many Successions of Hunting Seasons. *Actæon* has long Tracts of rich Soil; but had the Misfortune in his Youth to fall under the Power of Sorcery, and has been ever since, some Parts of the Year, a Deer, and in some Parts a Man. While he is a Man, (such is the Force of Magick) he only grows to such a Bulk and Fatness, which as soon as he arrives at, he is again turn'd into a Deer, and hunted till he is lean; upon which he returns to his human Shape. Many have been the Arts try'd, and many the Resolutions taken by *Actæon* himself, to follow such Methods as would break the Inchantment; but all have hitherto prov'd ineffectual. I have therefore, by Midnight Watchings and much Care, found out, that there is no Way to save him from the Jaws of his Hounds, but to destroy the Pack, which, by Astrological Præscience, I find I am destin'd to perform. For which End I have sent out my Familiar, to bring me a List of all the Places where they are harbour'd, that I may know where to sound my Horn, and bring 'em together, and take an Account of their Haunts and their Marks, against another Opportunity.

Will's Coffee-house, August 24.

The Author of the ensuing Letter, by his Name, and the Quotations he makes from the Ancients, seems a Sort of Spy from the old World, whom we Moderns ought to be careful of offending; therefore I must be free, and own it a fair Hit where he takes me, rather than disoblige him.

SIR,

'HAving a peculiar Humour of desiring to be somewhat the better or wiser for what I read, I am always uneasy when, in any profound Writer, (for I read no others) I happen to meet with what I can't understand. When this falls out, 'tis a great Grievance to me that I am not able to consult the Author himself about his Meaning; for Commentators are a Sect that has little Share in my Esteem. Your elaborate Writings have, among many others, this Advantage, that their Author is still alive, and ready (as his extensive Charity makes us expect) to explain whatever may be found in them too sublime for vulgar Understandings. This, Sir, makes me presume to ask you, How the *Hamstead* Hero's Character could be perfectly new when the last Letters came away, and yet Sir *John Suckling* so well acquainted with it Sixty Years ago? I hope, Sir, you will not take this amiss: I can assure you, I have a profound Respect for you; which makes me write this, with the same Disposition with which *Longinus* bids us read *Homer* and *Plato*. *When in reading* (says he) *any of those celebrated Authors, we meet with a Passage to which we cannot well reconcile our Reasons, we ought firmly to believe, that were those great Wits present to answer for themselves, we should to our Wonder be convinc'd, that we only are guilty of the Mistakes we before attributed to them.* If you think fit to remove the Scruple that now torments me, 'twill be an Encouragement to me to settle a frequent Correspondence with you, several Things falling in my Way which would not, perhaps, be altogether foreign to your Purpose, and whereon your Thoughts would be very acceptable to

Your most Humble Servant,

Obadiah Greenhat.

I own

Amhurst had served his purpose, his political friends made a compromise and deserted him. He died at Twickenham in 1742 of a broken heart and was indebted to his printer, Richard Franklin, who paid for his tomb.

Steele and Addison

But the two most important publications of this period, by far, were *The Tatler* and *The Spectator*. Since its launch on 12 April 1709 – as a thrice-weekly, two-page paper intended to cater for the urbane tastes of all those who frequented the coffee-houses – *The Tatler* had been in the hands of Richard Steele, and of the 271 issues until it ceased publication Joseph Addison wrote just forty-two.

Born in Dublin, Steele had been educated at Charterhouse with Addison and at Merton College, Oxford, from where he entered the Guards, becoming a captain and secretary to Lord Cutts, Colonel of the Coldstreams. Steele's first significant work was *The Christian Hero* (1701), where he displayed his missionary and reforming spirit. There then followed three comedies: *The Funeral* (1703), *The Lying Lover* (1703) and *The Tender Husband* (1705). Although to a degree prophetic, the plays came too early to succeed.[9]

In 1707, Steele was appointed gazeteer of *The London Gazette*, enabling him to have access to political news, but within two years he was able to launch *The Tatler*, thereby announcing a new style of journalism that was to develop into the modern weekly review. In the first issue, he announced that it was to include 'Accounts of Gallantry, Pleasure and Entertainment . . . . under the Article of White's Chocolate House; poetry under that of Will's Coffee-House; foreign and domestic news from St James's Coffee-House.' And it was the 500-odd coffee-houses that were to provide Steele with the bulk of his circulation – and with most of the sources of his information.

In Steele, *The Tatler* had the right man as editor and proprietor. Here was a scholar, a soldier, a wit and a person from the correct background: his viewpoint was that of a reasonable Christian gentleman, far removed from the savagery of Jonathan Swift. Nevertheless, Steele was acutely aware that his new periodical must be accepted by the readers of the coffee-houses, as he was to declaim: 'We writers of diurnals are nearer in our styles to that of common talk than any other writers.'

Two years later, on 21 May 1709, in *The Tatler*, he was to comment further upon his fellow-writers:

> The ingenious fraternity of which I have the honour to be an unworthy member: I mean the news-writers of Great Britain, whether Postmen or Postboys, or by what other name or title so ever dignified or distinguished. The case of these gentlemen is, I think, more hard than that of soldiers, considering they have taken more towns and fought more battles. They have been upon parties or skirmishes where our armies have lain still, and given the general assault of many a place where the besiegers were quiet in their trenches. They have made us masters of several strong towns many weeks before our generals could do it, and completed victories when our courageous captains have been content to come off with a drawn battle. Where Prince Eugene has slain his thousands Boyer [owner of the

> *Post-Boy*] has slain his ten thousands. This gentleman can, indeed, never be commended for his courage and intrepidity during the whole war. He has laid about him with inexpressible fury, and like an offended Marius of ancient Rome, made such havoc among his countrymen as must be the work of two or three ages to repair.

Despite its success, in January 1711 *The Tatler* ceased publication, its closure providing a huge shock for its readers, and causing playwright John Gay to comment: 'The coffee-houses realised that it had brought them more customers than all their other News Papers put together.'[10]

Within days of *The Tatler*'s demise, the indefatigable Mrs Baldwin had sponsored a *New Tatler*, edited by William Harrison, a young poet and protégé of Jonathan Swift. As the widow of Richard Baldwin, she had carried on the family business as publisher of *The Postman;* and its popularity had encouraged her to produce a French translation for distribution among the London Huguenots and for sale on the Continent. For the Whig Party, from October 1710 to August 1711, she issued on Mondays and Fridays *The Medley*, edited by Arthur Maynwaring, a member of the Kit-Kat Club, and assisted by Steele.

The *New Tatler* made its first appearance on 13 January 1711, and Swift, writing to his pupil and friend, Stella, reported: 'Today little Harrison's *New Tatler* came out. There is not much in it, but I hope he will mend. You must understand that upon Steele's leaving off, there were two or three Scrub *Tatlers* come out, and one of them holds on still and today it is advertised against Harrison's. I am afraid the little toad has not the true vein for it.' Swift's fears were well founded, for within weeks the periodical was in serious financial trouble and in May 1711 it ceased publication.

Although political reasons have been suggested for the demise of *The Tatler*, it is likely that Steele and Addison were more interested in producing a daily publication; and on 11 March 1711 they launched *The Spectator*, the aim of which was to 'enliven morality with wit and to temper wit with morality'. The paper was quickly accepted in the world of gracious living, 'inhabited by people living in Queen Anne houses and sitting on Queen Anne chairs; people who would ride in one of the 800 hackney coaches or 200 hireable sedan chairs'.

Co-partner in *The Spectator*, Joseph Addison was the son of the Dean of Lichfield, and, as noted, educated at Charterhouse with Richard Steele before Queen's College, Oxford, and Magdalen, where he was a Fellow from 1698 to 1711. A distinguished classicist, he soon attracted the attention of Dryden with his Latin poems. As a supporter of the Whig Party, Addison entered Parliament for Lostwithiel in 1708, and twelve months later was elected as MP for Malmesbury, remaining its Member until his death. In 1709, he was appointed Chief Secretary to the Lord Lieutenant of Ireland, and it was from there that he had sent suggestions and articles to *The Tatler*.[11]

Virtually a daily, *The Spectator* ran until 6 December 1712, and during this period 555 issues were produced, of which Addison was responsible for 274 and Steele for 236. In its first issue, Addison announced: 'Thus I live in the world rather as a Spectator of mankind, than as one of its species.' The number of coffee-houses in London had now risen to more than one thousand, and everywhere the paper was read and discussed; and as Addison wrote: 'About half-a-dozen ingenious men live very plentifully about this curiosity of their fellow-subjects.' *The Spectator* reigned supreme: the antics of Sir Roger de Coverley and his friends were greeted everywhere with delight; and, as conceived by Addison, Mr Spectator was the very epitome of the new journalist; a man who knew everything and everybody. From his lofty position, Addison could comment on the rest of the Press and their treatment of the news:

> They all of them receive the same advices from abroad, and very often in the same words; but their way of cooking it is so different that there is no citizen, who has an eye to the public good that can leave the coffe-house with peace of mind, before he has given every one of them a reading.

Addison could also quote Socrates in his leaders:[12]

> It was said of Socrates, that he brought philosophy down from heaven to inhabit among men; and I shall be ambitious to have it said of me, that I have brought philosophy out of closets and libraries, schools and colleges, to dwell in clubs and assemblies, at tea-tables and in coffee-houses. I would therefore in a very particular manner recommend these are my speculations to all well-regulated families, that set apart an hour every morning for tea and bread and butter; and would earnestly advise them for their good to order this paper to be punctually served up, and to be looked upon as part of the tea equipage

Steele, though, was more prosaic when discussing the advertisements in *The Spectator*:

> The advertisements are accounts of news from the little world, in the same manner that the foregoing parts of the paper are from the great. Here people find out where they may be furnished with almost everything that is necessary for life. If a man has pains in his head, colics in his bowels, or spots on his clothes, he may here meet with proper cure and remedies.

From the beginning, the paper had been a success, with daily sales of more than 3000. Every copy had many readers; and, because not all who wanted to read the paper could afford to buy it daily, it was collected and bound periodically – and a first printing of 10,000 copies of the bound volume was not unusual.

Unfortunately, the introduction by Parliament of a Stamp Tax on 1 August 1712 was to herald the end of *The Spectator*. Addison could comment on 31 July, in issue 445:[13]

> This is the day on which many eminent authors will probably publish their last works. I am afraid that few of our weekly historians, who are men above all others that delight in war, will be able to subsist under a Stamp Duty with an approaching peace. In short, the necessity of carrying a stamp, and the impracticability of notifying a bloody battle, will, I am afraid, both concur to the sinking of those thin folios which have every other day related to us the history of Europe for several years past. A facetious friend of mine, who loves a pun, calls this present mortality 'the fall of the leaf'.

Addison was to be correct, for within five months *The Spectator* had folded, the chief casualty of the government's Stamp Tax. In *The Spectator*, Addison had found his ideal literary form: the essay. He had raised it to new heights of subtlety and wit, and created a fictitious club presided over by Mr Spectator with the assistance of Sir Roger de Coverley and others, winning a host of admirers. Virginia Woolf was to be in no doubt over his merits: 'There still remains the fact that the essays of Addison are perfect essays . . . . undoubtedly it is due to Addison that prose is now prosaic – the medium which makes it possible for the people of ordinary intelligence to communicate their ideas to the world.'

As for the co-founders: on the closure of *The Spectator*, Addison penned his classical tragedy *Cato*, which was a big success on the stage. That same year he wrote for Steele's new periodical, *The Guardian*, and then, in 1714, revived *The Spectator*. However, it was not the success he had hoped for, running for just 80 numbers (556–635). Within months, Addison was to launch his political newspaper, *The Freeholder*, which lasted from 1715 to 1716. He then married the Countess of Warwick, and two years later retired from public office with a pension of £1500. Unfortunately, his final years had been marred by a quarrel with Steele. Addison died in 1719 and was buried in Westminster Abbey, lamented by Thomas Tickell in *The Death of Addison* and satirized by Alexander Pope as Atticus in *Epistle to Dr Arbuthnot*.

Steele's final years, though, were to be of mixed fortune:[14] in March 1713 he launched *The Guardian* as a professional, non-political journal. Once again he was assisted by Addison, who contributed articles, plus Berkeley, Pope and Gay. However, with circulation falling, it came to a sudden end in the October after Steele had fallen out with Tonson, his publisher. Within weeks, Steele had started *The Englishman*, a more political newspaper, and this was to be followed by *The Lover*, in the style of *The Spectator*, and *The Theatre*, a bi-weekly, which continued until 1720.

Seven years earlier, in 1713, Steele had been elected MP for Stockbridge, but his publication of articles in *The Englishman* and *The Crisis* in favour of the Hanoverian succession led to his expulsion from the House of Commons on 18 March 1714. Although the Press was now no longer under the control of the Crown, Ministers were able to take their revenge on individuals – this in spite of a spirited defence of Steele by future Prime Minister Sir Robert Walpole: 'The liberty of the press is unrestrained; how then shall a part of the legislature dare to punish that as a crime, which is not declared to be so by any law passed by the whole.'

However, with the accession of George I, Steele's fortunes changed, being appointed Supervisor of Drury Lane Theatre, and knighted in 1715. After issuing pamphlets against the South Sea Company, he produced his last comedy, *Conscious Lovers*, in 1722; and two years later, beset by debts, he left London and died at Carmarthen in 1729.

Although as an essayist Steele was overshadowed by Addison, he was among the first to associate himself with the emerging middle class; and may, rightly, be considered one of the founders of modern journalism.

The First Woman Editor

During this period, one of the closest rivals of Steele and Addison had been Mrs Mary de la Riviere Manley, known as 'Mrs Crackenthorpe, A Lady that knows everything'. Born in 1663, she was the daughter of Sir Roger Manley, a Royalist and Lieutenant-Governor of Jersey. A prolific author, in 1696 she published *Letters Written by Mrs Manley* and that same year had two plays produced: *The Lost Lover or the Jealous Husband* and *The Royal Mischief*.[15]

However, her best-known and most infamous work was her book, *Secret Memoirs and Manners of Several Persons of both Sexes from the Atlantis*; and as a consequence she was arrested on 29 October 1709 for 'defaming several persons of quality'. Released on bail, she was finally discharged by the Court of Queen's Bench the following February. The previous summer, on 8 July 1709, as editor, she had launched *The Female Tatler* – the first-known woman editor of the British Press. Following a row with Benjamin Bragge, her printer, from issue no. 19 production of *The Female Tatler* was transferred to Mrs Anne Baldwin, since she [Mrs Crackenthorpe] had been 'disengenuously treated' by Bragge. Here, indeed, was to be a fearsome combination.

The periodical was now in competition with *The Tatler*, but was published on 'contrary days'. Although *The Female Tatler* was first and foremost a gossip sheet, Mrs Crackenthorpe masked the text with high ideals. She was, in fact, one of the first 'agony aunts', as her advice in an issue of October 1709 showed:

> The young lady in the Parish of St Laurence near Guild Hall, that lately went into the Coffee House in Man's Cloathes with two 'Prentices called for a Dish of Bohee, smoak'd her Pipe and gave herself an abundance of Stroddling Masculine Airs, is desir'd to do so no more.

Despite being a success, *The Female Tatler* was not without its critics, especially among those who had been libelled, and late in 1709 Mesdames Baldwin and Crackenthorpe found themselves indicted by the Grand Jury of Middlesex, which declared that

> A Great Number of printed papers are continually dispersed under the name of *The Female Tatler* sold by A. Baldwin and other papers under other Titles .... which .... reflect on and scandously abuse several persons of honour and quality, many of the magistrates and abundance of citizens and all sorts of people.

Appearing before the Grand Jury, Mrs Manley informed them that 'if there had been any reflections on living characters the offence had been quite accidental'. And, with her being discharged, there the matter rested. The editor, though, was now proving a liability even for the redoubtable Mrs Baldwin, and early the following year the ladies dissolved their partnership. As for Mrs Crackenthorpe, she regretfully announced her retirement because of 'an affront offer'd to her by some rude citizens, altogether unacquainted with her person'.[16] For the remainder of its short life, until March 1710, *The Female Tatler* was to be conducted by 'A Society of Ladies'.

Mrs Manley was next involved in writing pamphlets for Jonathan Swift, and in June 1711 she replaced him as editor of *The Examiner*, a political weekly. Swift had resigned because of the threats from enemies he had made through his venomous pen. In his final issue (no. 45) Swift gave his reasons: 'Those little barking Pens which have so constantly pursu'd me, I take to be of no further Consequence to what I have writ, than the scoffing Slaves of old, placed behind the Chariot, to put the general in mind of his Mortality.'

However, following six months as editor, Mrs Manley became very ill; and on 26 January 1712 Swift, her main supporter, wrote: 'Poor Mrs Manley the Author is very ill of Dropsy and sore leg. The printer tells me he is afraid she cannot live long. I am heartily sorry for her; she had very generous Principles for one of her sort; and a very great deal of Sense and Invention; she is about forty, very homely and very fat.' Swift was to be proved wrong. Mrs Manley lived another dozen years, only to die in the office of her lover and printer, Alderman John Barber, on 11 July 1724 – a fitting end for the first woman editor.

Stamp Duty Introduced

Throughout the great days of *The Tatler* and *The Spectator*, the Press had been unfettered, but the good times could not last; and on 1 August 1712, in response to a plea from Queen Anne for a remedy to 'the scandalous libels in the Press', Parliament levied a Stamp Tax of a halfpenny on papers up to half-sheet, of a penny up to a sheet, and of two shillings on more than a whole sheet. Advertisements were to be taxed at one shilling irrespective of length.

Writing on 9 July, Swift commented: 'This Grub-street has but ten days to live.' Three weeks later he was to observe: 'Grub-street is dead and gone last week; no more Ghosts or Murders now for Love or Money . . . . *The Observator* is fallen, *The Medleys* are jumbled together with the *Flying Post*, the *Examiner* is deadly sick, the *Spectator* keeps up, and doubles its price. I know not how long it will hold.'[17]

However, the introduction of the Stamp Tax by Parliament did not have the desired effect of permanently reducing the sales of newspapers, as trade was increasing and with it the size and power of the commercial classes. Despite this punitive measure, by 1750 the combined circulations of newspapers had trebled. One immediate effect, however, had been a decline in the sales of daily newspapers and those of an essay-type nature. The demise of *The Spectator* had marked the end of an era, as few people were now prepared to purchase this type of publication: the future belonged to the thrice-weeklies such as *The Post-Man* (which were intended mainly for country distribution) and, above all, the weekly newspapers.

The Stamp Act of 1712, which was to be the basis of newspaper legislation throughout the eighteenth century, required that the sheets of paper should be stamped at the Head Office, Somerset House, The Strand, while they were still blank. Immediately before the Act's introduction, Addison wrote in *The Spectator* on 31 July: 'A sheet of Blank Paper . . . . must have this Imprimatur clapt upon it, before it is qualified to communicate anything to the Publick.' Its appearance was greeted by Swift in writing to Stella on 7 August: 'Have you seen the red stamp the press are marked with? Methinks, it is worth a halfpenny, the stamping of it.'

In an effort to bypass the Act, astute publishers took to issuing papers consisting of one-and-a-half sheets (six pages),[18] and so common was this between 1714 and 1724 that new legislation was introduced for George I on 5 April 1725. One result was that the proprietors of both the six-page journals and the thrice-weeklies were forced to raise their prices to *2d.* and *1d.* respectively and curtail the size of their papers to four pages. It did not take the printers long, however, to realise that there was an omission in the Act: the restriction on the size of the page. This led, increasingly, to a large number of four-page newspapers as half-sheets, from which was to evolve a change in the make-up of the page from two to three columns.

Despite these strictures, an unregistered Press continued to flourish, and it has been estimated that there were at least thirty such titles circulating in London during this period. This undergound Press has been cited by Samuel Negus, a government agent, who was himself a printer, with offices in Silver Street, City of London, as the principal cause of the 1715 rebellion and disturbances. And it was during this period that Negus wrote a letter to the Secretary of State, Viscount Townshend, in which he produced his *Complete and Private List of all the Printing-houses in and about the Cities of London and Westminster, together with the Printers' names, what Newspapers they print and where they are to be found.*

He divided the list into four categories: 'Those well affected to King George I of thirty-four printers, of whom he and James Roberts were two; Nonjurors [those who refused to swear allegiance] consisting of three names; said to be High Flyers, some 34 names; and Roman Catholics, just four people.' His list revealed:[19]

> Daily papers: *Daily Courant*, Buckley, Amen Corner; *Daily Post*, Meere, Old Bailey; *Daily Journal*, Appleby, near Fleet Ditch.
>
> Weekly journals: *Mist's Journal*, Carter Lane; *Freeholder's Journal*, Sharp, Ivy Lane; *Read's Journal*, Whyte Friars in Fleet Street; *London Journal*, Wilkins, Little Britain; *Whitehall Journal*, Wilkins, Little Britain.
>
> Papers published three times every week: *Post Man*, Leach, Old Bailey; *Post Boy*, James, Little Britain; *Flying Post*, Jenou, Giltspur Street; *Berrington's Evening Post*, Wilkins, Little Britain; *St James's Post*, Grantham, Paternoster Row; *The Englishman*, Wilkins, Little Britain.
>
> Half-penny Posts, three times every week: *Heathcote's*, Baldwin Gardens; *Parker's*, Salisbury Court; *Read's*, Whyte Friars in Fleet Street.

Following his breakdown of the London newspaper offices, Negus could also inform the Secretary of State that there should be 'no surprise at the present ingratitude and dissatisfaction of a rebellious sort of men. They have no way to vend their poison but by the help of the press. Thus printing houses are daily set up and supported by unknown hands.' Negus added: 'The country printers in general copy from the rankest papers in London, and thus the poison is transmitted from one hand to another through all his majesty's dominions.'

He concluded: 'It is impossible, my good Lord, to reduce the number of printers to what they once were; yet I would humbly inform your lordship there are many of them who give great offence and disturbances to the State, and who never have been brought up to that business and ought to be put down.'

Of the newspapers mentioned by Negus, *The London Journal* was one of the most outspoken against the government, evidenced by the Cato Letters which ran in 144 issues from November 1720 until December 1723. Written by John Trenchard and Thomas Gordon, the Letters covered many subjects, including the South Sea Bubble and an attack against a proposal to revive Press censorship because of the frequent libels and seditious opinions. In Letter no. 32, Cato wrote: 'As long as there are such things as printing and writing, there will be libels; it is an evil arising out of a much greater good . . . . I must own that I would rather many libels escape should the liberty of the Press be infringed.'

As for the printers – whether registered or not – all were held responsible for the legal contents of their papers. They considered it their duty not to pass on the names of any offending writers to the courts, even if they themselves would have escaped liability. The printing craft, generally, was very strict on this code, although in 1719 John Matthews, on the evidence of two of his apprentices, was found guilty of high treason in a publication.

The Sage of Fleet Street

The literary giant of the eighteenth century was, undoubtedly, Dr Samuel Johnson. Born at Lichfield in 1709, the son of a bookseller, he was educated at Lichfield Grammar School and Pembroke College, Oxford, but left after fourteen months without taking his degree. Following a short spell as an under-master at Market Bosworth, he entered journalism as a contributor to the *Birmingham Journal*, a weekly started by Thomas Warren in 1733, where he furnished 'some numbers of a political essay to the newspaper'. Two years later, Johnson married Mrs Elizabeth Porter, a widow twenty years older, and started a private school near Lichfield.[20] It was not a success, and in 1737 with David Garrick, one of his pupils, he left for London. Johnson's first work there was for Edward Cave, founder of *The Gentleman's Magazine*, writing essays, poems and Latin verse.

One of the capital's most prominent publishers, Edward Cave had been educated at Rugby School, from where he was expelled 'for robbing the principal's hen-roost'. He then went to London and was apprenticed to Deputy Alderman Collins, a well-known printer, but within two years Cave was sent to Norwich to manage and edit *The Norwich Courant*. Moving back to the capital, he married a young widow and became a writer on *Mist's Weekly Journal*, while at the same time acting as London correspondent for county newspapers at Canterbury, Gloucester and Stamford: this involved writing news-letters at one guinea each. One result, however, was that he and Robert Raikes, of *The Gloucester Journal*, were imprisoned for breach of privilege. A contrite Cave, having served just 10 days, paid a heavy fine and was duly released.

With enough money saved to buy a print shop at St John's Gate, Clerkenwell, Cave in 1731, under the imprint R. Newton, launched *The Gentleman's Magazine*. From the first issue it was a great success, and by 1739 had sales of more than 10,000. Much of this success was due to its political reportage, for in 1732 Cave had begun regular publication of parliamentary debates, thanks to his reporter William Guthrie, who had a prodigious memory.

By bribing the doormen, Guthrie was smuggled into the House of Commons, listened to the debate and then wrote his copy outside Parliament. The material was not normally published until the end of the parliamentary session, and care was taken only to use the initials of MPs. For eight years, Cave and Guthrie managed to report Parliament in this manner until it was treated as a breach of privilege – and as a result publication was prohibited, not only during Parliament but also any time afterwards. In June 1738, the House resolved that:[21]

> It is a high indignity to, and a notorious Breach of the privilege of this House, for any News-Writer, in Letters or other Papers .... or for any Printer or Publisher of any News-papers, or of any Denomination, to presume to insert in the said Letters or Papers, or to give therein any Account of the Debates, of other Proceedings of this House .... as well during the Recess as the Sitting of Parliament.

To get around this ban, parliamentary reports were now presented as the record of the proceedings in the Senate of Lilliputia, and the various speakers were provided either with Roman names or anagrams of their real names

In November 1740 Johnson began to report these proceedings, an arrangement which lasted until February 1743. And at a later date, when complimented on his coverage of a particular speech made by William Pitt, he told his dining companions that he had written the speech in Essex Street, off Fleet Street, adding:

> I never had been in the gallery of the House of Commons but once. Cave had interest with the doorkeeper. He and the persons employed under him gained admittance: they brought away the subjects of discussion, the names of the speakers, the sides they took, and the order with which they rose, together with notes of arguments adduced to the course of the debate. The whole was afterwards communicated to me and I composed the speeches in the form they now have in the 'Parliamentary Debates', for the speeches of that period were all printed in Cave's magazine .... I saved appearances tolerably well, but I took care that the Whig dogs should not have the best of it.

Apart from working on *The Gentleman's Magazine*, Johnson had also published in 1738 his poem *London*, a satire in imitation of Juvenal, and in 1743 his *Life of Mr Richard Savage*. Two years later, with the assistance of Dodsley, the bookseller and publisher, he embarked on his majestic *Dictionary of the English Language*; and from his new home in Gough Square, off Fleet Street – with the aid of six assistants – wrote the definitions of 43,500 words, illustrated by 118,000 quotations.[22] After eight years of 'harmless drudgery', it was published in two large volumes in 1755; and as a result he received his long-overdue Oxford MA and fame. (He was to become LLD, Dublin, 1765, and Oxford 1775.)

As a relief from the Dictionary, and partly for money, in 1750 Johnson had launched *The Rambler*, published twice a week at twopence, but its circulation was never more than 500 copies an issue and it lasted barely two years – evidenced by Lady Mary Wortley writing to Lady Bute on 23 July 1752:

> *The Rambler* is certainly a strong misnomer. He always plods in the beaten road of his predecessors, following the *Spectator* (with the same pace a packhorse would do a hunter) in the style that is proper to lengthen a paper . . . . I should be glad to know the name of this laborious author.

In the final issue, Johnson wrote: 'I never have been much of a favourite with the public.' Nevertheless, when reprinted in volume form, his essays were to achieve a considerable success. Johnson's next incursion into journalism was as a regular contributor to the *Universal Chronicle or Weekly Gazette*, and from 1758 to 1760 his *Idler* articles were to achieve great popularity. In one of his early pieces, 27 May 1758, discussing the Press, he wrote:

> The compilation of newspapers is often committed to narrow and mercenary minds, not qualified for the task of delighting or instructing, who are content to fill their papers with whatever matter is in hand . . . . The tale of the morning paper is told in the evening and the narratives of the evening are brought out again in the morning.

His comments on fellow-scribes on 11 November 1758 were equally scathing:[23]

> A news-writer is a man without virtue who writes lies at home for his own profit. To these compositions is required neither genius nor knowledge, neither industry nor sprightliness, but contempt of shame, indifference to truth are absolute.

In 1762, Johnson's efforts were rewarded with a Crown pension of £300 per annum; and the following year he met James Boswell in the bookshop of his friend, Thomas Davies, in Covent Garden. Within a matter of months, Johnson had founded his Club, whose members included Edmund Burke, Oliver Goldsmith, David Garrick and Joshua Reynolds. A later member was to be Boswell, whose *Life of Samuel Johnson*, published in 1791, gives a vivid account of those years: 'I talked of the cheerfulness of Fleet Street owing to the constant quick succession of people passing through it.' Dr Johnson: 'Why, Sir, Fleet Street has a very animated appearance, but I think the full tide of human existence is at Charing Cross.'

Now rightly a colossus in the literary world, Johnson's next work, published in 1765, was his edition of Shakespeare, in which he received aid from George Steevens. In 1773 he travelled with Boswell to Scotland and the Hebrides, recorded in *A Journey to the Western Islands of Scotland* (1755); and, following a visit to Wales in 1774 and to Paris the following year with the Thrales, in 1777 he began to write his final work, *The Lives of the Most Eminent English Poets* (1779–81). He was now estranged from Mrs Thrale, his close companion; and deeply saddened at this state of affairs he died at his home in Bolt Court in 1784, and was buried at Westminster Abbey.

As for Cave, Johnson's first publisher, in 1747 he had been in trouble once more, for printing accounts of the trial of Lord Lovat. On paying fines and begging pardon on his knees he was discharged with a reprimand. Meanwhile, from 1742 until 1748 he was also producing an occasional magazine, *Miscellaneous Correspondent*, and for Johnson *The Rambler.* A large man, Cave suffered from gout, and from 1736 took the waters at Bath for almost twenty years until his death at St John's Gate on 10 January 1754. He is buried at St James's Church, Clerkenwell.

A rival of Cave during this period was Henry Fielding, who between 1729 and 1737 wrote more than two dozen plays; and so popular was he with his anti-government satires – culminating in *The Historical Register for 1736* – that Prime Minister Walpole introduced the Licensing Act of 1737, allowing censorship by the Lord Chamberlain, thus effectively bringing Fielding's career in the theatre to a close.

Two years later Fielding, who had already written anonymously for Swift's *Craftsman*, launched the *Champion*, a thrice-weekly anti-Jacobite newspaper,[24] edited and largely written by himself between 1739 and 1740. 'I do not live within a mile of Grub Street,' he declared, 'nor am I acquainted with a single inhabitant of that place. I am of no party – a word which I hope, by these my labours, to eradicate out of our constitution.' Modelling the *Champion* on Addison's *Spectator*, he used a group of imaginery characters as writers, including Captain Hercules Vinegar, whose political articles were the main features of the journal. But, short of money, Fielding turned to studying for the law, and in 1740 he was called to the Bar, becoming a JP in 1748 and Chairman of the Quarter Sessions in 1749.

Nevertheless, Fielding did not abandon journalism. In particular he continued to publish his *True Patriot*, and in the first issue, 5 November 1745, vented his spleen on contemporary newspapers:[25]

> There is scarcely a syllable of TRUTH in any of them. If this be admitted to be a fault, it requires no other evidence than themselves and the perpetual contradictions which occur, not only on comparing one with another, but the same author with himself on different days. Second, there is no SENSE in them. Thirdly, there is in reality NOTHING in them at all. Such are the arrival of my Lord— with a great equipage, the marriage of Miss— of great beauty and merit; and the death of Mr— who was never heard of in life etc.

Unfortunately, the *True Patriot* was not popular with the public and closed after a few months. During this period, Fielding had also been busy as a novelist with *An Apology for the Life of Mrs Shamela Andrews* (1741), *The Adventures of Joseph Andrews and his Friend, Mr Abraham Adams* (1741), his masterpiece *The History of Tom Jones, a Foundling* (1749) and *Amelia* (1751) which, at the time, had the best sales of all his works.

In 1752, Fielding returned to journalism with his *Covent-Garden Journal*, which ran for eleven months; and its contents, apart from general news and essays, contained a column of reports from Bow Street Court, where he sat as a magistrate. Now suffering from asthma and gout, and on crutches, Fielding left for Portugal to recuperate, but he died at Lisbon in October 1754, and was buried there. Walter Bagehot later wrote of him: 'Fielding's essence . . . . was a bold spirit of bounding happiness.'

Another novelist who became involved in journalism at this time was Tobias Smollett. who, with the aid of Archibald Hamilton, headed a syndicate 'The Society of Gentleman' to launch the monthly *Critical Review* in 1756. Three years later, following a libel on Admiral Sir Charles Knowles, Smollett was fined £100 and imprisoned for three months. His next post was as editor of the *British Magazine; or*

Monthly Repository for Gentlemen and Ladies, before, at the instigation of Prime Minister Lord Bute, he launched the short-lived *Briton*.

Wilkes the Radical

During the 1760s two outspoken campaigns which were to have a profound effect on the Press were instigated: the first concerned John Wilkes, parliamentarian, libertine and publisher of *The North Briton*. As a journalist he was responsible for securing the tacit removal of the ban on reporting parliamentary debates; and he believed passionately in the right to criticize the government. His public victories were, perhaps, even more important: the vindication of the freedom of the electorate and the abolition of the general warrant, which specified the offence but not the persons to whom it was committed.[26]

Born in 1727 the son of a Clerkenwell distiller, he was educated at Leyden; and in 1757 was elected MP for Aylesbury. Five years later, with the assistance of Charles Churchill, he launched *The North Briton,* a six-page paper; and in the first issue, 5 June 1762, announced:

> The Liberty of the Press is the birthright of a Briton, and is justly esteemed the finest bulwark of the liberties of the country. It has been the terror of all bad ministries; for their dark and dangerous designs, or their weakness, inability, and duplicity, have thus been detected, and shown the public generally in too strong colours for them long to bear up against the odium of mankind.

Week after week he published scurrilous attacks on the Earl of Bute and the Scottish influence on the court of the newly-crowned George III. The attacks reached their peak on 23 April 1763, with the famous issue no. 45, in which Wilkes wrote a lengthy and highly damaging article on the King's Speech, for which he was arrested for libel on a general warrant:[27]

> Every friend of his country must lament that a prince of so many great and amiable qualities, whom England truly reveres, can be brought to give sanction of his sacred name to the most odious measures, and to the most unjustifiable declarations, from a throne ever renowned for truth, honour and unsullied virtue. I wish as much as any man in the kingdom to see the honour of the crown maintained in a manner truly becoming Royalty. I lament to see it sunk even to prostitution.

In all, 48 people – writers, printers, publishers – were arrested; and Wilkes, as an MP, issued a writ of *habeas corpus*. He appealed to the court in masterly fashion:

> My Lords, the liberty of all peers and gentlemen, and, what touches me more sensibly, that all the middling and inferior set of people, who stand most in need of protection, is in my case this day to be finally decided upon a question of such importance as to determine at once whether English liberty shall be a reality or a shadow.

Lord Chief Justice Pratt upheld the appeal of privilege, and Wilkes was released from custody to be borne back in triumph to Westminster to cries from the crowd of 'Wilkes and Liberty!' Wilkes and his co-defendants then sued the government, winning more than £100,000 in damages and expenses. However, the matter was not to rest there, for in the ransacking of Wilkes's house a copy of *Essay of Woman*, a pornographic parody of Pope's *Essay of Man*, had been found. The House of Lords ruled that it was 'a most scandalous, obscene and impious libel'; and moving the resolution was Lord Sandwich, a one-time member of the Hell-Fire Club with Wilkes, and the greatest rake of his day. On a previous occasion, Sandwich had received from Wilkes one of the most devastating retorts on record: 'Wilkes, you will either die of a pox or on the gallows,' Sandwich said. 'That depends, my Lord,' came the immediate response, 'whether I embrace your mistress or your principles.'

Found guilty of republishing *The North Briton* and of publishing *Essay of Woman*, and having been wounded in a duel, Wilkes departed for France, and in his absence was declared an outlaw. An attempt to burn copies of *The North Briton* outside the Royal Exchange led to a riot, with the law officers being roughly handled.

In 1768, Wilkes returned from exile, and, although technically still an outlaw, stood as MP for the City of London but was rejected. Standing next for Middlesex, he won by more than four hundred votes. Twice he was refused his seat; and the third time the government put up its own candidate, Colonel Luttrell, who was elected even though he polled fewer votes. London was now in an uproar and everywhere the sign '45' was to be seen. Benjamin Franklin noted that 'there was not a door or window to be found in the City that was not marked with the figure "45", and this continued here and there quite to Winchester which is sixty-four miles'.[28]

During this period of the Middlesex elections and his constant rejection, Wilkes was in jail, having been fined £1000 and sentenced to 22 months' imprisonment for the reprinting of no. 45 and the publishing of *Essay of Woman*. Even though incarcerated, his popularity with the people never waned, and as Edmund Burke so aptly observed: 'Since the fall of Ld. Chatham there has been no man of the Mob but Wilkes.'

If parliamentary parties could overrule the wishes of the people and install their own men, who were open to corruption and who would vote accordingly, then elections meant nothing. The mobs readily seized upon this and London was rife with excitement, reaching its peak with the Massacre of St George's Field on 19 May 1768, when a dozen rioters were killed by the military.

During the next six months, passions gradually cooled until Wilkes published in *The St James's Chronicle* on 10 December a copy of a most indiscreet letter sent by Lord Weymouth to the local magistrates before the massacre. This urged the use of troops 'when the Civil power is trifled with and insulted, nor can a military Force ever be employed on a more constitutional Purpose, than in Support of the Authority and Dignity of the Magistracy'. Making the most of the situation, Wilkes noted in his introduction to the letter 'how long the horrid Massacre in St George's Field had been planned and determined upon, and how long a hellish Project can be brooded over by some infernal Spirits without one Moment's Remorse'.

Wilkes was not alone in his fight, for in April 1769 William Beckford, the Lord Mayor of London, and other supporters launched *The Middlesex Chronicle or Chronicle of Liberty* 'to vindicate the cause of depressed liberty by exhibiting in full view of the people every measure that has already been taken and every attempt that may further be made'. The Letters of Junius, which had first appeared in the *Public Advertiser* on 21 January 1769 advocating a free Press,[29] were now also having an effect; and following a 'Letter to the King', 19 December 1769 (also reprinted in five other newspapers), the government prosecuted. Of the newspapers involved, two were found guilty, two were acquitted and two were not tried.

One result of the Junius trial was that the reporting of parliamentary debates increased – and with greater accuracy. To counteract this, on 5 February 1771 Parliament reaffirmed a resolution of 1738 prohibiting the publication of its proceedings. John Wheble, in the *Middlesex Journal*, and R. Thompson, of the *Gazeteer*, were scathing in their comments on this decision. Both printers were summoned to appear before the House of Commons charged with 'misrepresenting the speeches and reflecting on several members'. It seems as if the whole affair had been orchestrated by Wilkes, as neither person put in an appearance. The writ was now extended to cover *The St James's Chronicle*, *Morning Chronicle*, *London Packet*, *Whitehall Evening Post*, *General Evening Post* and *London Evening Post*.

As a result Baldwin, *St James's Chronicle*, and Wright, *London Evening Post*, were made to kneel in penance before the Speaker, the last ever to do so. Baldwin rose in silence, ostentatiously brushed his knees, and in an audible aside remarked: 'What a damned dirty House.' A month later, Wilkes took the case a stage further, allowing Wheble to be arrested by E.T. Carpenter, a fellow-printer in the City. He was then brought before Wilkes himself, as sitting magistrate, at the Guildhall, and discharged. A similar happening occurred with Miller, another publisher, who had been apprehended at the authority of the Speaker. At the Guildhall, Lord Mayor Brass, Alderman Oliver and Wilkes demanded on 'What authority could a citizen of London be arrested within the jurisdication of its magistrates?' The Speaker's warrant, they declared, was illegal.

It was now a direct conflict between Parliament and the City: the Lord Mayor and Alderman Oliver were arrested, found guilty of breach of privilege, and sent to the Tower. At the end of the session they were released, to the roar of a 21-gun salute, and escorted in triumph by more than fifty carriages to the Mansion House. To the crowds a great victory had been won: the Press was finally free; the right to report parliament was secured.

Letters of Junius

The second campaign of this period advocating more freedom for the Press was that conducted by Junius in *The Public Advertiser*. In a series of Letters from January 1769-January 1772, he attacked among others George III, the Duke of Grafton, Lord North and Lord Mansfield. Full of scorn and biting invective, the Letters upheld the Whig cause and even that of John Wilkes. Fortunately, only one Letter led to the prosecution of its publisher and printer Henry Sampson Woodfall: Letter XXXV (19 December 1769) addressed to George III:[30]

> Sire – It is the misfortune of your life . . . . that you should never have been acquainted with the language of truth, until you heard it in the complaints of your people. It is not,

> however, too late to correct the error. You could shelter under the forms of parliament, and set your people at defiance or your could Discard those little, personal resentments which have too long directed your public conduct . . . . Come forward to your people . . . . Tell them you are determined to remove every cause of complaint against your government; that you will give your confidence to no man who does not possess the confidence of your subject.

The Letter concluded in the most telling of phrases:

> The prince who imitates their conduct should be warned by their example; and while he plumes himself upon the security of his title to the crown, should remember that as it was acquired by one revolution, it may be lost by another.

At a trial held at the Guildhall before Lord Justice Mansfield, an ambiguous verdict was returned by the jury of 'guilty and publishing only' and Woodfall was acquitted. (Interestingly, one of the jury was a 30-year-old coal merchant, John Walter, who 16 years later was to found the *Daily Universal Register* – later *The Times*.)

Celebrating the victory, Junius wrote:

> Let it be impressed upon your minds, let it be instilled into your children that the liberty of the Press is the palladium of all civil, political and religious rights of an Englishman . . . . The power of King, Lords and Commons is not an arbitrary power. They are the trustees not the owners of the Estate.

The identity of the writer caused a great deal of contemporary speculation. Edmund Burke, considered a likely candidate, was to inform Charles Townsend (another possible) on 17 October 1771: 'You observe rightly that no fair men can believe me to be the Author of Junius. Such a supposition might tend to raise the estimation of my powers of writing above their just value.' Junius, himself, was to declare: 'I am the sole depository of my own secret and it shall perish with me.'

It now seems likely that the author of the Letters was Sir Philip Francis (1740–1818), who was educated at St Paul's School with Woodfall, and worked in the Secretary of State's Office and the War Office from 1756 to 1772. Two years later he became one of the four newly-appointed councillors to the Governor-General of India. He left India in 1780 and assisted Burke in preparing the charges that were to lead to the impeachment of Warren Hastings.

Francis Williams was later to write of Junius: 'Few men in the history of journalism have been blessed with a bolder or more biting pen; none with a publisher, Henry Sampson Woodfall, more ready to stand behind him.'

A keen supporter of Junius and Wilkes during those years was John Almon, who in 1770 was convicted and ultimately bound over for twelve months for selling a copy of *The London Museum* containing Junius' Letter to the King. In later years, he was to edit the works of Junius. Almon, though, was to be better known for his remarks in 1784, when as proprietor and editor of *The General Advertiser* he was tried for libel before Lord Mansfield: 'A man had better make his son a tinker than a printer. The laws of tin he can understand, but the law of libel is unwritten, uncertain and undefinable . . . . It is sometimes what the King or Queen please; sometimes what the minister pleases; sometimes what the attorney-general pleases.'[31]

As for Woodfall, in 1779 he was found guilty of publishing a libellous handbill, fined 5*s.* 8*d.* and imprisoned at Newgate for twelve months. Five years later, Burke sued him for libel, claiming £10,000 in damages. Although successful, he was awarded only £100. Woodfall could say in later years 'that he had been *fined* by the House of Commons; *fined and confined* by the court of the King's Bench; and *indicted* at the Old Bailey'. He sold his interest in *The Public Advertiser* in November 1793, and retired from business the following month, when his premises in Paternoster Row were burnt down. Throughout more than thirty years as editor/proprietor of *The Public Advertiser*, Woodfall had determined that his newspaper should be what 'its correspondents please to make it'. He was proud to say that he never paid his writers, nor took bribes to publish government information. He was appointed Master of the Stationers' Company in 1797; and died at Chelsea on 12 December 1805.

3

Launching *The Times*

BY THE MID-CENTURY, Fleet Street had undergone many changes – despite Wren's dramatic plan to make a canal of the foul-smelling Fleet River from as far as Holborn Bridge to the Thames having been turned down. Wren had also proposed a Thames Quay, which would have provided an attractive and much-needed river frontage. However, the building of the Mansion House in 1737 had meant the removal of the stock market; and to accommodate the displaced traders the City Corporation had arched over the Fleet River from Ludgate Circus to Holborn Bridge at a cost of £10,256.

Within a dozen years there would be a new bridge over the Thames at Westminster; soon the City Corporation would clear away the houses and widen London Bridge; and in 1769, after many delays, Blackfriars Bridge would be opened to traffic. Notwithstanding irate letters from Dr Johnson, the Fleet River was now covered as far as the Thames – and London had lost a golden opportunity. Between 1760 and 1767, the City gates were taken down, footpaths were properly laid, but everywhere there remained chaos in the streets; and as George Wendeborn was to write: 'More people are seen in London at midnight than in many considerable towns of Europe at noon-day.'

Nevertheless, London was still a volatile city, and, as been seen with the Wilkes affair, its people were easily swayed with oratory and skilful – even if sometimes misguided – leadership. In June 1780 the crowds found a new champion: Lord George Gordon, leader of the recently-formed Protestant Association; and for five days the City was subjected to mob rule, much destruction of property, and, ultimately, intervention from the Army. The origins of the Gordon Riots lay in the Catholic Relief Bill of 1778, which for those prepared to take an oath of allegiance offered the ordinary civil rights of a citizen, although there was no move to give full political status.

Since the time of the Stuarts, Irish immigration had been a feature of London life, but in the reigns of the Georges it had increased greatly. Unfortunately, it was believed that the immigrants brought with them a lower standard of living which often depressed the native Londoners' wages. Indeed, this hatred against the Irish labourer was one of the causes of the feeling against Roman Catholics, and merely provided a further strand to Lord George Gordon's rhetoric.

On 2 June 1780 some 60,000 people gathered in St George's Fields, Southwark, before marching to Westminster to present a petition. There, amid turbulent scenes,

Members were not able to leave the Houses of Parliament until 11 p.m., when the Brigade of Guards had managed to clear a path. In the next few days, several Roman Catholic churches were set on fire, which resulted in five of the rioters being imprisoned in Newgate. The authorities were tardy in examining the petition; and on the Tuesday night the mob reacted violently: Newgate Prison was sacked and set on fire, and all the prisoners freed.

Urged on by the cry of 'No Popery',[1] the mob now turned its attention to Fleet Prison, and within hours it was just burnt-out rubble, with all the prisoners having been released. From his father's house, six-year-old Charles Baldwin, a future owner of *The Standard*, saw Lord George at the head of the rioters passing through Fleet Street on their way to the House of Commons: they filled the street as far as he could see and numbered many thousands. In later years, he would recall how the family had packed up their valuables in fear of their house being burned. He saw the smoking ruins of Newgate, and remembered one of the Horse Guards shooting a rioter. Private houses in Fleet Street, Fetter Lane and Shoe Lane were set on fire; and one honest citizen climbed to the top of the spire of St Bride's Church to escape the rioters.

The troops were called out on the express authority of the King, and, as a first priority, were ordered to guard the Bank and the Mansion House. Having fired Fleet Prison, the mob was met at the foot of Fleet Street by the Guards, who, after a volley into the crowd, set to with the bayonet. Twenty mutilated corpses were left on the street and thirty-five other rioters were seriously wounded. In all, 210 were killed by the soldiers, 248 wounded and 135 taken prisoner, of whom twenty-one were hanged.

Among those citizens helping to beat back the mob was the redoubtable John Wilkes, who led a group of volunteers after houses in New Bridge Street had been set on fire and the tolls at Blackfriars Bridge plundered. When the riots had died down, Wilkes, in his capacity as Alderman of the Ward of Farringdon Without, sat at the Globe Tavern, Shoe Lane, examining and sending to prison the rioters brought before him. As for Lord George Gordon, he was tried and acquitted. However, after a series of hare-brained political schemes, he insulted the French government, and as a result spent the last five years of his life imprisoned in the Tower of London.[2]

Dr Johnson in his Letters to Mrs Thrale was to leave a graphic account of the riots:

> On Tuesday night they pulled down Fielding's house, and burnt his goods in the street .... leaving Fielding's ruins they went to Newgate to demand their companions who had been seized demolishing the chapel .... all the prisoners released and Newgate in a blaze. On Wednesday I walked with Dr Scott to look at Newgate, and found it in ruins with the fire yet glowing.
>
> On Wednesday they broke open the Fleet and the King's Bench, and the Marsalsea and Wood Compter, and Clerkenwell Bridewell, and released the prisoners. At night they set fire to the Fleet and to the King's Bench, and I know not how many other places; and one might see the glare of the conflagration fill the sky from many parts. The sight was dreadful .... There has, indeed, been a universal panic from which the King was the first that recovered.
>
> The public has escaped a very heavy calamity. The rioters attempted the Bank on the Wednesday night but in no great number; and like other thieves with no great resolution.

> Jack Wilkes headed the party that drove them away. Jack, who was always zealous for order and decency, declares that if he be trusted with power, he will not leave a rioter alive .... Such was the end of this miserable sedition from which London was delivered by the magnanimity of the Sovereign himself.

Pitt and the Press

Now, less than four years later – with the riots a distant memory – and with William Pitt the Younger having become Prime Minister in December 1783, London was served by nine daily newspapers, five of which were devoted to advertising: *Daily Advertiser*, *Public Advertiser*, *General Advertiser*, *Public Ledger* and *London Gazeteer*. The others were: *Morning Herald*, *Morning Post*, *Morning Chronicle* and the *Citizen's Morning Post*. Ten other newspapers appeared two or three times weekly: *London Evening Post*, *Lloyd's Evening Post*, the *General Evening Post*, the *Whitehall Evening Post*, the *London Chronicle*, *The St James's Chronicle*, the *London Packet*, the *Middlesex Journal*, the *London Courant* and the *English Chronicle*.[3]

London was now about to get its first true evening newspaper, and this duly appeared on 3 May 1788: the *Star and Evening Advertiser*, which sold for threepence, and which announced in its prospectus that 'It has long been subject of complaint that the number of Morning Prints tend rather to confound than to inform.' (As far back as August 1706, the *Evening Post* had been launched, but it was published on Tuesdays, Thursdays and Saturdays only, timed to catch the country mails that left London on those nights). The *Star and Evening Advertiser*, though, appeared nightly; and 'aimed to report the debates in parliament, cover financial matters while not forgetting the discoveries and improvements in the arts, sciences and even in dress'.

Within months, however, there was discord between Peter Stuart, the chief proprietor, and his partners, and in February 1789 he broke away to launch the rival *Stuart's Star and Evening Star*. This, though, was a failure and closed after just sixty-four issues. Stuart's next venture, the *Morning Star*, was also unsuccessful, and ceased within weeks.

George Crabbe, a doctor/cleric/poet, from Aldeburgh, Suffolk, had a few years earlier commented on the state of the Press in his ode, *The Newspaper*, published in 1785:[4]

> For, soon as morning dawns with roseate hue,
> The *Herald* of the morn arises too,
> *Post* after *Post* succeeds, and all day long
> *Gazettes* and *Ledgers* swarm, a motely throng.
>
> When evening comes she comes with all her train
> Of *Ledgers*, *Chronicles*, and *Posts* again,
> Like bats appearing, when the sun goes down,
> From holes obscure and corners of the town.

Even though there was such a choice of newspapers in London, Dr Johnson's observations of journalists some years earlier still held good: 'They habitually sold their abilities, whether small or great, to one another of the Parties that divide us; and without a wish for Truth or Thought of Decency.'

Politically, Johnson was correct, for the Press was now facing significant changes. The loss of Britain's American colonies in 1776, followed by Lord Cornwallis's surrender to Washington's forces at Yorktown on 19 October 1781, thus ending the American War of Independence, had ensured that the government of Lord North must fall. The Whigs, now in power, had been determined to stop the war and to restrict the interference of George III in the working of parliament. And William Pitt the Younger, as the new Prime Minister, was leading a party which for the first time since the Commonwealth was the result of a genuine uprising of public feeling.

However, the triumph of Pitt when taking office was to herald a critical change in the political control of the Press, for despite his efforts to secure newspaper support he was subjected to unprecedented journalistic abuse. Determined to overcome this, he began to use the funds of the Secret Service to buy off the Press; and he also persuaded government agencies to deny recalcitrant newspaper proprietors inside information and official advertisements. The government could also cause trouble at the Stamp Office, thereby effectively restricting newspaper distribution.

Pitt was certainly no friend of the Press, for in 1789 he raised the Stamp Duty to twopence and increased the advertisement tax to *2s. 6d.* (Since the initial taxes of 1712, there had in 1757 been increases in duty of one penny on all newspapers, whether printed on a half-sheet or a full sheet, while the advertisement tax was raised to two shillings. This was to be compounded in 1776 with a further increase in the Stamp Duty to three-half-pence.)

Now, in 1789, and not content with these increases, Pitt even made it illegal for people to hire out newspapers, making those found guilty pay a penalty of £5 for each offence. In addition to Pitt's bribing of editors and proprietors, a large number of journalists were in the pay of the Treasury, receiving sums which ranged from a few guineas for an article to as much as £500 per annum for special cases.[5]

Within months of taking office, Pitt had bought the support of five newspapers: three dailies – *Public Ledger*, *London Evening Post* and the *Morning Herald*; and two tri-weeklies – *The St James's Chronicle* and the *Whitehall Evening Post*. The money was paid to the newspapers through third parties, thus 'Mr Harris for Mr Longman to be divided between the editors of the *Ledger*, *Saint James*'s and the *London Evening Post* £300'. In the words of Charles Pebody:

> If Pitt's object in instituting prosecutions and imposing stamp duties was to put a gag into the mouth of the Press, he soon found that he might just as well have left the Press alone. He silenced the *Courier* by purchasing it exactly as it stood – plant, copyright, lease of the office, and everything upon the premises – by turning out the editor and staff, and replacing them with a corps who instantly transformed the *Courier* into an organ of Constitutional loyalty. He established the *Sun*, placed it under the editorship of one of the Treasury clerks, and retained Peter Pindar *upon* its staff at a salary which, if not paid out of the Treasury, was probably paid by private subscription among the Ministers themselves.

It was against this background – despite the government's efforts to assume control – that a vibrant Press was now emerging. 'There was much public support, and provided the challenges to authority were not too blatant it is instructive how far a disciplined and well commanded pen might go. Specialisation proved to be a valuable screen behind which every kind of critical faculty might find expression.'

However, although the Press was now politically free, it was still prey to the laws of libel, and, until Fox's Libel Act of 1792 restored to juries the right to decide upon every indictment whether the defendant was guilty or not guilty, newspapers were at the mercy of the judges. One of the first to be affected had been Henry Baldwin, owner of *The St James's Chronicle*, for printing a letter of 29 January 1794[6] addressed to the First Lord of the Admiralty, the profligate Earl of Sandwich, asking him what were his reasons 'for appointing a Man to Command one of His Majesty's Ships, who has behaved notoriously ill in a neighbouring Service and dismissed from it with ignominy?' The man in question was Captain John Elphinstone, who had been present at the capture of Quebec, had served as a rear admiral in the Russian navy and had been the subject of both English and Russian criticism. An angry Elphinstone sued in the King's Bench for the printing of a libel: a verdict of guilty was reached in barely fifteen minutes – and damages were set at £500 with £8 costs.

A newspaper owner for more than thirty years, Henry Baldwin, the convicted party, had been apprenticed to Mary Say as a printer before launching *The St James's Chronicle or the British Evening Post* as a thrice-weekly paper on 14 March 1761. Shortly before its launch, Baldwin had purchased from fellow-printer William Rayner *The London Spy*, *Read's Weekly Journal* and *St James's Evening Post or British Gazette*. *The Spy* and *The Journal* were merged to form a Saturday paper, and the *St James's Evening Post* became *The St James's Chronicle*. Baldwin then formed a joint stock company to secure financial support; and among the other proprietors were playwright George Colman, writer and wit Bonnell Thornton and actor/manager David Garrick.

As one of the most successful titles of the day, *The St James's Chronicle* was able to attract the finest writers including Oliver Goldsmith, William Cowper, Edmund Burke and Richard Brinsley Sheridan – and the meeting place of this 'phalanx of first-class wits' was the Bedford Coffee-house, Covent Garden. Thornton was to remark:

> This coffee-house is every night crowded with men of parts. Almost every one you meet is a polite scholar and a wit; jokes and *bon mots* are echoed from box to box; every branch of literature is critically examined, and the merit of every production of the theatres weighed and determined.

Both Burke and Sheridan were to be notable parliamentarians: it was Burke who first called the Press the Fourth Estate, at the House of Commons in 1774: 'There are three Estates of Parliament; but in the Reporters' Gallery yonder sits a Fourth Estate more important far than they all.' And it was Sheridan who in 1779 was to comment in his play *The Critic, or a Tragedy Rehearsed*: 'The newspapers . . . Sir, they are the most villainous – licentious – abominable – infernal – not that I ever read them – no, I make it a rule never to look into a newspaper.' However, he is perhaps better remembered for his speech on the Freedom of the Press which he delivered at the House of Commons in 1810:[7]

> Give me but the liberty of the Press, and I will give the minister a venal House of Peers, I will give him a corrupt and servile House of Commons, I will give him the full swing of the patronage of office, I will give him all the power that place can confer upon him to purchase submission and overawe resistance, and yet, armed with the liberty of the Press, I will go forth to meet him undismayed, I will attack the mighty fabric he has reared with the mightier engine, I will shake down from its height corruption, and lay it beneath the ruins of abuses it was meant to shelter.

The Big Four

Of the newspapers circulating during the premiership of Pitt, four in particular were to establish a firm hold on the reading public: the *Morning Chronicle*, founded in 1769; the *Morning Post*, 1772; the *Morning Herald*, 1780; and *The Daily Universal Register*, 1785.

Launched on 28 June 1769 by William Woodfall – whose elder brother, Henry was publisher of the *Public Advertiser* – the *Morning Chronicle* was renowned for its parliamentary coverage, led by Woodfall himself. Apart from being editor and printer: 'He could walk down to the House of Commons, with a hard-boiled egg in his pocket,[8] take his seat in the gallery, sit out the longest debate, and, then, returning to his printing office, sit down, and, without a single scrap of paper in the form of notes, write out fifteen or sixteen (small) columns of speeches!' Small wonder that he was known as 'Memory Woodfall' – and the leading parliamentary reporter.

In 1773, though, he was accused of taking £400 per annum from Fox and Sheridan to ensure that they were reported at greater length than Pitt and Dundas. 'He denied taking the money, claiming he was merely acceding to public interest. But when his patrons dismissed the charge as electioneering the worst conclusion was reached.' Aside from his parliamentary reporting, Woodfall was well known as a drama critic – not without its dangers. Adverse comments that had appeared in February 1776 on Garrick's performance led Woodfall to write: 'As the printer of the *Morning Chronicle* I am the servant of the public, their message-carrier, their mouthpiece.' Woodfall added that in the disturbances he had 'narrowly escaped being murdered'.

In 1779, he sold his interest in the *Morning Chronicle* and later set up an evening paper, the *Diary or Woodfall's Register*, but it was to be a short-lived affair, closing in August 1793; and during this period Woodfall was being subsidized by the government to the extent of £400 a year. In 1790, he had written to Mr Speaker Addington of his experiences and those of his colleagues: 'Softly, gentlemen, recollect you are going into the House of Commons and not a bear garden, The fact is nothing can counteract national character. John Bull in a crowd is always John Bull in a mob.' Woodfall died on 1 August 1803, and is buried in St Margaret's Churchyard, Westminster.

During Woodfall's editorship, his chief rival had been the *Morning Post*, launched on 12 November 1772 by a group of twelve men, including the founders of Christie's and Tattersall's, plus the Rev. Henry Bate, who was appointed editor. 'The newspaper of a hundred years ago was sold to a great extent by hawkers, and the proprietors of the *Morning Post* employed boys in livery, who blew a postman's horn at the corners of the most popular thoroughfares and sold the papers to all who would buy them.'

Paid four guineas a week, Bate was, undoubtedly, the star of his day: he believed that his paper should be witty, amusing yet salacious; and in the first issue he cheerfully carried an advertisement offering for sale a list of addresses of the 'ladies of the town' who lived in Piccadilly.[9] He was also not above selling 'puffs' and receiving payments for the suppression of news stories. The government was quick to take advantage of this in its defence of the Earl of Sandwich, and for a time the paper was popularly dubbed 'Lord Sandwich's Post'.

Known as the 'Fighting Parson' – for his duelling and, in particular, for an affray at Vauxhall Gardens in 1773 which had brought him much notoriety – on 25 February 1780 he accused the Duke of Richmond of opposing every measure for the defence of England and of providing the French with a plan of the Sussex coast. This was now a matter of honour, but, instead of a duel, which Bate, a skilled swordsman, would have welcomed, the Duke sued; and on 25 June 1781 Bate was sentenced to twelve months' imprisonment. (Judgement had been delayed until Fleet Prison had been repaired following the Gordon Riots in June 1780.)

Bate himself had severed his connections with the *Post* in the autumn of 1780, following a disagreement with his co-proprietors, and on 1 November he started the *Morning Herald*. A month later he asserted that its circulation 'is already increased to the very extensive sale of 3,000'. Once again, Bate was to be in the pay of the Treasury, and during the nineties he was receving an annual subsidy of £600.

In 1784, Bate had been named as beneficiary in the will of a relation, on condition that he adopted the surname Dudley. This he did; and three years later he was appointed curate of Bradwell. As a devoted follower of the Prince Regent, Bate was rewarded in 1812, when the Regent made him a baronet and five years later when he gave him a stall at Ely Cathedral. But Sir Henry Bate Dudley was soon being chased by bailiffs; and the threat to publish an embarrassing letter concerning the now King George IV led to his receiving a pension of £300 per annum from the government. Justice was done, however, when he died at Cheltenham on 1 February 1824, just three months after having received his first payment. His character was, perhaps, best summed up by a critic at the Royal Academy after studying Gainsborough's portrait of Bate and his dog: 'The man wants execution and the dog wants hanging.'

Apart from the successful launches of daily newspapers, one ground-breaking title of that period had made its debut in the late summer of 1779 when Mrs Elizabeth Johnson brought out the first Sunday newspaper, *E. Johnson's British Gazette and Sunday Monitor*. Modelled on the daily newspapers of that period, it contained the latest news, a summary of the week's main events, a religious column on the front page plus advertisements – and was 'designed to appeal to those who had neither money nor leisure for a daily paper'. Published near Ludgate Hill in the City of London, it was later to have its title shortened to *The Sunday Monitor*; and a decade after the launch Mrs Johnson could declare: 'Four thousand papers are published every Sunday morning in the cities of London, Westminster, etc., which circumstances give a most pleasing sensation to all Advertising Customers.'

Its success had been noted earlier, in 1786, when William Davies in his play *News the Malady* had written: 'The Sunday,'tis true, is upon the increase; the scheme is new, consequently entertaining; it kills a few hours of this dull morning and pleads an excuse for a preference of a coffee-house to a chapel-pew.'[10]

However, the most prestigious Sunday title to be launched was *The Observer*, which appeared on 4 December 1791 and continues to this day, the world's oldest Sunday newspaper. It was started by W.S. Bourne, an 'impecunious but resourceful Irishman', with an initial investment of £100. Published from 'No. 169, Strand, London', under its masthead it proclaimed that it was 'Unbiased by Prejudice – Uninfluenced by Party, Whole Principle is Independence – whole Object is Truth, and the Dissemination of every Species of Knowledge that may conduce to the Happiness of Society, will be dispatched from *London early on Sunday morning*, and delivered in every part of *Great Britain* with the utmost Expedition.'[11]

Bourne's intentions were high-principled and inspiring but he soon ran into financial problems. Bourne, having failed to sell the paper to an anti-government group, in 1794 his elder and more prosperous brother invested £1600 to keep *The Observer* alive. His efforts to sell the paper to the government were unsuccessful, but he did set up links with the authorities, which were to last until the middle of the nineteenth century.

Launching The Times

Of all the newspaper ventures, by far the most important occurred early in 1785 with the first issue of *The Daily Universal Register*, a paper of four pages, 'Price Twopence Halfpenny', principally designed to show the public a new technique of printing in which type represented words and syllables instead of letters. The paper's editor, printer and proprietor was John Walter, of Printing House Square. Having purchased the patent for the logographic process from Henry Johnson, he announced in May 1784 from the 'Logographic House, Blackfriars' that he had bought the printing house near Apothecaries' Hall – at one time the King's printing house – for the purpose of printing by the new process.

The son of a London coal merchant, he was himself in that trade from 1755 to 1787, being a founder and chairman of the London Coal Exchange; and from 1770 to 1782 was also an underwriter at Lloyd's Coffee-house. However, in 1782, due to the loss of shipping during the American War of Independence, he was declared bankrupt. He was later to write to Lord Kenyon: ' I subscribed my name to six millions of property but was weighed down .... by the host of foes this nation had to combat in the American wars.'

In May 1784, Walter wrote to Benjamin Franklin, at that time American Minister in Paris: 'I am going to publish a newspaper by my Plan' – initially as an advertising medium for his logographic printing business – and true to his word eight months

THE *Universal* DAILY *Register*

Printed Logographically — *By His Majesty's Patent*

NUMB. 1.] SATURDAY, JANUARY 1, 1785. [Price Two-pence Halfpenny.

The SIXTH NIGHT.
By His MAJESTY's Company

AT the THEATRE ROYAL in DRURY-LANE, this present SATURDAY, will be performed

A New COMEDY, called
The NATURAL SON.

The characters by Mr. King, Mr. Parsons, Mr. Bensley, Mr. Moody, Mr. [illegible], Mr. Wrighten, and Mr. [illegible]. Miss Pope, Miss Tidswell, and Miss Farren.
With new Scenes and Dresses.
The Prologue to be spoken by Mr. [illegible], jun.
And the Epilogue by Miss Farren.
After which will be performed the last New Pantomime Entertainment, in two Parts, called
HARLEQUIN JUNIOR;
Or, The MAGIC CESTUS.
The Characters of the Pantomime, by
Mr. Wright, Mr. Williamson, Mr. Burton, Mr. [illegible], Mr. Williames, Mr. Palmer, Mr. Waldron, Mr. [illegible], Mr. Chaplin, Mr. Phillimore, Mr. Walton, Mr. Alfred, Mr. Spencer, Mr. Chapman, and Mr. Grimaldi. Mrs. Burton, Miss Barnett, Miss Tidswell, Miss Burton, Miss Crawford, and Miss [illegible].
To conclude with the Repulse of the Spaniards before THE ROCK of GIBRALTAR.

To-morrow, by particular desire, (for the [illegible] time) the revived Comedy of the DOUBLE DEALER, with the favorite Masque of ARTHUR and EMMELINE.
On Tuesday the Tragedy of VENICE PRESERVED: Jaffier by Mr. Brereton, Pierre by Mr. Bensley, and Belvidera, by Mrs. Siddons; And on Friday the Carnelian. Massinger's Play of the MAID of HONOUR, (with alterations and Additions) is in Rehearsal and will soon be produced.

NINTH NIGHT. FOR THE AUTHOR.

AT the THEATRE-ROYAL, COVENT-GARDEN, this present SATURDAY, January 1, 1785, will be performed, a New Comedy, called
The FOLLIES of a DAY,
Or, The Marriage of Figaro.
With new Dresses, Decorations, &c.
The principal characters by Mr. Lewis, Mr. Quick, Mr. Edwin, Mr. Wilson, Mr. Wewitzer, Mr. [illegible], Mr. Thompson, and Mrs. Martyr; Mrs. Bates, Mrs. Webb, Miss Wewitzer, and Miss Younge.
With a new Prologue, to be spoken by Mr. Davies.
To which will be added, for the [illegible] time,
A new Pantomime, called,
The MAGIC CAVERN,
Or, VIRTUE's TRIUMPH.
With new Scenery, Machinery, Music, Dresses, and Decorations.
The Scenes chiefly designed by Mr. Richards, and executed by him, Mr. Carver, Mr. Hodgins, and Assistants.
The Overture, Songs, Chorusses, and the Music of the new Pantomime, [illegible] by Mr. Shield.
Nothing under Full Price will be taken.
The Words of the Songs, &c. to be had at the Theatre.

MR. WALTER returns his thanks to his Friends and the Public for the great encouragement and generous support he has already received from them in his new improvement in Printing, by the readiness with which they have subscribed to his intended publication of the works of some eminent Authors; and whilst he solicits a continuance of their favours, begs leave to acquaint them that by
The middle of January will be published,
In One Volume [illegible],
MISCELLANIES IN VERSE AND PROSE,
Intended as a Specimen of his Printing Types at the Logographic Office, Printing House Square, Blackfriars.—And by the beginning of February, the first volume, containing Watts's Improvement of the Mind, with an [illegible] written on the occasion, will be ready to be delivered to the Subscribers.

This Day is published, Price 6d.

PLAN of the CHAMBER of COMMERCE, King's Arms Buildings, Cornhill, London, which is open every day, for Consultation, Opinion, and Advice (verbal or in Writing) Mediation, Arbitration, Arbitration, &c. in all Commercial, Maritime, and Insurance Affairs, and matters of Trade in general; and the Laws and Usages relating thereto.—The Address is, To the [illegible] of the Chamber of Commerce, as above.
To be had of [illegible], Royal Exchange; J. Sewell, Cornhill; T. Whieldon, Fleet-street; W. [illegible], Holborn; and at the above Chamber.
Where may also be had, in one Volume Folio,
Mr. Weskett's COMPLETE DIGEST of the THEORY, LAWS and PRACTICE of INSURANCE; an entire new and comprehensive work, including all the adjudged Cases extant, with several never before printed; [illegible] from the Statutes, foreign Ordinances, and maritime Treatises; accounts of all the Insurance Companies, the Maritime Courts, the commercial and maritime Laws, the Law of Nations, &c. the whole forming (alphabetically) a new *Lex Mercatoria*.
"This Work has been compiled with great Care and Industry, by one who is evidently a Master of the Subject. It abounds with Proofs of extensive Reading, as well as mature Reflections, and judicious Remarks; and if the completest System of Information that has hitherto been composed be entitled to Praise, the present useful Digest must meet with the Approbation of the commercial World." Crit. Rev. Vol. 57, p. 413.—All the other Literary Journals speak in similar Terms of this Book; which had already been translated abroad.

This Day is published, in 3 Vols. Price 9s. sewed.
By the LITERARY SOCIETY,

MODERN TIMES; or The ADVENTURES of GABRIEL OUTCAST. A Novel, in Imitation of Gil Blas.
"Que regit [illegible]."
Printed for the Author, and sold by J. Walter, Printing-house Square, Black-friars; where may be had, gratis, the Plan of this Society, [illegible] for the Encouragement of Literature, who propose to print and publish at their own Risk and Expence such original Works as they may approve of, and give their Authors all Profits arising from the Sale.

MRS. KING begs leave to acquaint her Friends she opens her SCHOOL at CHIGWELL in ESSEX, on Monday, the 10th of January, for the EDUCATION of YOUNG LADIES; as she has always been accustomed to watch and improve the opening mind, hopes to give satisfaction to those who trust her with so important a charge.
Till the 10th of January Mrs. King may be spoke with at Mr. Kent's, [illegible] to his Majesty, in the Mews, Charing-cross.
N. B. Wanted an Apprentice and Half-boarder.

SHIP-PING
ADVER-TISEMENTS

For NICE, GENOA, and LEGHORN,
(With Liberty to touch at One Port in the Channel,)
The NANCY.
THOMAS WHITE, Commander,
BURTHEN 160 Tons; Guns and Men answerable. Lying off the Tower, and will absolutely depart on Saturday the 8th instant.
The said Commander to be spoken with every morning at Sam's Coffee-house, near the Custom-house; at Will's Coffee-house, in Cornhill; and at Exchange hours on the French and Indian Walk, or
WILLIAM ELYARD, for the said Commander,
No. 16, Savage Gardens.

Direct for LISBON,
The NANCY.
JOHN RACKHAM, Commander,
BURTHEN 300 Tons, Men answerable. Lying off Horslydown Chain; Seven-eighths of her Cargo absolutely engaged, and is obliged by Charter-party to depart on Saturday the 8th instant.
The said Commander to be spoken with every morning at Sam's Coffee-house, near the Custom-house; at Will's Coffee-house, in Cornhill; and in Exchange hours in the French and Indian Walk, or
WILLIAM ELYARD, for the said Commander,
No. 16, Savage Gardens.

For NICE, GENOA, and LEGHORN,
(With Liberty to Touch at One Port in the Channel.)
The LIVELY.
ROBERT [illegible], Commander,
BURTHEN 100 Tons, Guns and Men answerable. Lying off Iron Gate.
The said Commander to be spoke with every Morning at Sam's Coffee-house, near the Custom-house; at Will's Coffee-house in Cornhill; and in Exchange Hours in the French and Italian Walk, or
WILLIAM ELYARD, for the said Commander,
No. 16, Savage Gardens.

For CONSTANTINOPLE and SMYRNA, or SMYRNA and CONSTANTINOPLE,
(With Liberty to Touch at One Port in the Channel,)
The BETSEY.
ROBERT LANCASTER, Commander,
BURTHEN 200 Tons, Men answerable. Lying at Iron-Gate. Two-thirds of her Cargo engaged, and is obliged to depart by Charter-party, in all the present Month of January.
The said Commander to be spoke with every Morning at Sam's Coffee-house, near the Custom-house; at Will's Coffee-house in Cornhill; and in Exchange Hours at the French and Italian Walk; or
WILLIAM ELYARD, for the said Commander,
No. 16, Savage Gardens.
N. B. No Goods to be taken on Board the Vessel without an Order from the Broker.

NEW NOVELS

This Day are published, (in two Volumes, price 5s. sewed,)

THE YOUNG WIDOW; or, the HISTORY of Mrs. LEDWICH.
The HISTORY of Lord BELFORD and Miss SOPHIA WOODLEY, 3 vol. 9s. bound.
Printed for the Editor, and sold by F. Noble, in Holborn;
Where may be had lately published,
[illegible] Abbey, a Novel, 3 vols. 9s. bound.
The Woman of Letters; or, History of Fanny Belton, 2 vol. 6s. bound.
A Lesson for Lovers; or, History of Col. Melville and Lady Rachel, 2 vols. 7s. bound.
Literary Amusements, or, Evening Entertainer, 2 vol. 7s. bound.
Adventures of a Cavalier, by Daniel Defoe, 3 vols. 9s. bound.

E. RICKABY, PRINTER,
No. 13, Duke's Court, Drury Lane;

RESPECTFULLY informs his Friends and the Public in general, that the Partnership between him and Mr. Moore being entirely dissolved, he now intends to carry on every branch of the PRINTING BUSINESS upon his own account; and having purchased a complete assortment of the newest and best materials, is determined to pursue a Mode of Printing which he hopes will meet with the approbation of his employers.
N. B. Cards, Hand-Bills, Circular Letters, and all articles of the kind, accurately printed at a few hours notice, in a manner particularly neat, and at the lowest prices.
*** An Apprentice wanted.

To the Readers of the London Medical Journal
This day is first published, price 1s.

SYMPATHY DEFENDED, or, the first MEDICAL CRITICISM in London; written to improve the Principles and Manners of the Editor of the London Medical Journal: To which are added the Censure of the Treatise on Medical Sympathy, and a Postscript, an account of a premature Review in a late Number of the London Medical Journal.
By a Society of Faculties;
Friends to the Public and Enemies to Imposition.
"[illegible]
[illegible]"
Mart. Epig.
This pamphlet has been hitherto distributed gratuitously. The repeated applications for them, particularly from the country, have become so numerous, that the Society find themselves under the necessity of putting them into the hands of a publisher.
Sold by J. Murray, Bookseller, Fleet-street.

Nondum lingua suo dextra, peragit opus.
Mart.

SHORT-HAND, on the latest and most approved Principles taught by J. LAKEMAN, No. 11, [illegible] Alley, Bishopsgate Street.
It would exceed the limits of an advertisement merely to mention the various errors either in the plan or the execution of the different schemes of Short-hand hitherto made public, or to point out the peculiarities and excellencies of the present. Mr. L. therefore only begs leave to observe, that the approbation of many gentlemen well known in the literary world, and well versed in the Theory and Practice of Short-hand, expressed in stronger terms than delicacy will permit him to repeat, warrants him in saying he will be found a system of short and swift writing, more easy to acquire and retain, more expeditious, more legible and more regular than any ever yet offered to the Public.
The terms of teaching one Guinea, the usefulness of learning from letters.

To the Public.

TO bring out a New Paper at the present day, when so many others are already established and confirmed in the public opinion, is certainly an arduous undertaking; and no one can be more fully aware of its difficulties than I am: I, nevertheless, entertain very sanguine hopes, that the nature of the plan on which this paper will be conducted, will ensure it a moderate share at least of public favour; but my pretensions to encouragement, however strong they may appear in my own eyes, must be tried before a tribunal not liable to be blinded by self-opinion; to that tribunal I shall now, as I am bound to do, submit those pretensions with deference, and the public will judge whether they are well or ill founded.

It is very far from my intention to detract from the acknowledged merit of the Daily Papers now in existence; it is sufficient that they please the class of readers whose approbation their conductors are ambitious to deserve; nevertheless it is certain some of the best, some of the most respectable, and some of the most useful members of the community, have frequently complained (and the causes of their complaints still exist) that by radical defects in the plans of the present established papers, they were deprived of many advantages, which ought naturally to result from daily publications. Of these some build their fame on the length and accuracy of parliamentary reports, which unquestionably are given with great ability, and with a laudable zeal to please those, who can spare time to read ten or twelve columns of debates. Others are principally attentive to the politics of the day, and make it their study to give satisfaction to the numerous class of politicians, who, blessed with easy circumstances, have nothing better to do, than to amuse themselves with watching the motions of ministers both at home and abroad; and endeavouring to find out the secret springs that set in motion the great machine of government in every state and empire in the world. There is one paper which in no degree interferes with the pursuits of its contemporaries; it looks upon parliamentary debates as sacred mysteries, that cannot be submitted to vulgar eyes without profanation; political investigations it apprehends to be little short of treason, and therefore *wisely* abstains from them; it deals almost solely in advertisements; and consequently, though a very useful, it is by no means an entertaining paper. Thus it would seem that every News-Paper published in London is calculated for a particular set of readers only; so that if each set were to change its favourite publication for another, the contamination would produce disgust, and dissatisfaction to all; the politician would then find nothing to amuse him but long accounts of petty squabbles about trifles in Parliament, or panegyrics on the men and measures that he most disliked; or libels on those whom he most revered. The person to whom parliamentary debates afford unspeakable delight, would find himself bored with political speculations about the measures that the different courts in Europe might probably adopt; or disgusted with whole pages of advertisements, in which he felt no concern;—whilst the plain shop-keeper who wanted to find a convenient house for his business, and the servant who purchased his paper in hopes of seeing in it an advertisement directing where he might find a place to suit him, would have their labour for their pains, in perusing publications, filled with senatorial debates, or political essays and remarks, which would direct them to nothing less than the house or place they wanted.—A News-Paper, conducted on the true and natural principles of such a publication, ought to be the Register of the times, and faithful recorder of every species of intelligence; it ought not to be engrossed by any particular object; but, like a well covered table, it should contain something suited to every palate: observations on the dispositions of our own and of foreign courts should be provided for the political reader; debates should be reported for the amusement or information of those who may be particularly fond of them; and a due attention should be paid to the interests of trade, which are so greatly promoted by advertisements.—A paper that should blend all these advantages, and by steering clear of extremes, hit the happy medium, has long been expected by the public.—Such, it is intended, shall be the UNIVERSAL REGISTER, the great objects of which will be to facilitate the commercial intercourse between the different parts of the community, through the channel of *Advertisements*; to record the principal occurrences of the times; and to abridge the account of debates during the sitting of Parliament.

It is no less the interest of the proprietors of News-Papers, than of the public, that every encouragement should be given to advertising correspondents; yet this private interest of the proprietors is frequently sacrificed to the rage for parliamentary debates, to the great injury of trade; for the extreme length of these debates so greatly retards the publication of the News-Papers which are noted for detailed accounts of them, that the advantages arising from this species of intelligence, though highly acceptable in itself, are frequently over-balanced by the inconveniences occasioned to people in business by the delay. These inconveniences are great and many; it generally happens, that when either House of Parliament has been engaged in the discussion of an important question till after midnight, the papers in which the speeches of the Members are reported at large, cannot be published before noon; nay, they sometimes are not seen so early as soon; consequently parties interested in *sales* are essentially injured, as the advertisements, inviting the public to attend them at ten or twelve o'clock, do not appear, on account of a late publication, till some hours after.—From the same source flows another inconvenience; it is sometimes found necessary to *defer* sales, after they have been advertised for a particular day; but the notice of putting them off not appearing early enough, on account of the late hour at which the papers containing it are published, numbers of people, acting under the impression of former advertisements, are unnecessarily put to the trouble of attending.—It will be the object of the *Universal Register* to guard against these great inconveniences, without depriving its readers of the pleasure of learning what passes in Parliament.—It is intended, then, that the debates shall be regularly reported in it; but on the other hand, that the publication *may not be delayed* to the prejudice of people in trade, the speeches will not be given on a large scale; the *substance* shall be faithfully preserved; but all the uninteresting parts will be omitted. I shall thus be enabled to publish this paper at an early hour; and I propose to bring it out *regularly* every morning *at six* o'clock. The *Universal Register* will therefore have this advantage over the *Daily Advertiser*, that, though published as early, it will contain a substantial account of the proceedings in Parliament the preceding night, which is never to be found in that paper; and compared with the other morning papers it will be found to have the merit of containing in substance, what they give in long detail (which men in business cannot well spare time to read) and, nevertheless, of being published much sooner. These circumstances, it is hoped, will give the *Universal Register* at least an *equal* claim to public favour with the parliamentary papers, and the *trading* part of the metropolis, it is presumed, will find it their advantage to give it the preference.

An essential part of the plan of this new paper is, that, for the convenience of advertising correspondents, their favours shall, *to a certainty*, be inserted on the very *day* that they shall direct; provided they deliver them at the office in *due* time. For the *strict* observance of this rule, the credit of the paper shall stand pledged; and its pretensions to public countenance will be renounced, if this fundamental principle in its institution shall ever be violated, except in cases of absolute necessity, which human prudence cannot prevent.—And here I beg it may be understood that I do not make use of the word *necessity* as a reserve, under colour of which, I may, whenever I think fit, be released from my engagements; I mean by that word a necessity arising from accidents that sometimes happen in the printing business, and from which, the most careful man cannot, at all times, be secure. But so far from wishing to break from my engagements, I intend, whenever the length of the Gazette, Parliamentary Debates, &c. shall render it impossible for me to insert all the advertisements promised for the day, *in one sheet*, to print an additional half sheet, and publish it with the ordinary paper without any additional charge to my customers.—From the difficulty that people experience in procuring the insertion of their advertisements even in the *Daily Advertiser*, and particularly from the impossibility of obtaining an early insertion at some periods of the year, it may be presumed that this regulation will greatly recommend the UNIVERSAL REGISTER to public notice, and procure it support.

These, though in my opinion good, are not the *only* grounds on which I build my hopes of success. I flatter myself, I have some claim to public encouragement, on account of a great improvement which I have made in the art of printing. The inconveniences attending the old and tedious mode of composing with letters taken up *singly*, first suggested the idea of devising some more expeditious method. The cementing of several letters together, so as that the type of a *whole word* might be taken up in as short a time as that of a *single letter*, was the result of much reflection on that subject. But the bare idea of cementing was merely the opening, not the accomplishment or perfection of the improvement. The founts consisting of types of words, and not of letters, was to be so arranged, as that a compositor should be able to find the former with as much facility as he can the latter. This was a work of inconceivable difficulty. I undertook it however, and was fortunate enough, after an infinite number of experiments, and great labour, to bring it to a happy conclusion. The whole English language is now methodically and systematically arranged at my founts: so that printing can now be performed with greater dispatch, and at less expence, than according to the mode hitherto in use.

In bringing this work to perfection, I had not my own advantage solely in view; I wished to be useful to the community; and it is with pleasure I see that the public will derive considerable benefit from my industry; for I have resolved to sell the REGISTER *One halfpenny* under the price paid for seven out of eight of the morning later, on Saturday, 1 January, 1785, he launched his new title. Walter outlined his aims in the first issue:[12]

> *On his ambitions for the new paper . . .*
> To bring out a News-Paper at the present day; when so many others are already established and confirmed in the public opinion, is certainly an arduous undertaking. I nevertheless entertain very sanguine hopes that the nature of the plan on which this paper will be conducted will ensure it a moderate share at least of public favour . . . . A News-paper ought to be the Register of the times, and faithful recorder of every species of intelligence; it ought not to be engrossed by any particular object; but, like a well covered table, it should contain something suited to every palate.
>
> *On deadlines . . .*
> It generally happens, that when either House of Parliament has been engaged in discussion till after midnight, the papers in which the speeches are reported at large, cannot be published before noon. Consequently advertisers are injured, as the advertisements inviting the public to attend them at ten o'clock the next morning, do not appear till some hours after. It is intended, then, that the publication may not be delayed to the prejudice of people in trade. Parliamentary speeches will not be given on a large scale. The *substance* shall be faithfully preserved; but all the uninteresting parts will be omitted. I shall thus be able to publish this paper at an early hour; and I propose to bring it out regularly every morning at six o'clock.
>
> *And commitment to advertisers . . .*
> I intend whenever the length of the Gazette, Parliamentary Debates etc. shall render it impossible for me to insert in one sheet all the advertisements promised for the day, to print an additional half sheet, and publish it with the ordinary paper *without any additional charge to my customers*.
>
> *On new technology . . .*
> I flatter myself I have some claim to public encouragement, on account of a great improvement which I have made in the art of printing. This was a work of inconceivable difficulty. I undertook it however, and was fortunate enough, after an infinite number of experiments and great labour, to bring it to a happy conclusion so that printing can now be performed with great dispatch and at less expense.
>
> *On cover pricing . . .*
> I have resolved to sell the Register one halfpenny UNDER the price paid for seven out of eight of the morning papers; however I indulge a hope that this sacrifice which I make of the usual profits of printing, will be felt by a generous public; and that they will so favour me with advertisements, as to enable me to defray the heavy expenses.
>
> *On contributions . . .*
> Advertisements, Essays, real Articles of Intelligence, etc. to which great attention will be paid, will be taken in at the Office in Printing House Square, and for the greater convenience of the distant parts of town, at Mr. Searle's, Grocer, No. 55, Oxford-Street; Mr. Pratt's, Green Grocer, of Wapping.

The first issue contained a column of foreign intelligence, succeeded by ten lines of Court News and an *Ode for the New Year* by Thomas Whitehead, Poet Laureate; but there was no leading article. 'The issue devoted exactly three of its columns to news and three to the prospectus. There were ten columns of advertisements, including a back-page puff of the *Register* signed "Gregory Gazette"'.

Exactly three years after the launch, on Tuesday, 1 January 1788 – issue No. 940 – Walter announced in a one-and-a-half column prospectus that henceforth the paper would be titled *The Times*. All now seemed fair, but on 21 February 1789 he published two paragraphs – 'supplied to him, in accordance with the agreement by Mr Steele, Secretary of the Treasury' – criticizing George III's sons, whereupon the Prince of Wales and the Duke of York instituted libel proceedings. As a result of the first libel, Walter was fined £50, sent to Newgate Prison for a year, sentenced to stand in the pillory at Charing Cross for an hour and ordered to give good security of behaviour for seven years. Although the pillory was remitted, he served a total of sixteen months for the two libels, and was released on 7 March 1791.[13]

Nine months after the unfortunate libel there appeared in *The Times* on 26 November 1789 a letter from William Finey, the paper's editor:

> TO THE CONDUCTOR
>
> Being informed by many of my friends, that I am considered as the Author of that paragraph in *The Times*, reflecting on the Duke of York, for the publication of which Mr Walter received judgment on Monday last, I hold it necessary to declare, that it was not written, or caused to be written by me; and that I never saw it – or even heard of it – until it was published in the paper.
>
> Mr Walter, I am confident, will do me the justice to acknowledge, that I never did write, or cause to be inserted, any matter in *The Times* which has occasioned the Proprietor, Editor, Printer, or Publisher of that Paper, to be prosecuted.

Finey – not above taking payments for leaving out unflattering paragraphs – remained as editor until 1795. And as Stanley Morison was to write in his *History of The Times: 1785–1841*:

> From the beginning, readers of daily newspapers had enjoyed scandalous paragraphs. Topham and Bell in the *World* set a new standard in personal detraction which *The Times* exerted itself to surpass. There was money as well as entertainment in the system of paragraphing practised at this time. The subject was often informed previously by the journal's agent that a paragraph was in type, and it was hinted to him that the paragraph need not appear if a sum, known as the suppression fee, were paid. If the subject of the paragraph had not been reached before publication, a cutting was sent to him with a hint that room could be found for any 'statement'. Inclusion of the second paragraph was delayed until a payment, known as the 'contradiction fee', was forthcoming.

That same year as Finey's letter, 1789, a Mrs Wells, a well-known and notorious figure, married a Mr Sumbel, leading to offensive paragraphs in *The Times*. Mr Sumbel, having summoned the editor to his home, handed him a large parcel of notes, saying: 'Will that be enough?' Finey replied: 'Give me a few more and by St Patrick I will knock out the brains of anyone in our office who dare even whisper your name.'

As for the proprietor, John Walter continued to be involved daily with *The Times* until 1795. He then decided to spend more leisure at his home in Teddington, Middlesex, giving up direct control of the paper to his son William Walter, who was manager from 1795 to 1797. He then shared responsibilities with his brother John Walter II from 1797 until 1803 when John Walter II assumed sole charge.

The Printers Unite

During the final decades of the eighteenth century the growth in the number of daily newspapers had led to the journeymen printers banding together to negotiate with the proprietors; and in 1785 there had been the first confrontation between management and men. The number of master printers was then 124, who between them employed 500 compositors and 180 apprentices.

In pressrooms there were a further 200 journeymen and some 80 apprentices, while 180 journeymen worked as bookbinders. Dissatisfied with their wages, the compositors presented a petition, and in response the master printers held a meeting at the Globe Tavern, Fleet Street, on 25 November 1785, to consider the workers' eight proposals. Arising from the meeting, it was decided to appoint an *ad hoc* committee. There was, however, no direct negotation at this time, since the master printers did not believe that the men had a right to address them collectively; but from these discussions was to emerge the Compositors' Scale of Prices.

However, not all the negotiations between employers and employees were of such a friendly nature; and in 1786 the compositors failed to obtain an injunction against John Walter, proprietor of *The Times*, which would have forbidden him to set up as a master printer, on the grounds that he had not served an apprenticeship in the trade.

Six years later, on 12 March 1792, the printers formed the Phoenix: or Society of Compositors, designed as a Friendly or Benefit Society, which collected regular contributions, arranged meetings of delegates from distant offices, and, most importantly, tried to limit the number of apprentices. Within twelve months of its formation, in March 1793 there was presented an *Address of the Compositors of London to the Master Printers, with the Answer of the Masters* to discuss the subject of payment for the setting of type. The Address stated:[14]

> As we disclaim all proceedings militating against justice, or that are subversive of decent and respectful behaviour, we presume that any communication, which the present situation of the business renders necessary to be opened with our employers, will be received in a manner suitable to its importance, and with candour coinciding with its equity.

Two small additions to the existing piece-work scale were requested, with a reminder that the cost of living had risen since 1785. The Address, signed by 593 journeymen, concluded: 'The communication of your sentiments to the compositors in your office or in any manner agreeable to the masters in general, to the committee of compositors at the Hole-in-the-Wall, Fleet Street, on or before the first of March, will be gratefully received by your humble servants.'

By the end of the century, the compositors had decided that the time was ripe for amalgamation of the various factions, and in 1801 the Union Society was founded. Its purpose was to correct irregularities, and in the words of its charter: 'To endeavour to promote harmony between employers and the employed. By bringing the modes of change from custom and precedent into one point of view, in order to their being better understood by all concerned.'

However, the government, alarmed at the speed of revolutionary ideas from France, passed in 1799 and 1800 the Combination Acts, which made all journeymen's trade societies illegal, and provided for summary convictions of the offenders – and importantly these convictions could now be dealt with by magistrates. Within weeks of the first Act being passed, members of the Pressmen's Friendly Society, whose headquarters were at the Crown, near St Dunstan's, Fleet Street, and who had attempted to negotiate with the master printers on limiting the number of apprentices, were prosecuted for conspiracy. The prosecutor declared:[15]

> It was called a Friendly Society, but, Gentlemen, by means of some wicked men among the society it degenerated into a most abominable meeting for the purpose of conspiracy: those of the trade who did not join their society were summoned, and even the apprentices, and were told unless they conformed to the practices of these journeymen, when they came out of their time they would not be employed

Another case which won widespread attention was that of the nineteen *Times* compositors, who in 1810 were found guilty of 'conspiracy' and imprisoned, with one of their number, Malcolm Craig, dying in gaol. In reality, these two cases were the exceptions in the printing industry, for in most instances the masters were prepared to meet representatives of the men's societies in order to agree wages and conditions of employment. But it was not until 1825, largely through the efforts of Francis Place, that the Combination Acts were repealed.

Distribution and Production

Despite the punitive stamp and advertisement taxes imposed by the government and the constant political interference, the Press in England had continued to grow throughout the eighteenth century – from a figure of 2.5 million in 1713 to some 16 million by 1801. This is reflected in the number of stamped papers printed: 1713, 2.5 million; 1750, 7.3 million; 1760, 9.4 million; 1765, 9.7 million; 1775, 12.6 million; 1780, 14.0 million. In London, the number of titles had increased from twelve newspapers in 1712 to sixteen dailies by 1792.

For the proprietors based in the Fleet Street area, the main method of distribution was through the use of hawkers, who were normally allowed a penny margin on each paper, and given two papers in every quire. An interesting advertisement regarding hawkers had appeared in *The Times* on 15 April 1792:[16]

> An old established NEWS WALK to be disposed of that brings in £1 12*s*. per week clear profit; situate in the best part of London, and capable, with care and assiduity, of great improvement: such an opportunity seldom offers for an industrious person. Enquire tomorrow at No. 14, Portugal Street, Lincoln's-Inn-Fields.

The hawkers not only sold papers on the 'walk', they carried them round to booksellers, coffee houses, and the Post Office.

Throughout the first part of the eighteenth century, distribution of newspapers from London to the country had been a long-standing problem – despite the fact that four hundred Road Acts had been passed; and that in the next fifty years this figure was to exceed one thousand. The stage coach did not appear until mid-century and it was not until 1784 that the mail coach came into being. A daily coach service to most parts of the country was developed, and this was complemented by a steady increase in the number of cross-posts between provincial towns.

The man behind this innovation was Ralph Allen, who, as deputy postmaster for Bath, had designed a system of cross-posts for England and Wales; and from their introduction in 1720 to 1764 his profits were estimated at £12,000 a year. Known as the Man of Bath because of his munificence, he was a patron of Fielding and a friend of Pope, who refers to him in the Epilogue to the *Satires of Horace*:

> Let humble Allen, with an awkward shame
> Do good by stealth, and blush to find it fame.

Allen died in Bath on 29 June 1764, having been taken ill at Maidenhead.

From the seventeenth century, the Clerks in the offices of the Secretaries of State had acted as the main retailers of London papers, sending copies to the provinces at reduced rates. The role was held by six Post Office Clerks of the Road, whose responsibility was for services to different parts of the country, making them ideal agents for the traffic of London papers. Although not without their faults – including vulnerability to political bribery – the Clerks performed a useful function, and their services were used extensively. As an example, a parliamentary investigation revealed that in seven days during March 1764 the Clerks had distributed more than 20,000 London papers, mainly on Tuesdays, Thursdays and Saturdays. And by the end of the decade, it was possible for individuals whose names were registered at the Post Office to have their copies franked individually. There was a heavy demand for this service with Members of Parliament using the system, and by June 1789 the weekly number of newspapers posted had reached 63,177 compared with 12,909 for the Post Office Clerks and only 756 by the Secretaries' office.

Towards the end of the century, though, the Post Office was once again going through a financial crisis; and in 1787 it had set up the Newspaper Office to receive and sort all newspapers, made up in bundles according to districts. These bundles were distributed to the postmasters by the Clerks of the Road for the postal divisions of the country. Prior to this date, the newspapers had arrived at the Post Office late and 'in so wet a state as to deface the directions of many of the letters which were sent in the same bags'.

In 1796, a Bill was presented to the Commons 'for regulating the conveyance of newspapers'. The result was a curtailment of the role of the hawkers and the handing over of the monopoly to the already entrenched Clerks of the Road, who now, in effect, became wholesalers to the country postmasters; and the Post Office – with the exception of booksellers and hawkers in London – became the national distributing agency. From that year, newspapers were to be carried post-free. However, the Post Office was determined to keep a tight rein on the stamping of the newsprint sheets, as an article of 19 March 1798 pointed out:[17]

> *The* new Postmaster General, Lord Auckland, has begun very extensive reforms in that department. On Saturday night all the Newspapers were examined, to see that no writing was put upon the stamped sheets, so as to defraud the Revenue of postage. This is assuredly proper. No person has a right to abuse the privilege of free carriage which the Newspapers enjoy for the encouragement of the stamp duty by smuggling under the cover of private correspondence.

Although advances had been made in distribution, the production of newspapers had barely changed in one hundred years: compositors still stood at their frames, setting each character by hand in their sticks, before placing the justified lines of type on galleys, prior to being locked up in chases ready for printing on the wooden hand presses. In the final years of the century, there had been a small improvement with the introduction of the Stanhope iron press. However, this was still a manual operation – and press speeds seldom exceeded 250 copies per hour.

A survey at the time showed that 'frames cost 24*s*., with font cases, per pair, at the same price. A wooden demy hand-press £31. An iron Stanhope Press, a new invention, £73'. The price of paper – made from rags – cost £2 2*s*. for 500 sheets, yielding 1,000 copies. The old tax on double demy, the size used for newspapers, had been 8*s*. 4*d*. a bundle weighing 106 lbs: less than 1*d*. a pound. But the new duty – introduced in 1789 – was 2½*d*. a lb, which for a bundle of 106 lbs was 22*s*. 1*d*., an addition of 13*s*. 9*d*.

Since 1793, an increase in compositors' wages had brought the rates of full hands up to £1 16*s*., an extra 4*s*. 6*d*. since the introduction of the London Scale of Prices in 1785.[18] Supernumaries had received an increase of two shillings and were now paid 17*s*. a week. With the costs of the pressmen, flyboys and readers to be added, it is doubtful if the total weekly wages bill of a typical daily would be in excess of £65, and of this sum the Printer would have received £3 3*s*., which was the going rate.

Apart from paper and wages, other costs were relatively low, although the price of dipped tallow candles for lighting was 8*s*. 4*d*. a dozen; and founders' type had increased in price after August 1793, with pica at 1s. 1½*d*. and small pica at 1s. 3½*d*. a lb. Two-line letters cost 1*s*. 1*d*., leads (six to pica) 1*s*. 6*d*.

Rivals to The Times

Of the daily newspapers emanating from London at this time, two in particular – the *Morning Chronicle* and the *Morning Post* – were the chief rivals to *The Times*. In 1789, as noted, William Woodfall had sold the *Morning Chronicle* to James Perry, who also became the paper's editor – and as such was to be described by the Earl of Derby as a man 'who never employed his pen or his paper to undermine the civil and religious establishments of the country'.

Born in Aberdeen , Perry had entered Aberdeen University in 1771, but, because of his father's financial difficulties, had been forced to leave. He had then worked as a draper's assistant and later as an actor, but was told that his 'brogue unfitted him for the stage'. Following a brief spell as a clerk in Manchester, he moved to London in 1771, joining Richardson & Urquhart booksellers, writing for their newspaper, the

General Advertiser, at a salary of one guinea a week, while receiving an extra half-guinea for helping to launch the *London Evening Post*. He also acted as a special reporter, and during the courts martial of Admirals Keppel and Palliser sent up to eight columns of evidence a day to the *General Advertiser*.[19]

Now keenly interested in politics, in 1782 he launched the *European Magazine*, and for the next twelve months was to be its editor. He was then appointed editor of *The London Gazeteer*, and soon converted the paper, which had been little more than an advertising sheet for booksellers, into a forthright journal supporting Charles James Fox. One of Perry's first tasks was to engage young and 'impecunious barristers to report parliament, taking shorthand notes in relays, half-an-hour at a time' – thereby providing a full account of the debates the following morning.

A circulation war with the *Morning Chronicle* ended in 1789 with Perry taking over the paper – greatly assisted with a loan of £500 from his bankers, further monies from his friends, and by the Duke of Norfolk providing 'a set of palatial offices in one of his unlet houses, No. 332 The Strand'. Perry merged the two papers but kept the *Chronicle* title. As Ray Boston has written:[20]

> Once free of *The London Gazeteer*, a 'ministerial' paper heavily subsidised by the government, Perry steadfastly refused to take insertions and corrections from anyone; nor would he accept free theatre tickets in exchange for printing puffs. 'It will be essentially better,' he wrote to one theatre manager, 'for both of us to put an end to this pitiful arrangement and resolve in future to pay for admission to each other's premises.'

Throughout his editorship, Perry had numerous brushes with the authorities, and in 1792 he was charged with printing a serious libel, but, on this occasion, was found not guilty. Six years later, a reference to the House of Lords and the fact that 'dresses of the opera-dancers are regulated there' led to his imprisonment and a fine of £50. He still had the support of his friends, however, and on his release an entertainment was given in his honour at the London Tavern.

To achieve the success which his paper now had, Perry, in running the principal organ of the Whigs, was in touch with all aspects of life, and for a year acted as his own special correspondent in France at the time of the French Revolution. Perry 'may be said practically to have to created the profession of journalism'; and this was reflected by his hiring writers of the calibre of Samuel Taylor Coleridge, William Hazlitt, Leigh Hunt, Charles Lamb, Richard Brinsley Sheridan, Tom Moore – and John Campbell, afterwards High Chancellor of England. Thanks to Perry's fine business management, detailed news and in-depth parliamentary coverage he could report by 1810 that the paper was the largest of all dailies, with a circulation of more than seven thousand copies.

His independence was to continue to bring down the wrath of the Tory government and two years later, in 1812, he and his publisher, John Lambert, were charged with libel for reprinting an article which had appeared in Leigh Hunt's *Examiner*.

Apart from the *Chronicle*, other papers were charged, but it was Perry whom the government wished to see imprisoned. His case was called first: he defended himself brilliantly and was acquitted, leading to the actions against the other papers being dropped. The trial, though, was to take its toll, and in 1817 Perry gave up the editorship through ill-health, handing over to his assistant, John Black, to whom the paper was sold after Perry's death on 4 December 1821. Thomas Escott was to write of him:[21] 'The services rendered to his craft by this great editor and businessman will be better estimated if one contrasts the honour and authority secured by Perry for his vocation with the discredit and contempt in which he had first found it.'

The other leading paper of this period, the *Morning Post*, was also now under the direction of a Scot – Edinburgh-born Daniel Stuart, who was sent to London when aged twelve to join his older brothers in their printing business. One brother, Peter, in 1788 founded the *Star* and that same year Daniel took over from him the printing of the *Morning Post*. With the paper about to fold, he bought the *Post* for £600 in 1795; and for that received a house in Catherine-street, all the printing plant and a title – circulation only 350 copies per day – that was morally discredited.

Although extremely interested in the political events in France, and a man of radical views, Stuart, as editor, was determined to maintain a balance on the *Post*; and among the distinguished recruits who 'made the Paper cheerfully entertaining, not entirely filled with ferocious politics', were Coleridge, Lamb, Wordsworth and Southey. Lamb, who also acted as drama critic, at sixpence a paragraph, was later to write:

> The chat of that day – scandal, but, above all, dress – furnished the material . . . . A fashion of flesh, or rather pink-coloured hose for the ladies, luckily coming up at the juncture when we were on our probation for the place of Chief jester to S's Paper established our reputation in that line. Then there was the collateral topic of ankles. What an occasion to a truly chaste writer like myself, of touching that nick brink, and yet never tumbling over it . . . .

Lamb in his *Recollections of Newspapers Thirty-five Years Ago* also had much to say 'of the *Morning Post* and its offices, of its handsome apartments, of its rosewood desks, of its silver ink-wells, and of its bluff and genial proprietor'.

Coleridge, too, was to comment, although in a less flattering vein, writing with bitterness and disgust – 'disgust at the work itself, in which he wasted the pride and manhood of his intellect, without adding anything to his reputation'. However, he did concede that: 'The rapid and unusual sale of the *Morning Post* is a sufficient pledge that genuine impartiality with a respectable portion of literary talent will secure the success of a newspaper without the aid of party or ministerial patronage.'

Having already purchased the *Gazeteer*, in 1798 Stuart bought the *Telegraph*, with whom he had been in dispute, and subsumed it into the *Post*. With these mergers, plus editorial improvements in the paper, the *Morning Post* circulation 'rose with such rapidity that in a couple of years it is said to have been 7,000 a day, and the profits between £5,000 and £6,000 a year'. This increase in sales was to have a dramatic effect in the number of small advertisements, as Stuart was quick to point out: 'Advertisements act and react. They attract readers, promote circulation, and circulation attracts advertisements.'

In 1800 Pitt raised the Stamp Duty to 3*d*., and as a consequence Stuart daily reminded his readers: 'Price 6*d*. Price in 1783 3*d*. Taxed by Mr Pitt 3*d*.' The following year Stuart sold the *Morning Post* for £25,000. In 1796, he had entered the evening newspaper market when he bought the *Courier*, which sold for 7*d*. Recovering his health, Stuart now devoted his engergies to his evening title; and with the aid of Peter Street, first manager and later editor, plus Coleridge and Wordsworth, he increased the circulation of the *Courier* from 1500 to 7000. Stuart was to be involved until 1822, when he sold his interest in the paper and retired from journalism to live in the country.

Nelson and Wellington

During the early years of the nineteenth century the news was dominated by the war with France; and every battle, whether on land or sea, was religiously covered by the papers in the printing of the official despatches and translations from foreign newspapers. A flavour of the style is given in *The St James's Chronicle* of the two main conflicts:[23] Trafalgar and Waterloo.

News of the Battle of Trafalgar, 21 October 1805, did not reach London until 6 November; and the full despatch to the Admiralty from Vice-Admiral Collingwood, Commander-in-chief of His Majesty's ships and vessels off Cadiz, covered 2½ columns. In 12 pt single-column caps it is headed:

THURSDAY, NOV. 7
NAVAL INTELLIGENCE
The London Gazette
Extraordinary
WEDNESDAY, NOV. 6

The ever-to-be lamented death of Vice-Admiral Lord Viscount Nelson, who in the late conflict with the enemy fell in the hour of victory . . . .

On the last of the four-page issue there is a Postscript of a half-column:

DECISIVE VICTORY OVER THE
COMBINED FLEETS;
AND DEATH OF LORD NELSON

A fulsome tribute compares him with the Gods: 'He now lies with the Epaminonda's, the Leonidas's, the Abercrombys, and those heroes who most enjoy the sympathetic admiration of the human species through all ages.' The tribute ends: 'Even the ashes of such a man as Nelson are prolific. What British seaman, who recollects his name, will not endeavour to emulate his glory?'

For the remainder of the year, Nelson and Trafalgar are mentioned in every issue, including the Thanksgiving ordered by the King for December 5; and the despatch of Surgeon Beaty, who was present at Nelson's death. In his account, however, there is no mention of Nelson having said, 'Kiss me, Hardy.'

The Battle of Waterloo, on 15 June 1815, was covered in even more detail, for in the *Chronicle* issue of Saturday 17 June–Tuesday 20 June there was a Postscript headed:

IMPORTANT NEWS
COMMENCEMENT OF HOSTILITIES
MOST DREADFUL BATTLE

'The long looked-for contest has at last begun by Napoleon's making one of those furious and desperate attacks for which his campaigns are distinguished . . . .' The Postscript is only of a dozen paragraphs, and it ends on a note of doubt: 'Since writing the above we have heard that a telegraphic communication states the battle to have been fought, and the French have been obliged to retreat. We cannot vouch for this – the Messenger has not arrived.'

In the following issue, however, victory is confirmed; and the account covers four columns over pages three and four under a bold single-column heading:

GREAT VICTORY
OFFICIAL DOCUMENTS
The despatch brought by Hon. Major H. Percy
WELLINGTON'S DESPATCH
GAZETTE EXTRAORDINARY

'I send with this despatch two eagles taken by the troops in the action, which Major Percy will have the honour of laying at the feet of His Royal Highness . . .'.

The Postscript, which covers another two columns on the back page, is headed:

OFFICIAL CONFIRMATION
OF A
GREAT AND DECISIVE VICTORY

Due honour is paid to the Iron Duke and his troops in profuse praise, and the tribute ends: 'Nothing was wanting to complete the military fame of our illustrious Wellington but a decided victory over Napoleon.'

Although all England had welcomed the peace that followed Waterloo, it was not a country without its own internal problems. Between 1811 and 1813, the troubles with the Luddites, and the smashing of new machinery, had won great prominence in the Press; and in the very issue containing the obituary notice of Henry Baldwin, founder of *The St James's Chronicle*, there was a report of the hanging of Luddite trouble-makers at York.

The established Press was now complaining of the anarchists who dominated the weeklies and who were infiltrating the dailies: 'Inflaming the turbulent temper of the manufacturers, and disturbing the quiet attachment of the peasant to those institutions under which he and his father have dwelt in peace.' But the beginnings of the Industrial revolution were not just confined to the weaving machines of the North . . . .

Enter the Steam Press

At six o'clock on the morning of 29 November 1814, John Walter II, proprietor, went into the pressroom of his newspaper and astonished its occupants by telling them: '*The Times* is already printed – by steam.' Fleet Street had entered the industrial age. That same day, *The Times*' leading article proclaimed:[24]

> Our Journal of this day presents to the public the practical result of the greatest improvement connected with printing, since the discovery of the art itself. The reader of this paragraph now holds in his hand one of the many thousand impressions of *The Times* newspaper, which were taken off last night by a mechanical apparatus. A system of machinery almost organic has been devised and arranged, which, while it relieves the human frame of its most laborious efforts in printing, far exceeds all human powers in rapidity and despatch.

Walter informed his staff that there would be no redundancies as a result of this new press, except by natural wastage, but if 'any violence was attempted there was a force ready to suppress it'.

The inventors of the press were Friedrich Koenig and F. A. Bauer, who had come to London in the previous decade. The machine consisted of two single presses built symmetrically around a central inking system; later on, tape feeds and delivery systems were introduced to aid production. The great advantage of the press was that it could produce more than 1100 copies an hour, four times the output of the Stanhope hand press.

Less than a week later, on 3 December, Walter could inform his readers that with the press working with 'improving order, regularity and even speed', the paper was able to provide the very latest news, as had been particularly evident on the day of Parliament's recent adjournment:

> On such an occasion, the operation of the composing and printing the last page must commence among all the journals at the last moment; and starting from that moment, we, with our infinitely superior circulation, were enable to throw off our whole impression many hours before the other respectable rival prints. The accuracy and clearness of the impression will likewise excite attention.

For *The Times*, the introduction of the steam press meant that not only could the paper go to bed later, with up-to-the-minute news, but there was now no longer the need to duplicate the setting of formes, providing a saving in composing charges of between £2000-£3000 per year. By the use of the new press, more than seven thousand copies of an eight-page paper were produced every night; and this not only provided the opportunity for increased revenue from sales and advertisements, but it gave John Walter II independence from political parties.

Peace in 1815 had brought with it a slump, which, after the boom times of the war, was difficult for the working classes to appreciate; and always, in the background, there were the fears of the unknown, the social and economic changes that would be brought about by the coming of the Industrial Revolution.

It was a time of resurgence in radical journalism, but a journalism directed at the artisan and the labourer. It was crusading journalism with a purpose: to mould public opinion. Leading the fight was William Cobbett, whose *Political Register*, with its demand for parliamentary reform, was winning ready support from the working classes. Even though its price of almost one shilling for sixteen quarto pages was beyond the pocket of the average reader, working-men clubbed together to buy it and read it aloud in public houses. It was an immediate success, and Cobbett's idea was quickly followed by lesser imitations: *The Black Dwarf*, *The Gorgon*, *The Reformists' Register*, *The Republican*, *Weekly Commentary*, *Medusa*.

Born at Farnham, the son of a farm labourer, William Cobbett had served in the Army from 1784 to 1791, mainly in Canada. He resigned over injustices, and on leaving published a pamphlet denouncing military corruption. This led to his fleeing to hide on his farm in England, and then, because of the French Revolution, emigrating to the United States.

Cobbett left New York on 2 June 1800 on board the packet-boat *Lady Arabella*, bound for Halifax, Nova Scotia, and Falmouth, England. At Halifax he was given close to a hero's welcome, being entertained to dinner by the Governor, Sir John Wentworth, and feted by its leading citizens, who were still engaged in raising the $5000 dollars needed for his 'grossly unfair' libel action in New York (which he had already lost.)

He reached Falmouth at the beginning of July 'whereupon all the *gentry*, as they stiled themselves, went on shore and left us to get out of the ship as best we could . . . .' Cobbett then hired a post-chaise and drove his family to London – to find an invitation to dine at Mr Windham's (who was Secretary of War) 'and did dine with Mr Pitt himself, who was very polite'.

Within days he was offered by George Hammond, the Under-Secretary for Foreign Affairs, control of one of two daily papers, the *True Briton* (morning) or the *Sun* (evening), plus government money, to fight Jacobean propaganda. Cobbett refused the offer, but did start a daily paper of his own, the *Porcupine*, which lasted from 30 October 1800 until November 1801. And during this period, he bitterly opposed the peace treaty with France, resulting in a mob attacking his house and a troop of Horse Guards having to be sent to disperse them.

The following year, 1802, he founded and edited *Cobbett's Weekly Political Register*, which, with a few interruptions, was to continue until his death thirty-three years later. In 1802 he had also reprinted all his American writings, some twelve volumes, as *Porcupine*'s *Works*; and this was followed in 1804 with the launch of *Parliamentary Debates*, taken over eight years later by Hansard. Despite the high price, the *Political Register* was a success from its first issue; and with the paper firmly established Cobbett was able to live once more in the country. As editor, Cobbett was becoming more and more radical, and in June 1809 he published an article criticizing the practice of flogging in the Army. He was prosecuted by the government the following summer and found guilty. Sentencing was postponed for a few days; but despite an offer from Cobbett to cease publication of his paper he was fined £1000 and imprisoned for two years. On the day of his release, he was the guest of honour at a dinner for six hundred presided over by Sir Francis Burdett, MP for Westminster.

Still a radical, on 13 November 1816 Cobbett published his *Address to the Journeymen and Labourers of England, as well as Scotland and Ireland*, advocating the case for reform. The result was electric; and he was compelled to produce a cheap edition at twopence, with special discounts for quantities. Despite being dubbed 'Cobbett's twopenny trash', the circulation of his *Political Register*, produced in two editions, was to reach 40,000 copies a week. Worried at the popularity of Cobbett and his newspaper, the government hounded the news-sellers, and in 1817 suspended the Habeas Corpus Act. Taking fright, Cobbett left for the United States and was to remain there until 1819.

Peterloo Massacre

That same year, 1819, the Home Secretary, Viscount Sidmouth, declared that there was no difference between the established and more radical newspapers, saying that the 'Newspaper Press was a most malignant and formidable enemy to the Constitution to which it owed its freedom.' And it was Sidmouth, who in July 1819 instructed the Lord Lieutenant of Lancashire to take all measures thought necessary to preserve order, including the calling out of the Yeomanry in an attempt to control the Reformists. Within a month his instructions had been carried out to the letter, for in the August a meeting was held in St Peter's Field, Manchester, which was addressed by the radical Henry Hunt, calling for parliamentary reform.

Claimed by the organizers as the largest meeting ever held in England, a crowd of 50,000 was met by 400 constables, while, out of sight, the Manchester Yeomanry and the 15th Hussars were kept at the ready. After the reading of the Riot Act by the magistrates – mostly unheard – the Yeomanry arrested Hunt, and then lost complete control, charging the crowd with drawn sabres. The result was the Peterloo Massacre: more than a dozen killed, some 420 wounded; an event which has long lived unhappily in British social history.

During that long summer of 1819, two stories had dominated the newspapers: the Great Comet, visible from many parts of England, and the ever-increasing passions aroused by the Reformists. For many months, the growth of the Reformist Movement, with its meetings, marches and occasional riots, had been covered in depth by the Press. And on Saturday 17 July 1819 *The St James's Chronicle* in London noted the disturbances at Stockport in Cheshire; and in its leader commented that Viscount Sidmouth had on 7 July written to the Lord Lieutenant of Cheshire:[25]

> True bills of indictment had been found against Sir Charles Wolsely and Harrison, the Dissenting Minister, for speeches delivered by them at Stockport on 26th ult 'with intent to excite tumult and insurrection within the realm'. This is the right conduct to be pursued by the Government. The laws will be found abundantly strong: they only require to be called into action.

Four days later the Reformists – more than 20,000 strong – gathered at Smithfield, London, where they were addressed by Hunt. In a delicious phrase the paper reported the meeting, which 'included the idlers who came from curiosity and the pickpockets who attended professionally', had passed without incident.

But everything came to a head – producing a national outcry – on 16 August with the meeting and massacre at Peterloo, reported in great depth by John William Tyas, of *The Times*, the only London journalist present. In a striking and finely-written story – later lifted by most of the paper's rivals – Tyas followed the events, from the marchers arriving at the Fields at 10.30 a.m. until the charge of the Yeomanry four hours later:

> The first body of reformers arrived at the ground bearing two banners, each of which was surmounted by a cap of liberty. The first bore upon a white ground the inscription of 'Annual Parliament and Universal Suffrage'; on the reverse side: 'No Corn Law'. The other bore upon a blue ground the same inscription with the addition of 'Vote by Ballot'.

The gradual build-up to the horrors, with the drilling of the volunteers, included:

> A club of Female Reformers, amounting in numbers, according to our calculation, to 150, from Oldham; and another, not quite so numerous from Royton .... The later bore two red flags, the one inscribed *Let us die like men, and not be sold like slaves*; the other *Annual Parliaments and Universal Suffrage*.

Carefully, Tyas described the peaceful arrival of 'Orator' Hunt himself at the banner-bedecked waggon, whence he was to address his supporters. Immediately, there came an attempted arrest by the officer commanding the Yeomanry:[26]

> 'Sir, I have a warrant against you, and arrest you as my prisoner.' Hunt turned to the officer and said: 'I willingly surrender myself to any civil officer who will show me his warrant.' Hunt and Johnson, his associate, then surrendered to Joseph Nadin, leader of the constables. As soon as Hunt and Johnson jumped from the waggon, a cry was made by the cavalry 'Have at the flags!' and they immediately dashed not only at the flags which were in the waggon but those which were posted among the crowd, cutting most indiscriminately to the right and to the left in order to get them. We saw the Editor of the *Manchester Observer* being attacked .... another victim within five yards of us in another direction had his nose completely taken off by a blow of a sabre; whilst another was laid prostrate.
>
> Seeing this hideous work was going on we felt an alarm which any man may be forgiven for feeling in a similar situation. Looking around us, we saw a constable at no great distance, and thinking that our only chance of safety rested in placing ourselves under his protection we appealed to him for assistance. He immediately took us into custody and on saying that we merely attended to report the proceedings of the day he replied 'Oh! Oh! You then are one of their writers – you must go before the Magistrates.' To this we made no dissent.

Having been forced to spend the night in prison, Tyas completed his account the following morning, Tuesday the 17th. In the meantime, local reporters John Edward Taylor, later to found the *Manchester Guardian*, and Archibald Prentice, the future historian of the Anti-Corn League, had filed their stories to two London papers.

The report of the massacre and *The Times*' leaders caused an uproar throughout the nation, with public meetings, and subscription lists being opened for the victims. But for *The St James's Chronicle* and its new editor, Dr Stanley Lees Giffard, it was a different story. In a note of censure, he commented: 'Here *The Times* Reporter (who not being known has evidently lost his temper, and has obviously written under angry feelings which we feel should have been corrected and repressed by the editor of that paper).' Giffard continued:

> What has long been desired by every friend of order has at length taken place. The strong arm of the law has been put forth to put, we trust, a final stop to the assemblage of the ignorant and the seditious, which can produce nothing but evil, and which cannot be permitted under any form of Government, nor, indeed, in any state of social existence.

4

Plant here *The Standard*

ALTHOUGH STANLEY GIFFARD and his proprietor, Charles Baldwin, had in *The St James's Chronicle* denounced *The Times* and its new editor for that paper's reportage of the Peterloo Massacre, they were very much in the minority. For the 32-year-old Thomas Barnes, however, it was a different matter – he was soon to be feted. Many of his close friends 'who knew the brilliance of Barnes's scholarship, the extent of his reading and the ability of his pen' had believed that he would regret taking up the appointment of editor of *The Times*. They were to be proved to be so wrong; especially as others were quick to note that 'often he wrote so like a classically-educated prize-fighter'.

Educated at Christ's Hospital and Pembroke College, Oxford,[1] Barnes came to London in 1808 and quickly joined the literary circle of Hazlitt, Hunt and Lamb. Two years later Barnes became drama critic of *The Times* and within months had transferred to the paper's parliamentary staff. However, he was also writing for *The Examiner* under the pseudonym of Criticus; and many of these articles were subsequently republished as a book in 1815.

Launched in 1808 by James Henry Leigh Hunt, editor, and his elder brother, John Hunt, proprietor, *The Examiner* was a quarto-sized paper of 'Politics, Domestic Economy and Theatricals'. Owing allegiance to no party, but advocating liberal politics with courage, it became extremely popular but soon ran into trouble with the authorities: an article in 1811 on the savagery of military flogging led to a prosecution which was successfully defended. However, the following year, on 22 March 1812, an attack on the Prince Regent led to the brothers being fined £500 each and sent to prison for two years – Leigh to Horsemonger Lane and John to Coldbath Fields.

Notwithstanding, they continued to edit and manage *The Examiner* from their cells. Leigh Hunt was also able to entertain Lord Byron, Charles Lamb, Thomas Moore and Jeremy Bentham there. Moved to the infirmary, at the doctor's suggestion, he had a private apartment, complete with a piano, working library and green venetian blinds to hide the iron bars. 'Charles Lamb declared ironically there was no other such room except in a fairy tale.' Leigh and John Hunt were released from prison in February 1815.

It was during this period that John Walter II, proprietor of *The Times*, decided that he must have a new editor. Consequently, he authorized Barnes to write some leaders for the then editor, Dr John Stoddart. The brother-in-law of William Hazlitt, Stoddart was a fanatical anti-Bonapartist, and while his immoderate style of article went down well enough during the war he became an embarrassment after peace had been declared. Nevertheless, in 1814 he signed a six-year agreement at a salary of £1400 per annum; and for that he was to be in attendance every evening except Saturday, and when he was on his five weeks' holiday (even though Barnes was doing most of the editorial work.)

But the following year, on 15 November, Walter charged his editor with 'suppressing *news* against his own opinions'; and as a result decided to involve Barnes totally in revising and correcting Stoddart's leading articles. Stoddart remained as editor, despite continuing quarrels – 'the Doctor is with difficulty kept in order even by Walter and Barnes at the same time' – until 31 December 1816 when he was summarily dismissed.

Within two months, in February 1817, Stoddart, as editor, had started a rival paper, *The Day & New Times*; and in his initial leader revealed that he had been 'the person who had been for some time the writer of the leading article in *The Times* and who having left that paper now purposes to conduct the *Day* alone and without any restraint or hindrance whatsoever.' With unofficial backing from Carlton House, Stoddart's paper – its title shortened to *The New Times* in 1818 – continued until 1828; and his attacks on his former employer during those years were to make him the subject of ridicule, earning the epithet of 'Dr Slop'.[2] Many years later, Thomas Escott, writing about Stoddart, declared: 'The journalist who provokes a quarrel with his employer commits suicide.' Nevertheless, Stoddart was to flourish: he was knighted in 1826, and that same year appointed Chief Justice of Malta by his old friend the Prince of Wales, now George IV.

For Barnes, to assume the mantle of editor of *The Times* at the age of 32 was certainly a challenge; nevertheless he more than lived up to the role, and was to remain in charge until his death in 1841. Two early incidents were to mark his editorship: his argument in 1819 against the restriction of the Press that formed part of the 'Six Acts'; and his support for Queen Caroline during her trial the following year for alleged adultery. Thanks to *The Times*, huge public sympathy and the impressive defence of Lord Brougham the government dropped the charge. Sadly, Queen Caroline was turned away from Westminster Abbey at George IV's coronation, and died a few days later.

During his editorship, Lord Lyndhurst, the Lord Chancellor, was to remark: 'Why Barnes is the most important person in the country.'[3] As editor, Barnes was one of the first to appoint correspondents throughout the United Kingdom, and he made *The Times* the interpreter of public opinion. 'His achievement lay in the fact that he moulded the paper into the forceful organ that spoke for the nation.'

On 17 February 1827 the Prime Minister, Lord Liverpool, suffered a stroke and was forced to resign. Three people qualified as his successor: the Duke of Wellington, Sir Robert Peel and George Canning. In April, Canning was summoned by George IV to form a government, and the majority of the Old Tories who had been his colleagues for almost five years went into opposition. However, the Canning-led Coalition quickly won widespread approval from the public, which led Peel to remark that the Press was almost on one side. Charles Arbuthnott, another leading Old Tory, was also annoyed with the Press and hoped that some steps would be taken to secure at least one newspaper for the party.

Arbuthnott was particularly concerned that the reputation of the Duke of Wellington, who had recently given up command of the Army, for which he had been heavily criticized, should be restored. To this end he sought the aid of William Huskisson, President of the Board of Trade, and later to be the first railway casualty, when seeking reconciliation with the Duke. Huskisson, however, was not to be an ally, replying that 'he had never had any connexion with newspapers and was convinced that they had not been under any special influence since the formation of the new Government and that they had not been encouraged to speak disparagingly of the Duke'.

Attempts to turn *The Watchman* into a daily paper, and to save *The Courier* failed. The thoughts of Arbuthnott and his fellow Old Tories turned more and more to Charles Baldwin.

The Standard *is Launched*

At 2 p.m. on Monday, 21 May 1827, the hopes of Arbuthnott, Wellington and Peel were realized when the first edition of the new daily, *The Standard*, appeared. Charles Baldwin, however, had no intention of exposing his successful thrice-weekly *The St James's Chronicle* to five-nights-a-week production, as he later revealed:[4]

> I was not willing to risk the continuance of my old and valued journal; I preferred the heavier risks of establishing at my own expense and hazard, a Daily Evening Paper to be conducted on the same principles and by the same editor. I also engaged the assistance of Dr Maggin and other celebrated writers. The choice of a name then claimed our attention. The object was to make a stand against the inroad of principle; contrary to our Constitution in Church and State; a very appropriate motto was chosen by Dr Giffard, *Signifer, statue signum, hic optime manetimus* (Plant here the Standard Here we shall best remain) and on the 21st May, 1827, *The Standard* was reared, hauled as a rallying point, and was speedily followed by the raising of *Standards* in the Provincial and Colonial Conservative Press. Even Foreign newspapers have adopted the name.

As noted, the two men behind the launch of the *Standard* – Charles Baldwin and Dr Stanley Lees Giffard – had already achieved considerable success with *The St James's Chronicle*. The son of Henry Baldwin, Charles, had been bound to his father as an apprentice compositor on 7 July 1789, and 'So quickly did he attain the knowledge of the business that at 18 Mr Baldwin senior confided in him the entire superintendence of the working part of his establishment.'

In 1801, at the age of 27, Charles's efforts were rewarded when his father changed the firm's name to Henry Baldwin and Son; and later relinquished his two shares. By 1808, through gift, exchange and purchase, Charles Baldwin owned seven of the eight shares in the company, and with the death of Christopher Moody became sole owner.

Eight years later, he bought the rival *London Evening Post*, and then, in 1819, purchased the *London Chronicle* for £300 from Colonel Torrens and absorbed it into *The St James's Chronicle.*

For Baldwin and his editor, there were to be three principles that must be observed: opposition to Catholic Emancipation; opposition to parliamentary reform; and opposition to the repeal of the Corn Laws – and for the next twenty years they were to fight hard in these struggles. Initially, sales of *The Standard* were barely 700 per night, but within five years the circulation had risen to more than 1500; and with his other papers Baldwin was 'said to be worth upwards of £100,000'. Profits on *The Standard* alone were estimated to be between £7000 and £8000 per year; and, apart from *The Standard* and *The St James's Chronicle*, he was also the owner of the *London Packet*, which came out twice weekly, and the *London Journal* – 'all got up with scarcely any expense out of *The Standard*'. It was believed that his total income from newspapers was more than £15,000 a year.

The paper's editor, Dublin-born Dr Stanley Lees Giffard, had studied at Trinity College, taking the degree of LL.D before entering the Middle Temple, where he was called to the Bar in 1811. However, not making any progress as a barrister, he became a political writer on *The St James's Chronicle*; and after six years was appointed editor in 1819. Now, in 1827, he was chosen to edit *The Standard*, and within a matter of months was in trouble with the Duke of Wellington over an article, causing the Duke to exclaim: 'What can we do with these sort of fellows? We have no power over them, and for my part I will have no communication with any of them.' And three months later, on 16 March 1829, the publication of a letter from Lord Winchilsea, criticizing the Duke over King's College and Catholic Emancipation, was to lead to their fighting a duel at Battersea Fields. Fortunately, neither party was injured, and two days later Giffard published an apology in *The Standard*, plus the full correspondence – some eighteen letters. The final word on the matter, however, came some months later, from the Duke himself: 'The truth is that the duel with Lord Winchilsea was as much a part of the Roman Catholic question, and it was necessary to undertake it . . . . as was to do every thing else that I could do to attain the object which I had in view.'

The continuing outspokeness of Giffard meant that he was now a person to be reckoned with, but he was not without his critics as John Gibson Lockhart wrote in 1835: 'But McGinnis's [Maginn] superior in *The Standard* is a man of a different cast and calibre and he is really worth thinking of. He too is poor – often embarrased, and hence, irritable, sulky and dangerous.' Despite this criticism, Giffard was a proud man, and in 1828 had even refused a gift of £1200 from the Duke of Newcastle, who had been so impressed by one of the editor's leaders.[5] As the father of ten children, who in the autumn of 1840 was forced to send his family to France, to live on three pounds a week, this was self-sacrifice of the highest order.

Bright, Broken Maggin

The chief writer on *The Standard*, Dr William Maginn, had also been educated at Trinity College, Dublin, becoming an LL.D in 1819. Maginn is credited as being one of the first persons to call *The Times* 'The Thunderer'. In an article that appeared on 15 February 1830 in the *Morning Herald* he described *The Times* as 'The Great Earwigger of the Nation, otherwise the Leading Journal of Europe, otherwise The Awful monosyllable, otherwise The Thunderer – but more commonly called The Blunderer.'

A well-known figure in Fleet Street, Maginn had many friends, including Thomas Barnes of *The Times*, but it was to be Charles Baldwin whom he was to join for the start of *The Standard*. Maginn's brilliant writing and acerbic wit were features of the paper, and, although he wrote anonymously, his style was immediately recognizable and won him many admirers. One contemporary described him as: 'A bright Genius undoubtedly he was. He would write a leader in *The Standard* one evening, answer it in *The True Sun* the following day and abuse both in *John Bull* the ensuing Sunday.' One of his faithful friends was William Makepeace Thackeray, and he has described how his love of newspapers was fired by Maginn:[6]

> My interest in journals and magazines of all kinds had always been there – I knew and bought them all and had toyed for a long time with the idea of becoming somehow involved in them, either as a contributor – vain hope – or in the production which interested me almost as much. Does this surprise you? Then you don't know what an exciting business the putting together of a newspaper is. It does not just put itself through the letter box on its own – the print does not jump onto the page by itself and the pages do not cut and bind themselves alone and the illustrations aren't done on each copy by the artist – the whole process is extremely complicated and skilful and I am always astonished to this day that it can happen at all and at such speed. I remember being taken by my friend William Maginn to *The Standard* in London one Wednesday night where he showed me the mysteries I have outlined above and quite fired my imagination to have a hand in it all.

Thackeray has described his visit to *The Standard* offices in this passage from his novel, *Pendennis*:

> They were passing through the Strand as they talked, and by a newspaper office, which was all lighted up and bright. Reporters were coming out of the place or rushing up to it in cabs; there were lamps burning in the editor's room, and, above, the compositors were at work; the windows of the building were a blaze of light. 'Look at that, Pen,' Warrington said. 'There she is – the great engine – she never sleeps. She has ambassadors in every quarter of the world – her couriers upon every road. Her officers march with armies and her envoys walk into statesmen's cabinets. They are ubiquitous. Yonder journal has an agent, at this minute, giving bribes at Madrid; and another inspecting the price of potatoes in Covent Garden. Look! Here comes the Foreign Express galloping in. They will be able to give the news to Downing Street tomorrow: funds will rise or fall, fortunes will be made or lost – and Mr Doolan will be called away from his supper for he is foreign sub-editor.'

Apart from *The Standard*, Maginn was also contributing to *The Age* and to the radical *Sun*. But the years of heavy drinking were beginning to take their toll: 'He is a ruin, but a glorious ruin, nevertheless. Could he be induced to do so he would be the first man of the day in literature.' For a brief period, Maginn moved to the provinces where he edited *The Lancashire Herald*, a weekly published in Liverpool, but the lure of London and his friends was too much, and by 1841 he had begun his connections with *Punch*. Money, though, was to remain a problem, and, despite aid from the King of Hanover, Sir Robert Peel and Thackeray, he was thrown into Fleet Prison for debt. This did, not, however, prevent his contributing to *The Standard* and to *Punch*. Compelled to obtain his discharge as an insolvent, he emerged broken-hearted and in an advanced stage of consumption to live at Walton-on-Thames, where he died on 21 August 1842.[7]

The Reform Bill is Passed

With the Catholic Emancipation Act having received a reluctant royal assent on 13 April 1829, the way was now clear for parliamentary reform. The system at this time was full of anomalies: migration of the population to new industrial regions had created urban areas that were unrepresented, while leaving old constituencies with a handful of electors. Besides these rotten boroughs there remained the pocket boroughs where aristocratic patrons could secure the return of their nominees. As an example of this, the Duke of Newcastle, when his candidate was defeated at Newark, checked over the votes, and expelled every one of his tenants who had voted for the other person. His reason: 'Have I not got the right to do what I like with my own?'

Unlike Giffard on *The Standard*, Barnes, with his liberal outlook, had been a strong supporter of Catholic Emançipation, and was now a fierce fighter for parliamentary reform, evidenced by his leader on 29 January 1831: 'Unless the people – the people everywhere – come forward and petition, aye, thunder for reform, it is they who abandon an honest Minister – it is not the Minister who betrays the people. But in that case, reform, and Minister, and people too are lost.'[8]

It was against this background of malpractice and misrepresentation that, on 22 March 1831, Lord John Russell, for the recently-elected Whigs, introduced the first Reform Bill into the House of Commons; and after a heated struggle the second reading was carried by a majority of one. Macaulay has described the excitement of the moment: 'You might have heard a pin drop as Duncannon read the numbers. Then, again, the shouts broke out and many of us shed tears.'

For Giffard in *The Standard*, though, there was nothing but dismay: 'We neither like the policy, nor much rely upon the fidelity of gentlemen who blurb a measure upon a first or second reading, with the design of strangling it in committee. The Attorney General made exactly such a speech, as if it had been made elsewhere, ought to have been prosecuted by the Attorney General.'

William IV now dissolved Parliament and a general election took place. 'The Bill, the whole Bill, and nothing but the Bill' was the cry heard everywhere; and leading the cry was *The Times*, which proclaimed: 'Once again we warn them (the Boroughmongers) to desist – not only if they value their lives and happiness of theirs, for they are selfish to be moved by considerations, but if they value their own.' According to *The Standard* and *The St James's Chronicle* these words were an incitement; but, when the results were counted, seats which had been Tory-held for generations had changed hands – and the Whigs were returned with a majority of more than one hundred.

On 25 June 1831 Lord Russell again introduced a Reform Bill, and was successful by a large majority, but in early October the Bill went to the Lords, where it was thrown out in a night of high passion by forty-one votes. Less than two months later, on 11 December, William Cobbett was charged with publishing an article in the *Political Register* inciting labourers to acts of violence. Ever since his return in 1819 from the United States, Cobbett had fought for parliamentary reform; and for much of the decade he was to travel around England on horseback, when embarking on his political tours. The accounts of these trips were published in the *Political Register* and later in his famous collection, *Rural Rides*. Now, in July 1832, he was tried at the Guildhall for publishing the article, but the jury failed to reach a verdict, and the charge was allowed to lapse.

Within three months, in October 1832 the Reform Act was passed, leading the *Morning Post* to declare: 'We shall no longer regard [electoral reform] as an object of legitimate hostility, but, while, we watch its workings with deep anxiety, contribute to the extent of our humble means and our limited sphere to cause it to work well.' And one of the MPs in the reformed parliament was William Cobbett, newly-elected Member for Oldham.

The Murdered Editor

As the Tories' only champion among the evening papers, *The Standard*, plus the greater circulation of *The Times*, rendered insignificant the other two Tory newspapers, the *Morning Herald* and the *Morning Post*. The kindest words that one Tory critic could say about the *Post* in 1836 was that it was 'the pet of the petticoats, the darling of the boudoir, the oracle of the drawing-room and the soft recorder of the ballroom'.

Ever since Daniel Stuart had sold the *Morning Post* for £25,000 in 1803, the paper had for three decades been under the editorship of Nicholas Byrne, who had run into trouble with his coverage of the Queen Caroline case in 1820, leading to mobs smashing the front of the newspaper's offices. A man of strong convictions and a champion of law and order, Byrne was a keen supporter of the Tories and in their pay. Two attacks were made on his life, and the second was to be, ultimately, successful. In the centenary issue of the *Morning Post* on 2 November1872 it was reported:[9]

> One winter's night, or rather morning, nearly forty years ago, when Mr Byrne was sitting alone in his office, a man entered unchallenged from the street, and made his way to his room. He wore a crape mask, and rushing up to his victim stabbed him twice with a dagger. Mr Byrne, though mortally wounded, gave the alarm, and managed to follow his assailant to the street, but he escaped in the darkness of the night, and was never brought to justice.

Byrne did not die immediately, but lingered on; and in the issue of 28 June 1833 the *Morning Post* announced: 'DIED – Yesterday, June 27, after an illness of many months, in his 72nd year, N. Byrne, Esq., of Lancaster-place.'

Following his death, the editor and part-proprietor was C. Eastland Michele, who 'does not seem to have been a man of any great personal distinction', but he was instrumental in engaging a young Benjamin Disraeli as leader writer. As a businessman, Michele could show a profit of £42,000 a year.

The other true Tory newspaper, the *Morning Herald*, was owned by Edward Baldwin. The son of Charles, he was educated at Oxford University and then joined the family, mainly concentrating on *The Standard,* before, in 1834, purchasing the *Morning Herald* from the Thwaites family. At the time of purchase, circulation of the *Herald* was under 5000 copies, having six years earlier been 10,000.

In writing of the transaction, James Grant described Edward Baldwin as a thoroughly enterprising and enlightened trader in journalism, 'who two decades after Dudley's death bought the *Morning Herald* from the little group of fifth-rate capitalists to which it had gone'. Now with Giffard as editor – he simultaneously edited *The Standard* (sales 2950) and *The St James's Chronicle* (sales 4000) – Baldwin's first aim was to overtake *The Times.*[10]

The Radical Press

Aside from purchasers of the 'legitimate' Press, the time of the Reform Bill had also seen a great increase in the number of readers of unstamped titles; and in a blistering attack on 10 September 1833, Giffard in *The Standard* commented:[11]

> Everybody is aware of the miscellaneous multitude of cheap publications which the last two years have called into existence. Some of these have had very considerable sale; but we have evidence that all, without any exception, of an innocent and respectable kind, have been sold, not as cheap publications, but in collected numbers, at prices such as the upper and middle classes are accustomed to purchase. We need not hesitate to say, therefore, that those classes which have been the object of eleemosynary educated, have not availed themselves of the cheapness of innocent and respectable reading . . . . perhaps they have been reading – doubtless they have, and we are enabled, from an authentic source, to give some account of their reading . . . . It is a list of the unstamped publications in defiance of the law. With the late average sale of each:
>
> *The Poor Man' Guardian* – 16,000 circulation. This is printed by Hetherington, an Irish Papist and ex-student of Maynooth. *Destructive* – 8,000 circulation. Printed by the same. It is scarcely necessary to mention the principles of these publications; they are Jacobinical of the latest bloodiest dye. It will be remembered that Hetherington has preached the use of the dagger as an instrument of the revolution. *The Poor Man's Guardian* and *Destructive* circulate in Lancashire. *Gauntlet* – 22,000 circulation. The conductor is the notorious Carlile – his name is enough. *Cosmopolite* – 5,000 circulation. Editor, Destroisier. Principles, Owenite and Republican. *Working Men's Friend* – 7,000 circulation. Editor, Watson. Principles, Republican. *Crisis* – 5,000 circulation. Conductors, Mr Owen and Mr Morgan, author of the *Wrath of the Bees.* Mr Owen's name precludes the necessity of describing principles. *The Man* – 7,000 circulation. Conductors, Lee, the Chairman of Coalbath-field's meeting; and Petrie. Principles, Spencean and Republican. *Reformer* – 5,000 circulation. Principles, Republican and Revolutionary. Editor, Lorimer.

Giffard concluded his diatribe:

> These are the principal unstamped publications of London – the reading with *The Times* and *The Weekly Dispatch* of the educated democracy of the metropolis. Are men to be turned loose upon such garbage as this? In the country there are also unstamped newspapers – particularly at Leeds, Bradford and Manchester, etc., all taking their tone from the *Poor Man's Guardian* and the others, which we described as the penny press of London. These are the primitiae, the first fruits of the late active exertions on behalf of indiscriminate education.

Within three years the protestations of Giffard were to be heeded, and in 1836 the reduction of the Stamp Duty was hailed by the middle classes as a great stride towards the freedom of the Press. By reducing the difference in price between the stamped and unstamped, it led to the latter's decline. And as the *Northern Star* was to note: 'The reduction upon stamps has made the rich man's paper cheaper, and the poor man's paper dearer.'

Of the Radicals mentioned by Giffard, the two most prominent were undoubtedly Richard Carlile and Henry Hetherington. Born at Ashburton, Devon, in 1790, Carlile was apprenticed as a tinman before moving to London in 1813. And upon publication of the *Black Dwarf* four years later, Carlile borrowed £1 from his employer, bought 100 copies on 9 March 1817, and travelled around the capital selling them.[12] When the publisher was arrested, Carlile offered to take his place: 'I did not then see what my experience has since taught me that the greatest despotism of the press is popular ignorance.'

He then met W.T. Sherwin who had recently launched the *Republican*, soon to be re-named *Sherwin's Political Register*, which ran from April 1817 until August 1819. Sherwin wrote most of the text himself, also acting as editor and printer; but, planning to limit his liability, he agreed that Carlile should be publisher. Immediately, Carlile was in trouble, through reprinting the trials of William Hone – and defying the Attorney-General; and as a result Carlile was committed to King's Bench Prison for ten weeks and then released. His next brush with the law was in 1818 when he published the works of Thomas Paine – author of *The Rights of Man* – and was again arrested. Carlile was later to write:

> When I first started as a hawker of pamphlets I knew nothing of political principle, I had never read any of Paine's writings; but I had a complete conviction that there was something wrong somewhere and that the right application of the printing press was the right answer.

In January 1819 Carlile opened up at 55 Fleet Street, and that same month two further prosecutions were brought against him. He was imprisoned at Newgate but released on bail within a few days. While on bail yet another charge was laid against him – for publishing details of the Peterloo Massacre in Sherwin's *Political Register*. This did not prevent Carlile from assuming the editorship and reverting the paper to its old title, the *Republican*.

By the October of 1819, when he came up for trial, he faced six indictments. Nevertheless, Carlile reported the trial at some length, and there was a rush to buy

Daily Express building

Geoffrey Dawson and Neville Chamberlain

Peace for our Time, September 1938

The Times bombed

Northcliffe, Rothermere II, Rothermere I

Max Aitken and Beaverbrook

Hugh Cudlipp and Cecil King at 1968 IPC AGM

J.J. Astor

Ken and Roy Thomson

Bert Hardy, John Leese, Rothermere III

Donald Trelford

Bill Deedes

Kelvin MacKenzie and Rupert Murdoch, Wapping 1986

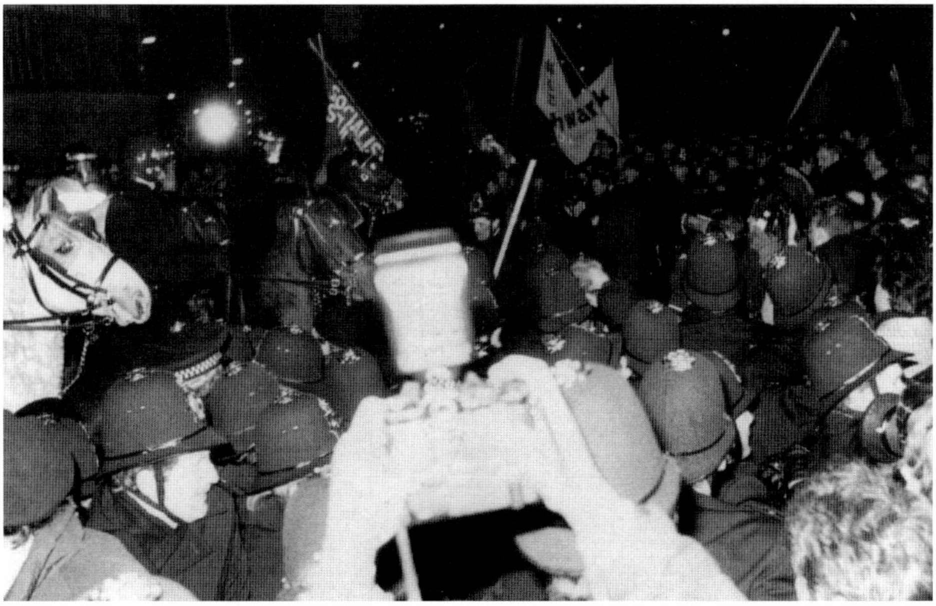

Pickets at Wapping

The Sunday Telegraph departs Fleet Street 1987

his publications. However, found guilty, he was sentenced to three years' imprisonment in Dorchester Gaol, fined £1500, his shop closed and his stock of seven thousand volumes seized, making it impossible to pay the fines. None of this, though, was to prevent Carlile from his cell publishing the *Republican*; and of the fourteen volumes produced until 1826 twelve were dated from Dorchester Gaol.

With Carlile in gaol, his wife Jane now decided to become publisher, but she, too, was prosecuted, and on 21 January 1821 was sentenced to two years' imprisonment. The next victim was her sister, Mary Ann, and in the July she was fined £500 and gaoled for twelve months for selling his work. Three members of the Carlile family were now in prison, but, thanks to his assistants, his shop remained open. Nevertheless, the authorities were to imprison several helpers, with sentences ranging from six weeks to two years. Matters came to a head in 1824 when nine assistants were tried and sentenced together with terms ranging up to three years.

In 1825 the Cabinet decided that the prosecutions against Carlile and his family should be discontinued. According to a manuscript note in St Bride's archives:

> Richard Carlile's shop was burned out in 1824, while its owner was in Dorchester Gaol, for what was called upholding the right of free discussion, but what the Law called selling blasphemous works. The Vicar and Wardens of St Bride wanted the site. Carlile offered to sell if the churchmen would secure his release. They saw the Prime Minister: Carlile was released: the site was secured.

The result was that St Bride's Church was now visible from Fleet Street.

And as for Carlile, upon his release he published *The Gorgon*, and from January 1828 until December 1829 edited a weekly, *The Lion*. Carlile was to clash once more with the authorities – when he objected to an assessment of church rates on his premises and refused to pay the fines. As a result he was sentenced to a further three years, bringing his time in prison to a total of nine years and four months. Carlile's determination to maintain a free Press won him sympathy and financial support from a host of allies, not prepared to take such risks; and as Cobbett was to remark: 'You have done your duty bravely, Mr Carlile, if everyone had done it like you, it would be all very well.' Any faults that Carlile had were to be forgiven for he had done more than any other in his day for the freedom of the Press.

The other prominent Radical of this period, Henry Hetherington, had, as noted, been a close friend of Carlile, and from the launch of his newspaper on 1 October 1830 was to be a thorn in the side of the authorities. In his opening editorial in *Penny Papers for the People*, yet another unstamped title, he declared: 'It is the cause of the rabble we advocate, the poor, the suffering, the industrious productive classes .... We will teach this rabble their power – we will teach them that they are your master, the industrious productive classes.'

In 1831, with his paper, having been suppressed, Hetherington started the *Poor Man's Guardian*, 'carrying not the little stamp duty but a black design of a printing press and the slogan Knowledge is Power'. The words 'Published in Defiance of the Law, to try the Power of the Right against the Might'[13] were printed below. As a weekly, the paper ran until 1835, and during those years many employees were imprisoned, the presses smashed and property seized.

Hetherington himself was one of the first to be imprisoned, and in 1834 was sent to Clerkenwell Gaol for publishing an unstamped paper, followed by another six months when he defied the law by continuing to issue the *Poor Man's Guardian* unstamped. This led him to write: 'Had I 20,000 lives I would sacrifice them all rather than succumb to such mean, such dastardly, such malignant reptiles.' He was prosecuted once more in 1834, but now in respect of a new, unstamped paper, the *Destructive and Poor Man's Conservative*. 'He was fined £120 for publishing the former journal but acquited on the other charge, thus scoring a victory that freed political sheets from the stamp duty.'

As a result, in issue no. 159 of the *Poor Man's Guardian* Hetherington was proud to proclaim: 'This paper, after sustaining a persecution of three years and a half duration, in which upwards of five hundred persons were imprisoned for vending it, was declared in the Court of Exchequer to be a strictly legal publication.'

Another Radical publisher of this period who suffered terms of imprisonment for his beliefs was William Hone. Born at Bath in 1780, he had failures in running a savings bank at Blackfriars, followed by a spell as a bookseller before in 1815 publishing the *Traveller* newspaper. Two years later, Hone launched the weekly *Reformists' Register,* priced twopence, but after just eight months he discontinued the publication because of the worries of 'a little business and a large family'. That same year he wrote three satires attacking the government: *The Late John Wilkes's Catechism of a Ministerial Member*, *The Political Litany* and *The Sinecurist's Creed or Belief*. The Attorney General immediately charged Hone with 'printing and publishing certain impious, profane and scandalous libels'.

Not being able to find the bail of £1000, he was sent to prison on 3 May 1818 and remained there for two months. But even while in prison Hone continued to write, informing his readers: 'I wrote my last *Register* at home in the midst of my family. Since then the Reign of Terror has commenced, and now I write from prison.' The ordeal began in the December; three times Hone was tried – and three times he was acquitted. His courage and ability in defending himself won much public sympathy and support from fellow-newspaper editors. As a result more than £3000 was raised by subscription, and Hone's accounts of his trials ran into many editions, while his parodies sold nearly ten thousand copies. William Wordworth, though, believed that 'The acquittal of Hone is enough to make one out of love with English juries.'

Hone was to live for another twenty-odd years, busy as a writer and publisher. In 1826, his *Every-day Book*, through initial poor sales, led to his being imprisoned for debt. But *The Political House that Jack Built*, with illustrations by his great friend, George Cruikshank, ran to 54 editions. Hone's last years, though, were to be marred by tragedy: in 1837, while working as a sub-editor on *The Patriot*, he suffered a stroke and was to be paralysed for five years before dying on 6 November 1842.

Repeal of the Corn Laws

Scandals apart, the talking points in the first decade of Queen Victoria's reign, since ascending the throne in 1837, were Corn and Chartism; and the reportage of these was extensively covered in the newspapers of the day – and none more so than in the *Morning Post*, *The Times* and *The Standard*. The first Corn Law had been introduced in 1804, when the landowners who dominated Parliament had sought to ensure their well-being by imposing a protective duty. Ten years later, a government committee had recommended that foreign corn should be imported free of duty only when the price of wheat had reached 80s. a quarter.

On 24 February 1827 the *Morning Post* published side by side 'Arguments in Favour of Free Trade' and 'Arguments in Favour of Protection',[14] but it was to be a further eleven years, following the formation of the Anti-Corn Law League in 1838, that the paper came out in support of the 'landed interest'.

In 1828, William Huskisson, President of the Board of Trade, had tried to relieve the distress caused by the high price of bread by introducing a sliding scale of duties. Now the economic conditions of the thirties were steadily worsening, with a major depression in 1839 followed by bad harvests and a potato famine in Ireland. All this led to the founding of the Manchester-based Anti-Corn Law League, which advocated Free Trade and, more especially, the abolition of duties on imported corn. Led by Richard Cobden and John Bright, it was the first great national radical movement, employing all the methods of well-organized agitation – mass meetings throughout Britain, lobbying of MPs, the use of the growing railway system plus the new penny postage to send pamphlets to every elector in the land.

Leading the fight for the League was *The Times*, 'which knew that the middle classes, i.e. public opinion, were in favour, and that only the squires opposed repeal'. But, ever consistent, *The Standard* supported the Corn Laws; and on 24 January 1839, Charles Greville, Under-Secretary of State, wrote:

> The question of absorbing interest is how the repeal or alteration of the Corn Laws and the declaration of war against them on the part of *The Times* has produced a great effect, and is taken as conclusive evidence that they cannot be maintained, from the rare sagacity with which the journal watches the turn of public affairs. Besides that, its advocacy will be of the greatest use in advancing the cause which it has already perceived was likely to prevail. The rest of the Conservative Press, the *Morning Herald*, *Post* and *Standard* support the Corn Laws, and the latter has engaged in single combat with *The Times*, conducted with a kind of chivalrous courtesy, owing to the concurrence of their general politics, very unusual in newspaper warfare, and with great ability on both sides.

Within weeks, the *Morning Post* had come out strongly against change:

> The manufacturing people exclaim 'Why should we not be permitted to exchange the produce of our industry for the greatest quantity of food which that industry will anywhere command?' To which we say, 'Why not indeed? Who hinders you? Take your manufacturers away with you by all means and exchange them anywhere you will, from

Tobolsk to Timbuctoo. If nothing will serve you but to eat foreign corn, away with you and your goods, and never let us see you any more![15]

On 7 May 1841, Thomas Barnes, editor of *The Times*, was operated on for a tumour, but died before the day was out, aged fifty-five. There was no obituary in his paper, just a bare few lines announcing the death: 'On the 7th inst., at his house in Soho Square, Thomas Barnes, Esq., in the 56th year of his age.' However, he was not to be forgotten by his rivals; and Leigh Hunt, in the *Examiner*, wrote: 'Of the great talent and energy of Mr Barnes the newspaper which he conducted for upwards of twenty years is the best evidence.'

The new man was to be John Thadeus Delane, who was aged only twenty-three when he assumed control. Educated privately and at Magdalen Hall, Oxford,[16] he joined *The Times* – where his father William Delane was manager – as a parliamentary reporter before becoming editor, a position he was to hold for thirty-six years. Despite his youth and lack of experience, Delane was the proprietor's first and only choice, but John Walter II fully intended to keep a watchful eye, as evidenced by this letter to a Conservative Party manager:

> In consequence of my conversation with you this morning, I made an immediate visit to my young friend [Delane] at Blackfriars. I there imparted to him, in a great degree, what had passed between us – and I thought it satisfactory to him, as I am sure it would have been to me in early days, that the Government communications should be made impartially – equally, fairly and impartially – to all the Government Journals, without any reference to their several sales, or their presumed influence upon that ground . . . . *The Times* and *The Standard*, the *Post* and the *Herald* should be upon the same footing.

By the late summer of 1841, Peel was once more Prime Minister and he was immediately confronted with the results of the poor harvests. He had long believed that if free trade in manufactured goods benefited the people then the time had come to apply the same principles to agriculture – and to repeal the Corn Laws. In this he was only echoing the opinion of the country, but he almost certainly underestimated the strength of opposition among his own Conservative Members of Parliament: not only was he offending their political principles but, as landed gentry, he was also hitting their pockets.

For Giffard, amid the political turmoil, it was yet another chance to pledge his allegiance to the Tory Party. On 31 August 1841, he wrote to Peel: 'I hope that in placing unreservedly at your command *The Standard* and the several other papers under my control I shall be thought to have no personal object nor other object other than the power of being useful to the country and of testifying my gratitude to you.' Within two days, Peel had replied: 'I will again communicate with you upon the subject of it when I am less harassed by business which presses for instant despatch.'[17]

The battle to repeal the Corn Laws was now about to enter its final stages, but Peel was still intent on opposing the demands of a more and more vociferous opposition. For Queen Victoria, there was the deep concern that political upheaval was about to be forced upon the country. And for months, people had been amused by the puzzle:

'Why are the Tories like walnuts? Because they are troublesome to *peel*.' It was now no longer amusing.

With the bad harvests continuing, increasing pressures from the populace and the growing importance of the Anti-Corn Law League, the subject of repeal was constantly being debated in the wet summer of 1842; and on 11 August Peel could write to his wife, Julia: 'Parliament will be prorogued tomorrow, We have unpleasant accounts from Manchester and that neighbourhood. Great rioting and confusion. The Anti-Corn Law League have excited the passions of the people and are among the first victims of their own folly. Read the account of last night's debate in *The Standard*.'

Still bitterly opposed – and especially since *The Times* had pledged its support to repeal – the *Morning Post* now decided to criticize its own party:

> Will their repeated discomfitures not induce the landowners of England to open their eyes to the dangers that beset them? What may be the causes of Mr Cobden's success? The primary cause is assuredly that which conduces to the success of Sir Robert Peel. Why, indeed, if Parliamentary landowners deem it honest and wise to support the author of the Tariff and of the new Corn Law should not the tenant farmers of England support Sir Robert Peel's principles when enunciated by Mr Cobden? . . . It is not, we fear, by such men as the present race of Parliamentary landowners that the deadly progress of the League is to be arrested.

Meanwhile, under Delane's editorship, the policies of *The Times* and *The Standard* had grown further and further apart – and their differences over Roman Catholicism and the repeal of the Corn Laws were now to be debated in even more passionate terms. The row over Catholicism was particularly apparent in the spring of 1845 concerning the Maynooth Grant – Peel's proposal to subsidize the Roman Catholic College at Maynooth out of public funds. On 5 May 1845 *The Standard* in a violent outburst declared:[18]

> To whatever motive our conduct may be ascribed we must warn all parents and teachers to keep *The Times* of this day from the eyes of the young persons under their control. The journal to which we refer has thought it not indecent or criminal to publish a cento of the worst extracts from the filthiest part of the most filthy books by which Roman Catholic priests are made to prepare themselves for the duties of the Confessional, and these extracts are either in plain English, or in such Latin that a school-boy or girl – for Latin is now properly a part of female education – can understand them . . . . Three years ago *The Times* was approaching the end of the only access of honourable and consistent conduct in its history; but we imagine that had been an access of some years' duration; we therefore thought well of *The Times* three years ago.

Events were finally to come to a head in the autumn of 1845 when the force of the Anti-Corn Law League, assisted by a devastating blight on the Irish potato crop, aroused a powerful clamour against the duties; and none was more vociferous than *The Times*. On 29 October it informed its readers: 'Once we might have declared a free trade in corn, now we must.' It then launched a fierce attack on Peel, and on 6 November demanded his resignation.

Cobden and Bright, in leading the fight for repeal, were now barn-storming the country; and on 28 November more than eight thousand of their supporters crowded into the Manchester Free Trade Hall. Bright was in devasting form, and *The Standard* quickly became a target for his invective: '*The Standard* . . . . has at last found out . . . . that no human being, no one of her Majesty's subjects must perish of hunger.' While these attacks on *The Standard* continued, the paper was, surprisingly, praising the Whigs – but these were Whigs who were against repeal. However, on 4 December *The Times* dropped its bombshell:[19]

> The decision of the Cabinet is no longer a secret. Parliament it is confidently reported is to be summoned for the first week in January; and the Royal Speech will, it is added, recommend an immediate consideration of the Corn Laws, preparatory to their total repeal. Sir Robert Peel, in one House, and the Duke of Wellington in the other, will, we are told, be prepared to give immediate effect to the recommendations thus conveyed.

To say this was a sensation is an understatement. In the words of Greville: 'The whole town has been electrified.' For *The Standard* the report could not be true, and there was an immediate riposte:

Atrocious Fabrication By *The Times*

> We are now, we rejoice to say, in a condition to give the most positive and direct contradiction to the statement of a proposed repeal of the corn-laws, which appeared in yesterday's *Times* . . . .

As the row raged on between the papers, Giffard wrote on 10 December:

> Let the protecting duties be abolished, and they must follow the corn-laws and the whole mass of British labour. We ask the artisan is he prepared for a reduction of half his earnings in order to have bread, perhaps two-pence in the four pound loaf cheaper? We will not go out of our own department to put the question. We ask the working printer will he be contented to exchange his present working conditions for twelve shillings a week wages, and bread at three halfpence a pound?

As a result of a Cabinet split, Peel had resigned on 4 December; and Lord John Russell's endeavours to form a government were to be a failure. The Queen again summoned Peel, and he at once agreed to accept the challenge. On 22 January 1846 the new parliament assembled, and Peel immediately announced his determination to repeal the Corn Laws as the only remedy to the famine in Ireland – but to *The Standard* leader writer it was 'next to impossible to believe . . . . that as the adviser of such an injunction Sir Robert Peel can contemplate such a change'.

The debate continued throughout the spring of 1846, and despite the bitter invective of Benjamin Disraeli and his cohorts, the joint forces of the Peelites and Whigs ensured a majority of ninety-eight over the Tory Protectionists at four o'clock on the morning of 16 May 1846. The *Morning Post* gave the result in its issue of the same day, and in its leader commented:[20]

> It is nothing but the veriest extravagance, truth-denying effrontery, or inflated self-conceit, that can lead anyone to maintain that the people at large are enamoured of this

> free-trade measure . . . . The labourers know well enough that the master manufacturer supposes that by admitting the competition of foreign labour in the production of food, the general price of labour in Great Britain will be beaten down, while ampler markets for manufacturers will be opened up in corn-growing countries.

A month later, the Duke of Wellington carried out his last service to Peel by steering the Bill through the House of Lords.

While the debate was raging over the Corn Laws, *The Daily News*, edited by Charles Dickens at a salary of £2000 per annum, had made its debut on 21 January 1846. From the outset, costs were deemed secondary, and a large staff, with corresponding salaries, was engaged, including Dickens's father, who was responsible for the parliamentary reporting. For those days, the first number of *The Daily News* was a remarkable feat of journalism. Dickens's opening article was followed by three others, all dealing with the Corn Laws. In his opening leader he commented on the strictures that the Press was facing:[21]

> The stamp on newspapers is not like the stamp on universal medicine bottles, which licenses anything, however false and monstrous; and we are sure the misuse of it, in any notorious use, not only offends and repels right-minded men in that particular instance but, naturally, though unjustly, involved the whole of the press as a pursuit or profession in the feeling so awakened and places the character of all who are associated with it at a great disadvantage.

Despite the success of the early issues, Dickens's tenure was to be brief, and he edited only seventeen numbers. On 9 February he wrote to John Forster, one of the chief leader writers, saying that he was 'tired and quite worn out'. Forster took over as editor; and to Dickens, now contributing a Letter from Italy, he wrote: 'God knows there has been small comfort for either of us in the *Daily News*' nine months . . . . I am beginning to get over my sorrow for your nights aloft in Whitefriars.' The strain, though, was to prove too much for Forster and he resigned to edit the *Examiner*.

Bitter Rivals

Since taking over the *Morning Herald*, Edward Baldwin's main preoccupation had been to recover the ground lost to *The Times*; and as a first step he decided to engage the best editorial talent available, almost regardless of cost – and one of his initial acts was to raise the honorarium paid for leading articles from three to five guineas. For the first few months, the paper, with its highly-paid staff, was running at a loss, but then the circumstances changed dramatically. In 1845, Great Britain was swept with railway mania, which led to wild speculation usually alternated with periods of panic:

> There was a perfect mania of railway companies and so great was the influx of long advertisements of new companies that the *Morning Herald* had sometimes a sufficient number to require not only a second sheet, but a supplement of four pages. This made the paper on each day on which it occurred consist of twenty pages, or 120 columns.

The advertisements were charged at one shilling a line – double that of the ordinary advertisements – and for a time Edward Baldwin was making clear profits of more than £3000 a week. This lasted for almost four months; and then came the railway panic, when the mania of forming new public companies suddenly and completely collapsed.

Not only had the *Herald* gained large sums from its advertisement columns but circulation had also increased; and during 1845 it had achieved a daily average of 6400 – the highest since 1837, when it had been 6000. But in the panic year of 1848 circulation dropped to 4800, and by 1854 had fallen to 3700.

On 17 November 1845 *The Times* had exposed the competing schemes,[22] showing that there were some 1200 projected railways seeking to raise more than £500 millions. While the boom lasted the papers waxed rich – but not the government. For the duty on these long advertisements was exactly the same as the dozens of smaller ones which had been left out for lack of space: one shilling and sixpence.

Baldwin, though, fondly believed that the good times would return and he continued to conduct his business in a most extravagant manner, even increasing the pay of his parliamentary reporters from five guineas to seven guineas per week – and all the while his circulation continued to fall. But for *The Times* it was now a different tale: in 1837 its daily average had been just 10,700, while in 1845 sales had reached 25,000. Two years later it was 29,000, and in 1852 it would exceeded 52,000 – twelve times that of the *Morning Herald*.

During the struggles of *The Standard* and *The Morning Herald* to wrest supremacy from *The Times*, one man was to prove the real stumbling-block, John Thadeus Delane. As noted, he had succeeded Thomas Barnes as editor in 1841, at the very young age of twenty-three, and was to retain that post for thirty-six years, with his brother-in-law, George Dasent, acting as assistant editor. During those years, Delane's career was that of his newspaper: he shrank from publicity, and was careful to preserve the impersonality of the role.

He rarely wrote a leader, but 'was the conductor of a brilliant editorial team and controlled by discussion, suggestion and revision'. Until then, no editor had been better informed; he was accepted at the best establishments; he stayed at the finest country houses; and he knew all the leading members of society. Richard Cobden remarked that Delane was to be seen dining at tables 'where every other guest but himself was an Ambassador, a Cabinet Minister or a Bishop'. Reaffirming this, Lord John Russell could inform Queen Victoria in 1854: 'The degree of information possessed by *The Times* with regard to the most secret affairs of State is mortifying, humiliating and incomprehensible.'

During his tenure, Delane saw thirteen changes of government; and his editorship did much to hasten the Repeal of the Corn Laws, the abolition of newspaper duty and the expansion of the telegraph system. In 1845, Delane had exposed the Railway Mania, even though *The Times* itself lost thousands of pounds in advertising revenue; and he was the first to describe, through the eyes of pioneering war correspondent [Sir] William Howard Russell, the extreme sufferings of the British troops in the Crimean War. Delane even went so far as to set up a relief fund for the soldiers.[23]

The outbreak of hostilities had given Russell the chance of a lifetime. He landed at Gallipoli on 5 April 1854, and within days his Letters from the Crimea were showing up the inadequacies of the British Army's administration. Given the full support of Delane, his Letters amounted to a serious problem for the Cabinet, ultimately leading to Lord Aberdeen's resignation as Prime Minister. Russell's descriptions of the Battle of Balaclava on 25 October 1854, where he used the phrase 'the thin red streak tipped with a line of steel' – afterwards wrongly interpreted as the 'thin red line' by Victorian writers – and his account of the Charge of the Light Brigade later that day are superb pieces of reportage: 'All our operations in the trenches were lost in the interest of this melancholy day in which our Light Brigade was annihilated by their own rashness and by the brutality of a furious enemy.'

The defeat, glorious as it was, is best summed up in the words of the French commander, General Bosquet, who was an astonished onlooker: '*C'est magnifique, mais ce n'est pas la guerre.*'

But it was to be Russell's Letters covering the winter of 1854–55, disclosing the deprivations and sufferings of the British Army which had the deepest effect. Despite criticism from Lord Raglan, the British commander, Sir Evelyn Wood believed that Russell had 'saved the remnants' of the army. Harold Herd, writing in his *March of Journalism*, published in 1952, was to say: 'Exercising boldly the right of criticism as well as disclosure *The Times* overturned one administration, brought about changes in another and secured the removal of the Commander-in-chief, Lord Raglan.'

Although often coming under attack from politicians, Delane was always quick to retort, his replies to Lord Derby in February 1852 and March 1854 being classic examples of his defence of freedom of the Press:

> The Press lives by disclosures; whatever passes into its keeping becomes a part of the knowledge and the history of our times; the statesman's duty is precisely the reverse. He cautiously guards from the public eye the information by which his actions and opinions are regulated . . . . We would hold ourselves responsible not to Lord Derby or the House of Lords, but to the people of England, for the accuracy and fitness of that which we think proper to publish.

Delane was to keep up his attacks on all that was wrong for another two decades until his retirement, aged fifty-nine, in 1877; worn out he died two years later. In a fitting tribute, one of his leader writers, the Rev. Henry Wace, was to say:

> In short the paper produced every morning was not a mere collection of pieces of news from all over the world, of various opinions, and of more or less valuable essays. It was Mr Delane's report to the public of the news of the day, interpreted by Mr Delane's opinions, and directed throughout by Mr Delane's principles and purpose.

Newspaper Costs

For all the newspapers operating during the mid-century costs were important; and an idea of the weekly expenditure of producing a daily newspaper was given by H.R. Fox Bourne in his *Fourth Estate*:

Editorial: Chief editor, £18 18*s*.; sub-editor, £12 12*s*.; second sub-editor, £10 10*s*.; foreign sub-editor, £8 8*s*.; writers (about four guineas a day) £25 4*s*.; sixteen parliamentary reporters, £86 7*s*. *Foreign*: Paris correspondent, £10 10*s*.; reporter for Chamber, £3 5*s*.; Paris Postage, £18 13*s*. Agents in Boulogne, Madrid, Rome, Naples, Vienna, Berlin and Lisbon, £26.

In addition it would be necessary to have paid correspondents in Malta, Athens, Constantinople, Hamburg, Bombay, China, Singapore, New York, Boston, Massachusetts, Halifax, Nova Scotia, Montreal and Jamaica. There would also be the need to employ reporters in Britain – either staff or linage – at, say, Dover, Southampton, Liverpool, Manchester, Leeds, Birmingham, Bristol, Dublin, Plymouth, Pembroke, Falmouth, Portsmouth, York, Wakefield, Chatham, Sheerness, Woolwich, Gravesend, Glasgow, Cambridge and Oxford. Cost of covering the various courts in London – Lord Chancellor's, Rolls, Bankruptcy, etc. – amounted to £25 a week, with a further £6 alloted for the provincial circuits. For reporting the London police courts a sum of £20 a week would be allowed.

The City salaries were given at £9 9*s*., and there would also be a need to subscribe to the *Stock Exchange Lists*, to Lloyd's, and the Jerusalem Coffee House. In addition, 'penny-liners' would cover the principal markets in London. Provision would also be made to cover the Royal Court, fine arts, sport and turf. A large number of foreign and provincial papers would be taken daily and these could total more than 150, plus copies of the *Hansard's Debates*, *Acts of Parliament*, *Votes of the House* and other parliamentary papers, *The London Gazette*, the *Coal Market List* and the *Packet List*.

To service the editorial staff, between fifty and seventy production personnel would be needed:

Printing: Number of men employed – printer, an assistant printer, a maker-up of advertisements, three readers, three assistant readers or 'reading boys', and about forty-five to fifty compositors regularly employed, also about eight or ten 'grass' men not regularly employed but who wait for engagement of work in place of regular hands who may be absent through illness or otherwise.

Time of working: Copy is given out by the printer from about half-past seven to eight in session of parliament time, and from eight to nine during the recess. The compositors are obliged to attend about three hours before the copy is given out, for the purpose of distributing the type used in the previous day's paper, which will be required for the night's work. Composition is usually closed about three o'clock; the men are usually occupied about ten hours in the office.

Wage rates: The printer earned between £5 and £6 per week; the assistant printer and advertisement man, £3 10*s*. to £4; the readers from £2 10*s*. to £3; assistant readers £1 1*s*. to £1 10*s*.; the compositors from £2 10*s*. to £3, averaged over the whole year. About four to six men were generally employed by the printer after the composition was closed, to assist in putting the paper to press. These men averaged between £3 10*s*. and £4 a week. There were 460 compositors working on the daily press in London, three-quarters of whom were men of superior intelligence, habits and respectability, a great improvement having taken place in the previous eight or ten years.

Machine room: Machinist and assistant, chief engineer and assistant engineer, sixteen men and boys to feed the machines and take out the paper, one wetter to prepare the paper. *Publishing room*: Publisher at five guineas a week, assistant and four or five errand boys. *Business management*: Secretary, cashier and accountant; three advertisement clerks, night porter, day porter and errand boy.

Total costs: Including rent, gas, wear and tear of plant, interest on outlay, plus other charges, were: editing, writing and reporting a double paper, during the Session of Parliament, £220; foreign and local correspondence, £100; printing, machining, publishing and general expenses, double paper, with occasional second or third edition; and an evening edition three days a week, £200. *Weekly cost*: £520

The Rise of Chartism

While *The Times* and *The Standard* had been continuing their bitter rivalry – especially with regard to being first with the news from abroad – Chartism had come to the fore by the end of the 1840s: universal male suffrage, annual parliaments, vote by ballot, payment for MPs, equal electoral districts and the abolition of the property qualification for MPs. A decade earlier, on 5 May 1838, the London Working Men's Association had published the *People's Charter* which had advocated the above six points. In spite of the introduction of the Reform Bill in 1832, the Industrial Revolution had produced a vast working class, of whom five out of six were left without the vote. As Disraeli so aptly wrote in his novel, *Sybil*: 'Two nations between whom there is no intercourse and no sympathy; who are as ignorant of each other's habits, thoughts and feelings, as if they were dwellers in different zones or inhabitants of different planets .... The rich and the poor.'

During this period, none had been more active in promoting the Chartist cause than the Rev. James Rayner Stephens, especially when addressing a meeting at Ashton-under Lyne; and quoted in the *Northern Star* on 6 January 1838:[24]

> If the people who produce all wealth could not be allowed, according to God's word, to have the kindly fruits of the earth which they had, in obedience to God's word, raised by the sweat of their brow, the war to the knife with their enemies, who were the enemies of God. If the musket and the pistol, the sword and the pike were of no avail, let the woman take the scissors, the child the pin or needles. If all failed then the firebrand – aye the firebrand – the firebrand I repeat. The palace shall be in flames.

On 5 January 1839 there was an early mention in *The Times* of Chartists, when reporting a meeting in Manchester 'of some 600 persons in support of the principles of Magna Carta, the Carta de Foresta and the Charter. The concern and surprise of *The Times* reflects the mind of the commercial and middle classes on the Chartist disturbances'. Later that year, on Tuesday 6 November, the paper could report the Chartist riots at Newport of the previous day:

> Newport, Monday, Eleven o'clock a.m.
> The Chartists have almost entire possession of the Town. There are 7,000 or 8,000 marched in from the hills and attacking the Westgate Inn, where the magistrates are sitting. I have heard 30 or 40 shots fired, and I learn that several of the Chartists as well as soldiers are killed. What the end will be God only knows; they are firing now. I write by post, but fearing the mail may be stopped I send this in addition.

The rioting was also covered in detail by *The Morning Herald* correspondent:

> Newport, Two o'clock
> The Chartists are in possession of the town. This morning alone about 8,000 of the most desperate, headed by Frost, the ex-magistrate and Chartist demagogue, marched into Newport from the hills armed with muskets, guns, pistols, pikes, swords and other offensive weapons (and, as I have been told, two small pieces of cannon) and commenced a violent attack on the Westgate Inn, where the magistrates were sitting. The military was promptly called out, and the attack was of the most ferocious and bloody character. They were obliged to fire upon them, and several have been killed, accounts vary between 10 and 20. I myself have seen several in our yard . . . . Besides the nine Chartists I have seen dead, I have since seen several whose wounds are such as would almost certainly prove mortal. The 45th soldiers acted bravely – they acted like men, and but for their noble exertions the town would probably by this time have been a mass of smoking ruins – they charged the Chartists and put them to flight in all directions, leaving several hundreds of their weapons in the street.

To *The Standard*, the reason for the riot was clear-cut: 'This is the fruit of the incendiary writing of 1831 and 1832, the natural and necessary result of letting loose the fierce passions of an uninstructed and indigent population, and of teaching them that their will ought to stand above the law . . . .'

Between 1840 and 1842, the Chartist movement was widely split, but a second massive petition was presented to Parliament in May 1842 and, as with its predecessor three years earlier, was rejected. Following this rejection, the movement had fallen under the influence of Fergus O'Connor, and now in 1848, the 'Year of the Revolution', the time was ripe to make one final demand. On 10 April, following a huge meeting at Kennington Common, a monster petition containing the Six Points was to be presented. Advocating that the ringleaders of the meeting should be prosecuted for treasonable conspiracy, *The Standard* leader writer commented:[25]

> Before taking leave of the Chartists and their description let us offer one other remark upon the audacious petition presented to the House of Commons. The petition is said to be the names of five and a half million signatures. The number would never be counted for it would take fifteen weeks of twelve hours a day to count so many, but, however closely written, five and a half million signatures would cover some tons of parchment, whereas the petition actually presented did not weigh more than a few hundredweight.

During the two days after the demonstration, clerks at the House of Commons had a chance to examine the petition, and on 13 April *The Standard* reported:[26]

> The whole number of signatures amounts to one million, nine hundred thousand; enough of all conscience, but no less than three million, seven hundred thousand short of Mr O'Connor' deliberations. The misstatements of the actual number of signatures, such as they are, is not, however, the most disgraceful part of this affair. The signatures are for the most part forgeries. The Duke of Wellington's name appears seventeen times repeated, the Queen and Prince Albert's name are again and again repeated; the like liberties are taken with the names of all distinguished public men of all parties; and in addition to those there is a huge miscellaneous muster of ludicrous, filthy and even impious and obscene designations under the form of names. Of the numbers of persons

> represented by *bona fide* names, an idea may be formed from the fact stated by a correspondent of *The Times* that one errand boy had signed the petition more than 1,250 times.

In the laughter and ridicule that followed, the days of Chartism were numbered and the movement died a natural death. Unlike the Anti-Corn Law League, it failed because of weak leadership, lack of co-ordination or contact with the trade unions, and because its objectives were not clear. Nevertheless, the four main Chartist demands were to be enacted within the next seventy years.

5

'Taxes on knowledge' repealed

WHILE *THE TIMES* AND *THE STANDARD* were engaged in their circulation battles, there had been an underlying theme which was affecting all newspapers – the 'taxes on knowledge' imposed by successive governments on advertisements, newspapers and paper. As far back as 14 June 1832 W.H. Bulwer-Lytton had moved resolutions in the House of Commons for the repeal of the principal taxes, saying:

> In 1829 the number of newspapers published in the British Isles was 33,050,000 or 630,000 weekly, which is one copy for every thirty-sixth inhabitant. In Pennsylvania, which had only in that year 1,200,000 inhabitants, the newspapers amounted to 300,000 copies weekly, or a newspaper for every fourth inhabitant. What was the cause of this mighty difference? The newspaper in one country sells for one-fourth of what it sells for in the other.

Daniel O'Connell, the Irish statesman, seconded the resolutions, but, sensing that they would not be accepted, they were withdrawn by the sponsors. However, in the following year, 1833, there was success when the advertisement tax was lowered from 3*s*. 6*d*. to 1*s*. 6*d*.; and three years later, on 14 September 1836, the stamp duty on newspapers was reduced from fourpence to a penny a copy, and a reduction on the duty on paper was also made. The government's decision to reduce the duty was primarily due to the increase in unstamped publications.

In July 1835 there had even appeared an unstamped daily title, the *Daily National Gazette*.[1] Although lasting barely a week, its arrival brought forth strong protests to Melbourne's government from *The Times* and the *Morning Post*, the later asking whether 'extensive newspaper properties, some of which have existed nearly a century, are to be left, by the callous indifference and shameful negligence of a Whig Government at the mercy of every ruffian who chooses to defy the law.'

As a result of these reductions in taxes 'the total circulation of stamped newspapers increased by approximately fifty per cent, rising from thirty-five and one half million copies in 1836 to over fifty-three million in 1838'.

Now, twelve years later, on 16 April 1850, Thomas Milner-Gibson – Liberal MP for Manchester, a one-time active member and speaker of the Anti-Corn Law League, a former Vice-President of the Board of Trade 1846–48, and currently President of the Association for Promoting the Repeal of the Taxes on Knowledge – introduced resolutions in the House of Commons calling for the repeal of the advertisement tax, the newspaper stamp duty and the duties on paper and imported books. In this, he had a powerful ally in Richard Cobden, who had argued:

> So long as the penny [tax] lasts there can be no daily press for the middle or working class. Who below the rank of merchant or wholesale dealer can afford to take in a daily paper at fivepence? . . . The governing classes will resist the removal of the penny stamp, not on account of the loss of revenue – that is no obstacle with a surplus of two or three millions – but because they know that the stamp makes the daily press the instrument and servant of the oligarchy.

Neverthless, despite the pleas of Milner-Gibson, Cobden and their supporters, the resolutions were defeated, with Lord John Russell, the Prime Minister, commenting loftily that he could give no countenance to any plans encouraging such abominations of popular education in England. However, Milner-Gibson was not to be beaten and within months had secured the appointment of a select committee to inquire into the working of the Newspaper Act. For *The Times*, it was to prove an unhappy experience; and its manager, Mowbray Morris, in appearing before the committee, was asked by Cobden if he did not think it desirable that cheaper papers should be available for the public. A disdainful Mowbray Morris replied that 'He had very little opinion of the sagacity of uneducated people'[2] and he believed that 'the production of newspapers should be limited to a few hands and be in the hands of parties who are great capitalists'.

Acting with alacrity, the committee reported before the year's end, and attention was drawn to:

> The objections and abuses incident to the present system of newspaper stamps, arising from the difficulty of defining and determining the meaning of the term news; to the inequalities and evasions that it occasions in postal arrangements; to the limitation imposed by the stamp upon the circulation of the best newspapers; and to the impediments which it throws in the way of the diffusion of useful knowledge regarding current events among the poorer classes, and which species of knowledge, relating to subjects which must obviously interest them, calls out the intelligence by awakening the curiosity of those classes.

The following year, 1852, Milner-Gibson once more tried to have the 'taxes on knowledge' repealed; and again was defeated, despite support from Gladstone – although Disraeli, as Chancellor of the Exchequer, 'defended the taxes as necessary evils'. But within months, in 1853, Milner-Gibson achieved his breakthrough: once more he had benefited from Gladstone, who 'had no wish to restrain any restraint whatever upon the Press for the sake of restraint and would be delighted to see the day when the duty on newspapers might be removed'. This time, Parliament voted for the advertisement tax to come to an end.[3]

Milner-Gibson's next move was to put forward a resolution declaring that in the opinion of the House 'the laws in reference to the periodical press and newspaper stamp are ill defined and unequally enforced, and it appears to this House that the subject demands the early attention of Parliament'. With a Liberal government – led by Lord Palmerston, a one-time leader writer on *The Observer* – in power, the way was now clear. On 19 March 1855 Sir George Cornewall Lewis, Chancellor of the Exchequer, introduced the Newspaper Duties Bill, 'which made it optional for every newspaper to issue all or any of its copies stamped or unstamped, the stamped copies having the privilege of transmission through the post'. Passed by 215 votes to 161, the Bill became law on 30 June 1855.

A delighted John Bright, who, with Cobden, had led the campaign in repealing the Corn Laws in 1846, could say of this success:

> I am willing to rest on the verdict of the future, and I am quite convinced that five or six years will show that all the votes of Parliament for educational purposes have been as mere trifles compared with the results which will flow from this measure, because, while the existing papers retain all their usefulness, it will call to their aid numbers of others not less useful, and while we enjoy the advantage of having laid before us each morning a map of the events of the world the same advantage will be extended to classes of society at present shut out from it.

For *The Times* – although there would be no material gain – the decision was approved, and Delane, in his leader, noted: 'We make a great stir about teaching everybody to read .... then we proceed to tax the first thing that everybody reads. But we have several times enlarged on the absurdity of a tax which, as it is a tax on news, is a tax on knowledge.'[4]

On 1 October 1861 the final 'tax on knowledge' fell, when Gladstone, once more Chancellor of the Exchequer, moved the repeal of the paper duty of 1*d*. per lb, despite opposition from Lord Robert Cecil, who was later, as Lord Salisbury, to become Prime Minister. He maintained: 'It was a prostitution of real education to talk of this tax upon a penny paper as a tax on knowledge. Could it be maintained that a person of any education could learn from a penny paper?'

For Milner-Gibson and his supporters the battle had been won – and the Press was finally free.

Colonel Sleigh and The Telegraph

With the 'taxes on knowledge' finally gone, there now appeared a rush of would-be newspaper owners, especially in the provinces. But by far the most important launch took place at 253 Strand, London, on Friday 29 June 1855, when Colonel Arthur Burroughes Sleigh, with the aid of his brother, William Campbell Sleigh, and Colonel Alfred Bate Richards, who became editor, brought out *The Daily Telegraph & Courier* as a means of pursuing a vendetta against the Duke of Cambridge, Commander-in-chief of the Army. Born in Montreal, Sleigh had become an ensign in the Second West India Regiment on 23 July 1842, transferring to the 77th Foot two years later. He sold out on 12 September 1848, but in 1852 was back in military service as colonel of militia, Prince Edward's Island. After starting the weekly *British Army Dispatch* – edited by Richards – which he later sold to a Major Walker for £900, he launched *The Daily Telegraph & Courier*, a four-page broadsheet, in a crowded market of ten daily newspapers. 'Taking advantage of the removal of the

Daily Telegraph & Courier.

No. 1.] LONDON, FRIDAY, JUNE 29, 1855. [TWOPENCE.

ENGLISH & FOREIGN LIFE ASSURANCE SOCIETY, 125, Oxford-street, near Cavendish-square, LONDON. Capital, £250,000.

[illegible]

SOVEREIGN LIFE ASSURANCE COMPANY, 48, St. James's-street, London. Established 1845.

[illegible]

METROPOLITAN LIFE ASSURANCE SOCIETY, No. 3, Princes-street, Bank.

[illegible]

AGE ASSURANCE COMPANY.

[illegible]

SOUTH AUSTRALIAN BANKING COMPANY.

[illegible]

BANK of AUSTRALASIA (incorporated by Royal Charter, 1835).

[illegible]

RAILWAY ACCIDENT INSURANCE.

[illegible]

SOLDIERS' FRIEND and ARMY SCRIPTURE READERS SOCIETY.

[illegible]

CRIMINAL REFORM.—PREVENTIVE and REFORMATORY INSTITUTION.

[illegible]

COUPONS ON FOREIGN STOCK.

[illegible]

MONEY LENT, in Sums from £30 and upwards.

[illegible]

CAPE of GOOD HOPE ALMANAC and DIRECTORY.

[illegible]

RAILWAYS in AMERICA and CANADA.

[illegible]

COLONIAL NEWSPAPER AGENCY.

[illegible]

LONDON and PROVINCIAL NEWSPAPER ADVERTISEMENT OFFICE.

[illegible]

SURGICAL and PATHOLOGICAL OBSERVATIONS.

[illegible]

HOMŒOPATHIC DOMESTIC MEDICINE.

[illegible]

HOMŒOPATHIC TREATMENT of INDIGESTION.

[illegible]

LONDON LABOUR and the LONDON POOR.

[illegible]

THE ELEMENTS of BANKING.

[illegible]

THE LIFE, REIGN, and POLICY of NAPOLEON III.

[illegible]

SCOTTICISMS CORRECTED.

[illegible]

MISTAKES of DAILY OCCURRENCE.

[illegible]

WORKS JUST PUBLISHED by WALTON and MABERLY.

[illegible]

ASTHMA.—Dr. LOCOCK'S PULMONIC WAFERS.

[illegible]

COLES'S ALGA MARINA.

[illegible]

HOW the POOR may be TAUGHT.

[illegible]

CONVERSATIONS on the TEETH.

[illegible]

ENGLISHWOMAN'S DOMESTIC MAGAZINE.

[illegible]

THE ENGLISHWOMAN'S DOMESTIC MAGAZINE.

[illegible]

ENGLISHWOMAN'S DOMESTIC MAGAZINE.

[illegible]

ENGLISHWOMAN'S DOMESTIC MAGAZINE.

[illegible]

SPURGEON and WHITFIELD.

[illegible]

A MEMORIAL of Mr. SPURGEON'S MINISTRY.

[illegible]

ORATORIOS.

[illegible]

HAMILTON'S MODERN INSTRUCTIONS.

[illegible]

MISS M. LINDSAY'S VOCAL COMPOSITIONS.

[illegible]

CHELTENHAM.—THE TELEGRAPH and COURIER.

[illegible]

NOTICE.—The TELEGRAPH and COURIER.

[illegible]

CROGGON'S PATENT ASPHALTE ROOFING FELT.

[illegible]

SLACK'S NICKEL SILVER.

[illegible]

SLACK'S NICKEL ELECTRO-PLATED.

[illegible]

SLACK'S TABLE CUTLERY and FURNISHING IRONMONGERY.

[illegible]

GENUINE COCOA.

[illegible]

KEATING'S COUGH LOZENGES.

[illegible]

COLT'S METALLIC FOIL CARTRIDGES.

[illegible]

COLT'S NAVY or BELT REVOLVER.

[illegible]

COLT'S HOLSTER, or CAVALRY REVOLVER.

[illegible]

CHUBB'S ILLUSTRATED LIST of LOCKS.

[illegible]

GENERAL NOTICE, PER TELEGRAPH and COURIER.

[illegible]

NEWSOM and CO.'S strong and useful Black, Green, and Mixed TEAS.

[illegible]

THE GOLD REVIVER.

[illegible]

THE GRESHAM PEN.

[illegible]

THE GREATEST CURIOSITY.

[illegible]

GENTLEMEN are invited to try WORTH'S.

[illegible]

THE 16s. TROUSERS reduced to 14s.

[illegible]

SUPERIOR HATS.

[illegible]

THE HAIR.—CHURCHER'S TOILET CREAM.

[illegible]

STAGG and MANTLE'S SILK MERCERY.

[illegible]

DRESSES, MANTLES, and TRIMMINGS.

[illegible]

TO LADIES.—SELLING OFF.—STAYS.

[illegible]

TO LADIES.—AVOID TIGHT LACING.

[illegible]

TO LADIES.—Why give such a high price for.

[illegible]

TO LADIES.—At W. CARTER'S, 22, Ludgate-street.

[illegible]

THE Proprietors of the LONDON GENERAL MOURNING WAREHOUSE.

[illegible]

MARK YOUR LINEN.—THE PEN SUPERSEDED.

[illegible]

BEDDING.

[illegible]

THE NEWLY-REGISTERED "FAMILY FIRE-ESCAPE."

[illegible]

CHARACTERS faithfully and scientifically delineated.

[illegible]

LATE DESPATCHES FROM THE SEAT OF WAR.

[illegible]

stamp duty from newspapers six weeks earlier, Sleigh published at the recklessly low price of twopence. *The Times* then cost sevenpence; and other leading journals such as the *Morning Post* five pence.'[5]

On 15 August, six weeks after the launch, Sleigh wrote to a mysterious George Dornbusch offering to transfer the entire control of the political portion of the *Telegraph & Courier*:

> To a committee to be chosen by the Rational Peace Party, and to whom I am willing to confer the right of nominating a Supervising Editor, through whose hand every article should pass, and by whom the policy of the paper should be guided. The terms are: 1st The Party to purchase from me for a sum to be agreed upon my paper, I retaining some shares, but these shares not to carry any right of power of interference on my part. OR, secondly, The Party, if they prefer this arrangement to the one of the purchasing as stipulated in the first clause to take say 4,000 copies daily, to be circulated all over the United Kingdom, a large number of which would, of course, be sold, and thereby the expenditure to a certain extent reimbursed; but that circulation to be guaranteed to me. I am agreeing to the same restrictive clauses as to the policy, supervision, editor, etc. In all matters I am equally willing to abide by such further terms as will thoroughly secure the *Telegraph & Courier* to the Party. I am dear Sir, Yours faithfully B.W.A. Sleigh.

In launching the paper, Sleigh had been assisted by two partners who had each provided £1500, but he soon bought them out. The first few issues were produced by Aird & Tunstall, Essex Street, off the Strand, but on 2 September the printing was moved to Joseph Ellis, 2 Northampton Terrace in the City, who threatened closure if the bills were not paid. Meeting Joseph Moses Levy, printer and publisher, who was also manager of *The Sunday Times*, Sleigh informed him of his predicament.

Levy agreed to print the *Telegraph & Courier* 'but only on condition that if the bills remained unpaid beyond a certain period the paper, its copyright and everything concerning it would pass to him by default'. Sleigh agreed, and Levy, and his son Edward immediately became involved in the running of the paper. With issue no. 45, published on 17 September, the decision was taken to drop *& Courier* from the masthead, and 'London was given its first, double-sheet, eight-page, morning newspaper at the sensationally low price of one penny'. And in the first issue of the revamped *Telegraph*, they could announce:

> There is no reason why a Daily newspaper, conducted with a high tone, should not be produced at a price which would place it within the means of every class of the community. The extension of the circulation of such a journal must prove beneficial to the public at large. If Artisan and Peer can alike peruse daily the same wholesome literary matter, produced by first-class writers, the general tone of society must benefit.

Within a week, it was reported that sales were in excess of any London newspaper except *The Times*; and as 'The Largest, Best and Cheapest newspaper in the world' circulation had reached 27,000 copies per day by January 1856.

Colonel Richards, though, was no longer the editor, having been dismissed on 31 December 1855. During his time on the *Telegraph* he had advocated the setting-up of a rifle corps throughout Great Britain as a precaution against invasion. As a result in

1858 he was elected secretary of the National Constitutional Defence Association, which, with War Office backing, was twelve months later to lead to an official circular authorizing the enrolment of rifle volunteers. Richards himself was responsible for enlisting more than one thousand men for the 3rd City of London Rifle Corps, being appointed its colonel. And from these small beginnings was to grow the Territorial Army, which in 1907 absorbed 337,000 volunteers.

Meanwhile, on 12 March 1856, Sleigh signed a lease at 253 Strand for 21 years at a rent of £220 per annum, and within five days the paper was published in a new and enlarged format. With the growing success, on 25 April Levy, intent on further financial involvement, gave Sleigh £3000 and took on the role of general manager. Within six months, on 1 September Sleigh had entered into a 50/50 partnership with Levy. And on 17 February 1857 Levy was in total control, when he purchased the remaining shares for a final payment of £2000 on the proviso that 'Sleigh was forbidden from publishing a penny paper within a 50 mile radius of the city of London'.[6]

A firm believer that journalism should be lively, Joseph Moses Levy, or JML as he was known, used to declaim of a dull paragraph: 'That sort of stuff is enough to sink a ship.' An erudite person, he had a wide circle of friends – including actor Sir Henry Irving and novelist Bram Stoker – and each week used to hold literary and musical receptions at his London home.

In 1857, to expand the *Telegraph*, he brought his brother, Lionel Lawson, a successful financier, into the business; and a series of interlinked trusts was created: JML held a quarter; his brother, Lionel Lawson Levy, a half; his son Edward, one eighth; and George Moss, superintendent of the printing business, the other eighth. With financial backing assured, the paper, through the engagement of first-class writers, grew from strength to strength.

By 1862, sales of the *Telegraph* were in excess of 140,000, and in 1876 it announced, once more, that it had the largest circulation in the world. JML was to live until 1888, and during his remaining years was to see the *Telegraph*, under the direction of his son Edward, open palatial premises in Fleet Street and continue to remain the leading daily newspaper.

JML's son, Edward Levy Lawson, was to become one of the great figures of the newspaper industry. Educated at University College School, London, he joined the family business as a teenager, and underwent a thorough training in all aspects of newspaper production; and branching out into journalism was to act as drama critic for *The Sunday Times*. One of JML's first decisions was to appoint the 22-year-old Edward to be in charge of the editorial department, although Thornton Hunt was nominally editor; and under Edward's guidance the paper was to develop at a great pace. He was undoubtedly the man who made the *Telegraph*, by widening the range of interest and by producing a newspaper that would appeal to a new and larger readership.

While he did not neglect the leading article, he laid down the principle that the paper could not have too much news; and he handled the news in a vivid and popular manner – so different from the more sedate fashion of the other broadsheets. He had a gift for finding new writers, and one of his first discoveries was George Augustus Sala, who in 1857 had been invited for an interview and immediately went and hired 'black camlet vest, profusely embroidered with beads and bugles of jet, a chocolate coloured frock coat and Blucher boots'. Thus attired, he joined the paper, and for the next thirty years was to be its star journalist. In the words of Ralph Strauss, his biographer:

> [Sala] was a heavy man, short and stoutish, and his face was blotched and coarse-featured; distinctly a florid person . . . . he had a striking feature [his nose] which, alike for its size, its peculiar contours, and its fiery hues, was destined to become Fleet Street's most famous landmark.

Sala's fame was made by his articles covering the American Civil War – ninety-three in total. He also reported Garibaldi's campaign in Italy, before sharply observing the early clashes of the Franco-Prussian War, where, in 1870, he was arrested as a spy in Paris. In later years he reported from Spain, Russia, Turkey and the United States. In November 1882 he helped to found the Press Club, becoming its first chairman; and, as one of the 'young lions' of the paper, was to introduce a style of florid writing, known affectionately as 'telegraphese'.[7]

In the words of Sir Philip Gibbs, the distinguished war correspondent: 'He remains in the memory of Fleet Street as one of its great characters, and as one of the best descriptive writers, who humanised the columns of a newspaper, and with a vivid pen dealt with most aspects of social life in Victorian England.'

Others who were to make their mark on the paper included Bennet Burleigh, W.L. Courtney and J.L. Garvin; and it was Edward Levy who sent H.M. Stanley to Africa to complete the discoveries of David Livingstone. As for Edward Levy's thoughts on parliamentary affairs, they were to be summed up in his: 'Politics are fearfully dull and it is no good forcing them when there is a superabundance of social matter immediately calling for attention'; and he regularly warned his staff against the 'unforgivable sin of lack of variety in the paper'.

In 1875, Edward Levy, in consideration of a deed of gift from his uncle, Lionel Lawson, assumed the surname of Lawson by Royal Licence. Politically, Edward (now Lawson) was an early supporter of Gladstone; as the GOM was to say: '. . . . that the only man who knew how to support a Minister in the London press was Lawson of *The Daily Telegraph*'. However, the Balkan Attrocities of 1876 were to cause a split between Gladstone and Lawson. This did not, though, prevent Gladstone from being 'constitutionally responsible' for obtaining a baronetcy for Lawson on 13 October 1892.[8]

Throughout the years, Lawson always took a great interest in the leaders: he was a meticulous craftsman, as James Macdonnel was to note in 1865: 'I shall sit with Mr Levy and be his confidential helper. Gradually, I shall be brought into contact with great people – statesmen, etc. – on the business of the paper.' Twenty-five years later, W.L. Courtney wrote on watching his chief: '. . . . at his best line by line, word by word, making erasions here, adding a sentence there, deleting, strengthening, building-up – and all the time explaining why he did this and what object he was aiming at'.

The Three-way Circulation War

Less than two years after the launch of *The Daily Telegraph*, there appeared in the spring of 1857 a short notice in *The Times* announcing the bankruptcy proceedings of Edward Baldwin – and with it the end of almost two hundred years of his family's involvement in the London newspaper world. With sales of *The Standard* barely 700 copies a day, there had been no way that Baldwin could have survived. The notice read: 'Edward Baldwin, Shoe-lane, printer, to surrender March 5 at half-past 11 o'clock, April 2, at the Bankrupt Court. Solicitors: Messrs Baker, Bowler and Peach, Grays-inn square; official assignee Mr Johnson, Basinghall-street.'

The new owner was to be James Johnstone, aged 42, a senior partner in a firm of accountants, and he bought *The Standard*, *The Morning Herald* and *The St James's Chronicle* three months after Baldwin's bankruptcy. Discussing the sale of *The Standard*, James Grant was to write:

> Mr James Johnstone, who had for many years held an official appointment of considerable pecuniary profit in the court, bought the newspaper property thus put up for sale. I am making no disclosure to which Mr Johnstone would object when I mention that the price which he paid for *The Morning Herald* and *The Standard* together, including what is called the 'plant' – presses, types, everything indeed, necessary for working the paper was £16,500.[9]

For the first few weeks the new proprietor continued to conduct *The Standard* and *The Morning Herald* in the same manner as Edward Baldwin, but finding that he was operating at a loss decided that drastic measures were called for. He, therefore, reduced the price of *The Standard* from fourpence to twopence, doubled the pagination to eight and on Monday 29 June converted it into a morning paper. The introduction of this new-style *Standard* now posed a direct threat to *The Times*. As Stanley Morison was to write in the official history of *The Times*:

> The ability with which the twopence *Standard* was conducted – Robert Cecil, later Lord Salisbury, was one of its leader-writers – contributed an undeniable threat to the supremacy of *The Times*. Even *The Daily Telegraph* considered the 2*d*. eight-page *Standard* to be a very desirable money's worth in comparison with its own four pages for 1*d*.

James Johnstone, however, was not content; and on 4 February 1858, 'the entire town and country trade was staggered by an announcement that *The Standard* was about to reduce its price to 1*d*. without any reduction in size'. Both *The Times* and *The Daily Telegraph* were now rightly concerned at the eight-page, one-penny *Standard*. *The Telegraph* realised that it must produce larger papers, and on 29 May 1858 announced that, with its new press room strengthened by one of the latest Hoe rotary machines printing eight pages at the rate of 15,000 copies per hour, an average circulation of 30,000 was being produced.[10] For *The Times*:

> It was clear that *The Daily Telegraph*, catering as it did for the 'million', affected *The Times*' sales very little, if at all. It was unfortunately only too sure, however, that *The*

> *Standard* was successfully competing with *The Times* almost on its own level – and at a quarter of the price. The Indian Mutiny assisted *The Times*, but days and weeks and months of a well-edited and well-produced penny *Standard* gradually brought down the sales of *The Times*.

Not content with his new-style *Standard* – and anxious to make full use of his recently-installed presses – James Johnstone now revived the evening edition, which had ceased publication three years earlier; and at 3 p.m., 11 June 1859, *The Evening Standard* was launched. Johnstone now also decided to start a Conservative evening entitled *The Evening Herald*, in conjunction with the long-established *Morning Herald*. Priced at twopence, it was not a success, even though much of the material was lifted from its sister paper, and it expired on 21 May 1865. As for *The St James's Chronicle*, which had for so many years been the bedrock of the Baldwin family fortunes, he sold it to Charles Newdegate, MP for North Warwickshire, who converted it into a weekly.

Unfortunately, in his bid to overtake *The Times*, Johnstone had overstretched himself, and in 1858 he had been pleased to accept Tory funds in the form of a mortgage on his premises and machinery. For this, he and Thomas Hamber, who had succeeded as editor, following the death of Dr Stanley Lees Giffard in 1858, were pledged to follow the party line. However, the paper's coverage of the American Civil War – where it supported the South – was to bring about a huge increase in circulation, and in October 1862 sales were more than 100,000 on special occasions with an average of 50,000 copies per day.

On 14 February 1874 Johnstone was featured in *Vanity Fair*'s caricature gallery of 'Men of the Day'.[11] The cartoon by 'Ape' simply entitled *The Standard* shows the proprietor, paper in hand, pointing to the daily average of 185,276. Unfortunately, Johnstone did not live long enough to enjoy the fruits of his labour; he died on 22 October 1876. In his will he directed that his friend William Mudford, who had replaced Hamber, should serve both as editor and general manager of *The Standard* as long as he desired.

The Quality Sunday Press

Thirty years after the launch of Mrs Johnson's *British Gazette and Sunday Monitor* in 1779, the number of Sunday newspapers had grown to almost twenty, and most, it was claimed, were fit only for 'shop boys and milliners' apprentices' and certainly not for 'decent houses'. As early as 1807, John Bowles, a Tory pamphleteer, could rail against these newspapers:

> No pains are spared to make their distribution as general and as public as possible. Besides the gross indecency of announcing them by the blowing of horns, whenever they obtain any extra-ordinary news, greengrocers, hairdressers and pastry cooks throughout the metropolis and its vicinity are furnished with signboards intimating that particular papers are to be sold at their respective shops and they are copiously provided with copies.

Now, forty years later, six newspapers dominated the Sunday Press: on the 'quality side' there were *The Observer* and *The Sunday Times* and on the 'popular front' were *Lloyd's Weekly News*, *Reynolds's News*, the *News of the World* and *The People*. Since its launch in 1791 *The Observer* had been owned by the Bourne brothers, but in 1814 the title was sold to William Clement, a former newsvendor; and two years later he was accepting monies from the government in return for supporting their point of view and for distributing free copies of the paper.

In giving evidence in a libel action (*Ward* v. *Clement*) in 1819, the deputy publisher, George Goodger, revealed that *The Observer* sold 10,850 copies on a Sunday, plus a further 2000 of its Monday print, all of which were stamped. He believed, however, that a further 10,000 unstamped copies were being given away. Postmen were sent some 200 copies of the paper, and were asked to distribute them free of charge. One postman said he 'was given two or three shillings for the trouble. He delivered them to the lawyers, doctors and gentlemen of the town.' Clement himself admitted that free distribution of *The Observer*, on behalf of the government, extended to Bath and Dublin.

Apart from owning *The Observer*, Clement was also the proprietor of *The Morning Chronicle*, *Bell's Life in London* and *The Englishman*; and it was said that he controlled ten per cent of all the newspapers published from London. One of his first acts was to appoint Lewis Doxat as editor and manager of *The Observer*, and – apart from a short spell on *The Morning Chronicle* – Doxat would remain in control until 1857.[12] Born in the West Indies, Doxat had joined the *Chronicle* as an office boy and remained there until 1804 when he moved to *The Observer*, the paper he served for more than fifty years.

In December 1821, with James Perry, proprietor of *The Morning Chronicle*, about to die, Clement bought the paper for £42,000, retaining John Black as editor. Clement immediately sent Doxat back to his old office as manager. However, Doxat's relations with Black were not cordial; but the strained partnership was to last until 1832 when Clement sold the paper to Sir John Stanhope for £16,500. Doxat then returned, full-time, to *The Observer*, and in the words of James Grant, the Press historian: 'Although he possessed a wide general knowledge and had a pleasant literary style, he never wrote a single line for the paper. He confined his activities to financial and editorial management control.'

Under the guidance of Doxat, the contents of *The Observer* gradually improved with increased editorial staff, new typography and the introduction of woodcuts, all of which became especially apparent in the coverage of the Cato Street Conspiracy. As a result of these changes, circulation of the paper doubled. William Clement died in 1852, as did George Dowling, the paper's chief reporter, who was alleged to have been in the pay of the Home Office for many years. Doxat, though, continued as editor until 1857, when he was succeeded by Joseph Snowe, whose championing of the North during the American Civil War caused the paper's circulation to fall – so much so that it was not until the 1870s that sales improved.

The paper was then owned by Julius Beer, who died in 1880, leaving it to his son, Frederick. Editors during those years were Edward Dicey and then H.D. Trail. In

1887, Frederick Beer married Rachel Sassoon, an heiress, who, as Rachel Beer,[13] edited *The Observer* from 1891 until 1905. In 1892 her husband bought *The Sunday Times,* and she was then to edit the two papers simultaneously. In an interview in *Pearson's Magazine*, she said that she intended to take a proprietorial and editorial interest in both titles, adding that *The Sunday Times* gave her a paper in which she could expound her Imperial views.

Years later her nephew, Siegfried Sassoon, in his book of memoirs, *The Old Century*, was to write: 'At that time both *The Observer* and *The Sunday Times*, which in those days were rather unobtrusive and retiring newspapers, belonged to Mr Beer, whose father had been a financier.' Each week in *The Sunday Times*, the leading article, headed 'The World's Work', was to be a platform for her thoughts and ideas; she was not content to edit a newspaper which just discussed the domestic, social and artistic scenes. And each Saturday, page proofs would be taken from the paper's offices in Portugal Street to her home in Mayfair for approval.

For the first two years of her editorship she was assisted by Arthur a'Beckett, but Mrs Beer was a well-known figure in her own right, being a member of the Institute of Journalists and of the Society of Women Journalists. Towards the end of the nineteenth century she was involved in one of the greatest-ever scoops for *The Observer*: the revelation that documents that had led to the conviction of Dreyfus for high treason had been forged by fellow-officer Esterhazy. Rachel Beer continued to edit *The Sunday Times* until 1897; and much later W.W. Hadley, a future editor of the paper (1932–1950), was to write:[14]

> She became first an occasional contributor to *The Observer*, and then its assistant editor and then – so Fleet Street believed – its editor. Her ambition still unsatisfied, she bought *The Sunday Times* in 1893 and edited it herself – this without relinquishing her position on the staff of *The Observer*. Journalists were amused by this wealthy slapdash newcomer who edited two rival journals simultaneously and wrote articles for both with equal assurance.

Launch of The Sunday Times

On 21 October 1822, under the proprietorship of Henry White, *The Sunday Times* was launched in opposition to *The Observer.* During a varied career, White had written for the *Courier*, *Morning Post* and *Sunday Review* before starting his own weekly in January 1806, *The Independent Whig*, whose circulation was to rise within two years from 2400 to 4200 copies a week. To William Cobbett, 'It was the most excellent Sunday paper.'

However, in June 1808, White and his printer were prosecuted for libel – the articles had been written by John Gale Jones and W.A. Miles – and convicted, White was sentenced to three years' imprisonment in Dorchester Gaol. During his incarceration, he remained the paper's proprietor and publisher, although it was managed by his son. In 1811, soon after White's release, a new prosecution was brought against him for an article written by his son which had appeared in September 1810. Charged with seditious libel, White defended himself and was found not guilty on 1 November

1811. The verdict was greeted as a victory for a Free Press, and his supporters, led by Sir Francis Burdett, raised more than £1000 to reimburse him for lost revenues.

Apart from Burdett, he had also received assistance from other Whig leaders; and as a result in October 1813 launched a weekly, *The Charles James Fox*. As for his other paper, by November 1820 sales of *The Independent Whig* had fallen to less than 1000 copies and White was declared bankrupt. But, once more, his supporters rallied round, and raised enough money for him to regain control. In 1821 he changed the title of his paper to *The New Observer*. This lasted for just two months before, in April 1821, it became *The Independent Observer*. There was to be one final change of name, when in October 1822 it was retitled *The Sunday Times*, and in the following January he sold the paper to a group led by Daniel Whittle Harvey, a lawyer and Radical politician, who represented Colchester in the House of Commons, plus John Chapman, who became editor.

White's death at Islington on 1 May 1828, aged sixty-nine, was met with mixed reactions. Radical politician Henry 'Orator' Hunt believed him 'a man of the most inflexible integrity . . . . a real friend to Liberty', whereas Francis Place, a leading Reformist, considered him a plausible rogue who preyed unscrupulously on public men. White himself had previously declared: 'Mine has been a life of persecution for my relentless hostility to Tory despotism and corruption.'

Meanwhile, within weeks of purchasing *The Sunday Times* from White, Harvey had run into trouble. On 9 February 1823 he published a libel on George IV, and eight months later, on 30 October 1823, was fined £200 and ordered to be gaoled for three months in the Marshalsea Prison. Once released, Harvey was soon introducing new ideas into the paper, through the use of wood-engravings; and as *The Pearl of Days*, the history of *The Sunday Times* (1972) was to note: 'He organised sporting and agricultural supplements, which were profitable for advertising and an enormous advertisement for the paper itself. He was a great believer in hard-hitting leading articles, and his use of the editorial "we". . . . must have annoyed Cobbett, who had his own detestation of leader-writers.' Cobbett had previously written:[15]

> The mysterous WE that they make use of, gives men an idea that what they are reading proceeds from a little council of wise men, who have been sitting and deliberating upon what they wish to put forth. Each paragraph appears to be a sort of little order-in-council; a solemn decision of a species of literary conclave.

After selling the newspaper at a profit, Harvey established the *True Sun*, 1833–37; the *Weekly True Sun*, 1833–39; and the *Statesman or Weekly True Sun*, 5 January–27 December 1840. The titles were not a financial success and Harvey was declared bankrupt. He was fortunate, though, in having the right friends: in 1839 he was appointed Registrar of Metropolitan Carriages, and the following year became Commissioner of the City of London Police, holding that position until his death.

From Harvey, the paper passed into the hands of A.J. Valpy, a bookseller, of Red Lion Court, off Fleet Street, who then sold the title to Henry Colburn, another but more important publisher, but it was to be a short association, for Colburn soon disposed of the title to John Kemble Chapman, a theatrical producer. For much of this period – 1828 to 1854 – *The Sunday Times* editor was Thomas Gaspey, who in his younger days had been a parliamentary correspondent on *The Morning Post*. Following him there was a succession of editors, including Joseph Knight: 'A worthy Bohemian, he was known as 'Good Knight', not because of his moral qualities but in recognition of the fact that he was always the last to leave any pub or club to which he had gained entrance.'

On 12 March 1856, *The Times* reported on a case between J.M. Levy, of *The Daily Telegraph,* and Messrs George and Thomas Lamb 'from completing or taking any further proceedings towards completing the sale of *The Sunday Times* to E.T. Smith'. In a letter dated 25 October 1854 and at a meeting a few days later it had been agreed verbally:

> That Levy should be engaged for the term of three years at a salary of five guineas a week to manage and conduct *The Sunday Times*; this salary to be increased to eight guineas a week as soon as the profits of the paper should be be increased to the extent of £1000 per annum and that the plaintiff should have the option at any time during the three years of purchasing a quarter of the paper for £2000.

Levy requested that George Lamb should now sign the document but this was not done.

However, towards the end of 1855, given the opportunity of acquiring *The Sunday Times,* Levy – fearing too much responsibility – refused. Some weeks later, hearing that the paper was now on the market, and having expressed surprise that his quarter share of the agreement was being overlooked, on 21 February 1856, Levy offered to purchase the title for £3000, to be paid in instalments. Four days later he was told by the Lamb brothers that they now had a better offer from a Mr E.T. Smith, licensee of the Drury Lane Theatre. Unfortunately Levy had not signed any documents, leading Sir W.P. Wood, Vice-Chancellor, in the High Court, to rule 'that the agreement had not been signed, and in his own view it had not assumed its actual completion. Thomas Lamb was in no way affected, nor was it necessary upon the present occasion to consider the position of Smith'.[16]

Within days, Smith was the new proprietor – and Levy could now direct all his energies to *The Daily Telegraph*. And under Smith and his editor, William Carpenter, *The Sunday Times* was able to give more space to the theatre, book reviews, racing and boxing.

By the late 1860s, *The Sunday Times* – now based in Leicester Square – was in the ownership of Edward Seale, a banker, and one of his first moves was to appoint a Unitarian minister, Henry M. Barnett, as editor. Edward Seale died in 1867, whereupon his son, Edmund, became principal proprietor until selling the title to the the Fitzgeorge family in 1881.

Six years later, *The Sunday Times* was bought by Miss Alice Cornwell as a present for the war correspondent, Phil Robinson, whom she later married and appointed editor. Born in Essex, she had studied with great distinction at the Royal Academy of Music, winning several gold medals and composing a number of popular songs. But, with the death of her mother in Australia, Alice Cornwell turned her attention to gold mining – and had the good fortune to make one of the richest strikes in Victoria: the Midas Mine at Sulky Gully, Ballarat. Known as the Princess Midas, she was a flamboyant figure in both London and Melbourne; and in an interview given in Victoria, she was to say:

> Yes I bought *The Sunday Times* . . . . When I purchased the paper it was only a scissors and paste affair, with hardly any original news. After being placed under the management of Mr Phil Robinson it began to be a splendid paper and when I left circulation was rapidly increasing. There are six Sunday newspapers in London, some of them having very large circulations. Two or three elderly ladies were rather shocked at my becoming proprietress of a Sunday newspaper, until I explained that the work was nearly all done on Saturday. One of the ladies thereupon determined to take the paper but not read it until Monday.

After running *The Sunday Times* for a period of five years, she sold the paper to Frederick and Rachel Beer, of *The Observer*, and devoted her energies to founding the Ladies' Kennel Association.

The Popular Sunday Press

The greatest increase in the newspaper market during the early years of the Victorian age, though, was to be in the popular Sunday Press. 'In 1821, the leading Sunday papers had each sold about 10–14,000; by 1843 they sold 20–55,000, and by 1854 as much as 110,000, which only twenty-five years earlier had been their aggregate sale.' Although the leading titles – with their mixture of sex, crime and gossip – were not launched until the 1840s, there had been attempts before to introduce a popular Sunday newspaper.

One early entrant had been *The Selector or Say's Sunday Reporter* published by Mary Vint (late Say), 10, Ave-Maria Lane, London, price *6d.*, started in 1796. Here was a woman publisher from a long-standing newspaper family, who had quickly realized the opportunities in the Sunday market, following the launch of Mrs Johnson's *Sunday Monitor* a decade earlier. In the issue of 8 October 1808, although most of the eight pages were devoted to news, she found room for a half-column on 'Female Fashion for October' and one-and-a-half columns on the theatre, including a review of *The Tragedy of Douglas*, featuring Mr C. Kemble and Mrs Sarah Siddons.[17]

Another early title had been the eight-page *The News*, price 8 ½*d.* and 'published at an early hour every Sunday by T.A. Phipps (the Proprietor) at No. 28, Brydges-street, Covent-garden, and distributed throughout the Metropolis, and within the Two-penny Post District, by Nine o'clock – *No advertisements of any description are inserted in this newspaper*'. In the issue of 24 December 1815 Phipps railed against the newsvendors and their insertion of handbills advertising rival titles:

> Our correspondent 'Equity' is not the only one who has animadverted on the practice of rival Newspapers availing themselves of the circulation of their more successful contemporaries to puff forth the merits of their respective publications. To persons not

> in the secret, it appears extraordinary, that, in the bowels of THE NEWS, should sometimes be contained that which if attended to, might prove the means of its disolution – In other words, that with THE NEWS should be delivered a hand-bill earnestly recommending Readers to take in some other Newspaper in its place. Their surprize will, however, cease when they learn that the enclosing of hand-bills in Newspapers is done by the Newsmen for profit, after they have purchased the papers at the different offices . . . . It must be acknowledged the practice we have alluded to is not the most honourable – however a Newspaper is not the only profession where a man, who, having attained to a good height on the ladder of profit and reputation, on looking down, sees half a dozen adventurers endeavouring to raise themselves to a similar altitude by laying hold of the skirts of his coat.[18]

Five years later, *John Bull* made its debut in November 1820, whose editor, on the recommendation of Sir Walter Scott, was to be Theodore Edward Hook. His paper was a mixture of politics and news, and had among its writers the well-known Dr William Maginn. Under Hook's guidance it was known for its wit, salaciousness and sarcasm; and sales quickly reached more than 10,000. As a precaution against libels, Hook engaged the unfortunate Mr Shackell as the 'legal lightning editor' – and it was he who was to serve two terms of imprisonment. Hook, though, was not only editor of *John Bull* for the first few years, but remained a contributor until his death in 1841.

However, it is as a practical joker that he was best known, and in 1809 he pulled off the famous Berners Street hoax. Hook had sent out more than four thousand letters to all types of people, ranging from chimney-sweeps to the Duke of Gloucester and the Lord Mayor of London, requesting them to call at a fixed time at the home of a Mrs Tottenham. The tradesmen were told to deliver articles of their merchandise – furniture, pianos, linen, jewellery, casks of wine, barrels of beer, clothes, hats and even wigs. The result was utter chaos, and the traffic of London was dislocated for most of the day.

As a result the Prince Regent declared that something must be done about Hook and he was sent to Mauritius as accountant-general at £2000 a year. Unfortunately, Hook was not a success in the post and came home two years later in disgrace, with a deficiency of 62,000 dollars in the treasury. Although there was no basis for criminal proceedings, Hook was held responsible, having his property in England seized. He was also imprisoned for making no effort to pay off his debt. Upon his release, he turned to journalism – and editorship of *John Bull*.[19]

Another early entrant in the popular field was John Cleave's *Weekly Police Gazette*, launched in 1834, which, with its mix of 'shocking crime' and police court reports, was to attain a circulation of more than 20,000 within a few years. However, it was to be *Lloyd's Weekly News*, originally launched on 27 November 1842 as *Lloyd's Illustrated London Newspaper*, that was to set the pace. Priced twopence, in the eighth issue the illustrations were dropped, the price increased to twopence halfpenny and the paper renamed *Lloyd's Weekly London Newspaper* (later shortened to *Lloyd's Weekly News*). Within twelve months, the paper was increased in size from eight to twelve broadsheet pages and the price again raised, to threepence.

In marketing his newspaper, Lloyd was one of the first to use research – albeit rather crudely – evidenced by his remarks to one of his managers in the 1840s: 'We sometimes distrust our judgment and place the manuscript in the hands of an illiterate person – a servant or a machine boy, for instance. If they pronounce favourably upon it we think it will do.'

Known as 'the father of the cheap press', Edward Lloyd,[20] the paper's founder, was born at Thornton Heath, near Croydon, and trained as a compositor at the London Mechanics Institute before, while in his teens, starting his own business. One of his early ventures had been *Lloyd's Stenography; or an Easy and Compendious System of Shorthand* in which the definitions were printed and the shorthand characters written by Lloyd himself.

From his Salisbury Square premises he next published song-books, followed by *The Penny Pickwick* (edited by 'Boz' [Charles Dickens] and illustrated by 'Phiz' [Hablot Knight Browne]), which brought, without success, legal proceedings for alleged libel from Charles Dickens, although the two were later to become good friends. Lloyd then launched *Lloyd's Weekly Miscellany* and *Lloyd's Weekly Atlas*; both were good sellers, but neither was a newspaper in the accepted sense. In 1840 he started the *Penny People's Gazette*; and two years later *Lloyd's Illustrated London Newspaper* (later *Lloyd's Weekly News*) edited by a Mr Ball followed by Dr Carpenter. Then, after the paper had been established nine years, Lloyd engaged Douglas Jerrold as editor at a salary of £1000 per annum.

Jerrold was lucky, for immediately on taking over in 1852 the death and funeral of the Duke of Wellington sent the sales to more than 150,000 per week, and the circulation continued to rise. Jerrold's tenure was to be brief, for he died five years later in 1857. The previous year, to provide for the increase in sales, Lloyd had introduced the Hoe rotary press – developed by Robert Hoe in New York in 1846 – which printed the newspaper from type, with each page being locked into a segment of the impression cylinder. As a further measure to secure production he established an esparto grass estate in Algeria to supply the raw material for his paper mill at Bow on the River Lea. He was to increase his paper-making capacity even further when he opened a huge factory at Sittingbourne, Kent, in 1877.

With the success of the *Weekly* assured, Lloyd had the previous year bought the *Daily Chronicle* for £30,000 and had set out to transform a small local daily into a national newspaper of the first rank. Originally a half-penny weekly, the *Clerkenwell News*, it was started in 1856, and was a successor to the *Business and Agency News*, a free advertisement sheet, launched a year earlier. It became a daily in 1869 under the title of the *London Daily Chronicle and Clerkenwell News*. On assuming ownership Lloyd declared that he would support the *Chronicle* for five years and then review the position. In that period he expended more than £150,000 and saw the *Chronicle* become a great and prosperous morning journal. Meanwhile, sales of *Lloyd's Weekly* continued to soar, approaching 900,000 copies in the 1880s; and when Lloyd died the magical figure of one million sales was almost in sight.

His successor was his son, Frank, who had joined the family business straight from school, working first at the Bow paper mill and then at the larger operation in

Sittingbourne, where he became manager. On his father's death in 1890 he took over the company as chairman and managing director; and his first step was to strengthen the editorial staff on both newspapers, *Lloyd's News* and the *Daily Chronicle*. The results were soon evident, in 1896 *Lloyd's News* became the first newspaper to reach a circulation of more than one million.

Enter George Reynolds

For much of that time the chief rival to *Lloyds's News* had been *Reynolds's News*, launched on 5 May 1850 as the successor to *Reynolds's Political Instructor*, which had made its debut the previous year.[21] The new paper was designed to attract an increasing Sunday market with a mixture of sensationalism and politics. It was an immediate success with the working classes; and as Wesley Perrins was to recall: 'My grandfather was one of a group of twelve men, who paid a half-penny each week to buy a copy of *Reynolds's News*. The men would gather once a week in the nailshop and my grandfather would read to them.'

The man behind the paper was George Reynolds, who had been born at Sandwich, Kent, and had entered the Royal Military Academy, Sandhurst, in 1828, leaving two years later to travel on the Continent, where he became fluent in French; and as a result published his *Modern Literature of France* in 1839. Turning to journalism, Reynolds worked for the *Monthly Magazine* and the *London Journal* before becoming head of the foreign department of the *Weekly Dispatch*, a position he retained until the mid-1840s. During this period, he had also been involved in the launch of two periodicals: *Teetotaller* (1840–41) and *Reynolds's Miscellany* (1846).

Although from a comfortable middle-class background, Reynolds was a 'dedicated' Chartist, and made his first public appearance as a political leader in Trafalgar Square on 6 March 1848. That same year, on 10 April, he was a prime organizer of the great Chartist gathering at Kennington Common, which, however, proved to be less threatening than had been feared – the presentation of a 'monster' petition to Parliament later that day (many of the signatures were forgeries) led only to laughter and ridicule. Nevertheless, Reynolds retained his interest in Chartism until 1856, when as his final act he chaired the Feargus O'Connor monument committee.

By the time of his death, circulation of *Reynolds's News* was more than 300,000 a week – and the market for a Sunday title catering for the artisan had been proven. Reynolds died at Woburn Square, London, on 17 June 1879; and although known as a Chartist in his early days his association with the movement had not been entirely altruistic. Many believed that Reynolds had embraced Chartism for the gains that he could achieve in his personal and business dealings. Karl Marx dismissed him as 'a rich and an able speculator'.[22]

Two years after the death of Reynolds, another newspaper entered the Sunday market: *The People*, launched on 16 October 1881 by George Armstrong and W.T. Madge. And for the National Unionist Party meeting at Newcastle there was delight to learn of this addition to the weekly Conservative Press and optimism that 'it will go far to break down the almost complete monopoly of the popular Sunday Press, at present enjoyed by the Radical Party'.

George Armstrong, one of the paper's founders, had led a most exciting life as a young man. When eighteen years old he left for India where he was gazetted to the 59th Bengal Native Infantry. Based at Amritsar when the Mutiny broke out, he was sent to Delhi to join the besieging force and appointed second in command of Stoke's Pathan Horse, a newly-raised regiment of irregulars. On the day of the great assault on Delhi, Armstrong, leading his force, was attacked by a Sepoy trooper, 'who dealt him a tremendous blow on the top of his bare head with a tulwar'. The rebel was cut down before he could deliver a second blow. Following a spell in hospital, Armstrong returned to action, but, not fully recovered, he was invalided home after the Mutiny had been quelled.

He left the Army in 1861 with the rank of captain, and five years later was appointed secretary of Westminster Conservative Association, doing much to assist W.H. Smith win his seat in 1868. So impressed was George Watney that he offered him a six-fold increase in salary if he would become head manager of his brewery. A surprised Armstrong accepted, and was a great success, but three years later, in 1871, he was invited to take over the management of the *Globe* at the same salary as he was receiving at Watney's.

Armstrong agreed, and by cutting costs was able to turn a loss of £5000 per annum into a profit within two years; and his reward in 1874 was complete control when he became proprietor and editor. With the expansion of the *Globe*, a move was made to 367 the Strand, and it was there, with the assistance of W.T. Madge, that Armstrong decided to launch a Sunday title, *The People*. Prior to becoming publisher of the *Globe* – a relationship that was to last almost fifty years – Madge had already gained a wide experience on West Country newspapers.

For seven years, *The People* had a struggle to avoid closure, until in 1888 it achieved its first big success. At two o'clock one Sunday morning, Madge was sitting in his office when he received a visitor, who told him that there had been a murder in Whitechapel. Having had the presses stopped, Madge took a cab to the East End and there saw the body of a woman, a victim of 'Jack the Ripper'. Madge then found that there had been a second 'Ripper' murder that night just eight minutes' walk away. Returning to the office at five a.m., he wrote his 'exclusive', with the result that *The People* had a complete sell-out. Not content with this, Madge, discovering that the newsprint stocks had been used up, went to the home of a newsprint supplier, who he learned was at church, and had him open up the stores. As a result, *The People* continued printing until late Sunday evening 'so that a record sale was achieved'.[23]

The Carr Family in Charge

Another well-known Sunday paper of this period was the *News of the World*, launched on 1 October 1843 by John Browne Bell, priced at 3*d*. with the statement 'Our motto is the truth, our practice is the fearless advocacy of the truth.' The son of John Bell, who in 1796 had launched *Bell's Weekly Messenger*, he had, following his father's death, started *Bell's New Weekly Messenger* in January 1832 and then *The Planet*, another Sunday paper, which lasted from 1837 until 1844. (These two titles were later to be merged with the *News of the World*.)

Within weeks of its launch, Bell was in difficulties with the London news trade, and a deputation met him in attempt to get him to increase the selling price of the *News of the World*. Bell's reply was brief and to the point: 'Gentlemen, I brought out a paper on which the trade had 1½*d*. profit. What have you done for it? You have pushed it – but you have pushed it out of existence. I have made up my mind and I shall adhere to the plans I have laid down.' Initially, the paper was printed and published from cramped premises at 30 Hollywell Street – now demolished – off the Strand. Then, in October 1852, with sales in excess of 100,000 the establishment was moved to 19 Essex Street.

> New machinery was installed [although] still hand fed they could produce 4,000 copies an hour; they required eight men to work each machine, four men to feed in the sheets of paper and four to take them off after printing. One side of the paper was printed on the first machine; the sheets were then fed through the second machine to print the the other side, after which they were folded by hand and counted.

Within two years of moving to Essex Street, the paper could claim the highest circulation in the world with 5,673,525 stamps issued by the authorities for 1854; but these were just copies sold, and the readership would have been much higher: 'The writer's grandfather lived at that time a few miles from Neath in South Wales, and it was his habit to drive into Neath every Saturday morning, purchase the *News of the World* when it arrived by train, and then sit in the trap and read the [Crimean] war news to the assembled crowd. This was the practice in many parts of the country.'

Following the death of John Browne Bell in 1857, 'having amassed a large fortune', the paper passed to his son John William Bell, a solicitor, who also acted as trustee to his younger siblings; and after his death in 1877 the estate was again divided, passing on to his two sons, Walter John Bell and Adolphus Bell. However, indecision in reducing the price of the *News of the World* to one penny to compete with its rivals led to a loss in circulation and sale to a consortium of families headed by Lascelles Carr, George Riddell and Charles Jackson.[24]

A Yorkshireman, Lascelles Carr, the new chief proprietor of the *News of the World*, had worked on the *Liverpool Daily Post* before joining the recently-launched *Western Mail*, Cardiff, in 1869. Within months, the owner of the *Western Mail*, the Marquis of Bute, had appointed him manager; and ten years later, Carr, in conjunction with David Owen, purchased the paper from the Marquis.

Under Carr, as editor-in-chief, the *Western Mail* soon became the national daily of Wales; and eight years later he started the *Evening Express*. When the *Western Mail* became a limited company, Carr was appointed editor-in-chief for life. In 1891 Carr became chief proprietor of the *News of the World*, the purchase price for the machinery, premises and goodwill being just £25,000; and on 24 May 1891 the first issue under the new regime was printed. As chairman, Carr swiftly brought in George Riddell, his lawyer from the *Western Mail*, to help run the new acquisition. Carr remained as chairman until 1897, when, following a series of family bereavements and in poor health, he resigned and settled in Paris. Ironically, in 1902, while on a visit to Hyères for the benefit of his health, he had a stroke and died the following day.

His nephew, Emsley Carr, was to edit the *News of the World* for fifty years, a Fleet Street record. Born in Leeds, he had been educated locally before joining his uncle on the *Western Mail*, learning the basics of journalism; and in 1891, at the age of twenty-four, was appointed editor of the *News of the World*. With company secretary George Riddell looking after the finances, the only two permanent members of the editorial staff, Carr and Bob Berrey, received £3 10*s*. and £2 a week respectively. Having inherited a circulation of 51,000, Carr was to see sales increase to almost 100,000 within five years.

Carr's close colleague, George Riddell,[25] had been born in Brixton and articled to a Bloomsbury solicitor, coming first in the English Solicitors' Examination of 1888. He abandoned law in 1891 for newpaper management, and in 1903 was appointed chairman of the *News of the World*. With most newsagents' shops closed on Sundays, Riddell built up a special network of agents to sell the *News of the World* in every village and town in Great Britain, and under his leadership the circulation rose from 60,000 in 1892 to more than 2,500,000 by 1917. On Saturday nights, he often rode on one of the vans taking copies to the railway stations, where he would hand out half-crowns to the porters who were responsible for putting the parcels on the trains. Apart from his managerial interests, Riddell also contributed to the paper's political and social columns.

Knighted in 1909, Riddell was a close friend and golfing companion of David Lloyd George, and was to be especially useful to the Prime Minister during the First World War in his role as an executive of the Newspaper Proprietors Association. He was rewarded with a baronetcy in 1918 and two years later was raised to the peerage.

However, despite its success, the *News of the World*, with its combination of sex and sport, did not find favour with everyone. One day, the legendary editor Arthur Greenwood ran into Lord Riddell at his club. Riddell said to him: 'You know, I own a newspaper.' 'Oh, do you,' replied Greenwood. 'It's called the *News of the World* – I'll send you a copy.' When they next met, Riddell asked: 'Well, Greenwood, what did you think of my paper?' 'I looked at it,' replied Greenwood, 'and then I put it in the wastepaper basket. And then I thought, if I leave it there, the cook may read it – so I burnt it.'

Reuters is Founded

The advent of telegraphy had meant that newspapers were now able to receive information weeks, days or hours faster than before, and this had led to a number of news agencies being started. The oldest of these, Reuters, dated back to 1851. Its founder, Julius de Reuter, was born in Hesse-Cassel, Germany, and began work as an office boy for his uncle, but came into contact with Professor Gauss, a scientist, who was experimenting with electro-magnetism. When the telegraphic line between Berlin and Aix-la-Chapelle was opened in 1849, Reuter set up an office in the latter town;

and to speed up his news service from Aix-la-Chapelle to Brussels he employed carrier pigeons which beat the usual rail service by some seven hours.[26]

Reuter came to London in 1851, when the Calais-Dover cable was laid, and opened an office at No. 1, Royal Exchange Buildings, where for several years he was mainly concerned with supplying financial and commercial information. But, during those early years, Reuter had also been aware of the inadequate coverage of foreign news in the London papers; and by 1857, through his own network of agents, he decided he could provide a better service. He first approached Mowbray Morris, manager of *The Times*, who told him, dismissively, that: 'They generally found they could do their own business better than anyone else.'

Not downhearted, Reuter next turned to James Grant, editor of the *Morning Advertiser*, offering for two weeks a free service of 'earlier, more ample, more accurate and more important information from the Continent than they at presently received from their own people'. If successful, the papers should then take the same service for £30 a month, some £10 less than they were presently paying. Reuter stressed that he intended to confine himself to just the facts – and accuracy and speed would be his watchwords. Other papers to take the service were: *The Standard*, *The Morning Herald*, *The Daily Telegraph*, *Daily News*, *Morning Post*, *Morning Chronicle* and *Morning Star*. As a result of this trial, Reuter was able to sign up most of the London dailies before 1860, and was to expand his service to the leading provincial newspapers.[27]

Reuters, however, was not the only news agency to provide a service on the Continent, for in the 1860s there were two main rivals: Charles Havas, in Paris, and Bernard Wolff, in Berlin. Following talks, they agreed that the world news outside North America should be divided among them, with Reuters becoming the leading member of the 'ring combination'. Next came the need to provide a faster service from America, and this was achieved with the laying of the first Atlantic cable in 1866. Before then, Reuter employed fast sailing yachts to meet incoming steamers from the United States off the Irish coast. The yachts would put into harbour at Crookhaven, and the news was then sent by way of Cork over a telegraph line laid down by Reuter, before onward transmission to London. Reuter was also involved with governments in the laying down of cable lines: he received a concession for a submarine telegraphic line between Germany and England; and he also acquired from the French government the right to construct and lay a cable between France and the United States.

Having converted his agency into a limited company in 1865, Reuter became managing director until standing down in 1878 to be succeeded by his son, Herbert de Reuter. Even then he remained on the board. Reuter had been made a baron by the Duke of Saxe-Coburg-Gotha in 1871, a title recognized by Queen Victoria twenty years later. He died in Nice on 15 March 1899. That same year saw the start of the Boer War, and Reuters' coverage – with correspondents on the Boer side as well as the British – was second to none. Under the direction of H.A. Gwynne, a future editor of *The Standard* and *Morning Post*, there were to be more than two hundred correspondents in the field, including a young Edgar Wallace.

The new head of the agency, Baron Herbert de Reuter, had been educated at Harrow, Balliol College, Oxford, and in Paris, where he studied music. At first he was reluctant to give up his music, but in 1875 he joined the firm as 'assistant manager without salary'. On his father's resignation three years later, he became managing director, and from then on Reuters was to be his main interest. In his *Reuters' Century* (1951), Graham Storey was to write that Herbert de Reuter was a man 'who loved words; and except for the official communication had a horror of the bare facts'. During his years in charge, he showed 'great initiative and intuition' in expanding the news service; and he was to remain in control of the agency until his death.

On Thursday 15 April 1915, while working late in the City, Herbert de Reuter received a telephone call informing him that his invalid wife, whom he had looked after for many years, had died suddenly. Heartbroken, he went home immediately, and three days later was found shot by his own hand in the summer-house. By his body was a letter addressed to the 'Spirit of my dear wife', which ended with two lines from Sophocles' *Oedipus Coloneus*:

> To go as quickly thither whence one has come
> is much the second best thing.

There was to be one further act in this Greek tragedy: in 1916 his son, Hubert de Reuter, who had worked for the agency in Turkey, Australia and Austria, before leaving to become a schoolmaster, was killed while bringing in British wounded under heavy machine-gun fire on the Somme during the First World War.[28]

6

The New Journalism

POLITICIANS WERE NOW BECOMING AWARE that not all editors could be manipulated, and there was also a consciousness of the phrase 'New Journalism'[1] introduced by the poet Matthew Arnold in the May 1887 issue of *Nineteenth Century* when discussing the *Pall Mall Gazette* and its contemporaries:

> It has much to recommend it; it is full of ability, novelty, variety, sensation, sympathy, generous instincts; its one great fault is that it is feather-brained. It throws out assertions at a venture because it wishes them true; does not correct either them or itself, if they are false; and to get at the state of things as they truly are seems to feel no concern whatever.

Although hardly ever exceeding a circulation of more than 10,000 copies, under the editorship of Frederick Greenwood the *Pall Mall Gazette* – launched on 7 February 1865 – had brought 'wit, lightness, urbanity and intellectual polish into journalism'. Described as 'the most dignified and influential figure in later nineteenth-century journalism', Greenwood based his editorial policy on good, vigorous writing; and he was able to attract such names as Matthew Arnold, Anthony Trollope and Sir Henry Main.

Despite these writers, the paper was not an immediate success; and Greenwood was later to declare 'that his craft was waiting for a breeze which no amount of whistling on the skipper's part seemed likely to bring'. But a series of articles by his brother James, under the pseudonym 'Amateur Casual', was to bring the paper to the public notice. His accounts of life as a down-and-out and the horrors of the casual wards of the workhouse provided graphic reading.

In 1875, after ten years as editor, Greenwood was given secret information that the Khedive of Egypt was about to sell his 177,000 shares in the Suez Canal to a French syndicate. Greenwood immediately told Lord Derby, the Foreign Secretary, who in turn informed Disraeli, the Prime Minister; and at a Cabinet meeting approval was given to purchase the shares for £4,000,000. As a result of this decision, Britain was to have a controlling interest in the Suez Canal for the next eighty years. Disraeli, in a letter to Queen Victoria, claimed the credit – and for Greenwood there was nothing. Despite Disraeli's snubbing of the editor, he held him in high regard, and was reported to have said: 'Whenever I read Greenwood, I feel myself in the grip of a statesman.' Greenwood continued to edit the *Pall Mall Gazette* until 1880, when on 29 April he wrote to Gladstone: 'My paper (I originated it & have carried it on uncontrolled through its fifteeen years of existence) has since the election been sold into the

THE
PALL MALL GAZETTE
An Evening Newspaper and Review.

No. 1.—Vol. I. *TUESDAY, FEBRUARY 7, 1865.* *Price Twopence.*

THE QUEEN'S SECLUSION.

A LITTLE paragraph appeared in the newspapers lately, to revive a hope which was to have been fulfilled to-day, and has not. "We "are informed that Her MAJESTY the QUEEN will open Parliament "in person next session:" this was the little paragraph—printed, too, in that authoritative large type which carries conviction straight into the minds of most newspaper readers. But somehow the herald who brought such good tidings from Court was little credited. The trumpet sounded—that we all heard; but no confirming echo answered it—not even in those hollow places in our own hearts where dwells the hope of what we much desire. The most timid inquirer hesitated to believe; and he whose faith in editorial announcements had hitherto been complete, found himself disturbed by a strangely courageous scepticism. Was the announcement authorized at all by any one? Had we not been told of journalists and politicians who endeavoured to achieve what they wished by declaring it already certain? These questions were asked by many people. The answer to the first one is that the QUEEN never at any moment intended to open Parliament this session—(here is our own authoritative large type to prove it)—and to the other, that if the trick was played, it was a trick which only a very few philosophers can muster morality enough to condemn. There may be some politicians of the fermentative platform kind who secretly rejoice that (if tried) it did not succeed, but they are not philosophers.

It is when we consider what these gentlemen *are* that we most regret the QUEEN'S long absence from what is called public life. If it were not for them, and if Her MAJESTY'S retirement were not brought home to us strongly *now*, when a Parliament is about to end and agitation to begin, we should say nothing about it. There are, indeed, other reasons for regret but none that we can think of which justifies the remonstrant tone in which some journalists have lately discussed the subject. What *would* justify such a tone is a state of things which does not exist. The Sovereign of England is not an autocrat, sold to cares and committed to responsibilities which must necessarily be neglected in the indulgence of personal sorrow. Her Ministers are able and honest; and, what is more—what is conclusive, in fact—the QUEEN is known never to neglect the real duties of her sovereignity. Their faithful performance goes on, and has always gone on; and while that is so, our concern that her grief also continues should cease with the sympathy of a loyal and home-loving people. Of such sympathy there cannot be too much. Taking it for a moment out of the region of mere human kindness where it were better left, we may go so far as to say there are sound political reasons why it should be encouraged; unless, indeed, the country has had enough of the great blessing which the QUEEN'S reign is said to have brought upon it ever since her rule began. We have all been lying under a mistake for twenty years if the nation has not been purified by an example of homely affection and of household faith in that place where example is so potent for good or evil—the palace. Some observers are of opinion, indeed, that a certain reaction against this beneficent influence has set in: be that as it may, we cannot think the reaction likely to be forwarded by the sincere and lasting sorrow of a wife for the loss of her husband; or by our respect for it.

There are some other considerations which have been almost as much forgotten as these. There is the fact that a monarch is still a human being; and that a people has no right to ask him to smile when his heart is ill at ease, or violate the most natural, most pious, most imperative instincts of his human nature in order to make a pageant. Again, our affection for the QUEEN, our deepest reverence for her, has grown out of the knowledge that she is not only a queen, but a good and most womanly woman: and yet how many people have considered that the very qualities they reverence in the woman have embittered the grief of the queen? We all understand what is meant by the "sacredness" of sorrow, and know that to turn our eyes upon one whose heart is deeply smitten, is to add to the pain a new and intolerable distress. This is so if you are happily unknown to all but a dozen people, whose gaze you easily can and do escape. But if you are a queen, then you cannot escape; your grief, which should be secret to be endurable, is known to all the world—talked of by all the world—gazed upon wherever you turn. And the more womanly you are, the more you are conscious of an observation which is scarcely the less painful for being sympathetic. Therefore we say Her MAJESTY'S seclusion is exactly what might have been expected of her position and her virtues; and that inasmuch as we respect them we must respect their natural consequences, nor forget that her retirement is the most natural one of all.

But this is not saying we wish the seclusion to continue. What we do say is, that with the fullest sense of what is due to Her MAJESTY, with the strongest inclination to take no part in the discussion of this subject, we cannot resist the suggestions of the ceremony of to-day. In brief, we cannot help speculating, not upon the regret or the disappointment of the nation at large on seeing another fair occasion for the QUEEN'S re-appearance amongst us pass by, but upon the satisfaction it may give that small, determined coterie of Americanized politicians who are so particularly active just now, and whom we shall behold still more active before another Parliament can be assembled. Who can doubt that they *do* find satisfaction in the QUEEN'S absence, once more, from the most important and significant of all State ceremonials? To be sure, they are not likely to acknowledge such sentiments. There are many bold speakers amongst them, and a carnival of declamation is fast approaching; but we do not suppose any demagogue so rash as to suggest the question yet awhile, that as the country gets on very well with a monarch in retirement (the Board of Trade returns will sufficiently prove it), why not abolish the monarchy altogether? We do not expect *him* to point out so soon that people may become so accustomed to the absence of a Sovereign from public business as to make them ready converts to Americanism and the democratic idea. But it is just because he is not likely to speak that we feel bound to speak for him—now, while the people are *not* quite accustomed to the QUEEN'S seclusion, and earnestly desire her back again. Perhaps the event of to-day was not the most fitting occasion for her return to public life; perhaps we may hope that when the new Parliament is called together, Her MAJESTY will come once more face to face with her people. If so, we shall all rejoice—all but those who are speculating hopefully now upon the probability that her seclusion may be confirmed by habit, and, who are perfectly prepared to turn it into a political argument.

Private letters from St. Petersburg and Moscow say that the example of the Moscow assembly, which has adopted by a very large majority an address in favour of a constitution, will be followed by the nobles of the other provinces of the empire. The proceedings at the Moscow assembly were published without being submitted to the consorship, and the printer of the journal in which they appeared is being prosecuted criminally.

The *Standard* published a letter yesterday from St. Petersburg, in which the writer, apparently an official, sets before the English public, with great complacency, the reasons current among Russian functionaries of all classes for discountenancing the courageous endeavours of the nobility to obtain the establishment of a representative assembly. Such an assembly would, of course, be a terror to the members of the public service, whose acts it could criticise, if it could not legally control them. This is just the good—perhaps the only good—that the Reichsrath has done in Austria. "But," say the functionaries and the democrats of the baser kind, "if a legislative body were to be formed by election "in the present day, only members of the aristocracy would be chosen, "for it is well known that they alone are capable of discussing political "questions. The merchants are careless about such matters, and the "peasants are steeped in the greatest ignorance." The functionaries, then, from fear of exposure, and the democrats from mere envy, would postpone the formation of political assemblies indefinitely, or what comes to the same thing, until the spread of education throughout the empire should raise the other classes to the level of the nobles! These views, in default of more plausible ones, have been adopted by the Russian Government, and we find them expressed with great earnestness in a paragraph which bears the following curious heading:—"The Moscow Nobility demanding a Constitution!"

How perverse on the part of the Russian nobility! So in ancient times the discontented Hebrews, in the sinfulness of their hearts, called out for a King! But the Hebrews *had* their King; whereas the Russian landed proprietors, with an autocrat, supported by a mass of bribe-taking officials on one side, and with hordes of newly-liberated serfs on the other, have no chance whatever of getting a constitution. A few of the leaders may have the privilege accorded to them of going to the East of Russia in their own carriages, and remaining there until further notice. The others will have to be silent; or they may have the same measure meted out to them which they were so glad to see meted out last year and the year before to the Poles.

hands of a thorough going party-man of Liberal views & is henceforth to be no erratic independent but to be printed as a supporter of your government.' According to J. Saxon Mills, the new proprietor, Yates Thompson, 'Managed to carry on by dipping into the accumulation of manuscripts left in the pigeon-holes by Mr Greenwood.' On 1 May, the *Pall Mall Gazette* announced that Greenwood 'will not be responsible for any political opinion after today'. Within a month, Greenwood, with backing of more than £100,000 – and further offers of 'five times over' – had launched the *St James's Gazette*, and taken with him many of his old staff. However, following financial problems, Henry Gibbs, the owner of *St James's Gazette*, had decided by 1888 to sell – to Edward Steinkopf, described as 'a vulgar loud-speaking German'.[2] Greenwood and his new proprietor soon fell out and within eight months he had resigned as editor. Nevertheless, it is as the launch-editor of the *Pall Mall Gazette* that Greenwood will be best remembered; and as Thomas Escott was to write: 'Trained under Thackeray – the title *Pall Mall Gazette* was taken from his *Pendennis* – Frederick Greenwood saw in his evening print the legitimate opportunities offered by the translation of the paper for which Pendennis wrote.'

Succeeding Greenwood as editor of the *Pall Mall Gazette* on 10 May 1880 – at a salary of £2,000 per annum – was John Morley, a Liberal politician and editor of the *Morning Star* in June 1869 until it was subsumed by its Liberal rival, the *Daily News*, a few months later. There then followed a decade editing the *Fortnightly Review* before joining the *Pall Mall Gazette*. One of Morley's first acts was to choose W.T. Stead as his deputy. It was a strange partnership: Morley so scholarly and austere; Stead a Christian with a mission to reform the world. Stead was to say of his editor: 'We disagreed on everything from the existence of God to the make-up of a newspaper.' On another occasion he was to write: 'No power on earth could command Mr Morley's interest in three-fourths of the matter that fills the paper. To him a newspaper was simply a pulpit from which he could preach.'[3]

Still determined to embark on a career in politics, in October 1882 Morley stood down as editor of the *Fortnightly Review*, and in a valedictory article described his style of editorship. The following year he was politically successful, being elected as Liberal MP for Newcastle-upon-Tyne, and within months he had resigned as editor of the *Pall Mall Gazette*. Years later, Morley was 'continually to reproach himself for having betrayed his true calling'. As a politician, though, he was to have a most distinguished career, becoming Chief Secretary for Ireland in 1886 and 1892, Secretary of State for India, 1905-10 (when he became Viscount Morley of Blackburn) and Lord President of the Council. With Morley having departed, the way was now clear for William Thomas Stead to assume the editorship. Born near Newcastle-upon-Tyne, Stead had been apprenticed as a clerk at a Newcastle merchant's office; and in his spare time wrote for the *Northern Echo*, Darlington, and in 1871, when aged only twenty-two, was appointed editor. But before taking up the post it was suggested that he see T. Wemys Reid, the experienced editor of the *Leeds Mercury*. Later, Reid was to say: 'For hour after hour he [Stead] talked with an ardour that delighted me . . . . Many a time since I have recalled that long night's talk when I have recognized in some daring development of modern journalism one of the many schemes which Stead flashed before my eyes.'

Before accepting the position, Stead insisted on three conditions: no Sunday working, control of his own writing and no wearing of a top hat. And to a friend he wrote: 'What a glorious opportunity of attacking the devil.' Earl Grey, a future Foreign Secretary, was to say of Stead: '[He] amused me to begin with. I found this provincial editor was corresponding with kings and emperors all over the world and receiving letters from statesmen of every nation. This struck me as odd and interesting.'

Much later, Viscount Morley in his *Recollections* was to say of Stead:

> We were lucky enough to induce to join us as assistant a man from the North of England, who, by sailing under his own flag, became for a season the most powerful journalist in the island. Stead was invaluable, abounding in journalistic resource, eager in convictions, infinitely bold, candid, laborious in sure-footed mastery of all the facts and bright with a cheerfulness and geniality that no difference of opinion between us and none of the passing embarrassments of the day could ever for a moment dampen. His extraordinary vigour and spirit made other people seem wet blankets, sluggish creatures of moral weakness.

A deeply religious Nonconformist, Stead saw journalism as a means of doing good and publicizing God's work. Brought up in a Puritan atmosphere, Oliver Cromwell was his idol; and in later years Stead was to say that the greatest compliment he had ever received was when Cardinal Manning said to him: 'When I read the *Pall Mall Gazette* every night it seems to me as if Oliver Cromwell has come to life again.' Stead first came to the attention of the public in 1876–77 with his Bulgarian atrocities crusade in the *Northern Echo*, and on a visit to London in connection with this he met Gladstone and other Liberal leaders; and as a result in 1880 was invited to become assistant editor of the *Pall Mall Gazette*. The coming of Stead – and especially after his replacement of Morley in 1883 – heralded a drastic renovation of the paper. They were quite different and Stead readily admitted that 'Morley and I had approached almost everything from a different standpoint'.

Upon taking over as editor, Stead immediately redesigned the paper, introducing[4] illustrations, larger headlines and crossheads to break up the previous columns of grey type. He was one of the first to employ women journalists; was very keen on in-depth interviews; and, above all, sought sensational scoops. The apostle of the New Journalism had arrived. In his paper, Stead exposed and dramatized the plight and conditions of the poor in London, forced the Gladstone government to send General Gordon to the Sudan, and sparked off the Press campaign to modernize and strengthen the navy. His assistant editor, Alfred Milner, later noted: 'It was such fun to work with him. He was a mixture of Don Quixote and Phineas T. Barnum.'

Having increased the paper's circulation from 10,000 to 13,000, Stead launched his famous campaign, exposing the white slave traffic. On 6 July 1885 he astounded his readers with the first of a series of sensational articles headed 'The Maiden Tribute of Modern Babylon'. Having learnt that the Criminal Law Amendment Bill for the raising of the age of consent (then only thirteen) was again to be defeated in the House of Commons, Stead decided to shock the conscience of the public by revealing the facts about the child victims of white slavery and child prostitution on the basis of his personal investigation in collaboration with the Salvation Army. He had told the Archbishop of Canterbury, the Bishop of London and Cardinal Manning that he intended to impersonate one of the men 'engaged in the traffic' to show how easy under the existing law it was to procure a young girl. He would, of course, not commit the actual offence. He introduced his first article with the statement that:[5]

> The report of our secret commission will be read today with a shuddering horror that will thrill throughout the world. After this awful picture of the crimes at present committed as it were under the very aegis of the law has been unfolded before the eyes of the public, we need not doubt that the House of Commons will find time to raise the age during which English girls are protected from expiable wrong.

As a consequence, he was attacked by rival newspapers – especially Mudford in *The Standard*: 'We protest the streets being turned into a market for literature which appeals to the lascivious curiosity of every casual passer-by, and excites the latent pruriency of a half-educated crowd' – and deluged with hundreds of letters of abuse; but the ensuing public agitation did compel the House of Commons to speed the Bill through its Second Reading, and on 10 August 1885, with some amendments, it was approved by the House of Lords.

Nevertheless, Stead suffered for what he had accomplished, for in his personal investigations he had omitted one precaution, thus making himself technically guilty of abduction. Exposed by *Lloyd's Illustrated Newspaper*, Stead was arrested, tried, and sentenced to three months' imprisonment.[6] He served his time (as a first-class prisoner) in Holloway Gaol, the first genuine rest from his editorial labours that he had been able to enjoy, as he cheerfully told his friends, and made use of his leisure to write an essay on 'Government by Journalism' for *The Contemporary Review*:

> I am but a comparatively young journalist, but I have seen Cabinets upset, Ministers driven into retirement, laws repealed, great social reforms initiated, Bills transformed, estimates remodelled, Acts passed, generals nominated, governors appointed, armies sent hither and thither, war proclaimed and war averted by the agency of newspapers.

John Morley when visiting his successor in Holloway found him 'him in a strangely exalted mood', especially when Stead told him: 'As I was taking my exercise this morning in the prison-yard I asked myself who was the man of most importance now alive. I could only find one answer – the prisoner in this cell.'

Five years later, in 1890, Stead left the *Pall Mall Gazette* to found *The Review of Reviews* as a digest of the chief reviews and magazines of the month and as a journal of opinion. In his new periodical, which was a great success, Stead continued to clash with authority, notably in his support of the Boers at the time of the South African War. Following visits to Russia, where he met Tsar Nicholas II, Stead inaugurated the Peace Crusade, and founded War Against War. He also attended the Hague Peace Conference, throwing himself into Arbitration propaganda. However, the launch of Stead's *Daily Paper* in 1904 was not a success, lasting only a few weeks.

Stead's time as editor of the *Pall Mall Gazette* was to be summed up by H.W. Massingham, writing in the *Leisure Hour* in 1892: 'Mr Stead, flamboyant, expansive, full of ideas transmuted by the rough and ready alchemy of an impressionable nature, a born sub-editor, a brilliant, though not faultless, writer, and a man of impetuously daring temperament . . . . when Mr Stead edited the *Pall Mall* it always sparkled with the salt of his personality.'

Stead was to die in 1912 in the *Titanic* disaster, having missed the greatest scoop of his life – and having left an indelible mark on English journalism.

George Newnes and Tit-Bits

A key figure in the New Journalism was George Newnes, considered by many to be the father of the movement: others were to adapt to it more successfully, but to him must go the credit for seeing its potential. The Education Act of 1870 had created a vast new reading public, with simple tastes and eager for enlightenment; and to meet this demand Newnes decided to launch a specialist newspaper.

As a thirty-year-old fancy goods representative in Manchester, Newnes was a great collector of snippets of information from newspapers. One evening while reading a paper at home he came across an exciting incident which was dramatically reported. He remarked to his wife: 'Now that is what I call an interesting tit-bit. Why doesn't someone bring out a whole paper made up of tit-bits like that?' 'Why don't you?' she retorted.

Armed with a scrapbook of cuttings, he published the first issue of *Tit-Bits* on 30 October 1881 – having raised much of the capital through opening a vegetarian restaurant.[7] Within six weeks, he had been offered £10,000 for the title, and six months later a London publisher was prepared to pay him £30,000. A new reading public eagerly purchased the periodical; and years later the *History of the Times* was to comment: 'That this penny paper of scraps culled by Newnes from odd sources was destined to modify in the most profound degree the intellectual, social and political tone of the Press as a whole.'

Newnes, a stickler for accuracy, would never allow an issue of *Tit-Bits* to appear unless he had proof-read every page. With a circulation of more than 300,000 in the first year, the paper was a financial success; and assisting him as the London manager was C. Arthur Pearson, who had won the position as a prize in a *Tit-Bits* competition. Among the freelance writers was a teenage Alfred Harmsworth, who was to remark:[8]

> The Board Schools are turning out hundreds of thousands of boys and girls annually who are anxious to read. They do not care for the ordinary paper.They have no interest in society, but they will read anything which is simple and is sufficiently interesting. The man who produced this *Tit-Bits* has got hold of a bigger thing than he imagines. He is only at the beginning of a development which is going to change the whole face of journalism. I shall try to get in with him.

In 1890, Newnes was approached by W.T. Stead to launch a new type of sixpenny magazine, the *Review of Reviews*. The magazine was a great success, but the relationship between Newnes and his partner was not a happy one, and within a few months Stead became the sole owner. Some months earlier, Newnes had told Stead that there were two kinds of journalism: 'The journalism of the *Pall Mall* upsets ministers, makes wars or prevents them, rebuilds navies and initiates new policies. It is very magnificent but it does not pay. There is another kind of journalism, the journalism of *Tit-Bits*. It does none of those magnificent things, but it gathers in the shekels.'

Two years later, writing in Stead's *Review of Reviews*, H.W. Massingham, who had edited the *Star* for just six months in 1890, was to say: 'New Journalism has contributed to give the Press a good conceit of itself, but it has not realised the fond hopes of those who imagined it was going to lead and direct the New Democracy. I wait for the coming of a man of riper culture, wider sympathies, and greater weight, before I will hail the journalist who can ride the whirlwind and direct the storm.'

The next venture for Newnes was to start an illustrated magazine with a picture on every page. While he was considering the launch, he had been approached by H. Greenough Smith suggesting the publication of a magazine containing translations of stories by well-known foreign authors. The result was that Newnes incorporated the idea with his own and started the *Strand Magazine*, with Greenhough Smith as editor. With success of the *Strand Magazine* assured, Newnes then launched the *Ladies' Field*, *Country Life*, the *Sunday Strand*, *Wide World Magazine*, *Woman's Life*, *Fry's Magazine* and *The Captain*.

On the political front, he had always been a keen Liberal and had been MP for Newmarket since 1885; and when the *Pall Mall Gazette*, under its new owner, William Walford Astor, changed its politics to support the Conservatives, Newnes immediately launched the *Westminster Gazette* – taking over many of the *Pall Mall Gazette* staff, including the editor, E.T. Cook, and J.A. Spender. In launching this evening newspaper, printed in bold type on green paper to 'rest the readers' eyes', he believed that 'the public would quickly accept a paper with only one edition a day, published at five o'clock, giving all the news and sub-edited with care'.[9]

Not all his launches, though, were to be successful: as a pioneer of illustrations, Newnes was convinced that the public wanted pictures. To prove his beliefs he brought out the *Daily Courier* in 1896, but the public thought otherwise, and the paper died within a few months. Newnes, though, had received his reward for supporting the Liberals and for launching the *Westminster Gazette* when he was created a baronet in 1895. He re-entered parliament in 1900 as MP for Swansea and represented that constituency until 1910.

A graphic account of Fleet Street during this time was to be given by Charles Pebody, one-time reporter on the *Morning Post* and editor of the *Yorkshire Post*, in his *English Journalism and the Men Who Have Made It* published in 1882:

> All around you, as you walk down Fleet Street today, are newspaper offices. The *Daily News* appropriates Bouverie Street. The *Daily Telegraph* monopolises Peterborough Court. The *Standard*, with its stately pile of buildings, towers above everything else in Shoe Lane. The *Morning Advertiser* holds possession of one side of the street, and the *Daily Chronicle* of the other. The *Times*' office stands in gloomy isolation under the shadow of St Paul's. It is almost the only morning newspaper that is published beyond the precincts of Fleet Street. The *St James's Gazette* blushes unseen in the seclusion of Salisbury Square, where Richardson at the end of the day read the proofs to a coterie of

> his friends over a dish of tea in the garden. The *Morning Star* used to be printed in Salisbury Square, *Lloyd's Newspaper* is still. But newspapers, as a rule, do not court the shade. It is not their fashion, if they blush at all, to blush unseen. They must live, if they are to live, in an atmosphere of publicity; and in Fleet Street you cannot turn either to the right or left without being challenged by a newspaper or a periodical of some kind. The place swarms with newspapers – religious newspapers, comic newspapers, sporting newspapers. There are newspaper offices in the cellars; there are newspaper offices in the garrets; and if there is a square foot of space to be found above the garrets, I should not be surprised to find a pale-faced correspondent writing against time and space for a Chicago or Cork newspaper.

And it was during this period, 1887, that young Ralph Blumenfeld, a future Fleet Street senior figure, arrived from New York and became immediately aware of the solemn appearance of the morning papers, all 'great heavy-sided blanket sheets full of dull advertisements and duller news announcements'. But with the New Journalism, a gradual change was taking place: the trend was towards snappier news stories; and for the politicians, long-accustomed to being reported verbatim, this was to be a bitter blow.

In November 1885 the Central Press Agency – founded in 1863 with the purpose of supplying feature pages in stereo form to provincial newspapers but now providing a news service – had announced new instructions on the coverage of politicians' speeches: Joseph Chamberlain, Lord Randolph Churchill, W.E. Gladstone and Lord Salisbury were entitled to verbatim reportage; Lords Hartington and Spencer to one column; and all others merited a half column or less. Even Churchill complained that his speeches were being cut in *The Times* and *The Standard*. According to Press historian, Stephen Koss: 'This was the most striking development in late Victorian journalism.'[10]

Parnell and The Times

Although 'the old journalism had a great tradition behind it, it was never, indeed, quite what its eulogists would have us believe. There never was a time when the feet of advertisers were not beautiful upon its staircases. There never was a time when the proprietor thought of his paper purely as a public institution. Indeed, the fact was rather that the proprietor was so much of a tradesman that he restricted himself to the commercial side of his venture'. And as Max Pemberton was to write:[11]

> There was nothing so conservative as the newspaper tradition of the time. Grave and reverend personages, who wrote leading articles in musty offices, continued to write them because they were grave and reverend. The editorial staff was organized upon the methods of the Civil Service.

Of the long-established members of 'the old journalism', *The Standard* and *The Times* had remained profitable for many years, but the final decades of the nineteenth century were to see a dramatic change in their fortunes.

Following the retirement of Delane from *The Times* in the autumn of 1877, Lord Beaconsfield was heard to ask: 'Who will undertake the social part of the business.

Who will go about the world and do all that Mr Delane did so well?' It was a shrewd question. Delane's successor was Thomas Chenery, a great linguist, who had been Professor of Arabic, Oxford University, before becoming a leader writer on the paper. However, his editorship was of a fairly short duration: he died in February 1884.

As a former foreign correspondent himself, Chenery had served the paper at Constantinople 1854-56; and under his editorship was determined to increase the overseas coverage. He had been especially fortunate in having Henri Stefan Opper de Blowitz as the Paris correspondent, who had been appointed by Delane in 1874, and who, within weeks of his taking over, had secured an exclusive interview with the new King of Spain, Alfonso XII.

The greatest triumph, though, for Blowitz was to be at the Congress of Berlin 1878,[12] when he had an exclusive interview with Bismarck, and surreptitiously secured a copy of the Treaty on 12 July 1878, the day before the Congress ended. With the aid of his assistant, Mackenzie Wallace, he was able to publish the Treaty – in total fifty-seven out of the original sixty-four clauses – in the later editions of Saturday's *Times*. Details of the story were then telegraphed back to Berlin just as the Treaty was being signed.

Proprietor of *The Times* during this period was John Walter III, who had joined his father in the management of the paper in 1840 and who had seven years later become sole owner. Known as the 'Griff' (short for griffin), John Walter III was a severe person with a high sense of responsibility; and, according to *The Times* official history: 'After his father's death he initiated articles and leaders only occasionally. But although Walter's leading articles were rare, his influence over the leader page was marked and constant.' He was also extremely interested in the mechanical production of the paper and in 1869 devised and introduced the Walter printing press.

In November 1880 George Earle Buckle joined *The Times* as assistant editor. Educated at Winchester and New College, Oxford, he was from 1877 until 1885 a Fellow of All Souls. Turning down an offer as assistant editor of the *Manchester Guardian*, he read law at Lincoln's Inn before joining Thomas Chenery, and four years later, following the latter's death, was appointed editor. Still under thirty, Buckle's main interest was in home politics, giving a general but critical support to the government of the day; but he had a difficult role to play when *The Times* became embroiled in the controversy over Home Rule for Ireland and the Parnell Affair.

On 18 April 1887 *The Times* – despite reservations from Buckle – published the second of letters purported to be from Charles Parnell, the Irish nationalist leader, which alleged that he had secretly connived at the Phoenix Park murders: the assassination of the Chief Secretary of Ireland and the Under-Secretary. In the House of Commons that evening, Parnell described the letter as a 'villainous and barefaced forgery'. On 13 September the following year, a Special Commission of three judges began enquiring into the Parnell Affair, which culminated in Richard Pigott's evidence. Under cross-examination, Pigott 'an old man with watery blue eyes and a white beard',[13] broke down. He later went to the flat of Henry Labouchere, the editor of *Truth*, and confessed what had happened; this was witnessed by George

Augustus Sala. A few hours later, Pigott fled the country; he was traced to a hotel in Madrid, but as his pursuers entered his room (No. 13) on 1 March 1888 he shot himself.

Although *The Times* withdrew the letters unconditionally, the paper stood by its allegations against Parnell made in the articles. As a result of the findings of the Commission, Parnell was exonerated from conspiracy in the murders and all the letters were declared forgeries. Buckle immediately offered his resignation, but it was refused by Walter. Costs for *The Times* were enormous: more than £200,000 plus a settlement of £5000 for Parnell's libel action in Scotland. Rejecting all offers of financial aid or the raising of a public subscription, Walter said that the paper should bear its own burden. The Commission sat for 128 days, more than 450 witnesses were examined; one counsel spoke for twelve days. The report, published in February 1890, filled more than seven thousand folio pages.

Notwithstanding *The Times* suffering heavily in the financial sense, it suffered less, perhaps, in authority than has sometimes been made out. The sudden shattering of confidence in its accuracy and reliability was only temporary.

Mudford in Charge

Meanwhile, at *The Standard* – following the death of proprietor James Johnstone on 22 October 1878 – the paper was now under the control of its editor. In his will, Johnstone had directed that his friend William Mudford should serve as both editor and general manager at a salary of £5000 per annum as long as he desired – a sum previously unheard of in Victorian journalism.

He had been brought up in a newspaper environment, as his father, also William Mudford, was owner of the *Kentish Observer* and *Canterbury Journal*. After acting as a 'stringer' for *The Standard*, he joined the paper in the 1860s, becoming a member of its parliamentary staff, and as an expert writer of Gurney's shorthand system was acknowledged as the best of the political team of twelve. In 1874, at the recommendation of Alfred Mould, head of the parliamentary staff, who had turned down the position, he accepted an offer from Johnstone to become editor.

As a journalist, he had been a popular man about town, but, on becoming editor, 'he was not to be seen at a dinner party or a reception, or any other social entertainment; he refused all the invitations which at one time were freely offered'. Hardly anyone entered Mudford's office except the principal members of his staff. Some leader writers claimed that they had worked for years on the paper without ever seeing his face. With his new power, Mudford became even more independent of political parties; and on 19 February 1880 he was in a position to inform Lord Salisbury:[14]

> The Editor of *The Standard* asks permission to return the enclosed telegram (just received from his assistant) which has been addressed to *The Standard* by Lord Salisbury's House Steward: The Editor of *The Standard* may, perhaps, be allowed to add that he is not in the habit of receiving telegraphic instructions from House Stewards: not even when they are in the Household of the Secretary of State for Foreign Affairs.

The American Press, in *The Nation* published in New York that year, said that the paper under Mudford although a professedly Conservative journal was not deterred 'from showing a certain independence with regard to its own party'. Gladstone, the Liberal leader, was also aware of the paper's importance: 'When I read a bad leader in *The Standard* I say to myself, Mr Mudford must be taking a holiday.'

Mudford had been fortunate in taking over a profitable business. Much money had recently been spent on modern machinery and in 1878 *The Standard*'s new building had been completed in St Bride Street. He had gathered together a first-class editorial team: G.A. Henty, Charles Norris-Newman and John Cameron were special correspondents of the highest order, and with leader writers such as Alfred Austin and Thomas Escott plus more than a dozen parliamentary staff *The Standard* was greatly admired for 'the port-wine flavour in the solid rhetoric of its editorial pages'. Add to this an excellent foreign service, and it was little wonder that *The Standard* in the mid-1880s was daily selling more than 250,000 copies.

However, in little more than a decade the paper lost its direction, saw its influence wane, and its sales surpassed by other daily papers. The basic cause of *The Standard*'s decline was not difficult to discern: the journal simply could not adapt to the changing patterns of the New Journalism. The paper continued in its unspectacular way of presentation, for Mudford was certainly not about to change the habits of a lifetime. R.D. Blumenfeld was later to recall those days:[15]

> There was Mudford, the editor of *The Standard*, the morning *Standard* of those days, the most authoritative, the most widely quoted, the best-informed and the least enterprising journal of its time. It made a great deal of money for the people of importance in the various capitals, and the old *Standard* went on undisturbed, unperturbed and unnoticing the changes of the world. Meanwhile, Mr Mudford, its editor, who in person was amiable and capable, and by reason of his studied anonymity a more or less mythical personage, looked benevolently on while his next-door neighbour *The Daily Telegraph* banged the drum, blew the whistle, rattled the bones and trumpeted the glad news from the second-storey window to the surging masses of top-hats passing up and down Fleet Street.

It was not a journalism with which Mudford wished to be associated, and he stood down on 31 December 1899, leaving the new century to his successor, Byron Curtis. Mudford retired to Westcombe Lodge, Wimbledon Common, where on 20 October 1916 he died from burns, his clothing having caught fire when he slipped into the fireplace. In its long obituary on William Mudford, *The Times* concluded:[16]

> His ear was not attuned to the modern voice; he did not move with the times; and in his arrogant confidence in the unmistakable ability of his newspaper he failed to recognize the inroads which his brasher rivals were making upon its prosperity. But he was one of the masters of older journalism; and as long as his hand was at the helm *The Standard* was a real force. How largely this was due to his own curious but capable individuality is shown by the rapid decline which set in after his retirement of the editorship.

The brashest of these new rivals was, almost certainly, the *Star*, edited by T.P. O'Connor and launched on 17 January 1888, which on its first day sold 142,600 copies, then a world record. Born in Athlone, O'Connor was educated at Queen's

College, Galway, and in 1867 joined *Saunder's Newsletter*, a Dublin conservative paper, as a reporter. Three years later he moved to Fleet Street, where, because of his fluency in French and German, he was appointed sub-editor on *The Daily Telegraph*, dealing with the Franco-Prussian War. Following a spell as a freelance, he next worked for Gordon Bennett Jr.'s *New York Herald* in its London office; and during this time also wrote, anonymously, in serial form a *Life of Beaconsfield*, which appeared under O'Connor's name as a book in 1879. The following year he was elected MP for Galway; and, combining politics with journalism, was then engaged by John Morley, editor of the *Pall Mall Gazette*, to write a nightly parliamentary sketch.

O'Connor founded the *Star* as a half-penny radical evening with a capital of £48,000, and as editor received £1200 a year. He declared that his newspaper would do away with the hackneyed style of obsolete journalism and that there would be no place for the verbose and prolix articles, which featured so prominently in other newspapers. 'The *Star* will be a Radical journal. It will judge all policy – domestic, foreign, social – from the Radical standpoint.' In that first issue, he set out his credo:

> We believe that the reader of the daily journal longs for other than mere politics; and we shall present him with plenty of entirely unpolitical literature – sometimes humorous, sometimes pathetic; anecdotal, statistical, the craze for fashions and the arts of house-keeping and now and then, a short, dramatic and picturesque tale. In our reporting columns we shall do away with the hackneyed style of obsolete journalism; and the men and women that figure in the forum or the pulpit or the law court shall be presented as they are – living, breathing, in blushes or in tears – and not merely by the dead words that they utter. Our ideal is to leave no event unrecorded; to be earliest in the field with every item of news; to be thorough and unmistakable in our meaning; to be animated, readable and stirring.

From the beginning, O'Connor had gathered together a first-rate team:[17] George Bernard Shaw wrote on music, Richard Le Galliene about books, A.B. Walkley on plays, and W.T. Hewart, later Lord Chief Justice, was its leader writer. Among the staff were more than a half-a-dozen young men destined to become Fleet Street editors: H.W. Massingham, the *Star* and later the *Daily Chronicle*; Ernest Parke, the *Star*; Thomas Marlowe, *Daily Mail*; W.T. Evans, *Evening News*; Sir Robert Donald, *Daily Chronicle*; Wilson Pope, the *Star*; James Douglas, *Sunday Express*; and Clement K. Shorter, the *Sphere*. 'Not only was it [the *Star*] the first genuine expression of the new journalism, it was its school and university. It bred editors. No less than eight first learned their trade on its staff: there was a time when you could hardly open an editorial door in Fleet Street without finding a *Star* man sitting behind the desk.'

Whereas other newspapers had been sober in their treatment of the news, this was not to be the style of the *Star* – especially in O'Connor's use of headlines: a wife murder at Stepney was headed 'Bullets for Mother', while a criminal who cut his throat in trying to escape from the police was described as 'A Scarlet Runner'; and a *Star* bill could announce: 'POPE – NO NEWS!' The paper was a strange blend of seriousness and flippancy. 'To the rather stodgy decorum of the old-established papers it opposed a curiously insincere rowdyism. The *Star* was really not at all vulgar. On its literary side it stood for the very opposite of vulgarity.'

Following differences with his partners, O'Connor resigned from the *Star* after three years, selling his interest for £17,000, which he later lamented as 'the greatest mistake I ever made'. In 1891 he started the *Sunday Sun*, subsequently called the *Weekly Sun*. Two years later – once his undertaking not to launch a rival to the *Star* had expired – he brought out *The Sun*, but although a bright and newsy paper it lacked financial backing and soon closed.

Succeeding O'Connor as editor of the *Star* was Ernest Parke, who had been sub-editor of the paper, and he was to remain in charge until 1908. In 1892 he had launched a companion paper, the *Morning Leader*, and was to retain the editorship of that paper until its amalgamation with the *Daily News* in 1912. Parke's editorship of two paper simultaneously was to be summed up by H. Simonis:[18]

> I well remember that Mr Ernest Parke, the editor of the *Star* and the *Morning Leader*, used to be at the office at 7 a.m. to see the *Star* leaders before going to press, and was also to be found in the same place at 10 o'clock in the evening to put the *Morning Leader* to bed. He never took a whole week's holiday, and as a result most of us did not care to go away either. Both by his example and kindly encouragement he got the best possible work out of all his men.

The Harmsworth Effect

Although the *Star* under T.P. O'Connor had made such inroads into the market – and had introduced thousands of readers to the New Journalism – it was to be a much younger Irishman, Alfred Charles William Harmsworth, later to be described as 'the greatest figure who ever strode down Fleet Street', who was to make the outstanding impact. Born near Dublin, the son of a barrister, he was brought to London as a child, when his father pursued his legal career. The family lived in the Hampstead area, and as an eighth birthday present Alfred was given a toy printing set by a family friend, George Jealous, editor of the *Hampstead and Highgate Express*. As he grew up he was allowed the freedom of the composing room of the *Ham & High*, something he would recall fondly forty years later.

At the age of thirteen, he entered Henley House School, whose headmaster was J.V. Milne, father of A.A. Milne, and there in March 1881 Alfred started the first school magazine. At this time he also began to undertake simple reporting jobs for the *Ham & High*; but, while Alfred was still only sixteen, his father died and he found himself head of the family. He now began to contribute to *Tit-Bits*, recently launched by George Newnes, and to the *Globe*, *St James's Gazette* and the *Morning Post*; and he was later to recall those times:

> As I went in and out of these newspaper offices I found that their organization was so constructed that one could never convey an idea to the men at the top. Contact with the staff was as a rule by postcard. There were rumours in Fleet Street about high and mighty personages who surrounded an Editor. And once I did get as near to these great gentlemen as to talk with the late most gifted and kindly George Augustus Sala, who

strongly advised me to having nothing to do with journalism. He had been at it for forty years.

Fortunately Harmsworth was to ignore that advice. In 1885, through ill-health, he had to leave London, and moving to Coventry joined William Iliffe. There, at the age of twenty, he became editor of *Bicycling News*, at a salary of £10 per month. After revamping the weekly, with shorter stories plus a gossip column – and showing an increase in circulation – he suggested to Iliffe that they should start a rival to *Tit-Bits*, under the title *Answers to Correspondents*.[19] Iliffe was not interested in becoming the publisher, but did offer to print the paper. With financial assistance from a Captain Beaumont, who put up £2000, in June 1888 Harmsworth was able to launch *Answers*. (Much of the research in finding the 'answers' was undertaken by his sister, Geraldine, in the British Museum.)

Through the use of simple competitions, short stories and interviews with famous people the paper began to be a success; and within a year his brother Harold, who had abandoned a career in the Civil Service and who was now the company's financial director, was able to state that sales were almost 50,000 and the paper was showing a small profit of £1097. 'He [Alfred] had at all times a stock of odd information in his head; he knew no Latin or Greek: he had very hazy notions of history; he was well acquainted with no modern language; the interest he took in science was that of a quick-witted child.' And as Charles Wintour wrote in *The Rise and Fall of Fleet Street*:[20]

> But the big breakthrough came when Alfred launched a competition for '£1 A WEEK FOR LIFE'.... The competitors had to guess the amount of bullion in the Bank of England on a certain day. (Again it was Alfred who had spotted a little paragraph in *The Times* giving a figure for the previous day.) But the key to success was that each entry had to be signed by five witnesses, none from the same address as the entrant. As the fame of *Answers* was thus spread, extra staff had to be hired to vet the postcards; Harmsworth brothers and sisters were roped in; and on the last day alone 295,000 entries were received, bringing the total up to 718,218. The sale of the Christmas issue which contained the name of the winner, one Sapper Austin of the Ordnance Survey in Southampton, exceeded 200,000 copies.

This was to be the nucleus of Amalgamated Press, and Alfred Harmsworth soon followed with such successful titles as *Comic Cuts* in May 1890 – 'Amusing without being vulgar' – and, despite a low cover price of ½*d*., its weekly sales of 300,00 soon made it more profitable than *Answers*. Next to appear was *Chips*, which was one of the first to feature comic strips, followed by *Forget-Me-Not*. In July 1892, two years after the launch of *Comic Cuts*, the Harmsworth brothers could reveal that their publications were now selling more than one million copies weekly: *Comic Cuts* 420,000, *Answers* 375,000, *Chips* 212,000 and *Forget-Me-Not* 83,000. In 1894, *Sunday Companion*, was added to the publications – and within a decade the paper was making £20,000 a year.

That same year, in the spring of 1894, Alfred and Harold Harmsworth decided that the time had come to enter the daily newspaper market; and as a consequence sent one of their staff, Houghton Townley, to speak to the owner of the *Islington Daily Gazette*. The proprietor was not interested in selling; but within months Alfred Harmsworth was approached by Kennedy Jones, news editor on the *Sun*, a halfpenny evening paper, launched and edited by T.P. O'Connor in 1893. In Jones's own words:

> Early information, received through a friendly publisher, that the *Evening News* was on the market enabled me to obtain an option on it. The sale price was £25,000. How was the money to be obtained? Alfred Harmsworth I only knew by sight. He was a man of my own age in his thirtieth year, with a reputation for enterprise. Here was Opportunity. A meeting was arranged. We came to terms. The *Evening News* was bought and a business partnership formed, which, before it was dissolved through my ill-health eighteen years later, had called into being the modern newspaper.

Although Harmsworth could see the potential in owning the *Evening News* he had doubts as to Kennedy Jones's credentials, as he noted a few days later when writing to his brother Harold:[21] 'Kay Robinson has not a very high opinion of Tracy and Jones. He says they have not got that reputation as journalists which they would like us to believe. He, however, fully believes that the *E. News* might be made to pay .... If we could pick the paper up for a song it would be worth our while to have it, but not otherwise.'

Nevertheless, on August 25 1894 Harmsworth took possession of the *Evening News*, with Jones and Louis Tracy, who had provided the information, each receiving a 7½ interest in the business and jobs on the staff, while Harmsworth held a controlling interest of 51 per cent. (Later, Tracy, who became a successful novelist, was to sell his shares – thereby missing out on thousands.) Strangely, the first copy under the new ownership, published on 31 August 1894, bore the imprint: 'Printed and Published for the Proprietors by Louis Tracy at 12 Whitefrairs Street, E.C., London.' According to Francis Williams in *Dangerous Estate*: '[Harmsworth] took it, met the *Evening News* proprietors, persuaded them to sell for £23,000 instead of £25,000 (£5000 was in cash the rest in shares) and launched into daily journalism.'

Started in 1881 by Coleridge Kennard, the paper had in thirteen years absorbed no less than £298,000, despite having a circulation of more than 100,000 copies; and prior to its sale 'had been managed at an increasing loss by H.H. Marks, the principal proprietor of the *Financial News* .... too busy to provide further editorial supervision. Marks nevertheless tendered a bid on behalf of himself and the executors of the Kennard estate.'

Now, in its first issue under his management, Harmsworth, as chairman, declared that the *Evening News* would: 'preach the gospel of loyalty to the Empire and faith in the combined efforts of the peoples united under the British flag'. He added that the paper would be 'strongly and unfalteringly Conservative and Unionist in imperial matters while sympathetic to labour at home'. On social issues the paper vowed to 'occupy an advanced democratic platform' and to be 'progressive in municipal reform'. Concerning Church matters, it would be non-secretarian.

With clever editing and proper cost control led by Harold Harmsworth – significant savings were made in the purchase of newsprint – profit on the first year's workings was £14,000. (There was even a profit after the first week of £7, 'which the proprietors expended on a banquet, themselves the guests, at Kettner's in Church Street, Soho'.) The paper now began to adopt a much bolder style of presentation: 'stories were allowed to flood the pages with black type and short paragraphs, giving the paper an excited, disordered look that not even the bloodiest crime had done before. There was no attempt to keep news and comment separate; patriotic sentiments flowed into the writing.' Commenting on those first days on the paper, Harmsworth was later to write:[22]

> After a hard day's work in editing, managing and writing for periodicals, my brother and I met Mr Jones night after night in the ramshackle building in Whitefriars Street in the endeavour to find out what was wrong with the *Evening News*, and why it was that a newspaper in which the Conservative Party had embarked between three and four hundred thousand pounds was such a failure. Our combined efforts soon discovered the faults in the *Evening News*. They were mainly – lack of continuity of policy (there had, I think, been eight editors) and lack of managerial control.

Editor of the *Evening News* was Kennedy Jones, a Glaswegian, who had entered journalism as a sixteen-year-old by contributing pieces on city life to a local paper, *Scottish Nights*, and for this he received ten shillings per article. A year later he was working as a sub-editor for the *Mercantile Age*, and from there left to join the *Glasgow Evening News* in a similar position. By the age of twenty-six, he had moved to the Midlands as assistant editor of the *Leicester Free Press*, and then joined the *Birmingham Daily Mail* in an executive role.

Having been refused a ten shillings rise, he left Birmingham for Fleet Street, where he arrived 'without a bob or a job'. By 1892, however, he was assisting in launching the *Morning*, which came out two days before the *Morning Leader*, but it soon died. From there he joined T.P. O'Connor for the birth of the *Sun* at £7 per week. Having been rejected by O'Connor in his effort to find a purchaser for the *Evening News*, he turned to Alfred Harmsworth. They were to become a profitable partnership. Discussing the ethos of an evening newspaper, Kennedy Jones was later to write:[23]

> The functions of an evening paper only begin when the busy day is well advanced. It is as a rule afternoon before news of the moment comes in; by 7 p.m. at the latest its sale is ended. It may also be said than an evening daily has to make itself in three hours – from 12.30 to 3.30 – and to sell itself in two hours – from 4.30 to 6.30. The very first essential for an evening journalist is exceptional quickness – quickness of perception, quickness of decision, quickness of execution – but if there be momentous events forward, comment on them has be guarded, as important news may come in just as the biggest edition goes to press, which may entirely alter the aspect of the case. The whole internal machinery of an evening newspaper office must be highly geared and in the smoothest working order, for in the publication of news in which there is keen interest seconds are golden.

Having made such a success of the *Evening News*, Harmsworth's intention now was to found a circle of morning newspapers, centring on London and looking to London for their news and opinions. 'This scheme seemed feasible and commercially sound

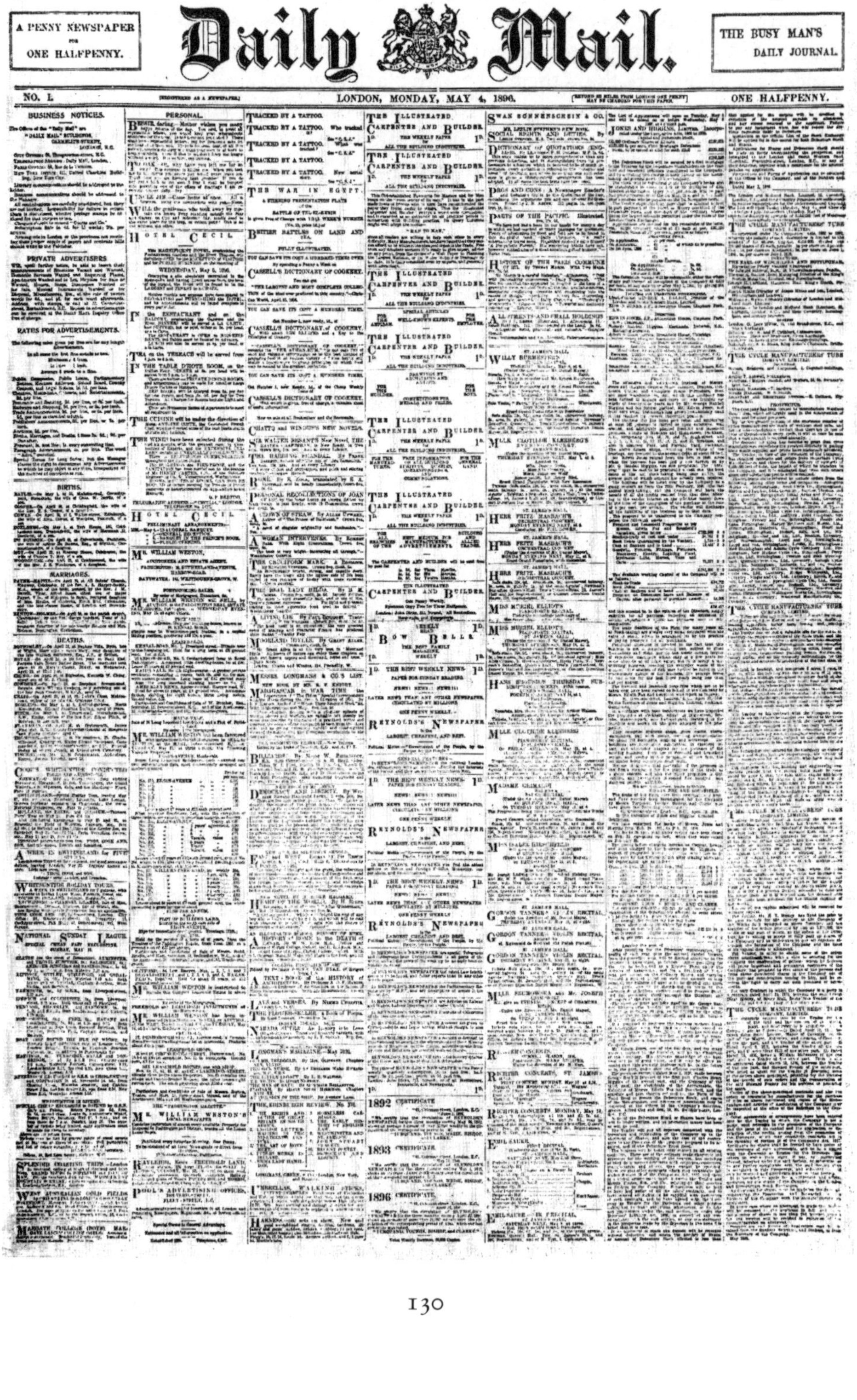

A PENNY NEWSPAPER FOR ONE HALFPENNY.

Daily Mail.

THE BUSY MAN'S DAILY JOURNAL.

NO. 1. LONDON, MONDAY, MAY 4, 1896. ONE HALFPENNY.

BUSINESS NOTICES.

PERSONAL.

TRACKED BY A TATTOO.

TRACKED BY A TATTOO.

TRACKED BY A TATTOO.

TRACKED BY A TATTOO.

TRACKED BY A TATTOO.

THE WAR IN EGYPT.

THE ILLUSTRATED CARPENTER AND BUILDER.

SWAN SONNENSCHEIN & CO.

HOTEL CECIL

PRIVATE ADVERTISERS

RATES FOR ADVERTISEMENTS.

BIRTHS.

MARRIAGES.

DEATHS.

in that it is possible to lease a private telegraph wire from the Government from 6 p.m. to 6 a.m. for the absurdly small sum of £500 a year, which included the pay of a trained operator at either end.'

Daily Mail *Launched*

With the *Evening News* having made a profit of £25,000 in year two – and having decided *not* to go ahead with the plan to ring London with morning titles – Harmsworth now determined to start a daily paper – and on Monday, 4 May 1896, the *Daily Mail* was launched, and was an immediate success with sales of 397,215. Prior to that first day almost fifty dummy issues had been produced at a cost of some £40,000. Kennedy Jones could say of the launch:

> I was born on May 4. It was an early ambition that if ever I helped to found a newspaper it should be born on my birthday. Fortune favoured. In 1896 May 4 fell on a Monday, which is the best day of the week for a new daily to be brought to bed, for it allows all Sunday for making ready. On Monday, May 4, 1896, the *Daily Mail* was born. It is my hope that when in 1996 its centenary is celebrated then shall K.J. be freshly remembered, and it will be recalled that had he lived to see that day he would have been 131 years old.

An eight-page broadsheet, the *Mail* proclaimed that it was 'A Penny Newspaper for a Halfpenny', and in his first leader Harmsworth announced:[24]

> But the note of the *Daily Mail* is not so much economy of price as concise and compactness. It is essentially the busy man's paper. It is no secret that remarkable new inventions have just come to the help of the Press. Our type is set by machinery, we can produce 200,000 copies per hour, cut, folded, and, if necessary, with the pages pasted together! Our stereotyping arrangements, engines, and machines are of the latest English and American construction, and it is the use of these inventions on a scale unprecedented in any English newspaper office that enables the *Daily Mail* to effect a saving of from 30 to 50 per cent, and be sold at half the price of its contemporaries.

For Alfred Harmsworth, it had 'meant working for two days and nights, actively editing the paper, planning pages, tasting news, running upstairs to the stone to supervise make-up; and when at last the presses were running and the whole building reverberated in the tremendous hour of the paper's birth he was besides them, watching the run, while the publisher brought him reports of the progress of sales'.

Within hours of the first copies reaching the streets – with white-coated newsvendors selling the paper as fast as they could get supplies – Harmsworth and Kennedy Jones knew that they had success on their hands; and as Jones was to relate:

> Early that morning – a perfect May morning, the sun over the horizon – I walked home, leaving the office after twenty consecutive hours' labour, with the printing machines purring away happily. In the afternooon I returned. 'How goes it?' I asked Alfred Harmsworth. 'Orders still pouring in,' he said, 'We have struck a gold mine.' He was right. We had struck a gold mine.'[25]

Although Lord Salisbury, the Prime Minister, could dismiss the *Daily Mail* as 'A newspaper for office boys written by office boys', it had certainly proved popular with the public – and was to be the vanguard of the New Journalism. One such supporter was former prime minister W.E. Gladstone: 'The *Daily Mail* appears to be a most interesting experiment, to which I give my heartiest good wishes' and from George Newnes, currently hitting severe problems with his new *Daily Courier* there had been a generous telegram – 'a wonderful halfpennyworth'.

Much later Alfred Harmsworth was to reveal to his long-standing friend, Max Pemberton, who had been the first roving reporter on *Answers*, how he came to launch the *Daily Mail*:[26]

> The success of the *Evening News* and the announcement of the project of the *Daily Mail* in no way shook the complacency of the great dailies. *The Times* went on its own mysterious way in the island of Printing House Square; the *Daily Telegraph* continued its gentle rivalry with the *Standard*; the *Morning Post* was aloof; the *Daily News*, political and literary, was the leading Radical organ; and the *Daily Chronicle*, under Mr Massingham, was the most brilliant and enterprising of all. Their lack of initiative, through which they had fallen from the highly competitive days of the 'sixties, and their subservience to Party were a direct invitation to the assault administered by the *Daily Mail* on Monday, May 4th, 1896.
>
> We prepared the battle by plenty of staff work. For months before May 4th we produced a great many complete private copies of the paper. In some of these, I remember, we inserted all sorts of grotesque features with which to delude any of the enemy who might be awake, and we saw to it that he got those copies. When we were digging the pits for the great rotary presses, a waggish enemy spy, who came over 'to see what those *Evening News* people were doing' was good enough to remark that they had an ominously big look and were large enough to swallow up all our arduous work in the establishment of many periodicals and the *Evening News* itself. 'Better be satisfied with what you have done,' he said.
>
> Like most successful things, the instant success of the *Daily Mail* was due to the combination of good luck and careful preparation. The good luck was the inertia of the London newspapers, none of which seemed to observe the writing on the wall in the reduction of French morning newspapers from ten to five centimes and the great public desire for more cable news. While the project of a complete morning newspaper at a halfpenny aroused comparatively little interest among those directly concerned (the proprietors of the penny morning newspapers and the owners of *The Times*, which had maintained its price of threepence since 1861) events proved that the public was vastly interested in the new development, and far more so than we anticipated.
>
> We had prepared for an issue of one hundred thousand copies. The paper chosen was, as now, exactly that used by penny morning newspapers. We were equipped with the very latest in mechanical appliances. Able young men from everywhere, having watched the progress of the *Evening News*, were offering their services. We thought that we had made every provision for every contingency, but the only lack of foresight shown, if I may say so with modesty, was in not anticipating the immense demand which resulted. The actual number of copies produced on the first day was three hundred and ninety-seven thousand two hundred and fifteen, and it became instantly necessary to commandeer various neighbouring printing establishments while more machinery was being made for us.

So successful was the *Daily Mail* that sales rose to more than 400,000 in 1898, to 500,000 in 1899, and at the close of the Boer War in 1902 were in excess of one million a day, the largest circulation in the world. Its launch, though, had been carefully noted by a young publisher – also with past *Tit-Bits* connections – and on 14 April 1900 he duly struck . . . .

7

The Greatest Hustler

ON 7 FEBRUARY 1900 the editor of *The Newspaper Owner and Modern Printer* received a letter from C. Arthur Pearson from his premises at 17 Tudor Street: 'If you think the matter of sufficient interest, will you be so good as to announce that I am going to produce a London morning newspaper in a few weeks' time? It will be called the *Daily Express*. Its price will be a half-penny. It will be owned by myself and not by Messrs. C. Arthur Pearson.' As good as his word, ten weeks later, on 24 April, Pearson launched the *Daily Express* – and for Alfred Harmsworth there was now the first direct challenge to his *Daily Mail*.

Pearson and Harmsworth had been rivals since 1890, and the success of the *Evening News* and, later, the *Daily Mail* had made Pearson more determined than ever to start a national newspaper. Even before the *Daily Mail* had been launched, Pearson had been planning a daily newspaper, but one designed for American readers in particular, with extracts from the main newspapers in the United States. He had even gone so far as to open offices near Fleet Street and to send A.W. Rider, one of his close associates, to New York to make the necessary arrangements. But costs were deemed too high and the project was abandoned.

Now, in his opening leader, as editor and proprietor, Pearson could announce that the *Daily Express*[1] 'will be the organ of no political party nor the instrument of any social clique . . . . Its editorial policy will be that of an honest Cabinet Minister . . . . Our policy is patriotic, our policy is the British Empire.' A seven-column, eight-page broadsheet, the *Express* was unusual in that it carried news on the front page – a two-and-a-half column account of an attack on the Boers near Bloemfontein. There was also a scoop in the first issue: a message from the Kaiser:

> Tell the British people that my first hope now and always is the preservation of international peace; my second, the consolidation and maintenance of good relations between Germany and Great Britain. Between these two nations no essential cause of difference exists nor should ever arise; between them there should be no rivalry other than friendly competition in furthering the economic and social progress of the people.

Among those assisting Pearson on the paper were Robert Dennis, managing editor; J.B. Wilson, later news editor; and a young Percival Phillips, a slim, fair-haired American, who had been sent to Europe by a Pittsburgh newspaper to report the Graeco-Turkish war while still in his teens. Sidney Dark was the theatre and literary critic, and later he was to write: 'There was nothing pretentious about the *Daily Express*. Pearson was anxious to produce a paper that the ordinary man could read. From the beginning no foreign words were allowed to be printed without translations, and he constantly urged his staff "never to forget the cabman's wife".'

After just a few issues it was apparent that the paper was a 'hit' with the public, and by the end of the first month had an average daily circulation of 232,374. Much of this was due to the war news from South Africa – including an exclusive interview with Paul Kruger, leader of the Boers – and this was especially evident in the issue of Saturday, 19 May, which celebrated the Relief of Mafeking in a 72pt caps main headline:[2]

WHEN SHALL THEIR GLORY FADE?
HISTORY'S MOST HEROIC DEFENCE ENDS IN TRIUMPH
THE BOERS' LAST GRIP LOOSENED
MAFEKING AND BADEN-POWELL'S GALLANT BAND SET FREE

Nevertheless, despite the satisfactory circulation figures, launch costs had been high, and on 6 June Pearson could inform his readers: 'We want to assure our well-wishers that the huge preliminary cost and enormous daily losses at present sustained were all foreseen and provided for. The *Express*, we assure them, is no more likely to cease to exist than is the *Mail* or the *Telegraph*.'

The man behind this new daily, C. Arthur Pearson, was still aged only thirty-four, having been born at Wookey, near Wells, Somerset, on 24 February 1866, the son of a country curate. He was educated at Winchester, and after leaving school was awaiting a promised position in a bank when he entered a competition in the recently-launched *Tit-Bits*. The prize was a position in the offices of that periodical at a salary of £100 per year. Pearson was declared the winner,[3] and within days, in September 1884, had joined George Newnes in Fleet Street, and by the following April, at the age of nineteen, had been appointed office manager.

Nine months later, Pearson was promoted manager and remained on the staff of *Tit-Bits* for a further five years. By that time, married and the father of two daughters, he found it increasingly difficult to live on his salary of £350 per year, and to increase his income began to work in his spare time as a freelance journalist. One of his earliest successes was an article entitled 'Light', which appeared in *The Standard* on 15 February 1889. When early the following year George Newnes and W.T. Stead launched the *Review of Reviews*, Pearson was appointed business manager. Because of this additional responsibility, he sought an increase in salary, but Newnes rejected the request, and on 30 June 1890 Pearson left – and three weeks later the first number of *Pearson's Weekly* appeared.

From the initial issue, with sales of more than 250,000, *Pearson's Weekly* was a huge success. Most of the first number was written by Pearson himself, who also acted as business manager. Launching the paper involved making a tour of the United Kingdom, visiting every newsagent of importance, often sleeping in third-class carriages, and writing on the train articles and stories which were posted to the London office. From *Tit-Bits* he had brought with him Peter Keary and Ernest Kessel, and

Daily Express

NO. 1. LONDON, TUESDAY, APRIL 24, 1900. ONE HALFPENNY.

Summary of News.

TUESDAY MORNING.

The Programme of THE DAILY EXPRESS will be found in the leading article on page 4.

On the same page Mr. Hesketh Prichard begins a most remarkable series of articles, descriptive of a visit paid by him for THE DAILY EXPRESS to Hayti, the Black Republic. Mr. Prichard's revelations will undoubtedly afford a world's sensation.

GOOD MORNING on the same page calls for no further description.

On page 6, under the heading FROM LONDON TOWN, will be found a selection from the London Letters of the great Provincial Dailies, published simultaneously by special arrangement.

THE NEW BRITANNIA on the same page is the first of a series of articles which it is believed will be of peculiar interest at this moment, referring as they do to the Commonwealth Bill of Australia and its far-reaching results.

Those who like serial stories cannot fail to be intensely interested in the one which Mrs. C. N. Williamson begins on page 6; and those who do not as a rule read serial stories could scarcely hope to find one better calculated to convert them to this practice.

As we are going to press we have orders for THE DAILY EXPRESS amounting to a million and a half of copies. It is an absolute impossibility to supply this unprecedented and entirely unforeseen demand, but we are doing our best.

The German Emperor, through our Berlin correspondent, sends a gracefully conciliatory message to the British people. His first hope is the preservation of international peace; his second, the permanent consolidation of good relations between Germany and Great Britain.

Lord Roberts telegraphs that reinforcements, consisting of the 11th Division, which were being despatched to General Rundle, were opposed by the Boers near Bloemfontein, and some fighting took place. The British casualties amounted to 25—mainly wounded.

There have been movements also in the Wakkerstroom district, where fighting is momentarily expected, and at Brandfort, where a British patrol retired with a loss of one killed and two captured out of a party of ten. A Boer report from Wepener says the British have lost considerably.

Lord Roberts reports as missing 23 men of the 1st Worcesters, who were sent to an outpost after dark.

Thirty-five of the Sunniside rebels captured by Colonel Pilcher were yesterday sentenced by the Supreme Court at Cape Town to five and three years' imprisonment. Mr. Solomon, the Attorney-General, who prosecuted, has stated that the Cape, and not the British Parliament, should appoint the Commission to try the rebels, or much irritation will be caused.

Ireland, already the conquest of the Queen, will be more than ever gratified by the intimation the "Express" correspondent sends us that the Queen will almost certainly revisit Ireland next spring instead of going to the Riviera. Her Majesty's health has been wonderfully benefited. The long-projected Royal residence in Ireland is now regarded as a certainty.

Her Majesty yesterday drove to

THE QUEEN WINS IRELAND'S LOVE

AND BETTER HEALTH THROUGH HER IRISH SOJOURN.

ERIN'S BRIGHT HOPES

FOR A ROYAL RESIDENCE AND YET ANOTHER VISIT.

"EXPRESS" DUBLIN CORRESPONDENT.

DUBLIN, Monday.

Ireland certainly suits the Queen. Everybody is saying how wonderfully well she looks—fresh and bright and alert, with a quick eye for every peasant who stands bare-headed by the roadside, and a sympathetic interest in the welfare of all the homely warm-hearted folk who, for the first time for so many years, are taking care of their Queen.

Her Majesty goes everywhere. Nor hail, nor rain, nor blizzard robs her of her afternoon drive. It may curtail the excursion; but it never postpones it.

"An' that proves," said the carman, with Hibernian logic, "that if she had always lived here she would have been a wonderful healthy ould lady." I submitted that her Majesty's health was rather wonderful as it is.

"Yes, that's thrue," he rejoined, "but if she had always lived in Ireland she would not have required to come to Ireland to improve it."

There was no answering this.

It is now believed in quarters where they ought to know that the Queen will certainly visit Ireland again next spring, instead of going to the Riviera. Nor is this all. The permanent Royal residence in Ireland, long hoped for and long denied, will, in all probability, now be established.

The Queen and her Irish subjects have come face to face, and are agreed that they would like to see each other oftener. With a Royal Prince in constant residence, and the gaiety and encouragement of Court life, Ireland hopes for the dawn of a golden day when her sons will all stay at home, and prosperity smile on the land.

COMPETITIVE COURTESY.

Tears of gratitude and pleasure were in the Queen's eyes when she met the cheering multitudes at the review on Saturday. She has done her best to see and be seen by all, and has not hesitated to drive through the crowded streets, although it is known that with the advance of years, she has acquired a dislike for noise.

She has visited all sorts of institutions, and has been at least as much interested in the lowly as in the high. She heard of the case of Michael Connor, who for 29 years was postilion to the Viceroys of Ireland, and now, in his old age, keeps a gate in Phoenix Park. She sent for Michael, and the old man called at the Viceregal Lodge yesterday.

Questioned by the Queen about his career, he told how he had driven every member of the Royal Family who has visited Ireland since 1858; and acted as postilion of the Sovereign's carriage when her Majesty opened the Victoria and Albert Bridge in 1881. After a few kindly words from the Royal Lady, Connor returned to his gate a proud and happy man.

There is in Ireland a body known as the Congested Districts' Board, which is trying to foster the growth of an industrial population in the poor districts. The people are taught to do knitting, needlework, and lace work—which is easy, for there are no quicker people than the Irish under the face of the sun.

They are also taught to stick at the work when they have begun it—which is difficult for the Board find a "want of steady plod-

FATAL FOREST FIRES.

TRAIN TRAPPED IN BLAZING WOODS.

"EXPRESS" CORRESPONDENT.

NEW YORK, Monday.

Northern Minnesota and Southern Manitoba are aflame with great forest fires, which have already destroyed many lives and millions of dollars worth of property.

A special train was run from Winnipeg into the region of the fires to-day to rescue those whose escape had been otherwise cut off by the rapid advance of the flames. The train was outrun by the flames, which closed around it.

The crew brought the special back to Winnipeg after the most thrilling experience in American railroading. The heat was deadly and the cars were on fire when the train passed out of the burning forest.

The flames are of such intensity that there is no hope of saving those whose escape has been cut off, or of recovering their bodies. Many towns have been wiped out in Minnesota, and the wood and lumber industries of Winnipeg are seriously crippled.

The spring has been exceedingly dry in the North-West, and unless there comes a heavy fall of rain the fire will spread until it has burned itself out.

Relief expeditions are being organised in the region around the forest fires, which cover many thousand square miles. The loss of life will never be fully known, owing to the extreme intensity of the heat, which in many cases completely incinerates the bodies. The Northwest has suffered from forest fires before, but the present conflagration covers a larger territory, and is more destructive of life and property than any hitherto experienced.

KAISERS' MEETING.

A CHECK TO RUSSIAN AND FRENCH DESIGNS.

"EXPRESS" CORRESPONDENT.

ROME, Monday.

A persistent rumour in political circles attributes the intention of Germany and Austria, with the concurrence of Italy, to negotiate an agreement with England, fixing the Anglo-German spheres of influence in Asia and Africa, and upholding, even by arms, the status quo of the Mediterranean.

It is generally supposed that the objects of this agreement will be to resist any encroachments in Turkey, and to guard against the aims of Russia in the Balkan States, and those of France in regard to Morocco and Tripoli.

General Baron von Loë, an aide-de-camp of the Kaiser, is in Rome, and has paid a visit to King Humbert.

His mission was to induce the King to send the Prince of Naples to the Berlin fêtes to celebrate the coming of age of the Prussian Crown Prince, and to emphasise the stability of the Triple Alliance. Baron von Loë informed his Majesty that the Kaiser would give a promise to visit Rome.

The King gave his consent, and arrangements will be made for the Prince of Naples to visit Berlin on May 6.

THE GERMAN EMPEROR AND THE DAILY EXPRESS.

GRACEFUL MESSAGE.

Good Relations Sought Between Germany and England.

THE "PIN-PRICKS" OF JOURNALISM.

"EXPRESS" CORRESPONDENT.

Berlin, Monday.

"I offer my good wishes for the success of the 'Daily Express,' which, as I understand, proposes to foster that most excellent of missions, the promotion of international goodwill.

"Tell the British people that my first hope now and always is the preservation of international peace; my second, the consolidation and maintenance of good relations between Germany and Great Britain.

"Between these two nations no essential cause of difference exists, nor should one arise; between them there should be no rivalry other than friendly competition in furthering the economic and social progress of their peoples."

HOW THE MESSAGE WAS GIVEN.

Such is the message, at once graceful, gracious, and important, which the German Emperor has caused to be conveyed to me through the medium of one of his most trusted Ministers.

Circumstances have brought me into relations of the most intimate and confidential character with those who are now the leading men in German politics, and as an old student of German affairs I could not help being profoundly struck with the differences, vastly for the better, which exist between the German Administration of to-day and that which practically came to an end with the retirement of Prince Bismarck.

I have consequently been favoured with prolonged and interesting interviews with Imperial Ministers—among others, Count von Bülow and Freiherr von Richthofen, respectively Minister and Under-Secretary of State for Foreign Affairs. In Germany these brilliant and fascinating diplomats are properly regarded with great respect, as enjoying, perhaps, a larger share of the Emperor's confidence than is given to any of his nominal advisers.

IMPORTANT SUBJECTS DISCUSSED.

To a journalist a specially pleasing feature of all these meetings was the unstinted candour with which my frank and, possibly, unconventional comments were always responded to. The war in South Africa and the striking differences of German opinion on the question; the position and attitude of the Press as factors in International politics; the industrial prosperity of the Fatherland, and the latter's rise as a great colonising and naval Power—these and many other topics formed the subjects of our conversation.

The Emperor's message to the "Daily Express" was communicated in the course of one of these interviews, and its publica-

THE WAR.

ANOTHER DIVISION TO AID RUNDLE.

ATTACK NEAR BLOEMFONTEIN.

MISHAP TO THE WORCESTERS.

ROBERTS'S NEXT MOVE.

CLEARING THE FREE STATE.

THE SHELVING OF WARREN.

We are doubtless on the eve of stirring events in South Africa, and, although they still tarry by the way, the storm may burst at any moment with decisive results. The whole aspect of affairs is in our favour, as will best be realised by a survey of the situation. In the centre at Bloemfontein Lord Roberts holds a great army, 60,000 strong, effective at all points, and rapidly becoming perfectly mobile, perfect in all arms, with an abundance of transport and stores. It may be confidently expected, when he resumes the offensive, to strike with overwhelming force. His line of advance will be by his right, to the eastward—that is to say, so that he may lend a hand to Buller, clear the Drakensberg passes, and open up the railway from Harrismith by Ladysmith to Durban and the sea. This will be the crucial operation of the war, for it will help and simplify the final advance by supplying a shorter line of communication.

Lord Roberts despatched the 11th Division, under Pole-Carew, to reinforce Rundle on the 22nd inst. (Sunday), and they made their way to Kareefontein, thirteen miles from Bloemfontein, without much opposition; but the fact that they were opposed at all shows that the eastern flank is closely infested by the enemy, and the fighting was not without some losses. Yesterday (23rd) Pole-Carew's mounted infantry seized the Leeuwkop Hill, three miles in advance, and the Boers retired precipitately, abandoning their rifles and ammunition. Leeuwkop is a short twenty miles from Dewetsdorp, so that another division is now close up in support of Rundle. The force at Dewetsdorp is evidently in the presence of an active enemy, as a patrol of the Worcesters sent to reconnoitre were sharply handled, and 23 men are missing.

Quiet reigns everywhere else in the theatre of war. Methuen's secure retreat on Boshof may be taken to imply that the relief of Mafeking is not within his rôle. It will be more probably effected by Carrington, who is fast gathering strength at Salisbury, 290 miles from Bulawayo by road, a distance that must take a week to traverse even by mounted men. When Bulawayo, the terminus of

Yeomanry and Mounted Infantry, and our guns drove the enemy away.

We are greatly extending our position.—Reuter's Special.

WAKKERSTROOM, April 22.

Our camp has now been extended to include the top of a hill just two miles south-east of De Wet's Dorp.

Our lines have been extended for a considerable distance to the south of the town.

The Boers are clearly visible, and are in great force.

All to-day there has been rifle firing between the outposts on each side from cover.—Central News.

FROM THE BOER CAMP.

REPORTS OF BRITISH LOSS ABOUT WEPENER.

THABA N'CHU (undated, probably per express rider to Brandfort, April 22), via Lourenco Marques, April 23.

Fighting continues day and night at Jammersburg Drift.

Robertson's lower mill is reported to have been taken yesterday afternoon.

The Cape Mounted Rifles lost 120 men out of 500, including Major Sprenger, Capt. Goldsworthy, badly wounded; Major Waring, slightly wounded; and Lieut. Bousey, seriously wounded.

Lieut. Joe Taplin was among the killed, as were also Sergeant-Majors Court and Ledham.

The following prisoners are now on their way to Pretoria: Capt. J. H. Little, Lieut. H. J. Steele, Sergt. Evans, Troopers Morton, Geddie, Fletcher, Cameron, Smith, and West, also Julius Weil's manager, Holberry, and Reuter's correspondent, Mr. Milne.

PATROL COMES TO GRIEF.

BRANDFORT, April 21.

(Via Pretoria, April 22.)

A British patrol, consisting of ten men, ventured near Brandfort to-day.

The Federals caused them to retire, killing one man and capturing two, including a Free-stater, who was leading the party.—Reuter's Special.

FACING METHUEN.

HIS COMMUNICATIONS SAFE.

"EXPRESS" CORRESPONDENT.

BOSHOF, April 23.

The Boers, who are in strength, are laagered six miles from Lord Methuen's force.

The communications between Boshof and Kimberley are open and safe.

The Northumberland Fusiliers celebrated St. George's Day with a match past Lord Methuen.

CAPE COLONY.

TREASON PUNISHED.

THE SUNNISIDE REBELS SENTENCED TO 5 AND 3 YEARS.

"EXPRESS" CORRESPONDENT.

CAPETOWN, Monday.

At the Supreme Court to-day, 35 rebels who were captured by Col. Pilcher's force at Sunnyside, received sentences of five and three years for rebellion and high treason.

The prisoners were brought from gaol to the court under a strong escort, the court was crowded, and the trial was followed

GENERAL.

BUSHMEN EMBARK.

SPIRITED ADDRESS BY N.S.W. GOVERNOR

GRAND PATRIOTIC DISPLAY

"EXPRESS" [illegible]

[illegible]

St. George's [illegible] manner worthy [illegible] which this colony [illegible]

The Imperial [illegible] and were given [illegible]

The people turned out in extraordinary numbers, exhibiting [illegible] patriotism. The ships in [illegible] and the various [illegible] Bay were arrayed [illegible] pleasure boats [illegible] sightseers [illegible] over the [illegible] harbour.

As the Bushmen, who were addressed by both the Governor and the Premier, went on board, they were cheered to the echo.

SYDNEY, April 23.

The New South Wales portion of the Imperial Bushmen, consisting of 750 officers and men, with 800 horses, embarked in the Armenian this afternoon. There was the same display of patriotic enthusiasm as on the occasion of the despatch of the former contingents.

Earl Beauchamp, the Governor, travelled from his country seat at Mossvale, and paid a special visit to the Bushmen at Rookwood immediately before their departure.

His Excellency, addressing the men, said that the colony was proud of them because of the sacrifices which they were making in order to uphold the honour of Australia. An affectionate admiration was felt for them throughout the British Empire, from her Majesty the Queen down to the humblest boy in the streets of London. The sympathies of all would go with them in the hardships they would be called upon to undergo.

He thought that the people scarcely realised how great a day that was in the history of Australia. For the first time Australians were leaving their native shores as soldiers in the pay of the Imperial Government. He hoped that on their return they would form the nucleus of a force which would be more permanent in its character than now appeared possible. He believed they would return, having added fresh lustre to New South Wales, to all Australia, and to our common race. He wished them God-speed and a safe return.

When the men reached the wharf Admiral Pearson, General French, the Archbishop of Sydney, and others delivered congratulatory speeches.

Mr. Lyne, the Premier of New South Wales, said the Imperial Bushmen had the same courage, loyalty, and ambition as those already at the front, and would behave equally well. Their bush instincts would be given full play in South Africa, and he felt sure they would take advantage of every opportunity afforded to them of giving a good account of themselves. On behalf of the Government and people he wished them every success. All the country asked was that they should go to the front and add lustre to Australian arms.

The Premier paid a high tribute to Col. Mackay, who commanded the Bushmen, and said that that day had been chosen for embarkation because it was St. George's Day.—Reuter.

CANADA OUTRAGE.

A NEW THEORY OF THE MOTIVE.

GRAIN TRADE LABOURERS IMPLICATED.

they helped to establish Pearson's Limited. His major financial supporter was a Stephen Mills, who provided Pearson with £3000 to launch the venture. Under the motto of 'To Interest, to Elevate, to Amuse', Pearson proclaimed that the *Weekly* would be of equal interest to men, women and elder children of every class, creed and profession. 'It will appeal to master and servant, rich and poor, to parent and child.'

Always a person with ideas for circulation-boosters, in the first issue of the *Weekly* Pearson offered free railway insurance policies of £1000 with each copy of the paper. There were also prizes for the person with the longest name and for the father of twins, and women readers were given the opportunity to win £100 a year for life and a good husband. The name of the first lady selected for the prize appeared in the Christmas issue, but she withdrew after having second thoughts, explaining that 'she had not seen any gentlemen from the photographs who had taken her heart by storm, and did not feel disposed to come to any decision without due consideration'. One of Pearson's finest stunts, though, occurred during an influenza epidemic. Travelling on the train to his office, he was told by a doctor that the best preventative for influenza was 'some stuff made from the eucalyptus tree'. Pearson immediately bought all the eucalyptus oil he could find and engaged a staff of fifty commissionaires to squirt the oil through scent sprays onto copies of *Pearson's Weekly* as they came off the presses.

One of Pearson's best schemes had been the 'Missing Words' competition, which, by the time it was declared illegal, was attracting almost half a million entries a week. Writing in his diary on Friday, 3 December 1892, R. D. Blumenfeld was to note:[4]

> I went to the Bond Street Police Court this morning with Arthur Pearson to hear Sir John Bridge, the chief magistrate, pronounce missing word competitions as illegal. This will be a blow not only to Pearson, who invented these competitions, but also to the Harmsworth brothers and George Newnes, who all base their fortunes on this style of weekly circulation getting. Pearson says at one time the replies came in so thick and fast with shilling postal orders that it was impossible to keep control. Office boys were found with their pockets stuffed with postal orders. Those that were crossed they shoved down the drains and choked them up. Pearson says that the Harmsworths must be making £50,000 a year clear. Three or four years ago they were poor.

The Man from Wisconsin

Pearson's colleague at Bow Street Magistrates' Court that morning, Ralph David Blumenfeld – always known as 'Blum' or RDB – was destined to become one of the Fleet Street's leading figures. Born in 1865 at Watertown, Wisconsin, USA, he was the son of Professor David Blumenfeld, founder of *Der Weltburger*, a German-language newspaper circulating in the mid-West. Blumenfeld began his newspaper career as a printer's devil, learning the case in his father's office before further training as a telegraphist. After repeated rejections from the *New York Herald*, he joined the United Press and was sent to London in 1887 to report on Queen Victoria's Golden Jubilee.

Shortly after returning to New York, he covered a major fire, writing a 2000-word piece for the *Morning Journal* at the bargain price of ten dollars – but with the offer of employment as a reporter for thirty dollars a week. James Gordon Bennett Jr, owner of the *New York Herald*, on one of his infrequent visits to that city, saw Blumenfeld's story and immediately took him on his staff. A few months later, Bennett, from his Paris mansion, where he ruled the *Herald* and his other titles, called Blumenfeld to say that he had appointed him editor of the New York *Evening Telegraph*, the night edition of the *Herald*, 'a job requiring a cold head and a heavy fist in dealing with . . . . reporters all much older and with more working guile'.

In September 1890, Blumenfeld was in Paris, but was ordered by Bennett to London to close down the English daily and Sunday editions of the *Herald*.[5] However, within a few months, the circulation was 60,000 and the paper was showing a small profit. Bennett's retort, by telegram, was : 'Congratulations on having made a profit at last. Stop the paper at once. Close the office. Dismiss everybody.' Blumenfeld remained in London for the next three years as the *Herald* correspondent until being sent back by Bennett to New York to supervise the construction of the new *Herald* building. Walking with Bennett along the Promenade des Anglais at Nice, Blumenfeld had objected to the site of the building and to the short thirty-year lease, bringing the reply: 'Never mind, Blumenfeld, thirty years from now the *Herald* will be in Harlem and I'll be in hell.'

With the job completed, he returned once more to London, but when Bennett criticized his news values and ordered him back yet again to New York, Blumenfeld rebelled and resigned. A friend of Ottmar Mergenthaler, the inventor of the Linotype, Blumenfeld secured an agency to the European manufacturing rights of the rival Empire typesetting machine and set up an office in Essex Street, off the Strand, and a factory in Batley, Yorkshire. At the same time, Bowchier Hawksley, Cecil Rhodes's solicitor, offered to sell him *The Observer* and *The Sunday Times* for £5000. 'There was, of course, not much lock, very little stock and you could not see the barrel' – so he refused.

With his typesetting machinery business failing, early in 1900 Blumenfeld decided to send a telegram to Bennett in Paris, seeking to rejoin the *Herald*. But fate was about to take a hand. That same afternoon he went to Carter's hairdressing salon at the Griffin in Fleet Street, left his silk hat with the courteous old hat-polisher, as was the custom, and relaxed in the barber's chair to have his hair cut. Just as he was beginning to doze, the person in the next chair spoke: 'I say, Blumenfeld, when are you going to give up your stupid, soul-destroying task of making and selling typesetting machinery and go back to your proper place on a newspaper?'

He turned his head and recognized Alfred Harmsworth, with a great towel around his head. Blumenfeld replied that he was debating whether or not he would apply to go back to the *New York Herald*. 'Come down to Tallis Street when you've had your hair cut,' he said 'and have a cup of tea and a cigarette.' Within an hour, Blumenfeld was being shown into the palatial office of Harmsworth, and at six o'clock was being presented to the editorial staff as the news editor of the *Daily Mail*.

Even from its earliest days, the *Daily Mail* had been a newspaper aimed at the growing number of women readers; and Blumenfeld made a point of being aware of the latest fads and fashions, as he was to note in his diary on 14 October 1900:[6]

> The fashion writers in the office are agitated about the suggestion that women's skirts should be shorter. They have gone about interviewing the managers of the great shops, and they are all against it. I have received a note from Paquin on this subject to the effect that short skirts are 'ungraceful and unbecoming and distinctly inconvenient.' He says that the skirt two inches off the ground is all right for dry weather, as it leaves both hands free but not so in muddy weather .... The short skirt, to be safely left alone in the muddy weather, says this fashion dictator, needs to be at least six inches off the ground; and who dares to wear it.

As a social commentator, Blumenfeld had a most perceptive eye and turn of phrase, noting a fortnight later:[7]

> Shopkeepers in the Burlington Arcade are again complaining about the obstruction caused at the Piccadilly entrance by young bloods from Tufnell Park, Acton and Tooting Bec, who congregate there after five o'clock in the afternoon, all dressed up in frock coats, highly polished hats and lavender gloves. They stand tightly wedged together, leaning on their gold and silver-mounted sticks, looking bored and imagine that they give the impression to passers-by that they are heirs to peerages and great estates and are just out for an airing. This afternoon I saw young X, one of our clerks, in the languid group, Now I know why he is always anxious to get away before five. A strange fad.

Dangers of Motoring

Blumenfeld was aware also of another fashion: 'A motor-car maker tells me that he will not be surprised if motor-cars are used in future as much as horses. The *Daily Express* has issued a warning on the dangers of motoring, for these are not to be handled on a casual acquaintance.' Having lived in London, on and off, for more than a decade, Blumenfeld moved in the right circles, and interviewed many of the leading businessmen. However, not all his forecasts were correct, as a meeting with American traction magnate Charles Yerkes, developer of the new Charing Cross, Euston and Hampstead electric underground, shows:

> He has secured the backing of some large American financiers to the extent of £30,000,000, and he predicted to me that a generation hence London will be completely transformed; that people will think nothing of living twenty or more miles from town, owing to electrified trains. He also thinks that the horse omnibus is doomed. Twenty years hence, he says, there will be no horse omnibuses in London. Although he is a very shrewd man, I think he is a good deal of a dreamer.

In the autumn of 1900, Alfred Harmsworth, who had long hoped to become owner of *The Times*, asked Blumenfeld if he would secretly bid for the paper on his behalf. Harmsworth had initially become interested in purchasing the paper some two years earlier; and 'in March 1898 .... came for the first time to Printing House Square and there learnt from Walter's lips that the sale to him of any share or portion would not be admitted'. Nevertheless, on 22 June 1898 Harmsworth noted that he had 'spent two hours in *The Times* offices discussing with Mr Walter negotiations in regard to the paper'; and on 27 July had dined with Moberly Bell, manager of *The Times*. Now, on 16 October 1900, Blumenfeld wrote in his diary:[8]

> Alfred Harmsworth came into my room at the *Daily Mail* office a couple of days ago and said: 'There is nothing I would like better in the world than to obtain control of *The Times*. I do not think they are getting on too well over there, and they might like to sell. If I went to them they would at once refuse me. Will you make them an offer instead? You know the Walters and they may care to deal with you. I've got a million pounds in Consols, and I authorise you to pay up to that sum. It will be a great coup if you can get it.' So I went to Printing House Square and saw Mr Godfrey Walter, with whom I had done considerable business in the past in the way of new typesetting machinery, and without beating about the bush made him an offer for control of *The Times*. He looked, and was surprised. I told him to consult his brother Arthur, the senior member of the family, and he agreed to let me know. As I went out he said somewhat naively: 'You are now associated with Harmsworth, aren't you?' I did not deny the soft impeachment. This afternoon I received a nice note from Mr Godfrey Walter, saying he had discussed the matter of my visit in the proper quarter, and he regretted etcetera. Alfred Harmsworth is disappointed, but he says 'Never mind. We'll get it sooner or later.'

The Times, however, was not the only newspaper on which Blumenfeld's advice was sought: on the morning of 28 October he received a call from W. Broderick Cloete, a land proprietor and racehorse owner, very much involved in South African affairs, who was keen to start a daily newspaper supporting an expansionist Empire. 'How much money are you prepared to lose?' Blumenfeld asked. 'Nothing. It would be a great success at once.' Blumenfeld told the would-be Press baron that he would need at least £300,000. 'Well,' he replied, 'Harmsworth says he only put down £10,000 for the *Daily Mail* four years ago, and I understand Arthur Pearson is already making money on the *Daily Express*, so why couldn't I do the same?' Blumenfeld smiled at this, for Pearson was reported to be losing £2000 a week since the *Daily Express* had been launched the previous April. 'Cloete was most persistent and rather vexed at my refusal to change my views, particularly after I showed him that all the Unionist papers are strongly imperialistic and there is no room for another morning paper.'

Early in 1902, Blumenfeld was approached by Arthur Pearson, whom he had known for more than ten years, to join the *Daily Express*, and following a meeting agreement was reached : £20 a week as foreign editor to start on May 1. Blumenfeld was later to write about his departure from the *Mail*:

> Cyril Arthur Pearson's point in journalism was great; his place as a public benefactor can never be minimised. It was in May 1902 when I succumbed to the blandishments of his ebullient and attractive personality, and took on my shoulders the responsibility of nursing an infant newspaper called the *Daily Express*. Pearson had all the initiative, the enthusiasm and the will to win, but while he knew a lot about weekly newspapers he was inexperienced in the direction of a great daily. The *Daily Express* had then not been going for long. Pearson was trying to find a place in the sun, which was, however, denied it by the fact that his opponent whom he sought to pull down was the young giant Alfred Harmsworth, who had four years' start with the *Daily Mail*. I had for long been observing young Mr Pearson floundering in heavy seas. He was the most lovable man I had met for many years, and I felt terribly sorry for him; so I decided to throw in my lot with the *Daily Express*.

When Blumenfeld told Harmsworth that he would be leaving the *Daily Mail* to join its rival, he leaned back in his armchair in a Napoleonesque attitude, looked at him for a full minute without moving a muscle, and then said:[9] 'Blumenfeld, you are the world's champion idiot. You are the most quixotic ass in Fleet Street. You've got the mind of a child. Of course, Pearson is a nice man. Of course he is a lovable character, but that will never get him or you anywhere.' Harmsworth paused briefly: 'You will break your heart trying to get that newspaper on its feet. It has no chance. How can it? Here we are with a circulation of 1,200,000. That is the limit of circulation. No other newspaper can ever reach that figure, and we have only got it because of the war which is going on.' Harmsworth concluded: 'Aside from that, no other paper can ever expect to reach the great heights that we have achieved without throwing away a million of money, and Pearson has not got it. I warn you. You will be back here in six months.'

Alfred Harmsworth was to be proved wrong.

Blumenfeld Takes Charge

Within weeks of joining the *Daily Express*, on 24 June 1902 – only days before the date set for the coronation of Edward VII – Blumenfeld was called out of bed early and told that the King was dying after an operation: 'I went straight to Buckingham Palace, and there met Arthur Pearson and Alfred Harmsworth, who were there ahead of me, waiting for information, having been bidden to the Palace for this purpose. The general public at that moment knew nothing of it. It appears that the King became suddenly ill last night, and Lord Lister, Sir Thomas Smith, Sir Thomas Barlow and Sir Frederick Treves were called in. Sir Frederick Treves performed the operation for what they call perityphilitis. I have never heard of it. Harmsworth says it is just plain appendicitis. This means that the coronation festivities will have to be postponed. There is consternation everywhere, as His Majesty is not out of danger.' The King recovered and the coronation, which had been postponed, was held on 9 August.

Working closely with Pearson was for Blumenfeld a heartening experience: no longer was he suffering the tantrums of an absent proprietor, such as he had endured with James Gordon Bennett Jr; and the *Daily Express* was proving a much greater challenge than had been the case at the *Daily Mail*. Blumenfeld was a happy man:

> In a daily newspaper you can turn on all the taps and keep them running day and night. The battle is incessant, never-ending. Victory and defeat go tearing into the vortex, first one, then the other .... The clang and clamour and crash and glamour, with the compensations of something achieved, appealed to Pearson's mind. Hence the *Daily Express*. This paper, which we confidently hope will ever retain the enthusiasm which he lighted, was the inspiration of Arthur Pearson .... The first years of the new paper, strenuous, uphill years, taxed even the superhuman energies of its producer, so that, without seeming to notice it, his eyesight began to suffer, and he was forced to forgo the excitements of the nightly battle which entailed work by artificial light.

In addition to his *Daily Express*, Pearson also owned the *St James's Gazette* as well as the *Newcastle Evening Mail*, the *Birmingham Gazette*, the *Birmingham Evening*

Dispatch and the *Leicester Evening News*.[10] However, with these ever-increasing pressures, he realised that the strain of personally editing the *Daily Express* was proving too much. More and more Pearson was relying on Blumenfeld, and within a few months of joining the paper he had been promoted to news editor and then editor – although for several years Pearson was to attend morning conferences and supervise policy. When Blumenfeld became editor the entire staff was just 350 'all housed comfortably in nice little cubicle rooms in Tudor Street'.

Pearson was now about to become involved in a major political campaign: on 23 June 1903, he roused Blumenfeld from a heavy sleep at 11.30 in the morning – he had been at the *Daily Express* office until 2.30 am. To quote Blumenfeld's diary:

> He was greatly agitated; had just come from Joseph Chamberlain, the Colonial Secretary, who had sent for him to discuss his new Tariff Reform proposals. Pearson did not, of course, know that Mr H.W. Wilson, of the *Daily Mail*, with his brother, Mr J.B. Wilson, of the *Daily Express* and myself had manoeuvred this interview between the Colonial Secretary and the hesitant proprietor. The interview was arranged through another Mr Wilson, who was Joe's secretary. Mr Chamberlain has not until now been able to secure the support of a single London daily, and we, who are ardent Tariff reformers, felt that it was time to see to the support of his plans, particularly since Alfred Harmsworth thunders away about 'stomach taxes'. We knew that if Joe once succeeded in talking to Pearson we would win. Pearson said to me: 'Get up. We are going to do big things. Your chaps have had your way, and I have promised Mr Chamberlain the support of the *Daily Express*.' So I got up, and after hurried preparations for the day went to the *Daily Express* offices to help in the preparation of a pronouncement to the effect that the paper would in future advocate Mr Chamberlain's policy.

That afternoon the Tariff Reform League was founded, with Chamberlain describing Pearson as 'the greatest hustler on record';[11] and a month later, on 29 July, with Pearson as chairman, the first meeting of the executive committee was held. Later, Blumenfeld was to write:

> Many will remember how at the beginning of the century the Liberal newspapers almost hypnotised a large section of the public into the belief that if tariffs were imposed on any kind of foreign goods, the British man would starve. During the Chamberlain campaign of 1903–6, the Liberals suggested through their papers, the *Daily News* and the *Morning Leader*, that tariffs would bankrupt England. We who believed in Tariff Reform produced by means of constant iteration and reiteration, mass thinking on our side.

Day after day, week after week the *Daily Express* proclaimed on its front page the slogan:

TARIFF REFORM MEANS WORK FOR ALL

A key figure on the paper, though, Sidney Dark, had a different point of view: 'The reform of the tariff was the only political measure in which Arthur Pearson was ever seriously interested. He was to be closely associated with the agitation to which Mr Joseph Chamberlain devoted the latter part of his political career, but it is interesting to note that Arthur Pearson was a protectionist before Mr Chamberlain, and the *Daily Express* anticipated the great political leader.'

A New Daily for Women

While Pearson and his titles had been heavily involved with Tariff Reform, on Monday 2 November 1903[12] Alfred Harmsworth launched the *Daily Mirror* as a sister paper for his successful *Daily Mail.* There was, however, to be a difference: edited by Mary Howarth – the earliest woman to be in charge of a national daily, at a salary of £50 per month – and supported by a 'large staff of cultivated able and experienced females', it was the 'First Daily Newspaper for Gentlewomen'. Backed by an impressive pre-launch advertising and marketing campaign – some readers received Pompadour-style hand mirrors – Harmsworth was convinced that the paper would be a success, saying: 'If there was anyone not aware that the *Mirror* was to be started he must have been deaf, dumb, blind or all three.' And in the paper's first editorial he wrote:

> I make no apologies or excuses for the *Daily Mirror*. It is not a hurried or unconsidered adventure. It is the result of a deliberate decision to add to the ranks of daily newspapers one that it is hoped will, by virtue of its individuality, justify its presence in those ranks. It is new, because it represents in journalism a development that is entirely new and modern in the world; it is unlike any other newspaper because it attempts what no other newspaper has ever attempted. It is no mere bulletin of fashion, but a reflection of women's interests, women's thoughts, women's work. The sane and healthy occupations of domestic life.

He added: 'All that experience can do in shaping it has already been done. The last feather of its wings is adjusted, so that I now only have to open the front door of the cage and ask your good wishes for the flight.' George Sutton, one of Harmsworth's closest colleagues, was also in no doubt of the paper's success:

> The hideous fashion plates will find no place in the *Mirror*. Our pictures will be studies from life, showing the dress actually being worn. Every recipe will be tested by expert chefs. We shall study the requirements of the girl bachelor, the use of the chafing dish – or cookery above stairs, as it is sometimes called – will be fully dealt with. Information on society functions will be provided by the people concerned, not merely professional reporters.

Priced one penny, first-day sales of the *Mirror* were huge, with three presses producing 265,217 copies, leading Harmsworth to remark that with enough printing presses he could have sold several million. The strain of producing the first issue, though, had been too much for some of the female staff, several fainting through stress, leading Harmsworth to provide champagne to lift their spirits. Harmsworth, however, had been over-confident. Circulation was down the following day to 143,000 and the decline – 100,000 after the first week – seemed unstoppable; within three months the *Mirror* was selling a meagre 25,563 copies daily and showing a loss of £3000 a week.

Drastic measures were now called for: Mrs Howarth returned to the *Daily Mail* features department, where she was in charge of the women's page. The new editor was to be Hamilton Fyfe, brought over from the *Morning Advertiser* by Harmsworth, who told him that he had learnt two lessons from the paper: 'Women

The Daily Mirror.

No. 1. MONDAY, NOVEMBER 2, 1903. One Penny.

PAQUIN, LTD.

Dressmakers, Milliners and Furriers to the Courts of Europe.

ROBES.
MANTLES.
TAILOR GOWNS.
AUTOMOBILE TOILETTES.
THE NEW "PAQUIN" CORSET.
TROUSSEAUX.
LINGERIE.
HATS, TOQUES.
BLOUSES.

Special Department for Choice Furs and Fur Garments of Exquisite Design at prices Exceptionally Advantageous.

MAYFAIR, 39, DOVER ST., LONDON, W.

REDFERN
– OF –
PARIS & LONDON

REDFERN CREATIONS!
New Models in all kinds of Dress for Day & Evening Wear

EACH MODEL an Original Study

DRESSMAKERS FURRIERS MILLINERS

26 & 27, Conduit Street.

DEBENHAM & FREEBODY.

Special Sale
OF
MANTLES and JACKETS,
Coats and Skirts
AT
ONE-THIRD TO ONE-HALF BELOW THE ORIGINAL PRICES.

COMMENCING TO-MORROW, and Continuing throughout the Week.

DEBENHAM & FREEBODY have purchased the Entire Stock of one of the best-known Manufacturers of High-class Mantles, Jackets, and Coats and Skirts at a reduction of from 33⅓ to 50 per cent. below the Original Prices. The whole of these Goods are of a particularly exclusive character, and have all been made for the Present Season.

For Full Particulars See
To-morrow's "Daily Mirror."

DEBENHAM & FREEBODY,
WIGMORE STREET, LONDON, W.

PETER ROBINSON'S, OXFORD STREET.

WE ARE SELLING TO-DAY THE STOCK OF
Messrs. FRYER & JACQUES,
of 18, BROOK STREET, NEW BOND STREET,
Comprising
LADIES', GENTLEMEN'S & CHILDREN'S HOSIERY, GLOVES, & UNDERWEAR AT ONE-HALF THE USUAL PRICES.

ALSO A SPECIAL SALE OF MANTLES, COSTUMES, PETTICOATS, BLOUSES, BLANKETS AND DOWN-QUILTS, AT REMARKABLY LOW PRICES.

PETER ROBINSON, LTD., OXFORD-STREET.

PRECIOUS STONES. JEWELLERY.

TIFFANY & CO.,
221 and 221A, REGENT STREET,
LONDON, W.

PARIS. NEW YORK.

SILVERWARE. FAVRILE GLASS.

A VISIT IS SOLICITED.

VICTORY'S
FURS.

ELEGANT — and — EXCLUSIVE MODELS.

STRICTLY MODERATE CHARGES.

162, REGENT ST., W.

READ PAGE THREE FIRST. ☞

NUMBER 1.

TO-DAY'S WEATHER.

Our special forecast for to-day is: Continuing changeable; fair at first, rain everywhere later.

Lighting up time for all vehicles, 5.32 p.m.

SEA PASSAGES TO-DAY.

English Channel and North Sea moderate; Irish Channel rather rough.

The Daily Mirror.

306th Day of Year. Monday, Nov. 2, 1903. 59 days to Dec. 31.

PAGE 3

1903.	Nov.					Dec.	
Sun. ...	...	8	15	22	29	...	6
Mon. ...	2	9	16	23	30	...	7
Tues....	3	10	17	24	...	1	8
Wed. ...	4	11	18	25	...	2	9
Thurs.	5	12	19	26	...	3	10
Fri. ...	6	13	20	27	...	4	11
Sat. ...	7	14	21	28	...	5	12

TO-DAY'S REFLECTIONS.

Our Venture.

Guest: Sir, this is a most excellent wine!
Host: I do not offer it to you as my worst.

The day on which a newspaper is first published is generally regarded as the day of its birth; but it might more truly be said that it is the chief moment and turning point of its life, for long before it is read by the public it has been read and studied by those who have designed and moulded it; daily, during months of infancy, it has been printed and published to a small world of ruthless critics, and every action of its life in the large world drilled and rehearsed in miniature. All that experience and preparation can do in shaping it has already been done, and the last feather of its wings adjusted; so that I have now only to open the door of the cage, and ask your good wishes for the flight.

I make no apologies or excuses for the *Daily Mirror*. It is not a hurried or unconsidered adventure. It is the result of a deliberate decision to add to the ranks of daily newspapers one that it is hoped will, by virtue of its individuality, justify its presence in those ranks. It is new, because it represents in journalism a development that is entirely new and modern in the world; it is unlike any other newspaper because it attempts what no other newspaper has ever attempted. It is no mere bulletin of fashion, but a reflection of women's interests, women's thought, women's work. The sane and healthy occupations of domestic life, the developments of art and science in the design and arrangements of the homes of all classes, the daily news of the world, the interests of literature and art—these will all be found equally represented beside those more intimate matters in which (fortunately for the decoration of this dull world) women still take an interest.

It may be asked, why, if this provision for feminine interests is so urgently needed as the immense demand for the *Daily Mirror* indicates, has it never been supplied before? Partly because it was never necessary, and partly because it was never possible. It was unnecessary, because the freedom, the education, the aims of women have only recently become wide enough to demand serious provision on so large and organised a scale; it was impossible, because it is only now that that increased breadth in interests makes it possible for me to find the large staff of cultivated, able, and experienced women necessary for the conduct of a suitable newspaper. But to-day that newspaper is a possible, an accomplished thing; and to-day, as finished and as perfect as for the moment we can make it, it passes from our hands to the hands of the public, with whom its future rests. We shall develop it in a hundred directions; it will gain in interest in proportion to the favour you accord it.

Feminine, but I hope not effeminate, the *Daily Mirror* is designed for men as well as women. Why not? The interests which it represents are surely as important to the world as those of finance, shipping, and sport, each of which have their representatives in the daily Press; and as I intend it to be really a mirror of feminine life as well on its grave as on its lighter sides, I venture to think that no man to whom the reflection and progress of human affairs are of interest need be ashamed to be interested in the *Daily Mirror*. For the rest, we hope to be entertaining without being frivolous, and serious without being dull; to utilise our space so that no diligent reader need be ignorant of any considerable, nor disgusted with any unnecessary piece of news; and so to distribute our matter that the transition from the shaping of a flounce to the forthcoming changes in Imperial defence, from the arrangement of flowers on the dinner table to the disposition of forces in the far East, shall be made without mental paroxysm or dislocation of interest. *Salve!*

Alfred Harmsworth.

Court Circular.

Buckingham Palace, Oct. 31.

His Majesty the King received the Right Hon. Sir Francis Plunkett (his Majesty's Ambassador at Vienna) and Mr. Arthur James Herbert (his Majesty's Chargé d'Affaires at Darmstadt and Carlsruhe) in audience to-day.

The Hon. Sir Schomberg McDonnell, Commodore Sir A. Berkeley Milne, Bart., R.N., A.D.C., and Captain G. Holford also had audiences of the King.

Sunday, Nov. 1.

His Majesty the King and the gentlemen in attendance were present at divine service in the Marlborough House Chapel this morning.

The service was conducted by the Rev. Edgar Sheppard, D.D. (Sub-Dean of his Majesty's Chapels Royal), assisted by the Rev. H. G. Daniell-Bainbridge, M.A. (Priest-in-Ordinary in Waiting).

The King visited Her Royal Highness the Princess of Wales at Marlborough House, and Her Royal Highness Princess Louise (Duchess of Argyll) and the Duke of Argyll at Kensington Palace this afternoon.

His Serene Highness Prince Louis of Battenberg visited his Majesty to-day.

Marlborough House, Sunday, Nov. 1.

The Princess of Wales attended divine service at the Marlborough House Chapel this morning.

The King will journey to Windsor to-day by motor car, and will lunch at the Castle, returning to London later in the afternoon. His Majesty will inspect the arrangements made for the reception of the King and Queen of Italy, and will also view several improvements which have been made at the Castle.

The King is expected to leave for Sandringham on Thursday.

The Queen attended divine service at Sandringham Church yesterday morning, accompanied by Princess Victoria and Princess Charles of Denmark.

The King went to St. James's Palace on Saturday morning to sit for the picture which is now being painted of him.

To-Day's News At a Glance.

Important plans for securing efficient national defence are announced on this page.

Professor Mommsen, the famous German historian, died yesterday.

Lady Spencer died at Spencer House, St. James's-place, on Saturday.

M. Sagouni, the murdered Armenian revolutionary, has been buried at Forest Hill.

Vice-Admiral Hugo Lewis Pearson has been selected as Commander-in-Chief at the Nore.

Reuter says the miners' strike at Bilbao, which caused riot and bloodshed last week, is at an end.

Fifteen persons have been killed and fifty injured in a railway accident near Indianapolis, U.S.A.

Miss Joyce Howard, second daughter of Lady Audrey Buller, was married on Saturday to Colonel Arthur Doyle.

Forty-eight persons, passengers and crew of the Japanese steamer Tokai-Maru have been drowned in collision with a Russian steamer.

The King has given Staff-Captain Rawson, of Portsmouth Dockyard, the Royal Victorian Order for smartness in docking the Victory after her recent collision.

The London Chamber of Commerce has issued a letter showing how inexpensive furs are "doctored" so as to resemble much more valuable skins.

At Manchester on Saturday Sir William Harcourt declared that the gospel of universal dearness was contrary to common sense. At Paisley Mr. Asquith described Mr. Chamberlain's policy as one of lop-sided preference.

The skating season at Prince's opened on Saturday.

The entire Chilian Cabinet has resigned, says Reuter.

Paris newspapers say M. Lepine, Prefect of Police, has resigned.

Between 1,300 and 1,400 borough councillors are to be elected in London to-day.

Miss Lilian Dorothea Devitt was married on Saturday to Mr. H. S. Pendlebury, F.R.C.S.

At Maidenhead the floods are so deep that many inhabitants can only leave their houses in punts.

1,900 London shops will devote a percentage of their receipts to-morrow to the King's Hospital Fund.

Miss Dorothy Grimston, youngest daughter of Mr. and Mrs. Kendal, was married on Saturday to Mr. Robert Meyer.

M. Papasoglu, reputed the wealthiest man in Bulgaria, has (says Laffan) fatally shot himself in the presence of his parents.

Two men and a woman, who are suspected of robbing and defrauding servants all over London, have been remanded at Southwark.

The evidence in a divorce petition by Mr. Arthur Douglas, of Manchester, showed that the husband forgave his wife three separate times.

An electric disturbance, felt only beneath the surface, seriously interrupted telegraphic communication between England, France, and America.

By the breaking of a lift-rope a workman fell eighty feet and was killed, on Saturday, at the Savoy Hotel extension, which is being carried out by American methods.

TO-DAY'S ARRANGEMENTS.

The Court.

The King dines in Hall as a Bencher of the Middle Temple.

Events of the Day.

London Municipal Elections.

Miscellaneous.

The Haydn Musical Society Dance at the Portman Rooms, 9.

Shoe and Leather Fair. Special exhibit of "adulterated footwear."

"A trivial talk on women." Lady Violet Greville at Norbiton Schools, Kingston.

President's opening address, Royal Institute of British Architects.

Society of Chemical Industry.—Various papers of scientific interest.

East India Association.—Modern history of trial by jury in India.

Royal Institution.—Work and Aims of the London University.

Stock Exchange Holiday.

12th Middlesex R.V. Regimental Dinner, Alexandra Rooms, Trocadero, 6.45.

Political.

Polling at Londonderry.

Mr. Walter Long attends the Dinner of the Association of Metropolitan Mayors and ex-Mayors.

Golf.

Finals of inter-county matches at Sunningdale (3 days).

To-day's Sales.

Peter Robinson's—Blankets and down quilts.

Thomas Wallis and Co.—Mantles, costumes, lace, trimmings, glass and Worcester ware.

Jones Bros. (Holloway).—Paris models, blouses, mantles, etc.

Nicholson's Ltd., (St. Paul's Churchyard)—Silks.

Music.

Popular Concert, St. James's Hall, 8.

Miss Marie Nichols' Violin Recital, St. James's Hall, 3.

Theatres.

Adelphi, "La Principessa Giorgio," 8.30.
Apollo, "The Girl from Kay's," 8.
Avenue, "Dolly Varden," 8.30.
Comedy, "The Climbers," 8.30.
Criterion, "Billy's Little Love Affair," 9.
Daly's, "A Country Girl," 8.
Drury Lane, "The Flood Tide," 8.
Duke of York's, "Letty," 8.
Gaiety, "The Orchid," 8.
Garrick, "The Golden Silence," 8.
Haymarket, "Cousin Kate," 9.
His Majesty's, "King Richard II.," 8.15.
Lyric, "The Duchess of Dantzic," 8.
New Theatre, "Mrs. Gorringe's Necklace," 8.35.
Prince of Wales's, "The School Girl," 8.
Queen's (Small) Hall, "The Follies," 3.15.
Royal Court, "The Tempest," 8.30.
Royalty, "Der Sturmgeselle Sokrates," 8.15.
Shaftesbury, "In Dahomey," 8.15.
St. James's, "The Cardinal," 8.30.
Strand, "A Chinese Honeymoon," 8.
Terry's, "My Lady Molly," 8.15.
Vaudeville, "Quality Street," 8.30.
Wyndham's "Little Mary," 9.

LATEST INTELLIGENCE.

THE NATION'S SAFETY.

ARMY AND NAVY TO BE OVERHAULED.

GREAT SCHEME OF REFORM.

IMPORTANT COMMITTEE APPOINTED.

We are able to-day to make an announcement of great national and Imperial importance.

The public will shortly be officially informed that a committee of three, with powers of the most liberal character, has been appointed for the reorganisation of the national defences.

The Committee will consist of one of our ablest admirals, one of our best generals, and a third member who will be a civilian.

It will superintend the re-organisation of the War Office, consider the organisation of the Navy, and bring two great services into harmony.

The civilian member will be Lord Esher.

The naval officer selected will be Admiral Sir J. Fisher, Commander-in-Chief at Portsmouth, and the officer mainly responsible for the new naval education plan.

The soldier will be selected from the following names:

The Duke of Connaught. | Lord Kitchener.
Sir H. Brackenbury. | Sir Ian Hamilton.
Sir W. G. Nicholson.

The revolutionary measure has been vigorously urged forward by his Majesty, and is meant as a real movement towards complete reform.

The work of the Committee is expected to occupy at least six months.

This intimation of the appointment of the Committee may be officially described as "premature" and "unauthorised," but the *Daily Mirror* is prepared to risk its future reputation as a news-organ on the substantial accuracy of the statement.

The appointment of this new Committee is a practical recognition of the severe criticism of the Commission which examined into the management of the South African War. It is a proof that the finding of that Commission is not to be left a dead letter by the Government.

What the Commission Said.

The verdict of the Commission on the war was that there were serious miscalculations as to the nature of the operations, that there was no plan of campaign, that there were deficiencies in stores, which were full of peril to the Empire, and that no steps had been taken since the war and up to the date of the report of the Commission, to provide for safeguard against the recurrence of such a scandal; that in the remount department "from first to last there was not the symptom of an idea in anyone who was responsible for its organisation that in time of war there would be necessity for expansion"; and that the War Office was organised in a manner which destroyed responsibility and prevented progress.

The danger of the position thus disclosed was declared to be extreme. According to Sir G. Taubman-Goldie, "only an extraordinary combination of fortunate circumstances, external and internal, saved the Empire during the early months of 1900, and there is no reason to expect a repetition of such fortune, if, as appears probable, the next national emergency finds us still discussing our preparations."

Lord Esher's Report.

Particular interest attaches to the special report of Lord Esher, which was appended to the general report of the Commission, and which showed what were and are still his aims. He insisted that the Secretary of State for War, Lord Lansdowne, must either have been guilty of neglect or have been in utter ignorance of the facts. Lord Esher advocated a re-organisation of the War Office on the same lines as the Admiralty, coupled with the virtual abolition of the office of the Commander-in-Chief. It is not certain, however, that such a measure would be a real improvement.

With Sir John Fisher at his back and an able soldier, Lord Esher is not in the least likely to make any serious mistakes, and a great gain, not only in efficiency, but also in economy, is certain to follow from the work of the new Committee.

The Task of the Committee.

Its first task will be to examine into the working of the War Office, and to draw up a scheme for the logical apportionment of the duties of that office. Ultimately we may hope

Continued on Next Page.

can't write and don't want to read.'[13] Assisting the new editor was Kennedy Jones. Both Fyfe and Jones now believed that 'the monstrous regiment of women' must go. Fyfe told his friends of the 'bloomers' being perpetrated: 'When a letter about French affairs was sent daily from Paris the original headline [French Letter] was written by a lady, set up in type but did not appear: it was changed to "Yesterday in Paris".'

Many years later, Hugh Cudlipp was to write in his *Publish and be Damned!*: 'There was a further delaying factor in production: the anxiety of compositors to make-up a page, and re-make up a page under the appraising eyes of elegant women in low-cut evening gowns who had just returned from the theatre to supervise the assembling of their works of art in the mechanical department.' To save the *Mirror*, Fyfe's first task was to dismiss the women, with three months' salary; and as he later wrote: 'They begged me to be allowed to stay. They left little presents on my desk. They waylaid me tearfully in corridors. It was a horrid experience – like drowning kittens.' The changes took place over one weekend; and as Reginald Pound and Geoffrey Harmsworth were to relate in their seminal *Northcliffe*:[14]

> On Friday night the woman editor's room was like a boudoir. By Monday morning the scene was transformed. Gone were the dainty wall mirrors, the chintz curtains and the Queen Anne chairs. Masculinity had taken over, surrounded itself with varnished deal office equipment and filled the room with pipe smoke and cynical laughter.

Fyfe now began to turn the *Mirror* into a bright picture paper, and sales began to increase accordingly. It was not, however, done without cost, and it was later estimated that more than £100,000 had been lost on the women's paper, while almost £20,000 had been spent on reorganization. This included new machinery in addition to the task of engaging and training a staff of news photographers at a time when press photography was in its infancy. Neverthless, a sanguine Alfred Harmsworth in the hundredth number, of 27 February 1904, published his famous signed article: 'How I dropped £100,000 on the *Mirror*.' He wrote: 'If the *Daily Mirror* had not failed, I would not have found out so promptly that the public wanted a picture paper.'

Key figures in this change were Arkas Sapt – who had shown how the *Daily Mirror* could print news pictures on a rotary press – Hannen Swaffer, picture editor; and a young Guy Bartholomew, who assisted him. A month after the relaunch, sales of the paper had reached 140,000 and within a year almost 300,000 copies per day.

Sapt, editor of one of Harmsworth's minor publications, had been aware that the *Daily Graphic* was already printing the occasional half-tone news picture, but at the very slow rate of only 10,000 copies per hour. Confidently, he told his Chief: 'I can double or treble that speed – and print on an ordinary Hoe press.' Harmsworth gave Sapt the go-ahead, and on 25 January 1904 appeared *The Daily Illustrated Mirror*, 'a paper for men and women, the first half-penny daily illustrated publication in the history of journalism', printing picture pages at 24,000 copies per hour.

As for Arkas Sapt, although having secured a contract on a commission – the more copies sold, the higher his pay – he was a man who lived beyond his means, forever being chased by creditors. When he left the *Mirror* he stupidly sold his interest in the company for a small figure – and consequently lost a fortune. One story sums up Arkas Sapt: debt collectors cornered him in Canon Street railway station, where, labelling himself like a piece of luggage, he concealed himself in the lost property office and sent the ticket to the *Mirror* by district messenger with a note saying: 'Come and get me.' The office sent the money.[15]

The Standard *For Sale*

Since the retirement of long-serving editor William Mudford on 31 December 1899, his successor had been Byron Curtis, for more than twenty years the chief assistant editor. Commenting on the appointment, Arthur Jameson, a contemporary, noted:

> In the hot race for honours in London journalism the prize is not always to the swift. There have been cases where pushing young men have risen rapidly to the editorial chair, have flashed like comets through the sky of Fleet street and have disappeared as quickly as they came, leaving few traces of usefulness behind. The biggest prize in London journalism is held by journalists to be the editorship of *The Standard*. The prize was won after 20 years' faithful service as sub-editor on that paper. Mr Curtis is a thin, wiry man, about 55, who possesses a knowledge of Parliamentary secrets and of political doings on the Continent that is coveted by every journalist in London.

Unlike Mudford, who disliked clubs, Curtis was a member of both the Carlton and Junior Carlton, ideal places in which to secure the attention of Conservative politicians. Curtis, quite rightly, regarded the editorship of *The Standard* as the most important in Fleet Street: he certainly did not believe that his paper was in any way inferior to *The Times*. In a sense he was following the principles of Mudford, who had been said to reign like some Eastern potentate over the paper. Thus, Curtis could say: 'I know I'm only a humble sort of fellow, but I've a jolly lot of power.' Blumenfeld, his close friend, was to write:

> All London bona-fide departmental Editors are naturally under the Editor-in-Chief and have access to him. It has not always been so. I recall the case of Mr Byron Curtis, the august and personally kind Editor of *The Standard*, Mr Mudford's successor, who was as inaccessible to the staff as the Dalai Lama. He used to come down to the Shoe Lane office after lunch and sit in his heavily guarded sanctum, write a few letters in his own hand to Cabinet Ministers and Bishops (*The Standard* was largely read by the clergy) and then go off to his Club in Pall Mall for tea. If you had an idea to offer you went to his room at your peril. The idea of offering ideas! In the evening after dinner, he came down, talked to his leader writers, waited to see the proofs of the leaders and took the 12.20 train from Blackfriars. Did the French republic blow up or there were likely to be some grave news later in the night, he took the 12.20 just the same, and the efficient Night Editor did the rest.

For the Johnstone family, now in charge of *The Standard*'s ailing fortunes, the heady days of Mudford, in his dual role as editor/manager, belonged to the past; and with sales of the paper continuing to fall the family decided that the time had come to sell. Secret negotiations were opened with the Hon. John Edward Douglas-Scott-Montagu, the future Baron Montagu, in April 1904, and within a month he had been approached by Alfred Harmsworth, who informed him on 4 May that he had heard the news at the opera the previous evening from a mutual acquaintance, Alfred Watson, editor of the Badminton Library.[16] Harmsworth then said that he had been trying to buy *The Standard* for the previous two years, and suggested that, through Montagu, he should purchase the title. If successful, he proposed that Montagu would became editor-in-chief, with full editorial powers, at a salary of £5000 per year. However, in the event of a government crisis, he, Harmsworth, reserved the right to veto the paper's policy.

By mid-summer, Castle & Co., solicitors for the Johnstone family, were demanding to know the names of Montagu's backers, and were pressing him to sign – but were met with silence: doubts now began to creep into the negotiations. Harold Harmsworth was then brought into the secret for the first time and told by his brother, Alfred, that they should hold off signing until the autumn, as he believed that there would be a slump in advertisement revenue and that the asking price for *The Standard* would fall. Harold had other ideas, and felt that the deal should be struck immediately.

While negotiations were temporarily at a standstill, there was a pleasant surprise for Alfred: on 22 June he could record that he had 'received official confirmation from Mr Balfour [Prime Minister] that Baronetcy had been conferred by the King. Wired news to wife at Sutton. Received congratulations from wife, Pearson & others who curiously enough knew in advance.' His wife replied immediately: 'My darling Sir Alfred, I must be the first to tell you how glad and happy I am to know that you have gained recognition for the hard work of years.'

On 21 July Montagu made an offer for *The Standard* and was rejected: within days, on 2 August, Castle & Co. responded; now Montagu felt that their asking price was too high. For the next three months, negotations went silent, but on 28 October Montagu entertained Balfour at Beaulieu. There he had an opportunity to inform him of his plans for the paper. 'He was greatly interested and promised his support if we were successful in obtaining *The Standard*.' But, even while Montagu was being assured of the Prime Minister's support, the prize was slipping away. That same day Castle & Co. had been trying to contact him with the news of another prospective buyer. It was not until late on the afternoon of 2 November that Montagu, returning from a day's shooting, was handed a telegram sent by his aide, Eleanor Thornton, urging him to return to London. Arriving at his office at the late hour of 10.20 p.m., he found it deserted and immediately left for the Beefsteak Club. There he was discovered by Miss Thornton who told him that Harmsworth now believed that there was another bidder for *The Standard* – probably C. Arthur Pearson – and he wished to counter this.

With Harmsworth out of London on business, Montagu could do nothing the following day, and it was not until 4 November that they were able to meet. Immediately after their discussions, Montagu left for Castle & Co., but it was already too late. Pearson had paid the Johnstone family the full asking price. A chastened Montagu, knowing that Pearson had not actually signed the contract, hastened to Downing Street to tell Balfour the news and to warn him that *The Standard*, under Pearson, could not be relied upon to support Government policy as it had in the past. However, the languid Balfour did nothing.

On 4 November 1904, Pearson duly bought *The Standard* and the *Evening Standard* from the Johnstone family. While Montagu had been nursing his hopes for the paper, Pearson had been laying his plans, and on 12 October had written to Tariff Reform leader Joseph Chamberlain:[17]

> *The Standard* is on the market and I have secured an option on it. The paper has, of course, gone down very much of late, but not too far to be saved from the total wreck which will befall it if it is left much longer under the present management. From the business standpoint it is conducted on old and extravagant lines by people with no knowledge of practical newspaper work. With the introduction of modern methods it is, I am certain, capable of being brought back to a state of prosperity and of regaining the influence which it has lost. *The Standard* among newspapers is like a free-fooder in the Cabinet. It is a powerful enemy in our ranks and very much more harmful than an open foe. In my judgment, *The Standard* has from the point of newspaper influence done far more to impede the course of Tariff Reform than any other paper. It has still a great hold among the sober thinking class and particularly among business men, for its commercial intelligence has always been looked upon as the very best.

Writing in his diary on Thursday 3 November, Blumenfeld noted:

> Arthur Pearson came into my room this afternoon and said that he had purchased *The Standard* and *Evening Standard* from the Johnstone family for £700,000. Pearson is heavily backed by men of wealth. *The Standard*, which up to three years ago was one of the most prosperous papers in the world, has lost readers and support owing to its policy of Free Trade. I went with Pearson over the establishment in Shoe Lane tonight and found it archaic and ill-equipped. There are men there who have drawn salaries for years without doing an adequate day's work.

When Chamberlain heard that Pearson had been successful, he wrote to him from Siena in Italy offering his congratulations. He noted the rumour that the purchase price had been £700,000. 'If this had been so it would have been the greatest deal that has ever been negotiated.'

On the day after the sale, 5 November, the *Daily Mail* commented 'that no alterations are contemplated in the price, appearance or general tone of the paper'.[18] The hand of Harmsworth was behind the article, which added that Pearson had bought *The Standard* as a business venture and not as a supporter of Tariff Reform. It said that although aged 38, he talks with the enthusiasm of a 25-year-old. The sum of £700,000 was given as the purchase price. A pleased Pearson wrote to Harmsworth that very day, thanking him 'for the nice things you say about me in this morning's *Daily Mail* and for the importance which you gave to my purchase of *The Standard*. It had been intended to complete the business next Tuesday or Wednesday, but the announcement in your paper made it necessary to complete it at once.'

E.T. Cook, a former editor of the *Pall Mall Gazette* and the *Daily News*, wrote in his diary that the purchase price of *The Standard* was 'not far short of £700,000 as opposed to Harmsworth's offer of £450,000. The present circulation is 80,000 and last year's profits were said to have been £10,000 – at one time £100,000.' According to *The History of The Times*, however:

> Pearson needed to bargain with the Johnstones. The price of *The Standard* property (£700,000 was originally asked) came down to £300,000. It then became necessary for Pearson to go out and find new money. *The Standard* Newspapers Limited, which was formed for the purpose of acquiring *The Standard* (morning and evening editions) and the *St James's*, has a capital of £350,000. Most of this cash was contributed by a well-known stockbroker, Sir Alexander Henderson, later Lord Faringdon, a fervent Tariff Reformer.

The official disclosure of the change of ownership was contained in a mere four sentences in the paper on the morning of 5 November:[19]

> *The Standard* passes today into the possession of Mr C. Arthur Pearson. The recent owners felt assured that, in disposing of their property to Mr Pearson, they are taking a step which will ensure the continuance of the traditions which have given *The Standard* the proud position which it has for so long occupied in the annals of British journalism. No alterations are contemplated to the price, appearance or general tone of the paper. The statement cabled from America yesterday that Mr C. Arthur Pearson is acting for the Tariff Reform League is untrue. The transaction is purely a business one, in which Mr Pearson is acting for himself alone, and neither the Tariff Reform League nor any other body or association has anything whatever to do with it.

The announcement, though, was met with strong criticism, the venerable Frederick Greenwood writing that the Press 'was running down into disgrace as deep as ever it stood in, or deeper. The new managers of Shoe Lane were behaving after the manner of the mudlarks . . . . under the hotel windows of Greenwich.' And from the young Liberal MP for Oldham, Winston Churchill, in a speech at Glasgow, there was to be further censure:

> Only last week had witnessed the capture of *The Standard* newspaper, that organisation of the middle classes which for so long possessed a character of its own. When the Great Free Trade controversy arose, *The Standard*, like the *Glasgow Herald*, by remaining perfectly true to the Unionist cause, also remained perfectly true to Free Trade. Few more articles upon the controversy had been more able, none more damaging to the Protectionists than those written by *The Standard*. They could not answer them. An easier method presented itself. £700,000 was found – I wonder where – *The Standard* passed into the hands of the champion hustler of the Tariff Reform League. The group of able writers who exerted so much influence is scattered. Their places are filled by scribes of a mammoth trust, and the protest of the last remaining Free Trade newspaper is silenced.

On 9 November, *The Spectator* published a long letter from Pearson in which he rebuked Churchill: 'It is my firm intention to preserve in every way the tone which has distinguished *The Standard* up to the present. My association with other publications does not prevent me from thoroughly appreciating the dignified role played by *The Standard* in the past, and I am determined to uphold the traditions of the paper in the future.' As a first step, on 17 November he announced that 'Mr H.A. Gwynne has been appointed Editor of *The Standard*. Mr Gwynne began his journalistic life as an unattached regular correspondent for *The Times* in Roumania . . . . Since the beginning of this year Mr Gwynne has been acting as Foreign Director of Reuters Agency.'

Harmsworth and The Observer

Although disappointed at not buying *The Standard*, Harmsworth continued to consolidate and expand his empire; and on 1 April 1905 the *Daily Mail*, *Evening News*, *Weekly Dispatch* and subsidiary publications became Associated Newspapers Ltd, with a capital of £1,600,000. A month later, on 3 May, he wrote in his diary: 'Purchased *The Observer*.' For £5000 he had bought the oldest Sunday newspaper, based at 125 Strand, with sales varying between 2000 and 4000 per week, summing up his 'prize' as 'lying in the Fleet Ditch'.[21] Harmsworth's first move was to offer the editorship – plus one-third interest – to J.L. Garvin, editor of the Tariff Reform weekly, *The Outlook* . Garvin turned down the offer. Harmsworth next approached L.S. Amery, of the *Times*, offering him twice his current salary plus a one-tenth share in the paper. But after prompting from G.E. Buckle, his editor, Amery decided to stay at Printing House Square.

Finally, Harmsworth offered the post – without any shares – to Austin Harrison, who was to remain with the paper for three years. During that period, Harrison 'conducted the paper with competence and emphasized with knowledge and ability the dangers to Britain in the activities of the German Empire.' Much later, Harmsworth could inform Garvin, with whom he had established a close relationship, that after buying the paper he was regarded as 'a D.F. for doing so'. From the first week of his ownership, Harmsworth was determined that changes to *The Observer* should be made slowly so that the 'old-fashioned clientelle of the paper' would not be frightened away. With the aid of his *Mail* colleagues, George Sutton and Evelyn Wrench, costs were strictly controlled. In January 1906, to coincide with the General Election, the price of the paper was reduced to one penny, but circulation barely increased. The first years of ownership were to prove difficult with losses of £12,000 for 1905–06 and £8000 for the following year, producing not enough money to pay for the paper's newsprint.

It was in May 1905, also, that – after realizing that the English-language, Paris-based *Daily Messenger* was a poorly-produced publication with a minimal circulation – he decided to launch the *Continental Daily Mail*. On hearing this Norman Angell, manager of the *Messenger*, 'nearing its last gasp', offered to sell him the title. Harmsworth, however, suggested that Angell should set up the *Continental Daily Mail*, saying: 'Will fifty thousand pounds be enough with a further fifty thousand in reserve? You can make three major mistakes and I shall not hold it against you. After that we'll see.' The first issue was published from 3 Place de Madeleine on 22 May 1905; and for Angell, a committed socialist, it was to be a relationship that was to last almost a decade.

A firm believer that armed agression was not an answer to settle disputes, in 1909 he wrote *Europe's Optical Illusion*, enlarged the following year to *The Grand*

Illusion, which quickly became a bestseller, with many readers believing that it was the first practical discussion of the futility of war. In view of the controversy, Angell resigned as editor of the *Continental Daily Mail* in 1912 to devote his engergies to his increasing commitments through lectures and articles. Above all, Angell was to be remembered as a pioneer of the League of Nations. He was knighted in 1931, and two years later was awarded the Nobel Peace Prize.

For Sir Alfred Harmsworth, Bart, the year 1905 was to end on a high note: on 4 December Balfour resigned from office and a Liberal government was formed, the former Prime Minister submitting his list of Resignation Honours the same day. The King approved the names, but added four of his own, including Harmsworth; and on 9 December it was announced that he had been elevated to the peerage, taking the title Lord Northcliffe. Balfour was to say to him: 'You are the youngest peer who has been created. I am very proud of you.'

The Proprietors Unite

It was during this time that the newspaper owners were in dispute with the trade unions over manning levels and payments for operating new machinery. The 'wind of change' had reached Fleet Street in 1892 when *The Globe* introduced Ottmar Mergenthaler's Linotype machine to the composing room.[22] The machine had initially been used in the offices of the *New York Tribune* in 1886. Three years later, the *Newcastle Chronicle* became the first newspaper in England to install the Linotype. *The Times* had used a Kastenbein composing machine in the 1860s, which like its rivals, the Thorne and the Hattersley, was designed to increase setting speeds, but not to reduce costs. The distribution of used type and the filling of racks still had to be done by hand. The Linotype was the breakthrough: operators could now set type at six times the speed of hand compositors – and distribution of the used matrices was automatic; the slugs of type were melted down after use.

Five years after *The Globe* installation, the Linotype was also in use at *The Daily Telegraph*, *Morning Post*, *Financial Times*, *Star*, *The Echo*, *News of the World*, *People*, *The Sunday Times*, *Evening News* and the *Daily Mail*. On *The Standard*, though, traditions died hard, and the paper was still set by hand. But this would change, for by 1902 there were 1172 Linotypes in use throughout the United Kingdom.

The coming of the Linotype was to bring about a difference in industrial relations, especially from the employers' side, as they could well see the advantages to be gained from the new technology. In 1893, the employers had rejected a claim from the London Society of Compositors which called for a revision of the old News Scale (payments for setting type matter). Understandably, the proprietors wished to agree a scale of prices for the new mechanical setting before negotiating the News Scale. Thoroughly alarmed at the advent of the new machinery, the London Society of Compositors issued a 'circular to the Workmen of the United Kingdom', which stated: 'If machinery is to be introduced, we claim a right to benefit by its introduction; but if it can only be made to pay at the expense of those who have served an apprenticeship to the trade, we submit that in such an event no real advantage is to be desired.' There were two main objectives for the Society: to retain a 'fair' share of work for hand compositors during the transition to mechanical setting and to obtain rates and conditions equable enough to deter Linotype operators from indulging in 'speed contests'.

In 1894 the first agreement – designed to run for twelve months – was signed between the Society and the newspaper proprietors.[23] The most important clause from the union side was undoubtedly: 'All skilled operators shall be members of the L.S.C., preference being given to members of the companionship into which the machines are introduced.' A jubilant union could claim that this clause of exclusive right of operation of a machine was unique in the history of industrial relations in Great Britain. Under the new pay scales, the earnings of Linotype operators were double those of hand compositors – even though the operator's average output was just 6000 ens an hour.

However, it was not only in Fleet Street that favourable terms had been agreed, for the Typographical Association, which represented provincial printers, could announce at its 1895 Delegate Meeting: 'It can be asserted unhesitatingly and without fear of contradiction that the Scale then agreed upon was from first to last most favourable to case and machine hands; and it has on more than one occasion been suggested that the employers' representatives were "caught napping" when assisting to frame it.'

For the next decade there were to be rumblings on pay structure between the London Master Printers (L.M.P.) and the L.S.C., and in May 1906 deadlock was reached on negotiations on overtime limits, night working and typesetting scales. Simultaneously, a dispute between unions and the L.M.P. at Hampton's, a printers situated in Chancery Lane, in which L.S.C. members and other unions' members had been given notice, was to lead to a special general meeting. There it was agreed that if L.S.C. members were not reinstated the Society would issue a strike ballot of all London compositors. As E. Howe and H.E. Waite were to write in *The London Society of Compositors, a Centenary History*:

> Alarmed at this prospect, a group of daily newspaper proprietors approached the union and agreed to withdraw from the London M.P.A. and conduct separate negotiations with the compositors on the understanding that the Society would not involve the daily newspapers in any dispute with the masters in the general printing industry.

As a result of this dispute at Hampton's – the men were subsequently reinstated – the proprietors of several London newspapers then met at *The Daily Telegraph* offices to discuss the position and form an independent organization for the purpose of dealing with matters of common interest.[24] On 23 July 1906 the Newspaper Proprietors Association was formed. Eight men were present at that inaugural meeting: H.L.W. Lawson, part-proprietor, *The Daily Telegraph*; John H. Lingard, manager, *Daily Mail*; H.H. Marks, editor, *Financial News*; Ernest Parke, managing editor, *Star*; C. Arthur Pearson, managing director, *Daily Express*; George A. Riddell, managing director, *News of the World*; G. Holt Thomas, joint managing director, *The Graphic* and *Daily Graphic*; and Neil Turner, general manager, *Daily Chronicle*.

Bidding for The Times

As for Pearson, he was now about to bid for *The Times*; and with the assistance of Sir Alexander Henderson, the financier and chief supporter of the *Daily Express* and *The Standard*, a meeting was arranged with the Walter family, advised by Lord Rothschild. As a consequence, on 1 January 1908 a printed memorandum setting out details of the sale of *The Times* was prepared. It was, however, provisional and would need the consent of all the proprietors. In the statement it was noted that Pearson held the ordinary shares in The *Daily Express* Limited and the deferred and ordinary shares in *The Standard* Newspaper Limited.

Pearson stipulated that his company had ordinary liquid assets equal to their current liabilties, and, between them, additional working capital of £20,000; that all these assets with the goodwill of *The Times*, the printing business, and all other assets in connection therewith owned by the Walters should be transferred to a new company. The capital was to be £850,000, and the price to be paid by the new company for the Pearson holdings was to be £150,000 in ordinary shares. It was also agreed that the character of *The Times* would not be changed and its prestige and position as an independent organ would be preserved and maintained:

> The political direction and the appointment of the more important members of the staff of the Company shall, subject to the absolute control of the Board, be vested in the said Arthur Fraser Walter and the said Cyril Arthur Pearson including the following viz; Editor, Assistant Editor, Foreign Editor, City Editor, Principal Leader Writer, Correspondents in Paris, Berlin, Vienna, St Petersburg, New York, Ottawa, Sydney and Melbourne.

Pearson, as managing director, was to receive a salary of £2,500 a year and commission upon profits after certain deductions had been made.[25] Four days later, Fleet Street was surprised to read in *The Observer* of Sunday 5 January 1908:

> THE FUTURE OF *THE TIMES*
>
> It is understood that important negotiations are taking place which will place the direction of *The Times* in the hands of a very capable proprietor of several magazines and newspapers.

Having lost out to Pearson with *The Standard* in 1904 – and bearing in mind his remarks to Blumenfeld two years previously – Alfred Harmsworth (now Lord Northcliffe) saw the opportunity to pay off Pearson and to secure *The Times*. Northcliffe was later to say: 'I put the paragraph in the *Observer* to expose the Pearson conspiracy.'

In its issue of 7 January 1908 *The Times* announced that negotiations were in progress with Pearson, who, as the proposed managing director, would reorganize the business side. However, the editorial character of the paper would remain unchanged and would be conducted on lines independent of party politics. That same day Northcliffe printed the story in the *Daily Mail*; and in one significant paragraph quoted Joseph Chamberlain: 'Mr Pearson is the greatest hustler I have ever known. He is a great believer in the strenuous life. It is one of the sayings that his success is due to the habit he contracted as a young man of never wasting time and always working with extraordinary speed.'

Northcliffe followed up the article with a telegram from the Ritz Hotel, Paris, where he was staying, addressed pointedly to C. Arthur Pearson, *The Times*, London:

> PLEASE ACCEPT MY WARMEST CONGRATULATIONS AND ADMIRATION FOR YOUR MOST SPLENDID JOURNALISTIC ACHIEVEMENT ON RECORD HAVE WRITTEN PERSONAL SKETCH OF YOU PROOF WILL BE SUBMITTED TONIGHT

By late morning, Pearson had received a wired proof of the article, which noted his achievements and his future plans. He was delighted, and that afternoon cabled Northcliffe:

> MY SINCEREST THANKS FOR YOUR MORE THAN KIND TELEGRAM AND FOR THE STATEMENTS ABOUT ME THAT HAVE APPEARED AND ARE TO APPEAR IN THE DAILY MAIL YOUR GENEROSITY IS OVERWHELMING AND I AM DEEPLY GRATEFUL

Following the despatch of the telegram, Pearson wrote a letter of thanks to Northcliffe:

> I trust that I may have an opportunity of showing one day how much I appreciate your action. Words are poor things in such cases and written words particularly so. Perhaps you will let me tell you how kind I think of you, one day when you return. Were all 'opponents' as generous as yourself, business life would be a good deal happier than it is apt to be.

On 7 January, Northcliffe sent Pearson a cable, requesting that he be interviewed for the *Daily Mail* on his forthcoming purchase of *The Times*. Pearson replied that all the publicity for him was 'rubbing things in too much' so far as the Walters were concerned, and from their point of view he did not want to be seen as pushing himself: 'Believe me, I very much appreciate all that you have done, and will be very glad, if you still think it worthwhile, to have a talk with the *Daily Mail* after I have been in *The Times* office a few days.'

That evening, a confident and relaxed Pearson took the chair at a dinner held in the Savoy of his key staff on *The Standard*. He assured them that he had not the slightest intention of stopping separate publication of *The Standard*. His staff were, quite naturally, elated and drank a toast to their proprietor, wishing him every success at Printing House Square. So sure was Pearson of victory that the Savoy chef had reproduced *The Times* clock in ice as a table centre-piece. However, even while *The Standard* staff were celebrating, Kennedy Jones, Northcliffe's key executive, and the man who had obtained the *Evening News* for the Chief, was already at work. After considering heading a consortium to bid for *The Times*, Jones turned to Northcliffe and sent the following telegram:[26]

ARE YOU PREPARED TO COME INTO A DEAL WHICH WILL UPSET NEGOTIATIONS EVENTUALLY ACQUIRING BUSINESS OURSELVES? PROFITS ON PAPER HAVE FOR EIGHT YEARS BEEN BELOW THIRTY THOUSAND SCHEME WOULD REQUIRE THREE FIFTY THOUSAND WHICH WE COULD BORROW AND PROMISES GOOD MONEY IN RETURN WOULD HAVE TO BE CARRIED THROUGH BY SOME BIG MAN OR SYNDICATE WHO COULD SAVE ORGANIZATION FOR EMPIRE SUTTON CAN START TONIGHT KAYJAY

The following evening, Jones was in Paris with Northcliffe – and the plans were laid to take over *The Times*.

At the period of Pearson's bid for *The Times*, there had been doubts expressed by the City, even though Sir Alexander Henderson was regarded as the main backer. The latest published figures for *The Standard* and the *Daily Express* for the year ended 30 June 1907 had shown a profit of £33,000, but a recent increase in advertisement rates on the *Daily Express* was expected to yield further profits of £15,000 before commissions. According to the auditors, the circulation of *The Standard* was decreasing and was 'not showing any indication of an increase in income'. There was even talk in Fleet Street that *The Standard* was on the point of closing; but with both papers being printed on the presses of *The Times* plant it was estimated that profits would be in excess of £50,000, and there would be significant sharings in costs.

Northcliffe, meanwhile, had by now also involved George Sutton, another of his key executives, in the secret bid for *The Times*, and suggested to him on 9 January 1908 that they stop the Pearson negotiations by a slightly superior offer, but let Pearson remain as managing director, 'under our guidance, in which case I think he would be an excellent one'. Northcliffe insisted that complete secrecy be maintained, as he did not wish Pearson to increase his offer.

For the next few weeks, Northcliffe played a very clever hand: he praised Pearson anonymously in *The Observer*: 'He is a little over forty, an adventurer', who has done 'well and sensational things'. On 3 February, Northcliffe wrote to his solicitors: 'I am desirous of purchasing *The Times* on behalf of myself and others, and I authorize you up to 30th June 1908 to negotiate for the purchase of the copyright thereof for any sum up to £350,000. I agree to be satisfied with the purchase at that price.' The next move for Northcliffe was to meet with Moberly Bell, the general manager of *The Times*. As usual, he came straight to the point: 'Well, Mr Bell, I am going to buy *The Times* with your assistance if you will give it; without it, if you will not.' In less than a week a deal had been struck.

Walter, having given a tacit approval to the Bell proposal, now had the task of informing Pearson that his offer must now fail. He had been surprised at the almost unanimous opposition from the other proprietors of *The Times*. A chastened Pearson realised that he could not now win, and reluctantly agreed to withdraw his name. With Pearson thwarted, Bell determined to have Northcliffe, still hiding under the anonymity of 'Mr X', accepted as the future owner of *The Times*.

However, despite having withdrawn from the negotiations, Pearson was not finished, and on 18 February told the Press Association that he was still interested in purchasing *The Times*. There were to be three rivals for the paper: Pearson; Miss Brodie-Hall, one of the minor proprietors; and Northcliffe, still shielding under the pseudonym of 'Mr X'. Late in the afternoon of 16 March, Bell telegraphed Northcliffe at Versailles:

GONE THROUGH AS WE WANTED

For Northcliffe it was exactly as he had predicted – and at £320,000 *The Times* was £30,000 less than had been allowed.

Within hours of losing his battle for *The Times*, Pearson, on 18 March 1908, was operated on for glaucoma.[27] Since childhood, he had suffered with his eyesight and had invariably worn glasses. There was little doubt that the long hours of travelling, while he had been building up his publishing empire – reading constantly in poorly-lit railway carriages – had now taken their toll. Unfortunately, following the operation he was never again able to see well enough to read or write. His doctors advised him to rest completely for six months, and he went to Frensham Place, his country home. Towards the end of the year he had recovered enough to enable him to travel up to Shoe Lane each morning to supervise his newspapers and to attend board meetings. However, within three months, the strain was proving too much, and Pearson realised that there was no hope of his sight improving.

8

Dalziel entrepreneur

IN THE SPRING OF 1909, Pearson set off on a walking tour through the Austrian Tyrol, and on his return to England became involved in establishing the first Imperial Press Conference. Held in London, it culminated in a great banquet at the Earls Court Exhibition Halls on 9 June 1909, with more than fifty overseas delegates in attendance, plus scores from Great Britain; and from this was to grow the Empire Press Union (now the Commonwealth Press Union) with Lord Burnham, owner of *The Daily Telegraph*, as president; Lord Northcliffe as treasurer; Pearson as chairman and Harry Brittain as honorary secretary.

With increasing blindness, the pressures were now proving too much for Pearson, and on 22 April 1910, after six years' struggle, he sold *The Standard* and the *Evening Standard* to Davison Dalziel; and began to take less and less interest in the *Daily Express*. Some twelve months earlier, in January 1909, *The Advertising World* had published tables showing the amount of advertising (in numbers of columns) of the London daily and evening papers:[1]

> MORNING: *The Times*, 1,126; *Daily Telegraph*, 1,571; *Daily Mail*, 1,223; *Daily Chronicle*, 719; *Morning Leader*, 426; *Daily Express*, 697; *Daily News*, 752; *Daily Mirror*, 600; *Daily Graphic*, 555; *The Standard*, 794; *Morning Post*, 770.
> EVENING: *Westminster Gazette*, 388; *Evening Standard*, 608; *Globe*, 378; *Pall Mall Gazette*, 398; *Evening News*, 609; *Star*, 231.

From these statistics, it was apparent that although the *Evening Standard* and the *Evening News* were almost equal in leading the way with the evenings, it was a different story with regard to the morning papers – and the number of *The Standard*'s advertising columns, at 794, was only half that of *The Daily Telegraph*, *The Times* and the *Daily Mail*. Here was reason for the great concern. Sidney Dark, in his biography of Pearson, wrote:[2]

> The army of newspaper readers were amply catered for by the half-penny newspapers, the *Daily Mail*, the *Daily Express*, the *Daily News* and the *Daily Chronicle*, and *The Standard* had fallen so far behind in its bad years that it could never be re-established as a serious rival to *The Times*, the *Morning Post* and *The Daily Telegraph*. The public interest in the Tariff Reform agitation was for all intents and purposes destroyed by the Radical victory at the General Election of 1906, and by the stroke which took Mr Chamberlain permanently out of the ranks of the fighting politicians.

> Arthur Pearson was a man of splendid courage, but he detested being beaten. His early career had been one long romance of success, and it bored him to be responsible for a publication which showed no signs of becoming a genuine financial proposition. He grew weary of the losing battle. He once said that every time there was a fog or an east wind *The Standard* lost at least one of its elderly readers, and that there were never any young readers to replace the veterans.

The new owner of *The Standard* and the *Evening Standard*, Davison Alexander Dalziel, has been described as 'one of the most amazing and facile personalities that ever went in and out of Fleet Street'. Born at Camden Town in 1854, he was to lead a varied and colourful life; and as a youth went to New South Wales, working as a reporter on the *Sydney Echo*; and after marrying Harriet Sarah Dunning, of the Exchange Hotel, Sydney, became a journalist in the United States.

In February 1886 he was sued by the Hanover National Bank of New York, who alleged that his purchase the previous year of the National Printing Company from C.H. McConnel was fraudulent, as was his subsequent sale of it to the Dalziel Printing Company of Chicago. Dalziel immediately issued a $100,000 counter-suit for libel, defamation and false swearing. Four years later, another bank, S.A. Kean, of Chicago, obtained judgement against Dalziel; and in the autumn he sailed for England, where, with American backing, he launched Dalziel's News Agency to challenge Reuters' supremacy.[3]

He immediately secured a coup when on 7 October 1890 he signed a contract with Moberly Bell, manager of *The Times*. Dalziel then tackled the provincial newspapers who were annoyed at Reuters' subscription rates; and in a clever ploy took half the subscription fee to his news service in cash and the residue in free advertising space which his agency then offered for re-sale. However, in 1892, Moberly Bell, having accomplished his task 'to infuse a spirit of competition into the Agencies', dismissed Dalziel to take the improved Reuters' service.

Dalziel then turned his attention to transport, forming the General Motor Cab Co. Ltd, and in 1907, following their success in Paris, introduced motor taxicabs to London, prompting him to write to *The Times* on 2 July 1907 'that a new English industry with immense prospects has been established'. The previous year he had stood as Unionist candidate for Brixton, losing after a close contest. However, by siting the General Motor Cab's huge garage in the constituency in 1907, he was victorious in the General Election of 1910, and was to represent Brixton for almost 17 years.

Always the entrepeneur, Dalziel in 1906 had founded the De Mello Rubber Company to develop 700,000 acres in Brazil; and he was also involved with the Liberian Rubber Corporation which had a monopoly in that country.

Now, in 1910, with the assistance of the Unionist Central Office – Arthur Steel-Maitland, the party chairman and part proprietor of *The Sunday Times* was heavily involved – he was to purchase *The Standard* and the *Evening Standard*. During the first year of his taking over, the papers made profits of £29,000, but the following year the figure was down to £16,000.

Within twelve months of Dalziel assuming control of *The Standard*, Max Aitken, the Canadian-born millionaire businessman and newly-elected Unionist MP for

Ashton-under-Lyne, was making approaches to buy the newspaper. On 9 March 1911 Rudyard Kipling wrote to Aitken and hoped 'very greatly' that he would be able to get *The Standard*, adding: 'I just pray your £10,000 cheque will soften his heart if he has one. Evidently he has no brains.' But Dalziel was in no mood to sell. Northcliffe, however, was pleased that Aitken had not been successful in his bid. Years later, Aitken was to recount how before he had entered journalism he had been instructed by Northcliffe: 'Spreading the old *Morning Standard* on the floor, he turned over page after page, paying no attention to the text: he examined and commented on the advertisement columns – he condemned the character of the advertisements. Then he declared: "This newspaper will die" and it did die.'

Departure of Gwynne

Almost from the onset, Dalziel's handling of *The Standard* had been a source of worry to the Unionists; and as Stephen Koss has written: 'Dalziel was an obliging backbencher with more money than experience.' And from the first weeks of Dalziel's proprietorship, there had developed an antipathy between him and his editor. Gwynne, very much his own man, told Dalziel that his place was in the boardroom and not in the editorial department of which Gwynne was head. From these differences there could really be only one outcome. Barely a year after Dalziel had taken over, Gwynne realized that he was in an intolerable position, and on 6 May 1911 he wrote to the Leader of the Tory (Unionist) Opposition:[4]

> My dear Balfour,
>
> I feel that I owe it to your uniform kindness and courtesy for me to tell you that I am about to sever my connections with *The Standard*.
>
> I have struggled hard to sink my personal likes and dislikes in order to retain control of a paper in which I might do useful work for the party and the Empire but there are differences of journalistic principles so wide between my present proprietor and myself that I am afraid they are quite insuperable. I have no objections whatever to Jews, nor have I any great dislike for financiers, but the combination of Jew, finance and shady methods is too much for me and I have to confess to a retreat in good order.

Less than a month later, Gwynne's resignation from the paper was imminent, and on 7 June he wrote to Bonar Law, a prominent Unionist and future Prime Minister:[5]

> My dear Law,
>
> I would not like you to see first of all in the press the announcement of my resignation. I am most anxious that you should not think I have been petulant or unreasonable in the matter. There are irreconcilable differences of principle involved which no sort of compromise could bridge over for any time. I have been willing to meet Dalziel reasonably but when I found that we were fundamentally opposed in our views as to the proper conduct of the paper I found it only right and just both for him and myself to retire.

Coincident with Gwynne leaving *The Standard*, the editorship of the *Morning Post* became vacant, when Fabian Ware was dismissed. Rudyard Kipling, an old friend of

Gwynne, wrote to Lady Bathurst, the *Post*'s proprietor, suggesting him as editor. On 7 July she offered Gwynne the editorship at £2000 a year, with one proviso: 'I want the Lords to be urged to resist at all costs.' According to Bernard Falk, Gwynne 'alone among newspapermen, living or dead, had edited two separate London "dailies" the same day. At 3 a.m. on July 17, 1911, he saw *The Standard* safely to press, and at 11 a.m. he was supervising the staff of the *Morning Post*. The interval he had spent in snatching a few hours' sleep.' (But see also Ernest Parke's editorship of the *Star* and *Morning Leader* simultaneously, Chapter Six.)

Gwynne was to edit the *Morning Post* for 26 years until it merged on 30 September 1937 with *The Daily Telegraph*; and for his long and distinguished services to journalism he was rewarded the following year when he was appointed a Companion of Honour.

To the end of his long life, Gwynne was to remain a master craftsman, never losing his integrity and honesty of opinion. In later years he wrote:[6]

> The Victorian era in journalism may have been dull, but it was very honest. Each newspaper hoisted its own flag, and it fought cleanly and honestly under it. They were hard hitters in their days but they were polite, impersonal and content to limit their criticisms to ideas rather than to persons. And, above all, they were outside the political arena and political temptations. Today this is all changed. Honours, preferments, promotion and participation in administration seem to be the ambition of proprietors and editors . . . . It is impossible to serve two masters. Either a newspaper, to the best of its ability, puts before its readers the truth, as it sees it, or it must deceive them. It is impossible to combine honesty of thought and personal ambitions. But above all, we should bear in mind the very great responsibilities we carry. I remember, when first I entered a newspaper office, being given a piece of advice by a very experienced old journalist. 'Do not forget,' he said to me, 'that a whisper in the editor's room becomes a roar when it has passed through the case room.'

Just prior to leaving *The Standard*, Gwynne had written to J.L. Garvin, editor of *The Observer*: 'I look upon a paper as a very sacred trust. Dalziel regards it as a money making machine and must therefore ruin it.' Time was to prove Gwynne correct.

Garvin and The Observer

On 12 January 1908 *The Observer* carried a short item on page one: 'Mr J.L. Garvin, late editor of the *Outlook*, will assume the editorship of *The Observer*.' Northcliffe, after previous failures, had got his man.

One of the most important figures in twentieth-century journalism, James Louis Garvin was born at Birkenhead in 1868, the son of an Irish labourer lost at sea when Garvin was aged only two. His first connection with the Press was as a news-boy for the *Liverpool Daily Post*, which gave him a craving to be a journalist. When his family moved to Hull, where his elder brother was a teacher, Garvin was employed as an insurance clerk and in his spare time taught himself French, German and Spanish. And while still a youth he began to write for the local daily, the *Eastern Morning News*, on such topics as Irish Home Rule, radical reform and imperialism.

In 1889, Garvin moved to Newcastle-upon-Tyne, where he joined the *Newcastle Chronicle*, edited by Joseph Cowen, as a proofreader but with permission to write editorials without payment. While still employed at the *Chronicle*, in 1895 he began to contribute political articles to the *Fortnightly Review*, edited by W.L. Courtney.

Four years later, with the aid of Courtney, Garvin joined *The Daily Telegraph* as a leader writer and special correspondent, which was to include a visit to India to cover the 1903 Durbar. His remaining stay on the paper was to be brief, for he was now asked to edit the Tariff Reform weekly, the *Outlook*. While editor, he was approached by Lord Northcliffe to take charge of *The Observer*, which he had recently purchased. Garvin, having just turned the *Outlook* into a sixpenny review, declined; but in the autumn of 1907 Northcliffe repeated the offer, saying that Garvin was the greatest journalist in the country and offering him a share in *The Observer*. Garvin replied to Northcliffe:

> Does my future then lie with you? . . . They tell me you tire of men and throw them over and would tire of me and throw me. At my time of life, I cannot afford to make a mistake or leave anything to chance. In spite of all they say, I am personally drawn to you and your creative genius fills me with amazement. I have dreamed for hours often and often of what might be done if I were your political right hand.

Notwithstanding his doubts, Garvin accepted the joint post of editor and manager on the condition that he was allowed 'to say my own say about politics and life, and men and women'. One of Northcliffe's first questions to Garvin had been: 'I suppose you will sack all the staff?' Garvin replied: 'No. I shall give them double the space.'[7] His other great policy was to be better known. 'He told Northcliffe that he would not give the public what they wanted. No. He would give them what they ought to have. So he began to produce a weekly newspaper that combined thoughtfulness with a high literary standard.'

From the outset, Garvin had three principles: 'To give the paper, above all, character; To resume in an age of tabloid journalism the full treatment of important subjects; To give the public what it needed, although at first, it did not want – the only real path to moral influence.'

His first scoop in *The Observer* was to publish on 2 February 1908 information on the Admiralty – surreptitiously supplied by Admiral Fisher, the First Sea Lord – on the need to face the growing German armed challenge. Fisher wanted to modernize the Navy with dreadnoughts and concentrate the fleet in the North Sea. Bitterly opposing him was the Home Fleet C.-in-C., Lord Charles Beresford, whose supporters called for an Enquiry. To set one up would have suggested Government mistrust of Fisher, who fed Garvin secret Cabinet information:

> As to the present First Sea Lord, not only is his professional imbecility proclaimed, his patriotism is scouted . . . . There will be no Enquiry. There can be none. If it were instituted, it is notorious that the strongest board of Admiralty we have ever had would instantly resign in a body to the infinite joy of the German nation . . . . As for Lord Charles Beresford, whose name unfortunately is always in the mouth of the panic-mongers, the issue is exceedingly simple. If any officer in high but subordinate

> position finds himself in disagreement with the policy for which the chiefs are responsible he must either acquiesce in the ordinary course of discipline or attest the seriousness of his position by resigning his command.

As editor, Garvin was to prove a success, raising *The Observer* circulation from a bare few thousand to more than forty thousand, but throughout this period there had always been a lack of funds to promote the paper. In the summer of 1910, Garvin visited Northcliffe at St Raphael, and one of his first requests was for more money. To quote Paul Ferris in his *The House of Northcliffe*: 'Northcliffe and "Garve" had an up-and-down relationship, with much warmth on both sides. Telegrams and letters flowed between them' as this from Northcliffe on 12 August indicates:

> DO NOT THINK ME CAVALIER BUT I LITERALLY CANNOT CONTINUE ON THE DIRECTORATE OF THE OBSERVER IF IT IS TO BE A PERPETUAL SOURCE OF WORK. I AM NOT THE LEAST INTERESTED IN IT FINANCIALLY AND ONLY CARE THAT IT AFFORDS THE EMPIRE A PEEP AT YOUR GREAT VISION. ONLY PLEASE DO KEEP THE COUNTRY INFORMED ABOUT GERMANY THAT UNKNOWN QUANTITY, CANADA AND INDIA . . . . AS TO GRIEVANCES LET THEM WAIT UNTIL I GET BACK. I HAVE MINE TOO. AT PRESENT I AM BESET FROM 7 AM UNTIL BEDTIME.

The first difference between them had been over the Lloyd George Budget of 1909, and that same year Garvin 'put his views in a pamphlet, *Tariff or Budget*, published by *The Observer* with an introduction by Joseph Chamberlain'. A firm believer in Tariff Reform, Garvin was to continue to be at odds with Northcliffe, who was used to exercising far more political power over his editors. The break came in 1911, when the newly-elected Max Aitken MP suggested that it would be best if the Unionists dropped their proposals on 'food taxes'. In support, the *Daily Mail* ran an editorial headed 'The End of the Tax on Food'.

Garvin stood firm, forcing Northcliffe to wire him: 'Either you get out or I do.' Northcliffe then wrote to Aitken: 'So far as I am concerned *The Observer* is nothing. It is everything to Garvin. Under no circumstances will I continue in *The Observer* with him. I am very fond of him, but I think he acted with great unwisdom.' There could be only one result to the impasse:[8] Northcliffe informed Garvin that he would not be dismissed but would be given three weeks to find a new owner for *The Observer*, 'who soon came forward in the shape of Waldorf Astor, the American millionaire who had recently become a Member of Parliament'.

Although the business partnership had now come to a close there was to be a continuing close friendship between Garvin, his wife and Northcliffe and his wife, evidenced by his remarks: 'It has been a horrible upset but the best solution as things are. Nothing will ever alter our affectionate friendship for you both.' Northcliffe responded in kind: 'I know that the association of these several years between ourselves and our sweet ladies had made us like and understand each other and I hope that both of your will adorn our future years.' One final letter from Garvin was to sum up his feelings:[9]

> The whole thing has been a bit desolating, but it would have been an utterly miserable business had it meant a severance of our friendship. That must never be. Yet how sorry I was and am to part with the old situation. I feel like an orphan. Enough that we may have had many a good hour together. You will always find me the same obstinate but staunch and fundamentally affectionate man.
>
> I am tired to death and rather feeling that no salt has any savour. Well, life is a queer business. It makes me laugh and it makes me sigh. Who will I talk shop with now? Let us try to be closer friends than ever; there's nothing now to interfere; but it may be long indeed before I have three more such vital years as those we have spent together,
>
> Ever and always,
> Your affectionate
> GARVE

The new owner, William Waldorf Astor, 'was more interested in getting Garvin as editor of the *Pall Mall Gazette* [which the family had owned since 1892] than in buying *The Observer*. If that was the only way it could be done, then he would buy *The Observer*, but he would buy it outright or not at all. The Astors never took partners'. On 5 April 1911 he purchased *The Observer* from Northcliffe for £45,000 – and Garvin, having been forced to give up his one-fifth shares in the paper, was now £9000 better off.[10]

Although William Waldorf Astor was the owner of *The Observer* and the *Pall Mall Gazette*, it was his son, Waldorf, who, with Garvin, was responsible for the paper's political policy. Educated at Oxford University, Waldorf was heir to a great fortune, and was Conservative MP for Plymouth. His wife, Nancy, who was to replace him as MP for Plymouth – after he had been elevated to the House of Lords – was in 1921 destined to become the first woman to take her seat in the House of Commons.

In January 1912, Garvin assumed the editorship of the *Pall Mall Gazette*, and one of his first acts was to resurrect the table of his predecessors and on it he affixed a brass plate with the following lettering:[11]

> This is the old Editorial Table of the *Pall Mall Gazette*, and the lineal descendant of Captain Shandon's, the first editor of that famous journal, whose beginnings are faithfully recorded by Thackeray in the chronicles of *Pendennis*. Upon this plain piece of furniture much history has been made. It was used daily from the year 1865 onwards by Frederick Greenwood, John Morley, W.T. Stead, Alfred Milner, E.T. Cook, F.E. Garrett and J. Alfred Spender until the year 1892 when it was found unworthy and with revolutionary ruthlessness was kicked out into the cold, a scarred and war-worn veteran to be sure, but still in robust health.

In inheriting a dull, badly-laid-out paper – at that time there were seven other London evenings – Garvin was to say: 'If the *Pall Mall Gazette* is to look as much as possible like a half-penny paper why should people not buy the *Evening News*?' Within days, he had rejigged the paper, drawing a comment from F.S. Oliver 'better arrangements, better articles, better paper, better ink'. Garvin's efforts, including his regular column, were to pay dividends, for by August 1914 the average circulation of the *Pall Mall Gazette* was almost 67,000 copies. There was to be further good news with *The Observer* figures – up from 57,000 in 1910 to more than 200,000 in the autumn of 1914.

Earlier that year William Waldorf Astor had decided to sell both titles – his son had only been 'loaned' the papers – and the chief contender was to be Gardner Sinclair, an Edinburgh printer. On 1 January 1915 Garvin was told that Sinclair would be in control by the end of the month. However, there was to be an unexpected reprieve: Sinclair fell ill and asked that he be released from the deal; and as a direct consequence Waldorf Sr. decided that he would no longer be involved, and, in a grand gesture, gave both papers to his son as a birthday present. Nevertheless, there was a proviso: no longer would any deficits be met by the Astor Estate Office. Waldorf and Garvin were on their own; and their first move was sell the *Pall Mall Gazette* – duly achieved in August – to Sir Henry Dalziel. Garvin, released of the *Gazette*, could now concentrate all his efforts on the growing *Observer*.

First Labour Daily

While Garvin and Astor had been busy with *The Observer*, others were about to launch the first daily in support of the fledgling Labour Party – the *Daily Herald*,which made its debut on 15 April 1912. Launched by George Lansbury and Ben Tillett, with official party backing, on a capital of just £300, it was to be dubbed 'the miracle of Fleet Street'.[12]

For more than a decade there had been calls to launch a Labour daily, the chief advocate being Keir Hardy, the elder statesman of the Party. In 1894, he had founded the weekly *Labour Leader* from the wreckage of *The Miner* and was to remain in editorial charge until 1903. Four years later he was to declare: 'The solid sermon and newspaper articles of even half-a-hundred years ago would not now be tolerated; not because of their dullness, but because of the mental effort to follow and understand them. A snippety press and a sensational public are outstanding marks of modern times.' Now, his dreams were to be realized.

To quote Huw Richards in his seminal *The Bloody Circus: the Daily Herald and the Left*:

> The *Daily Herald*'s outstanding characteristics were established from its first issue. It was financially and organistically anarchic and politically disinclined to take orders from anybody. While the first board of directors included moderate authority figures like veteran TUC secretary C.W. Bowerman, this was a reflection of its origins in trade union activism rather than an indicator of its political stance.

The previous year, on 25 January 1911,[13] during a dispute of London printers, the first issue of the *Daily Herald*, produced by the locked-out compositors, appeared 'putting the case for a 48-hour week in the trade and replying to the attacks of the employers'. In less than a week the paper could announce sales of more than 20,000, and with the reporting of general – apart from strike – news there was a growing conviction that the paper could become a regular occurence. However, lack of capital meant its closure on 28 April, but not before there had been a commitment to raise funds to relaunch as a permanent newspaper.

For the next twelve months, with dockers' leader Ben Tillett playing a leading role, a committee of prominent London trade unionists appealed for funds. One of the first to be involved, George Lansbury, had been elected Labour MP for Bow and Bromley in 1910, and the following year was asked 'over a cup of tea in the Commons' by Tillett to be a member of the appeals committee. Lansbury agreed, and, as chairman of the company, soon involved the paper in the fight for women's suffrage; and at the same time resigned from the House of Commons in commitment. He then fought the 1912 by-election as an Independent, but lost – and it was not until 1922 that he regained his seat as an MP. To quote Huw Richards once more:

> The committee believed that it could attain an 80,000 daily sale. This should ensure £7,500 a year in advertising income and financial stability. Initially appealing for £10,000 in start-up capital, they then adjusted their sights to £5,000 in five-shilling shares, saying they would not start until they received 20,000 applications. The paper would have a mixed record on promises about content. This promise on money was blatantly broken.

Nevertheless, the *Daily Herald* did proceed, setting up offices in Tudor Street, just south of Fleet Street. Rowland Kenny, hired as labour editor at £5 per week, was to describe those early days:[14]

> The one room was the Editorial Department. It contained either two or three tables, two chairs and a telephone on the floor in one corner and the day's newspapers. There was not a piece of copy paper or a pencil, blue or otherwise, nothing. So on my suggestion, Seed [secretary of the committee] slipped out and bought a parcel of scribbling pads and other material. Then we began to discuss our 'news service'!

The first editor, Sheridan Jones, soon left to be replaced by Charles Lapworth. During the early months of the paper, through a shortage of funds, there was crisis after crisis, and on 23 October management could say: 'We may come out again or we may not.' However, the paper did publish. Initial sales of the *Herald* had been estimated at more than 200,000, but circulation had soon fallen away; 'and at a meeting at Manchester in 1913 Lapworth and Tillet described how the furniture in the editorial office had to be bolted to the floor to prevent its removal by debt collectors'.

At the onset of the First World War, the paper continued to be in dire straits financially, and during the conflict was forced to reduce publication to a weekly pamphlet with a circulation of barely 40,000 copies. Its dwindling sales notwithstanding, the *Daily Herald* was still a potent force – its pleas for British workers to follow the Bolshevik examples almost led to its being suppressed by order of the Cabinet.

However, thanks to financial support of some £200,000 from the unions,[15] with the National Union of Railwaymen agreeing to act as newsprint purchasers, on 31 March 1919 the *Daily Herald* reappeared, with Lansbury as editor, who gathered around him one of the finest-ever editorial teams. Among his writers were George Bernard Shaw, Siegfried Sassoon, E.M. Forster and Havelock Ellis. Future contributors were to include Robert Graves, Aldous Huxley and Rose Macaulay. His Paris correspondent was Vernon Bartlett, and Will Dyson was the paper's cartoonist.

By 1922, even though circulation had reached more than 300,000, Lansbury knew that the *Herald* could no longer remain independent – 'The more copies we sold the more money we lost'– and having rejected a number of private offers for the title he turned to the Labour Party and the Trades Union Congress with the plan that they should run the *Daily Herald* as an official Labour paper. This was agreed, but later the TUC assumed complete control, 'relieving the Labour Party of all financial responsibility'. Hamilton Fyfe took over as editor, while Lansbury acted as general manger, retaining that position until his resignation in December 1924.

Launch of the Daily Citizen

Six months after the start of the *Herald*, another Labour newspaper made its debut, when in October 1912 the *Daily Citizen* was launched from Manchester with Frank Dilnot as editor. Previously he had spent ten years as a special reporter on the *Daily Mail*; and upon his editorship Northcliffe was to declare: 'I think it very essential to the welfare of this Empire that Labour should have a proper newspaper. We have the only representative Parliament in the world. I should like a really representative Press.'

Despite a claimed circulation of 220,000 copies, and extending its operations to London, within six months Dilnot was forced to call upon the trade union movement for further funding. As Stephen Koss was to write: 'Its socialism, as distinguished from its preoccupation with industrial affairs, was nebulous; and its relations with the parliamentary Labour Party were mutually uncomfortable.'

Opposed to the First World War, Dilnot in the *Daily Citizen*, during the first days of August 1914, could declare that Great Britain should not get involved in the 'wretched international intrigue' and should avoid this 'Diplomats' War'. Dilnot added: 'While fighting for peace, we must do what we can by organised effort, and in conjunction with the Trade Unions and the Co-operative Societies, to relieve some of the worst horrors of war.'

The paper struggled on until the following year; and on 24 February 1915 representatives of one hundred trade unions, meeting off Fleet Street, agreed to launch a shilling fund to raise £5000. Ramsay MacDonald, a future Labour Prime Minister, was the first to contribute, with twenty shillings, followed by Dilnot with a similar sum, but it was to be of no avail. The London office closed on March 13 and the final issue was printed from Manchester on June 5.

'And even after the abject failure of that venture after three years of unremitting effort and an expenditure of over half a million pounds, the Labour Movement still sought its answer to the capitalist press. . . .' Arthur Henderson, Labour Party secretary, was to say of its demise:[16]

> If resolutions could have saved the *Daily Citizen*, it would have had a long life. So far as the National Committees of the movement are concerned, I think every practical step has been taken to ensure the continuance of the paper. The plain, blunt fact is that the Labour Movement does not want a daily newspaper and is not prepared to regard such a weapon as necessary in the Labour fight.

As for Dilnot, he then left for the United States, where he was president of the Foreign Correspondents' Association. He returned to England in 1919 to edit the *Globe*. However, it was to prove a lost cause and 'in 1921 the oldest evening journal was amalgamated with the *Pall Mall Gazette*, which, two years later, merged with the *Evening Standard*'.

Hostilities Commence

On 3 August 1914, Bank Holiday Monday, Frances Evelyn, Countess of Warwick walked out onto the lawns of Easton Lodge, Great Dunmow, Essex, to preside as she did every year over the Annual Flower Show. 'The sun shone, there were record entries for flowers and vegetables and the gardens were crowded. The Essex Yeomanry Band played. In the evening there were fireworks.'[17] And within twenty-four hours, the memory of the last firework barely fading, Britain declared war on Germany.

Just six weeks earlier, on 28 June, Archduke Franz Ferdinand, heir to the Austro-Hungarian Empire, and his wife, Sophie, had visited the Bosnian capital of Sarajevo, and there were assassinated by eighteen-year-old Gavrilo Princip, a member of Young Bosnia, using a pistol supplied by Black Hand, the Serbian terrorist organization, dedicated to achieving independence for the south Slav peoples. That same afternoon, R.D. Blumenfeld, a resident of Little Easton, Great Dunmow, for almost a decade was visited at home by his near-neighbour, H.G. Wells, the distinguished novelist. Wells's son, Anthony West – his mother was Rebecca West – was later to write:

> My father's morale was at a very low ebb indeed by the end of June when the shot fired at Sarajevo started all Europe on its sickening slide into a general war. On the day on which Archduke Francis Ferdinand was assassinated, he went over to see his neighbour R.D. Blumenfeld, the expatriate American newspaperman who was editing the *Daily Express*, and they argued about what was going to happen. Blumenfeld thought that there would be a war but not a big one. My father told him that it would set the world alight.

Later that night, Blumenfeld as usual wrote up his diary, and noted: 'H.G. Wells came over to tea. While we were talking news came that Austria's Crown Prince and his wife have been assassinated by a Servian. That will mean war. Wells says it will mean more than that. It will set the world alight. I don't see why the world should fight over the act of a lunatic.' Others, though, believed differently, and the Austrians, insisting that the Serbian government had instigated the assassination, delivered an unacceptable ultimatum on 23 July.

All Fleet Street editors were now aware that the situation was deteriorating rapidly, and none more so than H.A. Gwynne, Blumenfeld's close neighbour and friend at Little Easton, and on 24 July he wrote to Lady Bathurst, his *Morning Post* proprietor, that the outlook in Europe was most grave. 'It looks to me as if Germany thinks her time has come to challenge France and Russia. We shall soon see the need for a strong fleet and ready army.'

Twice within the past decade war with Germany had almost come about. On 31 March 1905 Kaiser Willhelm II had landed at Tangier, riding through the streets on a white charger, and in a volatile speech had pledged the support of Germany for the Moroccans. This was in direct response to agreements signed in April 1904 between France and Great Britain and six months later between France and Spain providing for the eventual partition of Morocco. To settle the dispute an international conference of the Great Powers was held at Algeciras, southern Spain, in April 1906, resulting in an acceptance 'which authorized France and Spain to police Morocco under a Swiss Inspector General and which respected the Sultan of Morocco's authority'.

Notwithstanding this treaty, for the next five years Germany continued to eye North Africa, and on 1 July 1911 the gunboat *Panther* arrived at Agadir on the Atlantic coast of Morocco allegedly to protect their interests menaced by French expansion.

'Britain, however, was alarmed at this exercise of German naval power so close to Gibraltar and her vital trade routes; she feared that Germany wished to turn Agadir into a naval base'. On 21 July, speaking at the Mansion House, Lloyd George, Chancellor of the Exchequer, gave a warning to the Kaiser and the German people when he outlined the role of Great Britain if the crisis were to grow.

When the Kaiser heard from his ambassador of Lloyd George's speech he fired off a note of protest to Sir Edward Grey, the Foreign Secretary, but he was a good deal more put out to learn that the Chancellor's warning represented the considered opinion of the British Government. Talks with Germany to solve the crisis continued throughout the summer, nearly breaking down in September. However, the Germans ultimately conceded and agreement was reached in early November, giving the French rights in Morocco, and in return the Germans received two strips of territory in the French Congo. With agreement reached, the German navy withdrew – and for the British there was to be much 'closer co-operation between the War Office and the Admiralty'.

Now, in 1914, with Serbia rejecting the demands, Austria declared war on 28 July, thus precipitating the First World War. The increasing crisis on the Continent, with Germany ready to come to Austria's aid and Russia and France allied to Serbia, meant that an expansion in hostilities was only days away. And for Blumenfeld and his *Daily Express* it meant 'newspaper circulations were rising, but advertising going to bits'.

Within hours of Austria declaring war, Belgrade, the Serbian capital, was on fire, and while from some quarters there were clamours that Britain should not become involved in any conflict the *Daily Express* was urging the Liberal government to support France. In a powerful leader in the *Morning Post* on Saturday, 1 August, Gwynne was in no doubt as to Britain's position:[18]

> A prompt and whole-hearted decision on the part of His Majesty's Government might yet preserve the peace, and, if that is impossible, may determine the issue of the war. Englishmen are all agreed that this country must stand by France, which means, in the existing situation, standing by Russia also. The decision required is to announce plainly that such is British policy, and that a mobilization of Germany will be instantly followed by the mobilization of the British Navy, the Expeditionary Force, and the Territorial Force .... The French people in the hour of their trial are looking across the Channel for the encouragement to be derived from the palpable determination of England to make good her professions of friendship.

The following glorious sunny morning, Sunday 2 August, while the church bells of Little Easton rang summoning the villagers to prayer, Blumenfeld had a visitor: Herr Kurt Buetow, the German tutor of H.G. Wells's two sons. (He is the famous German tutor in Wells's war-time classic, *Mr Britling Sees It Through*.) 'He came to bid us good-bye, since he has been called home to Germany to take his place in the Army. He was very stiff and formal and polite, but evidently sorry to leave England.'

With such a heavy news day in prospect, Blumenfeld left immediately after lunch for London and Fleet Street. But before going to his office he decided to walk through St James's Park and there, near the German Embassy, met a dejected Prince Lichnowski, the German Ambassador. He turned to Blumenfeld, saying: 'I am afraid we can do no more. I have just seen Sir Edward Grey [Foreign Secretary] and you are likely to take sides with the French.'

Dawn the next morning, Bank Holiday Monday, was to herald another clear and beautiful day in London, and crowds, aware of the threatening crisis, thronged Whitehall and Trafalgar Square, forcing traffic to come to a standstill. At 3 p.m., as a brilliant sun shone through the windows of the Chamber, the Foreign Secretary, in a light summer suit and looking pale and haggard through worry and lack of sleep, rose to address a crowded and hushed House of Commons – so crowded that chairs had to be brought into the aisles – and he left Members in no doubt as to the course of action Britain must now take. All seats in the Diplomatic Gallery were filled, with the notable exception of two – those of the Ambassadors of Germany and Austria; and in the Strangers' Gallery, Field Marshal Lord Roberts, so long an advocate of military service in the columns of Blumenfeld's *Daily Express* and Gwynne's *Morning Post*, was an avid listener.

Grey began by reading out the plea from Leopold, King of the Belgians, to King George V asking for Britain to defend the integrity of Belgium. If Belgium fell to Germany, other Lowland countries would follow, and, finally, France. Grey continued: 'If the German Fleet came down the Channel and bombarded and battered the undefended coasts of France, we could not stand aside and see this going on practically within sight of our eyes, with our arms folded, looking on dispassionately, doing nothing!' His closing remarks were to prove electric: 'Let every man look into his own heart, his own feelings, and construe the extent of that obligation to himself .... If in a crisis like this we run away from those obligations of honour and interest .... I doubt whether, whatever material force we might have at the end, it would be of very much value in face of the respect we should have lost.'[19]

His words brought immediate support from the Tory Opposition and the Irish Members; and as they left the House of Commons, Winston Churchill, a bellicose First Lord of the Admiralty, asked Grey: 'What happens now?' He replied that they would send Germany an ultimatum to stop the invasion of Belgium within twenty-four hours. Later that eventful day, as dusk fell, Grey, in his office at Whitehall, had a visitor, J.A. Spender, a prominent Liberal journalist, and editor of the *Westminster Gazette*. Standing at the window, they watched the sun set on St James's Park and the lamps being lit in the streets below. 'The lamps are going out all over Europe,' Grey said. 'We shall not see them lit again in our life-time.'

For Blumenfeld, now busy attending to the latest war telegrams and despatching correspondents to the Continent ready for the forthcoming conflict, there was still time to note in his diary on that fateful day: 'Sir E. Grey leaves no doubt as to British course. Declares in Commons that he will fight if the French coast is harried. Mobilisation decided on. Crowds in streets, and the Germans are on the Belgian frontier.' A further entry, for Tuesday 4 August, confirmed his worst fears: 'Ultimatum sent to Germany to respect neutrality. It expires at midnight. Declined; so there is nothing for it. At midnight, Great Britain declared war on Germany. We are in it! How long?'

Within hours of the outbreak of war, a backlash against anyone with a German-sounding name became apparent: shop windows were smashed and allegations made against leading citizens. One such allegation was against Blumenfeld, American-born and since 1907 a British citizen. He was certainly not the man to take this lying down, and in a robust reply proclaimed on the front page of the *Daily Express*:[20]

> It has come to our knowledge that certain rivals, evidently smarting under the phenomenally successful competition of the *Daily Express*, are sedulously spreading false reports calculated to damage the prestige of this journal. For the benefit of the many of our readers who have written to us on this subject we beg to state that:
>
> The Chairman and Editor of the *Daily Express* is not and never has been a German. The paper on which the *Daily Express* is printed is not and to our knowledge has never been made in Germany. There is not one German on the staff of the *Daily Express*.
>
> We shall be greatly obliged if any reader to whom these false and malicious statements are made will kindly communicate to us details of such conversation, including the name or names of those making the statements, so that we may take steps to bring the spreaders of falsehood to book in the Court.

Defence of the Realm Act

From the moment that war had been declared, the War Office and the Admiralty, invoking the Defence of the Realm Act (DORA), had assumed charge of the newspapers, and in the words of Blumenfeld, 'politely but definitely told us that we were under control, [and] took pains to let us know of all the boiling-in-oil penalties that awaited us if we transgressed'. F.E. Smith, the newly-appointed Chief Censor, and Blumenfeld were old friends, so he hastened to see him at his office 'in a dusty, grimy room' in Whitehall. There he assured F.E. that he would make his task easy by not bothering him too much with matter for submission, 'and he in his turn amiably informed me that so far as he was concerned there would be no trouble and no delay.'

However, with the establishment of the Censor Office in the United Services building further down Whitehall: 'all the retired colonels who were too old to fight decanted into the Censors' department to play hell and demoralisation with every newspaper in the country . . . . The chaos, the delay in receipt of telegrams and consequent loss of time in the production of newspapers, the peremptory orders without explanation or reason, and the recriminations on both sides went on until the only thing left to either was the will to win the war, and on that we finally found a secure basis of compromise and eventual smooth working.'

F.E. Smith's role as Chief Censor, though, was to be of short duration, as within weeks of being appointed he was succeeded by Sir Stanley Buckmaster, who twice censured Blumenfeld owing to 'the refusal of one of my sub-editors to submit to a bone-headed military censor's ruling which I considered to be based on a false view of the situation, so that, after I had printed the dispatch which the Censor had forbidden, I laid myself open to the devastating penalties of the Defence of the Realm Act. I got off with a judicial wigging'. Blumenfeld, and other editors, considered DORA most objectionable, one clause giving to any officer in charge of a battalion the right to summary jurisdiction over any editor.

As far back as 10 July 1910 the Newspaper Proprietors Association (NPA) at its annual meeting had declared that the prime object of the Association 'was to guard against incursions upon their privileges by other members of the public, of which the Official Secrets Bill could be cited as an example'. The Hon. H.L.W. Lawson, chairman, was to tell members that: 'The Lord Chancellor had spoken to him informally with reference to the Official Secrets Bill and had expressed the hope that he would have the assistance of the Council because he did not wish to do anything which was opposed to the interests of newspapers.'[21]

Now, on 25 August 1914, Sir George Riddell, vice-chairman of the NPA and a founder member of the Press Bureau – 'a body charged with the task of ensuring that newspapers did not print information about the Army and the Navy which might be useful to the enemy' – could write in his diary: 'The Press is furious regarding the censorship arrangements. The Cable Censor's department is chiefly responsible. It has been created hastily and is officered by half-pay officers, many being of an antiquated type. I am carrying on a campaign to reform and hope to get fresh arrangements made. There has been a row in Cabinet, so I am told, regarding suppression of news and delay in publication.'

Gwynne, unlike his rivals, was to be more fortunate in his dealings with the Censor. On Friday 25 September, with other Fleet Street editors, he had received notification that all articles written by military correspondents plus maps showing dispositions and operations of the Allies must be passed by the Press Bureau Censor. Within forty-eight hours he replied to Sir Stanley Buckmaster:[22]

> I have throughout this war been a steadfast believer in a strict censorship and even before the Press Bureau was established I myself kept a most vigilant eye on everything that went into the *Morning Post*. I think you will find on inquiry at the Press Bureau that the *Morning Post* has not sinned in any way in respect of giving information which might be of use to the enemy . . . . I sincerely hope that in return for our assurance that nothing prejudicial to the Allies . . . . shall appear in the *Morning Post* you may see your way to trust our discretion . . . . I may say that I have frequently censored telegrams here in the office which appeared to me to have passed the eyes of the cable and telegram censors, and in every case I have tried my best to comply not only with the letter but with the spirit of the regulations of the censorship.

By return of post, in a letter marked Private and Confidential, Gwynne received approval from the Chief Censor: 'I am glad to say that there is no difference of opinion here as to the loyal and effective way in which you have guarded publication in your paper.' There was, though, a sting in the P.S.: 'In the event of a mistake occuring in your office you will I am sure understand that this letter will not acquit you of responsibility.'

A delighted Gwynne then informed Lady Bathurst: 'I am sure that you will be pleased and proud to know that the *Morning Post* has been exempted from Censorship. Of course all telegrams and cables are censored in the ordinary way but we alone of all the papers in England have not to submit our articles and descriptive accounts before publication.' A swift reply from Lady Bathurst led Gwynne to write once more: 'I am so glad that you are pleased that the *M.P.* is exempted from Censorship. That is a great tribute to all connected with the paper. It is, of course, confidential for if it was made public the Chief Censor's life would not be worth living.'

For Riddell, as the NPA representative, there were to be regular meetings throughout the autumn with fellow-members of the Press Bureau; and on October 28 – following the suppression of news of the sinking of *HMS Audacious* – he was to tell them:[23] 'the Press is in an irritable and dissatisfied state, and that it was just as well that this be understood by the official members of the Committee'. Less than a month later, on 20 November, he was concerned at the consolidation of the Defence of the Realm Act, writing: 'The drastic and unique provisions of this legislation have not attracted the attention they deserve. The legislation has taken place so rapidly that the measures have not been properly discussed. The press have been singularly ill-informed and lacking in criticism regarding a law which wipes out the Magna Carta, the Bill of Rights etc, in a few lines. We have got some alterations made but trial by jury still stands.'

So concerned were the newspapers, that an extraordinary meeting of the NPA was held on Wednesday 2 December when 'After discussion it was resolved to write to the Prime Minister urging that it should not be left to military authorities to decide the mode of trial for offences in regard to publicity, but that such cases should be dealt with exclusively by the ordinary criminal courts.' Following representations by the NPA and the National Union of Journalists to the Chief Censor, and later to the Prime Minister, Herbert Asquith, the regulation was altered; and 'the case of a person alleged to be guilty of what appeared to be a Press offence was to be referred to the Director of Public Prosecutions, the Lord Advocate, or the Attorney General for Ireland, instead of the competent naval or military authority.'

On 7 March 1915 Riddell could note: 'The Defence of the Realm Amendment Act passed its second reading. The Attorney General accepted my amendments. Amid the clash of this huge war the liberty of the subject seems a small matter, but in reality it is vital. We shall not always be at war.'

Churchill Under Attack

During the early weeks of the war, Churchill's conduct had been beyond criticism from some editors, evidenced by this exchange of letters with Blumenfeld, who wrote to him from the *Daily Express* office on 4 September:[24]

> Dear Mr Churchill, Every day for a month I have been wanting to write a few lines. But always I have been prevented by the great crush of work. But even at this late date, a month behind the time, I shall be discharging my duty to you by sending my best wishes and conveying to you a sense of unbounded admiration for having played your part so nobly. When you took over the Navy I wrote that you now had the opportunity to soar above party and that I believed you would; as I am glad for 'more reasons than many' that you are where you are.

A delighted Churchill replied two days later:

> I was very glad to get your letter, the more so because I heard from F.E. [Smith] that you felt some compunction about the attacks which the *Daily Express* has made on me during the last year. But really there is no need for this. I am a regular reader of your paper and have never seen any criticism which I did not think perfectly fair politics. Above all, there has never been anything so far as I am concerned reflecting on private and personal conduct. That after all is the line politicians and political journalists ought to draw. I have been greatly amused by many of your cartoons. Therefore pray banish from your mind any idea that there has been any breach between us.

However, the 'honeymoon' between Churchill and the Press was now about to come to an end . . . .

On 2 October Churchill left London in a special train bound for France,[25] but twenty miles into the journey the train was stopped, and he was called back to Whitehall, where, in the presence of Sir Edward Grey, he was asked by Lord Kitchener, Secretary of State for War, to go to Antwerp and rally the Belgians until British reinforcements arrived. At midnight, Churchill, dressed in the uniform of an Elder Brother of Trinity House, set off. An American correspondent in Antwerp described how at noon the following day Churchill in his car dashed up to the leading hotel, jumped out and charged through the crowded lobby with outstretched hands. 'It was a most spectacular entrance, and reminded me for all the world of a scene in a melodrama where the hero dashes up bare-headed on a foam-flecked horse, and saves the heroine.'

As two thousand Royal Marines arrived at Antwerp, untrained troops of the Royal Naval Division – at Churchill's insistence – were on their way from Dover as reinforcements. After touring the defences, Churchill offered his resignation as First Lord of the Admiralty so that he could take command of all British forces in the city. However, when Asquith read out Churchill's request to the Cabinet the next day, he was ordered back immediately. In the early evening of 6 October, a few hours after the arrival of the Royal Naval Division, General Rawlinson arrived from Ostend to take command. Later that evening, as the Belgian army began withdrawing, Churchill left Antwerp and was back in London the following morning, causing

Asquith to say: 'Poor Winston is very depressed, as he feels his mission has been in vain.'

Three days later, following a week of intensive fighting and heavy bombardment, the Germans entered Antwerp. The bill for the British was high: the Royal Naval Division suffered 57 killed and 158 wounded, with 936 being taken prisoner – and 1500 managed to escape to Holland where they were interned.

When Gwynne learned the truth of the debacle, he was appalled at the mishandling and the casualties, and in an article entitled 'The Antwerp Blunder' in the *Morning Post* of 13 October was at his most bitter, insisting that Churchill's attempt to defend Antwerp with a small force of Marines and Naval Volunteers must be held responsible. He continued:[26]

> Is it not true that the energies of Mr Churchill have been directed upon this eccentric expedition, and that he has been using the resources of the Admiralty as if he were personally responsible for the naval operations? It is not right or proper that Mr Churchill should use his position as Civil Lord to press his tactical and strategical fancies upon unwilling experts .... We suggest to Mr Churchill's colleagues that they should, quite firmly and definitely, tell the First Sea Lord that on no account are the military and naval operations to be conducted or directed by him.

Gwynne's savaging of Churchill over the Antwerp debacle caused a sensation in Fleet Street and was immediately reprinted, with permission, in the *Daily Mail*; and Thomas Marlowe, the paper's editor, went a stage further in his leader when he demanded that the public be told 'who is responsible for a gross example of mal-organization which has cost valuable lives and sacrificed the services .... not only of a considerable number of gallant young Englishmen but also of a considerable section of the Belgian Army'. Northcliffe, never an admirer of Churchill, ensured that, apart from the *Daily Mail*, *The Times* also made its protest.

A month earlier, following the retreat from Mons, Northcliffe, as leader of a powerful body of Press opinion, had commented forcibly on Churchill and other Cabinet members:

> What the newspapers feel very strongly is that, against their will, they are made to be part and parcel of a foolish conspiracy to hide bad news. English people do not mind bad news. Every man that I know regards Churchill as responsible for many of the initial evils of the Press Bureau, and he himself is aware of his own letter to me about *The Times* dispatch from Amiens, which was inserted in *The Times* by special request in writing of Mr F.E. Smith, who not only made the request but personally embellished and altered the article. My newspapers were held up in the House of Commons by Mr Asquith and others of having acted disloyally, and, in the House of Lords, by Lord Haldane, although they were well aware of the fact that Mr F.E. Smith asked *The Times* and my other newspapers to publish the article.
>
> Some things are more than flesh and blood can stand. So far as I am concerned, I propose to keep aloof from members of this government until the war is over.

On 14 October, while J.L. Garvin was defending Churchill in the columns of the *Pall Mall Gazette*, Gwynne once more went into the attack, including publication of a letter from Walter Long, Opposition Front Bench spokesman, stating that 'when the news first became public that the Marines had been sent to Antwerp there was, to my certain knowledge, a general and profound feeling of consternation'. Later that day, Gwynne wrote to Sir Stanley Buckmaster:[27]

> I feel I ought to speak to you quite plainly because, first of all, I have always believed in plain speaking, and secondly because I am sure you will not misunderstand or misinterpret what I say; and I may add, that I speak to you as Sir Stanley Buckmaster and not as Chief Press Censor. The expedition to Antwerp was, in my opinion, a very grave military blunder; but it was worse. Whoever was responsible for it sent men without any training to fight a skilled and powerful enemy .... My 'biting'criticism was directed against a gentleman who holds the position of First Lord of the Admiralty and who is therefore responsible for the safety of these Islands. This gentleman hurriedly, and I cannot help thinking, without due thought, organised this expedition to Antwerp. Within the last month he has left his work at the Admiralty to pay visits to the Army Headquarters in France, to Dunkirk, and to Antwerp. He was under shell fire at Antwerp. He took part in the details of the expedition and so, in my opinion, must have neglected the high office which he holds.

Two days later, Gwynne was able to inform Lady Bathurst that Churchill had received a rebuke from Kitchener over his handling of the Antwerp affair; and within hours of his letter to his proprietor Gwynne now took the almost unheard of step of writing to Prime Minister Asquith and five other members of the Liberal Cabinet – David Lloyd George, Sir Edward Grey, Joseph Pease, Reginald McKenna and Charles Masterman – declaring that what had happened at Antwerp was 'proof that Mr Churchill is unfitted for the office which he now holds, and I am firmly convinced that this country will be in a state of considerable disquietude, if not panic, unless a change is made at the Admiralty'. He concluded: 'I feel I have a duty as Editor of a paper to protest against this continuance in office of a man who has shown most signally his incompetence to hold this office at least in time of war.'

Despite support from Garvin in *The Observer* on Sunday 18 October[28] – 'Mr Churchill did his duty like a strong man and like a representative of the spirit of the British Navy, in advising the fight to the last that delayed the besiegers of Antwerp for a week ....' – the criticism from Gwynne in the *Morning Post* continued: 'What we desire chiefly to enforce upon Mr Churchill is that this severe lesson ought to teach him that he is not, as a matter of fact, a Napoleon but a Minister of the Crown with no time either to organise or lead armies in the field.'

With criticism continuing from most of Fleet Street's editors, Churchill now appealed to Sir Stanley Buckmaster for assistance, the Chief Press Censor replying: 'I have written to the Editor of the *Morning Post*, pointing out the unfairness of criticism to which in the public interest no answer can be made. To go further would I believe to be to court defiance and defeat.' Gwynne, however, was still determined to write a leading article in his paper, calling for the resignation of Churchill and for his replacement by a serving officer. Then came second thoughts, and on 20 October he wrote to Asquith, saying that he had decided against publication. Much later he was to regret this: 'I wish I had persisted in my original intentions of getting Winston out of the Cabinet. I believe I could have done it at the time.'

9

Enter Max Aitken

THE DEPARTURE OF C. ARTHUR PEARSON in 1910 through approaching blindness had meant that Blumenfeld, a director since 1908, was now running the *Daily Express*. In 1910, as noted, Pearson had sold *The Standard* and the *Evening Standard*, and within months was to dispose of his interests in the *Daily Express*. The following year, Pearson went with his wife to Vienna to consult Professor Fuchs,[1] a famed Austrian oculist. Pearson was told that he would certainly be blind within two years, and was advised to give up active business and put his affairs in order. His wife, not entirely satisfied, telephoned the specialist from their hotel and was told that the two years would probably be less than one year. Returning to their room, she found her husband lying on a sofa. 'I shall soon be blind,' he said, 'but I will never be a blind man. I am going to be *the* blind man.'

From that moment, Pearson determined to do all in his power to help the blind, and in October 1913 he joined the Council of the National Institute of the Blind, being appointed treasurer the following January. His first act was to raise £30,000 to equip the Institute's headquarters in Great Portland Street and to form an endowment fund for the production of braille books. With the active support of Sir Vansittart Bowater, the Lord Mayor of London, donations flooded in, and among the first were £1000 from Lord Northcliffe, £1000 from the future Lord Rothermere and £1000 from Pearson himself. So successful were Pearson's fund-raising activities that in only eight years he was to increase the annual income of the Institute from £8010 to £358,174.

In his appeal through the Press he said:

> I am venturing to make myself the mouthpiece of the many blind folk who will benefit by your kindly and able advocacy .... The lives of the blind – particularly the poor blind – are very dull and monotonous, and, short of restoring them to their sight, nothing can be given them of greater value than books .... I do not want these poor blind people to go on being content to sit with folded hands. I want those folded hands to be busy passing to and fro along the lines of Braille type, and these unimaginated minds to be filled with pictures of the great and wonderful world which their owners cannot see.

After George V had opened the Institute's new premises on 19 March 1914, Pearson immediately launched a world-wide appeal for funds; and ever conscious of the use of the media he was the first person to use wireless in this fashion. With the assistance of the Marconi Company the message was sent free to 'all on board British ships, and even sympathetic friends on ships flying other flags who are grateful they are not blind'.

This dramatic, first-ever appeal rightly earned Pearson columns of newspaper publicity and praise. One writer, Filson Young, was to comment:[2] 'I am glad that it was Arthur Pearson who thought of this dramatic way of helping his fund for providing books for the blind; it is worthy of the hustler as he was called in the days before he, too, entered the dark kingdom. It is the old touch, the grand manner asserting itself again.'

Headed by the King and Queen, this first campaign for books for the blind was a great success, winning the support of all the parties, with Arthur Balfour, Bonar Law, Lloyd George and Ramsay MacDonald figuring prominently. Less than six months later, following the outbreak of the First World War, Pearson, at the request of the Prince of Wales, transferred his activity and enthusiasm to the Prince of Wales's Fund, and in less than a year succeeded in raising more than one million pounds for families of serving soldiers and sailors.

But Pearson was now about to embark on his greatest venture – a venture that was to be recognized as his living memorial. Fom the opening of his first hostel for blinded soldiers early in 1915 he had found his true vocation – and St Dunstan's was born. On 26 March of that year the hostel was moved from Bayswater Road to St Dunstan's, a mansion situated in Regent's Park. The house belonged to Otto Khan, a New York banker, who had gladly placed it at Pearson's disposal free of charge. From the small beginnings of sixteen men being cared for, by the end of the war more than 1700 members were on his books, and he could proudly say that 'with practically no exception all the blinded soldiers and sailors of the British Imperial Forces came under my care'.

In recognition of his great work at St Dunstan's, Arthur Pearson was, deservedly, created a baronet in 1916, and the following year received the GBE. With the war over and St Dunstan's firmly established, Pearson was considering entering Parliament as a spokesman for the blind.

On the morning of 9 December 1921, he was awakened at 7.15 and, unaided, went to his bathroom. He had always insisted on preparing his bath himself, but the previous day he had mentioned that the enamelled bath had been rather slippery. This particular morning, apparently, he slipped forward, striking his head on the tap. Stunned, he fell face downwards into the water and drowned. Pearson normally breakfasted at 8.30, but with no sign of him at that time his secretary contacted his son, who went to the bathroom, where he found his father dead.

His death caused a great sense of shock throughout the country; and in his old paper, the *Evening Standard*, it was noted:[3]

> The career of Sir Arthur Pearson is at once a romance and a glory. This fight against the foe of physical darkness – a magnificent struggle – undoubtedly owed the major part of its success to the virile personality, the optimism, and the genius of a man who would never acknowledge defeat. He treated blindness from a new angle: he cut out entirely the word 'pity' and the word 'affliction', and insisted that blind people, above all others, must be cheerful, with a wide humorous outlook.

R.D. Blumenfeld, so long one of his friends, wrote in the *Daily Express*, the paper that Pearson had founded:[4] 'A man of achievement, strong, vivid, a radiant figure of energy, enthusiasm and human affection has come to a sudden and tragic end of his picturesque career. Arthur Pearson, the blind leader of the blind, whose death is regretted today, was one of those rare men who are born for a purpose and who, having achieved that purpose, are taken away as flaming examples of posterity.'

Sir Arthur Pearson was buried at Hampstead Cemetery, and the King and Queen, Queen Alexandra, the Queen of Norway and the Prince of Wales sent representatives. Members of the government, Commissioners from the Dominions and the high and the mighty from Fleet Street were there also to pay their final respects. But, above all else, there were hundreds of blind mourners, brought especially from all over the country, who gathered by the graveside.

> Never before had such a scene been witnessed at a public funeral. It enhanced, if that were possible, the pathos of Sir Arthur's tragic end. Guided gently by big guardsmen in grey overcoats and by nurses, they moved slowly past the grave in groups of two and three, arm in arm. Humbly dressed and smartly dressed, some wearing dark spectacles, some with the blank expression of the blind man whose eyes look normal, the sightless procession moved uncertainly in the December sunlight.

Enter Max Aitken

In the summer of 1910 – with Pearson having left Fleet Street to spend the summer with his family in Switzerland – Blumenfeld had been finding himself more and more involved in the management of the *Daily Express*; and, although the circulation of 425,000 was beginning to increase, out-of-date presses made it difficult to cope with any extra sales. Blumenfeld, heavily in debt to newsprint suppliers, had pledged all his financial sources and was now urgently seeking a backer. He was soon to meet such a man. In the September, he was invited to a political lunch given by Edward Goulding, MP for Worcester and a leading official in the Tariff Reform League, in honour of Arthur Balfour and Bonar Law. Other guests included F.E. Smith and Max Aitken. To quote Blumenfeld:

> Edward Goulding was the host and said to me: 'I have put you alongside a young Canadian, Max Aitken, who will probably interest you.' I found myself beside a comparative youth, carelessly dressed, with tousled hair, searing eyes, alternately hard and twinkling, and a large full-lipped mouth which made him look cold and forbidding in repose and extraordinarily attractive when it spread itself in a smile over his colourless face . . . . He began to stupefy me with a torrent of questions, flinging in a new one almost before I had answered the old . . . . He knew little or nothing about journalism, but by the time the luncheon was over he knew as much, if not more, or thought he did, than I, and then and there, though he did not say so to me, he determined to become a journalist.

Born on 25 May 1879 at Maple, Ontario, William Maxwell Aitken was the son of a Church of Scotland minister, and throughout his long life was never to lose his rasping Candian accent. As a youth he had held a series of jobs: selling newspapers, clerk in a lawyer's office, drug-store assistant, peddling insurance – and even starting a small newspaper, *The Leader*, from home, until his father put an abrupt stop to it when he discovered Aitken working on a Sunday.

As a young, forceful entrepeneur, he entered the expanding field of selling bonds and promoting companies and company mergers, and by 1907 was a dollar millionaire. He was not, however, without his critics, and his final deals – the formation of the Canadian Cement Company and the birth of the Steel Company of Canada – were to find him under severe attack. On 17 July 1910, Aitken and his wife, the former Gladys Drury, daughter of a Canadian general, left Montreal for New York and then England for new conquests and fortunes.[5]

Aitken, a small man, was ever a restless, crusading person, and his attitude can be summed up in the following: 'On the rockbound coast of New Brunswick, the waves beat incessantly. Every now and then comes a particularly dangerous wave that breaks viciously on the rocks. It is called "Rage". That's me.'

One of his first ventures upon arrival in England was to buy into Rolls-Royce; and it was there that he came into contact with Lord Northcliffe, who took a non-financial interest in the company. He informed Aitken that Rolls-Royce was like a 'delicate orchid' and he should not interfere. As a result, Aitken sold his shares, drawing from Northcliffe the remark that 'he was one of the straightest men in the country'.

Over that September political lunch, Aitken had also told Blumenfeld that he was intending to enter Parliament; and, true as his word, within weeks he had been selected as Unionist candidate for Ashton-under-Lyne, a Free Trade stronghold. Using his best business methods, Aitken reorganized the local party machine, undertook a most detailed canvassing and had all the voters card-indexed. His tactics were to be successful, and following the poll on 2 December 1910 he defeated his Liberal opponent by 4044 votes to 3848, a majority of 196. Blumenfeld was delighted and asked Aitken to tell the *Daily Express* how he had achieved his success. Aitken telegraphed back:[6]

VICTORY DUE TO BRILLIANT ORGANISATION AND TARIFF REFORM

Rudyard Kipling, a recent friend of Aitken, was also pleased at the victory: 'what specially cheered me is that you seem to have won out on straight business talk – pure Tariff Reform. Now you get fit and when you feel you are all right again take a fortnight or three weeks in Switzerland.'

With the strain of electioneering having proved too much, Aitken was to heed Kipling's advice, seeing his doctor who told him that he needed to recuperate in the South of France. Christmas for the Aitkens, therefore, was spent on the Riviera, and it was at Monte Carlo on 2 January 1911 that he began a professional association which was to have a significant effect upon his future. As he was descending the steps of the Casino he was approached by Blumenfeld with a recommendation from Bonar Law. More than ever, Blumenfeld now needed financial help. The Tory Party had offered to take over the *Daily Express*, but being a keen Tariff Reformer he was reluctant to accept. Late in December, Blumenfeld had consulted Law, a fellow-member at the Carlton Club. Blumenfeld was in an excellent position. Having been offered and turned down a knighthood for services to the Tory Party he had asked for membership of the Carlton, the exclusive bastion of Tory MPs and grandees. This was agreed and with Gwynne he thus became one of the first journalist members of the club.

Now Law told him: 'I know the man for you. Max Aitken is enormously rich. He knows nothing about newspapers and is not interested in them. But he wants to have a big political career, and he'll be glad of a paper which will back him.' Blumenfeld left at once for the South of France. Aitken listened to his story, walked over to the Hotel de Paris and wrote out a cheque for £25,000 as a personal loan. Many years afterwards Blumenfeld was to recall:[7]

> A month or so later [following the lunch with Aitken and F.E. Smith] I was standing on the steps of the Casino at Monte Carlo, chatting with Sir Gilbert Parker, when what we used to describe as a 'powerful automobile' (it must have been 15 h.p.) drew up, and out jumped our new MP, Max Aitken. He was vociferous in his greeting, and then informed me that 'you and I are going to do big things together'. I did not agree but I have found in the past twenty years since he and I have been associated that, even if I did not always agree, he generally succeeded in doing what he wanted to do. So we became close friends. We breakfasted and dined incessantly. I learned a lot about mergers and share-splitting and cement and Canada, and he learned more about people and journalism.

Two months after the Blumenfeld-Aitken meeting in Monte Carlo, Pearson, still on the Continent, had received a telegram on 17 March urging him to return to England. Upon arriving back in London, he immediately began talks with Aitken about selling his majority share in the *Daily Express*. Aitken informed Goulding that negotiations were coming to a head. That same month Goulding encouraged him, saying he hoped he would become 'Boss of the *Express*'; and, in late June, Goulding evidently thought Aitken had succeeded in buying the paper. 'I am very glad about the *Express* as I am confident that you and Blum[enfeld] can make it a great organ.'

As an MP, Aitken was not a success, rarely bothering to vote and conducting most of his intrigues in the committee rooms of the House of Commons. However, on 20 April 1911 he met Sir Alexander Acland-Hood, the Tory chief whip, who informed him that he had 'Two peerages, two P.C.s, two baronetcies and six knighthoods in his giving for the Coronation.' He offered a knighthood to Aitken 'for the purpose of rewarding me for services to come to the [Tory] Unionist party.'[8] Before accepting the knighthood, Aitken consulted Gwynne, still then editor of *The Standard*. Gwynne was later to recall:

> You rang me in 1911 and asked me most urgently to come and see you at the Hyde Park Hotel. I dropped everything and came. You showed me a letter from Asquith offering a knighthood and asked my advice as to the answer you should give. I thought that I had convinced you that it was best to refuse for we drafted a letter declining the honour. Later I learnt that the matter had been arranged some time before. Although now I am quite convinced that you were just having a lark, I thought then that you were doing a somewhat unfriendly thing.

Gwynne was in fact deeply hurt and refused to have any dealing with Aitken for years afterwards.

Despite the loan which Aitken had given Blumenfeld, the *Daily Express* was still in financial difficulties. 'Blumenfeld might be a lively politician, according to Aitken, the only editor of the time who was universally beloved. He did not know how to make his paper prosper. The leading shareholders, who were gradually taking over the paper from Pearson, were indifferent to its fate.'

For the next few years Aitken, among his many other activities, continued to support the *Daily Express*, although Blumenfeld remained the titular head. But on 15 January 1915 the paper was once more in trouble, owing £9000 in newsprint bills, and a receiver was about to be appointed. The suggestion that three safe Tory MPs should be chosen was turned down by Aitken, who successfully proposed the appointment of Blumenfeld as receiver. On 5 May 1916 he wrote to Walter Runciman, President of the Board of Trade: 'The *Daily Express*, in which I am interested, is short of paper. I should like to have the opportunity of discussing with you the means by which I could secure the release of a ship to bring over a cargo of paper from the mills of Price Brothers and Company Ltd. of Quebec.'

Blumenfeld has left an interesting account of those difficult days on the *Daily Express*:[9]

> I was wallowing about in the trough of the sea somewhere NNE by SSW of Ludgate Circus, two points to leeward of Fleet Street – in Shoe Lane to be exact. My good ship *Daily Express* was strong enough in hull and frame and steering gear and all that, but short of steam. Like the Mississippi steamer of note, she was underpowered and over-whistled, i.e., every time the whistle blew the engines stopped. My friend Aitken came along and showed me how to balance things and keep the steam pressure always on top. He also pointed at the chart, and indicated that I had been travelling along the old course, which was full of danger and storms and fogs, whereas he knew a short cut which would land my craft quicker and with greater ease.
>
> Then he became more and more interested, until one day he joined me on the Board, and from that time on there was no holding him. Away went his cherished desire to return to Canda and grow up with that country. He got the sniff of printers' ink in his nostril, and those who know what that means will understand everything went overboard. I have often observed that revitalising effect on men who were once connected with my trade. The moment their olfactory senses come into contact with that strange overpowering heaven-induced tank of ink and type and rollers and paste, their eyes twinkle, their nerves tingle, and the years slough off almost visibly.

Aitken was hooked, and later, as Lord Beaverbrook, he recalled with clarity his early days as a newspaperman and his decision to become involved with the *Daily Express*:[10]

> The first farthing I ever made in my life was selling one cent or half-penny newspapers in the little town of Newcastle, New Brunswick. Afterwards I consolidated the whole newspaper distribution of the village, but I was not satisfied. I felt I could do better.
>
> I became a newspaper publisher. I was the publisher and the sole proprietor of the paper, *The Leader*. I also set up the type. I stood at the case, and could do so now but for those new-fangled machines. Not only that but I ran the printing press, and I did it not by touching a button, but had to do it by turning a handle in the same way as you turn a

mangle. I did everything but distribute type after it had been used. That I would never do. It was too boring.

Talking of how he entered Fleet Street, he said:

> Then the same friend came to me and asked me to take an interest in another newspaper [he had previously been involved with *The Globe*, a London evening]. That paper was the *Daily Express*. That was in 1915 and we turned a £40,000 loss into a profit. It was a very good thing we did. But there were branches of the newspaper industry that came along, demanding more pay and remuneraton. Well, we managed to wriggle along until 1920.

Four years later in his book *Politicians and the Press* he once more returned to his acquisition of the *Daily Express*:

> I had for a number of years a considerable connection with the *Daily Express* of an indefinite character, but was never interested much. Towards the end of the war that newspaper wanted money very urgently to keep its supply of newsprint. Finally, the editor came to me and suggested that I could purchase the controlling shares in the newspaper for £17,500.

Before buying, he spoke to Lord Rothermere, who told him that to take the shares at this price implied a great deal of courage and he would need to devote a considerable amount of money and energy to the business. Aitken then consulted Lord Northcliffe, who asked him: 'How much are you worth?' 'Over five million dollars,' replied Aitken. 'You will lose it all in Fleet Street,' retorted Northcliffe.[11]

Northcliffe was to be sadly mistaken, for within a few months Aitken – now in full control – could proclaim himself a full-blooded journalist and chairman of the *Daily Express*. The power of Blumenfeld was on the wane.

Meanwhile, as the power struggle had been going on for the soul of the *Express*, Gwynne had been searching his soul: should he continue as editor of an influential Fleet Street daily, with an almost immediate access to the workings of the Cabinet, or should he resign and join the Army in France? In January 1915, Gwynne was almost fifty years old, and on the 11th he wrote to Lady Bathurst, posing a question:

> I have had it frequently in my mind to make a suggestion to you. I am a heavy expense to the paper and I have felt that, now that it is running well, I might without disadvantage leave it for a time. Suppose I go out to the Front. I have horrible mental struggles with myself as to my clear duty to my country just now and at times I have felt that my experience and knowledge of war could be better utilised at the Front . . .'

Gwynne was now in torment, and two days later he wrote once more:

> Frankly what I feel is this. I know I am doing a little for the country in the *M.P.* but I am *not* risking my life. When the time comes to go forward, my little influence with the Commander-in-Chief may persuade him that to move forward it is necessary to sacrifice many, many lives . . . . May I be allowed to go out when the advance takes place, if I can get permission?

Lady Bathurst, though, knew exactly where Gwynne's place should be – not in the trenches of France but at the office of the *Morning Post*, influencing the Cabinet

– and her letter brought an immediate reply from a more relaxed Gwynne on 15 January:[12]

> Your letter received today has quite convinced me where my duty lies and that is here. But you will I hope not misunderstand what I have been going through. Here I am fit, sound and able to walk men of 20 off their legs. I sit in an office and tell the public rich and poor that their duty lies at the Front. 'At the Front' means death or disablement or at any rate danger. And what danger do I run? It seems cowardly to me and yet I know you are right. But it is hard to sit still while other people are dying. Yet I know you are right and this is the last you'll hear of it all.

Within days of reaching agreement with Lady Bathurst, Gwynne had fired off a detailed nine-point memorandum to Asquith and the Cabinet, with a separate copy to Balfour, outlining his thoughts on the first six months of the war, and what steps now needed to be taken to break the stalemate in France. His thoughts, however, did not embrace the Eastern Mediterranean and the Dardanelles.

Dardanelles Disaster

On 2 January 1915 Field Marshal Kitchener wrote to General Sir John French, commander-in-chief British Forces in France: 'I suppose we must now recognize that the French army cannot make a sufficient break through the German lines of defence to bring about the retreat of the German forces from northern France. If that is so, then the German lines in France may be looked upon as a fortress that cannot be carried by assault, and also cannot be completely invested.' That same day, Grand Duke Nicholas, the Russian commander-in chief, called upon Britain 'for a demonstration against Turkey in order to relieve the pressure on the Russian armies fighting in the Caucasus'. To Kitchener and Churchill, who was looking at an alternative to 'sending troops to chew barbed wire in Flanders', the Russian request had merit – especially as Kitchener himself believed that 'the only place that a demonstration might have some effect would be in the Dardanelles'.

Within hours, Admiral Fisher – recently recalled by Churchill to be First Sea Lord, in succession to Prince Louis of Battenberg, who because of his German birth had been hounded out of office – brought forward his proposal: a bombardment by British warships of the Dardanelles forts, followed by a landing of 75,000 troops.

Early in February, therefore, a squadron of ancient battleships, plus the new dreadnought *Queen Elizabeth*, under the command of Admiral de Robeck, arrived off the Dardanelles, and the preliminary bombardment commenced, destroying the outer Turkish defences. A month later, on 18 March, the main onslaught began, but 'unfortunately our ships encountered an unsuspected minefield and three battleships were lost and three more damaged'. To the amazement of the Turks and their German advisers – now thoroughly demoralized and desperately short of ammunition – the British fleet withdrew, thereby missing a golden opportunity; and after consultation with General Sir Ian Hamilton, acting as an observer for Kitchener, de Robeck decided to wait until land forces arrived.

On 5 March, despite the risks involved, Asquith, Kitchener and Churchill had decided that a landing should take place. Fisher, though, with the naval action having been a failure, was now having second thoughts, and exactly a month later warned Churchill:[13] 'You are just eaten up with the Dardanelles and can't think of anything else! D – n the Dardanelles! They'll be our grave!'

To Gwynne, with his many years' experience in the past as a distinguished war correspondent, the Dardanelles campaign had all the makings of a disaster, as he explained on 12 April to General Sir Henry Wilson, an old colleague from the Boer War, now serving in France:

> The Dardanelles is the greatest horror of the lot. Antwerp was bad enough in all conscience, but the Dardanelles is worse, for we were all given to understand that with the dismissal of Louis of Battenburg the conduct of operations at the Admiralty was altogether changing; that here was a great, strong man, Fisher, coming in, who could stand no nonsense and would insist that the expert's point of view should prevail. Unfortunately, the exact opposite has happened .... Three ships were lost, very little achieved, and the Germans and the Turks put on their guard for all time. Now Johnnie Hamilton is cruising somewhere about there with a large force with an awful job in front of him, for how is he going to land at Enos? I do not quite know, and to tell you the truth I am looking daily for news of a disaster from that quarter.[14]

Alas, within less than a fortnight, Gwynne's forebodings were to become a grim reality: shortly before dawn on 25 April, Australian and New Zealand troops disembarked at Z Beach below the cliffs of Chunuk Bair on the Gallipoli Peninsula – and the land battle for the Dardanelles had begun. Despite heavy shelling from a Turkish battery, the troops pushed forward, and by late afternoon had reached the heights, where the enemy, short of ammunition, were beginning to withdraw. But the arrival of Mustafa Kemal soon changed the situation. Kemal knew that if the crest was not held the whole position on the peninsula could be lost.

Fighting continued throughout the day, and, with fresh troops and ammunition arriving, the advantage now swung towards the defenders as they sought to drive the Australians back to the beaches:

> Successive waves of Turks, hurling themselves on their adversary, were killed by machine-gun fire as they clambered over the bodies of the previous wave. More and more Australian wounded were falling back to the narrow beach. There was no rest, no lull .... while the rotting dead lay all around us, never a pause in the whole of that long day that started at the crack of dawn.

Meanwhile, thirteen miles to the south, at Cape Helles, British troops had been put ashore in perfect weather. 'For the first time in the twentieth century, a modern army landed on defended beach-heads in open boats.' As dawn broke, General Hamilton watched from his observation post aboard the *Queen Elizabeth*. However, within minutes the serenity of the early morning and the calmness of the sea were to be shattered:

> He could see men up to their necks in water, men falling as they ran, men pinned down on the beach. Standing by his side, Roger Keyes snapped his telescope shut – he could watch

> the scene no longer. They were taking a terrible beating. There was barbed wire in the surf, and men were shot hip-deep in water as they groped for their shears, and too many of the boats, under fire from concealed machine-gun nests, arrived on beaches carrying nothing but corpses. Landing at Cape Helles, the first seventy men of the Lancashire Fusiliers were bowled over to a man.

So tightly packed in the naval cutters were the Fusiliers that 'some continued to sit upright after they had been shot dead'. Almost 1000 men were to land at W Beach, and before it was secured six officers and 254 men had been killed and 283 wounded. For the Lancashire Fusiliers, it was to be a savage but proud occasion with six Victoria Crosses being awarded 'before breakfast'.

With the Gallipoli campaign having come to a halt, back at the Admiralty in London, Fisher undertook the step he had been threatening for the past few weeks. On 15 May he handed in his resignation, complaining that Churchill desired to be in charge of everything – from the Grand Fleet to the Dardanelles. Following talks with Asquith and Lloyd George, Churchill now wrote to Fisher, requesting that he withdraw his resignation and offering new conditions. Fisher, though, was unmoved; there could be no going back, and he replied:[15] 'YOU ARE BENT ON FORCING THE DARDANELLES AND NOTHING WILL TURN YOU FROM IT – NOTHING. I know you so well! . . . You will remain and I SHALL GO.'

Scandal of the Shells

Apart from the Dardanelles fiasco, the Cabinet was now also faced with fresh problems on the Western Front. Early in May, Northcliffe had visited Sir John French, commander-in-chief, British Expeditionary Force in France, who confirmed that there was a serious shortage of shells. And on Friday 15 May Colonel Repington, the paper's chief war correspondent, reported in *The Times* that 'the want of an unlimited supply of high explosives was a fatal bar to our success'.

The following morning in the *Daily Mail*, Northcliffe opened his attack on Kitchener when the paper splashed with the headline:

BRITISH STILL STRUGGLING: SEND MORE SHELLS

For the next few days, Northcliffe kept up the pressure; and on 20 May Tom Clarke, the paper's news editor, was to write in his diary:[16]

> About 8 p.m., Caird, unusually late for him, looked into my room and said: 'Have you read the leader? We are going to break some windows tomorrow.' I got a proof. The heading ran 'The Tragedy of the Shells: Lord Kitchener's Error.' We are in the midst of a Government crisis. The Chief says conscription has nothing to do with it, that it's due to the shell shortage and the feud at the Admiralty between Winston Churchill and Lord Fisher. . . . Northcliffe says it is well known that Kitchener preferred shrapnel, and made tons of it, when any expert could have told him that it was no good for breaking down trenches.

The leader written by Northcliffe himself left his 'face white and set', and he was to tell senior colleagues: 'The circulation of the *Daily Mail* may go down to two and the circulation of *The Times* to one – I don't care. The thing has to be done! Better to lose circulation than to lose the war.' He then ordered one contents bill for all editions:

KITCHENER'S TRAGIC BLUNDER

With the proof in his hands, Northcliffe took the leader into editor Thomas Marlowe's office, who, having read it, said: 'You realize, I suppose, that you are smashing the people's idol? It will make the public very angry. Are you prepared to take the consequences?' Northcliffe replied: 'I don't care twopence for the consequences. That man is losing the war.' In his leader, Northcliffe wrote:

> Lord Kitchener has starved the army in France of high-explosive shells. The admitted fact is that Lord Kitchener ordered the wrong kind of shell – the same kind of shell which he used largely against the Boers in 1900. He persisted in sending shrapnel – a useless weapon in trench warfare. He was warned repeatedly that the kind of shell required was a violently explosive bomb which would dynamite its way through the German trenches and entanglements and enable our brave men to advance in safety. The kind of shell our poor soldiers have had has caused the death of thousands of them.

Even though editor Geoffrey Robinson of *The Times* had informed Northcliffe that he was not in full accord with the attack, this had not deterred the Chief. But Marlowe's comment that the leader would make the public angry was to prove correct. To quote Tom Clarke once more:[17]

> The Chief's comment in the paper this morning, when his leader attacking Kitchener fell like a bombshell on an amazed England, was that the verbose author of the leading article looked liked getting the paper in trouble. He certainly does. All day the telephones have been buzzing with protests from readers, and intimations that they will never buy 'our damned rag' again. The view of people in the office is that the Chief did not realise last night the size of the gun he was firing. Hundreds of abusive letters and telegrams are coming in. Copies of *The Times* and the *Daily Mail* were burned on the Stock Exchange this afternoon. The evening papers castigate us furiously. There is some alarm that public feeling may boil over, and so tonight there is a special police guard at Carmelite House, and all the gates are locked.

With an irate public not buying the paper, sales of the *Daily Mail*, which had been 1,360,00 copies on the day of the attack on Kitchener, fell within less than a week by 238,00 copies, leading Northcliffe to declare: 'I've had a hard time of it these last few weeks. They would take away my property, if they could, and put me in the Tower.'

For Northcliffe, there was to be no support from the other papers, Blumenfeld writing in the *Daily Express* on 22 May that an 'attack on Lord Kitchener helps Germany'. And even Garvin in the *Pall Mall Gazette* and *The Observer* was critical, causing Northcliffe to declare to Robinson: 'I hope you will speak to Mr Astor about the way he spends money in attacking me. I shall certainly retaliate on the Astor family in *The Times* and the *Daily Mail*.'

Northcliffe's leader – hindsight tells us that it was the most important of the First World War – was not to bring down Kitchener. However, with the combined pressures of the Dardanelles fiasco, the resignation of Admiral Fisher and the shell shortage in France, Bonar Law could inform Asquith that, unless changes were made, the Conservatives would no longer support the Government. On 17 May, therefore, Asquith wrote to his Ministers, asking for their resignations. He had agreed that a Coalition Government should be formed. Bonar Law, however, was adamant on two points: Churchill must leave the Admiralty and Haldane should not remain at the War Office. And for Kitchener? He was still to continue as Secretary of State for War.

But there was to be one new appointment: David Lloyd George as Minister of Munitions. And as Frank Owen was to write that prior to the appointment[18] 'Neither the number nor the calibre of the requisite guns and machine-guns had been assessed; no sum had ever been worked out of the ammunition required to feed those guns.' Lloyd George would soon change that.

Meanwhile, on hearing the news of Churchill's departure, a delighted Gwynne wrote to Lady Bathurst on 18 May:[19]

> Thank heavens W. Churchill is going. This is the very best news I have heard for a very long day and I confess that I am very cock-a-hoop. Last Saturday [15 May] Fisher handed in his resignation. He complained that Churchill wanted to take everything away from the Grand Fleet for the Dardanelles .... The Prime Minister accepted his resignation. But Bonar Law who heard it on Sunday immediately went to Lansdowne and between them drafted a letter to the Prime Minister saying that they could not allow this. They also expressed their desire that the Government should be reconstructed.
>
> I don't like Coalition but I cannot see how it is possible to refuse such a proposal. I don't care a hang for a party if only this war can be successfully carried out. The only way to get this Government out is by a general election and that would be worse than letting the Germans get to Calais. So I see no other alternative but to help, always provided that the ministry is purged of the rotters.

Although Gwynne was not enamoured at the idea of a coalition, nevertheless he was prepared to give his full support, as he confirmed in writing on 24 May to Walter Long, the Conservative MP and creator of the Union Defence League in 1907:

> As you know, I have never liked the idea of the Coalition; but I think from the time the Government asked us to cooperate a refusal was impossible, as it would have put the Unionist Party altogether in the wrong. I am going to support the Coalition for all I am worth now, because there is nothing between that and destruction. I shall leave all my criticisms and only put forward suggestions.

During all the trauma of the Cabinet reshuffle and subsequent Coalition, one man – a backbench MP but now a serving officer – had played an increasingly important role. His name was Max Aitken. Within weeks of war having been declared, Aitken, with the rank of lieutenant-colonel, had sailed to France with the Canadian Division, becoming his country's Record Officer, and, eventually, eye-witness at the Front. His initial reporting – and as a Canadian he was, seemingly, exempted from much of the British censorship – was his coverage of the battle of Ypres in April 1915:

> The Canadians wrested from the trenches, over the bodies of the dead and maimed, the right to stand side by side with the superb troops who, in the first battle of Ypres, broke and drove before them the flower of the Prussian Guards. Looked at from any point, the performance would be remarkable. It is amazing to soldiers, when the genesis and

composition of the Canadian Division are considered .... It consisted in the main of men who at the outbreak of war were neither disciplined nor trained.

They suffered terrible casualties. For a short time every other man seemed to fall .... The 4th Canadian Battalion at one moment came under a particularly withering fire. For a moment – not more – it wavered. Its most gallant Commanding Officer, Lieutenant-Colonel Birchall, carrying, after an old fashion, a light cane, cooly and cheerfully rallied his men, and at the very moment when his example had infected them, fell dead .... With a hoarse cry of anger they sprang forward (for, indeed, they loved him) as if to avenge his death .... After a hand-to-hand struggle, the last German who resisted was bayoneted, and the trench was won.

His description of the battle was to win approval from the Canadian government, and he ensured that there was wide publicity of his country's troops in action – especially in the American newspapers. Aitken then started the first newspaper devoted exclusively to the troops, *The Canadian Record*, with a free distribution of 250,000 copies.

Now, in May 1915, with Fisher having resigned and Churchill's position in jeopardy, Aitken, in France, received an urgent message from Bonar Law, his Party Leader, to return to London. Aitken's role was to tell Churchill, officially, that his time at the Admiralty was over. Aitken was later to recall the occasion:[20]

Churchill was on the Tuesday night I saw him at the Admiralty a man suddenly thrown from power into impotence, and one felt rather as if one had been invited to 'come and look on fallen Anthony'. What a creature of strange moods he is – always at the top of the wheel of confidence or at the bottom of an intense depression.

Looking back on that long night we spent in the big silent Admiralty room till day broke, I cannot help reflecting on that extreme quality of mind which marks Churchill above all other men – the charm, the imaginative sympathy of his hours of defeat, the self-confidence, the arrogance of his hours of power and prosperity. That night he was a lost soul, yet full of flashes of wit and humour.

For Churchill there was just the consolation prize of Chancellor of the Duchy of Lancaster, and a few days later he paid his first visit to Aitken's home at Cherkley, near Leatherhead, Surrey. 'With him he brought an easel and paints – he had recently begun his hobby – and a despatch box full of papers, containing, he told Aitken, the justification of his Dardanelles policy.'

Meanwhile in Fleet Street, with Fisher and Churchill out of the Admiralty, there was now a growing demand for Admiral Lord Charles Beresford to be put in charge. Blumenfeld, a friend of many years' standing, however, advised him to bide his time; and on 22 July the admiral replied:[21]

I am taking your advice, sitting absolutely still, and saying nothing. We all know the enormous waste going on in Government departments, particularly in the War Office .... and the Admiralty with regard to the frightful expenditure incurred by Churchill, which is still being pursued by building ships for the Dardenelles to carry low trajectory guns, after the experience of the *Queen Elizabeth*. You have got a copy of my letter of last April to Asquith, which, if the advice tendered in it had been taken, the battleships sunk in the Dardanelles, and the *Lusitania*, would have been above water at the present time.

> I am writing a letter to Mr Gwynne, as you are the only two strong supporters that I have in the Press.

The following week, there was a note to Blumenfeld from Nina, Lady Beresford: 'Are you all insane that at a moment like this you do not propose Lord Charles for the Admiralty? Excuse my strong language but if ever there was a moment for him it is the present one.'

However, despite the best efforts of Blumenfeld and Gwynne, Lord Beresford was not to achieve his life's ambition . . . .

Murdoch's Damning Report

Throughout that long, hot summer, conditions in Gallipoli remained attrocious; and, in the August, Captain Keith Murdoch, a former journalist from the Melbourne *Age*, arrived there – sent by Andrew Fisher, the Australian Prime Minister, to investigate problems with the forces mail. Meeting Ellis Ashmead-Bartlett, who was reporting for the Fleet Street papers, he was soon told of 'his carping denigration of the British strategy at Gallipoli' and the lack of leadership by the generals. After seeing for himself the misery of the trenches, Murdoch cabled back his first impressions to the Australian newspapers:[22]

> For five months they have lived on a solitary desert spot where every day brings its new test of sinew and every night its new test of courage: where no one is safe from wound and death and no physique is proof against the physical trials. It is only a strip of shell-torn beach and cliff and gully, with deep hat-high saps leading from place to place, and all life dependent upon the protection afforded by sand bags . . . . I have given only a bare impression of life at Anzac . . . . Life that is spiritual, mental and physical pain. I have not exaggerated – far from it. No one at home can image what it is. It is worse than any picture conjured by inexperienced, peaceable Australians.

Murdoch believed that an immediate withdrawal was essential; and his views concurred with those of Ashmead-Bartlett, who gave him a secret letter to take to Prime Minister Asquith. However, General Hamilton, having been told by H.W. Nevinson, of the *Manchester Guardian*, alerted the War Office to intercept the letter at Marseilles.

Arriving in London on 21 September 1915, Murdoch went immediately to *The Times* office at Printing House Square, and there composed an 8000-word letter for the Australian Prime Minister 12,000 miles away.[23] The next day, lunching with Geoffrey Robinson, editor of *The Times*, he told him of the horrors of Gallipoli, which he had now revealed in his letter. 'The unfortunate expedition has never been given a chance. It required a great leader. It required self-sacrifice on the part of the staff as well as the sacrifice so wonderfully and liberally made on the part of the soldiers. It has done none of these things.' Robinson persuaded him to repeat the contents to the chairman of the Dardanelles Committee, Sir Edward Carson, who then passed it to Lloyd George.

With the assistance of Lloyd George and Northcliffe the report went before the Cabinet and on 30 September Northcliffe wrote to Murdoch: 'If I were in possession of the information you have involving as it does the lives of thousands of your compatriots and mine I should not be able to rest until the true story of this lamentable adventure was so well known as to force immediate steps to be taken to remedy the state of affairs. The matter has haunted me ever since I learned about it.'

Ashmead-Bartlett, now back in London, wrote a damning article on the Dardanelles fiasco in the Sunday edition of *The Times*, and together with Murdoch then began lobbying for General Hamilton's dismissal. The Dardanelles Committee met on 14 October – and Hamilton was sacked. Within forty-eight hours, Northcliffe had written to Sir Edward Carson:

> At the risk of incurring your perpetual displeasure, I cannot refrain from again writing to you about the Dardanelles . . . . Ever since I saw you a few days ago I have had further news of fresh horrors . . . . It requires no imagination to realize that the Dardanelles tragedy, which the Australians and New Zealanders are determined to reveal to the world, will be for all time a theme of universal discussion.

Some eight weeks later on 12 December the successful evacuation of Gallipoli began; and at the Royal Commission that sat the following year, with Ashmead-Bartlett and Murdoch as key witnesses, it was concluded that the campaign had been a mistake – a mistake that had cost 252,000 casualties.

Churchill, meanwhile, had resigned his post on 11 November, and at a final appearance in the House of Commons four days later dealt in detail with his involvement in the Dardanelles campaign:

> I did not make a plan. Not a line, not a word, not a syllable that was produced by naval and expert brains have I combated with the slightest non-expert interference. But I have approved of the plan. I backed the plan, I was satisfied that in all the circumstances that were known to me, military, economic and diplomatic, it was a plan that ought to be tried, and tried then.

Within days, Churchill, now a major in the Oxfordshire Yeomanry, was on his way to the Western Front, and after meeting Sir John French at his headquarters was attached to the 2nd Grenadier Guards to gain experience of trench warfare.

Demise of The Standard

In December 1914, Arthur Steel-Maitland, Chairman of the Conservative Party, wrote to Bonar Law, his new leader, saying that it looked as if *The Standard* with the *Evening Standard* was coming to grief. He rated the *Evening Standard* a good property and the morning *Standard* a bad one. As Stephen Koss has written:

> Davison Dalziel had taken control of this dual concern in 1910, with a heavy investment from Sir Alexander Henderson. Since then, Henderson had been kept at arm's length and had grown very sore. Dalziel found himself 'in the strait', and his silent partner was disinclined to bail him out. Instead, Henderson had discussed the whole position with Steel-Maitland.[24]

Less than a week later, on 23 December, Steel-Maitland wrote once more to Bonar Law reaffirming the political need that the 'object is to keep the *Evening Standard* in your hands. The morning *Standard* can be dropped without loss'. He added that 'a good evening is a strength to a morning paper'. Lady Bathurst might be induced to publish the *Evening Standard* in tandem with the *Morning Post*. He believed that Gwynne should now put pressure on his proprietor, but not too strongly, otherwise she would 'tend to turn down anything'.

At this time, the circulation manager of *The Standard* and the *Evening Standard* was B. M. Hansard, who had recently joined from the *Daily Mail*, and he was to leave an interesting account of those days:[25]

> There was no hurry and no excitement. *The Standard* was very old, and as its readers died, so the circulation fell. It was dying fast. *The Evening Standard*, carrying the morning paper on its back, left the staff weary and worn. There was no life in the place and precious little money.
>
> We had two batteries of presses, one for the *Standard* and the other for the *Evening Standard*, and it was a nerve-wracking sound when the presses of *The Standard* started to revolve. It sounded like so much old iron whirling round in tin cans, and I thought that at any time, the presses might fall to pieces. Those of the *Evening Standard* were more modern and produced a very good sheet. A printing schedule did not exist – the papers went to press when the editorial department thought fit.
>
> I was in charge of what had been two of the greatest papers in London. My first attention was *The Standard*. I took it over with a very doubtful circulation of 40,000, with the *Evening Standard* about 45,000. At the end of the month, by concentrating on *The Standard*, I had increased its circulation by something like 5000 copies a day, but the *Evening Standard* had gone back.

Profits on the company had fallen from £29,000 in 1910 – the year Dalziel had taken over – to £12,000 in 1912. And advertising receipts for *The Standard* for the first six months of 1914 had been £52,298, but within a fortnight of the outbreak of the First World War had dropped from £2075 to £757 per week. Hansard, in recalling those days, was to write: 'The position of *The Standard* had become serious. Dalziel to help the financial landslide started the *Daily Call* as a competitor to the *Daily Mirror*. It had no hope or chance of success. It simply accelerated bankruptcy. Dalziel had divorced the *Evening Standard* from the parent company and had purloined it as his personal share of the wreck.'

Now, at Christmas 1914, Gwynne met Henderson, who expected to 'come into control of *The Standard* on New Year's Day, owing to Dalziel's default in the payment of debentures'. Following this, Gwynne spoke to Lady Bathurst and suggested that the morning *Standard* should be allowed to die but that the '*Evening Standard* which is a first class paying proposition should be taken over by you and run by you as an evening paper'.

Bonar Law, too, believed that there was merit in the proposal and he told Gwynne that 'he thought the idea worth considering and that he would be glad to talk it over with you or Lady Bathurst'. Henderson also had his reasons, the chief one being that he was afraid the newspapers might fall into the hands of Northcliffe. However, despite the efforts of Gwynne, Steel-Maitland, Henderson and other prominent Tories, Dalziel was to retain control of the titles until, in the late spring of 1915, Fleet Street was stunned to learn that Edward Hulton Jr had become involved.

The Man From Manchester

The son of Edward Hulton, he was educated at St Bede's College, Manchester, and left, aged sixteen, in 1885 to work in every department of the family firm. Edward Hulton Sr's story is one of the great romances of newspaper lore. He was the son of James Hulton, a self-employed tinplate worker, who owned a small foundry in the Ancoats area of Manchester.[26]

When Edward was aged only twelve, the foundry burned down and his father left, penniless, for America never to return. Now responsible for his mother and five sisters, young Ned sold newspapers on the street for 2*s.* 6*d*. per week, telling her that one day he would fill her apron with gold sovereigns. It was even said that if customers did not pay their paper bills he would dance in clogs outside their homes until the debts were paid.

From selling newspapers, he spent some years, as a youth, printing the contents bills of the *Manchester Guardian*. Always interested in horses and betting – he had even issued a racing sheet in his spare-time – in 1871, aged twenty-three, he joined forces with E.O. Beackley, a wealthy cotton broker, who had been impressed with Hulton's study of form. With Beackley's advance of £100, he bought a printing press, and from a cellar in Spear Street, Manchester, launched a four-page sheet called the *Prophetic Bell*, produced on a shoe-string. Hulton not only edited the paper but published his tips under the pseudonym of 'Kettledrum'. It quickly became a success among the working classes of Lancashire and within four years the *Prophetic Bell* had become the *Sporting Chronicle* – a paper which was to last for more than a century. The increasing interest taken by the public in cricket and football now decided Hulton to start a weekly paper devoted to amateur sport of all description. The new publication, *Athletic News*, was launched in 1875, and once more Hulton had gauged accurately the tastes of the public.

A decade later, and now an increasingly-important proprietor, he launched his biggest gamble, the *Sunday Chronicle*. That same year, 1885, Hulton took his son Edward away from school and set him to learn the newspaper business. Bernard Falk, later to be a legend in Fleet Street, has left a vivid account of those days:[27]

> Old man Hulton, after looking me shrewdly up and down his beard, decided that I would be a better recruit for the newly started *Evening Chronicle*. 'We are doing well with the *Sporting Chronicle*, the *Sunday Chronicle* and the *Athletic News*, but my boy Teddy says time has come for an "evening". He may be right and he may be wrong, but Teddy is a good boy. I suppose I shall have to give him £25,000 to play around with.'

The first issue of the *Evening Chronicle* appeared in May 1897 and despite strong opposition was soon firmly established. Following the success of their half-penny evening paper, towards the end of 1899 Hulton and his son started the *Daily*

Dispatch, a half-penny morning, which quickly won a place among the leading provincial newspapers. To service all his newspapers, he built a magnificent office at Withy Grove, Manchester, which for many years was to remain the largest printing complex in Britain. And from there more than five million newspapers were produced each week – a far cry from his early days, still remembered by some of his employees, when the only printing machine he owned was a single four-feeder and the distribution staff consisted of a man with a hand cart.

In 1904, Edward Hulton died, leaving an estate of £557,000 and the largest newspaper empire outside Fleet Street. There was, however an immediate family difference, and two of Edward junior's sisters, Aggie and Theresa, disagreeing with his lifestyle and its possible effect on the business, withdrew their support and money. He was fortunate, though, to retain the assistance of his two other sisters, Maggie and Mary.

With his papers all succesful, in 1905 Hulton took over *The Umpire*, for long the main rival to the *Sunday Chronicle*. Despite his new obligations as head of the family firm, Hulton continued to follow his main outside interests, horse racing and greyhound coursing, and in 1908 won the Waterloo Cup with his Hallow Eve, at odds of 1000 to 15.[28] Two years later, he registered his racing colours as H. Lytham, using an assumed name so that his mother would not hear of it.

Much influenced by Northcliffe's re-vamped *Daily Mirror*, in 1909 Hulton launched the *Daily Sketch*, an illustrated newspaper, from his Manchester offices, but within a few months he had moved it to the recently-vacated *Daily Express* building in Tudor Street, to the south of Fleet Streeet. There, under the editorship of James Heddle, the paper's picture coverage was excellent, and it secured outstanding reportage of the sinking of the *Titanic*, the suffragist tragedy at the Derby; and, later, some of the first pictures of the Irish Rebellion.

In 1912, Hulton built a modern office at the corner of Shoe Lane and Plum Tree Court, with the intention of keeping this plant running seven days a week. He therefore embarked on producing a London edition of his already successful *Sunday Chronicle*, but opposition from London composing chapels prevented this happening. The plan had been to send down some pages from Manchester in matrix form, thus saving the cost of a second setting, but the compositors demanded they should be paid for these pages. On 28 March 1915, therefore, Hulton launched *The Illustrated Sunday Herald*. Hulton was to say of the launch 'that apart from being an entirely new departure, it probably caters for a new set of readers'. Among its writers were Hilaire Belloc, H.G. Wells, Jerome K. Jerome and R. Blatchford.

Two months later, Hulton extended his empire when he purchased the *Evening Standard* from Davison Dalziel. It was noted that the change of ownership did not involve any disturbance in the staff. It was intended that the paper would still sell at a penny and, for the time being, would continue to be printed in its old home until plans had been finalised for a move higher up Shoe Lane.

William Colley has left an interesting account of the first moves by Hulton in taking over the paper:[29]

> One early morning while sitting alone in a large room engaged on the Notes and News column, there entered a smart, alert man wearing glasses. He had a Scottish accent and a pleasing voice . . . . Seeing I was unoccupied, after delivering my column, he said: 'You are Colley? I'm Heddle.' We shook hands. 'We are taking the *Evening Standard* over, you know, lock, stock and barrel . . . . The end of April or May at the latest.'

By the end of that summer, the *Evening Standard* was still being produced in the offices of its morning namesake, although there was now no connection between the two titles. It was noted that 'Messrs Hulton and Co., who bought it from Mr Dalziel for £50,000, are waiting for new machinery in order to print in their *Daily Sketch* offices. This delay means a bit of good fortune for *The Standard* and brings the proprietor a substantial sum per week.' The final move to the new premises came at five o'clock on a Saturday afternoon, and by the following Monday the staff were in their new premises. There they joined their colleagues on the other Hulton newspapers: *Daily Dispatch*, *Illustrated Sunday Herald* and *Daily Sketch*. Hulton believed that when he purchased the *Evening Standard* from Dalziel it had been handicapped for some time by the serious financial position of the morning *Standard*. He considered that with extra expenditure on the editorial and production sides the paper could respond and he hoped that 'an evening of the highest class may be established and maintained'.

Meanwhile, conditions at *The Standard*, still owned by Dalziel, continued to deteriorate. A change in format was ordered, and its pages were cut to a 'more convenient size': 'It was as if *The Times* came out suddenly, the size of *Answers*. The paper lost in a night the look of authority and the atmosphere of high responsibility.' It continued to exist during 1916, but gradually staff left and were not replaced.[30]

> The year 1916 had turned. On many nights the staff of *The Standard* assembled not knowing whether the paper would be published tomorrow or not. They waited about until Thompson, the editorial chief, had been to the City to endeavour to obtain money to carry on another day. For the staff, the position was dreadful: for *The Standard* tragic. Thompson was a hero, but, alas, he failed. On my visits from the *Evening Standard* I saw the empty rooms and many vacant chairs. Life slowly ebbed. A sort of newspaper continued until the early months had passed, when suddenly, although it had been expected, the long history of *The Standard* ended.

On 16 February 1916 *The Times* announced that *The Standard* was to be sold by auction: 'Notice is given in our advertisement columns that, by order of the Court, the goodwill and copyright of *The Standard* newspaper will be offered for sale by public auction by Messrs. Walter Phelps and Son at Anderton's Hotel, Fleet Street, at 3 o'clock on February 23.' History was about to repeat itself; for the second time in less than seventy-five years the paper was to be sold, but this time there was to be no James Johnstone to act as a last-minute saviour.

The auction was to prove a failure, with only one bid of £100 – later increased to £200 – for the copyright of the paper. With the improved figure deemed unacceptable, the lot was withdrawn, the auctioneer stating that the vendor would now be prepared to deal privately with any intending purchasers. However, despite the lack of interest at the auction, *The Standard* managed to struggle on for a further three weeks, thanks to the efforts of a group of Welsh businesssmen. The head of one of Cardiff's largest fleet of steamers, W.J. Tatem, then undertook to find funds for a short period, but with costs running in excess of £1000 per week he was unable to find other backers to support him.

On 17 March, *The Times* announced as its lead on page 5:[31]

THE STANDARD PUBLICATION SUSPENDED
AN HONOURABLE CAREER

> *The Standard* newspaper has suspended publication, but we are asked to state that the necessary steps have been taken to preserve its copyright. The disappearance of this old-established newspaper will be regretted, not only by the world of journalism, but by a wide circle of readers of newspapers. For several years *The Standard* had been struggling against troubled waters. High hopes were raised two years ago when the paper was altered in size and form and seemed for a while to thrive, but these hopes were finally destroyed when the newspaper's goodwill, copyright and plant were put up for auction three weeks ago and failed to draw anything like a satisfactory offer.

A graphic account of *The Standard*'s last hours was to be given by J. Maynard Saunders, night editor, in the 1 April 1916 issue of *Newspaper World*:[32]

> It was ten p.m. The paper had been dead fifteen minutes. The editor had bidden his farewells, and the staff – editorial, sub-editorial and printing – had been dismissed. But all through the evening work had gone on in every department for the possible production of the paper next day; the copy prepared and headlined had been dispatched to the composing room in readiness for the word that should set the machinery in motion. But instead of the 'carry on' there came the 'dismiss'. Yet so hard was the realization thereof, that a quarter of an hour after the departure of the last compositor the head printer came to the night editor, who was clearing his desk, to ask: 'I suppose all that copy on my desk is no good now?' To him there came the sad reply, 'No, it's all cancelled matter now.'
>
> The paper had existed for nigh on one hundred years – a power at home and abroad. The night editor himself had survived two changes in the proprietory and three editors and this was the end. But none had cause to be ashamed on the matter of their death. They formed but one of the many business casualties in journalism owing to the war. For four nights the staff had come in on the sporting chance that there would be a paper on the morrow. On three the morrow had seen the old journal appear. But the strain had been great. On one of the nights the 'line' was not on until 8.45 instead of at 5.30 owing to the uncertainty of the outlook; on another night – the agony was prolonged to a quarter to ten. Then it was that the strain became well night intolerable, for the question arose: Could the paper then be produced in time to catch the trains?
>
> Up to that hour was shown, in all its wonderful efficiency, the rigid discipline of a newspaper office. Everything revolved except the wheels of the composing machines – the Parliamentary sketch writer sent up his sketch – it was to be received, sub-edited and sent to the composing room; so with the the notes of the Lobby correspondent; the Parliamentary report came in and as it arrived it was dealt with and cut to the space which had been alloted to Parliament at the editorial conference in the afternoon.

> The editor was available for consultations; the leader writers had their subjects and only waited the word to begin. In one of the theatres the paper's representative was making notes of an important new play of which he was to write a notice – for the morrow's paper. He, poor innocent, ventured between the acts to telephone to the office for the latest news of the internal situation. The night editor, anxious to relieve the strain he dare not show before the staff, bade him sharply to have his copy prepared, paper or no paper, or stand the consequences the next day.
>
> Even the messenger boys, under the compelling eye of the head messenger – a man of forty years' experience – did not dare question the futility of their half-hourly pilgrimage with copy to a composing room which was in idleness and semi-darkness. Then came a summons to the night editor to attend his editor, who, in words husky by emotion, declared that the fight was over and there would be no paper on the morrow. He was bidden to tell the staff and to say that the editor would take his farewell of the printers and then of the sub-editors.
>
> Later, standing at the printer's desk, with the printers forming a dense semi-circle before him, in the semi-glow of lowered lights, the editor told of the efforts which he and others had made to carry on the paper and how their efforts had come to naught, and of the great sorrow for the older members of the staff. It was a very manly and moving speech. Then spoke the Father of the Chapel, who, on behalf of the printers, bore testimony to the excellent relations which had always existed between that department and the heads of the office. He was followed by the chief stone hand – a man of 41 years' service on the paper.
>
> Thus ended a sad and historic evening in the newspaper world. It is doubtful if more than one other journal in London can show such records of service among its staff, for there passed out of Fleet Street that night men who had found their daily occupation on the paper for sixty, fifty, forty and thirty years.

As for Dalziel, for the remainder of his life he was to be closely connected with the International Sleeping Car Company. Created a baronet in 1919, he was raised to the peerage in 1927, and when he died the following year he left £2,199,220. William Colley was to write: 'That Shoe Lane [*The Standard*'s headquarters] had caused him anxiety and financial loss I have no doubt, but his wider domain of business stood him well and he passed away with a "seven-figure fortune". His gratitude to all who did him the smallest service was ever in evidence.'

10

Brothers from Wales

WHILE *THE STANDARD* had struggled for months before finally ceasing, there had been much activity on *The Sunday Times*, and on 6 June 1915 a one-inch down-page paragraph in the paper announced that 'The controlling interest in *The Sunday Times* has been acquired by W.E. and J. Gomer Berry, of the firm of Ewart, Seymour and Co. Limited, Windsor House, Kingsway W.C., publishers.'

The new owners were two Welsh-born brothers. William, born in Merthyr Tydfil, was one of three brothers, each of whom was to become a peer: Seymour, the eldest, who became Lord Buckland, was an industrialist with large interests in steel mills and collieries, and died as a result of a riding accident in 1928; while Gomer, like William, was to become a Press magnate. William Berry himself had entered journalism, aged fourteen, after an essay he had written had been praised by William Hadley, editor of the *Merthyr Express*. 'The boy must become a journalist,' Hadley proclaimed, and soon took him on as an apprentice for four years.

Upon becoming a journeyman, William, now aged eighteen, went to London to work on the *Investors Guardian* at thirty-five shillings a week,[1] and within days was covering the annual meeting in 1898 of Harmsworth Brothers, owners of magazines. And so impressed was Alfred Harmsworth of the coverage that he offered him a job. William declined but was suddenly sacked 'over a difference of opinion'. Concealing the fact from his family in Wales, he was out of work for four months before becoming a reporter with the Commercial Press Association.

However, seeing a gap in the market – and with the loan of £100 from his elder brother – he launched the weekly *Advertising World*, most of which he was at first to write himself, as well as selling the advertisements and laying out the pages. From a shared third-floor office in Fleet Street he was working sixteen hours a day; and with the paper making a small profit he brought his younger brother, Gomer, aged sixteen, from the Merthyr home; and while William concentrated on the editorial Gomer devoted himself to the advertising and business management.

David Linton, archivist of The History of Advertising Trust, was later to tell the author: 'The strength of the *Advertising World* over both its independent contemporaries lay in its all-round coverage; agencies as well as advertising, news of personalities as well as businesses – hence a focus for the burgeoning social side, and prestige of advertising.'[2]

By December 1902, the *Advertising World*, with a ninety-two page issue, was in profit; and in the following spring a new member of staff was engaged, Edward Hart, the young nephew of the magazine's printer. And he was to leave a vivid account of those early days:

> It was Bill Berry who engaged me. We had dined overnight with my uncle. In his office the next morning Bill took me by the arm and said: 'Now we'll go along and see my young brother Gomer. You'll be working mostly with him.' Bill, by the way, was shamelessly Bohemian in dress. A double-breasted blue serge suit hung from him like a sack. But Gomer, the 'outside' man, was a stickler for appearance.
>
> My first impression of him is that he had his brother's blue-black hair, strong white teeth and the pallid complexion and lilting accent of the Rhondda Valley mining town they had so recently left to seek their fortunes in Fleet Street. Gomer, to appear older, had begun to cultivate a moustache. He was faultlessly attired in the mode of AD 1903; black frock-coat, narrow white vest-slip, high stand-up collar, immaculate cuffs (detachable), neat tie-pin. His buttoned patent-leather boots, I learned later, cost 10s 6d. He got them from an American chain store which polished them free at any of its branches. That was the price, too, of his glossy topper – ironed free at any of the Cuthbertson branches. Gloves and umbrella, of course, and a blue melton overcoat with black velvet collar.
>
> I recall that as we entered his little sparsely furnished office he rose from behind the cheap table that served as desk, shook hands and offered his brand-new silver cigarette case. Both brothers were chain smokers. They favoured Gold Flake at 5d for twenty.

On 11 September 1909 the Berry brothers launched *Boxing*, which was to be an immediate success; and from an initial print figure of 100,000 soon reached more than 250,000 copies per week. And in the first issue they could declaim: 'For a long time boxing journalism was regarded as little removed from gutter journalism and it was with recognition of this fact that we ventured to issue the paper. Gt. Britain needs MEN, will always need MEN, and we know that the best nursery in which men can be cultivated is the boxing ring.'

Two years later, in December 1911, the brothers sold *Advertising World* for £11,000 to a syndicate led by J.A. Ackerman, a future associate general manager of *The Times*. For the next few years, *Boxing* plus the ownership of *Health & Strength* and the *Penny Illustrated Paper* was to keep the brothers busy – and profitable.

One day early in 1915, through his boxing contacts, William Berry was lunching with fight promoter James White at the National Liberal Club, when they were approached by West de Wend Fenton, owner of the *Sporting Life*, who said that he had an option to buy *The Sunday Times* and was Berry interested?[3] After protracted negotiations with the principals, who included Sir Leander Starr Jameson; Sir Basil Zaharoff, the armaments 'king'; and Sir Arthur Steel-Maitland, chairman of the Conservative Party; the Berry brothers, in the face of strong opposition, were able to purchase the paper for £80,000, most of which they had to borrow; and with a circulation of just 30,000 – some 170,000 behind Garvin's *Observer* – they were to face a difficult task.

With just a small editorial staff, William Berry was to be heavily involved, and his early days as owner of *The Sunday Times* were to be described by his son, the future Lord Hartwell:[4]

> Though he had titled himself Managing editor, [he] acted as chief sub-editor on Saturdays. All his life he saw sub-editing as the key role on a newspaper – the task of evaluating (copy-tasting), checking, arrangement, allocation of stories to particular pages; the power to see the possibilities in the seemingly dull, to develop them or have them developed; to downgrade and condense as more important items came in; to discard the woolly; to tell a story in arresting sequence; to signpost in cunningly worded headings in pleasantly contrasting types.

Daily Chronicle *Sold*

Within two years of purchasing *The Sunday Times*, the Berrys were to be involved in discussions to take over the leading Liberal paper – the *Daily Chronicle*. However, there were to be problems.

The man at the centre of these problems was Sir Robert Donald, editor of the paper for more than twenty years. Earlier described by Northcliffe as 'a first-class reporter, as accurate as a stop watch', as an editor he believed that his role should not be that of a 'writing editor', rather that he should delegate and plan the contents of the paper and its future policy. After a few years in charge, Donald was asked to accept the added responsibility of editing the Sunday paper, *Lloyd's Weekly News*, as well as the managing directorship of the group's United Newspapers Ltd, with complete editorial responsibility, subject to following Liberal policy.

Very much a social person, Donald made a point of making contact with all the leading politicians and businessmen, and was a regular at fashionable functions. Nevertheless, he was invariably back in the office before midnight to pass proofs of the main editions before they went to press. He was also very much an innovator, and for the 1906 General Election had screens erected in the Aldwych and Fleet Street, which conveyed the latest results to the waiting thousands. And for readers who requested the service, each received a personal telegram giving the result of any constituency as soon as the news had been received in the *Chronicle* office.

A far-seeing person, in 1913 Donald was to address the Institute of Journalists on the future of wireless news: 'People may become too lazy to read, and news will be laid on to house or office, just as gas and water are now. The occupiers will listen to an account of the news of the day, read to them by much improved phonographs while sitting in the garden.'

The following year, the *Daily Chronicle* was at its peak, moving into a new building with increased production facilities. However, much of the new press-room capacity was not then needed, for the coming of the First World War meant that pagination had to be restricted from twelve to four pages.[5]

Politically, Donald and Lloyd George, now Prime Minister, had always been close, and in 1917 on the editor's recommendation Lloyd George created the Department (in 1918, the Ministry) of Information with Donald as Director. Once the department had been set up and running successfully, Donald withdrew, but that same year a rift grew between the two men. Donald had appointed General Sir Frederick Maurice, the recent Director of Operations at the War Office, as his military correspondent, and his remarks in a letter to *The Times* accusing the Prime Minister of lying about Britain's military strength incensed Lloyd George. And within weeks, Donald had published an editorial praising the British commander-in-chief, 'Well done, Haig!' This, too, brought down the Premier's wrath.

On 11 May, Sir George Riddell, vice-chairman of the Newspaper Proprietors Association, met with Lloyd George, who complained of Donald's behaviour:[6]

> He asked if I knew the reason. I said there were four possible: (1) That he is endeavouring to procure from the Liberal Party money to purchase the *Daily Chronicle*; (2) That he is anxious to obtain a Privy Councillorship and thinks the best method is by attacking LG; (3) That he is actuated by vanity. He thinks that he brought down the last Government by a ratting article which he published and which was repeated by the *Westminster Gazette*, and he may be anxious to repeat his exploit; (4) He may be actuated by personal pique because LG has choked him off calling and telephoning on Sunday.

Lloyd George answered: 'He is an unreliable fellow and a vain creature whose vanity is always likely to lead him astray.'

Lord Beaverbrook (Max Aitken had been ennobled in 1916) was now intent on putting together a syndicate to buy the *Chronicle*, and for this he would assume control, plus £20,000 commission – but would guarantee that the paper would support Lloyd George for five years. Among those whom he had approached were the Berry brothers, who, if they were to be involved, sought 'complete commercial control'. Liberal MP Sir Henry Dalziel, owner of the *Pall Mall Gazette* and *Reynolds News*, and a keen supporter of Lloyd George, was also expressing an interest in leading a syndicate.

But there was to be a proviso, as F.E. Guest, the Coalition Liberal Chief Whip, was to write: 'One last matter . . . . the Berrys have an opportunity of selling *The Sunday Times* – to Max Aitken – [for £200,000]. I have agreed with them that they shall *not* do this until our deal is through. This leverage is very important as Max can help or hinder us greatly, though indirectly.' There was to be no deal; and many years later William Berry [now Lord Camrose] was to write: '*The Sunday Express* saw the light of day in 1918 after abortive negotiations between Lord Beaverbrook and myself, whereby *The Sunday Times* might have passed into his ownership.'

Discussions Continue

Meanwhile back in 1917 there had been further discussions between the Prime Minister and Riddell on 23 June; and later that evening, in a long entry in his diary, Riddell noted the day's events:[7]

> We talked of the *Daily Chronicle*. Donald asked me to call upon him today, which I did. He told me an interesting story, casting a curious light on the ways of politicians and journalists. Some months ago, Guest, with Donald's connivance, approached Lloyd, the chief owner of the *Chronicle*, with a view to purchase. The name of the purchaser was

> given as Lord Leverhulme, who was to be associated with two or three other supporters of Lloyd George. Later, Donald discovered that Beaverbrook was the real purchaser and that Leverhulme's name had been used without his sanction. Thereupon, Lloyd broke off the negotiations. The price was to have been £450,000 (the existing debentures and preference shares) plus £900,000 for the ordinary shares, making in all £1,350,000, but the tangible assets were to be valued at £750,000. However, Lloyd declined to see Beaverbrook under any circumstances.
>
> Donald continued: 'I don't quite know how far LG was involved in all this, but there is no doubt that he was in the scheme and that he was plotting to hand over the *Daily Chronicle* to Beaverbrook, who is a very dangerous man calculated to do LG serious injury. That is why I am unfriendly to LG. That is why I attack him in the DC. I can do what I like with the paper. Mr Lloyd never interferes.'

Armed with this information, Lloyd George reiterated that he was still determined that Donald should be got rid of, adding that he placed no reliance on the editor. For Riddell, though, the main threat appeared to come from Beaverbook:

> [He] is a dangerous fellow. He is consumed with ambition and is seeking to secure domination over *the* Press. He is very close with Rothermere and on friendly terms with Northcliffe. He is busy cultivating Hulton, he owns the *Express*, he is trying, as Minister of Information, to ingratiate himself with the colonial Press whom he has invited to a conference, and if he could get control of the *Chronicle* he would be one of the most powerful men in the Kingdom.

Agreeing, Lloyd George believed that Beaverbrook wished to be the power behind the throne and pull the strings. The Prime Minister then had some comments in general about the Press: 'I admit that the combination you describe would be uncomfortable, but I don't believe that the newspapers have the power they think they possess. A prominent man can always defend himself and often put the newspapers in the wrong.'

There was to be further dialogue between Lloyd George and Riddell on September 4, when the Prime Minister told him that Frank Lloyd now wished to sell the *Daily Chronicle* for £1,100,000. 'The profits are about £200,000 p.a., of which £130,000 is payable in excess profits duty. It seems that Sir Henry Dalziel now has an option until October 1 . . . . . To return to Beaverbrook, one ground of complaint is that LG has excluded him from the *Chronicle* deal.'

Less than a month later, as planned, on 1 October 1918, Lloyd George gained 'full control of the editorial policy through Sir Henry Dalziel, who will in effect be his agent'. Donald, who had previously nurtured ideas of owning the *Chronicle*, immediately resigned. Frank Lloyd, his recent proprietor, was to write: 'Throughout the twenty years there has never arisen a shadow of shade between us, and I shall carry to the grave the memory of your loyal support and friendship.'

Donald's forced leaving, plus the the underhand purchase of the *Chronicle*, led to a wave of indignation. *The New York Times* could say: 'No British editor in recent times had so wide a respect from leaders in the various fields of thought and action.'[8] At a lunch given in his honour, H.A. Gwynne, editor of the *Morning Post*, declared: 'Mr Donald and I have never seen eye to eye on any great question of politics, but I have never yet met a man in journalism for whom I have had a greater respect.' J.A. Spender was to agree: 'We may only express our hope that in like circumstances we may be able to follow his example.'

Despite his disappointment at losing the *Chronicle*, for Donald there was to be reward seven years later when he was made a Knight Grand Cross of the British Empire for his work in setting up wireless stations throughout the Empire. During the 1920s he had also helped to organize the British Empire Exhibition at Wembley in 1923 and had been a much-travelled chairman of the Empire Press Union. He never attained another national editorship, but was involved with directorships of various provincial newspapers. He died in 1933 and at his memorial service at St Bride's Church, Fleet Street, his one-time colleague, E.A. Perris, could say of him: 'He was a just man, a considerate man, and a born leader. I never knew him weaken in his principles or fail those who worked for him and loved him.'

For the Berry brothers, there was to be consolation when early in 1919 they bought the *Financier and Bullionist*, the smallest of the financial papers. This, however, was to be exceeded in the November when they purchased the *Financial Times*, the market leader, from shipping magnate Sir John Ellerman. An added advantage of buying the *Financial Times* was that the deal brought with it the St Clement's Press, printers of *The Sunday Times*. 'Now in charge of the *FT*, William Berry became chairman, Gomer Berry, vice-chairman, and for the day-to-day running of the paper they brought in the experienced R.J. Barrett as managing director and managing editor, though C.H. Palmer remained acting editor.'[9]

A week later, the *Daily Graphic*, the oldest daily picture paper, with a sale of 80,000 was bought – along with the weekly *Graphic* and the *Bystander*. This sudden surge in newspaper ownership was to lead Northcliffe to remark: 'I enquired about the Berrys. They are quite respectable.' And to Wareham Smith, his advertisement director, the Chief was to remark: 'I hope these Berry people are all right. I admire them but they have not the experience of running a group of newspapers. It is a fearful strain.'

Rewards for the Proprietors

One aspect of the First World War had been the links between newspaper proprietors and the Government; and, following the resignation of Asquith on 6 December 1916, an early task of Lloyd George as Prime Minister had been to invite Northcliffe to join the Cabinet. Northcliffe's reaction was typical: 'Ah-h, wouldn't they like to get me out of Fleet Street! It would ease the pressure on their papers. Would not they like it? I prefer to sit in Printing House Square and Carmelite House.'

Meanwhile his newspapers continued their attacks on Germany – attacks which were bring forth retaliation, when on 25 February 1917 a German destroyer shelled his home at Elmwood on the Kent coast near Broadstairs. Northcliffe was to have a narrow escape, as he reported to his staff at the *Mail*:[10]

> [At] 11.30 my house was lit up by some 20 star shells from the sea, so that the place was illuminated as if by lightning. Shrapnel burst all over the place, some of it hitting the

> Library in which these notes are prepared every day, and killing a poor woman and baby within 50 yards of my home and badly wounding two others . . . . the Authorities have no doubt that my house was aimed at and the shooting was by no means bad. I understand that the destroyer was three miles out.

Four months later – following a 'reconciliation' with Lloyd George – Northcliffe was on his way to the United States as head of the British War Mission, arriving in June, and 'went through the great heat wave of July and August of that year. His activities can hardly be measured in words. I myself [Lloyd George] attribute the illness from which he suffered upon his return to the tremendous demands upon his energies during these strenuous months upon the other side'.

Northcliffe was to declare: 'I am in America because I have been a continual eye-witness at the War on its various fronts, at the War behind the battle line, and in . . . . the most serious part of the War, the home front, the war with politicians. I am here because I want to tell Americans something of the many blunders we made.'

Now described by Americans as 'the most important man in England', he remained there until the November, and on his return to London was delighted when made a viscount by the King and to receive 'in glowing terms the thanks and congratulations of the Cabinet'.

Anxious to use the services of Northcliffe once more, Lloyd George now proposed that he should join the Government as first Air Minister. On 15 November Northcliffe declined, saying: 'I can do better work if I maintain my independence and am not gagged by a loyalty that I do not feel towards the whole of your Administration.' Early in 1918, though, the Prime Minister was to be successful when Northcliffe accepted the role of Director of Propaganda against Enemy Countries, working from Crewe House, London – described by the Germans as the 'Poison Gas Factory' with Northcliffe as the 'King of Lies'.

Later, Northcliffe was to meet up with his old friend, Blumenfeld, at Crewe House, during the seven months when he was in charge. Blumenfeld was to recall:[11]

> I had not seen him for many months. The change in the man was too great to be unnoticed. There was a look about him which showed the effects of adulation in America, the never-ceasing floods of flattery, the stories of how he had forced Asquith out and Lloyd George in, the David who had defeated the Goliath Kitchener in the shell-shortage scandal; and the thousand and one pleasant-hearing tales of his public courage, his incorruptibility, his sense of duty and his complete sacrifice to the war – all had been ladled out to him with the inevitable effect of causing him to believe that it was all true and that he was the sole instrument appointed to bring glory to his country and its cause.

For Northcliffe, there was just one more task he wished to undertake: to be an official delegate at the Peace Conference to be held in Paris. But for Lloyd George the answer was a blunt 'No'. Ten years later, Lloyd George was to reveal the background:[12]

> He came to think he was indispensable for the settling up of the peace at least. That was a malignant idea for any man to get, and, as with others before him, this conviction of his indispensability destroyed the balance of Northcliffe's judgment. I had put up with him

for four years. It had to come – the row – when he wanted to dictate to me. One could not allow him to dominate the Prime Minister. Northcliffe told me he was going to Paris for the Peace Conference, and suggested that he should be put on the Peace Delegation. I told him there had been some misunderstanding, and that there could be no official position for him on the delegation. He had obviously expected otherwise and he flared up at me like Vesuvias in eruption. He was in a terrible temper, so I just had to tell him to 'Go to hell!' That's how I broke with Northcliffe.

His brother, Harold, too, had played an important role in the war: he became director-general of the Royal Army Clothing Department in 1916 and the following year was appointed Air Minister. As such he was charged with amalgamating the Royal Flying Corps and the Royal Naval Air Service. This was duly achieved on 1 January 1918. The war, though, had been a bitter experience for him, as two of his sons lost their lives. Harold Harmsworth was created a viscount in 1919 and resumed his interest in newspapers.

Another Press baron with strong political links was Max Aitken, who for his 'wartime services to Canada' had in 1916 received a baronetcy; and later that year, in the December, the resignation of Asquith had led to Lloyd George assuming office. Having been used by Lloyd George to secure the Premiership, Aitken was confident that he would secure a post in the new administration, probably as President of the Board of trade.

However, on 9 December Lloyd George wrote to Aitken offering a peerage: 'There are two or three important business departments which have no representatives in the House of Lords and therefore no spokesmen. Would you allow me to recommend your name to the King for a Peerage. You could answer for these departments in the H.L.' By return, Aitken replied: 'My dear Prime Minister, I am grateful to you for your offer and I shall be glad if I can be of any help to you in the way you indicate.' That same day, Bonar Law added his thoughts: 'My dear Max, I hope you will accept L.G.'s offer, Yrs. A.B.L.'

Not everyone, however, was pleased at the news, and one of the severest critics was George V, who did not 'see his way' to approve since he did not consider that the 'public services of Sir Max Aitken called for such special recognition'. Practising journalists were strong in their opposition to the new peer, and Leo Maxse, in writing to Bonar Law, noted:[13]

We are all terrified of having men like Max Aitken . . . . thrust upon us. Gwynne also had grave misgivings, as he said to Edward Goulding: 'I didn't make any comment about Aitken's Peerage in the *Morning Post* because I did not want to foul the nest of the new Govt. Just when they were starting. I'm not sure I've done right.'

Nevertheless, despite these criticisms, Aitken was ennobled, mainly due to Lloyd George's insistence. He had informed Lord Stamfordham, the King's private secretary, that any refusal would 'place him in a position of great embarrassment' and asked him to discuss the matter with Bonar Law, as the announcement had already been made unofficially. A reluctant King George gave way, but insisted that any future honours should not be offered until he had been informally consulted.

On 18 December 1916, in the visitors' book at his Cherkley country home, there appeared the following entry: 'Beaverbrook formerly W.M. Aitken'. The small boy from Maple, Ontario, had finally arrived .... For Fleet Street's latest Press baron the time had come to take stock of his new property, and for Beaverbrook, seemingly no longer required to act as a political go-between, the first task was to purchase a thousand tons of newsprint from Northcliffe at favourable terms.

Beaverbrook was later to write: 'I claim to have become a full-blooded journalist just before the general election of 1918.' Earlier that year, on 10 February 1918, Lloyd George invited Beaverbrook to become Minister of Information. As such, he made a great feature of inviting the editors of newspapers in the Dominions and in neutral countries to visit Britain: 'But no editor in the world was satisfied to leave England unless he could say that he seen Mr Lloyd George.'

Despite criticism in a House of Commons debate on 5 August when propaganda was discussed, Beaverbrook remained in office until 21 October when he resigned his post through ill-health – and was immediately operated on for a glandular swelling on the neck.

Free of office, Beaverbrook could once more turn his energies to the *Daily Express*. Bonar Law, though, suggested that he should remain in politics or, if he must, run an official Tory newspaper. 'No. In politics I am bound – for no man can really be a politician without submitting to the necessary trammels of the party,' Beaverbrook replied, 'In the Press, on the contrary, I am free and can work from the outside .... I never mean to hold a public office again except during a period of war.'

Launching the Sunday Express

On 29 December 1918 Lady Diana Manners (later Lady Diana Cooper) started the presses for the first issue of the *Sunday Express*.[14] Despite assurances by Blumenfeld that the new paper would cost only a few thousand pounds to launch, this figure was to prove woefully inaccurate; in the first two years it cost Beaverbrook almost £500,000, and he was to spend another £2,000,000 before it moved into profit.

Although Blumenfeld edited the first issue, he did not see working seven nights a week as his role. A succession of top editorial people were then engaged to direct the paper, but none lasted for long. Beaverbrook later wrote: 'The corpses of *Sunday Express* editors were spread up and down Fleet Street in every direction.' For a short time he even edited the paper himself, but found the constant conferences and planning too restrictive; and it was not until John Gordon, a dour Scotsman from Dundee, took charge that the *Sunday Express* began to establish its own identity.

Unlike most Press barons, who preferred to remain anonymous, Beaverbrook used his new paper as a platform to expound his views. In 1921 he wrote twenty-five articles; in 1922 thirty-five articles; in 1923 twenty-four articles; and in 1925 ten articles. Talking of those early years, he was later to say: 'I sometimes used to go out into my garden and shake myself like a dog .... I always wrote off the very considerable sums I had invested in, or advanced to the *Sunday Express* as a potential total loss.'[15]

Meanwhile, because of an unparalleled run of luck with its racing tips, the circulation of the *Daily Express* had begun to rise dramatically; and in the month of June 1920 sales soared from 530,000 to 701,000. But because of the heavy involvement of the racing fraternity, many regular readers were unable to obtain their copies, and it was almost with a sigh of relief that the paper's luck ran out with the horses, and by the year's end the circulation was able to settle down at 550,000 copies per day.

The previous four years had seen a hard battle to raise the paper's figures from 350,000 to 550,000, but the growth in sales had caused a consequent pressure on advertising space. Despite the pleas to put advertising on page one, Beaverbrook would have none of it. He was to be proved correct in his decision, for the more dramatic presentation of news on the front page was now helping to push the circulation over the 600,000 mark. Demand continued to soar, and by August 1922 , with sales of 942,591, certain restrictions had to be put into force. Beaverbrook was to comment:

> It may seem astonishing that a newspaper should be compelled to check its production, but let any man consider the practical proposition. The publication of every additional copy involved us in a loss. It compelled expensive arrangements for extra printing facilities outside our own office, and for handling and despatching the newspaper. It was necessary to start printing in our own office and to close the formes of type against extra late copy hours before the proper time. In spite of precautions the *Daily Express* was frequently late for delivery to the newsagents. Then came a further difficulty. By November 1922, it had become absolutely necessary to produce a sixteen-page newspaper. The growth in the sales had increased the demand for advertisement space, and this in turn created a further need for news space.
>
> But the consequence was to magnify the difficulties of producing the number of copies the public wanted. For the production of a sixteen instead of a twelve-page paper slowed down the rate at which several of the printing presses could turn out their sheets by nearly 50 per cent. It became necessary to ration the output of the *Daily Express*. I remember that in one single evening we took a decision which cut down the numbers of an issue by 30,000 copies – and this out of sheer necessity.[16]

Labour Problems

Meanwhile at the *Daily Mail* there was increasing concern with Northcliffe's health: he was becoming more and more subject to megalomania. In 1921 he went on a round-the-world tour; and a series of articles which he wrote were republished as *My Journey Round the World* the following year. His symptoms had been apparent on the first leg of the journey: 'while crossing the Atlantic aboard the *Aquitania* he ordered the *Mail* to print the menus of all its dining rooms every day'.

In March 1922, Northcliffe, with Sir George Sutton, one of his most senior executives, travelled to Pau among the French Pyrenees for a short holiday, but it was soon to be interrupted by a telegram from his brother, Harold, Viscount Rothermere, which gave details of an impending dispute with production staff over wage demands. To Northcliffe, who had always been a benevolent proprietor, this was anathema, saying 'that if they tried to dictate how he should run his business, he would fight them'. He added: 'But I am not likely to join combinations of rich men

Hawker

Boswell and Dr Johnson

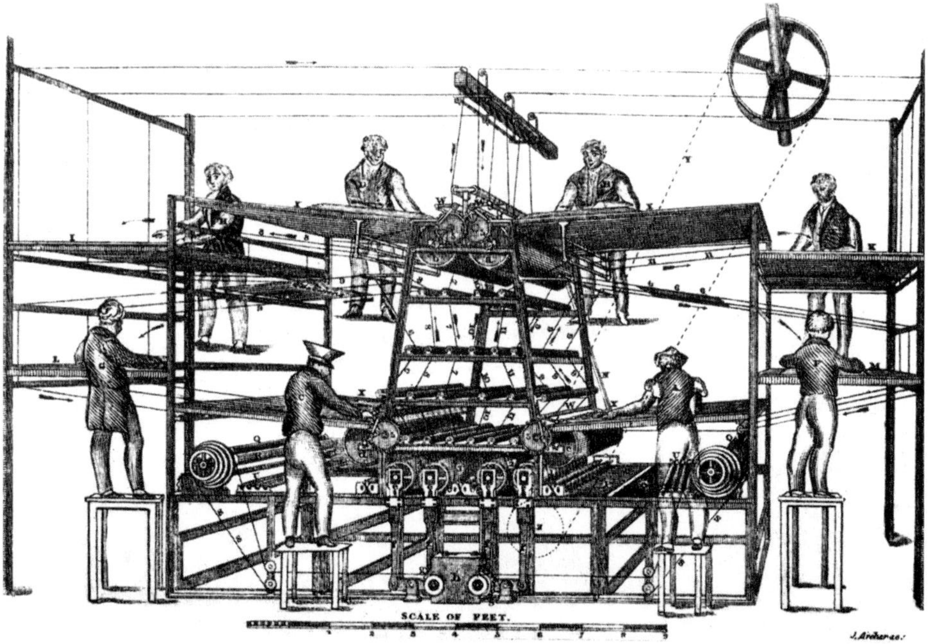

The Times printing press

J. Wilkes

Thomas Barnes

J. Delane

Rachel Beer

Sub-editors' room, *The Times*

Inside *The Times* publishing

Fleet Street, 1896

Northcliffe

J.L. Garvin

E. Hulton snr

Viscount Camrose

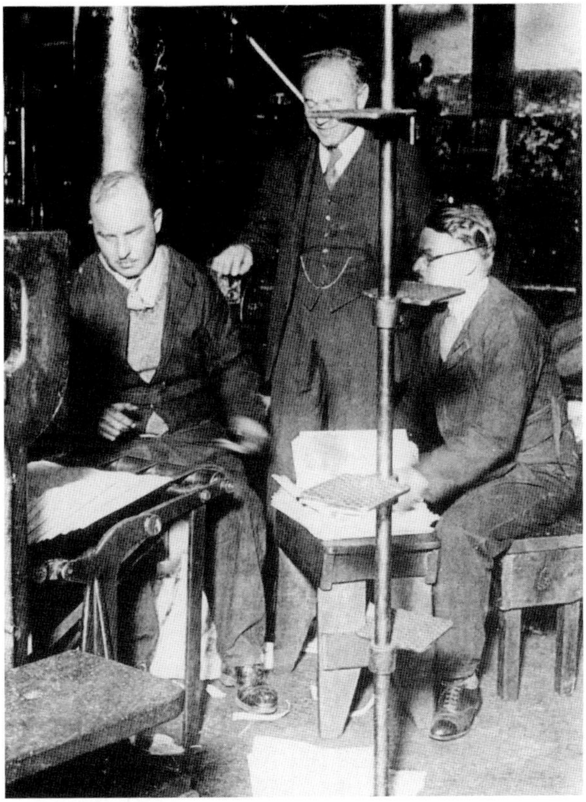

Beverley Baxter and Beaverbrook in the *Sunday Express* pressroom during the General Strike, 1926

The Times special edition

Prime Minister Ramsay MacDonald starts *Daily Herald* presses

for grinding down poor men.' Here he was referring to the new Fleet Street proprietors who were not journalists like himself – 'but who regarded newspapers as an extension of the commodity markets'. In one of his favourite phrases, he described them as 'Monsters of the Fleet Street deep'.

Nevertheless, on Saturday, 25 March, Northcliffe, still at Pau, sent a telegram to Viscount Burnham, chairman of the Newspaper Proprietors Association:[17]

> HAVE SENT FOLLOWING TO ISAACS BEGINS AM INFORMED RIGHTLY OR WRONGLY THAT YOU HAVE GIVEN IMPRESSION THAT I AM IN FAVOUR OF INCREASES IN WAGES OF MEMBERS OF NEWSPAPER UNIONS AS OPPOSED TO MOVEMENT FOR REDUCTIONS FULL STOP WHAT I SAID TO YOU IS WHAT I SAID TO FATHERS OF FEDERATED CHAPELS AT CARMELITE HOUSE THAT QUOTE NO INCREASES IN WAGES OR CHANGES IN CONDITIONS WOULD TAKE PLACE AT PRESENT UNQUOTE FULL STOP I SHOULD OPPOSE ANY SCHEME FOR UNJUST INCREASES AS VIGOROUSLY AS I FOUGHT THE RECENT STRIKE IN DAILY MAIL OFFICE INTO THE DEVELOPMENTS AND RESULTS OF WHICH YOUR MEMBERS IN THEIR OWN INTERESTS SHOULD I SUGGEST MAKE INQUIRY FULL STOP AM COMMUNICATING THIS MESSAGE TO MY STAFF AND OTHERS CONCERNED NORTHCLIFFE ENDS = HOTEL GASS ON PAU =

To quote Pound and Harmsworth once more:

> His attitude to labour relations had become that of an autocrat whose benevolence of intention was too often expressed in impulsive action .... Insisting that every printer should be able to own a car, he upset the balance of wage negotiations .... [and] as a generous contributor to the Printers' Pension Corporation, he demanded that its benefits should be made available to unapprenticed men of the National Association of Operative Printers & Assistants [NATSOPA]. He held that Fleet Street competition was entirely domestic, involving no outside rivalries. Therefore, he maintained high wages for printers did not affect the nation's external trading position.

With the dispute dragging on, T.E. Naylor MP, of the London Society of Compositors, wrote to Northcliffe offering his services as a mediator. In reply, Northcliffe stated: 'We in Great Britain invented trade unionism. Its name stands high before the world. I have often said in public that I could not produce these great number of newspapers without trade unionism. Throughout the whole of my career my relations with compositors, which began at the age of fifteen and a half, have been most pleasant.'

His behaviour, though, was now causing concern among his fellow-proprietors; and on 6 April, Riddell – now Lord Riddell, having been ennobled in the 1920 New Year's honours – noted in his diary: 'Northcliffe returns today, and on his arrival Burnham and I are to see him about the affairs of the NPA generally – Northcliffe's action in regard to labour having caused serious difficulties.' However, one of Northcliffe's first acts was to telephone George Isaacs, secretary of NATSOPA, asking him to call as soon as possible. There at Northcliffe's London home, 1 Carlton Gardens, Isaacs confirmed that there was a move by the proprietors to demand wage cuts. 'Isaacs also told him that he had asked the Newspaper Proprietors Association for dividend particulars before he could agree to any discussion of the cuts.' Northcliffe was in complete agreement.

On 3 May – disenchanted with the other newspaper owners, and still angry at the Council debating whether or not to reduce printers' wages while he had been abroad – Northcliffe resigned from the NPA, leading W.J. Evans, editor-in-chief of the *Evening News* and a close friend and colleague for thirty years, to opine that the Chief's resignation had been a grave error. He was also concerned that the personal negotations with 'that man Isaacs' had 'dulled our reputation'.[18]

Nevertheless, within days Northcliffe had published his threepenny pamphlet, *Newspapers and their Millionaires*, which was scathing about his fellow-owners, 'the sacred caste' of the Newspaper Proprietors Association. Northcliffe had dictated the pamphlet while at Elmwood his country home; and as Paul Ferris was to write:[19]

> This was the first public evidence, for anyone who chose to read it carefully, that Northcliffe's mind was straying. It rambled on about Press proprietors who had made their money elsewhere, and said rude things about their newspapers. Its message was that planned wage reductions in Fleet Street must not take place; dismay at the prospect of newspapers in the hands of industrialists, instead of journalists, seemed to be the underlying thought. But the message was clouded and confused.

Northcliffe began: 'Every now and then the question of the ownership of newspapers becomes a topic of public discussion, and doubtless new legislation is required in Britain.' He added: 'Journalists had no objection to capitalists coming to Fleet Street and owning newspapers and so creating employment, but I object to being a member of a Combination in which capitalists ignorant of Fleet Street dictate terms to those who have spent their lives trying to understand the complex question of a newspaper.'

For many of its readers, the pamphlet had hit the right note, among them being Clifford Sharp, editor of the *New Statesman*, who wrote that 'Lord Northcliffe is perfectly justified in poking fun at his millionaire colleagues', adding that 'journalists of all political colours are almost driven to pray for more Northcliffes'. A delighted Northcliffe was quick to respond on 25 May:

> Dear Mr Sharp, I notice your kind comments on my work. You ask why my newspapers are technically excellent. The explanation is very simple. There is not the bullying and sacking in my offices that take place elsewhere. Indeed, I am afraid there are many old passengers in our boat. We pay three times the salaries paid elsewhere. We have a bonus system. We give pensions. No man works more than five days a week. You know how muddly people are. Many people think I am a Jew, a Roman Catholic, that I am extremely eccentric, that I drink and the rest of it. My boast is that I have never lost a good man yet.[20]

However, not all persons were in accord with Northcliffe's pamphlet, among whom was fellow-proprietor and journalist Sir William Berry, who, in a public speech, after praising the Chief as the leading newspaperman, declared:

> I do not think in his recent criticism he has been fair to his fellow proprietors. After all there is 'the mysterious Mr Fish' [news editor, *Daily Mail*]. He is a very earnest and

> enthusiastic gentleman regarding the proposals and reforms he brought forward, and we have to remember that he is the Mr Fish acting on behalf of Lord Northcliffe's organisation, who proposed that the proprietors should negotiate with the unions. I have to remember that five out of the eight unions consented to a reduction, and it follows, therefore, that the proprietors as a whole, acting as the NPA, would have no very selfish motive in proposing the readjustment of the terms of the men.

For F.J. Mansfield, general secretary of the National Union of Journalists: 'The stand resolutely maintained by Northcliffe that "there is no case for a reduction in the wages of our daily printers, and as regards what are called the Northcliffe journals there will be none," saved the position for the unions, and there was no wage cut either for printers or journalists.'

Death of Northcliffe

While these negotiations had been proceeding, throughout the summer Northcliffe's condition was worsening; he was becoming more and more mentally deranged, leading Lord Riddell to seek Lloyd George's opinion. The Prime Minister replied: 'I should describe him as a great journalistic Barnum. He had the knack of divining what the public wanted, say a white elephant, and of seeking one out and getting it into his menagerie. Northcliffe did many good things, but the truth is that he had a bad effect on the public mind.'

On 17 June, Riddell played golf with Lloyd George at St George's Hill; and to quote from his diary:

> He talked much about Northcliffe's serious illness, and speculated as to what would become of his papers if he gave up. LG said: 'In that case I must get friends of mine to acquire *The Times*, otherwise it might get into the hands of Beaverbrook or someone else who would make things difficult.' LG said that if the reports concerning Northcliffe were true, it was a tragic business, and that he felt sorry to see him end in this way.

Less than two months later, on 14 August 1922, at the age of fifty-seven, Northcliffe died. Finding noise unbearable, 'Victor, the 9th Duke of Devonshire, let Northcliffe build a wooden chalet on the roof of his London house in the quiet of Carlton Gardens' and it was there – 'attended round-the-clock by three male nurses' – that the Chief passed away. His final wish, dictated to his doctor, had been: 'In *The Times* I should like a page reviewing my life-work by someone who really knows and a leading article by the best man available on the night.' He was not to be disappointed: Wickham Steed, the editor, did him proud:[21] 'His [Northcliffe's] bequest was his example in seeking steadfastly his country's welfare and in pursuing with fearless independence the ends he thought right. Such will be the aim of this journal which during fourteen years has kept in view the great objects he served.'

Throughout his long years as a proprietor, Northcliffe had taken a great interest in all facets of newspapers and justifiably lived up to his informal title the Chief. *The Manchester Guardian* was to say: 'As a material force there has been nothing in journalism to compare with him.' R.D. Blumenfeld in the *Daily Express* was to write of his long-time friend:

> The classes enfranchised in the late nineteenth century at last found a medium of instruction in public affairs and a method of making their opinions felt – not once every five or six years but continuously from day to day. Such an achievement ranks Northcliffe finally among the makers of history.

And in the words of Lord Beaverbrook: 'He was the greatest figure who ever strode down Fleet Street.'[22]

Following Northcliffe's death, his younger brother Harold (Viscount Rothermere) assumed control of Associated Newspapers, including the *Daily Mail*, *Sunday Dispatch* and *Evening News*. However, because of the death duties on Northcliffe's estate, *The Times* was put up for sale. Despite bidding £1,350,000, Rothermere failed to keep the title in the Harmsworth family, losing to John Jacob Astor, who secured the paper for £1,580,000. Astor's first move was to re-engage Geoffrey Dawson in place of Wickham Steed and to give independence back to the editor.

Dawson was born Geoffrey Robinson (he changed his surname to Dawson in 1917, following a family inheritance) and in January 1911 had met Lord Northcliffe, chief proprietor of *The Times*, who offered him a place on the paper. The following year, aged thirty-seven, Dawson was appointed editor, and he was to retain that position until early 1919. As a result of Dawson supporting the new Liberal government – and Lloyd George in particular – Northcliffe wrote on 25 January 1919: 'I beg you to do either one of two things – endeavour to see eye to eye with me, or relinquish your position.' Five days later, Dawson replied: 'I shall be only too willing, as you know, to give up the Editorship of *The Times* when the Proprietors desire it.' Dawson was as good as his word, and resigned the following month, going back to Oxford, where he became estates bursar of All Souls. He remained there until returning to *The Times* as editor on 1 January 1923.

As for the new proprietor, John Jacob Astor had been born in New York and educated at Eton and New College, Oxford, before joining the Life Guards in 1906. He had fought in France during the First World War, losing his right leg. In 1918 he was given Hever Castle by his father and the following year inherited a fortune. Entering politics, Astor was elected Unionist MP for Dover and held that seat until 1945. As controlling proprietors, Astor, nine shares, and John Walter IV, one share, formed a holding company; and set up a committee of trustees which had a veto on the transfer of the shares. The trustees were the Lord Chief Justice, the Warden of All Souls, the President of the Royal Society, the President of the Institute of Chartered Accountants and the Governor of the Bank of England.

And Rothermere? Some years later, in a reflective mood, he was to opine: 'I have never had any regrets about losing *The Times*, for common sense dictated that I should decrease, not add to my worries.'

Hulton Sells His Empire

In September 1923, Sir Edward Hulton, who had been made a baronet two years earlier for services during the war, was considering selling his newspapers. He had been dogged by ill-health for more than twenty years; and all his life had been 'tormented by the Puritan urge to get up early and work hard. He was a conscientious worker to an almost pathetic degree, being too suspicious to delegate.' Hannen Swaffer was to write of meeting him at Ascot and offering congratulations on his improved appearance: 'You are wrong,' replied Hulton. 'I am dying and I am the most miserable man on earth.'[23]

By the early 1920s E. Hulton & Co. Ltd, a private company, owned eight newspapers, including the *Evening Standard*, *Daily Sketch*, *Manchester Evening Chronicle* – plus three Sunday titles. The average circulation of the morning papers in the first six months of 1920 was 1,267,343; of the evening papers 868,639; and of the Sunday and weekly papers 4,518,349. Despite a loss in 1920 of £216,433, average profits before tax for the previous five and a half years had been £377,702; and profits for 1922, which included fifteen months of the *Empire News*, were £818,438.

Initially, Hulton had decided to sell his chain to the Berry brothers, and in April 1923 negotiations were at an early stage when their lawyer fell ill. Lord Rothermere, fresh from purchasing his brother's newspapers, now entered the fray, but Hulton would not sell to him. Never one to miss an opportunity, Beaverbrook now saw his chance and suggested to Rothermere that he should buy the newspapers on Rothermere's behalf, taking the *Evening Standard* as commission. Rothermere agreed. Beaverbrook started with one great advantage: as a near neighbour of Hulton he was a close friend, and his Cherkley estate was within walking distance of Sir Edward's home at Downside, near Leatherhead.

On 28 September 1923 Beaverbrook learned that the Berry - Hulton deal was to be signed three days later, on 1 October: 'The price was to be £6 million with an immediate down payment of £300,000.' It was an easy matter, therefore, for Beaverbrook to stroll through the french windows of Hulton's home to greet his friend lying ill in a ground-floor bedroom. Hulton needed little persuasion to sell his newspapers for £5 million. Beaverbrook wrote the details on a sheet of Midland Bank writing paper, and Hulton scrawled 'I accept' and signed it:

> The family had been ready to stop Beaverbrook entering the bedroom on the grounds that Hulton was too ill. They were horrified to find the note, and at once rang the Midland Bank to check on Beaverbrook's resources. The bank replied that Beaverbrook had no account with them, but within 20 minutes the manager rang back to say that the sum would be met. Beaverbrook had hurried home, and telephoned his friend, Reginald McKenna, former Chancellor of the Exchequer, and now chairman of the Midland Bank.[24]

He had asked McKenna if the bank would honour his cheque for one million pounds. With McKenna's assurance, Beaverbrook remitted the amount with the balance to follow within a week. But, even before the final payment had been made, the ever-astute Beaverbrook had sold the package to Rothermere, deducting the *Evening Standard* as his commission.

Ever prescient, on 3 October 1923 H.A. Gwynne, editor of the *Morning Post*, wrote to Stanley Baldwin, the Prime Minister, that he had heard 'on good authority that Beaverbrook is in with Rothermere in the purchase of the Hulton concerns'. On less good authority, Gwynne informed Baldwin that Lloyd George was behind the deal and that he had 'declared that he was coming back to sweep the country on an Empire policy'.

Ten days after the purchase, Beaverbrook was interviewed by the bureau chief of the *New York Times*:[25] 'He [Beaverbrook] dropped around to see Hulton late at night. There he was shown all the documents necessary for the sale of Hulton Press.' Beaverbrook then told the bureau chief: 'Of course there was Berry and it was just worth trying him, so information was conveyed to him that he could if he liked have the rest of the publications, but Berry did not seem to grasp the idea and said nothing.'

> Lord Beaverbrook then thought of Rothermere. It was common gossip that he was not satisfied with the position of his newspapers in Manchester, and it had even been rumoured that he was about to start a northern daily. Lord Beaverbrook called him up on the telephone and told him in his own offhand manner the proposition he had to offer and Rothermere equally nonchalantly accepted without ringing off. That is the inside story of the biggest newspaper deal that Fleet Street has ever known.

Less than a fortnight later, on 14 October, Beaverbrook was able to announce that he was in control of the *Evening Standard*. He kept 51 per cent of the company and the Daily Mail Trust took 49 per cent, paying for it with 40,000 of their shares. As A.J.P. Taylor was to write:

> It is true that he now had a well-balanced empire – a morning paper, an evening paper and a Sunday paper. But the *Evening Standard* did not fit in with the pattern he had previously created . . . . More probably, he welcomed the *Evening Standard* as something different. Those who thought that Beaverbrok could only inspire one kind of newspaper did not grasp the many-sidedness of his nature. He wanted political influence. He wanted mass circulations for some of his papers on the Northcliffe pattern. But he also wanted fun, and the *Evening Standard* provided an outlet for his excessive radicalism.[26]

With the sale of his newspapers, Hulton retired from full-time business and gave £75,000 to be distributed among his staff. For a time he lived in Cannes, but returned to London and then to his Surrey home, where he died aged fifty-six on 23 May 1925.

Some months after securing the Hulton empire, Rothermere was to say that the purchase of the papers had been based on commercial considerations:

> My whole and sole object was to obtain for the shareholders of the *Daily Mirror* and the *Sunday Pictorial* the control of two newspapers from which they had most to fear, the *Daily Sketch* and the *Sunday Herald*. I foresaw that unless I did this my newspapers might possibly have to fall under the skilful direction of Sir William Berry.

Notwithstanding his comments, in the spring of 1925 Rothermere sold all the Hulton papers – including the Withy Grove printing works – to the Berrys, except for the *Evening Standard* (51 per cent of which Beaverbrook had retained for himself), the *Daily Sketch* and the *Sunday Herald*. For this, Rothermere received £5,500,00 – a profit of £1,800,000. The following year, the Berry brothers bought the *Newcastle Chronicle*, the Glasgow group – *Daily Record*, *Evening News*, etc. – plus dailies in Aberdeen, Cardiff and Sheffield.

Not content, in 1926 the brothers' group, now known as Allied Newspapers, went on with Edward Iliffe to acquire the Amalgamated Press from Sir George Sutton, who was acting as executor of Northcliffe's will. The Amalgamated Press comprised more than one hundred periodicals, plus printing works at London and Gravesend, and the Imperial Paper Mills in Kent. And to satisfy the huge demand for newsprint generated by their daily titles, the following year Allied Newspapers purchased the paper mills of Edward Lloyd Ltd, the largest in the world.

11

The General Strike

EVER SINCE THE FIRST WORLD WAR there had been unrest in the coalfields, and by the summer of 1925, with exports falling, the industry was losing one million pounds a month and more than four hundred pits had been forced to close – and it was estimated that almost half the coal being mined was at a loss. To meet this crisis, the owners announced drastic new terms, including a wage cut to 1921 levels. Naturally, these terms were rejected by the Miners' Federation of Great Britain, and its leader, A.J. Cook, called on the Trades Union Council (TUC) for support. With the threat of a national strike looming, the Prime Minister, Stanley Baldwin, and his Conservative government with reluctance agreed to pay the coal industry a subsidy in support of existing pay and profits for nine months.

That autumn, on 30 November 1925, Beaverbrook wrote to Arthur Brisbane, the American newspaperman and long-time confidant of Blumenfeld:

> Churchill goes on his amazing course . . . . He seems to arrive at no fixation in his views. It was really his influence which secured the passage of the Coal Subsidy – a measure which was the absolute negation of everything which he had been preaching for six years past – surrender to the very forces which he had been denouncing as the public enemy.

During the nine-month moratorium, Sir Herbert Samuel, a former Liberal Home Secretary and now chairman, Royal Commission on Coal Mining Industry, headed an inquiry into the industry's needs; and in March 1926 the Samuel Report was published. Its recommendations included national agreements, rationalization of royalties, and sweeping reorganization and improvements. But all this was to be in the future. Its only immediate proposal was a pay cut. A.J. Cook, the miners' general secretary, was in no doubt that the proposal should be rejected, coining the phrase: 'Not a penny off the pay, not a second on the day.'[1]

Throughout April negotiations dragged on, and when Baldwin asked Herbert Smith, the Yorkshire miners' leader, if he would make some concessions to persuade the mine owners to make some in their turn, the reply was to the point: 'Nowt doing. We've nowt to give.' At the end of the month, the miners' union, with chief support from the dockers and transport unions, voted overwhelmingly for the TUC General Council to conduct negotiations with the Government or call a General Strike. 'Talks turned on whether the Government would continue the subsidy for a few weeks while plans to reorganise the industry were drafted. When reorganisation was started, the miners might then consider temporary pay cuts.'

However, with agreement almost reached, on 1 May a million miners were locked out by the coal owners, bringing an immediate response from the TUC – despite the conciliatory efforts of Transport & General Workers secretary Ernest Bevin – that 2½ million workers would strike in sympathy if assent had not been reached by 3 May.

David Lloyd George, leader of the Liberal Party, who was speaking in Cambridge that day, attacked the Conservative Ministers for taking their time in the face of the oncoming strike, declaring: 'All talking and no tackling.' He considered that the imminent General Strike was not a conspiracy but a lunacy into which an ordinary trade dispute had been allowed to drift by those in power. He added: 'But apart from the merits of the dispute, every citizen will feel it is his duty to support the Government of the day in the maintenance of order and in the organizing and facilitating of essential service. The country must come first, always and all the time.'

That same day, Saturday 1 May, the *Evening Standard* commented in its leader column on the possible strike:[2]

> A coal stoppage is a frightful disaster and an act of stark unreason. But if the miners decline to work under certain conditions, they have, after all, the right to do so. It is an entirely different matter if other trades seek to compel the Government to subsidise miners' wages by the threat of a general paralysis of trade and communications. Such action goes far beyond the limits of an industrial dispute . . . . Such action would be an attempt to dictate to the nation, and those who took it would have no reason to complain if the nation through its organ, the Government, reacted against it with the utmost vigour. It may be hoped that a sane spirit will prevail . . . . but if trouble of the kind does come the Government will have the nation behind it resisting any attempts to force it to surrender.

In the afternoon, Beaverbrook was summoned to the offices of the *Sunday Express*, where the fathers of the chapel were objecting to a government advertisement appealing for strike-breakers. He rang up Lord Birkenhead, who urged concessions. Winston Churchill, Chancellor of the Exchequer, though, was all for making a stand, saying: 'Close it down. You can afford it.'[3] Beaverbrook compromised by removing a few words from the advertisement. The *Sunday Express* was saved, but a statement in the leader – written by Blumenfeld – left readers in no doubt that a General Strike must fail.

During the weekend, negotiations continued at Downing Street between the Government and the TUC, and by midnight on Sunday 2 May agreement was in sight. Then came news from the *Daily Mail* that pressure from some unions was preventing publication of a leading article denouncing the miners. Upon hearing this, the Government immediately broke off negotiations, and Prime Minister Baldwin retired to bed. When a worried TUC delegation sought further information, they found the house in darkness. Leo Amery was to record in his diary that members of the Cabinet had assembled in Churchill's room at 9.30 p.m., then at 11 o'clock 'news arrived that the *Daily Mail* had been suppressed altogether by the printers because they did not like the leading article. We already had information that in the *Sunday Express* and other papers' articles had been considerably censored or ripped out. This turned the scale.'

Meanwhile, in the *Daily Express*, taking an almost conciliatory approach, Blumenfeld had written a leader which the workers were prepared to print. At the *Daily Mail*, its editor, Thomas Marlowe, had run into trouble because of his outspoken comments. Many of the production staff objected and sought to intervene. The editor refused – and the paper was not published.

Nevertheless, Beaverbrook was determined to print his papers, even if it meant giving way, and in his own words: 'I should have been perfectly prepared to go on publishing at almost any cost . . . . even though the actual editing of the *Evening Standard* was interferred with by the Fathers of the Chapel.'[4] The paper did appear on 3 May, but in a much-reduced size of eight pages – and cuts were made to the leader to placate the chapels. However, a statement did appear on page 1 giving details of the stoppage at Associated Newspapers:

THE DAILY MAIL

The editor of the *Daily Mail* has issued the following:

The Natsopas (National Society of Operative Printers and Assistants) at Carmelite House took exception to the leading article which had been prepared for publication in the *Daily Mail on* Monday, May 3, under the heading 'For King and Country' and demanded that alterations should be made by the editor, who refused to comply.

They were supported by the machine minders, the stereotypers and the packers. Several unions, including the compositors, the process workers and the telegraphists, declared that it was not within their province to discuss the policy of the newspaper, and resolved to carry on their work in the usual way.

The Natsopas and the members of the unions supporting them ceased work and consequently there will be no issue of the *Daily Mail* from Carmelite House this (Monday morning).

While the first copies of the *Evening Standard* were being produced, further down Shoe Lane – a narrow thoroughfare which led into Fleet Street – the National Union of Journalists' chapel of the *Daily Express* was in continuous session awaiting advice from Union headquarters as to whether journalists were on strike or not. The reply was that 'it was proper for journalists to assist in the maintenance of a flow of news by helping in the production of makeshift newspapers . . . . so long as the people who produce them cannot permanently displace the mechanical workers who are on strike'.

Volunteer society girls now ran the switchboard, under the leadership of Lady Louis Mountbatten and Mrs Jean Norton, while Lady Beaverbrook herself was in charge of the canteen.[5] Among the journalists employed that Monday was a young Francis Williams, a future editor of the *Daily Herald*, who has left a fascinating account of those hours in his *Nothing So Strange*. He was standing with his closest friend, Thomas Darlow, later to die as a war correspondent, looking out of the newsroom window when he heard loud shouting. As it turned into the *Express* loading bay, a lorry laden with newsprint and drawn by a pair of huge and handsome

Clydesdales was the centre of an angry crowd, some of whom were throwing stones, causing the horses to gallop off. To quote Francis Williams:

> 'They can't treat horses like that,' I shouted, and with Darlow at my heels raced down the stairs. We found the lorry halted some way down Shoe Lane. The horses were still panting. The driver had climbed down from his high seat much shaken and was looking indecisively about him. 'I'll take them,' I said. Brushing aside his protests I seized the reins from his hands and after talking to the two Clydesdales with the gentle cooing note my father used when any animals of his were frightened climbed up to the driver's seat as though to the manor born – and indeed in some measure I was. 'Come along then,' I said, and turning them round proceeded steadily back to the *Express* with Darlow walking purposefully alongside.
>
> The crowd was still there. But overawed either by my professional look on the driver's box or Darlow's size they let us through quietly and with a loud 'Whoah there' I brought the lorry to a halt with a stylish flourish to a rattle of cheers from the *Express* windows. I climbed down, gave the two Clydesdales a gentle rub on their soft velvety noses, told them what fine fellows they were, handed them over to the driver, who had followed inconspicuously on foot, and walked modestly into the *Express* building with Darlow.
>
> No sooner were we in the newsroom than we were seized by the Assistant News Editor and rushed to the lift. 'The Beaver wants to see you,' he said and we shot up to the top floor. Lord Beaverbrook was sitting, one leg under the other, in a deep armchair, three telephones on a side table by his right hand, his hair tousled, his tie large and floppy . . . . A couple of the society lovelies who had hurried to help the *Express* to keep the revolution at bay were lounging on a couch near a table laden with drinks. When we came in Beaverbrook leapt from his chair. 'Good-day to you,' he said, advancing on us with outstretched hands. He scarcely came up to Darlow's chin, but he seemed to loom over both of us. 'That was well done,' he said in his famous Canadian rasp. 'Have some champagne.' We each had a glass of champagne and when we had drunk it he turned to the Assistant News Editor, who seemed to have been left out when the champagne was being poured, and barked, 'Are these young men on your staff?' 'No, sir,' said the Assistant News Editor, regretfully I thought, 'they work for the Sunday.' 'Tell Innes he should be proud of them,' said Beaverbrook. 'Tell him to give them a rise.' He swung back to us. 'See you get it,' he said. 'Good-bye to you.'[6]

Churchill Meets the NPA

Under the direction of Sir William Joynson-Hicks, the Home Secretary, troops were being put on alert to provide protection for food convoys; and in the ten regions into which the country had been divided special constables were being sworn in. Among the points agreed by the Home Secretary and his committee – with Churchill playing a key role – was that national newspapers should cooperate in the publication of an emergency news-sheet. On 3 May, at one o'clock, Churchill at the Treasury informed editors and proprietors, including Lord Burnham, of *The Daily Telegraph*; Lord Riddell, of the *News of the World*; Major J.J. Astor, of *The Times*; and Esmond Harmsworth, of the *Daily Mail*, that it was essential that a powerful, reliable broadsheet should be produced, saying, 'Something must be done to prevent alarming news from being spread about and there is no reason why it should not be done as well as possible.'[7]

The broadsheet, continued Churchill, should be produced by volunteers; and if any damage were to be done by 'amateurs' to the presses or Linotypes then the owner of that newspaper, after the strike was over, would be reimbursed. Lord Burnham told Churchill that the proposed paper should be a Government publication and not under the aegis of a proprietor; and to Lord Riddell's query as to the policy of this paper, Churchill replied: 'Obviously, mainly of news, speeches, etc, also recruiting going on . . . . it should have a leading article, not violently partisan, but agreeable to the great majority of the people on our side.'

He concluded: 'It is for us to take responsibility for all things including requisitioning the premises. We want you to help the Government by producing the paper. We take full responsibility for it and for distributing it. We want you to think out a scheme and to decide what Government help is necessary. We want the newspaper to be produced, edited and distributed as far as possible, with all the help we can give, by the people who are accustomed to do it. If we print the thing we would not know all the ramifications. Without your help it is impossible.'

Major Astor noted in his diary: 'He [Churchill] explained that in view of the fact that the Printing Trade is among the first to be called out, it is essential that at any rate one newspaper should be maintained and asks for suggestions. He says the most desirable way is, of course, for the paper if possible to do it themselves, either singly or jointly.'

However, with no decision having been reached when the meeting broke up, it was decided to reconvene at the NPA headquarters at 3 p.m.

Before then, a fired-up H.A. Gwynne, editor of the *Morning Post*, in response to a note from J.C.C. Davidson, the newly-appointed Deputy Chief Civil Commissioner, had taken matters into his own hands, replying:[8]

> I was positively ashamed of my colleagues this morning at the NPA meeting. They are quite wrong and Churchill and you are right. 95 per cent of our compositors, stereotype hands and machine men are dead against the strike, and I have not the slightest doubt that in this office I could get volunteers to turn out a Government four-page paper to the extent of our machinery. But it would have to be accompanied by a definite promise from the Government that the men would not suffer for their patriotism. What they most fear is that they would lose the superannuation benefits which will accrue to them when they have done their work. And if this could be settled I have no doubt in my mind – and I speak after consultation with some of the mechanical staff – that we could run this joint paper with the greatest ease.
>
> I am not going to the NPA meeting this afternoon but I have spoken with our Manager who will be there and he is going to propose that as far as we are concerned we are ready to help in the production of a four-sheet bulletin paper to the extent of 100,000 a night to begin with.
>
> Churchill was absolutely right about the leading article and Riddell quite wrong. It is not sufficient to have mere news and proclamations and speeches. You ought to have every day a leader with a patriotic appeal by our very best writers. The way out of the difficulty would be that you acting for the Government should instruct whoever is to write the article as to what line he should follow and there will not be the slightest difficulty.

The British Gazette

Published by His Majesty's Stationery Office.

No. 1. | LONDON, WEDNESDAY, MAY 5, 1926. | ONE PENNY.

FIRST DAY OF GREAT STRIKE

Not So Complete as Hoped by its Promoters

PREMIER'S AUDIENCE OF THE KING

Miners and the General Council Meet at House of Commons

The great strike began yesterday. There are already signs, however, that it is by no means so complete as its promoters hoped. There were far more trains running than was the case on the first day of the railway strike in 1919.

The King received the Prime Minister in audience at Buckingham Palace yesterday morning.

Reports from all parts of the country indicate that satisfactory arrangements have been set up for recruiting. Volunteers came forward in large numbers in London and all the important provincial centres.

STRIKE LEADERS' MEETINGS.

The strike leaders have made no move, and the next step is with them.

The Executive of the Miners' Federation held a meeting yesterday morning at their headquarters. There was practically no business, and the officials then went to Eccleston-square, where the General Council of the Trades Union Congress were holding a meeting.

From Eccleston-square the whole Council, together with Mr. Herbert Smith, Mr. Cook, and Mr. Richardson (the miners' officials), went to the House of Commons. Mr. Ramsay MacDonald and Mr. Arthur Henderson had gone there half an hour earlier.

During the afternoon the full miners' Executive was sent for to the House of Commons to hold a conference with the General Council of the Trades Union Congress, and the miners and the Trade Union Congress special committee afterwards returned to Eccleston-square for a further meeting.

SPIRIT OF PUBLIC SERVICE.

Reports reaching the Government yesterday morning from the various areas into which the country is divided show that labour generally is quiet.

Recruiting stations have been opened in most parts of the country, and large numbers of volunteers have already enrolled.

RECRUITING STATIONS.

The following recruiting stations for volunteers in the London area are open:

Hornsey Area: Finchley Urban District Council Offices; Enfield U.D.C. Offices; Uxbridge U.D.C., and Harrow U.D.C.

Leyton District Area: Woodford U.D.C. Offices; Waltham Cross U.D.C.; Ilford U.D.C.; and Leyton U.D.C.

Hammersmith Area: Marylebone Town Hall; Ealing U.D.C.; Kensington Town Hall, Sutton U.D.C.; and Westminster City Hall.

Bethnal Green Area: The Guildhall; Hackney Public Library; Islington Old Town Hall; and Stoke Newington Public Library.

Wandsworth Area: Lambeth Town Hall; Wandsworth Town Hall; Richmond Town Hall.

Greenwich Area: Woolwich—22, William-street, Woolwich; Deptford—Paradise and Union-road, Deptford.

Kingston Area: Kingston Town Hall; Wimbledon Town Hall; Epsom Rural District Council Offices.

Croydon Area: Catford Town Hall; Croydon Town Hall; Bromley Urban District Council Offices.

In the Home Counties stations have been opened at:

Watford.	Sittingbourne.
St. Albans.	Lewes.
Colchester.	Eastbourne.
Chelmsford.	Hastings.
Hayes.	Tunbridge Wells.
Chatham.	Brighton.
Rochester.	Guildford.
Gravesend.	Woking.
Dartford.	Reigate.

NEVER-ENDING QUEUE

The wooden huts in the courtyard of the Foreign Office were besieged yesterday by an eager crowd anxious "to do their bit." In the never-ending queue were representatives of every walk of life, fairly evenly divided between men and women.

Inside the huts the officials and their volunteer helpers had a hard time of it, with never a minute to look up from their work or to cease their reiteration the questions. "What can you do? What are you willing to do?" The answer to the first part of the question was usually something to do with motors, and the answer to the second question [illegible] variably "anyt[illegible]

... the bareheaded motor-bicycle type to the newsboy and the van boy.

A casual inquiry as to what one of the latter was willing to do met with a unanimous cry from everybody in the vicinity, "Anything." "That," remarked the patient policeman at the door, "is the right spirit, and the sort of spirit we have had here in large quantities for the last two days."

Outside in Downing-street, the Police managed to keep the roadway fairly clear, but in Whitehall half a dozen mounted men had their work cut out to keep the curious on the move. Everywhere, however, good temper prevailed.

A MUSHROOM TOWN

The services of some of these volunteers were manifested in Hyde Park which, closed to the general public, controls the milk supply of London. In a night the familiar green stretches had changed into a mushroom town of ordered activity. Huts and tents had sprung up, each with an appropriate notice as to the occupation housed inside, and each in charge of competent staffs, who took to their unaccustomed duties with marvellous rapidity. One of the officials in charge of the milk pool stated that the organisation was almost perfect. "When you consider the circumstances," he said, "something in the nature of a miracle has been achieved."

The commissariat arrangements for the vast number of men and women who pass through the park during the day and night are in the hands of the Y.M.C.A., who, in a huge marquee, never cease supplying hot drinks and hot food at the minimum price.

The milk lorries themselves form one continuous line from end to end and side to side of the Park. They bring the milk in from the farms, report to the transport officials, and receive instructions as to its distribution in London. Yesterday everybody seemed cheerful and hopeful, but quite prepared, if the worst came to the worst, to carry on their new activities indefinitely.

LONDONERS' TREK TO WORK.

On foot, squeezed into cars, standing in vans, riding pillion, pedalling on cycles, swarming Citywards by every road and route, London came yesterday morning doggedly and cheerfully to work.

Whoever has struggled along the choked highway to Epsom Downs on Derby Day may form a mental picture of the "first day's strike pilgrimage to the east of Temple Bar. The congestion was as bad, and the temper of the people was as good.

No newspaper came to many houses to tell whether the conflict had at the eleventh hour been averted, but to read the news one had only to look out of the window. The streets with their press of private vehicles, with their streams of walkers settled to a long and steady stride, and, with never a sign of red omnibus or clanging tram, told emphatically as print that the great general strike had begun.

Every thoroughfare was a one-way street—to London. The luxurious limousines and the drab and coughing relics of pre-war motoring crept along side by side in the crowded fraternity of the road. At every crossing the police beckoned on the unending line, and their task was made easy, because every man and woman at the wheel drove with consideration and a new courtesy.

In the inevitable blocks and jams, conversation rose above the throbbing of the engines. "How long will it last?" "They say that the Government—" And there was much of the unwonted chaff that invariably is exchanged when two or three Englishmen are gathered together. "Was that Mr. Ford's first sample?" demanded a lorry driver stuck level with a sorry machine whose radiator oozed little rivulets. "Never mind," retorted the anxious owner, "it moves, and"—indicating three laughing girls in the back seat—"I've a better cargo than you."

Every now and then there was something to cheer—a pirate 'bus carrying two and a half times its legal complement; a gallant driver adding yet another tired pedestrian to his overburdened car; a trim party of bluejackets marching out of Chelsea Barracks; an antiquated horse-brake with "Liverpool-street" chalked on its crazy sides. With invincible good-humour Londoners extracted satisfaction out of the very difficulties of their slow trek to town.

Many firms sent vans to bring in from the suburbs the most essential members of their staffs. Typists and girl clerks [illegible] cheerfully, confident of a lift, and it [illegible] few of these were dis[illegible] everybody got to [illegible] weary, and [illegible] nevertheless [illegible]

FOOD SUPPLIES

No Hoarding: A Fair Share for Everybody

The Government is endeavouring to see that every person has a fair share of food and it is therefore of the greatest importance that every member of the public should assist in maintaining a fair distribution of supplies. They should do this by refraining from buying more than their usual quantities of foodstuffs.

Retailers should co-operate in securing a fair distribution of their stocks.

Bakers generally are holding satisfactory stocks of flour and coal.

The Executive Committee, appointed by the London Provision Exchange, unanimously agreed that all market prices established on Friday last for all kinds of butter, cheese, bacon, ham, and lard shall remain the maximum prices until further notice.

In some parts of the provinces there seems to be an inclination to put up prices, partly caused by a certain amount of panic buying, which, however, is being checked by the traders and Co-operative Societies themselves.

Some fish has been sent to London from Lowestoft by sea.

Milk services are being well maintained.

MILK DISTRIBUTION

Control of Supplies in the Metropolis

The Deputy Chief Civil Commissioner's Office yesterday issued the following from the Board of Trade:

The Milk Distribution (Emergency) Order, 1926, dated 3rd May, 1926, made by the Board of Trade under Regulation 3 of the Emergency Regulations, 1926.

The Board of Trade, in exercise of the powers conferred upon them by Regulation 3 of the Emergency Regulations, 1926, and of all other powers them thereunto enabling, hereby make the following Order:

(1) Every person owning or having power to sell or dispose of any milk within the Metropolitan Police Area of London shall as and when required by the London Milk Pool Committee, place such milk at that Committee's disposal.

(2) Infringements of this Order are summary offences under the Emergency Regulations, 1926.

(3) This Order may be cited as the Milk Distribution (Emergency) Order, 1926.

H. A. PAYNE.
A Secretary to the Board of Trade.

LAW COURTS AT WORK

Judge on the Duty of the Public

All the Judges in the Probate, Divorce, and Admiralty Divisions took their seats at the appointed time yesterday morning. Several King's Bench Judges were able to proceed with the trial of actions, but others had to delay proceedings because of late arrivals. Mr. Justice Horridge, in releasing a waiting jury, asked them to be in attendance at a quarter-past ten on Wednesday morning.

"It is a public duty," he said, "and we must do the best we can."

When Mr. Justice Lawrence arrived late he said he had been two hours and a half coming. Mr. Justice Hill stated that it had taken him two hours to travel from Wimbledon.

Mr. Justice Astbury said he did not propose to take any action in which the witnesses lived at any substantial distance. It would be a gross injustice to do so.

The spacious yard on the western side of the Law Courts resembled a huge garage, being packed with motors and motor-cycles.

G.P.O. SERVICES

Restrictions on Telegrams and Letters

The telephone and postal services are becoming so congested that delays will be inevitable unless messages and calls are considerably reduced.

Accordingly the public should avoid sending telegrams or making telephone calls unless of an urgent nature.

No foreign or colonial parcels will be accepted and no letter or inland packet over the weight of eight ounces will be allowed.

There will not be a delivery of parcels in the London postal area.

THE KING RECEIVES THE PREMIER.

The Prime Minister had an audience of the King at Buckingham Palace yesterday morning. He and his colleagues of the Cabinet were within call, and most of them attended the meetings of the two Houses, but no occasion arose for a Council nor for a meeting of the Negotiating Committee of the Cabinet.

Until the general strike is called off by the Trade Union Congress leaders nothing can happen. This is a condition precedent to any reopening of negotiations.

One result of the receipt of telegrams and telephone messages from the constituencies was that many members expressed the view that the Government ought to [illegible] so-called peaceful picketing [illegible] members [illegible]

HOLD-UP OF THE NATION

Government and the Challenge

NO FLINCHING

The Constitution or a Soviet

When King and People understand each other past a doubt,
It takes a foe and more than a foe to knock that country out.
Kipling.

"Be strong and quit yourselves like men."

The general strike is in operation, expressing in no uncertain terms a direct challenge to ordered government. It would be futile to attempt to minimise the seriousness of such a challenge, constituting as it does an effort to force upon some 42,000,000 British citizens the will of less than 4,000,000 others engaged in the vital services of the country.

The strike is intended as a direct hold-up of the nation to ransom. It is for the nation to stand firm in its determination not to flinch. "This moment," as the Prime Minister pointed out in the House of Commons, "has been chosen to challenge the existing Constitution of the country and to substitute the reign of force for that which now exists. . . . I do not believe there has been anything like a thorough-going consultation with the rank and file before this despotic power was put into the hands of a small executive in London. . . . I do not think all the leaders who assented to order a general strike fully realised that they were threatening the basis of ordered government and coming nearer to proclaiming civil war than we have been for centuries past."

FEW LIGHT HEARTS

"There are few light hearts in England to-day," he reminded the House. "The only people who are happy in this situation are those who envy us or who hate us, because they see the home of democratic freedom entering on a course which, if successful on the part of those who enter on it, can only substitute tyranny. But I have confidence in the character of our people, that we will see these troubles through."

Mr. Baldwin has rightly re-echoed the statement made by the late Socialist Minister of Labour (Mr. Tom Shaw) only two years ago, who, when asked whether the Government would give full protection to men who worked during disputes then in progress, said, "Yes, unhesitatingly, the Government will do all it possibly can to maintain public utilities." To that Mr. Baldwin added the assurance of the Government in the present crisis: "No man who remains at work shall be prejudicially affected afterwards."

The Government, as the Chancellor of the Exchequer has pointed out, would gladly have made sacrifices provided there had been a reasonable hope of securing agreement. Organised labour claimed the right to strike as a means of getting a concession in trade disputes. "But that," he declared, "is an entirely different thing from the concerted, deliberate, organised menace of a general strike in order to compel Parliament to do something which it otherwise would not do."

THE CHOICE

"The country and Parliament, which represents the nation, is confronted quite simply with the choice either of being ruined or of submitting to pay very large sums of the taxpayers' money to one particular trade which they do not think justified. . . . I cannot conceive any Parliament worthy of the name, let alone the oldest and strongest Parliament in the world, which would so completely abrogate its position, which would submit to such dictation without making every exertion and undertaking every expense and running every risk, and taking every measure in its power that circumstances may require."

Mr. Churchill pointed out that either the nation must be mistress in its own house, or suffer the existing Constitution to be fatally injured, and endure the erection of a Soviet of Trade Unions with the real effective control of our economic and political life. The Chancellor, however, foresees the nation's triumph in the struggle. "No one," he declared, "can doubt what the end will be, but from every point of view, including our duty in the interests of the working classes of this country, we are bound to face this present challenge unflinchingly, rigorously, rigidly, and resolutely to the end."

He summed up the position as it now stands. "There is no question of there being a gulf across which no negotiator can pass. Anyone can approach the Government who has authority and can parley with them. The Trades Union Congress have only to cancel the general strike and withdraw the challenge they have issued, and we shall immediately begin with the utmost care and patience with them again the long, laborious task which has been pursued over these many weeks of endeavouring to rebuild on economic foundations the prosperity of the coal trade. The door is closed, but, while the situation remains what it is, we have no alternative whatever but to go forward unflinchingly and do our duty."

Meantime it is strong, and qui[illegible]

COMMUNIST LEADER ARRESTED

Mr. Saklatvala, M.P., Charged at Bow Street

SEQUEL TO MAY DAY SPEECH

Mr. Shapurji Saklatvala, the Communist Member of Parliament for North Battersea, was arrested at his house, St. Alban's Villas, Highgate, on Monday afternoon on a warrant charging him with inciting the public to commit a breach of the peace during a speech which he made on May Day in Hyde Park.

He appeared before Sir Chartres Biron at a special session of the Bow-street Police Court yesterday afternoon, and was remanded on bail until Thursday on the undertaking that he would make no public speeches in the interval, except in the House of Commons.

Mr. George Lansbury, M.P., and Mr. Ben Spoor, M.P., drove up to the Court after the adjournment and each of them went surety for Mr. Saklatvala in £100. Mr. Saklatvala entered into a recognisance on his own behalf of £100.

Mr. Saklatvala was first arrested on Monday by Chief Inspector Parker, of the Criminal Investigation Department of Scotland Yard. He consented to say where he could be found when required, and was immediately released to go to the House of Commons. He was subsequently taken into custody at his house yesterday morning.

Mrs. Saklatvala was present in the public gallery of the Court with a number of sympathisers.

Sir Travers Humphreys and Mr. E. Clayton appeared on behalf of the Director of Public Prosecutions, and Mr. W. H. Thompson appeared for Mr. Saklatvala.

Sir Travers Humphreys asked the Magistrate to take the same course in this case as was taken in the well-known case of Lansbury and Riley—that of requiring the defendant to enter into recognisances to keep the peace and to give such sureties as the Magistrate might think proper.

GOVERNMENT'S VIEW

"It is the view of the Government that their first duty is to keep law and order," continued Sir Travers. "Last Saturday in Hyde Park the defendant made a dangerous and inflammatory speech, which was most improper at the present time.

"The defendant could have been charged under the new Emergency Regulations, but it was decided not to adopt this course, since these are the first proceedings to be taken in the present state of affairs."

Detective-Sergeant Arthur Davies, who had taken a shorthand note of Mr. Saklatvala's speech, then gave evidence. Among the extracts from the speech read in Court were the following:

"The Union Jack has for generations done nothing but protect fools and rogues."

"We want to tell the Army boys that they must revolt now and refuse to fight, and then they will be the real saviours of their homes and the workers. I want the Navy boys to march beside them."

At this point Sir Travers Humphreys remarked that the speech was one inciting the forces to abandon their duty.

Sir Chartres Biron—"It is very curious language if it was really used."

Mr. Thompson then applied for a remand, stating that he had only just been instructed and had still to prepare the defence.

SPECIAL CONSTABLES

Appeal to Capable Citizens in London to Enrol

An "appeal to capable citizens" to join the Metropolitan Special Constabulary Reserve and assist the Metropolitan Police in the maintenance of law and order during the present emergency is issued by Sir W. T. F. Horwood, the Commissioner of the Metropolitan Police.

The appeal is specially made to citizens not exceeding 45 years of age, to undertake these duties "which are one of the most important obligations of citizenship, and are incumbent upon those who set a value on loyalty to their King and Country and to the cause of good and orderly government."

Every effort will be made to minimise as far as possible interference with ordinary occupations. Those who enrol will only be called for duty if and when the Commissioner regards their services as requisite for the protection of the Metropolis. They will be released when the present crisis is over, though if they wish they may continue in the Special Constabulary Reserve.

Special constables who are injured in the execution of their duty, and widows and children in case of death, will be granted pensions allowances or gratuities.

It is desirable that a citizen should enrol at the enrolment station nearest to his own home.

Owners of motor-cars and motor cycles who are willing to attest as special constables and to drive their own vehicles should apply to the Commander, A.A. Section, 27-28, Long-acre, W.C. 2.

RESERVE OF OFFICERS

The Deputy Chief Civil Commissioner's Office issues the following:

The War Office states that there is no objection to officers of the Reserve of Officers offering their services to local organisations for the maintenance of order and vital services.

Those who do so will inform the local authorities of their potential military liability, which has priority over all other liabilities. Those whose services are accepted by local authorities with this proviso will inform the Under Secretary of State, the War [illegible] tating, the nature and [illegible] appointments.

THE "BRITISH GAZETTE" AND ITS OBJECTS

Reply to Strike Makers' Plan to Paralyse Public Opinion

REAL MEANING OF THE STRIKE

Conflict Between Trade Union Leaders and Parliament

A few words are needed to explain the appearance of the "British Gazette."

There are at present two quite different disputes which are holding up the country. The first is the stoppage in the coal industry. This is a trade dispute which could be settled in the ordinary way. The Government have already paid a subsidy of twenty-three millions to give time for this industry to put its affairs on a sound basis. They cannot, however, continue paying out between two and three millions a month of the taxpayers' money to the employers and workers in one particular trade.

Moreover, exporting coal at a loss to our rivals only increases their unfair competition with British manufactures. Lastly, if we go on subsidising our export coal Germany and other rivals will have to do the same. Thus every nation will be impoverishing itself in uneconomic competition. The coal industry must, therefore, come on to an economic basis.

The Coal Commission has shown how this can be done. The Government have accepted their proposals, and will carry out the recommendations affecting the State, even where this particular Government does not agree with them. But the owners and the miners must do their part as well. The owners have agreed to nearly everything recommended by the Commission; and it is certain that the small part to which they have not yet agreed would never be allowed to be the sole block to the scientific reorganisation of the Coal Industry.

NO ADVANCE ON JULY.

The miners' leaders have not, however, made the slightest real advance towards an acceptance of those recommendations of the report which call for any sacrifice from them. In spite of the nine months' breathing space which has been obtained, or the twenty-three million pounds of public money which has been spent, or the fact that even with the subsidy there have never been less than a hundred thousand miners unemployed in the coalfields, the leaders remain in exactly the same position as they were in last July. This may be natural, and one cannot help sympathising with the miners themselves in their difficulty. But it is no use making these difficulties worse by prolonging the subsidy or trying to carry on the coal trade month after month at a heavy loss.

All three parties—Government, owners, and miners—ought to accept unreservedly the whole of the Recommendations of the Coal Commission. And if they do, and when they do, the Government, apart from doing its share, will not refuse a helping hand. So much for the trade dispute which has caused the stoppage of the coal industry.

On the top of this has now come a second dispute. The Trade Union leaders, having failed to induce the miners to make any concessions, have felt bound, nevertheless, to support them. They have, therefore, declared a General Strike and called out millions of men in carefully selected vital trades throughout the country. This has for the time being paralysed the whole business of the nation and prevented this crowded island from earning its daily bread by manufacture and commerce.

PROSPERITY AT STAKE.

If the general strike is prolonged for many weeks the prosperity of Great Britain will be ruined for probably as many years. Our foreign rivals will eagerly supplant us in overseas markets. Unemployment, which had just dipped below the million, will rise again to unprecedented heights. Unemployment insurance and all the working class funds will be exhausted, and hard times, such as were not known even during the worst of the war, will descend for a long period on the whole community.

The Trade Union leaders believe that this threat will compel the Government to grant [illegible] prolong [illegible] of the sub[illegible] pear[illegible]

... policy, no better than drinking salt water to relieve thirst. No one has pointed this out more strongly than the wiser and more responsible Labour leaders.

If Parliament were to allow its considered judgment to be overborne under the cruel assault of a general strike, the economic disaster would only be a par[t] of a much greater disaster. It would [be] definitely established that the w[ielders] of a general strike which the [Trade] Union leaders at present wield [are ir]resistible. These men, although it [is cer]tainly not the object of the great [major]ity of them, would in fact becom[e] masters of the whole country, a[nd the] power of government would [have] passed from Parliament into [their] hands. This would involve the [final] supersession of Parliament and [the] representative institutions whic[h] have established in our island after [a thousand?] hundred years of struggle, whic[h] have preserved almost alone amon[g] nations of Europe, and which ar[e the] foundation of our democratic freed[om].

NO SECTIONAL DICTATION

Instead of the representatives of the nation duly elected on a franchise almost universal, our rights and destinies would be in the hands of a body of men who, however well meaning most of them may be, represent only a section of the public and have derived no authority from the people comparable to that of the House of Commons. We must never forget, even in the heat and height of this struggle, that we are all fellow citizens. But the democratic State cannot possibly submit to sectional dictation. It is bound to defend and assert, no matter at what cost, the national and constitutional authority.

While, therefore, there is plenty of room for negotiation and a spirit of compromise about the coal trade, there can be absolutely none about a general strike. That is not a dispute between employers and workmen. It is a conflict between the Trade Union leaders and Parliament. And that conflict must only end, and can only end, in the decisive and unmistakable victory of Parliament. This victory his Majesty's Government is definitely resolved to secure.

Ample force to preserve the laws and the life of the nation is at the disposal of the State. But force is not the instrument on which a British Government should rely. We rely on reason, on public opinion, and on the will of the people. In this crisis the organisers of the general strike have made it their first care to paralyse public opinion by breaking down and muzzling the newspapers on which the whole people have been accustomed to rely for information about what is going on at home and abroad.

DANGER OF RUMOURS.

Nearly all the newspapers have been silenced by violent concerted action. And this great nation, on the whole the strongest community which civilisation can show, is for the moment reduced in this respect to the level of African natives dependent only on the rumours which are carried from place to place. In a few days, if this were allowed to continue, rumours would poison the air, raise panics and disorders, inflame fears and passions together, and carry us all to depths which no sane man of any party or class would care even to contemplate.

The Government have therefore decided not only to use broadcasting for spreading information, but to bring out a paper of their own on a sufficient scale to carry full and timely news throughout all parts of the country.

The *British Gazette* is run without profit on the authority and, if necessary, at the expense of the Government. It begins necessarily on a small scale, and its first issue cannot exceed 700,000 copies. It is proposed, however, to use the unlimited resources of the State, with the assistance of all loyal persons, to raise the circulation day after day [illegible] provides [illegible] and [illegible] information and a guar[illegible]

> I am rather ashamed of my profession at the present moment, because it is bound up with jealousies and fears when England is at stake, and my suggestion to you is that if you have any more disagreements you should calmly commandeer one of the offices – and I should be happy to be commandeered myself – and bid us to produce so many papers and the thing will be done.
>
> Please tell Churchill that I admired his attitude this morning, and that he was perfectly right. There is not the slightest difficulty in getting out and distributing a sheet such as you want, and later on we ought to be able to produce between us a really good paper.

Initially, Gwynne believed that the *Morning Post* presses could print 100,000 copies a night and that within seven days this figure could increase to more than 400,000. The Government was quick to seize upon the offer, and at 11 o'clock that night Sir Malcolm Fraser, a former colleague of Gwynne at *The Standard*, with David Caird, publicity officer at the War Office, arrived at the *Post*'s offices, 1 Aldwych, to take control. Gwynne immediately suspended all *Morning Post* production and offered his complete cooperation. Within less than an hour, Churchill appeared with Sir Samuel Hoare, and 'the two Ministers stayed until three in the morning, helping to supervise the transfer'.

The following afternoon, Tuesday 4 May, the General Strike having begun, Churchill returned to the *Morning Post* offices and was told by Gwynne that his Linotype operators and stone-hands had been forbidden by their union, the London Society of Compositors, to produce the government's new paper, named by Sir Samuel Hoare the *British Gazette*. Churchill immediately telephoned Beaverbrook for assistance, and was asked to meet him at the *Express* in Fleet Street, fifteen minutes' walk from the *Post* offices. With Beaverbrook's approval, Churchill asked Sydney Long, works manager of the *Express* and one of the fastest Linotype operators in Fleet Street, if he would help to produce the *British Gazette*. Long agreed and brought with him his two senior overseers.[9] On arriving at the *Post* offices, Long discovered that only five of the fourteen columns of the *Gazette* had been set. As he began setting the remaining columns, further production personnel were introduced onto the paper including Alfred Hawkins, chief stereotype overseer of the *Daily Mail*. Gwynne, who remained in his editor's chair, was fortunate that his editorial staff had decided not to go out on strike and were assisting in producing the paper – even working in the press and publishing areas.

Churchill, who was revelling in the situation and, mistakenly, urging the men for greater efforts, contacted John Reith, managing director of the BBC, just before the presses started at 11 p.m., asking for the sound of the *British Gazette* being printed to be broadcast. The tall, aloof Reith refused. By 6 a.m. on Wednesday 5 May, Gwynne's initial forecast of 100,000 copies had been more than doubled – with a print figure of 230,000. An observer of that night's work was P.J. Grigg, principal private secretary to Churchill, who later wrote: 'I discovered the great man sitting in solitary contemplation by the rotary presses. With a wave of his arm he directed my attention to the inexorable mechanical power rolling out newspapers which would, a few hours later, be distributed all over the country.'

Although Churchill had been unsuccessful in his request to Reith, the Prime Minister, Stanley Baldwin, was to receive much more co-operation from the BBC, and he broadcast to the nation on three occasions, saying that he was longing, working and praying for peace but would not surrender the safety and security of the British Constitution: 'You placed me in power eighteen months ago by the largest majority accorded to any party in many, many years. Have I done anything to forfeit that confidence: cannot you trust me to ensure a square deal for the parties – to secure even justice between man and man?'

Trouble at Printing House Square

Meanwhile, Major Astor at *The Times* was also feeling the effect of the General Strike. On Monday 3 May the last issue of the paper, under its normal conditions, had been produced. In his diary he noted:[10]

> At PHS [Printing House Square] met the FOCs [fathers of the chapel], 'Situation beyond us. Part as friends and hope to meet as such before long. *The Times*, being above party or class, does not recognize the right of anyone to dictate policy or course of action and will carry on – so far and as long as possible – goodbye and good luck.' (Loud applause.) (Tongue in cheek.)'

With the strike having started at midnight, many of the production workers were now without means of transport as buses and trains had stopped running. Having been informed that more than one hundred production staff were stranded, Astor had his chauffeur drive some home in his car and had 'the remainder sent home in reserve motors which had not been required to carry papers'.

The next night – with no printers to man the presses – a much-reduced *Times* was produced on six Multiliths, but only 48,000 of this issue, known as the 'Little Sister', were run off, all of which were sold in the London area. However, this did give management time to bring in retired personnel and volunteers to man a rotary press for the following night, Wednesday 5 May. It was not without its trauma, as some hardcore strikers set fire to newsprint in the basement. This did not prevent the paper from coming out, with help from the management working in 'strange' areas, including Major Astor assisting in the stereo department, and W.W. Casey, a future editor of the paper, casting the plates:

> With an occasional ebullience of molten metal, and a certain overlapping of effort, the plates were cast and trimmed. One hardly dared watch operations on the Printing Machine – but we all did, greatly to the annoyance of Tanner, upon whom the strain appeared considerable. Allah was with us. The machine worked. The baby was safely delivered.[11]

And, as the society paper, Astor had no trouble in attracting the 'top' people to assist, including six Members of Parliament, and a bevy of titled ladies: the Duchess of Sutherland; Violet, Duchess of Westminster; Viscountess Massereene and Ferrard; Lady Mauren Stanley – all in the Transport Department, with backing from Viscountess Maidstone and Lady Diana Duff-Cooper in the Subscription Room. 'A

The Times

No. 44263. London Wednesday May 5. 1926 Price 2d.

WEATHER FORECAST. Wind N.E.; fair to dull; risk of local rain.

THE GENERAL STRIKE.

A wide response was made yesterday throughout the country to the call of those Unions which had been ordered by the T.U.C. to bring out their members. Railway workers stopped generally, though at Hull railway clerks are reported to have resumed duty, confining themselves to their ordinary work, and protested against the strike. Commercial road transport was only partially suspended. In London the tramways and the L.G.O.C. services were stopped. The printing industry is practically at a standstill, but lithographers have not been withdrawn, and compositors in London have not received instructions to strike. Large numbers of building operatives, other than those working on housing, came out.

The situation in the engineering trades was confused; men in some districts stopped while in others they continued at work. There was no interference with new construction in the shipbuilding yards, but in one or two districts some of the men engaged on repair work joined in the strike with the dockers.

Food:-Supplies of milk and fish brought into Kings Cross, Euston and Paddington were successfully distributed from the Hyde Park Depot and stations. The Milk & Food Controller expects it will be possible to maintain a satisfactory supply of milk to hospitals, institutions, schools, hotels, restaurants and private consumers. Milk will be 8d. per gallon dearer wholesale and 2d. per quart retail today. Smithfield market has distributed 5,000 tons of meat since Monday.

Mails:- Efforts will be made to forward by means of road transport the mails already shown as due to be dispatched very shortly from London. The position is uncertain and the facilities may have to be limited to mails for America, India & Africa.

At Bow Street Mr. Saklatvala, M.P., who was required as a result of his Hyde Park speech on Saturday to give his sureties to abstain from making violent and inflammatory speeches, was remanded for two days on bail.

Full tram and (or) bus services were running yesterday at Bristol, Lincoln, Southampton, Aldershot, Bournemouth, Chelmsford and Isle-of-Wight, and partial services in Edinburgh, Glasgow, Liverpool, Leeds, Northampton, Cardiff, Portsmouth, Dover, N.Derbyshire and Monmouthshire.

Evening papers appeared at Bristol, Southampton, several Lancashire towns and Edinburgh, and typescript issues at Manchester, Birmingham and Aberdeen.

The Atlantic Fleet did not sail on its summer cruise at Portsmouth yesterday. The men went on shore duty.

Road & Rail Transport:- There was no railway passenger transport in London yesterday except a few suburban trains. Every available form of private transport was used. A few independent omnibuses were running, but by the evening the railway companies, except the District and Tubes, had an improvised service. Among the railway services to-day will be:- 9.30 a.m. Manchester to Marylebone 9.30 a.m. Marylebone to Manchester; 10.10 a.m Marylebone to Newcastle; 9 a.m Norwich to London; 9 a.m King's Cross to York; 5 p.m. King's Cross to Peterborough; 9 p.m. Peterborough to King's Cross. L.M.S. Electric trains between Watford and Euston and Broad Street will maintain a 40 minutes service. On all sections of the Metropolitan Railway except Moorgate to Finsbury Park, a good service will run to-day from 6.40 a.m. The Underground hope to work a six minute service on the Central London Line to-day from 8 a.m. to 8 p.m. between Wood Lane and Liverpool Street. The following stations only will be open:- Shepherds Bush, Lancaster Gate, Oxford Circus, Tottenham Court Road, Bank, Liverpool Street. A flat fare of 3d will be charged.

The Prime Minister had an audience of the King yesterday morning.

There was no indication last night of any attempt to resume negotiations between the Prime Minister and the T.U.C.

The Government is printing an official newspaper, "The British Gazette" which will appear to-day, price 1d. It will be distributed throughout the London Area.

Volunteers for the London Underground Railways and for L.O.G.C. omnibuses should communicate with the Commercial Manager's Dept. 55 Broadway, S.W.

The Prince of Wales returned to London from Biarritz last night travelling from Paris by air

"THE LITTLE SISTER."

Governor-elect put in some strenuous shifts as a packer in the intervals of packing his own boxes for the Antipodes.'[12]

> Relations with pickets, in spite of the odd scuffle, remained friendly. They contained to be sustained with sandwiches and beer from the staff canteen and the Chairman [Major J.J. Astor] noted that 'they always touched their caps' to him as he passed the lines. In mid-week those with money owing were paid out, Astor and Captain Shaw [Astor's political secretary] acting as pay cashiers.

The close links between staff and management were apparent, when two days after the fire in the newsprint basement, the Chairman received the following resolution:

> That this meeting of *The Times* Compositors' Chapel (in full meeting assembled) abhor the attempted crime of arson as reported to us by our Father, and we cannot believe that any worker on *The Times* in whatever capacity could be associated with such a vile and unconstitutional action, considering the happy relations that have existed between us in the past.

A similar position on the lack of production facilities existed at the *Evening Standard*, where negotations with the chapels had broken down, as J. Wilson, the company chairman, would not agree to 'publishing at any price'. Beaverbrook offered to return to meet the men, 'but the directors demurred'. As the principal shareholder but not a director, 'I had no right to give a direction or an order though I had made my opinion clear.' With the production staff now out on strike, plans were put in hand to issue emergency editions, and these were to range from a two-sided mimeograph on foolscap paper to a small, four-page tabloid letterpress complete with pictures; but, because of using a variety of small printers in the Clerkenwell district, different mastheads were printed on the same editions.

Meanwhile, at the *Morning Post* offices, a lack of newsprint was threatening production of the *British Gazette*, particularly as the TUC's newly-launched *British Worker* – started in opposition – was using *Daily Herald* stocks. To counter this, Sir Malcolm Fraser, on behalf of the Government, commandeered all the *Daily Herald* newsprint, even interfering with the ink supplies. The Government were determined to hinder production of the *British Worker* at every opportunity – and the first night's production was to set the scene, as the paper's second issue, dated Thursday evening, 6 May, revealed:[13]

> HOW THE 'BW' CAME OUT
> A Sudden Police Raid – and After
> AMAZING SCENES
>
> Eight o'clock last night. A hundred difficulties had to be overcome. But they had been overcome. And the *British Worker* was all ready for printing. The last line of copy had been sub-edited and set. The last stereo plate had been made and fastened in place on the presses. All was ready. The big crowd of members of the Distributive Section of the Paper Workers' Union, who had been waiting outside with their cars and cycles, very patiently, for three hours and more raised a cheer.
>
> Then – from the half-finished new *Daily Mail* building across the street emerged a policeman – two policemen – five – ten – twenty – fifty or more. Round the corner a dozen

mounted men. They pushed the waiting workers from the front of the office, and held them by a cordon 50 yards away. Then a number of plainclothes men, headed by a detective inspector, entered the building and ordered that the machines should not be started.

Mr Robert Williams [manager] saw the inspector, who explained that they had a warrant from the Home Secretary to search for and seize all copies of the *Daily Herald* of 4 May, all material used in producing it, or which might be used in producing any document calculated to impede measures taken for the maintenance of essential services.

It was quickly made clear that what really interested them was less the *Daily Herald* of May 4 than the *British Worker* of 5 May. The inspector requested that a dozen copies of the paper should be run off for submission to the City Commissioner. If the Commissioner approved, we could go ahead. If not – he was sorry, but – He went off with the copies, leaving some of his men in charge. They were very courteous, the whole staff in very good humour, and the crowd beyond the police cordon magnificent in its quiet orderliness.

Meanwhile, a member of staff had gone to Eccleston-square. The General Council – which is, of course, in permanent session – at once considered the situation. Mr Ben Turner, Mr Bowen and Mr Citrine came up to represent the Council on the 'scene of action'. Mr Pugh and Mr Poulton hurried off to the House to inform the Leader of the Labour Party. After a short consultation with Mr MacDonald and Mr Henderson, the latter got at once in touch with the Government. While these conversations were going on word came that the ban was lifted.

The same message came to Carmelite-street. 'You can go ahead,' said the officer in charge with a smile. The machines were started. Word was passed to the waiting crowd, who greeted it with cheer after cheer. And the police moved on while staff and crowd sang *The Red Flag*. The crowd organised its own 'police', who made an avenue for the cars to roll up, load, and drive away amid echoing cheers. That was the final scene. It was the climax of a strenuous two days.

On Tuesday the news that the Government was going to produce a strike-breaking sheet with 'volunteer' labour at the *Morning Post* office decided the General Council to issue its own strike bulletin. Representatives of the printing unions came to Eccleston-square and agreed. On Wednesday morning we got to work. A staff was mobilised. The work went forward as swiftly as possible. A difficulty here, a difficulty there, and then a difficulty somewhere else caused delay. But bit by bit we got through the troubles, and then – enter our friends the police. But in spite of it all we printed and distributed 320,000 copies. Today we hope to do better.

Churchill Demands Newsprint

The commandeering of newsprint for the *British Gazette* was now to lead to trouble with proprietors and editors of national newspapers, a vociferous protest coming from Geoffrey Dawson, editor of *The Times*. On 7 May he wrote to the Prime Minister:[14]

The second letter, received this morning, formally commandeered for the Government all newsprint of a certain size in the possession of *The Times*. The broad effect of this action is to threaten the suppression of *The Times* and presumably also every other newspaper which is endeavouring in the face of great difficulties to maintain its daily existence . . . .

> I feel bound to add that if the real purpose of this commandeering of newsprint is to limit by general action the amount available for the TUC and their organ, then the policy seems to be equally disastrous.

In his columns, Dawson objected strongly to Government interference, and refused to say how many tons of newsprint he had in stock. He then told the authorities that he intended to print only 80,000 copies of an emergency foolscap *Times*; but within a week production had risen to 405,000 copies nightly, with distribution centres having increased from two to 142. Nevertheless, on 11 May the Government took eighty-nine reels, and in the circumstances, feeling that the only hope lay in publicity, *The Times* published the following on 12 May:

> THE GOVERNMENT AND 'THE TIMES'
>
> A considerable quantity of the stock of paper available for printing *The Times* was seized by order of the Government yesterday for the use of the *British Gazette*. In taking this action the Government are of course acting entirely within their emergency powers; but the matter raises afresh the question, to which no clear answer has yet been given by Ministers in the House of Commons, whether their policy is to encourage or to hamper, and possibly even to prevent, the production of the regular independent newspapers of the country.
>
> Mr Churchill, who is in charge of the *British Gazette*, stated on Monday that 'in the twinkling of an eye the newspaper Press went completely out of action' a week ago. It becomes necessary to state, therefore, in the interests of accuracy, that *The Times* has at no time been out of action, that its circulation has been steadily increased throughout the last week, and that the number of copies actually sold (and not merely printed) yesterday morning was more than 50 per cent greater than the normal average maintained before the general strike began.

However, the biggest row over newsprint supplies was to concern Churchill and his close friend Beaverbrook, who at the end of the first week of the strike – with agreed non-interference from his striking production staff – intended to bring out a full-size *Daily Express*. This did not suit Churchill, who not only meant to requisition the newsprint but also threatened to impound the *Daily Express* premises.

For Blumenfeld and Beaverbrook, it was Churchill 'in one of his fits of vainglory and excessive excitement'. Knowing that only Joynson-Hicks, the Home Secretary, could sign the requisition order, Beaverbrook defied Churchill and there was an awful row between the two men. When approached by Churchill to sign the order, Joynson-Hicks refused; and Beaverbrook was later to comment:[16]

> I remember once a terrible scene with him when he was in a position of uncontrolled power and authority in dealing with public affairs which closely concerned me. If any other man living had used such outrageous language to me as he did on that occasion I should never have forgiven him. Churchill on top of the wave has in him the stuff of which tyrants are made.

Having written to Churchill in a friendly manner: 'I have in the premises two hundred tons of newsprint. It would be necessary to leave us in possession of this supply. Otherwise plans would be impeded', Beaverbrook was surprised at the immediate response:

> We are trying to solve the newsprint difficulty as quickly as possible. The rapidly increasing circulation of the *British Gazette* will make the paper shortage very acute. We are expecting to publish over three millions tonight, and we shall probably have to requisition every scrap of newsprint which is available and suitable. I hope, however, that by the middle of next week our supplies will be coming forward well, and I hope it may be possible to help both you and Rothermere to start then. I hope you will not attempt to do so beforehand, as it would then be necessary for me to release all the key-men that Rothermere's people have contributed and this would gravely cripple the Government organ during the days when its influence may be indispensable to the successful termination of the crisis.
>
> I have in confidence told Sir Malcolm Fraser of the position and of your wish, and have asked him to facilitate your resumption on or after Wednesday, the 19th, if the newsprint situation can possibly be adjusted. We are also training understudies for all the key-men sent us by the *Daily Mail* as well as the three splendid fellows you so kindly lent us at the beginning.

Beaverbrook once more wrote to Churchill, but this time in a more conciliatory mood, though taking care to mention the sacrifices he had made:

> Very many thanks for your letter. Our only anxiety is to break the General Strike. We have made immense sacrifices to this end and I personally guaranteed the employees of this office who took on the task of producing the *British Gazette* at a time when no other London newspaper, except the *Morning Post*, was giving material assistance.
>
> In addition we have not hesitated to give supplies from this office and any other assistance in our power. The *Evening Standard* paper reserves have been freely diverted to the *Morning Post* office. Notwithstanding all the sacrifices we have made, we are prepared to go to any lengths.
>
> Therefore, if it is absolutely necessary for the Government to take the small supplies of newsprint at the *Evening Standard* for the purpose of printing the *British Gazette*, we will assist you to get it out of the office premises. I ought to explain, however, that this will be a very difficult task and the paper (just over 200 tons I am told) will not be worth to you the effort that you put into its removal.
>
> As to the key-men at the *Morning Post* office, whose services you so generously acknowledge, we are prepared to get on without them for the present, but would be glad to have them as soon as possible.

Despite the assurances given, Churchill believed that Beaverbrook now intended to produce normal editions of the *Daily Express*, *Sunday Express* and *Evening Standard*, and at a Cabinet meeting on the evening of 11 May he gave full vent to his feelings, as Leo Amery was later to record in his diary:

> This let loose Winston in a magnificent tirade on the wonders achieved, and the selfishness of the Press in wishing to increase its circulation at the expense of others during the crisis, the impossibility of letting go at the moment without unfairness to one or other newsaper and ended with his determination to suppress the *Daily Express* if, as they intended, they started an evening paper in the next four days.

Struggled Manfully

Throughout the early days of the strike, Beaverbrook's newspapers had struggled manfully to produce one-sided news-sheets, giving their full support to the Government; and on Thursday 6 May the *Evening Standard* announced:[18]

> THE GENERAL STRIKE WILL FAIL
> The Trade Unionists know it is failing. Every good citizen should help to make it fail quickly by standing firm and giving support to the authorities.
> TAKE NO NOTICE OF RUMOURS AND DO NOT SPREAD THEM

That same day in the *Daily Express* Blumenfeld in his leading article concluded:

> All great issues are simple. This is a great issue and it can be expressed in a sentence. It lies between a Parliamentary Government elected by a large majority of the nation for *the purpose of Government* and a Council of Trade Unions elected by a small minority of the nation – less than one tenth for entirely different purposes. *Everyone who believes in democracy must support Parliamentary Government.* Political creeds for the moment are in abeyance. There is only one issue – the constitution of the country or the Trade Union Congress. This is no moment for niggling distinction and fine criticism. Make your choice on the one broad question.[19]

Meanwhile, also on 6 May, the *British Gazette* declared that the Armed Forces of the Crown would receive the full support of the Government 'in any action that they may find it necessary to take in an honest endeavour to aid the Civil Power'. George V was appalled at this, and through Lord Stamfordham, his private secretary, stated: 'His Majesty cannot help thinking that this is an unfortunate announcement, and already it has received a good deal of adverse criticism.'

Lloyd George, too, realized that this was a time for calm, as he reflected in an article for the United Press Association, an article which brought accusations of his sympathizing with the strikers. Dismissing these charges, Lloyd George quoted in its concluding paragraph:

> Up to now it is in essence an industrial dispute over wages, unfortunately complicated by this 'sympathetic strike'. There is no revolutionary purpose animating the Union leaders who are now in charge. There has so far been no bloodshed. There has been no interference with property, and no personal violence. The whole influence of the strike leaders will be exerted in the interests of law and order. Let us trust that a settlement will be reached whilst calm and restraint are being maintained on both sides. There are grave risks in the whole situation. I put my faith on British coolness and in the British Parliament.

That same day, in the issue dated Saturday, 8 May, Blumenfeld discussed the question of Press censorship: 'Day by day publicity is triumphing over those who sought to muzzle the Press in order to hide the futility of the General Strike. The newspapers could have bought permission to resume work by surrendering their independence. They refused. They are meeting their difficulties without any aid from the unions, and with steady success.'

Blumenfeld was now working seven days a week and during the afternoon of Saturday, 8 May, when the General Strike was at its most bitter, he turned his attention as editor-in-chief to producing the *Sunday Express*. And among the small editorial team was 21-year-old Arthur Christiansen, destined to become one of the *Daily Express*'s greatest editors, who was working as a novice sub-editor on the paper. Running operations, as he he been doing for the past week, Blumenfeld 'took off his black coat and wrapped a white apron around his middle to become Head Printer for the day'. Sydney Long, the Works Manager, fresh from his labours on the *British Gazette*, was the one and only Linotype operator. The chief sub-editor was assigned to the machine room. Christiansen and W.T. Maxwell were the two sub-editors. And as Christiansen was to write later:[20]

> It seemed comically ironic to me that afternoon when Blumenfeld, the Editor-turned-Printer, kept returning copy to myself and to the other sub-editor with instructions to smarten up our first paragraphs and get active verbs into our headlines. 'Blum' was always a finicky stylist. It was he who started the 'Do's and Don'ts', a manual of newspaper grammar and style. As Head Printer he nearly gummed up the works by refusing to hand out our copy to be set into type until it had been approved to the last word.
>
> It was lucky for 'Blum' that Sydney Long was a brilliant Linotype operator – he could set a column of type without a single literal and at such a fantastic speed that in his pre-managerial career he took home more money on piece-rates than the star reporters or even the leader-writers. In every respect Long was in splendid form that day. Having set the type, he assembled the pages. Having supervised the stereo-making, he got the presses rolling. He not only overseered his departmental overseers, he bullied the great Blumenfeld into a feeling that it was easier to be an editor than to be a head printer.

With the first edition safely off stone, Christiansen and the others were relaxing with a cigarette, while waiting for early copies, when into the newsroom walked Beaverbrook, accompanied by James Douglas, the editor; Tom Innes, managing editor; and Fred Doidge, general manager. When Christiansen's turn came to be introduced, everyone seemed to have forgotten his name. 'I got a firm, dry handshake and a meaningful stare, but not a word passed between us. I remember that stare very well.'

Meanwhile, similar pressures were also being felt at *The Daily Telegraph*, and as Lord Burnham was to write in his history of the paper, *Peterborough Court*:[21]

> With overseers and others working we could have produced a full-size four-page paper in Peterborough Court but when Winston Churchill came down to the office with his plans for the *British Gazette* he was promised all available labour. So *The Daily Telegraph* for the first few days published tabloid editions printed in a number of non-union jobbing shops and distributed by an emergency organization with commendable efficiency. Before the end of the strike, work was resumed in Peterborough Court.
>
> One night, Robertson, the stereotypers' overseer, a thorough trade unionist, obviously and deliberately strike breaking, was standing in the foundry after all the plates for the night's edition had been cast. I was carrying plates to the presses. A life-long member of the Stereotypers' Society, he had hardened his heart to work with non-unionists, but he

could not cross the line of another union, and Robertson said to me, 'I wish I could help you with that but it's a Natsopa job.'

Interference with the Gazette

Despite the whole-hearted co-operation of Gwynne, production of the *British Gazette* at the *Morning Post* offices had not been without its difficulties, the main complaint being the interference of Churchill in production matters. This was to lead to a letter from Gwynne – without mentioning Churchill by name – to Davidson, the Deputy Chief Civil Commissioner, on 6 May:[22]

> I think now that we have got over the initial difficulties of bringing out the *British Gazette* that steps should be taken to regularise the position and to get order out of disorder due to the novelty of the task and the suddenness with which we were obliged to embark on it.
>
> My position as I understand it is this. I and my editorial staff have been commandeered with the rest of the *Morning Post* who remain on duty to bring out the *British Gazette*. I edit the paper with the aid of my editorial staff to the best of my ability, but I realise that in this matter I am merely producing the paper and expressing no opinions, and have no right to express them. All that I am concerned with is the production of as good a paper as possible. I realise that you have the last say through yourself or your representative, Mr Caird, in everything that goes into the paper, and I accept without question any decision as to the matter which is to appear. I produce the best that we are capable of, and it lies with you and your department to decide what shall or shall not appear.
>
> So far the arrangement has worked without the slightest friction between myself and your representative, Caird. We have produced the *British Gazette* under very trying circumstances, we are by no means satisfied that we cannot produce a much finer paper. In order to do this, however, it is essential that all orders, communications, instructions and suggestions from the Government should come through one channel, and that channel would naturally be you and your department.
>
> I would ask you most urgently to insist that all Government departments who have communications to make to us should send them through your department as quickly as possible. The paper has been most seriously delayed for the last three issues owing to the fact that communications have been sent in at such a late hour.

Realizing the seriousness of the complaint – and the veiled hint at Churchill's interference – Davidson immediately wrote to the Prime Minister:[23]

> The failure to some exent in the details of the distribution of the *British Gazette* has been due entirely to the fact that the Chancellor [Churchill] occupied the attention of practically the whole of the staff who normally would have been thinking out the details. Of course he was anxious, but it was unfortunate that he tried so persistently to force a scratch staff beyond its capacity. So long as he does not come to the *Morning Post* offices tonight the staff will be able to do what it is there to do, viz. organise the printing, the production and the distribution of the *Gazette*. I must depend on you, and the staff are relying on me, to find some means of preventing his coming. By all means let him put what pressure he can personally upon Sir Malcolm Fraser, who is in general control, and the Stationery Office by interview or letter, but the technical staff should be left to do their job. He rattled them very badly last night. He thinks he is Napoleon, but seriously

> enough the men who have been printing all their life in the various processes happen to know more about their job than he does.

Three nights later, taking heed of Davidson's warning – and urgent messages from Gwynne to the Cabinet that Churchill should be barred from the building: 'he butts in at the busiest hours and insists on changing commas and full stops until the staff is furious' – Baldwin paid a visit to the *Morning Post* offices, where Gwynne introduced him to Sydney Long and the other Fleet Street production volunteers making up the *British Gazette*.

Gwynne was pleased at the Prime Minister's morale-boosting visit, but Churchill's attempt at taking control of the *British Gazette* was still a problem, as Gwynne conveyed the following morning, 10 May, to Lord Percy, a director of the *Morning Post* and Minister for Education, who, as the Government representative, was dealing with the Lobby at the House of Commons:

> Since the beginning of the strike I sit in my office with the Treasury telephone at my elbow and am a kind of liaison officer between the Government and the paper. Winston has been my most frequent visitor, and, between ourselves, he has been a bit of a nuisance, for he is constantly coming in and dictating articles, some of which I have to cut. And then the fun begins.

For Gwynne and his staff, though, their problems were about to come to an end, as on Wednesday, 12 May, the *Evening Standard* announced:[24]

> BREAKING UP
>
> Important developments in the crisis are possible today. It seems clear that the leaders of the strike realise that it is failing and talks were initiated by them last night with the object of finding a speedy way out.

After meeting in the morning, the TUC General Council decided that it could no longer support the miners, and arranged to see Baldwin shortly after noon at 10 Downing Street, where Arthur Pugh, the TUC Chairman, told the Prime Minister that the strike was being called off immediately. Walter Citrine, a fellow-TUC delegate, who was with Pugh, later recorded in his diary:

> While we were talking, Churchill, Baldwin and Steel-Maitland [Minister of Labour] were pacing rapidly up and down the garden, talking animatedly. There was no sign of jubilation amongst them, and Pugh muttered to me: 'I saw Churchill a few minutes ago, and he said, "Thank God it is over, Mr Pugh."'

The immediate act for Churchill was hold hold a meeting of national newspaper editors at the Treasury where he informed them that the next issue of the *British Gazette* would be the last, adding: 'There was always the possibility that a further appearance might have a bad effect on the relations between newspapers and their employees.' Churchill then wrote to Gwynne praising him for all the co-operation that he and his staff had given over the past fortnight. Gwynne, now in a far more amiable mood, thanked Churchill, writing the next day: 'You have been kind enough to say nice things about our humble efforts here to bring out the *British Gazette*. May I lay at your feet my tribute of admiration at your wonderful energy and your marvellous powers of seeing a thing through.'

For *The Times*, the end of the General Strike was to be quite an occasion – the first afternoon edition in its long history. With the official announcement at 1.10 p.m., a special edition of 83,000 copies was on the streets at 2.50 p.m. And as *Strike Nights in Printing House Square*, its privately printed account of the strike, stated:

> It was, of course, a *tour de force*, an experiment not to be repeated too often. But the hundred minutes had been utilized to the full. There, prominently displayed, was the complete official statement. There, too, was a leading article, rapidly recast to meet the new situation. And there, by a strange Providence, was a skeleton staff just sufficient to set and cast and print the paper, and a body of volunteers prepared to distribute it.

The following day, Thursday 13 May, the eighth and final issue of the *British Gazette*, with a circulation of 2,209,000 copies, was published; and in it Churchill wrote: 'The *British Gazette* may have had a short life; but it has fulfilled the purpose of the living. It becomes a memory; but it remains a monument.' For the volunteer staff of the *British Gazette* there were to be awards in the King's Birthday Honours, Sydney Long, so much the power of strength in production, receiving the O.B.E. Gwynne himself declined all honours.

Not everyone, however, applauded the cause; and for Lloyd George the *British Gazette* was 'a first-class indiscretion clothed in the tawdry garb of third-rate journalism'. The most vicious attack, though, was in the *New Statesman* of 15 May:[26]

> One of the worst outrages which the country had to endure – and to pay for – in the course of the strike, was the publication of the *British Gazette*. This organ, throughout the seven days of its existence, was a disgrace to the British Government and to British journalism – in so far as British journalism can be said to have had anything to do with it. It made no pretence of impartiality; it exaggerated, distorted or suppressed news, speeches and opinions for propagandist purposes. It was full of solecisms, half-truths and trivialities. It was supposed to be supporting the authority of Parliament, but it gave us nothing worth calling a report of the proceedings either of the House of Commons or of the House of Lords. For that we had to go to *The Times*. It [the *Gazette*] was, in fact the most incompetently edited paper we have ever seen, and we cannot wonder that even journalists who were in full sympathy with the Government's attitude should have refused to serve under Mr Churchill in producing such stuff. It boasted in its final issue of its gigantic circulation, but it did not say that this was largely achieved by the pushing of unsolicited copies in our letter-boxes. Moreover, the offence of its appearance was aggravated by the wholesale commandeering of newsprint. It was scandalous that *The Times* should be deprived of its paper supplies in order to enable Mr Churchill to poison public opinion. We can only offer our gratitude and our congratulations to *The Times* for the struggle which it made in face of this robbery, and for the way in which it selected the comparatively small amount of news it was able to print, and maintained its best traditions of truthfulness and impartiality.

On 17 May, with the strike finally over, the *Evening Standard* published a bumper 16-page issue; and in his leader, E.R. Thompson, the editor, looked back on the dispute:

> Today the nation begins work once more, after an interruption of its activities which in many respects has had no parallel since the Great War. If we must survey with some

> ruefulness the result of the fortnight's folly we can yet start on the task of making good with some sense of relief if the situation is no worse. A fortnight ago, in the course of an article which was prevented from reaching the public, we wrote: 'The General Strike must fail, as it has always failed.' The nation has won, the costly lesson, it is hoped, has been duly digested. Let recrimination cease, and all classes settle down, on terms of amity and mutual respect, to make good the damage of the great folly.

Afterwards, Beaverbrook told his old friend Tim Healey: 'I think everybody enjoyed the strike – on both sides – volunteers and pickets alike. It was treated in a holiday spirit; and the pickets outside the *Daily Express* office were quite as amused as the amateurs working the mechanical side of the newspaper within. I am almost inclined to favour the idea of having a General Strike once a year by law.'

And for the Newspaper Proprietors Association, following the return to work of the strikers, an agreement was signed with the fourteen leaders of different unions.[27] In five short clauses the agreement ruled out interference with the contents of newspapers. It included the usual provision against victimization; it established the right of management to employ, promote or discharge members of staff, and excepted private secretaries and managers of departments (not engaged in production) from being obliged to belong to any union; it prohibited the holding of union meetings during office hours; and, finally, it recognized the strict observance of agreements as a matter of honour affecting each individual.

The failure of the General Strike left the miners deserted once more, and it was to be another seven months before in November 1926 they were forced back by hunger on the worst possible terms. The eight-hour day was imposed by law, and wages were back to the low point they had been in 1921, and in some places back to the level of 1914. Lack of support from the TUC had left a legacy of disaster for the miners. Baldwin, though, was very much the man of the hour and praise was heaped on him for his skilful leadership and successful conclusion to the strike. Beaverbrook took a much more sardonic view, writing on May 24: 'The laudations which are being poured on Baldwin are pure hysteria. I have worked with him intermittently at one time for ten years at a stretch, and he is a man absolutely without a mind or a capacity to make one up.'

12

Burnham sells the *Telegraph*

ON 1 JANUARY 1928 Viscount Burnham (Harry Lawson) sold *The Daily Telegraph* to Sir William and Gomer Berry (later Lords Camrose and Kemsley) and Edward Iliffe (later Lord Iliffe) and at the same time resigned as chairman of the Newspaper Proprietors Association. Discussing the sale, Lord Camrose was later to write:[1] 'Harry Lawson had not the journalistic flair nor indeed the same interest in newspapers that his father had . . . . and concerned himself more with public causes than he did with the paper.'

Born in 1862, Lawson was educated at Eton and Balliol College, Oxford, where he was secretary of the Union. At Balliol, he had been told by Jowett, the Master: 'Your father owns a great newspaper. There is nothing to beat the job at hand. You must go to it.' With his father, Edward Levy Lawson, becoming a baron in 1903, Harry Lawson was made manager-proprietor of *The Daily Telegraph*, a position he was to hold until selling the paper in 1928, when he was appointed a member of the Indian Statutory Committee.

Initially, Lawson was more interested in politics than journalism and became Liberal MP for West St Pancras at the 1885 general election – and at twenty-two was the 'baby' of the House. He lost his seat in 1892, but won a by-election at Cirencester the following year before being defeated in 1895. He later became a Unionist and represented the Mile End division of Tower Hamlets until succeeding to the barony in 1916.

A keen member of the Territorial Army, he commanded the Royal Bucks Hussars from 1902 to 1913, rejoining his regiment at the outbreak of war in 1914. Lawson was made a Companion of Honour in 1917, created a Viscount that same year and appointed GCMG in 1927. Among the many government committees on which he sat, he is probably best remembered for his work in education, helping to formulate the Burnham scales.

In 1922, Lawson in deciding to replace the out-of-date printing machinery had – against technical advice – insisted that the paper should be the same size as before, some three inches longer than any other London daily. Although the printing improved, the paper was still difficult to handle. And, with the circulation dropping to 84,000 in 1927, and bearing in mind his age and many outside interests, Lawson, as absolute controller, decided to sell. He, therefore, wrote to Sir William Berry, editor-in-chief of *The Sunday Times*, asking him if he 'would be interested in trying [his] hand with a daily newspaper of the same character'.

Following two meetings – the first, through a mix-up in booking, held in the billiards room of the Oxford and Cambridge Club – agreement was reached that Sir William, with his brother, Gomer, and Edward Iliffe, all partners of Allied Newspapers, should take over the *Telegraph* on 1 January 1928 for £600,000, with a further £600,000 on a low mortage, which was paid off four years later. Immediately prior to the new ownership, on 31 December 1927, Sir William – described as 'that rare being: an imaginative Celt without nerves' – addressed the entire staff at the Memorial Hall, Farringdon Street, with Arthur Watson, the managing editor, in the chair. And as he was to write many years later:[2]

> Lord and Lady Burnham were both in tears at the meeting and a number of staff were in the same condition. To many of them the future seemed black as they had no knowledge of what violent changes the new proprietors might have in mind. Happily there were none of that character and those made were gradual and not drastic at any time. I persuaded Colonel Fred Lawson to remain as General Manager. He had been on the paper a number of years and knew everything there was to know about the *Telegraph*. Incidentally, it used to be said that he was one of the few people who really knew their way about the old extensive but mystifying buildings and that when his uncle [Viscount Burnham] attempted to show visitors round he always lost his way. If he had succeeded to control, instead of his uncle, I doubt very much if the Telegraph would have ever reached the position where a sale was necessary or desirable.

And as Charles Wintour was to write of Sir William Berry in *The Rise and Fall of Fleet Street*:[3]

> He took the view that the *Telegraph*'s problems arose not from the staff but from lack of organisation and poor equipment. There was no news editor or news desk; there was no cuttings library. The handful of special writers, usually in frock coats, produced their columns with careful penmanship. And at night the paper was edited by a night editor and five assistants who worked in dignified silence in a large club-like 'library' with horsehair sofas and chairs; the woman's page editor sat behind a curtain, and decorously went home early. There was no proper financial control. A large sum would be needed to modernise the machine room.

Camrose – he had been raised to the peerage in 1929 – had duly taken notice of the problems; and with his fellow-proprietors was to knock down the old offices in Fleet Street and replace them with new premises at a cost of £320,00. Simultaneously, under the direction of Fred Lawson, new presses, costing £250,000, were installed by the autumn of 1930, enabling copies to be printed at the modern cut-off. Following this, it was possible to see the gradual editorial improvements, with a much bigger coverage of news – not 'being seduced by the allure of features'; and within months, still selling at twopence, the *Telegraph* circulation was in excess of 100,000.

The decision was then taken to halve the price to one penny. On Monday 1 December this duly took place: the results were soon apparent and within months circulation had doubled to more than 200,000. Each year, sales of the paper were to increase, and by the end of the decade the *Telegraph* was selling 750,00 copies daily.

Major-General Viscount Burnham (Fred Lawson had succeeded his uncle to the title in 1933) would later write of Camrose: 'He was not only proprietor but editor-in-chief. He brought to his task considerable equipment, not only a knowledge of the world, organizing ability and business training, but a practical experience of editorial organization and control of newspaper production.'

Morning Post *Absorbed*

In January 1937, the Berry brothers and Lord Iliffe decided, amicably, to split their partnership. Lord Camrose took over the shares of the others in *The Daily Telegraph*, Amalgamated Press and the *Financial Times*; and in return resigned from Allied Newspapers and Kelly's Directories. Gomer Berry – now Baron Kemsley – assumed control of *The Sunday Times*, *Sunday Graphic*, *Daily Sketch*, plus a number of provincial dailies, making him the largest newspaper proprietor in Britain. Lord Iliffe, who had been created a baron in 1933, took control of Kelly's Directories and was to remain in charge until the end of 1938, when he sold Kelly's back to Camrose and Kemsley, along with his other remaining interests in the companies.

Apart from the amicable splitting-up with his brother and Iliffe, for Lord Camrose the year 1937 was also notable, with his taking-over the *Morning Post*. Although it had sales of more than 100,000, the *Morning Post* – the oldest newspaper in London – had suffered financially for a number of years. Having been sold by Lady Bathurst in 1924 to a combination headed by the Duke of Northumberland, even a reduction in price two years later to one penny had not brought the expected increased circulation, which could have meant additional advertising revenue.

Now, in the spring of 1937, matters were about to come to a head; and as Viscount Burnham was later to write:[4] 'Colonel Ivor Fraser, general manager of the *Morning Post*, told me that it was in financial straits and asked me to approach Lord Camrose to discover whether he would be interested in its purchase.' On 31 May, therefore, Lord Camrose met Major J.S. Courtauld, chairman of the *Morning Post*, and H.A. Gwynne, its editor, ten days later. A first offer of '£220,800 (£4) a share but payable only in 3½ per cent notes redeemable over five years' was rejected; but on 15 July the shareholders accepted the new offer of '£193,000 in cash (£3.15 a share) plus £20,000 of directors' loans to the company'.

Less than a fortnight later, on 28 July, the directors of the *Morning Post* announced that they had reached agreement with Lord Camrose, and that the transaction would take place on 27 August. There was, though, to be a delay; and it was not until 30 September 1937, that the *Morning Post* appeared for the last time. And in that issue, Gwynne, who had been editor since 1911, was to give an account of the paper's final days:[5]

> It will be seen from the announcement on another page that the *Morning Post*, as a separate paper, appears for the last time in the present issue. Henceforth, it will be

combined with the *Daily Telegraph*, thus closing a life story which has extended continuously for more than a century and a half.

For a long time the *Morning Post* has fought a losing battle. In the fierce stress of present-day competition, new readers have been difficult to get and the advertising revenue has suffered accordingly. This has told its story in a steadily increasing annual deficit, culminating in the year ending 30th June last – a year in which financial and industrial conditions showed a decided turn for the better – with a loss of over £40,000.

The high costs of production which a London daily newspaper must face today – costs which are shortly to be magnified by a steep rise in the cost of newsprint and by other causes – and the ever-increasing service which is demanded from a modern newspaper must militate heavily against an organ whose appeal is necessarily a limited one.

In the light of these facts, the continued publication of the *Morning Post* as a separate newspaper presented difficulties which it has been found impossible to overcome.

The control of the combined *Daily Telegraph* and *Morning Post* by Lord Camrose assures the continuance of clean and responsible journalism, in an independent newspaper, unassociated with any combine. Amalgamation with the *Daily Telegraph* assures the necessary resources and experience which have enabled that paper to make such remarkable strides in the last ten years, and which will continue to be exerted in the interests of the *Daily Telegraph* and the *Morning Post*.

Gwynne retired with a pension of £5000 per annum – his current salary – and the following year, for his long and distinguished services to journalism, he was appointed a Companion of Honour.

Not all readers of the *Morning Post*, however, were in agreement with the merger, Margot Asquith, widow of the Liberal Prime Minister, writing to Gwynne: 'It is *terribly* sad that yr. fine old true blue Tory paper is going to those rich & colourless Camroses. I never agree with a *word* it says, but it has *character* – wh. few papers have, & above all *courage*, wh. no paper has.'[6]

But for Lord Camrose, the merger was a triumph: more than 100,000 *Post* readers were to accept the *Telegraph* – and that paper could show an October figure of 'in excess of 630,000'.

Liberal Papers Merge

Some six seven years earlier, on 2 June 1930, there had been another major merger, *The Times* announcing that 'last night after a week-end during which various rumours about the future of the *Daily Chronicle* had been current in Fleet-street', the following authorized statement was issued by the Press Association:

After to-morrow morning, Monday June 2, the *Daily Chronicle* and the *Daily News* will be published as a single newspaper under the title of the *Daily News and Chronicle*. The amalgamated journal will include all the leading features of both papers. The combined circulation of the two papers is over 1,000,000 and this fusion will create a great Liberal newspaper with a circulation comparable to the largest in the country.

> The *Daily News*, which was founded in 1846 with Charles Dickens as its first editor, is at present owned by News and Westminster Limited, of which the controlling shares are held by the Daily News Trust, created by the late Mr George Cadbury. The *Daily Chronicle*, which was started in 1855 under the title of the *Clerkenwell News*, is at present owned by United Newspapers Limited, control of which is in the hands of the *Daily Chronicle* Investment Corporation. Arrangements have been made for the transfer of the copyright of both papers to a new company.[7]

At the same time the following announcement of the 'fusion' appeared in the *Daily News and Chronicle*:

> We have to announce . . . . that these two great Liberal papers have joined forces and will from to-day be combined in a single newspaper. Under modern conditions, newspaper production is a highly organised and costly enterprise which must be carried out on the largest possible scale if popular daily journals are to give their readers the fullest and best news service, deal adequately with politics, commerce, art, literature, drama, sport and other matters of public interest, and also offer to advertisers a wide publicity. Indeed, rationalisation is as necessary in journalism as in any other great industry, and though there are fewer morning newspapers published in London than there were 30 years ago their number even to-day is larger than it is in New York.
>
> The *Daily News* and *the Daily Chronicle* have both from their foundation been working on parallel lines, have been animated by the same social ideals, and have stood for the same political principles. It will be the endeavour of the *Daily News and Chronicle* to maintain the traditions which it inherits from both its parents. Its influence will be exerted in support of a progressive Liberalism at home and of peace and cooperation in international affairs.
>
> It is our intention that readers of both papers shall continue to find in the new journal the features to which they have been accustomed. Moreover, the pooling of resources covering the entire world will ensure a news service of supreme efficiency. Readers of the *Daily News* will appreciate that in the amalgamated paper they will have the advantage of news on the front page.

With this merger of the two most prominent Liberal titles, the Cadbury family – whose connections with the *Daily News* had stretched back to Edwardian days – were now in charge of the combined newspaper.

The first of the family to have been associated with the *Daily News* had been George Cadbury. Born in Birmingham in 1831, he had been educated at a Quaker school in Edgbaston, and then worked for Joseph Rowntree of York, before joining his father's firm in Birmingham. Following the death of his father, George Cadbury and his elder brother, Richard, took over the company and five years later became the first to manufacture unadulterated cocoa. With business expanding, in 1879 the firm moved to Bournville, four miles from Birmingham, where in 1899, after his brother's death, George Cadbury founded the Bournville Village Trust, providing well-designed housing for his employees.[8]

Early in 1901 – already the owner of ten weekly newspapers in the Birmingham area – Cadbury headed a syndicate which bought the *Daily News* to espouse the Liberal cause and to oppose the war in South Africa. When the other syndicate members dropped out, Cadbury was left as sole proprietor, and wrote to C.P. Scott on 20

December 1901: 'The *Daily News* ought to be a power for peace in the South of England as the *Manchester Guardian* is in the North . . . . I believe that the only change for the *Daily News* would be for one individual practically to have unlimited control.'

Once committed, Cadbury realized that the paper needed a strong editor and engaged A.G. Gardiner. Under his leadership, 'the paper gained an unsurpassed reputation for literary merit', its writers including Arnold Bennett, G.K. Chesterton, Joseph Conrad, John Galsworthy, Henry James, Rudyard Kipling and John Masefield,[9] plus a young, cigarette-smoking Winston Churchill as a part-time leader writer, who presciently ended one article: 'Where is the statesman to be found who is adequate to the times?' Twenty years later, looking back on his editorship, Gardiner was to write: 'Cadbury had taken up the business as his duty, and had no intention of benefitting financially from it, even if the results were satisfactory. It was his determination not to take any profits which might come from the paper but to devote them to the schemes in which he was interested.'

In an effort to increase circulation, Cadbury had reduced the price of the *Daily News* to a halfpenny, while also now printing in Manchester – and at the same time handed over control of the business to his third son, Henry Cadbury. Although circulation increased, losses on the paper remained high, but this did not stop him from expanding the business even further, with the purchase from the Rowntree family of the *Morning Leader* – which he merged with the *Daily News* – and the *Star*, the popular London evening paper. To his son, Laurence, then at Cambridge University, he wrote: 'It was evident that the *Star* with betting news and pleading for social reform and for peace, was far better than the *Star* with betting news and opposing social reform and stirring up strife with neighbouring nations.'

As a Quaker, Cadbury's philosophy was apparent 'from a letter he wrote to accompany the deeds of the Daily News Trust, founded in 1911, to control the papers through its holding of a majority of the ordinary shares of the Daily News Ltd.':

> I desire, in forming the Daily News Trust, that it may be of service in bringing the ethical teaching of Jesus Christ to bear upon National Questions and in promoting National Righteousness; for example that Arbitration should take the place of War, and the Sermon on the Mount, especially the Beatitudes, should take the place of Imperialism and of the military spirit which is contrary to Christ's teaching that love is the badge by which Christians should be known.[10]

Now in his seventies, Cadbury decided to stand down and transfer control to trustees. He died in Birmingham on 24 October 1922; and that same year, Henry Cadbury 'broke with Lloyd George after his refusal to join forces with Asquith'. However, the *Daily Chronicle* – controlled by Lloyd George's political fund (see also chapter nine, p.199–202) – now came under the ownership of Lord Reading, recently Viceroy of India, and Sir Thomas Catto, of Morgan Grenfell.

With the *Westminster Gazette*, originally an evening paper until bought by Lord Cowdray, who in 1921 converted it into a morning title, backing the Liberals, there were now three dailies competing for the same readership. It was to be another seven years, though, before the first step was taken into consolidating the Liberal market when, in January 1928, the *Daily News*, circulation 600,000, merged with the *Westminster Gazette*, 300,000. And unusually for such a merger there were to be no circulation losses.

A key figure in this merger was Walter Layton, editor of *The Economist*, who had turned down the editorship of the *Daily News*, but had agreed to become a member of the board, 'charged with responsibility for editorial policy and an investigation into the newspapers finances'. A distinguished economist, Layton had played a prominent part in the First World War, serving in the Ministry of Munitions before becoming a member of the Milner Mission to Russia in 1917 and the Balfour Mission to the United States that same year. For these services he was appointed CBE and became a Companion of Honour in 1919.

Now, in 1930, hearing that the *Daily Chronicle*, as part of the United Newspapers group, was in receivership, Layton was to play a key role in merging the title with the *Daily News*. As David Hubback was to write: 'Although the holding company, the Daily News Ltd., owned only 36½ per cent of the equity of the *News Chronicle* against the *Daily Chronicle*'s 50 per cent and the *Westminster Gazette*'s 13½ per cent, control, by a trustee agreement, was firmly in the hands of the Daily News trustees.'

The five trustees were: Laurence Cadbury, chairman of the Daily News Ltd.; Walter Layton, chairman of the News and Westminster Ltd., the company set up after the *News*'s merger with the *Gazette*; Lord Cowdray, vice-chairman of the News and Westminster Ltd; Bernard Binder, chairman of United Newspapers; and Jack Ackerman, managing director and vice-chairman of United Newspapers.

With Layton in full editorial control of *News Chronicle* (the result of the merger between the *Daily News* and the *Daily Chronicle*), sales of more than 1,400,000 – and the paper in profit – he was surprised to receive a note of advice from Henry Cadbury:[11]

> I should like to emphasise the fact that I think whereas the actual time given in a newspaper office should not be very great – say 4 or 5 hours on any one day – I do feel it is essential that one's mind should be free to think things out, to see the tendency and trend of affairs, to be ready to switch off on to something quite new and fresh, and to sense quickly what the public is really thinking about. This kind of thing cannot be done by frequent attendances at the Reform Club. Indeed, I think that the Reform Club is the negation of any succesful newspaper enterprise.

For Layton, who never did join the Reform Club, and who was apt to spend up to twelve hours a day at the *Chronicle* office, this advice was hardly necessary.

With the paper now worth more than £1 million, in November 1936 the Cadbury family were able to buy out the other shareholders for £582,000; and for the next twenty-five years they were to reap the dividends of a successful business.

Circulation War

One man, more than any other, was to be responsible for the 1930s Circulation War: Julius Salter Elias, born at Birmingham in 1873. Moving to London with his parents, he delivered morning papers for his father's newsagent's business in Hammersmith; and, at the age of thirteen, was a shop-boy in a Holborn jewellers before, in 1894, when unemployed, joining Odhams Brothers, a small printing firm. He started there at twenty-five shillings a week, and, with his insatiable appetite for work, was soon promoted manager, and four years later was made a director.[12]

With the expansion of their business, Odhams were able to purchase a prominent site in Long Acre, off the Strand, where Elias, now working eighty hours a week, was determined to fill the presses. He believed that the way to expansion was first in print and then in ownership of journals; and as an initial step in 1896 purchased *Table Talk*, the house journal of the Hotel Cecil.

Two years later, Odhams Brothers became Odhams Ltd, a private company which lasted until 1912, before going public. During this period, Elias had endeavoured to obtain the contract to print *Tribune*, a national daily, and the following year, 1907, he even tried for *The Times*. But in neither instance was he successful. However, in 1906 Odhams had produced the first issue of *John Bull* for Horatio Bottomley. A hard-hitting penny weekly, whose main purpose was to expose abuses and rogues, it soon ran into the first of many libel cases, in which Odhams were joint defendants with Bottomley.

In 1920, Elias was appointed managing director of Odhams, and that same year Bottomley sold *John Bull*, but remained its editor. Twelve months later, Odhams, suspicious of Bottomley's Victory Bonds, parted company, and in May 1922 a disgraced Bottomley was imprisoned. For Elias, there was now the challenge of raising further financial capital and of increasing the circulation of *John Bull* which had fallen from 1,700,000 to barely 200,000 copies. Turning the weekly into a family paper, he employed such diverse writers as Arnold Bennett and Field Marshal Lord Haig.

Apart from taking over *John Bull*, Elias had recently bought *Picturegoer*, *Kinematograph Weekly* and *Sporting Life*; and, to keep the huge rotary presses running, in 1925 Odhams acquired a Sunday paper, the *People*, from Colonel Grant Mordern. Under the editorship of Hannen Swaffer, with sales of 300,000, it was losing heavily; but within three years – partly through free life insurance to new readers and other promotional stunts – the circulation was to reach three million. For the newly-appointed editor, Harry Ainsworth, it meant that he was now the highest paid in Fleet Street; and for Elias it meant every Saturday in the office until eight p.m. – and orders that he could be phoned at home any time.

The next step in Elias's plan was to utilize the partly-occupied presses during the week, leading Odhams in 1929 to take over the Labour Party's *Daily Herald*, and as a result Odhams owned 51 per cent and the Trades Union Congress 49 per cent. Progress, initially, was slow, with circulation hovering around the 300,000 mark; and despite the efforts of Ernest Bevin and other Labour Party leaders in helping the *Herald* reach the one million mark, it was still not profitable. Elias now realized that the circulation needed to be more than two million daily.

His plan was simple: to provide free gifts to potential *Herald* readers. And as *The Economist* was to say:[13] 'It began with the giving away of relatively inexpensive objects such as, in a previous age, used to be given away with a pound of tea.' Dozens of canvassers were engaged by the *Herald* – many of them former naval officers – 'glad to earn £3 or so a week touting from door to door'.

Soon the *Daily Express*, 1,693,000; *Daily Mail*, 1,845,000; and *News Chronicle*, 1,400,000; were to be involved in the circulation battle. Political and Economic Planning – an independent non-party group – following a three-year programme could note in its *Report on the British Press*:

> Some 50,000 canvassers were recruited and armed with a selection of merchandise ranging from cameras, fountain-pens, mangles and tea-kettles to silk stockings, flannel trousers and even gold wristlet watches. These they offered to astonished housewives in return for an undertaking to become registered readers for two or three months. Naturally a brisk trade developed in these household necessities and luxuries. It was said (perhaps apocryphally) that a whole Welsh family could be clothed from head to foot for the price of eight weeks reading of the *Daily Express*.

Cost for all the newspapers was high, the *Herald*, for example, paying out £1 to each reader who promised to take the paper for ten weeks at 1*d*. per day. This was a state of affairs that could not exist; and at a special meeting of the Newspaper Proprietors Association, chaired by Lord Riddell, Elias was warned that if the *Herald* continued on its course the other newspapers would out-bid him. Agreement was soon reached: there would be an immediate ban on free gift schemes, nothing would be offered to readers at below cost, and canvassing should continue only on free insurance and competitions.

The uneasy peace was to last until March 1933, when the *Daily Herald* offered its readers a sixteen-volume set of the works of Dickens – originally sold at four guineas – for just eleven shillings plus ninety-six coupons, Elias even mentioning that at that price the paper was making a small profit on each set sold. This was too much for the other newspaper proprietors, who met him at the Savoy Hotel. Beaverbrook demanded that the sets of Dickens be withdrawn. Elias refused, saying that the offer had already been made to the *Herald* readers. An angry Beaverbrook turned on him: 'Elias, this is war – war to the death. I shall fight you to the bitter end', and drawing an imaginary sword ran it through him.

There was to be immediate retaliation from the *Daily Express*, *Daily Mail* and *News Chronicle*, all beginning to offer sets of Dickens' novels – and for Beaverbrook and his *Daily Express*, it was to result in a loss of £18,000 in selling at 10*s*. apiece 124,000 sets of Dickens that had cost 14*s*. 4*d*. each.[14]

In June 1933 the four newspapers concerned were believed to be spending from £50,000 to £60,000 a week between them on free gifts and canvassing. Writing in the *Evening Standard* on 30 June 1933, Sir Emsley Carr, editor of the *News of the World*, estimated that 'the whole mad campaign cost Fleet Street more than three million pounds'. If proof were needed, it had been announced that canvassing in the first six months of 1933 had cost the *Daily Express* nearly £350,000, and between March and June 300,000 readers were added at a cost of 8*s*. 3*d*. a head; but it was 'noteworthy that the *Daily Express* lost a quarter of a million readers as soon as it ceased intensive canvassing, evidence of the artificial nature of a heavily canvassed circulation'.

Notwithstanding these readership losses, Beaverbrook was to be successful: the circulation war had affected Elias adversely, and in 1937 he was ordered into the London Clinic. Although delighted to be made a baron that year, he was not pleased to learn that his battle had been lost to the *Daily Express*, which, at 2,329,000, had long passed the *Daily Herald*, struggling to maintain its 2,000,000 figure.

To a lesser degree, the circulation war was to continue throughout the 1930s, until on 2 February 1938 the newspaper proprietors held informal talks, and 'while an immediate pact is unlikely, it is significant that preliminary exchanges are taking place'. However, within months there were to be far more pressing problems – and with the coming of war all canvassing, prizes, insurances and free gifts were ended by agreement.[15]

Rise of the Daily Mirror

While the popular broadsheets – *Daily Express*, *Daily Herald*, *Daily Mail* and *News Chronicle* – had been involved in their circulation war, on the tabloid front there had emerged one title, the *Daily Mirror*, which was about to have a huge impact on the market. Rothermere having sold his holdings on the Stock Exchange, ownership of the *Daily Mirror* was now more widely spread, but circulation still hovered around the 720,000 mark.

However, through the efforts of Guy Bartholomew, editorial director, the stance of the paper was about to change, appealing to the masses with bright snappy stories, big pictures and bold headlines. Bartholomew was in the van of popular journalism; and the arrival in 1935 of young journalists such as Hugh Cudlipp, William Connor (Cassandra) and Peter Wilson meant that the *Mirror* was laying down the foundations of its future success. Hugh Cudlipp was later to write of those days:

> *The Daily Mirror* was at that time Fleet Street's most identifiable lame duck, quaintly Conservative in its politics; circulation around 700,000 losing 70,000 customers a year through death or boredom, with a musty odour in its wedding-cake edifice in Fetter Lane. There were nose-tapping, rib-digging plans to – well, nobody knew quite what, but there I was in August 1935 at the barricades of the tabloid revolution. The story is well-known of how a phoenix rose rambunctiously from the ashes propelled by Bartholomew's erratic regime, Cecil King's forward thinking and the brilliance of a dozen adventuresome young men lured by the rumours of a *Mirror* revival that would make the American 'populars' look like Wesleyan hymn sheets. In reality, instead of a proprietor's chattel for turning profits to indulging political caprice, in the phrase of the historian A.J.P. Taylor: 'The English people at last found their voice.'

Born at Cardiff in 1913, Hugh Cudlipp was the youngest of three Welsh brothers, all of whom were to edit national newspapers in Fleet Street: Percy, the *Daily Herald*; Reginald, the *News of the World*; and Hugh, the *Sunday Pictorial*. Leaving school, aged fourteen, Hugh Cudlipp became a junior reporter on the expiring *Penarth News*; and after five years in provincial journalism he arrived in London aged nineteen as features editor, *Sunday Chronicle*, then features editor, *Daily Mirror*.

Two years later, in 1937, he was appointed editor of the *Sunday Pictorial*, at the age of twenty-four, the youngest in Fleet Street.[16]

Guy Bartholomew – the key figure in the *Mirror*'s new look – had joined the paper in 1904, just weeks after its launch. His initial post, at thirty shillings a week, was in the new photo-engraving department, producing half-tone blocks for Hannen Swaffer, the flamboyant picture editor. Bart's talents were soon recognized; he secured many pictorial exclusives, and on one occasion, after covering a royal tour, processed the engraving blocks on a steamer in mid-Channel so as to be first with the pictures back in Fleet Street.

In 1913, at the age of twenty-eight, he was appointed art director of the *Daily Mirror*, a role which called for hiring special trains, engaging aeroplanes, and developing with his assistant Macfarlane the Bartlane process for transmitting pictures across the Atlantic. Throughout the twenties he continued to exert considerable influence on the paper's editorial style and in 1934 was promoted to editorial director. 'Bartholomew's true role was in the creation of the *Daily Mirror* in the mid-thirties. It was the paramount newspaper achievement in the twentieth century so far, and success has many fathers.'

To quote Bill Hagerty in his seminal *Read All About It! 100 Sensational Years of the Daily Mirror*:[17]

> From the moment he gained that control, but especially throughout 1934, Bart attacked with ferocity the stuffy image the *Mirror* had managed to construct for itself during Rothermere's reign. The prudish schoolmarm that the paper had become was summarily sacked and a jolly jack-the-lad, sensible but cheeky, supportive but a terrible tease, hired in her place. Had the word entered the lexicon by then, Bart's new *Mirror* could have been described as streetwise. It was also fun, with strip cartoons as a constant ingredient in the editorial mix.

The final member of the triumvirate, Cecil Harmsworth King, was the nephew of Lord Northcliffe; after Oxford University, where he read history, he joined the family firm, working on the *Daily Record*, Glasgow, before moving to the advertisement department of the *Daily Mail*. Following three years with that paper, he transferred to the *Daily Mirror*, 'then a genteel Tory organ', and in 1929 was appointed a director of the paper. He became editorial director of the *Sunday Pictorial* in 1931, and throughout the 1930s was to play a key role with Bartholomew in converting the *Daily Mirror* into a bright and breezy tabloid; and in 1937 was instrumental in appointing Hugh Cudlipp as editor of the *Sunday Pictorial*.

Much later, Cecil King was to comment on that period: 'Our best hope was to appeal to young, working-class men and women . . . . If this was the aim, the politics had to be made to match. In the depression of the thirties, there was no future in preaching right-wing politics to young people in the lowest income bracket.' And for Francis Williams, editor of the rival *Daily Herald*, the *Mirror* displayed 'a frenzied gusto in dredging the news for sensational stories of sex and crime and a complete lack of reticence in dealing with them'.

Finally, to quote Bill Hagerty once more: 'The revolution – conducted by Bart with advisers J. Walter Thompson, the American-owned advertising agency, at his elbow and the towering advertising director, Cecil Harmsworth King, emerging from his dynastic background to lend his not inconsiderable weight in support – continued apace.'

Beaverbrook Forges Ahead

Unlike other owners, Beaverbrook disdained involvement in the regional press. Instead he continued to develop the *Daily Express* and the *Sunday Express* into profitable concerns, building new offices in Fleet Street, Manchester and Glasgow. He believed in ploughing the profits from his newspapers back into the business. His reporting staff was second to none, and every major capital city had an *Express* man in attendance. Under the guidance of Sidney Long, production director, money was spent freely on the best machinery – and, as a result of all this activity, circulation of the *Daily Express* rose to 1.6 million in 1930.

On the editorial side, the venerable R.D. Blumenfeld stepped down as editor of the *Daily Express* in 1929, and was succeeded by Beverley Baxter. Born in Toronto, Baxter had worked as a piano salesman while training to become a concert pianist. During the First World War he had served as a lieutenant with the Canadian Expeditionary Force; and after demobilization, while returning to Canada, took part in a ship's concert. Beaverbrook, sailing on the same vessel, sent him a note: 'I have heard you sing. More than ever I advise you to take up journalism.'[18]

Heeding Beaverbrook's advice, Baxter joined the *Daily Express* in 1920, and two years later was promoted managing editor of the *Sunday Express*. He was promoted further in 1924 when he was appointed managing editor of the *Daily Express* under Blumenfeld. And it was during this period that Beaverbrook engaged E.J. Robertson, another Canadian, in a managerial role. He had met Robertson as a hotel receptionist while working his way through college; and Beaverbrook was known to relate with relish how 'I carried the *Daily Express* to greatness with the aid of a bell-hop and a piano tuner.'

In 1929, Baxter became editor and a director of the *Daily Express*; and as A.J.P. Taylor was to write: 'Baxter was the only editor in Fleet Street who regularly appeared in the office late at night in tails and white waistcoat after a visit to the opera or some grand party.' For Baxter, though, it was not altogether a happy relationship with his proprietor, and in July 1929, following a row with Beaverbrook, he sought – and was offered – the role of editorial director with the Inveresk Company, at a salary of £10,000 per annum. Beaverbrook, on hearing this, saw Tom Clarke, a senior executive on the *Daily Mail*, at his Cherkley home on Sunday 28 July. Clarke was later to write that he was offered £6000 per annum to edit the *Daily Express* and to give full backing to the Empire Crusade (see chapter thirteen). In Clarke's words: 'Maybe I was a fool. The salary was double that I was getting. I could doubtless have arranged to terminate my agreement [with the *Daily Mail*] .... but it never occurred to me to suggest it.'[19]

With Clarke having turned down the job, and Baxter's move to the Inveresk Company not proceeding, the *status quo* was preserved; but for the coming months there was to be increasing tension between Baxter and Beaverbrook. For instance, on 4 September 1930 Beaverbrook could complain: 'The *Daily Express* is not nearly as good as it was. Don't think that is the view of the public. It is the view of your own old colleague. The energy is gone. The initiative does not exist any more.'

Baxter's opinions were now differing more and more from those of Beaverbrook, and, with the introduction of a young Arthur Christiansen to the London office, he realised that he was about to be replaced as editor, and in September 1933 resigned.

The new man, Arthur Christiansen, destined to be the paper's greatest editor, was born in Wallasey, Cheshire, and educated at the local grammar school before, at the age of sixteen, joining the *Wallasey and Wirral Chronicle* – and within two years, through his linage activities, was earning more than his editor. After three years at the *Chronicle*, Christiansen moved to the *Liverpool Evening Express*, and in 1925 became the paper's London editor. On Saturdays, though, he worked as a casual sub-editor on the *Sunday Express*, and was soon taken on the staff as news editor, and then in 1928 promoted to assistant editor.

In the early hours of Sunday 5 October 1931 Christiansen was given the opportunity that would go down in Fleet Street folklore. Called out of bed at one a.m., with the news that the R101 airship had crashed in France, he dashed back to the office within twenty minutes to organize four special editions, arrange box-outs and lay on extra trains for the anticipated increased circulation. For the *Sunday Express*, the disaster was the scoop of the decade, and for Christiansen a phone call from Beaverbrook: 'You have secured a wonderful feat of journalism. I am proud to be associated with a newspaper on which you work.'[20]

Beaverbrook was not to forget that night, and in 1932 he sent Christiansen to Manchester to edit the northern edition of the *Daily Express*, then bringing him back the following year to London as assistant editor. Within months, he had replaced Baxter as editor; and many years later Christiansen was to write in his autobiography, *Headlines All My Life*:

> They placed [with me] George Gilliat, an elderly journalist who had been editing the *Evening Standard* for some years. It was made clear to me that Gilliat was the senior, and that while I was to run the paper, his decisions on all matters must be recognised. This arrangement seemed fair enough. Gilliat interfered as little as possible and was such a kindly, diffident man that I had no difficulty in getting my own way . . . . [He] was withdrawn from the scene six weeks later and went into happy retirement. I was therefore Editor. But nobody can give me the exact date in December 1933.[21]

The results were to be soon apparent: by the mid-1930s, the *Express*,with a circulation of 2,200,000, could claim the world's biggest daily sale. Beaverbrook was to say of this period: 'We appealed to the character and temperament which was bent on moving upwards and outwards.' The aims were simple: 'More life; more hope; more money; more work; more happiness.'

Throughout his long editorship of 24 years, Christiansen was the man who led popular British journalism; and his marrying-up of attractively-written articles, tight sub-editing and sharp layout – plus a reporter at every major event at home and abroad – ensured that the *Express* was the most-read newspaper in the land. He said of his role:

> Show me a contented newspaper editor and I will show you a bad newspaper. Throughout my years of office I was brooding, carping, despairing, doleful, self-critical, snarling, suspicious, tendentious, wary – and so on, right through the dictionary. I praised extravagantly and kicked unmercifully. I was also praised and kicked in the same measure.

Christiansen was not just a master craftsman who revolutionized the face of popular newspapers. He never ceased his quest for capturing the mood and the needs of his readership. He communicated directly with his staff each day through the famous editorial bulletin which he dictated to his secretary before lunch and which appeared on the notice board in the afternoon. Lavish in his praise, caustic in criticism, the daily bulletin reflected Christiansen's general principles in running a successful popular newspaper.

Cyril Aynsley, a long-serving senior editorial executive during those years, was to write:[22]

> By constantly reminding his staff of the importance of maintaining 'the common touch' he was also reminding himself, aware that living in the West End could breed a dangerous isolationism. He personalised the contact between newspaper and reader in two mythical figures The Man on the Promenade at Rhyl and The Man in the Back Streets of Derby.
>
> The Man on the Rhyl Promenade says: 'What's this Chateau and garlic stuff in the *Daily Express* today? My champagne touch is a bottle of Guinness and a plate of winkles.' Or the Man from Derby asks: 'What is the Civil List? and 'What is the Privy Purse?'

Himself a perfectionist, Christiansen demanded perfection from everybody, evidenced by another of his bulletins: 'It is journalistic fashion to concentrate on the first paragraph of stories. I believe in that. But I believe just as emphatically in the perfection of the last paragraph.'

By the end of the decade, with a circulation of 2,329,000, the *Daily Express*, producing from its 'black-glassed buildings' in London, Manchester and Glasgow, was the most popular of all the dailies; and was the one paper on which most journalists craved to work. Christiansen was to say that only two journalists – A.J. Cummings and Ian Mackay, both of the *News Chronicle* – had turned him down.

Undoubtedly, a major part of the secret of the paper's success lay in the chemistry between its editor and its proprietor, as Christiansen himself was to write: 'I was not a political journalist. My proprietor was a journalist and a political animal. The policies were Lord Beaverbrook's, the presentation mine.'

For Beaverbrook, though, despite his undoubted triumph as a newspaper magnate, there was to be no such success in politics; and his Empire Free Trade Campaign – supported by Rothermere – was deemed a failure, even bringing down the wrath of Prime Minister Stanley Baldwin.

13

Prerogative of the harlot

FROM THE AUTUMN OF 1923, when Beaverbrook sold the Hulton newspapers to Rothermere, links between the Press barons had grown closer – both having one common enemy: Conservative politician Stanley Baldwin. On 22 November, within weeks of the Hulton sale (noted in chapter ten, p.210–212), Rothermere had written to Beaverbrook asking if he 'could purchase an interest in your newspapers'. Almost by return, Beaverbrook replied: '. . . . of course I would like you to purchase an interest in Express newspapers. Nothing would give me greater pleasure than to work in co-operation with you and, indeed, with the *Daily Mail*.'

Ever-conscious of the attacks from Beaverbrook and Rothermere, on 18 May 1924 the *People*, then an independent Conservative newspaper, published a long interview with Baldwin, latterly Prime Minister, in which he revealed his contempt for the Press lords:[1]

> I am attacked by the Trust Press, by Lord Beaverbrook and Lord Rothermere. For myself I do no mind. I care not what they say or think. They are both men that I would not have in my house. I do not respect them. Who are they? . . . This Trust Press is breaking up. The *Daily Mail* is dead; it has no soul. Northcliffe, with all his faults was a great journalist, with a spark of genius. But this man!

The controversy was now to gain further coverage, evidenced by a quatrain that was to circulate in official circles:

> When round for public works we look,
> Two pressing jobs at once appear:
> To dam for ever Beaver Brook
> And drain the mud from Rother mere

And as Tom Driberg was to write: '*The Morning Post*, characteristically, published a rendering of this into Latin Sapphics':[2]

> Herculem quisquis studet aemulari
> Purget Augeae Rotheris lacunam
> Castorisque infanda premat perenni
> Flumina claustro

Even Herbert Morrison, a future Home Secretary, contributed to the row, when writing an open letter to Beaverbrook and Rothermere in *London News*:

My Lords,

You're a bright pair of lads, aren't you?

Has it ever dawned on you that nobody in Great Britain is doing more to destroy the influence of the Press than you two specimens of the Lloyd-Georgian aristocracy?

I am, My Lords,
Yours for Socialism,
Herbert Morrison

Labour are Successful

By the spring of 1929 the Conservative-dominated Parliament elected in October 1924 had almost run its course, so Baldwin decided to ask for a dissolution. Under his leadership, the Conservatives hit upon the slogan 'Safety First'. Labour, though, believed that they alone could cure the increasing problem of unemployment. The electorate were to agree; and following the poll of 31 May, Labour were to be succesful with 287 seats, followed by the Conservatives 261 and the Liberals 59. For Beaverbrook, it was the desired result, writing to Lord Birkenhead: 'I rejoiced in Baldwin's downfall. I wanted the defeat of the Government because I believe it was bad.'

Within days there was to be a dramatic move, when G. Ward Price, writing in the *Daily Mail* – with Rothermere's blessing – put forward the premise that at the forthcoming National Conference of Conservative Associations there should be a motion to depose Baldwin and elect Beaverbrook as leader. Ward Price wrote: 'His peerage could be only a temporary handicap, since the reconstruction of the Upper House, with the abolition of the hereditary principle, must soon make it possible for all peers to sit in the House of Commons.'

For Gwynne and his sardonic leader writers this was too good a chance to miss in the *Morning Post*:

> Here, indeed, is an argument which might reconcile the Conservative Party to the abolition of the hereditary principle – that it might set free Lord Beaverbrook from the only obstacle – the obligation of his caste – which prevents him from becoming their leader. At last we have an adequate reason for reconstructing the House of Lords.

Beaverbrook was now becoming more and more involved in his pet project: Empire Free Trade, and on 24 October 1929 he published a penny pamphlet setting out his credo:

> The foodstuffs that we need in this country could all be raised either on our own soil or in the British Dominions, Colonies or Protectorates. The coal, machinery and textiles that the increasing populations of our new territories overseas demand could be supplied by the mines and factories of Great Britain and its Dominions.

Within days of its publication, he was in discussion with Neville Chamberlain and, later, Stanley Baldwin, having been urged to work through Parliament in his efforts to secure Empire Free Trade.[3] Beaverbrook, however, had a poor opinion of both politicians, writing to William Hearst, the American newspaper magnate: 'Churchill should be their leader. But the Conservatives will have none of him. He has served too many parties. If Baldwin is dismissed Neville Chamberlain will take his place. He is as bad as Baldwin.'

Nevertheless, two months later, on 5 January 1930, now writing in the *Sunday Pictorial* – another Rothermere title – Ward Price, after attacking Baldwin for having given the vote to 'millions of flappers who promptly helped to put the Socialists in office', returned once more to the need for a replacement:

> The conviction is fast spreading among Conservatives that their next leader must be found outside the established hierarchy . . . . the name of Lord Beaverbrook becomes steadily more prominent . . . . *There is no man living in this country today with more likelihood of succeeding to the Premiership of Great Britain than Lord Beaverbrook.*

A few days later, at a public luncheon, a delighted Beaverbrook could declaim that Rothermere was 'the greatest trustee of public opinion we have seen in the history of journalism'.[4]

Events were now moving fast, and on 17 February 1930 Beaverbrook, with the ever- increasing backing of Rothermere, launched the United Empire Party. For the *Daily Mail*, it was the *only* story; and during the next twelve days the rise of the new party dominated the paper: readers were informed that the nation was undergoing a dramatic change, and daily thousands of followers were registering their approval.

Beaverbrook, with £70,000 and Rothermere, in close support, now launched a fighting fund of £100,000, and swiftly placed display advertisements in all the leading newspapers, forecasting that at the next election the United Empire Party would 'contest half the seats in the country'. There was to be an exception, the *Morning Post* refusing to accept the advertisement.

However, after just three weeks, Beaverbrook stood down from the party – mainly due to a speech by Baldwin at the Hotel Cecil on 4 March, which pledged that if he were to be returned to power he would hold a national referendum on food taxes. Beaverbrook wrote that it would not now be necessary to contest the Conservatives. Although subscriptions were being sent back, Rothermere was determined that the United Empire Party should continue, announcing that 'more than half of those whose subscriptions to the Party had been returned had sent the money back again'.

The 'truce' was to last just a month, when on 4 April Beaverbrook criticised Baldwin for a leaflet put out by Conservative Central Office, adding that it was 'one in a chain of events which have gradually made the present position extremely difficult'. For C.P. Scott in the *Manchester Guardian*: 'The true explanation is that Lord Rothermere has at long last succeeded in opening Lord Beaverbrook's eyes to the fact that March 4th marked a Baldwin, not a Beaverbrook, victory.'

Determined to pressurize Beaverbrook and Rothermere, Baldwin now called a meeting of the Conservative Party at Caxton Hall, London, taking the opportunity to launch a savage attack on the Press lords:[5]

> I have been very busy working for the party, making speeches all over the country. While I have been away a good many have been at work 'queering my pitch'. I can use that expression to you as I can the expression 'playing the game'. I cannot use it to that section of the press, because those words would convey no meaning to them . . . .

> There is nothing more curious in modern evolution than the effect of an enormous fortune rapidly made, and the control of newspapers of your own. The three most striking cases are Mr Hearst in America, Lord Rothermere in England and Lord Beaverbrook. It seems to destroy the balance – the power of being able to suppress everything that a man says that you do not like, the power of attacking all the time without there being any possibility of being hit back; it goes to the head like wine, and you find in all these cases attempts have been made outside the province of journalism to dictate, to domineer, to blackmail.

Baldwin then told the meeting of a request from a Beaverbrook representative that 'his lordship would want to be consulted on certain offices in the government if they were to become allies'. There was to be one final damning indicitment: the reading by Baldwin of a letter sent by Rothermere to a Conservative supporter laying down conditions for supporting the leader. Rothermere was demanding to know Baldwin's policy and to obtain the names of some ten of his most prominent colleagues in the next government. To Baldwin, this was the final insult: 'I repudiate it with contempt and I will fight that attempt at domination to the end.'

During the summer months, the campaign had gone quiet – Beaverbrook had been in Russia with Arnold Bennett – and it was not until 30 October 1930 that Vice-Admiral Taylor, the first of the Empire Crusade candidates, fought a by-election, and thanks to the support of Beaverbrook – and eleven members of his household staff at Cherkley as canvassers – was successful by 941 votes over the official Conservative candidate. A shock defeat for the Tory Party leadership revealed that there were now serious divisions. To quote Paul Ferris:[6]

> The Conservatives were so anxious about the newspaper threat to the party leadership that they considered starting a new evening paper of their own,and might have done so if anyone would have put up the eight hundred thousand pounds it was estimated to cost.

Indeed, dissent in the party's ranks meant that by early 1931 Baldwin's position was now in question; and on 25 February Sir Robert Topping, the chief Conservative agent, wrote to Neville Chamberlain urging the need for a new leader. And less than a week later, on 1 March, Chamberlain faced Baldwin with the letter, afterwards noting in his diary: '4.30. S.B. has decided to go at once.'

St George's By-election

In Baldwin's terms, 'at once' did not mean immediately, but it was to be Beaverbrook, ironically, who was to save the day through his intervention in a by-election at St George's, Westminster. This was an impregnable Conservative seat, and it was to become a straight issue over Baldwin's leadership. Following the refusal of two prominent Conservatives to support Baldwin, the party looked to Duff Cooper, a former Member for Oldham, who, with his wife, Lady Diana – a close friend of Beaverbook – were two of London's leading socialites. Opposing him was to be Sir Ernest Petter, an industrialist from the West Country, backed by Beaverbrook and Rothermere.

Beaverbrook rightly considered that the primary issue of the by-election was over the leadership of the Conservative Party: 'If we win this fight, the Conservatives will select a new leader and take up our policy and we'll all live happily ever after.' Even before the fortnight's canvassing began, Beaverbrook, 'in the friendliest manner', tried to dissuade Duff Cooper from standing: 'He felt that I should lose, that my support of Baldwin, who would have to retire, would do me no good in the party.' In his autobiography, *Old Men Forget*, Duff Cooper left a memorable account of the contest:

> Servants have little time to read a newspaper in the morning, but if they do cast an eye on one in the West End of London it will almost certainly be either the *Daily Express* or the *Daily Mail*. In the afternoon when they have more time at their disposal they will turn to the *Evening News* or the *Evening Standard*. These four papers were my chief opponents, and every issue of them was devoted to damaging my cause. The only other evening paper, the *Star*, was neutral, as was the rest of the press with the exception of the *Daily Telegraph*, which gave me support.

Speaking at sixteen venues and paying all Petter's expenses, Beaverbrook fought hard for his candidate; and there was to be support from Lord Castlerosse, in an article in the *Evening Standard* entitled 'Enjoying himself in St George's':[7]

> The inhabitants of the West End are having a golden age. 'City Lights' turned the limelight on them, and there is ending an election which has even put 'The Circus' into the shade. Sir Philip Sassoon made the mistake in going to Berlin with Charlie Chaplin: he should have stayed here in London, where the fun is far more furious. To have a vote in St George's today invites fame. I have been asked out to dinner by people, who, ordinarily speaking, would offer me but an occasional cup of prussic acid.

On 18 March 1931, at an eve-of-poll meeting, Baldwin spoke for Duff Cooper at the Queen's Hall and there his speech, bringing out the months of frustration and indignation, was on the theme of persecution by the Press; and it was to be developed relentlessly:[8]

> I have said little. It is not worth it. I am going to say something today. The newspapers attacking me are not newspapers in the ordinary sense. They are engines of propaganda for the constantly changing policies, desires, personal wishes, personal dislikes of two men.
>
> What are their methods? Their methods are direct falsehood, misrepresentations, half-truths, the alteration of the speaker's meaning by publishing a sentence apart from the context, such as you see in these leaflets handed out outside the doors of this hall; the suppression and editorial criticism of speeches which are not reported in the paper. These are methods hated alike by the public and by the whole of the rest of the Press . . . .
>
> I have used an expression about 'insolent plutocracy'. These words appeared in the *Daily Mail* of yesterday week: 'These expressions come ill from Mr Baldwin, since his father left him an immense fortune which, so far as may be learned from his own speeches, has almost disappeared. It is difficult to see how the leader of a party who has lost his own fortune can hope to restore that of anyone else, or of his country.'
>
> I have one observation to make about this. It is signed 'Editor, *Daily Mail*'. I have no idea of the name of that gentleman. I would only observe that he is well qualified for the

> post which he holds. The first part of that statement is a lie, and the second part of that statement is by its implication is untrue. The paragraph itself could only have been written by a cad. I have consulted a very high legal authority, and I am advised that an action for libel would lie. I shall not move in the matter, and for this reason: I should get an apology and heavy damages. The first is of no value, and the second I would not touch with a barge-pole.
>
> What the proprietorship of these papers is aiming at is power, and power without responsibility – the prerogative of the harlot throughout the ages.

The crucial final sentence was the work of Baldwin's cousin, Rudyard Kipling, and long before Max Aitken's first friend when he arrived in England. Harold Macmillan, who had been present at the meeting, was to write: 'For once in his life Baldwin was angry.' And for Duff Cooper, the last-minute intervention of Baldwin meant that the result was no longer in doubt – he was elected with a majority of 5700. Less than a week later, when he took his seat in the House of Commons, 'Mr Baldwin walked on my right – a rare honour to be accorded by the leader of the party. He knew how important the result of the election had been to him.'[9]

As Hugh Cudlipp was to write: 'Of permanent significance, the baleful influence of proprietorial journalism was diminished. The personal prestige of Beaverbrook and Rothermere as Press barons, which rarely extended beyond mutual genuflection, plummeted: so did their power, though not their pride or arrogance.'

Abdication Crisis

In the autumn of 1935, while a growing tension was emerging with Germany and Italy, the health of George V continued to deteriorate. On 9 December he received Anthony Eden, the Foreign Secretary, at Buckingham Palace and had discussions concerning Italy and Abysinnia, and possible conflict. Less than a fortnight later the King travelled to Sandringham to spend a traditional Christmas with other members of the Royal Family. He was now unwell, and on 17 January 1936 made his final, almost illegible, entry in his diary: 'A little snow and wind'. That same day the Prince of Wales flew to Sandringham: 'The air was clear; and as the semi-circle of the Wash came slowly into view, leaden grey under the winter sun, a sudden impulse made me signal the pilot to make a wide circle around the estate. Here was my father's home, a place he preferred to palaces . . . . It was impossible to believe that his life might be coming to an end.'

On 18 January the King's condition worsened, and the following morning the Prince of Wales drove to 10 Downing Street to inform Stanley Baldwin, the Prime Minister, that the King's death was imminent. He was met by Mrs Baldwin who invited him to join them at her birthday tea. When the Prince had finished telling the Prime Minister the grave news, Baldwin murmured his sympathy, adding, almost wistfully: 'I wonder if you know, Sir, that another great Englishman, a contemporary of your father's, died yesterday. But, of course, Sir, you have a great deal on your mind. I should not have expected you to know that it was Rudyard Kipling, my first cousin.'

At 9.25 p.m. on 20 January Lord Dawson, the King's physician, drafted a notice for the waiting Press at Sandringham: 'The King's life is drawing peacefully to its close.' For more than fifty years the King had kept a diary in his careful script, but the final entry is in the handwriting of Queen Mary: 'My dearest husband, King George V, was much distressed at the bad writing above and begged me to write his diary for him next day. He passed away on January 20th at 5 minutes to midnight.'[10]

Among the many messages of sympathy from world leaders was one from Adolf Hitler, the German Chancellor: 'The news of the death of His Majesty has deeply grieved me. I beg your Majesty to accept my and my Cabinet's sincere sympathy and the assurance that the whole German nation mourns with the great loss of the Royal Family and the British nation.' In Doorn, the Netherlands, it was reported: 'The ex-Kaiser had been aroused from his sleep shortly after midnight to be told of the death of King George V in accordance with special instructions given to his household before he went to bed. He expressed the deepest regret at the sad tidings.'

While George V was deeply mourned, there were also tributes to the new King Edward VIII; and in the House of Commons the Prime Minister could declare: 'Congratulations to our new King as he takes his place in the long line of his distinguished ancestors .... He has the secret of youth in the prime of age.'

Enter Mrs Simpson

Now, in the autumn of 1936, a crisis which had long lain dormant at last broke out into the open. For a number of years, the future Edward VIII had conducted a close relationship with Mrs Wallis Simpson, an American lady, married to an Englishman and living in London. Newspaper proprietors and editors – like so many politicians – were aware of the stories circulating in the American Press; but the general public was in complete ignorance.

Early that summer, a young William Deedes, then a reporter on the *Morning Post*, was asked by his editor, H.A. Gwynne, to obtain cuttings from overseas newspapers on the relationship, which could then be passed on to the Prime Minister. To quote Deedes:[11]

> Gwynne, who had been editor since 1911, was close to Baldwin .... Which of them initiated the request for cuttings I was not told and have never known. The slips were not difficult to gather. I worked through Hachette, the international booksellers and distributors. Some periodicals – including, I seem to recall, *Time* magazine – had been cut or blacked before I could lay hands on them. (This was not, as some will readily surmise, the work of ministers, but a precaution taken by distributors against possible writs for defamation.) I submitted the bundle. Word came back: the Prime Minister tells Gwynne that he must have more time. History confirms that this was his tone at the period.

On 27 October 1936 at the Ipswich Assizes, Mrs Wallis Simpson was granted a decree nisi by Mr Justice Hawke on the grounds of adultery by her husband, Mr Ernest Simpson, for an act of adultery committed at the Hotel de Paris, Bray, in the preceding July. The suit was undefended. To quote Deedes:

> The christian name of the lady at the Hotel de Paris, though this does not appear in history books, was Marigold. I never met her, but I heard enough from colleagues attending the case to form an impression. I have always vizualised Marigold as a figure straight out of A.P. Herbert's satire on divorce in those days, *Holy Deadlock*. I see her, even now, sitting fully clothed and knitting in the room of the gentleman concerned while the lurking detectives took appropriate notes.

Harold Nicolson was to write in his diary:[12] 'Mrs Simpson has now obtained her divorce, and there are very serious rumours that the King will make her Duchess of Edinburgh and marry her. The point is whether he is so infatuated as to insist on her becoming Queen or whether the marriage will be purely morganatic.'

Eleven days before the divorce proceedings – with the foreign newspapers ready to cover the case in great detail – Edward VIII, through Mike Wardell, a close friend and chairman of the *Evening Standard*, had approached Beaverbrook for assistance:

> At my request, Max Beaverbrook came to the Palace on October 16. I told him frankly of my problem. I had no thought of asking him to use his influence on other newspaper publishers for the purpose of hushing up the news of the imminent divorce proceedings. My one desire was to protect Wallis from sensational publicity at least in my own country. Max heard me out: 'All these reasons,' he said, 'appear satisfactory to me – I shall try to do what you ask.' Without delay he began a prodigious task, unique in the annals of Fleet Street, where the the mere suggestion of censorship offends.[13]

Beaverbrook's account was basically similar:

> The King asked me to help in suppressing all advance news of the Simpson divorce, and in limiting the publicity after the event. He stated his case calmly and with great cogency and force. The reasons he gave for his wish were that Mrs Simpson was ill, unhappy, and distressed by the thought of notoriety. Notoriety would attach to her only because she had been his guest on the *Nahlin* and at Balmoral. As the publicity would be due to her association with himself, he felt it his duty to protect her.

Following the meeting, Beaverbrook immediately contacted Esmond Harmsworth (a director of the *Daily Mail*, Lord Rothermere's heir and a close friend of the King), and Sir Walter Layton, in charge of the *News Chronicle*, writing also to newspaper associates in Dublin and Paris. To Percy Cudlipp, editor of the *Evening Standard*, who had asked if details of the divorce should appear in the paper, Beaverbrook had replied: 'Publish.' But, following the King's intervention, Mrs Simpson's divorce received only brief formal reports and went though unnoticed by the public. 'The *Morning Post* [published] a 10-point paragraph, the *Daily Telegraph* ran to twenty-two lines but on an away news page, sandwiched between "Colonel accused in private" and " Boy with a mania for silk stockings".' And for *The Times*, editor Geoffrey Dawson was to note in his diary of 27 October:

> It was the day that the Simpson divorce went through at the Ipswich Assizes. They had rung me up from the office one night when I was out to ask how this now imminent event was to be chronicled in *The Times*, and I pointed out the perfect model – a paragraph with one headline – in the recent divorce of Mrs 'X'. This was all in fact that the English law permitted, and so we acted when the time came.

With the King giving no indication that he intended to marry Mrs Simpson – and her solicitor, Theodore Goddard, an old friend of Beaverbrook, confirming this – Beaverbrook left for America. 'And I believed it,' he was later to write. 'The sole purpose of the application to you is to escape as far as possible the publication of unjustifiable gossip concerning the King.' While a sanguine Beaverbrook was en route to the United States, the crisis deepened. The King was now even more determined to marry Mrs Simpson – and retain the throne.

On 11 November, Dawson met the Prime Minister at 10 Downing Street and asked him how long the King's affair could be kept out of the Press. Baldwin, however, could not offer any advice. Meanwhile, Gwynne was pressing Baldwin, saying: 'The Press could not continue to keep silent unless assured that the Government had the matter in hand.' Baldwin could reply only that he and a close circle of senior Ministers were 'keeping a watch on the situation' – but he had not raised the matter with the Cabinet.

Six days later, on the morning of Monday 16 November, Gwynne and Dawson met at the Bath Club. Gwynne, the ever-forceful Welshman, 'was in favour of simultaneous common action by the newspapers when the time came and of direction by the Government'. Dawson, however, pointed out the inadvisability of presenting such a united front; nevertheless he left the meeting certain that the *Morning Post* would act only in concert with the other national newspapers.

That same day, Baldwin was summoned by the King to Buckingham Palace, who told him:[14] 'I understand that you and several members of the Cabinet have some fear of a constitutional crisis developing over my friendship with Mrs Simpson.' Pulling deeply on his pipe, the Prime Minister confirmed that he and his senior Cabinet colleagues were disturbed over the prospect of the King marrying someone whose former marriage had been dissolved by divorce. 'I believe I know,' he said, 'what the people would tolerate and what they would not. Even my enemies would grant me that.'

Leading Society Light

One of the key social personalities of this time, 'Chips' Channon, MP for Southend, but, more importantly, a leading light in London society – and a confidant of the King – has left in his diaries an absorbing account of the crisis. On 21 November he noted:

> London is suddenly seething with rumours: sinister, unlikely rumours .... Mr Baldwin has spoken separately to all the Cabinet, telling them that he had seen the King, and had with all respect protested at his association with Wallis, and declared that unless the King promised never to marry her, his Government would resign. He gave the King three weeks in which to make up his mind .... Beaverbrook is rushing across the Atlantic in order to help him .... [he] apparently sailed ten days ago for America en route for Arizona in the hope of curing his asthma, and was bombarded all the way over with cables and appeals from the King to return urgently. The crossing in the *Bremen* was bad and Beaverbrook, tired and ill, cabled back that he would return in a few days' time, after a short rest in New York. The King cabled through his solicitors that it was urgent, and that there was not a moment to be lost and Beaverbrook sailed seven or eight hours after his arrival in the same ship.[15]

Two days later, on 23 November, Esmond Harmsworth was received by the Prime Minister at 10 Downing Street. It was not a happy occasion; and much later Baldwin was to recall:

> I told him that he and his paper did not really know the mind of the English people: whereas I *did*. And I explained to him that a morganatic marriage would mean a special Bill passed in Parliament; and that Parliament would *never* pass it. Harmsworth said: 'Oh, I'm sure they would. The whole standard of morals is so much more broadminded since the War.' I replied: 'Yes, you are right: the ideal of morality . . . . certainly *has* gone down since the War: but the ideal of Kingship has gone *up*.'

Meanwhile, newly-arrived from New York, and having heard of the Cabinet meeting, an agitated Beaverbrook hurried to Buckingham Palace: 'Sir,' he exclaimed, 'you have put your head on the execution block. All that Baldwin has to do now is to swing the axe.' Beaverbrook asked the King if he had seen the cables which Baldwin had sent to the governments of Australia, Canada, New Zealand, South Africa and the Irish Free State: 'Do you recommend the King's marrying morganatically? Or if the King insists upon marrying, do you recommend abdication?' To the King's reply of 'No', Beaverbrook urged that he should stop their being sent. 'I am a Canadian. I know the Dominions. Their answer will be a swift and emphatic No.'

Less than a fortnight later the storm broke – and from a most unexpected quarter. On 1 December 1936 the Bishop of Bradford, the Right Reverend A.W.F. Blunt, made a startling speech in which he referred to the coming Coronation and the King's unawareness of his 'need of Divine grace'. It needed only this criticism to bring the affair into the open. The story was picked up by the provincial newspapers, led by the *Yorkshire Post*, still under the control of A.H. Mann, a former *Evening Standard* editor. Not only was the Bishop's speech reported in full but there were also strong condemnatory leaders. 'Dr Blunt must have had good reason for so pointed a remark. Most people are by this time aware that a great deal of rumour has been published of late in the more sensational American papers.'

Having received the first press agency report of the Bishop's speech, Beaverbrook at once telephoned the King who was taken by surprise. 'What are the London papers going to do?' I asked him. 'They will report Dr Blunt's speech.' 'With editorial comment?' 'No,' he answered, 'that will be reserved until the results of tomorrow's Cabinet meeting are available.' The gentlemen's agreement in Fleet Street lasted less than twenty-four hours. Led by *The Times*, the facts were printed in detail for the first time. Dawson was later to write:[16]

> In the late evening [December 2] as I was struggling with the paper he [Baldwin] rang me up twice himself – the only time, I think, to say that His Majesty was worrying him to find out, and if necessary stop what was going to appear in *The Times*. He understood that there was to be an attack on Mrs Simpson and 'instructed' the Prime Minister to forbid it. In vain S.B. had explained that the press in Britain was free, and that he had no control over *The Times* or any other newspaper. When he spoke to me, full of apologies, the second time, it was to say that the King would now be satisfied, and leave the Prime Minister alone, if the latter would read the leading article to him. Could I possibly let him see it for the sake of peace? By this time, as I told him, the paper was just going to press,

> but towards midnight I sent a proof of the leader by messenger to Downing Street and heard no more about it. S.B. – with Tommy Dugdale and all the other faithful staff who were supporting him – were able at last to go to bed.

With the Press having broken its silence at long last, for the majority of the country there was now almost a total disbelief that their King should be determined to put his throne at risk. There swiftly grew a faction in support of the King, and in London crowds paraded through the streets, singing 'God Save the King', and assembling outside Buckingham Palace all night. 'After the first shock the country is now reacting, and demands that their King be left in peace.' In the House of Commons, on 4 December Baldwin could add nothing to his statement of the previous day; but later on that evening he drove down to Fort Belvedere, near Windsor, to see the King once more.

Beaverbrook, ever eager to help his King, was revelling in the drama and could tell 'Chips' Channon: 'Our cock would be all right if only he would fight, but at the moment he will not even crow.' Channon ventured: 'Cocks crow better in the morning.' 'Not this one,' Beaverbrook retorted.[17] During the next few anxious days, the King's friends – led by Beaverbrook and Churchill – fought desperately to save the situation, but time was not on their side. On 7 December, Mrs Simpson left for Cannes after issuing a statement:

> Mrs Simpson throughout the last few weeks has invariably wished to avoid any action or proposal which would hurt or damage the King or the Throne. Today her attitude is unchanged, and she is willing, if such action would solve the problem, to withdraw from a situation that has been rendered unhappy and untenable.

Only the *Daily Express*, *Evening Standard*, *Daily Mail* and *Evening News* supported the King, the *Daily Express* even announcing 'End of Crisis'. *The Times* and *The Daily Telegraph*, though, were determined that the King should abdicate.

Matters came to a head on 10 December: at two o'clock on a grey winter's afternoon, to a crowded House of Commons, the Speaker, through tears, announced that the King had renounced his Throne, the first abdication since Richard II in 1399. That same evening, the King – now Prince Edward – made his moving abdication speech, a speech in which the hand of Churchill was clearly visible. When Churchill had left the King, there had been tears in his (Churchill's) eyes. 'I can still see him standing in the door, hat in one hand, stick in the other.'

Listeners throughout the world were much moved by the broadcast in which he said: 'But you must believe me when I tell you that I have found it impossble to carry out the heavy burden of responsibility and to discharge my duties as King as I would wish to do without the help of the woman I love.' On hearing those words, Churchill, at Chartwell, wept once more.

Following the broadcast, now as the Duke of Windsor, he left by car for Portsmouth, where at midnight, through the fog, he boarded a waiting destroyer, the *Fury*, for France and exile – and the woman he loved.

The final word must rest with Dawson, editor of *The Times*, who wrote in his diary: 'And there the crisis was brought to an end. The Abdication Bill went though all its stages on the Friday morning (December 11) so rapidly that when I looked in at the House of Commons after lunch there was no one left in Westminster and the Duke of York was already King George VI.'[18]

Munich and Appeasement

To most intelligent people, it was not just a question of if there were to be a war, but when would it begin: since the mid-1930s the demands of Hitler had become more and more insistent. From the Nuremberg Rally in September 1934, when the slogan of the Nazi Party was first heard, *Ein Reich*, *Ein Volk*, *Ein Führer* (One Realm, One People, One Leader), there could be only one ending: the reunification of the German-speaking peoples. The first move was to be the reoccupation of the Rhineland; and, transgressing the Treaty of Locarno, four German brigades crossed the Rhine in March 1936 with secret orders to withdraw if the French took military action. There was to be no resistance, leading Baldwin to announce: 'If there is one chance in a hundred that war might result, I cannot commit Great Britain.' This statement was to win the approval of Edward VIII, who had 'urged his ministers not to act'.

Throughout the 1930s, one voice more than any other was to speak out against Hitler and his grandiose plans. That man was Winston Churchill and his platform was the *Evening Standard*, even though in his earlier articles he was to adopt a more circumspect point of view. Churchill made his debut on 13 March 1936, only days after the German occupation of the Rhineland, and was to comment:[19]

> There has rarely been a crisis in which Hope and Peril have presented themselves so vividly and at the same time upon the world scene. When Herr Hitler last Saturday repudiated the Treaty of Locarno and marched his troops into the Rhineland he confronted the League of Nations with its supreme trial and also with its most splendid opportunity. If the League of Nations survives this ordeal there is no reason why the horrible, dull, remorseless drift to war in 1937 or 1938, and the preparatory piling up of enormous armaments in every country, should not be decisively arrested.

Eighteen months later, on 15 September 1937, he wrote: 'I declare my belief that a major war is not imminent, and I still believe there is a good chance of no major war taking place in our time.' He was to return to this theme two days later:

> I find myself pilloried by Dr Goebbels' Press as an enemy of Germany. That description is quite untrue . . . . no one has a right to describe me as the enemy of Germany except in war time. We cannot say that we admire your treatment of the Jews or of the Protestants and Catholics of Germany . . . . To feel deep concern about the armed power of Germany is in no way derogatory to Germany.

To Churchill, it was the power that Mussolini with his fascists was now wielding in Italy that was causing concern, and the following month he wrote in the paper: 'It would be a dangerous folly for the British people to underrate the enduring position in world history which Mussolini will hold; or the amazing qualitites of courage, comprehension, self-control and perseverance which he exemplifies.'

Ever since becoming Prime Minister, Chamberlain had believed that the Foreign Office, under Anthony Eden, was too anti-German, hence the visit by Lord Halifax to Hitler at Berchtesgaden in November 1937. Early the following year, Chamberlain proposed to open discussion with Mussolini to obtain a general agreement in the Mediterranean, including the recognition of the Italian conquest of Abyssinia. This was too much for Eden, who forthwith resigned on 20 February[20] – the same day Hitler, in addressing the Reichstag, 'reaffirmed the identity of German and Italian attitudes and goals to Spain'. Much later, in his memoirs, Eden was to comment: 'A leading democracy in negotiating with a militant dictatorship must not go cap in hand in search of fresh negotiations to cover long-standing differences unless there is evidence that the dictator is going to carry out the engagements he has already undertaken.'

The new Foreign Secretary was to be Lord Halifax, who, as Lord President of the Council, had not been burdened by a government department, and he could say of Eden's departure: 'Confidence faded as misunderstanding grew, so that at the end the parting was unavoidable.'

Meanwhile, writing in the *Evening Standard* on 4 March, Churchill noted: 'They [the Austrians] could now probably face a plebiscite . . . . under fair conditions without fear.' However, no one could tell 'what the reaction of Nazi Germany will be, or what new shattering blows impend upon a small unhappy state'. Two days later in *The Observer,* editor J.L. Garvin, discussing any possible involvement by Britain, was in no doubt as to what should be done: 'Is it imagined for a moment that Austria itself is a harmonious unit? It is riven with discord. A powerful section passionately demands closer union with the Reich. Conflict would mean civil war. It is a family issue within the German race. We have nothing to do with it.'

A little over a month later, on 10 April, a Nazi-controlled plebiscite recorded a vote of 99.75 per cent in favour of the *Anschluss* – the unification of Austria and Germany had been achieved. As George Steiner was to write: 'When Nazism came home to Vienna in the spring of 1938 the welcome accorded it exceeded in fervour that which it had received in Germany.' And to quote Geoffrey Cox:[21]

> The next day ecstatic crowds lined the streets to see Adolf Hitler drive in triumph into the city which had rejected him as a failed artist and casual labourer twenty-five years earlier. A huge crowd packed the space in front of the Imperial Hotel. When Hitler appeared on the balcony, a triumphant, smiling figure in the same type of brown shirt uniform he had worn at Nuremberg, every arm went out in salute. I raised my own with them. To have done anything else would have been suicide, for no passport, no claim to be a foreigner could have stood a chance against the hysteria which filled the air.

In London, Churchill was becoming more and more aware of the impending conflict, and was now directing his attention to the growing crisis in Czechoslovkia; and, although advocating that the German-speaking minority should be granted equal citizenship, he welcomed the declaration that France should satisfy its Treaty obligations if Czechoslovakia were to be attacked. 'A further declaration of the intentions of the British Government in such an event must come soon.' However, Churchill's column was now out of line with Beaverbrook's thinking – and in early April he was given one month's notice. Much later, Peter Howard, *Daily Express* leader writer, was to comment:

> Churchill sat by himself in the moonlight, or almost, it seemed in the sunset of a career which had somehow missed greatness. His war song against the Nazis was almost a solo. Just the same he sang it fortissimo in the columns of the *Evening Standard*. Meanwhile, my boss, Lord Beaverbrook, was advocating the cause of Splendid Isolation .... He was entirely opposed to Mr Churchill's big idea.

Another proprietor viewing Germany anxiously was Lord Kemsley. Although owning Britain's largest newspaper group, Kemsley reserved his main attention for *The Sunday Times*, where he was fortunate in having the mature W.W. Hadley – his erstwhile boss from Merthyr days – as editor. In the weeks before Munich, during the time of the Appeasement, Kemsley was in regular contact with the Government through Hadley's sessions with the Prime Minister and through his own private meetings. 'Indeed, Kemsley was the only newspaper proprietor whom Chamberlain confided in and trusted.' Halifax, likewise, was aware of the extreme importance to the Government of the'big group of provincial press owned by Lord Kemsley'.

During the long hot summer of 1938, while holiday crowds were flocking to the seaside and Len Hutton was breaking batting records at the Oval, trenches were being dug in Hyde Park and gas masks were being issued by the thousand. But for Beaverbrook, who still believed in staying out of any European conflict, life remained good, as he reminded Edward Grigg on 20 June: 'As we have isolation in fact, although not in name, I have not much to complain about.' So confident was Beaverbrook of a continuing peace that on 1 September he announced in the *Daily Express*: 'There will be no European War.' This phrase, and subsequent similar headlines, was to be used time and time against him by opponents – even appearing in Noel Coward's film, *In Which We Serve*.

However, despite his apparent confidence, Beaverbrook did write to Lord Halifax, the Foreign Secretary, on 16 September, saying: 'Newspapers are all anxious to help the Prime Minister and to help you. But they are greatly in need of guidance. A Minister should be authorized to have direct contact with the newspaper.'[22]

Inevitably, the newspaper which attracted the most attention as a source of influence and opinion during those dark days was *The Times*, which was once more under the editorship of Geoffrey Dawson, with Robin Barrington-Ward as his deputy. During his second editorship (1923–1941), Dawson was very much an Establishment figure and his handling of Appeasement, especially during the Munich Crisis, was to earn him much criticism.[23] Dawson, along with Sir Neville Henderson, J.L. Garvin and Lord Lothian were members of the 'Cliveden Set', a term invented by Claud Cockburn in his publication *The Week* to describe the group of 'appeasers who regularly visited the Waldorf Astors either at Cliveden or at their London house in St James's Square'.

In 1937, Dawson had written: 'I do my utmost, night after night, to keep out of the paper anything that might hurt their [the German Government's] susceptibilities.' A leader in the spring of 1938 suggesting the secession of the Sudetenland to Germany was to bring an angry riposte from his co-proprietor John Walter IV: 'In contemplating the dismemberment of Czechoslovakia as a measure of justice to the Sudetan Germans, our leader writer made no allusion to the flood of injustice and cruelty that would certainly overwhelm the minorities, thus handed over to the tender mercies of Messrs. Hitler, Goering and Goebbels.'

Now, six months later, with Hitler pressing strongly his claims on Czechoslovakia, Europe was on the brink of war; and on 7 September *The Times* published a leader which put forward the case for dismemberment of Czechoslovakia.

> Drafted by Leo Kennedy, the text was hurriedly revised by Dawson [the editor] who regarded it 'as a very mild suggestion and one that had been constantly made before, that no avenue should be left unexplored which might lead to settlement of the Sudetan question' .... Dawson believed that this leading article, 'which caused so much hubbub', did good rather than harm.

The offending leader declared:

> No Central Government would still deserve its title if it did not reserve in its own hands Defence, Foreign Policy, and Finance. There does not appear to be any dispute about this principle in the minds of the Government or of Herr Henlein; and if the Sudetens now ask for more than the Czech Government are apparently ready to give in their latest set of proposals, it can only be inferred that the Germans are going beyond the mere removal of disabilities and do not find themselves at ease within the Czechoslovak Republic. In that case it might be worth while for the Czechoslovak Government to consider whether they should exclude altogether the project, which has found favour in some quarters of making Czechoslovakia a more homogeneous state, by the secession of that fringe of alien population who are contiguous to the nation with which they are united by race. In any case the wishes of the population concerned would seem to be a decisively important element in any solution that can hope to be regarded as permanent, and the advantages of Czechoslovakia becoming a homogeneous state might conceivably outweigh the obvious disadvantages of losing the Sudeten German districts of the borderland.

It was not, however, a point of view shared by the Government, which issued a statement 'that a suggestion appearing in *The Times* this morning to the effect that the Czechoslovakian Government might consider as an alternative to their present proposals the secession of the fringe of alien population in their territory in no way represents the view of His Majesty's Government'.

Britain – and Europe – were by this time awaiting Hitler's speech,[25] to be made at Nuremberg on 12 September. On that day as its page one lead, the *Evening Standard* announced:

> Sir Neville Henderson, British Ambassador in Berlin, saw Herr von Ribbentrop, German Foreign Minister, at Nuremberg today .... Sir Neville sought to convince Herr von Ribbentrop that Britain, as the Prime Minister had stated in the House of Commons, could not finally remain disinterested in the event of a general European conflict. Herr von Ribbentrop, it is believed, was previously reluctant to accept the prospect of joint action by Britain and France if peaceful methods fail.

From Nuremberg the news was bad: Hitler had staked his claim; the Czechs now declared that they would not budge, 'and the French say they will march if one inch of Czech territory is violated'. With war seemingly imminent, Chamberlain took the dramatic step of telegraphing Hitler for an urgent meeting. His request was granted and on 15 September, at the age of sixty-nine, he took his first flight – to Berchtesgaden. David Low's cartoon in the *Evening Standard* showed an airborne Chamberlain, with the caption 'STILL IN THE AIR. PEACE: It all depends on where we come down doesn't it?'

Duff Cooper was later to write in his diary:

> At the cabinet meeting on September 17 .... the Prime Minister told us the story of his visit to Berchtesgaden. Hitler struck him as 'the commonest little dog' he had ever seen .... After ranting and raving at him, Hitler had talked about self determination and asked the Prime Minister whether he accepted the principle .... From the beginning to the end Hitler had not shown the slightest sign of yielding on a single point.

In this highly-charged atmosphere of impending war, while huge processions were marching down Whitehall crying, 'Stand by the Czechs' and 'Chamberlain must go', Beaverbrook was writing in the *Daily Express*: 'Britain never gave any pledge to protect the frontiers of Czechoslovakia .... no moral obligation rests on us'. Days later, on 28 September, with the navy already mobilized, the Prime Minister rose in the House of Commons to give his verdict on recent events: 'Hitler had declared that his mobilization will begin today at two o'clock.' He cleared his throat and paused, before telling the Members that he had telegraphed both Hitler and Mussolini that morning. He then read the message and said: 'That is not all. I have something further to say to the House': Hitler had invited him, along with Benito Mussolini and Edouard Daladier, the French Prime Minister, to go to Munich the following morning.

The next day, 29 September, at dawn, the whole Cabinet was at Heston Airport to see off the Prime Minister. There was to be no success, however, from the meeting with Hitler: Sudetenland was to be ceded to Germany, and Polish and Hungarian claims for frontier adjusments were to be made at the expense of Czechoslovakia. And all frontier fortifications, along with more than a third of the population, were to be transferred to Germany. When these changes had been made, all four of the Powers represented at Munich agreed to guarantee the rump of Czechoslovakia against unprovoked aggresion.

For Chamberlain it was to be his hour of triumph; and from the moment, on 30 September 1938, when he stepped off his plane at Heston waving his scrap of paper and averring 'Peace for our time' it was to be a glorious return to Downing Street and the admiring crowds. As Lord Halifax later wrote: 'That drive from Heston is perhaps worth recording. It was not easy to talk at all, for flowers were being thrown into the car, people were jumping on the running board, seizing his hand and patting him on the back.'

The following morning, in the *Daily Express*, Beaverbrook, who like other British Press barons had met Hitler, was to announce: 'Britain will not be involved in a

European war this year or the next either' – a headline which was to haunt him for the next twenty years.

One person anxious not to upset Anglo-German relations at this time was Walter Layton, editor-in-chief of the *News Chronicle*. Often he would insist on cuts to any story that might offend the *status quo*. This came to a head on the day Chamberlain announced 'Peace for our time'.[26] Ivor Bulmer-Thomas, the *Chronicle*'s leader writer, was later to say: 'We discussed and discussed from every angle, while edition after edition went out without any leader on the subject....' And editor Gerald Barry was to comment that 'his recollection and that of my colleagues is that during the critical days of that humiliating period we were obliged to hold our horses and, if I may mix metaphors, back-pedal'.

Throughout the following six months, an uneasy peace hung over Europe; and it has been said that the Ides of March (15 March) 1939 marked the beginning of the end of 'a low dishonest decade'. Chamberlain, however, still refused to face the fact that Hitler was once more casting his eye on Czechoslovkia: on 9 March 1939 he called representatives of all the Fleet Street newspapers to a private conference at 10 Downing Street, and told them that the international situation had much improved. He added that as a result of the Munich Agreement there were high hopes of reaching political, economic and military understanding throughout Europe, and as a first step he intended to call a disarmament conference later that year.

Realistically, the editors had greeted Chamberlain's statement with astonishment, for their correspondents in Prague and Berlin had daily been informing them of an impending German invasion. They were to be proved correct, for less than a week later the Munich Agreement was in tatters. On that day, 15 March – while Chamberlain was on a fly-fishing holiday with fellow-Conservative Sir Joseph Ball – Germany annexed Czechoslovakia. Beaverbrook's comments on the invasion were: 'Our Government could never have defended Czechoslovakia, and the combination of races could never have worked together in their common defence against Germany. The structure was bound to fall as soon as the weight of reality was imposed upon it.'

On 27 July 1939 Kemsley visited Hitler in Germany and was to tell the Führer that 'far more notice was taken of him [Churchill] abroad than in Britain' and that 'Mr Churchill had been unfortunate in his campaigns on at least four occasions in the past ....' Kemsley could also inform Hitler that, as the owner of a large group of British provincial newspapers, he ensured whole-hearted backing for Chamberlain, and that the Prime Minister still attached 'tremendous importance to the documents signed between him and Hitler at Munich'. However, in view of the deepening crisis, plans to involve Dr Otto Dietrich, the German Press chief, in an exchange of articles in the *Daily Sketch* and German newspapers came to nothing, Kemsley having been asked by the British Government on 28 August to hold back publication.

For Francis Williams, editor of the *Daily Herald*:[27]

> The time between Munich and the declaration of war was, I suppose, the worst ever lived through by those who had not been old enough to feel the full weight of the First World War. We knew that war was certain. We were ill-prepared for it and expected it to be

> indescribable in horror. By an unfortunate coincidence a film based on H.G. Wells' *War in the Air* [*Things to Come*] had been showing at the cinemas at the time of Munich and had added a macabre horror to the sight of slit trenches being dug in the parks by the light of acetylene flares as darkness fell.

Meanwhile, Beaverbrook, having sailed for Canada on 5 August – and into retirement, firmly convinced that his newspaper days were over – told waiting reporters at Quebec: 'I would not be here if I did believe that war was imminent.' E.J. Robertson, managing director of the *Daily Express*, was far less sanguine, and with the signing of the Nazi-Soviet Pact on 23 August told him that war was imminent and that he should return to England. 'At this point German plans called for the invasion of Poland on 26 August.' And as Franklin Reid Gannon was to write:[28]

> Neville Henderson [British ambassador] came to Berchtesgaden on the 23rd to deliver a letter from Chamberlain written after the Cabinet of the 22nd, which had discussed the announcement of Ribbentrop's departure [he had been withdrawn as German ambassador to Britain], and determined resolutely to honour its commitments: 'If the case should arise, they are resolved, and prepared, to employ without delay all the forces at their command, and it is impossible to foresee the end of hostilities once engaged.'

Back in England once more, Beaverbrook was greeted with the news that Germany had invaded Poland: Hitler's plan to annexe Danzig and the Polish Corridor was now being put into effect, and by the end of the first day, 1 September 1939, more than one million troops had attacked Poland. At six o'clock the following evening, a hushed House of Commons heard Neville Chamberlain say that His Majesty's Government would be bound to take action unless the German forces were withdrawn. From the Labour Opposition there was complete agreement. Less than twenty-four hours later, Great Britain was at war. Chamberlain had informed Parliament that a further communication had been given to the German Government at nine o'clock that morning asking for an assurance that their forces would, as previously requested, suspend their advance into Poland; if a satisfactory assurance to this effect had not been received by eleven o'clock a state of war would exist between the two countries.

At 11.15 a.m. Chamberlain broadcast to a waiting nation. No satisfactory assurance had been received: 'Consequently this country was now at war with Germany.' He told the House of Commons: 'This is a sad day for all of us, but to none is it sadder than to me. Everything that I have worked for, everything that I have hoped for, everything that I have believed in during my public life, has crashed into ruins.'

14

Fleet Street at war

WITH WAR HAVING BEEN DECLARED, one of Chamberlain's initial moves was to invite Winston Churchill into the Cabinet to serve as First Lord of the Admiralty. For Beaverbrook there was to be no place; instead he was sent to the United States to find out what President Roosevelt thought about the conflict. One of Beaverbrook's last acts before leaving was to inform E.J. Robertson, his managing director, of the need for American support. On 19 September Robertson replied:[1] 'A written instruction has been given to Christiansen [*Daily Express*], Gordon [*Sunday Express*] and Frank Owen [*Evening Standard*] that Mr Kennedy [the American Ambassador] is not be criticised in the columns of our papers, but that he is to receive favourable comment.' For Viscount Camrose, proprietor of *The Daily Telegraph*, though, there was to be the appointment of chief assistant to Lord Macmillan, the Minister of Information and Controller of Press Relations, until he (Camrose) announced in the House of Lords that he 'had organised himself out of a job'.

In the spring of 1940, the war at sea continued, but in western Europe there was virtual stalemate. The storm was to break, however; and on 9 April the Germans invaded Norway, where the intervention of British forces ended in a humiliating withdrawal. Almost a month later, on 7 May, a two-day debate began in the House of Commons to discuss the fiasco. The first day was notable for the intervention of two speakers from the Conservative benches: Roger Keyes came to the House wearing his uniform of Admiral of the Fleet, a gesture which dramatically enhanced his speech; but the main attack came from Leo Amery, who, in quoting Oliver Cromwell, seemed to sum up the feelings of the members. He told the Prime Minister: 'You have sat too long for any good you have been doing. Depart, I say, and let us have done with you. In the name of God, go!' For Chamberlain, the signs were ominous; and in a division forced by the Labour Opposition forty-one supporters of the government voted against him and sixty abstained.

During the early hours of 10 May, German armies invaded the Netherlands and Belgium. That same day, Kingsley Wood led a revolt against Chamberlain within the Cabinet, and, with the Labour leaders also refusing to serve under Chamberlain, that afternoon Churchill became Prime Minister. Past differences forgotten, Beaverbrook was once more established as Churchill's intimate adviser, dining with him on that momentous day. And one of the first acts of the new Prime Minister was to appoint Beaverbrook as Minister of Aircraft Production.

Beaverbrook's Finest Hour

For Michael Foot, then deputy editor of the *Evening Standard*, they were critical times, as he was to recall:[2]

> In those first weeks we had another interest, too. Right up till the moment when Hitler's tanks smashed through the Ardennes, Beaverbrook had continued to exercise his perpetual, erratic, inescapable surveillance over the newspaper; he was the editor-in-chief and everyone inside the office knew it. Then, one fine memorable morning, peace descended. The blitz was just about to burst upon us in all its fury. All Beaverbrook's improvising energies were devoted to the task, night after night, for weeks on end.

Meanwhile, the battles in Europe were at a critical stage, and after five days of fighting, and the destruction of Rotterdam, the Netherlands capitulated. This was followed on 28 May by King Leopold of the Belgians surrendering his country. With the remnants of the British and French armies encircled at Dunkirk, after constant attack from massed Panzer divisions and devastating German air power, there seemed to be little hope. But on the fateful weekend of 31 May–2 June an armada of little ships crossed the Channel to evacuate the British army from the beaches; and in an epic operation more than 250,000 British and 100,000 French soldiers were saved.

On the afternoon of 31 May Michael Foot, Frank Owen, and Peter Howard, leader writer, *Daily Express*, met to discuss the news.[3] They blamed the debacle directly on Chamberlain and his colleagues and decided to write a book in which they would take to task the neglect of these men. Their book, *Guilty Men*, proved to be a sensation, selling more than 200,000 copies in three months.

Beaverbrook was now about to enter his finest hour, and his appointment as Minister of Aircraft Production was just the shot in the arm that the Royal Air Force needed. In the savage withdrawal from France, RAF fighter strength had been badly mauled, and aircraft were at a premium. In his official report, Lord Dowding, head of Fighter Command throughout the Battle of Britain, wrote:

> I saw my resources slipping away like sand in an hour glass . . . . The effect of Lord Beaverbrook's appointment can only be described as magical and thereafter the supply situation improved to such a degree that the heavy aircraft wastage which was later incurred during the Battle of Britain ceased to be the primary danger.

Years later, Dowding informed Lord Templewood (formerly Sir Samuel Hoare): 'The country owes as much to Beaverbrook for the Battle of Britain as it does to me. Without his drive behind me I could not have carried on during the battle.' To Beaverbrook, the man who only nine months before had sailed into retirement, it was the challenge of a lifetime, and he ran his enterprise as he ran his newspapers: all was high drama. Throughout that summer of cloudless days, while he led the crusade for more aircraft, his son Max was flying as a fighter pilot. Each evening, Beaverbrook would be on tenterhooks until he had received that very important telephone call from his son to say that he had survived another day. Family pride, quite rightly, had not prevented Beaverbrook from writing to Harold Balfour, Under Secretary of Air, on 30 May: 'Max Aitken is nerveless. He should be given some squadron at once. His promotion is long overdue. And he can carry any burden.'

The proof of Beaverbrook's success is contained in a memo written to Churchill on 2 September 1940, in the midst of the Battle of Britain:

> On May 15th last there were 884 aircraft available for operations in the Squadrons – excluding Lysanders. Now there are 1,325, excluding Lysanders. There is an increase of about 450 to 500 in operational aircraft in operational units. So it will be seen that the RAF has drawn from the Aircraft Ministry nearly a thousand operational machines since your Government was formed, for the purpose of strengthening units. In addition all casualties had to be replaced. And 720 aircraft were shipped abroad. 'Nobody knows the trouble I've seen.'

Churchill minuted: 'I do.' By 15 September the Battle of Britain was reaching its climax, and on that fateful day the number of German aircraft shot down over south-east England totalled 185. But for Beaverbrook the incessant pressures of working seven days a week, and suffering many sleepless nights, had brought on fresh attacks of asthma, and on 30 September he offered his resignation. Churchill, however, would not hear of his resigning, and it was not until 1 May 1941 that Beaverbrook's pleas were finally heeded, when he was immediately appointed Minister of State. This was to be no sinecure: in the September he visited Moscow, when he and Averell Harriman led an Anglo-American Supply Mission, and in the December he accompanied Churchill to Washington.

Despite his new role in government, Beaverbrook had not entirely forgotten his newspapers, and on 24 September, on his way Russia, he wrote to Robertson, outlining his thoughts on the *Daily Express*:[4]

> I have been reading the paper. You should improve it. It is not nearly as valuable a paper as you could give at the present time. You should have much better foreign correspondents, and a good deal more attention should be paid to the foreign service of the paper. Your centre page article ought now to be more informative and it should have same valuable contribution from abroad – really valuable, written by men who are trained to see and have a reputation for doing so. Add more – a good deal more – to your editorial charges. Give up now the popular presentation of small events. The front page should be a document of the war. You do not want any more net sales, and you should make no popular appeal whatsoever. Here is an opportunity for you young fellows to build up the greatest newspaper in the world – the greatest ever imagined. On your net sale you can build so soundly and so well. All this must be done with serious thought. And when the decision has been taken and the line settled, it will be still more difficult to sustain.

A mixed decade

For Rothermere, the thirties had been a mixed decade: there had been his alignment with Beaverbrook in the failed Empire Free Trade Movement, his brief involvement with the Blackshirts, plus his friendship with Hitler . . . .

Rothermere's support of the British Union of Fascists (the Blackshirts) – led by Sir Oswald Mosley – lasted from January to June 1934; and early that year, on 8 January, on the leader page of the *Daily Mail*, under a heading HURRAH FOR THE BLACKSHIRTS, he proclaimed that it was 'the Party of Youth'. Italy and Germany were 'beyond all doubt the best-governed nations in Europe today . . . . We must keep up with the spirit of the age. That spirit is one of national discipline and organisation.'[5]

And almost a fortnight later, on 21 January 1934, writing in the *Sunday Pictorial* – another title in which he had a major interest – Rothermere was to assert that the British Blackshirt Movement was 'one hundred per cent constitutional and national. Persuasion, not violence, will be its path to power . . . . Nor is there the slightest ground believing that the Blackshirts are, or ever will be, antagonistic to such bodies as the Jews, Trade Unions or The Freemasons.' A delighted Mosley was to say of Rothermere: 'He was an ultra-patriot. He was in a state of terror that the Empire would be lost, so he would back anyone who looked like a strong boy.'

After providing the Blackshirts with a substantial sum, the next move by Rothermere, at a cost of more than £70,000, was to set up a cigarette company, even taking on a manager from Imperial Tobacco, and to use the movement's hundreds of branches as selling points. He told Mosley: 'Either we are going to do a lot of business, or the tobacco companies are going to pay us a large amount of money not to do business.' Rothermere was to be wrong on both counts: pressures from advertisers in the *Daily Mail*, already incensed at the paper's increasing involvement with the Blackshirts, hardened further when they heard of the plans to set up a cigarette company. A furious Mosley blamed Rothermere for changing his mind, saying that his brother (Northcliffe) would have filled the streets with contents bills saying: 'Jews Threaten British Press.'

Rothermere's friends were now advising him more and more that consorting with the Blackshirts was a drastic mistake; and on 7 May he wrote to Beaverbrook: 'I intend to tell Mosley that if he attacks you I shall drop the Blackshirts. You are my greatest friend and this is the least I can do.'[6] Within days, the relationship between Rothermere and Mosley was to come to an end, the catalyst being the Olympia riot of 7 June. With more than twelve thousand packed into the hall, it was reckoned to have been the largest-ever indoor meeting held in Great Britain. Outside, the ticket-holders – 'including peers, MPs and affluent fellow-travellers of the Right who attended in Rolls-Royces and evening dress' – were greeted by hundreds of angry demonstrators from the East End, supported by large groups of Communists.

The meeting started late, with the Leader – bathed in searchlights and surrounded by bodyguards carrying Union Jacks and fascist banners – being greeted with frantic shouts of 'Mosley' and thousands of upraised arms in the fascist salute. Within minutes of his attempting to speak, mayhem raged as Blackshirt 'volunteers' ejected with considerable force the dozens of Communists who had infiltrated the meeting.

For Mosley that was the beginning of the end; and an exchange of letters the following month with Rothermere was to bring their relationship to a close.

Hitler's Admirer

Apart from his brief flirtation with the Blackshirts, Rothermere had for the past three years been an admirer of Hitler and the National Socialist Party in Germany; and on 24 September 1930 in a 3000-word signed despatch from Munich, 'the birthplace and power house of Nazism', he had told *Daily Mail* readers:

> With the same vigour as they have developed their bodies by physical culture, with the same energy as they have worked long hours at factory, office or farm, these young Germans have organised themselves to take an active part in their country's affairs. They have discovered, as, I am glad to know, the young men and women of England are discovering, that it is no good trusting to the old politicians. Accordingly, they have formed, as I should like to see our British youth form, a Parliamentary party of their own.
>
> Under Herr Hitler's control, the youth of Germany is effectively organised against the corruption of Communism. It was with some such purpose that I founded the United Empire Party in England, for it is clear that no strong anti-Socialist policy can be expected from a Conservative Party whose leaders are themselves tainted with semi-Socialist doctrines.

Rothermere was to return to the theme on 10 July 1933, six months after Hitler became Chancellor. Datelined 'Somewhere in Naziland' and headed YOUTH TRIUMPHANT, he urged 'all young British young men and women to study closely the progress of the Nazi regime in Germany'. He believed that Hitler and his followers had been ill-treated in the British Press:[7]

> They have started a clamorous campaign of denunciation against what they call 'Nazi' atrocities which, as anyone who visits Germany quickly discovers for himself, consist merely of a few isolated acts of violence such as are inevitable among a nation half as big again as ours, but which they have generalised, multiplied and exaggerated to give the impression that Nazi rule is a bloodthirsty tyranny.

Just days before the article appeared, Hitler had written the first of more than a dozen letters to Rothermere, a correspondence which was to extend from 22 June 1933 until early 1938. (Copies of the letters were passed on to key members of the Cabinet and senior MPs; and in May 1935[8] Rothermere could inform Ramsay MacDonald, the Prime Minister, that 'If in the emergency days an informal, semi-official conversation between him and me can serve any national purpose, I place my services at the disposal of the Government.')

Christmas 1934 had seen Rothermere in Germany meeting the Nazi leaders; and a seasonal article in the *Daily Mail* described 'his conversations with Hitler in his office, or beside a red log-fire as the winter dusk came down'. For Hitler, this growing friendship with the Press lord was to lead to his saying: 'Rothermere is one of the very greatest of all Englishmen. He is the only man who sees clearly the magnitude of this Bolshevist danger. His paper is doing an immense amount of good. I have the greatest admiration for him.'

Nevertheless, despite these glowing words, Rothermere *was* aware of the growing threat from Germany, as he had confided to J.C. Davidson, Chancellor of the Duchy of Lancaster, just two months earlier on 7 October: 'Personally I have no doubt that he [Hitler] and his ruthless associates intend immediately he has command of 30,000 or 40,000 aeroplanes to wage an aerial war against France and ourselves if we stand with her. Such a war might put our very existence at stake.'

Six months before his letter to Davidson, in March 1934 Rothermere met directors of the Bristol Aeroplane Company and told them that he wished to have built an executive plane faster than any other. Despite initial opposition, the plane had its test flight on 12 April 1935. Not satisfied, Rothermere had new engines installed, giving a speed of 307 mph, eighty miles faster than any fighter in the RAF. In August 1935, the plane was presented to the RAF by Rothermere on behalf of the *Daily Mail*, and by the spring of 1937, one hundred and fifty Bristol Blenheim bombers – as the plane was now dubbed – were in service with the RAF.

Throughout the final months of the decade, conflict loomed ever closer, and on 2 August 1939 Rothermere wrote to von Ribbentrop, former German ambassador to Great Britain, and now back in Berlin, one of Hitler's confidants:

> I have never known the British people more warlike than they are today. They are talking as they did at the outbreak of the Great War and the Boer War. The rearming of the country has been wonderfully well-done; worthy of the best periods of British history. And this has given the people much confidence.

Von Ribbentrop's reply was to the point:[9]

> .... of one thing I am certain: if these two countries should ever clash again, it would this time be a fight to the very end and to the last man. And this time every German conscious of the tremendous power of these 80 million people behind one man and of Germany's powerful allies is convinced that this would end with German victory.

My Dear Max

Now, nine months later, on 15 May 1940, within hours of Beaverbrook having been appointed Minister of Aircraft Production, Rothermere was to telegraph from the South of France:

> MY DEAR MAX OVERJOYED AT LAST SOME GOVERNMENTAL USE HAS BEEN FOUND AT THE CRITICAL JUNCTURE FOR YOUR GLITTERING ABILITIES .... QUITE PREPARED TO HELP YOUR DEPARTMENT OTHER SIDE WITHOUT SALARY TRAVELLING EXPENSES OR CLERICAL EXPENSES FOR DURATION OF WAR IF NECESSARY STOP

Beaverbrook replied immediately: 'I WILL WANT YOUR SERVICES IN AMERICA AND HOPE YOU WILL GO THERE AT ONCE.'

That summer, Rothermere, 'now elderly and a sick man', left for the New World, Beaverbrook having asked him to provide a report on the aircraft manufacturing facilities in Canada – 'a topic on which Beaverbrook was already fully informed by his knowledgeable Canadian friends'. Lord Halifax, the Foreign Secretary, however, wished Rothermere to be recalled, especially before his impending visit to the United States. Beaverbrook replied: 'I do not know where Rothermere is. I think he is already in the United States. In any case he is an old man.'[10]

Rothermere was, indeed, in the United States, and during the last fortnight of June 1940 had been in St Luke's Hospital, New York, undergoing tests. For the next few months, though, he was to continue his visits in Canada and the United States until leaving in late October for Hamilton, Bermuda. Within hours of his arrival, a doctor had been called, who, diagnosing dropsy, advised an immediate transfer to the King Edward VII Memorial Hospital, and it was there that he died on 27 November, being buried the following day at St Paul's Churchyard, Paget, Bermuda.

Two years later, in November 1942, Beaverbrook paid his respects, and was to write to the new Lord Rothermere, Esmond Harmsworth: 'In Bermuda last Sunday I visited your father's grave. He was great in vision, courage and loyalty. We do not make friends easily when old age overtakes us.'

Sir Emsley is Honoured

Despite the war, on 1 May 1941 a banquet – attended by 150 people – was held at the Dorchester Hotel to celebrate Sir Emsley Carr's fifty years as editor of the *News of the World*. His late colleague, R. Power Berrey, was to recall the early years: 'In those days there were only two members of the editorial staff – [Sir] Emsley and myself. If Sir Emsley happened to be called away suddenly, I found all sorts of queer jobs falling my lot. I did the book reviews, the leaders, the interviews, the sub-editing, the illustrations, and even the racing notes.'

Carr had taken over as chairman, following the death of Lord Riddell on 5 December 1934. Despite requesting that there should be no mourning, a memorial service was held at St Bride's, Fleet Street; and Lord Beaverbrook was to say of Riddell: 'Only a man of great attainment could have achieved the results which made his services to the Press so substantial and so honourable. He gave more than his purse; he gave time and care, the dearest gifts of a busy man.'

After raising the money in the City, Carr was able to buy Riddell's shares for £1 million. As Stafford Somerfield, a future editor of the paper, was to write: 'He was already editor, and, if you judge an editor's success by his paper's circulation as many proprietors do, Emsley Carr was the greatest. Not only the editor who lasted longest, he was the editor who sold most newspapers.'[11]

Among the guests at Carr's celebrations in May 1941 was Winston Churchill who had been a frequent contributor to the paper. The Prime Minister was to say: 'When things are not at their best in this country, it is to the journalist that people turn for inspiration.' And J.J. Astor, chairman of *The Times*, unveiling a portrait of Carr, remarked with relish: '*The Times* and the *News of the World* are not in competition. They publish on different days.'

Another guest, Cecil King, was to describe the occasion in his diary: 'The Prime Minister, who greeted me, looked white and drawn, but had a marvellous ovation from those present . . . . made a short speech and was present for at least one and a half hours. Even the King and Lloyd George sent telegrams!'

In his long career, Carr had been chairman of the Press Gallery, 1929–30; and on two occasions, 1932 and 1933, had been President of the Institute of Journalists. He was knighted in 1918. During his editorship, Carr had established the right to sell newspapers in Scotland on Sunday, and had pioneered competitions as circulation-boosting schemes. And at the time of his death on 31 July 1941, aged seventy-four, circulation of the *News of the World* was more than 4,400,000 copies. Carr was to say of his paper: 'The *News of the World* is a human document representing the daily life of the average man – not neglecting the more serious problems, but also touching on the lighter forms of life, bringing humour, brightness and humanity into everyone's existence.'

The new editor was to be Percy Davies, 'unassuming, white-haired and usually seen in morning coat and pin-striped trousers', who had entered journalism in 1910 as a reporter in Swansea on the *South Wales Daily Post*, edited by David Davies, his father.[12] He then joined the Welch Regiment (TA) and was to serve in France and Italy during the First World War as a major in the XIth Corps Cycle Battalion. Called to the Bar of Gray's Inn during 1919, that same year he became a sub-editor on the *News of the World*, rising to deputy editor, 1933, and a director two years later, before succeeding Carr. Apart from being editor, Davies was also elected chairman, but in October 1943 was persuaded to relinquish the latter post, remaining on the board as vice-chairman.

Departure of Garvin

While Sir Emsley Carr had been, justifiably, feted for his fifty years' leadership, just twelve months later another long-serving editor, J.L. Garvin, was about to depart after thirty-four years in charge of *The Observer*. Throughout the thirties, Garvin had been in favour of negotiations with Germany, but only from a position of strength; and in July 1937 had welcomed the appointment of Neville Chamberlain as Prime Minister, a leader who had 'the right instinct for the main things in foreign affairs'. Twelve months later, he privately noted the 'hysterical reception for Chamberlain, the saviour of peace'.

Now, early in 1942, a difference began to emerge between Garvin and his proprietor, Waldorf Astor. Garvin believed that Churchill should continue to be both Prime Minister and Defence Minister. Waldorf Astor was opposed; and that same year David Astor, introduced 'Forum', a new feature, to the paper. The second son of Waldorf and Nancy Astor, David had been educated at Eton and Balliol College, Oxford, before entering journalism in 1936 on the *Yorkshire Post* under the editorship of A.H. Mann. During the Second World War, David Astor was to serve as a captain in the Royal Marines, and was a liaison officer for Lord Mountbatten. In June 1944, he took part in a special operations jump into France and was wounded. He was later awarded the Croix de Guerre.

Although David Astor, after coming down from Oxford, had wished to join *The Observer*, there had not been any sense of welcome from the editor; and writing to Garvin on 9 December 1937 his father could say: 'Do let me know what you think of David – I have always hoped that at some time he might train or come into the 'Observer'.' From Garvin there was silence.

Since the 1920s, Garvin had been living at Beaconsfield, Buckinghamshire, some twenty-five miles from *The Observer* offices off Fleet Street; and it was from his home that he had mainly edited the paper. To quote David Ayerst:[13] 'Secretaries and messengers shuttled between London and Beaconsfield, and once a week there was an expedition to London when business could be transacted in Tudor Street before or after an editorial lunch on the top floor. Its purpose was not to plan the paper but to develop a corporate sense.'

In the words of Stephen Pritchard: 'The modern quality Sunday newspaper is a descendant of Garvin's post-First World Creation. He recast the paper, making strict divisions between news and comment, introducing new layout and typefaces. He recruited a staff of eight talented people and 15 contributors and between them they produced 24 to 36 pages a week.'

In January 1941, Garvin – having refused earlier offers of a knighthood – was made a Companion of Honour, but, within a little more than a year, his world was to undergo a dramatic change. As Joanna Anstey and John Silverlight wrote in *The Observer Observed*:

> On 15 February 1942, *The Observer* published a Forum piece, entitled 'What's Wrong?', which called on Churchill to give up his role as Defence Minister. Astor claimed that Garvin had passed 'What's Wrong?' at proof stage. However, on 22 February Garvin published a leading article, entitled 'To Win the War', which denounced the idea. Garvin's contract expired on 28 February and Astor decided not to renew it. *The Observer* of 1 March was produced without Garvin. The leader in that issue paid tribute to Garvin's achievements as editor and was almost certainly written by Astor.

Garvin's departure was to be covered extensively in the Press, and in a short interview given to the *Daily Mirror* he was to say: 'My last article speaks for itself. I live only to prosecute the war to a successful conclusion. I think I should die if I ceased writing.' Within hours, Garvin was to receive offers from other Fleet Street titles. He chose the proposal from his old friend Beaverbrook to join the *Sunday Express* as the 'star' columnist at a salary of £10,000 per annum. Garvin was thrilled, as he revealed in this letter from his home at Gregories, Beaconsfield, to E.J. Robertson, managing director of Beaverbrook Newspapers:[14]

> 13 March 1942 – Dear Mr Robertson, I shall be delighted to meet you and my other coming colleagues next Thursday, March 19, at the Savoy. Will your secretary phone me whether 1, 1.15 or 1.30? Many thanks for fitting up the private wire. It has been

> everything to me here. I am never late with my copy when the time of delivery is given. From here by car the copy gets to the *Sunday Express* office in one hour.

For Garvin, the next few years were to be a golden period. Apart from regular contact with Beaverbrook, there were weekly lunches with E.J. Robertson at Claridge's or the Connaught – plus meetings with the Prime Minister and Field Marshal Smuts. He was very much in the 'inner circle'. To give an example:[15] 'July 2nd, 1943: My dear Robertson: I am astonished to get a reply-paid telegram from Mr Churchill asking me to lunch at No. 10 next Wednesday. So of course I had to reply "yes" though to my regret it puts off our meeting.'

Garvin was to remain with the *Sunday Express* until 1945, when, after a lapse of forty years, he went back to write for *The Daily Telegraph*. His final article appeared in the paper on 16 January 1947 and a week later he was dead. The following day, Churchill paid his respects in the *Telegraph*: 'Jim Garvin [was] a friend of fifty years in whom courage, generosity and faithfulness shone in private and in public life as they shine in few.'

Many years later, David Astor was to comment on the aftermath of Garvin's departure: 'As far as there was an editor in those dreadful weeks, it was me in my lunch-hour.' On the staff of Combined Operations Headquarters, based in Richmond Terrace, off Whitehall, Astor could attend to *The Observer* only in his spare time. Nevertheless, by the autumn of 1942, he had made sweeping changes, and on 1 November news appeared on the front page for the first time; and in that same issue he announced the paper's credo:

> *The Observer* is not a party paper. It is tied to no group, no sect, no interest. Its independence is absolute. But merely to stand alone, challenging and bracing as that attitude may be, is not enough. One must also stand for a system of ideas and for a pattern of constructive reform . . . . the first task is to end the mad competition of nations by a worldwide control, a control not static but susceptible always to necessary changes. The second is to destroy the social injustices of an ill-balanced society without creating a sluggish conformity and dull inertia. In our rebuilding we shall drive at the old Athenian ideal of seeking beauty without extravagance while pursuing new ways of efficiency and mastering the machine which has so often been the oppressor, rather than the liberator, of mankind. That, in broad outline, must be the ideal of a dynamic, democracy. It is also the policy of this paper.

Daily Worker *Suspended*

Early in 1941 the *Daily Worker* was suspended – the first such instance since the *Globe*, a London evening, was banned for a fortnight in November 1915 for 'baldly stating that Kitchener had departed as the result of an altercation with his civilian colleagues'. To quote Stephen Koss: 'Beaverbrook, withholding the incriminating fact that he had been one of the editor's informants, later recalled that "when the errant newspaper was closed down the plan to change War Secretaries was closed down with it".' Kitchener continued as Secretary of State for War; but an indignant Charles Palmer was forced to quit as editor of the *Globe* – even threatening to sue

Dudley Docker, his proprietor, for 'allegedly counselling him to attack Lloyd George on behalf of Kitchener'.

Now, a quarter of a century later, another national newspaper was to suffer the same fate. Since its launch on Wednesday 1 January 1930, the *Daily Worker*[16] – with its slogan 'Workers of the World Unite!' included in its masthead – had long been the mouthpiece of the Communist Party and the working classes; and, in its first issue, could lead with:

WOOLLEN WORKERS TAKE THE FIELD
MASS STRIKES AGAINST
WAGE REDUCTIONS
Police Attack Pickets
ALL WORKERS SOLID AND
DETERMINED TO FIGHT

But down page in column one there was a four-paragraph story in small headlines – SIXTY DEATHS IN CINEMA FIRE: Many Children Amongst The Victims – telling of a fire which had broken out at a Paisley cinema, near Glasgow.

Under the editorship of William Rust, the paper had long been a thorn in the side of the authorities; and throughout its first decade had relied on the generosity of its readers in contributing to the Daily Worker Fighting Fund to keep the title alive. Now, during the early summer of 1940, the paper was becoming more and more unacceptable to the Government, leading the *Daily Worker* editorial board to issue a statement, headed 'Those in High Places Fear Us', which outlined threats to the paper's newsagents and sellers.

On 10 July Herbert Morrison, the Home Secretary, wrote to the editor threatening to suppress the paper under Regulation 2D, unless it stopped 'publication of matter calculated to foment opposition to the prosecution of the war'. In response to a query from Professor Haldane, chairman of the board, he was told that 'no reference could be given to particular items to give you guidance'.

While there continued to be an uneasy peace between the Home Secretary and the paper, the *Daily Worker* was proud to announce the launch of the Scottish *Daily Worker* from its Glasgow plant on Monday 11 November. Even though the paper was printed on a flat-bed press, and maximum circulation was just 14,000, there was a three-hour advantage for Scottish readers over the London production.[17]

With circulation now slowly increasing, the next move from the paper was the calling of a People's Convention, to be held in London on 12 January 1941. However, a month before, on 10 December, speaking in the House of Commons, Beverley Baxter, the former *Daily Express* editor, was calling for the suppression of the paper. And on 20 December the Home Secretary, in attacking the Convention as a Communist gathering, gave a hint that he might ban it under the Defence Regulations.

Notwithstanding these threats, the Convention was held, 'overflowing the big hall of the Royal Hotel to fill two others'. Support was immense: more than 2200 delegates representing 1,284,000 workers, including 665 delegates from 497 trade organizations and 471 delegates from 239 factories.

MONDAY, SEPTEMBER 7, 1942

PASS THIS ON TO A FRIEND—

Daily Worker

LATE EDITION

—TEN READERS FOR EVERY COPY!

No. 3431 MONDAY, SEPTEMBER 7, 1942 ONE PENNY

STALINGRAD BEATS OFF ANOTHER MASS GERMAN ASSAULT

Von Bock's South-West Drive Fails

VON BOCK'S SECOND AND GREATEST MASS ONSLAUGHT AGAINST THE HEROIC CITY OF STALINGRAD HAS BEEN SMASHED AND THE RESISTANCE OF THE DEFENDERS IS STIFFENING, ACCORDING TO A DESPATCH FROM MOSCOW LATE LAST NIGHT.

Though the situation must remain grave while 50 German divisions with thousands of tanks and planes are ceaselessly battering at the gates of the city, the drive from the south-west has failed, cables Reuter's special corresp ondent, that was confirmed by the Moscow communique yesterday:—

"All German attempts to break through to the city are meeting with staunch resistance from Soviet troops," it was reported. "During the past 24 hours the Germans have made four attempts to attack one fortified sector, all of which were unsuccessful.

From JOHN GIBBONS
Daily Worker Special Correspondent

MOSCOW, Sunday night.

THE great Stalingrad battle rages with undiminishing intensity. With first grey steaks of dawn German Junkers and Messerschmitts come over in their hundreds trying by bombing and machine-gunning to pulverise Soviet defences.

"Yesterday's fighting was characterized by several heavy tank attacks launched simultaneously from different directions.

At one point south-west of the city, German units supported by a hundred tanks delivered seven successive but fruitless attacks against Soviet positions.

True there was a period when it seemed that the enemy had been successful. That was when his battering ram of tanks made a breach in the defences and German mobile units began to stream through.

Danger was averted by a skilful Red Army move. The advancing enemy infantry were attacked from either wing, while the tanks were caught in a concentrated fire from Red Army Mortars.

Many of the panzers were put out of commission, and the mobile infantry, cut off from their tan ksupport and having lost heavily, were forced to retreat.

Zhukov Presses On West of Moscow

On the Moscow front General Zhukov continues to storm the German "winter line" fortresses, and it is officially announced in Moscow that several more populated places have been taken, causing the Germans big losses in man power and equipment.

In the Caucasus two major battles are raging which may decide the fate of the great naval base of Novorossisk and the oilfields of Grosny.

Novorossisk is besieged by armies advancing from the north-west and north-east.

While the Germans claimed yesterday that the invasion forces from the Crimea which landed on the Taman Peninsula north-west of Novorossisk had now mopped up the whole of the western tip of the Caucasus, the Soviet communique spoke of defensive engagements against strong enemy forces

RIVER FORCED

Fifty-five miles from the Grosny oilfields the Germans have forced a passage of the Terek River at Mozdok, but a battle of annihilation is going on at the bridgehead.

Soviet Tank Unit Struck At Full Speed

From HAROLD KING
Reuter's Special Correspondent

MOSCOW, Sunday night.

It is known to-night that one of the most tremendcus mass assaults ever staged in modern warfare has been beaten at the south-western outskirts of Stalingrad by a Soviet tank unit which drove at full speed into the flank of the panzers and their infantry support.

The German Commander first threw all his weight into a drive on the city from the north-west.

When the out-numbered defenders stood their ground and broke the panzer spearhead, Von Bock swung his forces to the south-west, and for four days his empetus has been irresistible. Now for the second time the Germans are checked.

The climax of this second battle came after wave on wave of Luftwaffe planes had bombed the Soviet lines unmercifully for two hours. Then hundreds of tanks raced forward, vastly outnumbering the Russian forces.

Wheeling suddenly an outnumbered Soviet tank force let loose with their cannon and machine-guns against the oncoming motor vehicles, sending lorry after lorry crashig in a heap of twisted and blazing metal.

The German tanks tried to turn to meet the new menace, but by that time the remainder of the German motorised infantry had fled, leaving their tanks to be plastered by Soviet anti-tank guns and anti-tank rifles.

The defeat of this attack enabled Soviet troops in neighbouring sectors to recapture several strongholds.

HOLD FIRM

North-west of the city the Russian lines are also holding firm despite repeated German attempts to drive on Stalingrad along the right bank of the Volga.

But evidently Von Bock still has enormous reserves at his disposal. German troops are standing in a deep echelon along many miles behind the front line, ready to be thrown in to replace battered battalions.

Some panzer divisions which started the offensive a week ago have now been reduced to 60 or 70, but new tanks are arriving in a steady steram.

Harry Pollitt's Appeal

I APPEAL on behalf of the Central Committee of the Communist Party to every member and Party organisation to now set the example in the way we all work for the success of the Daily Worker.

The Daily Worker is our fighting tool. We are all going to prove we know how to use it. How to apply it to very job we are on. It is a tool that every worker, skilled and unskilled, man or woman, can use.

It can be used by every man and woman, because it is the people's paper fighting a people's war for a people's victory and a people's peace.

Malta Gunners Greet Us

How to Win the War

DAILY WORKER'S POLICY

The following declaration of the aims of the Daily Worker has been adopted by the Editorial Board:

ON this historic day of re-publication the Daily Worker thanks all those in the Labour, trade union, co-operative and democratic movements whose magnificent support not only succeeded in removing the nineteen months' ban, but also very considerably strengthened the unity of the people in the fight for victory over Fascism.

The Daily Worker, which belongs to you who made its rebirth possible, solemnly pledges to repay all you have done by the service it will give in the struggle to destroy the Hitlerite enemy.

We shall speak for Britain, for a virile national unity, firmly buttressed by a united working class.

We shall speak for the millions of ordinary folk, the men and women in industry and the services, whose toil and courage and sacrifice will bring victory and the new world of security.

The people want the truth; we shall give it to them.

Increasing Output

They want the selfish exposed, the pro-Fascists hounded from office, the vested interests vanquished: we shall be fearless and without mercy in attacking those obstacles to Britain's victory.

The Daily Worker pledges itself to make its special concern a mighty increase in the production of all war materials essential for victory.

It will stimulate output competition between factory and factory throughout Britain's industries and fight to remove every obstacle to increased production, no matter from which quarter it arises.

The Daily Worker will support the work of the production committees and uphold the principles of trade unionism.

The Second Front

The people want to know how to win the war within this fourth year: we shall tell them. This is our policy.

1 **Open the second front in Europe immediately. Support without reserve every measure to keep the second front supplied with arms, material and manpower so that it is carried through to victory.**

2 **Strengthen the alliance of the United Nations and the unity within the nations. Sustain the heroic Red Army and the Soviet people whose fight has saved humanity from barbarism. Send them the arms and material they require.**

3 **Re-open negotiations with India. Recognise India's right to National Government, representing all sections of the Indian people, able to mobilise them in armed struggle against Fascism.**

Day in and day out this newspaper will do its utmost to achieve the full mobilisation of the country's resources. The Daily Worker says:

MOBILISE every able-bodied man and woman for war service in the armed forces, civil defence and industry. No evasions to be tolerated.

SPEED the training and placing of women in all industries to release large numbers of men for the armed forces.

RAISE wages for lower-paid workers, especially women, so that greater production can be obtained.

INCREASE the pay of Old Age Pensioners to 30s. a week flat rate.

ABOLISH the Means Test.

REDUCE with the utmost strictness the consumption of fuel. ADOPT without delay a fuel rationing scheme that will give priority to vital war industries and small householders.

RATION all commodities at fixed prices within reach of the lowest paid workers. Penal servitude, instead of fines, for Black Marketeers. Abolish all inequalities in the distribution of food.

INCREASE pay for men in armed forces to 5s. a day basic rate, from which 2s. can be allotted to dependants. Proportional increases for women in the services. INCREASE allowances for serving men's wives to £2 a week, 10s. 6d. a week for every child under 14 and 16s. for every child between 14 and 16 still at school.

PROMOTE more men from the ranks. Remove barriers standing in the way.

(Cont'd on Back Page, Col. 5)

American Solidarity

Five hundred dollars have been cabled to the Daily Worker by Earl Browder, Secretary of the U.S. Communist Party, as a practical gesture of American workers' solidarity.

Drive Rommel Back From Our Minefields

ROMMEL'S Africa Corps has now been pushed back west of our minefield on the Egypt battlefront through which they advanced a week ago.

Two panzer divisions and other German and Italian units have suffered severe losses, states yesterday's Cairo communique.

The enemy did not penetrate our main defensive system at any point, in spite of every effort.

WILLKIE'S TOUR

Mr. Wendell Willkie, after touring the Egyptian front yesterday said:—

"My impression is that what has taken place here today and the preceding days has removed the desert threat to Egypt.

"The battlefield I have seen (he added) is an object lesson in the necessity for more material. You could use it as a classroom for Americans. I wish all Americans could have had my experience."

R. F. Roland, Reuter's Special Correspondent in Cairo, says: "Pursued without rest by the Eighth Army's mobile columns, Rommel is to-night back where he started in his latest attempt to smash through to the Nile Valley. Since the Axis troops began their retreat, Allied land and air forces have hammered them ceaselessly by day and night."

£50,000

£5,254 19s. 2d. in ten days! This is the record sum into our Fighting Fund since the lifting of the ban.

A grand response—but we need every penny. The Daily Worker has got to run for six weeks without income against an expenditure running into thousands of pounds.

On top of this we must complete the purchase of our press which replaces our Cayton Street works destroyed by the nazis.

We need £50,000 to give the Daily Worker a firm start.

* * *

The Fund letters make wonderful reading. What enthusiasm and confidence! Thanks for all the amounts, large and small. Many shop stewards are organising big collections and setting target figures. An example to follow.

* * *

And now let us introduce you to George Allison, who to-day takes over the Fund Drive from Violet Lansbury. We are very, very sorry to say good-bye to our Violet, but her command of the Russian language has called her away for vital service elsewhere.

All supporters of the Daily Worker know Geoorge Allison and the fine job he has done in the fight against the ban. He is going to do the same job on the Fund.

Write to GEORGE ALLISON Fighting Fund, Swinton House, 324, Grays Inn Road, W.C.

Hungary Blacks Out

Following the Russian air raids on Hungary, the Hungarian Minister of the Interior has ordered a black-out throughout the whole country, says Reuter.

Back in action — after suspension

For the *Daily Worker* of 14 January, the Convention was, naturally, the main news story – and, following its success, the paper now announced plans to stage a further twelve regional conferences. This was a situation that could not be tolerated by the Government; and on Tuesday 21 January 1941 Herbert Morrison called the Newspaper Proprietors Association to a meeting, announcing that he had that day 'issued the necessary Orders under Defence Regulation 2D for the suppresion of the *Daily Worker* with which was coupled *The Week*, a duplicated news-letter issued personally by Claud Cockburn'. After lunch that day, the Home Secretary then met all Fleet Street editors and informed them of his decision. To quote William Rust:[18]

> Early that evening Det.-Insp. Whitehead led a posse of Special Branch men, and supported by uniformed police who surrounded Clayton Street in due form, raided and seized our offices and formally carried out the suppression. There were the usual searches and questionings. And, since Mr Morrison had thoughtfully added a separate Order under Defence Regulation 94B that the newspaper's rotary presses should be sequestered until leave had been obtained from the High Court, they were sealed and placed under police guard. Parallel operations were carried out that same evening at the offices and plant of the Scottish *Daily Worker* in Glasgow.

Just twenty-four hours earlier, a defiant *Daily Worker* in its final leader, headed 'We Accuse the Government', had alleged that the crisis in war production was 'due to the reckless profiteering and incompetence of the ruling class . . . . The *Daily Worker* can prove that more working hours have been lost in certain factories as a result of mismanagement than in all the strikes of recent months.'

That same day as the suppression, Herbert Morrison justified his decision in the House of Commons:

> This action has been taken not because of any recent change or development in the character of these publications nor because of the appearance therein of some particular article or articles, but because it is and has been for a long period the settled and continuous policy of these papers to try to create in the readers a state of mind in which they will refrain from co-operating in the national war effort and may become ready to hinder that effort.
>
> Since the end of September 1939, when the *Daily Worker* reversed its policy, it has refrained from publishing anything calculated to encourage co-operation in the struggle which this country is waging against Nazi and Fascist tyranny and aggresion; and has by every device and misrepresentation sought to make out that our people have nothing to gain by victory, that the hardships and sufferings of warfare are unnecessary and are imposed upon them by a callous Government carrying on a selfish contest in the interests of a privileged class.

Defending the Government's decision, *The Daily Telegraph* in its leading article declared:[19]

> Freedom of opinion and discussion in the Press are at the foundation of democratic institutions; and the long hesitation of the Government to interfere even with the injurious activity of the *Daily Worker* is a recognition of the fact. But this is no case of ordinary criticism of the Government, which is the birthright of any citizen of a democratic country.

> This organ of Communism has existed to serve not British but alien ends by the systematic publication of matter intended to prevent the nation's survival by disabling its prosecution of the war. It is propaganda as hostile to this country as that of Goebbels himself, and as continuous. Its dominant purpose has been to make mischief, to sow tares at a time when the nation, whose tolerance it has so constantly abused, is engaged in a life and death struggle with an enemy who shows no tolerance himself. If the *Daily Worker* had attempted to carry on its subversive work in Germany, it would not merely have been suppressed. Those responsible for its publication would most likely have been beheaded.

The *Daily Mirror*, however, thought differently, as Cecil King's diary entry of 21 January reveals:[20] 'We got wind of this on Friday last and anticipating this move which will be announced tonight, we included this morning a cartoon and a leader making it very clear that we deplored this blow at freedom of the Press. It will be interesting to see what sort of press it gets tomorrow.'

Six days after the suppression, the House of Commons debated the issue on a motion by Aneurin Bevan, Labour, and Sir Richard Acland, Liberal; and although the sponsors disassociated themselves with the policy of the *Daily Worker* they felt protest was necessary against the use of 2D. The most forthright defence of the paper, however, came from William Gallacher, Member for West Fife:

> One of the reasons for its suppression is that the *Daily Worker* has exposed day after day the rotten profiteering and the corruption in the ruling class, especially among the employers, especially when they are paid cost plus .... *The Daily Worker* day after day has exposed the disorganisation of the factories and the fact that it is the employers who are responsible for it and the failure to get effective production.

When the vote was taken, 297 MPs supported the Home Secretary, while just eleven were opposed.

It was to be nineteen months before the *Daily Worker* was allowed to resume publication, and during that period there had grown a vociferous protest against the suspension. Prominent among the protestors had been H.G. Wells and George Bernard Shaw: 'It would have been far more sensible to suppress *The Times* and the other papers which have for years carried on, and are still carrying on, a campaign of insult, calumny and clamour for a capitalist united front against Bolshevism.'

For Rust it was a case of keeping the *Daily Worker* and its principles in the public eye through involvement in monthly broadsheet specials and the weekly pocket-size *Commentary on Current Political Events*. Support continued to grow for resumption, and on 28 May 1942, at the Labour Party Conference – in defiance of the National Executive – comrades voted to lift the ban by 1,244,000 to 1,213,000. Pressure was to mount further with a National Deputations Day on 29 July, when 1500 delegates from more than 300 constituencies besieged the House of Commons. And for all those protesters there was a copy of the *Daily Blank*, 'a four-page full specimen showing what the *Daily Worker* would have been like if it had appeared the previous day'.[21]

With the Co-operative Congress – membership 8,700,000 – also opposed, plus the Scottish Trades Union Congress and likely disapproval at the forthcoming TUC

Conference scheduled for Blackpool in early September, the Government now realized that it was time to rescind the ban. On Wednesday, 26 August, therefore, the *Daily Worker* editorial board were informed that the Home Secretary 'has this day revoked the Order.'

Some ten days later, on 7 September, the *Daily Worker* – having had its previous premises blitzed and now printing on a twenty-year-old rotary at the London Caledonian Press, Swinton Street, Gray's Inn Road – made its reappearance; and such was the demand that there were orders for more than 500,000 copies. However, because of newsprint rationing, the first-day circulation was confined to just 75,000. For editor William Rust, his greatly-improved paper 'must become the most consistent exponent of national unity, based on working-class unity'.

Daily Mirror *Under Threat*

One other newspaper, the *Daily Mirror* – far more important in terms of prestige and circulation – was now to incur the wrath of the Government. For months, the *Daily Mirror* and its sister paper, the *Sunday Pictorial*, had vented their 'criticisms of the Army and the political leadership'. Only weeks previously, the loss of Singapore on 15 February 1942 had brought a stinging rebuke from the *Pictorial*: 'There are too many ministers definitely not of the stuff of which war-winners are made. And the country cannot afford political passengers.'

In an exchange of letters between Cecil King and Churchill, the Prime Minister had complained of 'a spirit of hatred and malice against the Government .... which surpasses anything I have ever seen in English journalism'. Following a meeting at 10 Downing Street and further correspondence there had emerged 'an uneasy truce'. However, the publication on 6 March 1942 of a Zec cartoon – destined to be the most famous of the Second World War – showing a torpedoed sailor adrift on a raft in a black empty sea almost led to the *Daily Mirror* being banned. The caption, written by Cassandra (William Connor) read: 'The price of petrol has been raised by a penny. Official.'

An incensed Churchill now suggested that Morrison, using Regulation 2D – which provided for instantaneous suppression of a newspaper on the edict of the Home Secretary – should shut down the *Mirror*. Morrison, however, with the backing of Beaverbrook and Brendan Bracken, Minister of Information, was totally opposed, suggesting that the paper should be given a final warning. Churchill demurred, and Morrison then ordered the *Mirror* chairman, John Cowley, and editor Cecil Thomas to see him.[22]

For almost an hour, Thomas and Bartholomew, the paper's editorial director, deputizing for Cowley, were forced to endure a tirade from Morrison:

> First, Zec cartoon for instance .... 'very artistically drawn. Worthy of Goebbels at his best.' To Thomas: 'Only a very unpatriotic Editor would pass that for publication.' He turned to Bart: 'Only one with a diseased mind could be responsible for the *Daily Mirror* policy.' Morrison then criticised an editorial 'which was no more than a ridiculous exaggeration in words about a Blimp'.

To quote editor Cecil Thomas: 'He reminded us he had closed one paper and said it would be a long time before it was opened. "And that goes for you, too. You might bear that in mind. If you are closed, it will be for a long time." No further warning would be given. "We shall act with a speed that will surprise you".'

From the rest of Fleet Street – with the exception of *The Daily Telegraph*, which gave a guarded approval to the Government's action: 'The examples given by Mr Morrison of the sort of publication that has given rise to his warning will be enough for any reasonable mind' – there was much support for the *Daily Mirror*. To quote a few examples:

> *The Times*, 'yesterday's reminder to one newspaper will in no way deter the rest from the discharge of their duty'; *Daily Express*, 'the offending newspaper should have been prosecuted before the Courts and thus given the opportunity to defend itself'; *Daily Herald*, 'denounced the Government interpretation of the Zec cartoon and warned Churchill and Morrison that it was amid the twilight of compulsory censorship that Petain and Laval had contrived to do away with legitimate Government in France'.

Herbert Morrison, in his reply, told fellow-Members of Parliament:[23]

> The cartoon in question is only one example, but a particularly evil example, of the policy and methods of a newspaper which, intent on exploiting an appetite for sensation and with a reckless indifference to the national interest and to the prejudicial effect on the war effort, has repeatedly published scurrilous misrepresentations, distorted and exaggerated statements, and irresponsible generalizations . . . .
>
> As it is possible that some of the persons responsible for the publication of such matter have not realised that it is within the ambit of Regulation 2D, it has been thought right in the first instance to take action by way of warning. I have seen those responsible for the publication of the *Daily Mirror*, and I have made clear to them the considerations which I have outlined to the House. A watch will be kept on this paper, and the course which the Government may ultimately decide to take will depend on whether those concerned recognise their public responsibility and take care to refrain from further publication of matter calculated to foment opposition to the successful prosecution of the war.

For Aneurin Bevan, who some fifteen months earlier in the suspension of the *Daily Worker* debate had argued fiercely for the independence of the Press, this was a further opportunity to launch an attack on the Home Secretary:

> I do not like the *Daily Mirror*, and I have never liked it . . . . I do not like that form of journalism. I do not like the strip-tease artists . . . . But the *Daily Mirror* has not been warned because people do not like that kind of journalism. It is not because the Home Secretary is aesthetically repelled by it that he wants it. I have heard a number of honourable Members say that it is a hateful paper, a tabloid paper, a hysterical paper, a sensational paper, and that they do not like it. I am sure the Home Secretary does not take that view. He likes the paper. He is taking its money.

As Bill Hagerty was to write:[24] 'And Bevan waved a batch of Morrison's *Mirror* cuttings in the air. It was a cheap shot and a foolish one. Morrison immediately responded with: "If the honourable Gentleman wants to be personal so is somebody closely connected with him." Perhaps it had momentarily slipped Bevan's mind that his wife, Jennie Lee, had the previous year become political correspondent of the *Mirror*.'

The controversy caught the attention of George Orwell, who, writing in his diary, noted: 'Terrific debate in the House over the "affaire" *Daily Mirror*. A. Bevan reading numerous extracts from Morrison's own articles in the *D.M.*, written since war started, to the amusement of Conservatives who are anti-*D.M.*, but can never resist the spectacle of two Socialists slamming one another.'

Fleet Street Under Attack

For some nine months from September 1940 until May 1941 Fleet Street was under almost nightly attack from the Luftwaffe; and recording those events was Gordon Robbins, former day editor of *The Times* and chairman of Benn Brothers, in his invaluable *Fleet Street Blitzkreig Diary*.

The air raids commenced on September 20 1940 when the *Evening Standard* offices in Shoe Lane suffered a direct hit from a large calibre bomb. This struck a 15,000-gallon water tank on the roof wrecking it and the tower, and penetrating the composing room, where considerable damage was done. The huge volume of water cascaded down ten flights of stairs into the basement; there the engineers and machine minders worked valiantly to 'bail out' the pressroom which was under two feet of oily water.[25]

The *Standard* was fortunate in that Tom Blackburn, the general manager, and A.L. Cranfield, the managing editor, together with a number of executives were sleeping on the premises, and were thus able to take immediate steps to contain the damage and maintain production. The *World's Press News* later reported that the editorial and composing activities were transferred to the *Daily Express* building at 121 Fleet Street, and printing was started on the south side of the river, with the result that no delay whatever was caused in production.

The prompt steps taken and the fact that the ensuing edition carried a cartoon by Low showing that a bomb had suffered damage by contact with the *Standard* building drew from Churchill a congratulatory telegram: 'Bravo, *Evening Standard*.' Throughout those almost nightly raids, Beaverbrook, when not required at the Ministry, would return to his specially-fortified flat high in the *Standard* building, from where he could see at first-hand the efforts of firewatchers in their battle against the incendiaries. And on the odd occasion he would even by joined by Churchill.

Less than a week later, on 25 September, *The Times* building was hit by heavy-calibre bombs, just as the presses were rolling with the first edition. Due to the supreme efforts of the staff only eighteen minutes' production time was lost. To quote Harold Herd:

> No one was more than slightly hurt. It was the main building facing Queen Victoria Street that was struck, all the front rooms – which housed the editorial, managerial and advertisement departments – being wrecked. But though internal damage was severe, the fabric itself stoutly resisted the bombardment. Windows were smashed, the famous clock disappeared and the building showed its wounds, but otherwise the solid structure withstood the test. The plant and the machinery escaped damage.

Later that day, editor Dawson received a letter from Neville Chamberlain at the Privy Council Office: 'Just a line to send you my sympathy upon your misfortune in being bombed and to congratulate you upon getting to press all the same. It is a great achievement, but only what one expects from *The Times*.'

Throughout the following month, the nightly air raids continued, as Dawson noted in his diary on 12 October: 'Another whopping bomb dropped just outside the office about 11.00 p.m. (the previous evening), bursting gas and water mains. It looked like the inferno . . . . flames ascending from one end of a huge crater and a waterfall at the other!' Churchill was now to congratulate Major Astor and his staff on their dedication in producing the paper. But the greatest praise was to come from the *New York Times*:[26]

> The London newspapers of these terrible days are in themselves documents that deserve to be treasured. They explain how millions in London have been able to endure a month of terror from the skies . . . . To look at the unchanging front page of *The Times* one would hardly know that London was being bombed, apart from a pathetic death notice now and then, telling friends that some man, woman or child had died 'owing to enemy action' . . . . With such a spirit the free Press of England is now writing a chapter of courage and devotion which will take its place among the finest records of the newspaper profession.

Although newspapers were prepared to assist rivals who had suffered bomb damage – the *Daily Mirror* was a prime example, having made plates for the *Daily Sketch*, when it had no gas, and blocks for the *Evening News*, when it was without water – there was the occasional bitterness, as Gordon Robbins was to reveal in his diary entry of 4 October: 'Plummer, the Assistant Manager of the *Daily Express*, came to see me this morning with the idea of renting part of our shelter at night for sleeping accommodation for twenty-five or thirty members of their staff for whom they cannot find room in their building.' Three days later, on 7 October, Robbins was to write:[27]

> A curious bit of bother arose over our agreement to the request of the *Daily Express* . . . . The *Express* provided each man with a palliasse, and, when the regular occupants of the public part of the shelter saw preparations going on for the reception of an entirely new company, there was some murmuring. On Saturday evening there was talk in the bar of 'The Kings & Keys' of a procession of protest to the Guildhall and the *Express* men being stoned when they entered the shelter. None of these things happened, but there was some unpleasantness, which the housekeeper dealt with tactfully.
>
> The malcontents, however, took up the question again on Monday morning, and I received this telegram which gave their argument in a nutshell: 'RESERVING SHELTER EXPRESS MEN UNFAIR WOMEN, CHILDREN, AGED. PLEASE RECONSIDER. VAUGHAN.' At the same time, two determined-looking women waited upon the *Daily Express* people with the same complaint and also went to the Guildhall.

The matter *was* resolved, but 'the arrangement is subject to reconsideration at any moment'.

The raids of 1940 were to reach their climax on Sunday 29 December, when St Paul's Cathedral narrowly escaped destruction but for St Bride's Church it was total devastation. The Verger, Leonard Morgan, was to leave a graphic account of that night:[28]

> The year has gone beyond recall, with all its hopes and fears to play on the bells. It was a natural choice but it has a prophetic irony. The bells rang for the last time over a darkened Fleet Street (blackout was at 5.27 p.m.). The congregation, some forty or so, attended the last evensong. After the doors were locked, they all went home – but not to bed. Few Londoners had any sleep that night. 'The dome of St Paul's,' said *The Times*, 'seemed to ride the sea of fire like a great ship lifting above the smoke and flame the invoilable ensign of the golden cross.' But below the smoke there were no noble metaphors. Only steel being melted, stone being calcined, a city being consumed.
>
> A bomb, or maybe bombs, pierced the roof of St Bride's, and the inside was soon ablaze. Good neighbours from the Press Association, Reuters and the Press Club rushed in, grabbed what they could – including the brass lectern which tradition said had already been rescued from the same blazing church nearly three hundred years before. St Bride's famous bells fell in molten ruin but the steeple in which they hung had its night of greatest glory, for though flames were ravening out from its every opening it stood, a triumphant affirmation of Wren's engineering mastery.

The Daily Telegraph building was also to come under attack, when dozens of incendiaries started fires, gutting the women's page editorial department, but those which penetrated the composing and machine rooms were swiftly dealt with. Nevertheless, gas and electricity failed, 'neighbouring buildings caught fire and one next door, in Wine Office Court, was so gutted by flames that it collapsed, burying a fireman and a soldier beneath the rubble'. Despite the fires, the presses continued to roll – and the print figure was completed. And in nearby Gough Square, Dr Johnson's House suffered heavy damage, though, fortunately his chair and a number of first editions were saved.

The *News Chronicle*, too, suffered badly; and as S.J. Taylor in her *The Reluctant Press Lord*, quoting Bill Benbow, was to write: 'The bomb landed in the building, and we stood and watched. I've never seen a scene like it in my life. As the flooring gave way under the intense heat, machinery on the fourth floor fell through the various floors, creasing a great inferno in the basement of the *News Chronicle* building. It was an awe-inspiring sight.' And that same night, just yards away on the roof of the *Daily Mail* building, photographer Herbert Mason was to capture the most iconic image of the war: St Paul's Cathedral through the smoke.

Bill Needham, the legendary advertisement director of the *Daily Express*, was a regular firewatcher during the Blitz, and was to leave a graphic account in his *50 Years of Fleet Street*:

> There was plenty of excitement. Bombs fell all around us. London, for a period, endured fires in some area or another almost each night of the week. It was always a toss-up whether the next bomb would be ours. One bomb did hit the *Daily Express* building. Fortunately it was not a blockbuster which would have blown the entire premises to bits. But it did set fire to the old wooden-floored and largely wooden-walled original offices with one entrance in 8, Shoe Lane and another at 23, St Bride's Street.

The closest shave, though, was a 1250 kilogram parachute mine suspended from wires outside the *Daily Express* main entrance, 121, Fleet Street:

> In the half light of the stars and a dim moon, Strube, the cartoonist, saw only just above or on the surface of the road, a hideous oblong metal shape attached to a parachute which had wrapped itself round the overhead power cable of the street light. One cable had snapped with the result that the oblong had fallen on its side and not on its nose. Had it done so the entire *Daily Express* building would have been blown to rubble. The building was vacated and within minutes we all left for the *Evening Standard* office at the other end of Shoe Lane. Shortly afterwards those double-dyed heroes, The Bomb Disposal Squad, arrived. The mine was defused and taken away.

The nightly air raids were to continue throughout the spring of 1941, with one of the heaviest being on Wednesday 16 April. This time the area under attack was the City Road area, where the *Daily Worker* offices and plant – still banned from producing – were completely gutted by fire. Editor William Rust was to tell of the raid in a leaflet, *Bombed and Banned*:[29]

> The building, originally a tea warehouse, had wide timber floors and very little steel work. It burnt like a match box, despite the heroic efforts of the staff present (two firewatchers, the regular night watchman and two machine-men) to stem the flames. Bombs had been raining down since 9.30 p.m., and the incendiary bomb which finally struck the building fell at 1.30 a.m. It lodged in a space between partition walls, where it was inaccessible. Firemen arrived on the scene struggling bravely with the difficulties of water supply, in a narrow street where flames spouted from side to side. Local people, citizens of Hoxton and St Luke's, bore a hand, although their own defenceless homes were threatened. But all the efforts to save the building were in vain. There is little or nothing to salvage from these ruins of what was once a highly efficient printing plant. No compensation will be paid by the Government until after the war.

On 10 May 1941 – a day when Deputy Führer Rudolf Hess was parachuting from a Messerschmitt near the Duke of Hamilton's estate in Scotland, on a bizarre personal peace mission – the raids reached their climax, when the Luftwaffe launched its final major attack, the most destructive of the Blitz. There was a full moon, and the Thames had a low ebb tide, a favourite bombers' combination. 'Two thousand fires were started, three thousand people were killed or injured, all but one main-line station were put out of action, and the House of Commons was destroyed.' In the City, the Law Courts and the Tower of London were seriously damaged, while in Fleet Street dozens of fires were raging, with fifteen blazing on or around the *Daily Mirror* offices. Very much involved that night was Cecil King, then general manager of the *Sunday Pictorial*, who was to leave a vivid description of the fight to save the offices:

> When I got back I found that we had been delayed over starting printing again, because the electric current had failed and the metal pots in the linos had gone cold; all the lights had gone out. However, after a ten-minute interval they came on again and efforts could be made to get the paper out. I left at 6.30 when all danger to the offices from nearby fires seemed to be well over.

Also under attack had been the *Morning Advertiser* whose offices were burned out, leading to an edition being missed. Other buildings which had been hit included the Newspaper Proprietors Association offices in Bouverie Street, the nearby old *Daily*

News building and the old *News of the World* building across the way. 'Production of the *News of the World* continued and distribution was effected with a delay of not more than a couple of hours.'

The blaze that night was visible to the German bombers more than 150 miles away; and in the City 1436 were killed. As Philip Ziegler was to note in his *London at War*:[30]

> Though nobody suspected it, dared even hoped it, the blitz was over – 30,000 houses had been destroyed or badly damaged, more than 20,000 civilians killed, fifteen Wren churches wrecked. There was still trouble in plenty to come, still major air-raids, as well as the V1s and V2s, but the intensity of the raid of 10 May was never to be repeated.

15

Shortage of newsprint

FOR THE NATIONAL PRESS the most urgent problem from the first month of the war had been the shortage of newsprint. Prior to hostilities, the Press had used some 22,000 tons per week – a figure that was to fall to just 4300 tons in 1942. In September 1939 the Newspaper Proprietors Association (NPA) agreed that pagination should be greatly reduced:[1]

> Daily papers except *The Times* and *Telegraph* to be limited to 12 pages for the 6th and 7th September, thereafter to 8 pages. *Daily Telegraph* to be allowed to exceed these sizes by the amount of classified advertising. Sunday papers to be limited to 16 pages. Evening papers to be limited to 8 pages or 16 pages for the *Evening Standard* [tabloid]. The Sunday papers to be a maximum of 16 pages with the exception of the *Sunday Times* and the *Observer*.

The NPA also imposed a ban on newsbills and circulation promotions – and sale or return of copies was discontinued.

Two months later, it was reported at an NPA Council meeting that representatives of the newspaper industry had met the Minister of Supply to discuss the shipment of newsprint and pulp from Canada, and at that meeting it was suggested that there should be a small advisory council set up, consisisting of four consumers, a chartered accountant plus four representatives from the newsprint companies. One suggestion, however, not put to the Minister was that 'stocks of newsprint in the country should be requisitioned at cost price for redistribution to all papers'. This proposal was to bring about a mixed reaction from Fleet Street owners.

A week later, on November 21, at the NPA Council meeting, E.J. Robertson, managing director of Beaverbrook Newspapers, was to rebut rumours putting his company's stocks at 80,000 tons:[2]

> The facts are that at the end of last week the Express Newspapers had in this country 29,560 tons of Canadian and Newfoundland newsprint or just over eight weeks' normal consumption. One month's normal supply for the Express group is 15,500 tons. Average weekly supplies from English mills at the present time are 1000 tons per week, or just over 50 per cent of the contract tonnage from English mills. (In 1938 total consumption of the Express group – *Daily Express*, *Sunday Express*, *Evening Standard*, *Evening Citizen* (Glasgow) – was 187,000 tons, 95,000 tons of which came from Canada, 92,000 tons supplied by English newsprint manufacturers.)

As a gesture to the newspaper industry, the *Daily Express* was 'prepared to fall back on accumulated stocks, thereby allowing newspapers without stocks to build up one month's normal supply.' There was to be further progress on Friday 15 December, when, at the behest of the NPA, the first meeting of the Newsprint Advisory Council took place; and for the next six months this was to be the key factor in allocating newsprint to the industry. But it soon became apparent that there was a need for a much more structured organization – and in the spring of 1940 this was to come about.

The establishment of a more formalized organization was to become even more necessary when, through the German occupation of Norway in April, the flow of Scandinavian newsprint came to an abrupt halt. Frank Waters, manager of Express Newspapers in Scotland, wrote in his diary of 28 April: '[Newsprint] has become rarer than gold. Sizes of paper have been further limited to 8 pages [broadsheet]. Now actually embarrassed by extra sales. Like many other things newspaper life has become so standardised and stereotyped that originality will count for nought. That for a newspaper is pure hell.'

On 10 May 1940 – the day German armies invaded the Netherlands and Belgium and Churchill succeeded Chamberlain as Prime Minister – members of the NPA met at their offices, 6, Bouverie Street, to discuss the urgent problem of newsprint. (Since the announcement in October 1939 that newsprint was to be £17 per ton the following six months had seen further rises, and in June 1940 the cost was to rise to £22 per ton.)

As the minutes reveal, this was to be the most important meeting that the NPA had held, and the only occasion when Lord Beaverbrook was present. Other Press barons attending included: Lord Camrose, *The Daily Telegraph*; Lord Kemsley, *The Sunday Times*; Lord Southwood, *Daily Herald*; the Hon. Esmond Harmsworth, *Daily Mail*; Sir Emsley Carr, *News of the World*; Sir Walter Layton, *News Chronicle*; and Major the Hon. John Jacob Astor, *The Times*. Each newspaper 'made themselves liable for £100,000'.

The initial move was to appoint Lord Beaverbrook as chairman with Esmond Harmsworth as deputy chairman, but within hours Churchill was to nominate Beaverbrook as Minister of Aircraft Production – and for the remainder of the war Esmond Harmsworth was to be chairman of the newly-formed Newsprint Supply Company (NSC). The first steps taken were to set up two shipping companies and purchase the *San Rafael*, 8600 tons, and the *Kainalu*, 9400 tons, at a price of $60 to $65 dollars per ton. A week later it was agreed to secure a further vessel, *American Oriole*, 8600 tons, at a cost of $600,000. Within days, though, it was reported that the *Humber Arm*, on charter, had been sunk by a submarine, and that 'the loss of this vessel would throw back the shipping programme by at least three weeks'.[3]

The bad news was to continue, when it was learned that the *Geraldine Mary*, one of the NPA's chartered vessels, inward bound with newsprint, had been sunk and another outward-bound chartered vessel was also feared lost. Not deterred, it was decided that the company should approach the Ministry of Shipping for approval to purchase a vessel to replace the *Geraldine Mary*. However, in October 1940 the NSC reported that an application to acquire two more ships had been turned down by the

Ministry of Shipping. 'One large and a few small charters had been secured, but freight accommodation was difficult to secure.' By the end of the year more than 50,000 tons of newsprint had been destroyed by enemy action, while stocks in hand amounted to 207,000 tons, of which 189,000 tons were with the newspaper companies, the balance being mill stocks.

Difficulties in securing newsprint were to continue throughout 1941, and on 21 February, in an effort to ease the situation, it was announced that the Newsprint Supply Co. were negotiating to purchase the *J.B. White*. But less than a month later, it was learned that the *Huff* was considerably overdue on her journey to Canada and must be considered a total loss; and that the *J.B. White* had been sunk with a cargo of 4500 tons of newsprint. 'Thirty-seven out of thirty-nine of the crew had been landed.'

There was to be further bad news when it was found out that the *Esmond* had been severely damaged by enemy action and would be out of commission for some time.

From the authorities there was to be no help, with Sir Kingsley Wood telling the NSC 'that the Government could not at present facilitate the company's proposed arrangement to acquire ships to replace those recently lost'.

Stern measures were now necessary to trim consumption; and with a reduction of 5900 tons per week – 17 per cent – this meant that from Sunday 13 April 'London morning papers would have to produce three 4-page and three 6-page issues per week instead of two 4-page and four 6-page issues and Sunday papers 6-page issues'. Lord Camrose, however, declared that *The Daily Telegraph* would maintain its size of six pages, and effect the economy by means of a lesser circulation:[4]

> In contradistinction to other penny papers, *The Daily Telegraph* will, therefore, be maintained as a six-page paper. To do this means, unfortunately, a substantial reduction in the number of copies which can be printed, with the newsprint available. The war has led to a spirit of co-operation unknown in normal days, and we hope that in this spirit those readers who are fortunate enough to get their copies regularly will share them, wherever practicable, with less fortunate friends . . . . Far better that five people should read a *Daily Telegraph* true to its character and traditions than that six should read what could in four pages be, at the best, only an approximation to it.

There was to be further bad news on Friday May 23 1941, when it was reported that the *Rothermere* – shortly after completing its one hundredth voyage – and the *Esmond* had been torpedoed. These latest sinkings had meant that 25,000 tons of newsprint had been lost en route at sea, with the arrival of some 300,000 tons. With only the *Dodge*, 4000 tons of newsprint, having berthed safely at Manchester and no further shipments expected for another two months, there was now a need for even more control, and as a result it was announced that from June 11, 'all 1*d*. morning and evening papers would keep to a maximum of four pages, standard size (eight pages tabloid size), and the *Daily Telegraph* to six pages'.

Amid all the gloom, however, there was to be one brief glimmer of light: the announcement that 'The stevedores at Manchester and Liverpool having agreed to work two reels per sling instead of one hitherto, it was expected that a considerable improvement in the rate of discharge of vessels would be forthcoming.'[5]

For the remainder of the year, there was to be an improvement in operation – no further vessels were lost, although the *Dodge* and *Pachesham* were damaged on their last voyages, necessitating delays of six and two weeks respectively. But, as for the recent request to purchase further vessels, on 12 December the Ministry of Shipping sought to commandeer two of the company's existing vessels for the Ministry of Transport for six months in 1942! And there were to be further newsprint shortages in 1943, necessitating *The Daily Telegraph* in the January to reduce to just four pages, and a consequent reduction in leaders from four to just one.

Advertisement Difficulties

The dearth of newsprint and the consequent reduction in paper sizes meant that 'there was a sharp fall in [large] display advertising and a switch to small advertisements, which further reduced the proportion of advertising revenues of the national dailies from 60 per cent of income in 1938 to only 30 per cent in 1943'. As an example, in the first year of the war, the *Evening Standard*, through pagination being depressed, showed a dramatic drop in advertising revenue of more than £200,00 to a low of £347,645.

There was, though, to be an unexpected benefit for the less-profitable titles. Advertisers unable to be accommodated in the more popular papers were now forced to take space in those with smaller circulations. The Advertising Association, which ran its own campaign, reminded its members 'that goodwill was a valuable asset needing to be sustained by advertising'.

So great was the demand from advertisers that Lord Camrose decided that *The Daily Telegraph* should run 'A' and 'B' editions, enabling twice as many advertisements to be carried but reaching only half of the full circulation. This was particularly beneficial to members of the public placing small advertisements – births, marriages and deaths, especially – for, although the probable readership was reduced by fifty per cent, the advertisement did appear. (After the war the period of waiting increased at one point to eight weeks.)

The chief advertiser during the war years was undoubtedly the Government, which, using its special discount of 2.5 per cent, between March 1940 and June 1945, through its 34 different departments, spent more than £9,500,000. Unlike the 'normal' advertisers who were limited to maximum sizes of 5 in. × 2 cols, government agencies could take spaces up to 11 in. × 3 cols. And as T.R.Nevett was to note:[6]

> Most important were the National Savings Committee, which during this time, spent some £2,250,000, and the Ministry of Food, with £2,000,000. These two placed their advertising direct, but in the case of other departments it was cordinated by the Ministry of Information . . . . The public were told about ration books, gas-masks, identity cards and air-raid shelters. They were asked to walk more, save more, spend less, and say nothing . . . . Salvage was to be conserved, fornication avoided.

Until the Paper Control Order no. 48, of March 1942, there was no restriction on the amount of advertising carried by newspapers. However, from that date, limits were imposed which declared that the maximum advertising space in morning or Sunday newspapers should not exceed 40 per cent and 45 per cent in evenings. One result was that newspapers could now charge more for their advertisements, evidenced by Bill Needham, advertisement director of the *Daily Express*, being able to ask more than £10 a single column inch compared with £6 10*s*. in 1939. His colleague, editor Arthur Christiansen, was to comment on the small-size papers:

> Immediately war broke out the *Daily Express* had been reduced from twenty-four pages to twelve; then to eight, then six, until, when the blitz on London began, we were working on only four. It was then that we really learned what compression meant: thirty items to a page was the rule and if we fell below that number there was an inquest.

With no new products being launched, it was a case of well-known firms keeping their brand-names in the public eye – and newspapers were the main medium 'gaining in prestige through their relative scarcity and their association with important news'. The fact that there was a desperate shortage of newspapers meant that readers were now being asked to share copies.

Newspaper advertising in the war years was to follow a predictable pattern, and as E.S. Turner was to write:

> Boot-polish firms brought out the comic sergeant major to commend their wares; girls balanced military hats, not always at military angles, on their shampooed locks. Soon the cry was go easy with –, please use – sparingly. . . . [but] by the war's end some of the public had grown exasperated at the constant reminder of goods which were not in the shops.[7]

Reuters' Shares are Purchased

While the shortage of newsprint had presented a major problem to the industry, early in 1941 the Newspaper Proprietors Association had been faced with another complication – whether or not to take a major shareholding in Reuters. Sixteen years earlier they had turned down an offer to purchase fifty per cent of the shareholding. Now the offer was to be renewed.

For much of the time, following the suicide of Herbert Reuter in 1915, the company had been under the control of one man: Roderick Jones, the Agency's former manager in South Africa, who became the first non-family head. To escape a hostile take-over the company returned to private ownership the following year, with Jones and Mark Napier, the chairman, forming a group to buy the entire shareholding; and Reuters Telegram Company became Reuters Limited. Subsequent to the death of Napier in 1919, Jones was appointed the principal proprietor and chief executive.

For Reuters, the First World War was to pose great difficulties: the business from private telegrams was no longer profitable; the cost of reporting the conflict was high; and the company was accused of being under the influence of the British government. Since Jones was also head of the Department of Propaganda at the Ministry of Information, for which he was later knighted, this was a charge difficult to deny.[8] In fact, Reuters and the British government had reached an agreement under which the agency transmitted a service of Allied communiques and official news. This was financed by the authorities but kept separate from Reuters' own services which aimed to provide balanced reporting of the conflict, including coverage of German war communiques.

As head of Reuters between the two World Wars, Jones ran the business as an autocracy; and although the company needed government subscriptions he believed that 'Reuters could work *with* the British government, so long as it was seen not to be working *for* it; he was careful not to ask for subsidies'. In May 1925 Jones, as chief shareholder, offered a majority interest in the Agency to Britain's newspapers: half to the Press Association (PA) representing the provincial papers and half to the Newspaper Proprietors Association. Three years earlier, he had received tacit approval from Lord Burnham, chairman of the NPA, and Lord Riddell, vice-chairman; and on 31 March 1922, four months before his death, even Northcliffe had given his blessing:[9]

> Go ahead with your plans. I am with you. I'll go in with you. I don't want to make money out of the thing. I have made all the money I want. But I believe in Reuters and I believe in you; and I will do anything to assist you in carrying out these ideas of yours. Make it a broad scheme. Fit in all the papers you can and all *shades* of opinion.

On 27 October 1925 the NPA and the Press Association, under the chairmanship of Lord Riddell, held a joint meeting to which Jones was invited. There he was told that 'the ostensible criticism was financial'. Five days later, on 2 November, Lord Riddell advised Jones that his revised 'offer would not win the acceptance of the NPA who were almost heatedly hostile to the equality in the ownership of Reuters as between the London newspapers on the one hand and the remaining newspapers of the United Kingdom on the other, so long as I refused, as I did, to modify the insistence upon equality'.

Within an hour of leaving the meeting he was to receive a phone call asking whether he would meet the Press Association committee at once, and there was told that the Association wished to accept his proposal including taking up the shares offered to the NPA. On 31 December 1925, therefore, Jones sold 55 per cent of his Reuters shares to the Press Association – and for that received £160,00 with a ten-year contract at a salary of £300 per year as chairman, £4200 as managing director, plus £2000 representation allowance and ten per cent commission on profits over £13,000.[10] Five years later the Press Association purchased the remainder of Jones's shares and became the sole owner.

In the autumn of 1937, with war impending, Sir Roderick Jones approached Neville Chamberlain, the Prime Minister, in secret for financial assistance to transmit the Reuters news service. Three months later, in January 1938, the Foreign Office noted: 'Sir Roderick has throughout been most anxious that this grant-in-aid should not be represented publicly as implying any government interference in Reuters.' Now, one year after his meeting with Chamberlain, he was delighted when the initial government subsidy of Reuters transmission from Rugby and Leafield began on 22 September 1938 – the day Hitler invaded the Sudetenland; 'and in the year 1939 to

1940 the Ministry of Information calculated that the company had received £64,000 for "propaganda purposes" from the Treasury'.

On 12 September 1939, at a Reuters board meeting, new director William Haley, of the *Manchester Evening News*, asked Jones if there had been any influence by the Foreign Office. Jones vehemently denied that there had been. But less than eighteen months later, on Tuesday 4 February 1941, feeling that Jones had compromised Reuters in his dealing with the British government, the PA directors forced his resignation. Haley was to write that if Sir Roderick had not stood down he would have proposed:[11]

> That his fellow Directors, having heard Sir Roderick Jones's explanation of the circumstances in which when on September 12, 1939, he sought and obtained the authority of the Board to enter into the contract of 1939 with His Majesty's Government he failed to disclose to the Board that it was Lord Perth's proposal that the arrangements set out in Paragraph A of Lord Perth's letter of August 24, 1939, should be an integral part of the arrangements, are of the opinion that this information was material to the Board's proper appreciation of the implication of the Agreement, and therefore that they can have no future confidence in him as a colleague or a representative and Resolve that he be called upon to resign his offices as Chairman and Managing Director forthwith.

Following his sudden departure, on 12 February at an NPA Council meeting 'the resignation of Sir Roderick Jones from the Chairman and Managing Directorship of Reuters was discussed, and it was agreed that endeavours be made to ascertain the reasons for the changes'.[12] Within days, Sir Roderick had approached members, saying that 'the London newspapers must intervene at once and arrest the processes that were threatening to encompass Reuters; in other words they must have a share not inferior to that of the Provincial newspapers'. His memo concluded: 'While this would entail the splitting up of the Reuter shareholding between the Provincial newspapers (Press Association) and the London newspapers (Newspaper Proprietors Association) it would not be detrimental to the Provincials.'

Armed with a memorandum from Jones, on 8 April Lord Rothermere, on behalf of the NPA, made a formal presentation to the Press Association. There was, however, to be a three-and-a-half hour interruption: 'a 1250-kilogram landmine was caught suspended in the trolley-bus wires outside the front door of Reuters and the Press Association at 85, Fleet Street'.[13] Fortunately, following evacuation of the building, the bomb was rendered harmless. Rothermere in his presentation stressed that with the ever-increasing encroachment of the American news agencies there was a need for independence and increased efficiency; and ended with a motion that the PA should sell 50 per cent of its shares to the NPA. But before making the proposal, Rothermere explained what could happen he were to receive a negative reply:[14]

> If common agreement cannot be found we would have to ask Reuters to disclose to us what steps are being taken to organise the collection of news in the present German-controlled countries and elsewhere. Agencies that are now mere puppets of their governments must be suspect for many years and we should have to know the sources of foreign news so that we could determine whether we should remain as subscribers or

organise our own news collecting and distributing agency, or make other arrangements. We doubt if the provincial newspapers have the experience necessary to satisfy us who have our own representatives in all parts of the world.

Following the presentation, the Press Association decided to open discussions, and throughout the summer regular meetings were to be held, until it was agreed that the Fleet Street newspapers should purchase 50 per cent of Reuters at £4 10*s*. a share – the price paid by PA in 1930 to Sir Roderick Jones for the stock which they did not already own, a total of just under £170,000. On the instructions of Beaverbrook, though, the *Daily Express* decided not to buy shares, but would still continue to use and pay for the Reuters News Service. (It was not until the closure of the *News Chronicle* in 1960 – discussed in chapter 17, p. 331–335 – that the *Daily Express* took a shareholding.)

From the Press Association directors there had been a mixed response, and on 8 September the motion was passed by just five votes to two, with the Consultative Committee agreeing by the narrower majority of seven to five. One fierce opponent of the proposed sale was Samuel Storey, MP, of Portsmouth and Sunderland Newspapers, the recently-appointed chairman of Reuters. The following month, on 17 October, 66 members of the Press Association 'filed into the [Reuters] conference room overlooking the burned-out shell of St Bride's Church for what was to be a tense meeting'. And there, following a full day's debate, R.A. Gibbs, of the Luton *Evening Telegraph*, one of Storey's supporters, proposed that the sale should be to individual Fleet Street proprietors, thus leaving the Press Association in control. This was rejected by 43 votes to 17. James Henderson, of the *Belfast News-Letter*, then called for a poll which resulted in defeat by 5204 votes to 2272. To quote Donald Read in *The Power of News The History of Reuters*: 'The Storey party always maintained that this majority had been obtained only thanks to votes representing the provincial editions of London newspapers, and of provincial titles within the London newspaper groups.'

Storey, though, was not finished, and on 22 October, five days after the PA meeting, he sponsored a debate on Reuters in the House of Commons as 'a matter of extreme public importance and urgency', and was to accuse the NPA of 'tactics ranging from "plain unfriendly" to "domineering" and "contemptuous" of the Press Association itself'. Alarmed at the thought that the NPA would control the Reuters partnership, he said: 'The trustees will not even hold shares in Reuters Limited or the income arising from the shares. They will appoint the directors but they can only appoint those persons who have been nominated to them by the shareholders.'

Brendan Bracken, the newly-installed Minister of Information, and an experienced newspaperman as chairman of the *Financial News*, believed that someone should have spoken up for 'the bold, bad barons of Fleet Street'. He considered that there was no reason to expect the NPA to behave dishonourably, maintaining that 'the future of Reuters was the concern of the Press not of the Government. It was for the Press, through Reuters, to put its house in order.' He added:[14]

It is extremely unfair to the Newspaper Proprietors Association to regard them as a lot of greedy bandits who are anxious to doctor the news for the benefit of their readers. They are no such thing. And, if they were, why did not the Press Association, who have sold these shares to these supposed scoundrels of Fleet Street, take that into account before this great protest?

Less than a week later, on October 28, 1941 at a Reuters board meeting, Storey was formally removed as chairman; and the following day it was announced that the Press Association and the Newspaper Proprietors Association were now equal partners of Reuters, the NPA having paid £168,768 for 37,504 shares.

The Editors Depart

In December 1940 Fleet Street's youngest editor, Hugh Cudlipp, of the *Sunday Pictorial*, boarded a train at King's Cross bound for Richmond, Yorkshire, to join the Royal Corps of Signals at snow-bound Catterick Camp. In his pocket he carried a letter from the paper's military correspondent, Major-General J.F.C. Fuller: 'You will find the Army a strange change after an editor's office; but I am convinced that you did the right thing in joining up. This war, won, lost or drawn, is the greatest experience of your generation.'

In 1942 Cudlipp was posted to Sandhurst for officer training, and passing out as an infantry subaltern joined the 5th battalion Royal Sussex Regiment. Weeks later he was bound on a troopship for Suez, and during the two-month voyage, with the aid of half-a-dozen soldier/compositors, turned out a daily newspaper:[15]

> The creaky menu machine had never produced anything more meaningful than the menus, but by the time we reached Freetown, our first brief stop, *Ocean News* was a two-page daily. Before we reached our second stop at Cape Town we were supplying our captive customers with a four-page special on Sunday in colour. I had discovered a mass of old travel brochures. The comps and I cut out the coloured pictures of beautiful cruising girls with a razor blade and stuck them with paste (flour and water from the Army cooks) into the white spaces we arranged in *Ocean News*.

Disembarking at Suez on 1 July 1942, within days Cudlipp was serving as a platoon commander during the defence of the El Alamein line. Six months later, in January 1943 on a visit to a summit conference at Casablanca with President Roosevelt, Winston Churchill, noticing the American *Stars and Stripes*, realized that there was no British equivalent; and through Harold Macmillan, Minister of State in Algiers, decided that there should be a forces newspaper. The only choice as editor was Hugh Cudlipp, who was given complete freedom in his selection of staff, contents and policy – with direct access to senior officers. In his autobiography, *Walking on the Water*, he was to write:[16]

> I undertook to deliver a report at 10.00 hours at AFHQ the next morning, and sat up all night typing it on faded, war-bedraggled mauve notepaper in a small bedroom in a hotel in the company of some indigestible salami sandwiches, a bottle of tepid *vin rose*, and some black dried-out cigars I had picked up in Marrakesh. They burnt with a crackle and exuded the stench of saltpetre.

Having managed to secure volunteer journalists, Linotype operators and compositors from nearby Army units – and, with the help of Sergeant Reg Thackeray, a French-speaking former sub-editor on the *Manchester Guardian* foreign desk, diverting a load of newsprint to the paper – the first issue of *Union Jack* was printed on 21 March 1943, on the presses of the *Dépêche de Constantine*. Initially published three times a week, it soon became the 'Daily Newspaper for the British Services'.

A week after the launch, Cudlipp flew to London 'to lift any material from the British newspapers free of charge and to lay on news and picture services'. And it was during his visit that he was asked to broadcast on the 'triumphant desert campaigns of the Eighth Army':

> The last time I saw the valiant Eighth Army was at the approaches to the Mareth Line. Then I was ordered to fly to the other side of Africa to launch a newspaper for the British fighting forces. 'Union Jack' we called it, for we were feeling mighty proud. The first story we had to print was EIGHTH ARMY STRIKES AGAIN. And that made us feel prouder still.

The next morning, there was a phone call from Beaverbrook: 'Do you know who this is? The Prime Minister and I listened to your Eighth Army broadcast last night and Winston thought it was great stuff. Good-bye to you.'

Following on the *Daily Mirror* style, Cudlipp ensured that the *Union Jack* was bold and punchy, and among former colleagues who were to assist him were sports writer Peter Wilson and columnist William Connor (Cassandra). To quote him again:

> *Union Jack*'s second and third productions appeared in Algiers and Tunis in September, and the peak was reached in the first half of 1945 with five separate editions, plus *Eighth Army News* which came under my wing in April 1944, plus a twelve-page weekly magazine titled *Crusader*. In addition, improvised Battle Editions were published for short periods during swift advances by the Army.

As a lieutenant-colonel, he was demobilized in 1946, having been awarded the OBE in the preceding year.

Owen in Control

While Hugh Cudlipp was bound for Egypt, in the summer of 1942 Frank Owen resigned his editorship of the *Evening Standard* to join the Royal Armoured Corps as a trooper – and was to end the war editing the Forces newspaper, *SEAC*, the 'All Services Daily Newspaper of S.E. Asia Command'.

In May 1943 Admiral Louis Mountbatten, worried at the morale of the troops under his command – and aware of the success of the recently-launched *Union Jack* in North Africa – was keen to start a similar paper and asked Brigadier Mike Wardell, a senior member of his staff: 'Where do I find an editor?' Wardell replied: 'The man you need is Frank Owen.' Having been Owen's managing director at the *Evening Standard*, he was well aware of his merits. Years later, in the final issue of *SEAC*, dated Wednesday 15 May 1946, Mountbatten was to write:[17]

> I knew that if we were to fight a campaign of indefinite duration, thousands of miles away, we should all need to feel that we were still in touch, not only with what was

> happening in the world at large but also with what was going on at home. We are used to reading different newspapers and we have very varied tastes and opinions so it was obvious that the paper would have to carry light articles and serious articles, frivolous cartoons and general knowledge tests and sports news. Most important of all it would have to be edited as fairly and impartially as possible and it would have to be our own paper in which we could air our views. All this would have been comparatively easy with an unlimited paper supply, but as we should certainly be limited to four pages this attainment of all these objects presented a problem. I decided that the man to solve our problem was Frank Owen. When I managed to trace him, he had just blossomed from a trooper RAC to a fully-fledged cadet and was with difficulty persuaded to abandon his ambition to be a second lieutenant in a tank. I told Frank Owen what I needed. I authorised the Editorial Staff to express their own opinions in the 'Good Morning' column, or in reply to correspondents, but on no account to inject them into other parts of the paper.

It was to be more than six months, though, before agreement was reached allowing the newly-commissioned second lieutenant Frank Owen to leave for the Far East; and on 10 January 1944, under his editorship, *SEAC* was launched from Calcutta. On his way out to India, Owen's ship, the battleship *Renown*, had called at Gibraltar, where he met Hugh Cudlipp's brother, Reg, who was later to say: 'Frank took a lot of interest in my publications. He must have been impressed and asked if I could join him on *SEAC* . . . . and within three months I was on my way to Calcutta.'

From the first issue, *SEAC* was a success, leading Air Chief Marshal Sir Philip Joubert, Mountbatten's deputy chief of staff for information, to write:[18] 'It is hard to say what the troops appreciated most: Owen's pungent leading articles that frequently got him – and me – into trouble with the War Office, the sports news or the Jane cartoon.' Printed on the presses of *The Statesman*, the four-page tabloid soon reached a circulation of more than 30,000 copies which were airlifted to 14th Army headquarters in Burma before being distributed to the troops in the front line – and, on many occasions, to the Chindits operating deep behind Japanese positions.

On 2 September 1945 Japan formally surrendered on the battleship *Missouri* in Tokyo Harbour, and within days *SEAC* was being produced in Singapore. In the vanguard was Peter Eastwood, later managing editor of *The Daily Telegraph*. His initial role with *SEAC* was that of chief sub-editor, 'but never one to neglect small levers of driving power, he became the paper's driving force, and eventually succeeded as editor'. His first move on landing was to commandeer a Hudson Tourer and proceed to the offices of the *Straits Times*, which had just put to bed a Japanese paper, to produce the first Singapore edition of *SEAC*. Within weeks, Eastwood had been demobbed personally by Mountbatten to launch the *Singapore Free Press*, an afternoon paper, and was to remain in charge for several months until returning to England.

Meanwhile, back in Calcutta, Owen realized that India was now less important as the *SEAC* base and quickly left to set up his headquarters at Raffles Hotel, Singapore, while publishing from 127 Cecil Street – and it was from there that the final edition was printed on 15 May 1946 – the last of 852 issues. Owen himself was already demobilized as a lieutenant-colonel, OBE, and was to join the *Daily Mail* as a columnist in June 1946.

Field-Marshal Sir William Slim, commander of the 14th Army in Burma, was later to write in his *Defeat into Victory*:[19]

> An innovation was to be the publication of a theatre newspaper, *SEAC*. One day I was told that its editor designate was touring the Army area and had asked if I would see him. A hefty-looking second-lieutenant was ushered into my office and introduced as Frank Owen. I had strong views on Service Newspapers, and sat the young man down for ten minutes while I explained to him exactly how his paper should be run and what were an editor's duties. He listened very politely, and said he would do his best, saluted and left. It was only after he had gone that I learned he had been one of the youngest and most brilliant editors in Fleet Street and had characteristically thrown up his job to enlist at the beginning of the war. *SEAC* under his direction – and Admiral Mountbatten wisely gave him complete editorial freedom – was the best wartime service journal I have ever seen. It – and Owen himself – made no mean contribution to our morale.

Foot Takes Charge

His successor as editor of the *Standard* was the paper's leader writer, 28-year-old Michael Foot, a sufferer from asthma and therefore not fit for military service, who has left a most interesting account of his war-time editorship:[20]

> For two years since the departure of Frank Owen for the forces, I had the enthralling job of editing the paper which he above all others had created, the war-time *Evening Standard*, the *Standard* in its very greatest days I naturally contend, although it has had some other great ones since. The war, as one of its minor by-products, raised the quality of British journalism as a whole and especially London journalism in a manner which has never been properly and collectively acclaimed. For one thing, the profit test, advertising pressures, were overnight tossed out of Fleet-street's bomb-threatened windows, and there prevailed instead a genuine competition of merit to use the precious supplies of newsprint to serve the common interest of the hour.

Beaverbrook, from the beginning, had realized the potential of the young Foot and was determined to aid his career: 'You and I are the last two Radicals.' He was not, though, prepared to share his services with any other title. Being short-staffed, Kingsley Martin had asked if Foot might be allowed to write the occasional article for the *New Statesman*. On 18 November 1942 Beaverbrook replied:

> If the newspaper opened the door, it would swing very wide. The newspaper pays Foot nearly £4000 a year. If he were to do similar work for another paper, the directors would ask 'Is Beaverbrook losing his punch?' Is he going down the valley where all the newspaper men before him have gone? And they might be right.

Encouraged by the huge success of his *Guilty Men* some two years earlier, Foot now wrote a sequel, *The Trial of Mussolini* by 'Cassius'.[21] This time, however, he could not rely on the support of Owen and Howard, and his authorship was not to remain secret for long. Beaverbrook was not amused and told Foot that he could be either an editor or a pamphleteer but not both at the same time. Foot had also been in trouble with his proprietor in securing a scoop with the publication of the Beveridge Report, much to the dismay of Churchill and his Cabinet.

A clash was inevitable: Foot resigned as editor, though for a number of months he continued to write editorials until in June 1944 he decided that even this was too much, informing Beaverbrook:

> Your views and mine are bound to be more irreconcilable. As far as this Socialist business is concerned my views are unshakeable. For me it is the Klondyke or bust, and at the moment I am doubtful whether I am going the right way to Klondyke. There does not seem to be much sense in my continuing to write leaders for a newspaper group whose opinions I do not share and some of whose opinions I strongly dissent from. I know you never ask me to write views with which I disagree. But as this works out it is good business neither for you nor for me . . . . Your kindness to me has given me great advantages in this world. I do not forget them. But I am sure it is right for me to make a change and I dearly hope you will understand my reasons.

Censorship and Information

On 14 October 1935 the Committee of Imperial Defence agreed that a sub-committee should make preparations for the establishment of a Ministry of Information in war time. Bearing in mind the 'virtually unanimous hostility of Lord Beaverbook's Ministry of Information in 1918',[22] it was felt that any new department should not be just a propaganda vehicle, but should project the British viewpoint overseas.

Less than three years later, on 29 June 1938[23], following the unification in the spring of Germany and Austria – and with war looming – Esmond Harmsworth, Chairman of the NPA, could tell his Council that he had seen the Air Minister who had asked for the support of London newspapers for the air expansion scheme. And a fortnight later, he could report that an invitation had been received by the NPA to act on an Emergency Committee.

There was now to be a continuous dialogue between the Government and Fleet Street, and on 14 September it was learned that Sir John Anderson, Home Secretary, had met NPA representatives and proposed a draft secrecy guidance on the Government's policy. 'The vice-chairman reported that he had been approached by the authorities on certain subjects, particularly censorship, but was unable to divulge any information at present.'

A fortnight later, on 28 September, under the heading 'News production in the event of war', the NPA Council agreed that unless the crisis had passed, a special session should be held on Friday afternoon. Fortunately for Fleet Street and the nation, Chamberlain's meeting with Hitler at Munich the following day was a 'success'. But in reality, it was just a respite . . . .

There were to be further discussions between the Government and the NPA during the next six months, culminating in a gathering on 9 March 1939, when Chamberlain called representatives of all Fleet Street newspapers to a private conference at 10 Downing Street, and told them that the international situation had much improved. Within less than a week, though, Chamberlain's hopes were in shatters: on 15 March, as noted, German troops entered Prague – and Czechoslovakia had ceased to exist as an independent nation – an event (detailed in MI5 secret files released on 1 March 2005) – that was to bring from Rothermere 'a very indiscreet letter to the Führer congratulating him on his walk into Prague'.[24]

Even though Chamberlain had recently met with proprietors and editors, he and his Government had long been making preparations. For example: 4 January 1939 – letter from Sir John Anderson re details of National Service; Home Office commmunication re newspaper production in war time; 25 January – Further meetings and letter to Sir Samuel Hoare, Lord Privy Seal; P&KTF protection of staff in air raids; 15 March – Chairman reported that he had met Prime Minister, 'who had promised to consider representations submitted'. Reported that newsprint stock had been submitted for inclusion in the Board of Trade scheme for insurance of stocks of essential commodities.

There was to be anger, though, at an NPA Council meeting on 8 May when the Chairman referred to a letter sent to members by the editor of the *World's Press News* asking for details of emergency publication arrangements. 'Agreed that no information be given and that speculation on this score by the publication was to be deprecated.'

As the news from Germany worsened, so communication between the authorities and the NPA increased, all discussed at the fortnightly Council meetings. For instance, on 20 June, it was agreed to appoint the Chairman and Vice-Chairman to the revived Admiralty, War Office, Air Ministry and Press Committee. Less than a month later, members were informed of negotiations with the Ministry of Information and that 'Oliver Stanley [President, Board of Trade] had intimated the probablity of newspaper raw material stocks being included in the government war insurance'.

On 28 July the Chairman reported on correspondence between himself and the Ministry of Information regarding proposed broadcasts of news at frequent intervals throughout the day in the event of an emergency. It was agreed 'that the government had the right to broadcast official communications at all times'. It was also agreeed that the Chairman should accept an appointment at the Ministry of Information in the event of an emergency. A little over a month later, on Friday 1 September, Germany invaded Poland; and that same day a Special Council Meeting of the NPA was held to discuss 'Emergency Matters'.

Meanwhile, Prime Minister Chamberlain had appointed Lord Macmillan to take charge of the Ministry of Information, a person who was not a government minister and was without any knowledge of the Press. The result was chaos; and 'after only five days of war the National Executive of the National Union of Journalists passed a resolution expressing grave concern at the failure of the Ministry of Information to provide the public with adequate news of the war'. Macmillan, though, survived until 4 January 1940, when he was replaced by Lord Reith, the first Director General of the BBC from 1927 to 1938. He, too, was not a great success – and one of Churchill's initial moves when becoming Prime Minister was to replace him with Duff Cooper.

Bracken in Control

For some, the role of Minister of Information was to be much desired; and on 25 March 1939 Brendan Bracken had written to Beaverbrook concerning the position:[25]

> If war comes and the organization described by [Sir Samuel] Hoare [Home Secretary] starts up any newspaper man would covet the job you outlined. As I am what is called an able-bodied man my duty in times of war must be to go off with the soldiers. No one knows better than I how incompetent a warrior I shall be. But there will be lots of prentice recruits. I am most grateful for the suggestion you made. It will be the best of jobs for somebody.

Notwithstanding the criticism levelled against him in the First World War, some six months later, on 30 October 1939, Beaverbrook himself, in a letter to the Home Secretary, turned down the job, saying: 'I really do not want to be Minister of Information. The Ministry has now been stripped of its function and appears to me to be nothing more than a minor department, and a discredited one at that. I would have been the best man for the job at the outset. I have the experience in journalism and propaganda.'

With Beaverbrook having refused – and, as noted, Lords Macmillan and Reith not proving satisfactory – the decision was taken in the summer of 1940 to appoint Duff Cooper, a former First Lord of the Admiralty, who had resigned over Munich. His tenure, like his predecessors was to be brief, a few short months; and in the summer of 1941 he was appointed Resident Cabinet Minister, Singapore, fortunately being recalled to London, as chairman, Cabinet Committee on Security, just prior to the Japanese occupation. Bracken had taken office on 20 July 1941; and as someone who had been in magazines and newspapers for almost twenty years he was well qualified for the position.

Born in Tipperary, he had been sent by his widowed mother to a sheep station in New South Wales, returning to Ireland in 1919. He then left for England, where he became a prep school teacher.[26] In 1922 he met J.L. Garvin, who awakened his abiding interest in journalism, and the following year was introduced to Winston Churchill. This was the start of a devoted friendship on Bracken's part, even though Mrs Churchill was to deplore the influence of the 'three Bs' on her husband – Birkenhead, Beaverbrook and Bracken.

That same year, Bracken was invited by Major J.S. Crosthwaite-Eyre to take over the editorship of the monthly *Illustrated Review*, soon to be renamed *English Life*. For the next three years, Bracken ran the magazine at a loss until it was sold in 1926, when he launched the *Banker*. Elected to the board of Eyre & Spottiswoode in 1928, he purchased on their behalf the ailing *Financial News*. A young man in a hurry, Bracken was described by Oscar Hobson, City editor of the *Manchester Guardian*, as someone on the make, using all his talents and charm to rise up the ladder as quickly as possible.

Following the purchase of the *Financial News*, Bracken went on a spending spree, acquiring the *Investors' Chronicle*, the *Practitioner*, *Liverpool Journal of Commerce* and a half-share in the *Economist*. In 1929, when Churchill was Chancellor of the Exchequer, Bracken was elected Conservative MP for North Paddington; and, apart from his business affairs at the *Financial News*, Bracken, a bachelor, led a very busy social life, for which he was later to be caricatured as Rex Mottram in Evelyn Waugh's *Brideshead Revisited*.

With the advent of war in 1939, Bracken became Churchill's parliamentary private secretary at the Admiralty, remaining with him when he became Prime Minister in May 1940. A privy councillor, as Minister of Information, and with his wide publishing background he quickly won the respect of Fleet Street and the BBC as he defended their freedom. Now, in July 1941 his old friend Beaverbrook wrote to him:

> In the ordinary way, it would be looked on as sarcastic or even an unfriendly act to offer a man congratulations on becoming Minister of Information. In your case this is not so. You are going to make a great success in this office. Your gifts of imagination and energy will be given a scope they have never enjoyed before. And the glory you win will be all the brighter because it shines in a dark and dismal sky.

He was quick to reply, writing by return from the Ministry of Information:

> Your letter was a great encouragement to me. I have no illusions about this job. And I would not have taken it without your backing. You know all that need be known how to run this Ministry. And I shall be wanting your help, you will curse the day that your pressed me to come here! For you are already overworked, and have little time for the affairs of other Departments.

And to his old friend, J.L. Garvin, thanking him for his congratulations, Bracken could reply: 'This is one of the toughest jobs which has ever fallen to the lot of man! And I think that in a short time I shall be joining the happy band of ex-Ministers of Information.'

From the first day, his appoinment had been welcomed by Fleet Street, Beaverbrook telling Frank Owen, then editor of the *Evening Standard*, that the new Minister should be given every assistance and he was to provide the co-operation that had been withheld from Duff Cooper. Bracken, however, preferred as a rule to work through proprietors rather than editors. (His participation in the Commons debate on Reuters, discussed earlier, is a good example.)

For Duff Cooper, the newly-deposed minister, there was to be the appointment as Chancellor of the Duchy of Lancaster and the Prime Minister's representative in Singapore, but for his deputy at the Ministry of Information, Harold Nicolson, the former *Evening Standard* diary editor, there was to be just a position as one of the BBC's governors. 'He was deeply shocked and saddened. He was wounded by the curtness of the Prime Minister's letter. He felt that he had been sacked . . . .'[27]

Bracken's new department had been planned in 1936 and was 'brought into being two days before the war, and grew in four weeks from a staff of twelve to a notorious 999'. As Philip Knightley was to write in *The First Casualty*:[28]

> In Britain there was an outcry. The Ministry of Information with its staff of 999, was the target for most of the criticism, especially when statements in the Commons revealed that

> only forty-three of the staff had been journalists. The previous employment of other information experts ranged from a professorship of music to a professorship of world Christian relations. The newspapers were vitriolic. The *Daily Express* said that soon Britain would need leaflet raids on itself to tell its own people how the war was going on.

Strangely enough, another name had been mentioned as a contender for the post: Arthur Christiansen. Support had come from A.J. Cummings, political editor of the *News Chronicle*, and Bob Cruikshank, editor of *The Star*, who wrote that whenever people were dismissed at the Ministry of Information, 'some expert on Egyptian Hieroglyphics is appointed to take charge of British publicity in the Straits Settlement; the late Vice-Consul at Timbuctoo, for whom a job must be found, because he is Lady Bracknell's nephew, is appointed Director-General of Relations to the Collar and Tie Trade Papers'.

In putting forward the case for Christiansen, they appealed to Churchill: 'You who are so great a journalist . . . . would understand better than anyone else, if only our words could reach you, that *journalism* demands above all things, *journalists*, and news requires *newspapermen*.' Christiansen was flattered at the comments, but realized that there would have been no way that Beaverbrook would have allowed his release from the *Daily Express*; and besides: 'I was a journalist, and the politicians would have devoured me.'

Ministry's Early Days

Based at Senate House, London University, the Ministry of Information – 'Minny' to journalists – had in its earliest days been wracked with indecision. For instance, on 12 September 1939, following the announcement on Paris Radio that the British Expeditionary Force had landed in France, the War Office censor, at 9 p.m. acknowledged the fact and gave the go-ahead for the nationals to print the news. But as Richard Collier was to write:[29]

> Then at 11.30 p.m., when the main editions of Fleet Street papers were already in trains en route to Scotland and the provinces, the War Office abruptly backtracked. The landing of the BEF was still top secret. Newspaper trains already under way must be halted. Posses of police hastened to Paddington, Euston and King's Cross stations to haul bales of later editions from railway vans. Long after midnight, phones all over London rang urgently as editors and proprietors, roused from their beds, lobbied their favourite Cabinet Ministers. At last, at 2.30 a.m. on 13 September, the War Office accepted defeat. The landing – and existence – of the BEF was now official.

For the correspondents with the British forces in France, censorship was so strict that despatches, which had to be passed by four different authorities, could take up to two days to reach Fleet Street – and in every instance reporters had to be accompanied by a conducting officer.

Following these early incidents, censorship throughout the war was voluntary, and the appointment of Rear-Admiral George Thomson, a retired submariner, as Chief Censor, was to bring about a more open policy: 'the more truth was told, the higher stood morale'. However, any infringement of the D-Notices sent daily to editors could lead to either 'imprisonment or suppression of the newspaper itself'. Christiansen believed that he must have received some five thousand D-Notices before the end of the war in Europe; and was to note: 'I read them on the day they arrived, had them copied for departmental heads, stuffed them into a locked drawer and [in August 1945] made a bonfire of the lot.'

On 6 June 1944 the Allied invasion of Europe had at last begun. 'An immense armada of more than 4,000 ships, with several thousand smaller craft has crossed the Channel,' said the Prime Minister. Within days, Hitler had launched his secret weapon, the VI flying bomb (doodlebug), the first landing on British soil at Swanscombe, near Gravesend. Herbert Morrison, the Home Secretary, arranged with the Ministry of Information that the Press should publish no information about the attack, the War Cabinet concurring that no statement should be made until the enemy had made it public, or until the extent of the attack made a statement necessary.

Beaverbrook, who had long been aware of the threat, was to declare: 'Duncan Sandys strongly supported the view that Peenemunde was building V1s and V2s [rockets]. Cherwell opposed the notion that rockets would fall in Britain.' Before the launching-sites were finally overrun, during the ten-week campaign several thousand rockets had landed in southern England, killing six thousand civilians.

By the autumn of 1944 Bracken considered that the Ministry could begin to wind down, and as Charles Edward Lysaght was to write: 'As victory drew nearer the press was less willing to accept voluntary restrictions on its freedom. With their teams of war correspondents and the aid of military communiques they did not feel the need for the Ministry's news distribution services.' In May 1945, following the end of the war in Europe, Bracken resigned.[30]

16

Press Council proposed

ON 19 APRIL 1946, the annual delegate meeting of the National Union of Journalists at Liverpool passed a resolution from R.A. Smith (Manchester) urging the Government to appoint a Royal Commission on the Press of Great Britain. He was seconded by Preston Benson, of the Central London Branch, who said: 'In the last fifty years there has been widespread exploitation of the right to print. This long development of commercial newspapers, with millions of circulation, has reduced news to the quality of entertainment, and the gathering, reporting, discussing and commenting on news has lost its social interest.'[1] There were to be five areas which the union wished a commission to investigate:

> 1. Ownership, control and financing of national and provincial newspapers, newsagencies and periodicals; 2. Extent to which the growth of powerful chains of newspapers was creating a monopoly of ownership; 3. Ability of independent national and local newspapers and periodicals to withstand increased competition from syndicate companies; 4. Influence of financial and advertising interests on the presentation and suppression of news; 5. Dispersion and suppression of essential facts in home and foreign news.

Ten days later, Prime Minister Clement Attlee (Labour), who had defeated the Churchill-led Conservatives in the previous summer's general election, was asked if he had examined the resolution. His reply was brief and to the point: 'I have given my careful consideration to this proposal, which, however, I do not see my way to adopt.'

There was to be a pause, until on 10 July Churchill tabled a motion in the House calling for an enquiry before the BBC charter was renewed. This was the opportunity for Labour MPs, with journalistic backgrounds, to put down an amendment 'that steps should also be taken to investigate the ownership and control of the Press'. Within twenty-four hours Michael Foot and Haydn Davies, with the backing of more than a hundred Labour MPs, had tabled a further motion.

Less than a fortnight later, on 22 July, Herbert Morrison, Home Secretary, who was to delare that 'neither he nor His Majesty's Government would be a party to any interference with the liberty of the Press', received a deputation from the NUJ and assured them that he would report their concerns to the Prime Minister. There was to be no further movement until on 29 October Haydn Davies, seconded by Michael Foot, moved the following resolution:[2]

That, having regard to the increasing public concern at the growth of monopolistic tendencies in the control of the Press and with the object of furthering the free expression of opinion through the Press and the greatest practicable accuracy in the presentation of news, this House considers that a Royal Commission should be appointed to inquire into the finance, control, management and ownership of the Press.

Davies added:

We have watched the destruction of great newspapers. We have watched the combines buying up and killing independent journals and we have seen the honourable profession of journalism degraded by high finance and big business. The only freedom today is the freedom of the newspaper proprietors. They have the perfect closed shop with the highest entrance fee in industry.

In support, Michael Foot declared that as a journalist he thought there had been a 'serious decline in the quality of British journalism in the past 40 years'. This decline he attributed to the dwindling of the power of editors and to the encroachment of proprietors. 'Today very few of the editors' names are known to the public and many of them are little more than cyphers.'

Opposing the motion, Sir David Maxwell Fyfe (Conservative) said that 'the British Press shone forth as an example of freedom and independence' and he would remind them of the journalists' song:

The Pope can launch his interdict,
The union its decree,
But the bubble is blown and the bubble is pricked
By us, and such as we

He added that the motion had made four suggestions: (1) There is a growth in monopolistic tendencies in the control of the Press; (2) There is increasing public concern at this; (3) Free expression of opinion through the Press is limited; (4) That the accuracy of news is open to challenge. 'The House had heard no word in the speeches about the strength of these imputations . . . .'[3]

Nevertheless, following a debate of nearly seven hours and a free vote – in which NUJ members Tom Driberg, Douglas Jay, J.P.W. Mallalieu, Patrick Gordon Walker and Maurice Webb played prominent parts – the motion was carried by 270 votes to 157; and on 26 March 1947, the Prime Minister announced the names of the sixteen members of the Commission, while also stating the terms of reference:

With the object of furthering the free expression of opinion through the Press and the greatest practicable accuracy in the presentation of news, to inquire into the control, management and ownership of the newspaper and periodical Press and newsagencies including the financial structure and the monopolistic tendencies in control, and to make recommendations thereon.

Under the chairmanship of Sir William David Ross, Provost of Oriel College, Oxford, sixty-one meetings were to be held, 38 of them devoted to the collection of oral evidence from a total of 182 witnesses. Among the key witnesses was Aneurin

Bevan, Minister of Health, who declaimed: 'It is the most prostituted Press in the world, most of it owned by a gang of millionaires.'

There was little doubt that the Labour government had been concerned at the manner in which the Press had supported the Conservatives in the recent election. And this was a point emphasized by former *Standard* editor Percy Cudlipp, by this time occupying a similar role for the *Daily Herald*, when he chaired a meeting on 27 November 1946. The main speaker was the veteran Socialist, Kingsley Martin, who stressed: 'That our serious newspapers with a comparatively small circulation have a political influence quite out of proportion. The vast circulation press had nothing like a political influence to its circulation.'

For the proprietors, the chief witness was to be Beaverbrook, who was quick to comment on any threat to his newspapers; and to E.J. Robertson, his managing director, on his Soundscriber (an early form of tape-recorder) he was to say:

> I will be glad to hear about the Royal Commission on the Press which is one of the Government Agencies in the persecution of newspapers. Sorrow, sorrow ever more. There is nothing I can say about it except to bow my head in misery. It wouldn't be a bad thing if the Socialists cut off all newsprint entirely. I don't care Mr Robertson what the Government tries to do to us. The intention is without doubt to persecute the press, but let the effect of that persecution fall more heavily upon the government press than upon the independent newspapers. Now the way to carry the situation to a conclusion is to refuse to increase your selling price, tighten your belt and let the suffering and misery descend upon the wretches who supported the Socialists in the last election.[4]

As one of the early witnesses to be called before the Commission, Robertson put up an impressive performance before its members. Particular attention, though, was paid to the White List – a list of persons whose names were not to be mentioned in any of Beaverbrook's newspapers.

The star witness was Beaverbrook himself, who spoke on 18 March 1948, and had a field day. It was particularly agreeable for him to score off his old antagonist, Lady Violet Bonham Carter, and he made the most of his opportunity. What he said was no novelty. He had mentioned it many times before in his newspapers, but it apparently surprised the Commission:

> I ran the paper purely for propaganda, and with no other purpose .... In order to make propaganda effective the paper had to be successful. No paper is any good at all for propaganda unless it has a thoroughly good financial position. There is a strong, stern rule, and the most tremendous attempt .... to carry the rule into effect. But we do stumble. It is terrible how we stumble; it is heartbreaking sometimes.

Discussing the lists, he continued: 'Some people call it a black list. In the *Evening Standard* it is called the cautionary list, and in the *Daily Express* office it is called the warned list.' On the question of giving directives to his editors he remarked that it was really advice.

Journalists' Training

For Lord Kemsley – thanks to his personal assistant, Denis Hamilton – appearing before the Commission gave him the opportunity to put forward his proposal for the tutelage of journalists, which was to be developed as the Kemsley Editorial Training Plan. To quote Hamilton: 'Having started as the chief whipping boy of the Royal Commission – owner of the "gramophone press" in Herbert Morrison's phrase – Kemsley emerged the standard bearer of his profession.'[5]

The plan comprised four parts: three for editors, executives and qualified members of staffs, and one covering regular courses for juniors and new entrants. And with the full backing of Kemsley 'the whole programme was steaming along' by the time the Commission discussed recruitment and training in its report:

> The problem of recruiting the right people into journalism whether from school or from university and of ensuring that they achieve the necessary level of education and technical efficiency is one of the most important facing the Press . . . . The problem is the common interest and the common responsibility of proprietors, editors and other journalists.'

The report of the Royal Commission – total expenditure £21,442 – was not published until 29 June 1949; and in the words of Stephen Koss: 'The commissioners were defeated by their own prodigious industry, which produced a mound of indigestible and sometimes contradictory material.'

David Astor, in *The Observer*, on 3 July wrote: 'That newspapers are capable of inaccurate reporting was nicely demonstrated last Thursday, when almost every popular newspaper summarised the findings of the Royal Commission on the Press in a manner favourable to themselves. No one who relied on these papers for his information could have guessed that much of the Commission's report was unfavourable to our industry or profession.'

But for Hugh Cudlipp: 'The Royal Commission on the Press displayed a shrewder, broader-minded insight into the secrets of popular newspapers. Though critical of other aspects, the Commission described the mass circulation journals as remarkable value for money.'

Press Council Proposed

The 180-page report, with 183 pages of appendices, concluded that:[6]

> It is generally agreed that the British Press is inferior to none in the world. It is free from corruption: both those who own the Press and those who are employed on it would universally condemn the acceptance or soliciting of bribes . . . . The present degree of concentration of ownership in the newspaper press as a whole or in any important class of it is not so great as to prejudice the free expression of opinion or the accurate presentation of news or to be contrary to the best interests of the public.

The commission's final, and most important, proposal was that:

THE FREEDOM OF THE PRESS

Key: 1957 – *Daily Mirror*, Cecil King; *News Chronicle*, Lord Layton; *Daily Express*, Lord Beaverbrook; *Daily Mail*, Lord Rothermere II; *Daily Telegraph*, Michael Berry (later Lord Hartwell); *Sunday Times*, Lord Kemsley; *The Observer* –; *The Times*, Gavin Astor

> The Press should establish a General Council of the Press consisting of at least 25 members representing proprietors, editors, and other journalists, and having lay members amounting to about 20 per cent of the total, including the chairman, nominated jointly by the Lord Chief Justice and the Lord President of the Court of Session, who, in choosing the other lay members, should consult the chairman. The chairman, on whom a heavy burden of work will fall, should be paid.
>
> The objects of the General Council should be to safeguard the freeedom of the Press; to encourage the growth of the sense of public responsibility and public service among all engaged in the profession of journalism – that is, in the editorial production of newspapers – whether as directors, editors, or other journalists; and to further the efficiency of the profession and the well-being of those who practise it.

On 29 July 1949, a month after the publication of the report, Parliament approved the motion by Herbert Morrison 'That this House, having taken into consideration the report of the Royal Commission of the Press, would welcome all possible action on the part of the Press to give effect to the Commission's conclusions and recommendations.'

It was to be another four years, though, before the main recommendation of the Commission – the setting-up of a Press Council – came into being in 1953. It was not, however, received with favour by everyone, Cecil King saying: 'The idea was very unwelcome to Fleet Street, but one was eventually set up under Lord Astor of Hever [proprietor, *The Times*]. This had no outside membership and to my mind served no purpose. So I refused to let our people take part.'[7]

Inadvertently, Cecil King's 'people' were to be involved, for at its inaugural meeting in the June the Press Council was required to adjudicate on the findings of a front-page poll undertaken by the *Daily Mirror* as to whether Princess Margaret and Group Captain Peter Townsend should be allowed to marry – readers had voted 67,907 to 2235 in their favour. And the result of the first deliberation? The *Mirror* was heavily criticised by the Council, deprecating the paper's poll as 'contrary to the best traditions of British journalism'.

Although the proprietors had not been enamoured with the idea, at its meeting in May the NPA had drawn up a list of possible members who would be sitting on the Press Council under the proposed chairmanship of Lord Astor. The list revealed:

> Managerial – Lord Rothermere II, Associated Newspapers; Lord Burnham, *Daily Telegraph*; E.J. Robertson, Express Newspapers; Stuart McClean, Associated Newspapers; T. Blackburn, Express Newspapers; W. Emsley Carr, *News of the World*; Cecil King, *Daily Mirror* and *Sunday Pictorial*; W. Surrey Dane, *Daily Herald* and Odhams Press; Cyril Hamnett, *Reynolds News*; Frank Waters, *News Chronicle*.
> Editorial – Guy Schofield, *Daily Mail*; John Marshall, *Evening News*; Charles Eade, *Sunday Dispatch*; Henry Clapp, *Daily Sketch*; Harry Ainsworth, *The People*.

However, prior to the first meeting, Lord Rothermere, Lord Burnham, E.J. Robertson and Cecil King withdrew their names.[8]

Newsprint Shortage Continues

Despite constant overtures from proprietors and unions to successive Labour and Conservative governments, it was not until the end of 1956 that newsprint rationing came to an end. Certainly, during the war – with a cut-off in supplies from Scandinavia and the sinking by U-boats of newsprint vessels from Canada – there had been a justifiable case, but not with the coming of peace. One outspoken critic, in conversation, was Louis Heren, a future deputy editor of *The Times*:[9]

> If there was any time in recent history when the public needed to know what was going on, it was in those post-war years .... There was no alternative source of information to the press, but British-made newsprint was actually exported while broadsheets were reduced to eight pages .... It was a form of censorship. Politicians who routinely blathered on about freedom, democracy and a well-informed electorate were only too happy to keep the press on a lease, to tame it if it could not be suppressed .... There could be no other explanation; as was pointed out at the time, only an additional £5 million a year was needed to buy sufficient extra newsprint.
>
> The consequences for the press were grave. Unlike other industries, it was denied the opportunity to expand its market. Recruitment was greatly reduced, and a generation of journalists was lost. Those who were employed were denied space in which to develop. A generation of readers grew up not knowing what a good newspaper had to offer when it had the space. The serious-minded were denied full reports of great events, parliamentary debates, white papers and other essential material. The artistically-inclined had little idea of what was happening on the stage, in publishing and in the galleries apart from scrappy reviews. Sports fans got little more than the results.

In January 1946, a joint deputation of the newspaper organizations and the PKTF, representing twenty print unions, met Prime Minister Attlee; Sir Stafford Cripps, Chancellor of the Exchequer; and Herbert Morrison, Home Secretary; and were told unequivocably that they 'must quite understand that a 16-page paper is some years off'.

Previously, the deputation had stressed that the case for more newsprint was based on two essentials: the need for giving an adequate service of news and information on current events; and the need for providing full employment in the industry. It was pointed out that during the war – despite enemy air raids – not one Fleet Street newspaper had missed an edition; and it was further shown that whereas British newspapers were restricted to four-page issues, 'Australian titles were issuing 12 to 20-page sheets, and India, South Africa and New Zealand were giving from 6 to 10 pages'. It was also estimated that some five thousand employees would be returning from the Forces to Fleet Street, but, even with the pensioning-off of older persons, jobs could be found for only two thousand.

Four months later Sir Walter Layton, chairman, *News Chronicle*, and vice-chairman the Newsprint Supply Co., speaking at the first post-war luncheon of the Newspaper Society – at which the Prime Minister was chief guest – said that British newspapers are today using newsprint at the rate of 300,000 tons a year, compared with nearly one and a quarter million tons before the war. 'A return to pre-war consumption is not in sight, and we shall do very well if we are able to reach 12-page papers in the course of the next three or four years.'

He added that the foreign exchange required for British newspapers on a 16-page basis would be at present prices equal to the total of the American loan in a hundred years. 'We are only asking for a fraction of the foreign exchange that is spent on American films.'

Daily Mail *Jubilee*

While Sir Walter and the Prime Minister were debating newsprint shortages, on 5 May 1946 the *Daily Mail* celebrated its golden jubilee, and chief guest at its glittering banquet was Winston Churchill, who proposed the toast of the paper:[10]

> I remember lunching at Londonderry House on the day when the *Daily Mail* first came out, and Alfred Harmsworth sat as the guest of honour at a very small party – a very remarkable man, a man of great influence and independence. In a free country where enterprise can make its way, he was able to create this enormous, lasting, persuasive and attractive newspaper which had its influence in our daily lives and with which we have walked along the road for 50 years.
>
> Today what have we? A new chapter was opened in journalism when the *Daily Mail* was founded and scores of millions of people became newspaper readers who had not been attracted by the older forms of journalism. We live in a wider world with a much larger public. What is our Press today? It is a free Press; it is a decent Press.

Replying, Lord Rothermere II, in discussing the growth of the *Daily Mail*, made a point of mentioning the current strictures on newsprint: 'But it had something of which everybody here who is a newspaperman would be jealous – it was of eight pages. Eight pages in 1896 – four pages in 1946.' He added: 'It is a very serious thing for the country and for the newspapers that we are confined to so small a space. It is too small a space to give the news so that people can understand the momentous changes which are taking place today.'

His comments were to be echoed by Lord Beaverbrook, in proposing 'The Freedom of the Press':[11]

> *Freedom from competition*: For of course circulations are fixed by the shortage of supply of newsprint. There is no longer any competition for sales.
>
> *Freedom from advertising revenue*: 'There is so little space that there is no room for advertising.
>
> *Freedom from newsprint* – and with the universal shortage of raw materials, a refusal to take our national share of the world production of newsprint will exclude us altogether from the newsprint market.
>
> *Freedom from enterprise*: What might be called private enterprise. It is prohibited to start any new papers.

Two months, later, following ratification of the £937,000,000 American loan to the Government, talks were held between officials and the Newsprint Supply Company to permit increases, if desired, to six-page papers on alternate days; and in the House of Commons, Hugh Dalton, Chancellor of the Exchequer, 'expressed the hope that the Government would be able to arrange for the purchase of a limited supply'.

And for Sir Keith Murdoch, the Australian publisher, chairman of the Commonwealth delegation to the Imperial Press Conference in London, there was the belief that Britain's newsprint position could improve, 'but it cannot make a serious recovery until more newsprint is available'.

However, there was to be good news in August when the Government announced that from midday, 22 September 1946, broadsheets would be allowed to publish six-page issues on alternate days, but there would be, as agreed with the NPA, restrictions on sales promotion: (a) canvassing for the purpose of obtaining orders for copies; (b) providing free or paid-for insurance of their possessions for readers; (c) the supply of free copies or gifts.

A month later, on 24 October, although pleased at the recent increase, Sir Walter Layton was to comment:

> In 1938, the British newspapers consumed approximately 1,250,000 tons of newsprint. Fifty per cent on that puts annual consumption at about 2,000,000 tons. Two million tons for Britain is nowhere in sight, even if there is quite a big expansion in production. Our ambition has to be limited to one million tons, which means a maximum of 12 pages by 1950. This would be reached as follows: 1947 – six pages (compared with the present five); 1948 – eight pages; 1949 – ten pages; 1950 – twelve pages.[12]

Despite the gloomy picture painted by Sir Walter, newspaper groups had already been looking into launching new titles. One of the first was the *Financial Times*, which in the July had announced its intention of publishing a new paper 'as soon as extra newsprint was available'. Its columnist 'Observer', in his paper's 'Men and Matters', was to write: 'Plans are ready for the starting of several new Sunday papers in London and I shall be surprised if there are not at least two evening papers started here as soon as paper is made available.' And according to 'Brutus', writing in the *Recorder*, if newsprint were available, 'two morning newspapers, one Socialist evening paper, one right-wing evening newspaper and three Sunday newspapers' were planned in 'London alone'. All this, though, was pure speculation, for in the event no new titles were to be launched.

With the price of newsprint in 1947 – when available – at nearly £40 a ton, almost four times the price paid in 1939, *The Times* now decided to seek other means of providing the raw material on which to print their papers. But it was not until 1 December 1949, that a 25-year agreement (renewable after 20 years) was signed with Townsend Hook, a company which produced paper with an enhanced finish. For this improved stock – extra weight and consequent freight charges – *The Times* were now having to pay 15 per cent more than for normal newsprint. But as the management were to say: 'Quality of print means more to *The Times* than to any other newspaper.' And the plan was that when Townsend Hook could produce enough mechanical stock, *The Times* would go over entirely to this supplier.

Meanwhile, on 22 March 1954, in a leading article, editor Sir William Haley was to launch a fierce attack on the newsprint restrictions:[13]

> The Government's hesitation implies that they are in doubt whether it may be reasonable or not to sacrifice the freedom of the Press to publish as much as it wants for the sake of 0.4 per cent of annual dollar expenditure. Such hesitation is unworthy – and the doubt unintelligible. The Press should have been at the head of the list for freedom, not at the tail, and it will be to the Government's lasting shame if control of the newspapers becomes the sole *raison d'être* of the Minister of Materials. It is time for the Government to show they no longer rate the service of public opinion so far behind the enjoyment of tobacco, sweets and Hollywood films.

Twelve months after Haley's leading article, *The Times*, having gone over completely to the enhanced stock, resigned its share from the Newsprint Supply Company's pool. It proved to be an unfortunate decision, for in 1956 newsprint controls were lifted and 'the paper found itself obliged to pay for [the next] twenty years some 20 per cent more for its paper than any other newspaper'.

Camrose Sells the FT

While the war in the Far East still raged, in June 1945 Viscount Camrose sold the *Financial Times* to the owners of the *Financial News* for £743,000 – and was later to admit it had been his biggest mistake. Writing in his *British Newspapers and Their Controllers*, he was to say in 1947:[14]

> Competition between the *Financial Times* and the *Financial News* was keen but the circulation of the former was materially greater than that of the latter. Both lived on the same kind of revenue – mainly prospectus advertisements and the reports of company meetings – and there was sometimes not enough to go round when affairs in the City were not prospering. This proved embarrassing in the depression which followed the 'boom' of 1928–29 and both the owning companies had to pass their Preference dividends. The amalgamation has permitted the use of a better newspaper and should ensure for it a prosperous future.

Launched by James Sheridan and his brother on 13 February 1883, the *Financial Times* had soon ran into trouble, not being able to pay the printer's bills, leading Horatio Bottomley, of MacRae, Curtice & Co., to take over the paper. He became a director and was appointed chairman on 13 July 1888 but left within a few months to found the Hansard Publishing Company.

The first editor, at £6 a week, was Leopold Graham, and as David Kynaston was to say in the official history of the *Financial Times*: 'He had no notion of writing and was poorly educated, but he had a smattering of common French phrases and a real understanding of company promoting and speculative City business.'[15]

With Bottomley gone, Douglas MacRae became chairman and remained in control until 1901. His successor, Francis M. Bridgewater, was to remark: 'To speak of the career of the *Financial Times* for the first few years as chequered would be to describe it in favourable terms.' Bridgewater was to be chairman 1901–1915, being succeeded by Sir John Ellerman, the chief proprietor, and four years later, in October 1919, he sold the paper to Wiliam and Gomer Berry.

Its rival, the *Financial News*, launched and edited by Harry H. Marks, was known initially as the *Financial & Mining News*. It made its debut on Wednesday 23 January 1884, priced one penny, and consisted of four small-sized pages. Marks was to remain as proprietor until his death in 1916. He had, however, handed over the editorship to Ellis Powell in 1909, who was to remain in control until 1920. Later editors were: W.A. Domain, William Lang, Sir Laming Worthington-Evans, Sir Edward Hilton Young, Oscar Hobson, Maurice Green and Hargreaves Parkinson (1938–45).

In the spring of 1945 negotiations were to take place between Camrose, owner of the *Financial Times*, and Brendan Bracken, the *Financial News* chairman. During the war, Camrose and his brother, Lord Kemsley, had agreed that should either wish to sell the other would have first opportunity. (Kemsley believed that he should have had first refusal.)

Taking a key role in the negotiations was Garrett Moore, the future Earl of Drogheda, who, following a chance meeting with Bracken, had joined the *Financial News* as an advertisement salesman. By 1939 he had become deputy to Bracken; with the onset of the Second World War he joined the Royal Artilliery before, in 1942, being seconded to the Ministry of Production.

In the autumn of 1944 Bracken told Moore to make a formal offer for the *FT*, and was told that the price would be 'upwards of the 30 shilling market price', or in excess of £750,000. With the *FT* showing an excellent profit for 1944, Camrose declared in March 1945 that the purchase price would now be two guineas per share – and this was accepted on 15 May. To hasten through the deal, Camrose, who owned 70 per cent of the *FT* stock, had agreed to buy out the other shareholders while also providing a 'bridging loan before the *Financial News* could raise all the money'. And to quote David Kynaston once more:[16]

> Moore was greatly helped by Camrose himself, who did everything he could to ease the FN's path. . . . A great man with a large, disinterested mind and deeply committed to the well-being of the press as a whole as well as his own particular ventures, he must have known that one combined paper would ensure the future of daily financial journalism whereas the continuing existence of two might not.

On 30 September 1945 the final issue of the *Financial News* was published and the following day it was merged with the *Financial Times*. As the new part-time chairman, Bracken attended the Coleman Street offices only once or twice a week. While deliberately not interfering with editorial policy, his column 'Men and Matters' appeared every Monday. Bracken's management style was welcomed by Hargreaves Parkinson, the new editor, who in his first leader declaimed:

> Never have readers been so avid for guidance on everything bearing on full employment, inflation, taxation, the future of Government controls and similar problems. It is the objective to which the *Financial Times* proposes to devote its energy, experience and authority, as its contribution to the task of national reconstruction.

Parkinson remained editor until 1949 and died the following year, worn out before his years; and in a tribute Brendan Bracken was to say that 'few men had done more than he did to heighten the standards of financial journalism'.

Four years later, on 15 June 1954, in a Southampton hospital, Lord Camrose passed away, aged 74. His was one of the great successes of the British Press. As an employer he was a model to the industry and has been summed up admirably by Lord Drogheda, a former member of his staff: 'He was the best of the lot for fairness, firmness and inspiration.' *The Daily Telegraph* then came under the control of his second son, Michael Berry (the future Lord Hartwell).

As for Bracken, apart from his *Financial Times* interests, he was also chairman of the Union Corporation; and with the return of a Conservative government in 1951 Churchill offered him a cabinet post. Bracken declined, but the following year accepted a viscountcy.

In February 1957 S. Pearson Industries Ltd, under the chairmanship of Lord Cowdray, assumed control of the *Financial Times* for £720,000 through purchasing just over 50 per cent of FN Ltd, which controlled 51 per cent of the *FT*. Considering that the *FT* the previous year had made £550,000 pre-tax profits, Pearson had secured a bargain. Bracken, who remained as chairman, wrote to Beaverbrook on 4 February:[17]

> For many years the control of the *Financial Times* has been under the shadow of death duties. If anything happened to Oliver Eyre the paper would have to be sold. One of the Cowdray private Trusts has offered a price far above the market value and I strongly pressed for acceptance. The Eyre family will make a profit. I don't make a cent but that does not worry me. A good business is the ownership of the *FT*. Ellerman made a big profit by selling to Camrose. He made a much bigger profit selling to the Eyres. They make twice as big a profit by selling to Cowdray.

Beaverbrook, though, was not pleased, replying five days later: 'I am sorry that Cowdray has bought the *Financial Times*. It would have been much better in the hands of the Eyre family.'

Unfortunately, Bracken's tenure as chairman was to be brief: an inveterate smoker, he became ill with cancer of the throat and died on 8 August 1958. In his obituary notice in *The Times*, Sir Geoffrey Crowther wrote: 'He mastered the very difficult act of being a newspaper proprietor. His editors once appointed and trusted knew that they had in him the perfect shield against pressures and influences.' For his colleagues, he was to remembered in the naming of the new *Financial Times* building 'Bracken House'.

Kemsley Sells His Empire

As a loyal friend and supporter of Neville Chamberlain, Lord Kemsley had been disgusted at the revolt of Conservative backbenchers on 9 May 1940, which led to the fall of the Prime Minister and his succession by Winston Churchill: '[I] would have liked to have had the power to subject the unruly elements for a couple of days to German discipline . . . . the overwhelming mass of the people regard the hysteria of your critics with contempt.' Unlike his brother, William (Lord Camrose), he was not a close friend of Churchill.[18]

In 1943, he changed the name of his company to Kemsley Newspapers. His brother was later to write: 'He is perhaps more of a believer in personal journalism than I am. Each of the papers in the group now carries under the title block on the front page the words, "A Kemsley Newspaper". This is a practice known in America but never used here before.'

With the coming of peace, Kemsley, having been made a viscount in 1945, was anxious to retain his position as the leading publisher of newspapers in Great Britain. In 1948, he owned the following nationals: *Daily Graphic*, *Daily Dispatch*, *Sporting Chronicle*, *Sunday Times*, *Sunday Graphic* and *Sunday Empire News*, plus the *Daily Record* in Glasgow and morning and evening titles in Aberdeen, Blackburn, Cardiff, Glasgow, Manchester, Middlesbrough, Newcastle, Sheffield and York with a score of weekly newspapers. Combined circulation of these titles was more than 9,300,000: Sunday papers 5,730,000, morning papers 2,150,000 and evening papers 1,422,000.

The pride of Kemsley's many newspapers was, undoubtedly, *The Sunday Times* and he was determined that it should continue to grow in stature. He, therefore, through his personal assistant Denis Hamilton engaged the best editorial talent. Hamilton, a former junior reporter on the *Evening Gazette*, Middlesbrough, had served throughout the Second World War as an officer in the Durham Light Infantry. A survivor of Dunkirk, in the winter of 1944 he was awarded the DSO while acting as CO in the Duke of Wellington's Regiment in the fighting between Nijmegen and Arnhem; and ended the war, at the young age of 26, as commanding officer of the 7th Duke's.

On demobilization, he returned to the Newcastle *Chronicle* office as a senior reporter and feature writer, but within weeks was summoned to London to work for Lord Kemsley.[19] There, one of his first efforts, as noted, was to introduce a graduate training scheme for the group; and in 1950 he was appointed editorial director. Hamilton also became involved with *The Sunday Times*, and in 1958, through his war-time service under Montgomery, was able to secure the Field Marshal's memoirs for the paper, one of the first of the 'big reads'. These were to prove a decisive factor in the circulation war with *The Observer*.

The expenditure and effort on *The Sunday Times* was soon to become apparent: sales of the paper rose from 263,000 – the figure when Kemsley took over the paper in 1937 – to more than 885,000 when, in 1959, he sold out to Roy Thomson.

In 1952, Kemsley had begun to run down his empire and that year had sold the *Daily Graphic* to the second Lord Rothermere and was then to merge two of his Sunday titles, the *Sunday Chronicle* and the *Empire News*. Next on the list was the *Daily Dispatch*, which was absorbed by Cadbury's *News Chronicle*; and the *Daily Record* was then sold to the *Daily Mirror* group. Apart from this mass clearance, Kemsley also dabbled in commercial television, and in 1955 with impresario Maurice Winnick and retailer Isaac Wolfson had won the franchise for weekend broadcasting in the Midlands and North of England. However, Kemsley withdrew – and a golden opportunity was lost. To quote Denis Hamilton: 'Kemsley would have become, without doubt, the greatest newspaper and broadcasting magnate in the land.'

With the disposal of so many titles, *The Sunday Times* became even more precious to Kemsley; and his concern deepened when in September 1956 the paper's circulation was briefly passed by that of *The Observer*. As *The Times* was to say in his obituary: 'Like the friend of Dr Johnson who published the *Gentleman's Magazine*, he could not look out of the window without thinking of his newspaper.' Nevertheless, in 1959, owing to pressures on his other titles, recent labour troubles – the refusal at *The Sunday Times* of the nineteen different unions and sixty-five chapels to rationalize was an example – and having had to dig deeper into the family reserves, he decided to sell the whole group including *The Sunday Times* to Roy Thomson.

Kemsley asked £15 million for his empire, but, after a fortnight's secret negotaions, settled for £5 million. Kemsley himself received £3.5 million – and his parting gift to Hamilton, who had served him so well for a dozen years, was a photocopy of the cheque. Hamilton was later to write: 'I looked at this thing and I looked at Lord Kemsley, and I said: "Well thank you very much. It's a very interesting souvenir."'

Following the sale of his newspapers, Kemsley moved out of the public eye, and died eight years later in a Monte Carlo hotel on 6 February 1968.

A Licence to Print Money

The new owner of the Kemsley Group, Roy Thomson, had been born in Toronto, Canada, in 1894, and as a young man had been a clerk, farmer and motor supplies dealer.[20] In 1928 he became a radio salesman in Ottawa, and three years later, in Ontario, founded a radio station. This was followed by another in 1933, at Timmins, plus the purchase of the *Citizen*, an ailing weekly paper – so the foundations of his media empire were to be laid. By 1944 Roy Thomson owned eight radio stations plus many local newspapers.

Two years after his wife's death, in 1953 he arrived in Edinburgh and for £393,750 purchased *The Scotsman* from the Findlay family, who had owned the paper since its launch in 1817. There was one proviso: 'In the first place I had to promise that I would never sell the paper to an Englishman.' There his two lieutenants were to be James Coltart and Alastair Dunnett, as editor. But it was to be almost ten years before *The Scotsman* moved into profit.

In 1954, Thomson had taken an interest in two Canadian television stations, which led to his making a bid for the franchise for commercial television in Scotland. He was to be successful, and later described the venture as 'a licence to print money'. One of the persons who had turned down Thomson's offer to join in the bid was Beaverbrook, who told him: 'I'm a newspaperman and I'm not interested – and nor should you be.'[21] It was to be a big mistake, for in the eight years in which Thomson held 80 per cent of the shares in Scottish Television – before being forced by the ITA to reduce its holding ultimately to 25 per cent – its share of the profits was £13 million.

Having been rejected twice by Lord Kemsley in his attempts to purchase the *Press & Journal*, Aberdeen, in 1959 Thomson was, to his surprise, offered the Kemsley

Group. He accepted, and, as noted, for the sum of £5 million became the owner of three national Sundays including *The Sunday Times*, thirteen provincial dailies, plus several weeklies and a provincial Sunday. The negotiations had not been without their problems, and there was always the thought that the news might leak out. This was to lead Thomson to telephone Beaverbrook and explain the position. His reply was most reassuring: 'Roy, I'm with you all the way.'

One of his first acts after acquiring *The Sunday Times* was to install new presses; and on 29 October 1961 he appointed Hamilton as editor. This was to prove an inspired choice. The following year, under Thomson's guidance, he was responsible for launching the first Sunday newspaper colour magazine. Within six years he had increased the circulation to 1,400,000, and in so doing developed the 'Insight' team of investigating journalists, and added new sections to the paper.

During the 1960s, Thomson was to expand his regional newspaper group (TRN) by launching evening newspapers using the most up-to-date technology of computer typesetting and web-offset printing. The first of these evening papers – planned to surround London – was at Reading, and this was swiftly followed by the launch of newspapers for Watford and Luton, both emanating from Hemel Hempstead. There then followed a half-share in the *Evening Mail* for Slough and Hounslow produced at Westminster Press's plant at King & Hutchings, Uxbridge. (Of these four titles, only the evening at Reading is still in existence.)[22]

Apart from his newspapers, Thomson, with the aid of first-class managers such as James Coltart, Sir Gordon Brunton, Sir Eric Cheadle, Sir Alastair Dunnett and Sir Denis Hamilton, ventured into other fields in Great Britain and overseas. There were to be Thomson Yellow Pages, Thomson Travel and a large investment in North Sea oil. Having become Baron Thomson of Fleet in 1964 he was appointed GBE six years later and in 1975 published his autobiography, *After I Was Sixty*, having in 1960 written a chapter, 'The next ten years' in *Fleet Street: the inside story of journalism*.

Buying The Times

On 30 September 1966 it was announced that a new company had been formed: Times Newspapers Limited, to own and publish *The Times* and *The Sunday Times*. The new owners were Thomson Newspapers, and the board would comprise four Astor nominees plus four Thomson nominees with four independent national directors. Kenneth Thomson, Lord Thomson's son, became joint president with Gavin Astor, the son of John Jacob Astor; and Denis Hamilton was appointed editor-in-chief and chief executive.

For more than forty years, *The Times* had remained in the Astor family, headed by John Jacob Astor; and some of his finest moments came during the Second World War, when he played a key role in the military defence of the City of London. As colonel of the Press Battalion of the Home Guard, formed from all the Fleet Street newspaper offices, he was asked to assume operational responsibility for the City Defences Committee.

Apart from his newspaper, he had many other interests, being President of the MCC in 1937, first chairman of the Press Council from 1953 to 1955, and President of the Press Club 1935–64. In the 1956 New Year Honours List he was made a baron 'but pondered the offer of this for some time to make sure in his own mind its acceptance would not compromise the independence of *The Times*'.

Following service in the Second World War, Astor's sons, Gavin and Hugh, became more and more involved in the business, and in 1959 Gavin was appointed chairman and his brother vice-chairman of *The Times*. Three years later the 1962 Finance Act made assets abroad liable to estate duty, and therefore applied to the Astor Trust in New York. Having found it legally impossible to resign from the Trust, and to safeguard his children's inheritance, Astor decided with great reluctance to live abroad, moving to France; and he died at Cannes on 19 July 1971.

Eight years earlier, when Gavin Astor had become co-chief proprietor of *The Times* with John Walter IV, one of his first acts had been to purchase Walter's 10 per cent holding for £250,000; and Astor was to remain chairman until 1966.[23] During this period, he wrote in *The Times House Journal* that, like any other business, *The Times* must operate profitably:

> But the measure of its success ought not to be purely commercial. It is a peculiar property, in that service to what it believes are the best interests of the nation is placed before the personal and financial gain of its Proprietors. One of the great strengths of *The Times* today is that the Editor is known beyond all doubt to have absolute independence in the editorial content and editorial policy in the paper and is answerable only to the Chief Proprietors of *The Times* who alone are responsible for his appointment. Thus the Proprietors have the influence without the power, while the Editor has the power without security.

Astor, who died in 1984, was to remain joint president of Times Newspaper Ltd. until 1981. He had also played a prominent part in other newspaper affairs, being a director of Reuters 1955–61 and President of the Commonwealth Press Union from 1972 until 1981, when he was made an honorary life member.

His brother, Hugh, who had served as a lieutenant-colonel in the Intelligence Corps during the Second World War, joined *The Times* in 1947 as assistant Middle East correspondent and was wounded that year in a burst of gunfire while reporting from Palestine. He was elected to the board of *The Times* in 1956 and became deputy chairman three years later, resigning in 1967 on the merger with *The Sunday Times*. He was chairman of The Times Trust from 1967 to 1982.

Gavin Astor's warning of the increased costs of producing *The Times* meant that in May 1966 serious consideration had been given to merging with the *Financial Times*, under Sir William Haley as chairman and Gordon Newton as editor.[24]

Born in Jersey, William Haley's career had been meteoric. After joining *The Times* as a shorthand typist/telephonist in 1919, he transferred to the *Manchester Evening News* as a reporter. Within three years he was chief sub and by 1930 was managing editor and a director, and from 1939 until 1943 was joint managing director of the Manchester Guardian and Evening News Ltd. During this period he was also a director of Reuters and during the war years travelled to the United States on special missions for the government.

In September 1943 Haley was appointed editor-in-chief of the BBC, and the following year succeeded Sir Robert Foot as Director-General. He was to remain with the Corporation until 1952 when he became editor of *The Times*; and in an early memorandum outlined the three tenets of the paper: (a) a journal of record; (b) a daily paper which plays a useful part in the running of the country, and (c) a balanced, interesting and entertaining paper for intelligent readers of all ages and classes.

Under his editorship, the paper broadened its scope. More space was given to the arts – music, theatre, painting; women's features were extended and cartoons introduced. Little wonder that Beaverbrook could say: 'Haley changed *The Times* into a real paper.' And, to the horror of many, on 3 May 1966 news was introduced to the front page. In its leader, Haley could declaim:

> The same people have produced today's issue as did yesterday's. They will produce tomorrow's. They will continue to have the same sense of responsibility and the same standards. They will at the same time use all their professional skill to make *The Times* more comprehensive, more interesting, more explicit, more lucid. *The Times* aims at being a paper for intelligent readers of all ages and classes. The more it can have of them the better. Some people have expressed the dark suspicion that one of the reasons *The Times* is modernising itself is to get more readers. Of course it is. And we shall go on trying to get more readers for as long as we believe in our purpose.

Aware of the strength of *The Daily Telegraph*, whose circulation at more than one million copies was four times that of *The Times* and the ever-increasing threat of *The Guardian*, throughout the summer of 1966 serious negotiations had continued between *The Times* and the *Financial Times* at a possible merger – the plan being that a combined newspaper would contain the news from *The Times* and a business section from the *Financial Times*. However, the offer put forward by Lord Cowdray's advisors was not acceptable by *The Times* management and discussions foundered.

At this point, Sir Denis Hamilton, chief executive of *The Sunday Times*, was approached by Kenneth Keith, the Astors' financial adviser, to ask if Lord Thomson was still interested in purchasing *The Times*. For three years, Thomson had been seeking to secure the paper, and in 1963 had even made an overture to Lord Astor in the South of France,[25] suggesting 'a loose form of association [which] might include the sharing of machinery and other services'. Astor was not amused – and there was complete rejection. Despite this, during the following months Thomson and Hamilton were to hold a series of meetings with Gavin Astor and other *Times* executives.

Now, in the summer of 1966, to quote Thomson: '*The Times* people had completely changed their attitudes and their opinions. The fact was that they were losing nearly sixpence on every copy sold, and with an increased circulation but no increase in advertising revenue, the loss was all the greater, about £225,000 a year in fact.'

With Thomson in Canada, Hamilton put forward a package that was acceptable to the Astor family – 'and the Monopolies Commission if, as seemed certain, the deal was referred'. For 85 per cent of the new company's stock – at a maximum cost to himself of £3,300,000 – with Astor receiving a 15 per cent share, Thomson was to be successful, pledging to maintain *The Times* for at least twenty-one years, and thereby ensuring its editorial independence.

As expected, the purchase was referred to the Monopolies Commission, and appearing before them Thomson said that he anticipated losing more than £5 million before the paper broke into profit. As he was to declare in his autobiography:[26]

> Not once but many times I told them that I was only taking on *The Times* because I reckoned its rescue and restoration to health would be a worthy object and perhaps a fitting object for a man who had made a fortune in newspapers . . . . The financial arrangement was that in the first place *The Times* losses would be shouldered by *The Sunday Times*. If *The Sunday Times* were to make too little profit in any one year to cover those losses, then my son and I would forego enough of the dividends which would be due to us on our 78 per cent of Thomson Organisation shares.

New Editors Appointed

Approval was given by the Monopolies Commission on 22 December 1966, and less than a fortnight later, on 1 January 1967, Times Newspapers Limited came into being. At the first board meeting, on 14 January, Hamilton, as chief executive and editor-in-chief, put forward his nominations for editors: William Rees-Mogg, his deputy on *The Sunday Times*, was to be the new editor of *The Times*; and Harold Evans was to succeed Hamilton as editor of *The Sunday Times*.[27]

Educated at Charterhouse and Balliol College, Oxford, where he was President of the Union in 1951, William Rees-Mogg began his journalistic career on *The Financial Times* the following year and remained there until 1960. During this period he was chief leader writer, 1955–60, and assistant editor, 1957–60. He then joined *The Sunday Times*, and was successively City editor, political and economic editor and deputy editor, 1964–67, before being appointed editor of *The Times* in 1967, a position he was to retain until 1981. In its official history, *The Times* could say of his editorship:

> Rees-Mogg believed as a matter of principle in letting his gifted men express their personalities and views with a minimum of interference, even though he might not always agree with a particular piece. Rees-Mogg valued good talk and instituted regular weekly meetings in his room with a wider audience than the daily leader conference, over which he presided, symbolically at ease, in a rocking chair.

Harold Evans, the new editor of *The Sunday Times*, was born in Manchester, becoming a reporter on a weekly newspaper at Ashton-under-Lyne before serving in the RAF 1946–49. On demobilization he returned to the paper ahead of entering Durham University, 1949–52. He then joined the *Manchester Evening News*, becoming a leader writer and assistant editor. 'A Harkness Fellowship allowed me to study foreign policy for two years in the United States at Chicago and Stanford Universities; while there I also worked on American newspapers and filed reports for *The Guardian*.'

In 1961, he was appointed editor of the *Northern Echo*, Darlington, and soon made a name with his campaigning journalism, exemplified by his asking for an official inquiry into the hanging of Timothy Evans; and it was also at Darlington that his work on newspaper design began to attract attention. Five years later, Harold Evans became chief assistant to Denis Hamilton, editor of *The Sunday Times*. He was then appointed managing editor before becoming editor. As such he brought together a fine team of writers; and once more led with his investigative journalism, including sanctions busting in Rhodesia and the thalidomide case.

Despite the ever-increasing troubles with unions – discussed in chapter eighteen – Thomson was to support *The Times* financially until his death. Unlike many other proprietors, Thomson believed in giving his editors complete freedom and would not interfere with their policies. In his pocket he carried a card which declared:

> I can state with the utmost emphasis that no person or group can buy or influence editorial support from any newspaper in the Thomson group. Each paper may perceive this interest in its own way, and will do this without advice, counsel or guidance from the central office of the Thomson Organisation. I do not believe that a newspaper can be run properly unless its editorial columns are run freely and independently by a highly skilled and dedicated professional journalist. This is and will continue to be my policy.

Thomson died on 4 August 1976; and Sir Denis Hamilton was to say of him in the *DNB*: 'He was a self-taught genius with a balance sheet, who could discern trends, strengths and potential weaknesses.' *The Times* in a tribute could note: 'He was utterly generous and utterly reassuring. Editor Harold Evans in a *Sunday Times* leader wrote 'Lord Thomson was not a journalist, but he was the best friend journalism ever had . . . . above all, there was his homely regard for truth, the source of journalism's moral energy and the precept we love and remember him by.'

Thomson was also a modest man. His method of travel from his home in Fulmer, Buckinghamshire, was a car to Uxbridge then catching the tube to King's Cross, where he was driven to *The Sunday Times* offices in Gray's Inn Road. And it was quite common on his tube journey for him to share his newspapers with fellow-travellers.

In 1979, former Prime Minister Harold Macmillan unveiled a plaque in the crypt of St Paul's Cathedral. The simple message read: 'He gave a new direction to the British newspaper industry. A strange and adventurous man from nowhere, ennobled by the virtues of courage and integrity and faithfulness.'

17

The *Mirror* triumphant

AS EDITORIAL DIRECTOR and later Chairman of the *Daily Mirror*, Guy Bartholomew was to see its circulation rise from 732,000, when the paper adopted its new-style tabloid format in January 1934, to more than 1,500,000 at the onset of the Second World War; and as Hugh Cudlipp was to write:[1] 'Bart's true role [was] in the re-creation of the *Daily Mirror* in the mid-Thirties: it was the paramount newspaper achievement in the twentieth century so far, and success has many fathers.' Cecil King thought that Bart was: 'Amusing and at times brilliant, but a dreadful man to work for.'

While sales of the *Mirror* increased dramatically during the War – it was the most popular newspaper of all with British troops – Bart and his editor, C.E. Thomas, had been condemned by the Government over the Donald Zec cartoon and threatened with the paper's closure (see chapter 14, p. 279–281.) Apart from involvement with the *Mirror*, for three years Bart had directed a secret newspaper for submarine crews, entitled *Good Morning*; and in 1946 for his work on the project he was awarded the OBE.

For several decades, Bart was a lunch-time regular at El Vino wine bar in Fleet Street; Cudlipp again:[2]

> He stood with his back, on the same spot, whisky in hand, apparently oblivious to all except his henchman who would report the comings and goings of others, especially of his executives, disclosing who was in their circle. Laughter among his staff returning from a liquid lunch elsewhere would die away as he passed by. Working on a popular newspaper was fun, but not while he was around.

Despite his managerial style, Bart could look back with some pride at a *Mirror* circulation of more than 3,500,000 copies; and three years later, in 1949, he had the satisfaction of the paper overtaking the *Daily Express* with sales of more than 4,000,000, making it the most popular daily in the western world. And as chairman he also played a considerable part in expanding the *Daily Mirror* and *Sunday Pictorial* companies through the growth of their overseas investments in the United States, West Indies, West Africa and Australia. Cecil King, a key figure in this, was to write: 'The firm's excursion into Australia had the same cause as our investment in Nigeria; there was no chance of expansion in the newspaper field in the UK because of newsprint rationing, if for no other reason, so expansion overseas was the only way out.'

In late 1949, Bart, still angry at Hugh Cudlipp for leaving the *Mirror* to join Cecil King on the *Sunday Pictorial* in 1935, and now even more so since its sales had passed those of the *Mirror*, fired him as editor – and the cause, inadvertently, was King himself. In Nigeria to check on the company's *Daily Times*, King had flown on from Lagos to Enugu, where he learned that more than a dozen miners had been killed in a riot. 'Piecing together the story from anyone who had been present at the shooting', he eventually cabled the account to the *Pictorial*, where it arrived at 10 o'clock on Saturday night, 18 November, when the presses were running on the final edition after union stoppages. Cudlipp, deciding that a riot in far-away Nigeria was not newsworthy, spiked the story. Later, he was to say: 'On that particular Saturday night we were publishing a spectacular issue . . . . and were running late . . . . Enugu was not close to our readers' hearts or to mine. It wouldn't have sold an extra copy.' For Bart, it was the moment he had been waiting for and, upon King's return to London, he fired Cudlipp.[3]

Within hours of his dismissal, Cudlipp had received an offer from Beaverbrook Newspapers, and in reply to King's letter of commiseration, 'regretting that we shall be working together no more', he wrote:

> There is nothing I can say about Bartholomew's appalling behaviour that hasn't already been said by almost everybody who matters in Fleet Street. I have never had such fan mail, and I doubt if any other has. This at least was some comfort. Bartholomew fires me with all the subtlety accorded to a tenth-rate sub-editor who turns up late on the first morning of a month's trial. And then I get this cable from the proprietor of a firm for which I have never previously worked:
>
> MILLAR DAILY EXPRESS LONDON FOR HUGH CUDLIPP. IT IS WITH ENTHUSIASM THAT I WELCOME YOU TO OUR HOUSE WHERE YOU WILL BE HAPPY AND CONTENTED STOP I HAVE SOUGHT YOUR COMPANIONSHIP FOR LONG. BEAVERBROOK . . . .
>
> We have, as you say, had a great deal of fun with the 'Pictorial' together – and we *did* pass the 'People'. Perhaps we could meet in the New Year when the dust has settled.

And from Arthur Christiansen, editor of the *Daily Express*, there was a letter of welcome: 'As you know, I have been trying to tempt you to our side of the Street for years and years, and I take it as a high compliment to our friendship that you made contact with me. I will do everything possible to make your life in the *Express* outfit happy.'

But for Bart, who was to remain chairman for the next few years, time was running out. More and more his abrasive style of management and excessive drinking was ceasing to find favour with his fellow-directors, and in December 1951 Cecil King led a successful boardroom revolt. Told of his dismissal by Philip Zec, Bart, now 67, broke down and wept for twenty minutes 'after which they both drank a bottle of whisky together'. It was to be four days, though, before a distraught Bart resigned, leaving with a cash payment of £20,000 and a pension of £6000 per annum. On 21 December the *World's Press News* announced:

> A resignation which has occasioned surprise in Fleet Street by reason of its unexpected nature took place last weekend when H. Guy Bartholomew relinquished his

> chairmanship of the *Mirror* and *Pictorial* companies. In an official statement issued by the respective companies it was said that the resignation had been accepted with regret. Mr Bartholomew, aged 67, wrote that his advancing years and an earnest desire to promote the advancement of younger men had moved him to this decision. He would, however, remain as a director, until the end of the financial year. Cecil Harmsworth King has been elected chairman of both companies in his stead.

'The King revolution, dramatic and irreversible, marked the movement of the *Mirror* Group into a new and successful phase which King was to control and dominate'; and as he was to tell an interviewer: 'I only had one real battle and that was when I wanted to get rid of the previous chairman. One year later he was on the streets and I was chairman.'

For the new chairman – 'he prides himself on his ability to take the long view and choose the right men' – his first act was to write to Hugh Cudlipp at the *Sunday Express*, where he acted as managing editor to John Gordon, the paper's long-serving editor: 'Let's get together and make a dent in the history of our times.'[4] And for Cudlipp? There was to be a return to his old job as editor of the *Sunday Pictorial*, before being appointed editorial director of both the *Daily Mirror* and the *Sunday Pictorial* (he was never editor of the *Mirror*). Many years later, Geoffrey Goodman, labour editor of the *Mirror*,was to say:[5]

> The Fifties and Sixties were the decades of the Cudlipp revolution. Cecil King as Chairman, Hugh as Editorial Director. We are talking about a period that was, is, light years away from where we are today. Television, then, was still in its infancy; post-war newsprint controls were just being relaxed; the advertising market was way back in its Petticoat Lane status, growing in confidence to be sure, like the stall traders of the East End. But it was a different world. Those of us at that time in the early Fifties, back from the war, were still working our way back into Civvy Street, as well as Fleet Street. Still trying to find our post-war feet.

The Imprisoned Editor

In 1948 Bart had chosen Sylvester Bolam to succeed C.E. Thomas, the *Mirror*'s longest- serving editor, 1934–1948. A graduate of Durham University, Bolam began his career as a reporter on the *Newcastle Journal* in 1926; and after further experience as a sub-editor moved to Manchester, where he joined the *News Chronicle*. In 1936 he came to Fleet Street – and the *Daily Mirror* as a sub-editor at eleven guineas a week; and during the Second World War was, initially, joint night editor with Ted Castle before being appointed deputy editor.

When Bolam became editor, it was the period of a national emotional swing to the Left, and the hope of a better post-war world for the masses – crystalized by the *Daily Mirror*. Bolam could say later: 'All this was due to the inspiration of Bartholomew and the sense of purpose he created in the young men around him. I freely acknowledge the debt I owe him.' And one of Bolam's first acts upon assuming the editorship was to announce in a front-page manifesto: 'The *Mirror* is a sensational newspaper. We make no apology for that. We believe in the sensational presentation of news and views, especially important news and views, as a necessary and valuable service in these days of mass readership and democratic responsibility.'

Although sales of the *Daily Mirror* were now in excess of the *Daily Express*, his editorship was not without its problems, for in March 1949 the *Daily Mirror* – despite a police cautionary notice – published a number of statements concerning the Haigh acid-bath murder case, including the headline THE VAMPIRE CONFESSES. The *Mirror* was fined £10,000 and Bolam – who was not present when the offending article was published (it was amended for later editions) – after being admonished by the Lord Chief Justice, Lord Goddard, who 'had never seen such a contempt of court',[6] was sent to prison for three months. During his spell in Brixton, he was visited by Bartholomew, Cudlipp and Zec, who arrived in a chauffeur-driven Rolls-Royce and wished to discuss editorial business with him. As Bartholomew was to say: 'I bet that's the first and last formal meeting of newspaper directors ever held in jail.'

The only Fleet Street editor of the twentieth century to be so incarcerated, Bolam was later to say of his experience: 'The point about Brixton is that most executive journalists never get time to think. If you have eighteen hours a day by yourself for three months you have a valuable opportunity for reaching objectivity, for clearing your mind, for setting your sights. It was a most valuable experience.' After serving his sentence, he returned to the *Daily Mirror* as editor, but left in January 1953; he died suddenly while smoking a cigarette after breakfast three months later, on 27 April 1953.

His successor, nominated by Cudlipp, was to be Jack Nener; and, agreeing, King wrote: 'It is becoming clearer every day that the *Mirror* is drifting badly under Bolam. Nener is a good old warhorse with the qualities of courage and energy (and God knows the paper needs them) but he could not hold down the editorship without a great deal of help from you.' Jack Nener had entered journalism, aged fourteen, as a five-shillings-a-week apprentice on the *South Wales Daily Post*, Swansea.[7] He was to edit the *Daily Mirror* from 1953 until 1961, and take sales of the paper to more than four million copies a day. Tony Miles, a future chairman of the group, was to say:

> He was a man around whom newspaper legends had grown .... If Hollywood had asked a casting agency to supply someone to play a tough tabloid editor, a character like Jack Nener would have been sent along as the man most suited to the role. All the ingredients were there: crinkly silver hair, dapper bow tie, gravelly voice, gruff warmth, volcanic temperament. He was also a damned good editor.

The highlight of Nener's editorship was the Coronation Souvenir issue on 7 June 1953, when the paper sold an incredible seven million copies, the largest-ever figure by a daily newspaper in Great Britain. The lowlight was, probably, two years earlier, when on Election Day, Thursday 25 October 1951, in support of the Labour Party, the front page asked in bold headlines – with an accompanying drawing of a revolver by Jack Dunkley – 'WHOSE FINGER? Today YOUR finger is on the trigger. VOTE FOR THE PARTY YOU CAN REALLY TRUST. The *Daily Mirror* believes that party is Labour' This, one of the *Mirror*'s most famous front pages, was to lead Churchill to sue for libel. The case was settled out of court with Churchill receiving £1500 plus costs. Despite the *Mirror*'s backing, Labour lost the election and the Conservatives were victorious with an overall majority of seventeen.

Five years later there was to be another major libel case, when the American entertainer, Liberace, took exception to comments in Cassandra's column. The case, which was heard at the Royal Courts of Justice in 1959, cost the *Mirror* £8000 in damages and £27,000 in legal costs, leading Liberace to say: 'I cried all the way to the bank.'

Always direct, in January 1958, during a heated public debate on intrusion by the Press, Nener had written in the *Mirror*: 'This is a vigorous, outspoken newspaper. We will not hesitate to expose the buffooneries of public personalities when it is in the public interest to do so .... But we believe that news obtained at the cost of personal distress is not worth printing.' On his retirement in 1961, Nener and his wife, Audrey Whiting, one of the paper's leading writers, moved to the South of France, remaining there until 1970, when through ill health he returned to England. He died in 1982.

The Cudlipp Era

For almost twenty years the working relationship between Cecil King and Hugh Cudlipp had been close. King was to tell the Shawcross Commission: 'There is no policy committee. There are only two of us – Cudlipp and myself.' And much later Cudlipp was to write:[8]

> Cecil King took great care to supplement my street wisdom with wide-ranging dialogue, required reading, travel and discoursing with the world's leaders. When Lord Goodman [future chairman of the Newspaper Publishers Association] was making his solicitor's views of the human race even 'rounder', assuring his clients that he was 'on his way', I was benefitting by personal pow-wows with every Prime Minister from Churchill to Callaghan, flying to Tokyo to meet Mr Sato, to Delhi for a two-hour teach-in with Indira Gandhi (from whom I caught Asian 'flu), asking for Mr Soldatov at the Soviet Foreign Affairs Ministry in Moscow, walking nervously past the lions in the Palace courtyard at Addis Ababa on my way to chat up the Lion of Judah, touring Africa, and discussing the war in Vietnam off-the-record with the US President. I particularly enjoyed a jovial confrontation with Mr Khrushchev at a caviar and vodka nosh-up in St George's Hall, the Kremlin.

For Cudlipp, one of his first tasks on being appointed editorial director was to consider the growing threat from the launch of commercial television in 1956. Fortunately, King, with his advertising and financial background, had decided to take a stake in ATV, the company which served the London area. Both Cudlipp and King realized that commercial television would be the greatest danger to the mass-popular newspapers, of which the *Mirror*, with sales of five million, was undisputed market leader. They were to be so much more far-seeing than Beaverbrook's son, Max Aitken, when as Chairman he introduced his company's 1958 report:[9]

> It must be understood that the Beaverbrook Group is not engaged in television activity. We have been asked to go into television, but we have always taken the view that the *Daily Express* and television are in different fields, and that to attempt to engage in both at the present time could only damage the interests of the newspaper. It may be that time will test the judgement and confirm the decision .... Commercial television is not a medium suited to the presentation of many important products. There are instances in which results have been most disappointing and as the novelty of television wears off these examples are likely to increase rather than diminish.

As a means of countering the threat from commercial television, Cudlipp decided that the *Mirror* – unlike its main rival, the *Daily Express*, with its middle-aged readership – should concentrate more and more on youth; and on 12 October 1959 the paper splashed: New Mirror ... sparkling NEW ideas, NEW features, NEW contests, NEW writers. 'The blurb read: 'Sit back folks. Just look – and listen.' The *Mirror* was 'Gay ... Buoyant ... and moves with the times.' Abetting Cudlipp from 1961 in this move towards a more youthful readership was Lee Howard, who was to remain as editor for almost a decade. Following service during the Second World war in the RAF with Coastal Command, he transferred to the Operational Film Production Unit, winning the DFC in 1944. There, as a navigator/cameraman, in a Mosquito fighter-bomber flying at barely 50 ft., he filmed the results of the successful Dambusters Raid. On demobilization he joined the *Daily Mirror* picture desk, and was subsequently editor of the *Women's Sunday Mirror* in 1959 and then of the *Sunday Pictorial* in 1959 before assuming editorship of the *Mirror*.[10]

Known by his trademark of shirt-sleeves and bright red braces, Howard had none of the frenetic pace of his predecessor, Jack Nener; and he was in the words of Hugh Cudlipp aware 'that it was news that sold the *Mirror*, not views, entertainment, not policies'. He was married first to Sheila Black, the distinguished *Financial Times* writer, and then to Madelon Dimont, the *Mirror*'s Rome correspondent. Lee Howard died at Rome in November 1978, aged 64, and as Tony Miles was to write in the obituary: '[He was] one of those remarkable men who now and again emerge in Fleet Street and leave a legend behind them.'

So successful had been the Cudlipp format that on Tuesday 9 June 1964 'the *Mirror* was able to announce a world record average daily sale of five million copies – a readership, it claimed of 14 million, which meant that one in three of every adult in the country was now seeing the paper'. To celebrate the success, the *Mirror* threw a party at the Royal Albert Hall – and among the thousands attending were the Beatles. As Bill Hagerty, the paper's historian, was to write:[11]

> The 'sixties' did not really begin until 1963 – the *Mirror* worked hard to keep up with it. Sometimes the paper's capability to understand and adapt to social change had all the appearance of competitors in a three-legged race struggling not to be left behind by a champion sprinter, but efforts were made to embrace the new youth culture with pages devoted to rock and roll, mod fashion and teenage angst.

Meanwhile, chairman King, from his ninth-floor suite in the *Mirror*'s new building at Holborn Circus – built at a cost of £11 million and occupied since 1961 – was now presiding over a publishing group comprising twelve British newspapers, including two national dailies and two national Sundays, eleven overseas titles, 75 consumer magazines, 132 trade and technical journals plus interests in book publishing, printing and television – all of which constituted IPC (the International Publishing Corporation Ltd).

One of King's first tasks, in November 1955, had been to take back printing of the northern copies of the *Mirror* and *Pictorial* to Manchester, on the Kemsley-owned presses at Withy Grove. Not content, that same month – after protracted negotiations – he led the takeover of the *Daily Record* and *Sunday Mail* at Glasgow. And four years later, in the autumn of 1959, King, looking to widen the company's operations, bought for £18 million Amalgamated Press from Michael Berry (the future Lord Hartwell), owners of *Woman's Weekly*, *Woman and Home*, plus Kelly-Iliffe *Directories* and Imperial Paper Mills. Just prior to the deal, King telegraphed Cudlipp on a visit to Russia: 'Thinking of buying Uncle's old business in Farringdon Street stop. Cable your views but deal may have to be completed swiftly.' With Amalgamated Press showing profits of just £1 million a year, King felt that, through the efforts of the *Mirror* marketing department and by keeping a firm grip on production costs, the company could be turned around. Others at the *Mirror*, however, thought differently.

Nevertheless, King was now in a takeover mood; and twelve months later Odhams, the other magazine publishers, with printers, bill-posting – and, importantly, newspapers – came on the market. There was now to develop a two-horse race for the titles; for, apart from the *Mirror* group, Roy Thomson was also involved, and when King saw Thomson on television saying that no one could afford to make a counter-bid he offered 55*s*. for Odhams shares which were then valued at 40*s*. on the market. When King improved his offer to 63*s*. a share, valuing Odhams at £35 million, he was successful.

There was, however, to be one huge proviso. Appalled at the idea of two Labour-supporting titles, the *Daily Mirror* and the *Daily Herald*, being owned by one company, with the possibility of the latter title being subsumed by the *Mirror*, King was forced to agree that the *Herald* would be kept alive for seven years – a decision to be known to wags as 'King's Cross' – and that the paper's editor, John Beavan, should remain.

Christiansen Departs

While the *Mirror* had been making such strides, the strain of six-day-a-week editing the *Daily Express* was now about to take its toll on Arthur Christiansen, and in July 1956, while staying with Beaverbrook at his proprietor's residence, La Capponcina, near Monte Carlo, he suffered a heart attack. For the next few months, while he was recovering, his place was taken by Ted Pickering, deputy editor. Born at Middlesbrough, Pickering had entered journalism on the *Northern Echo*, before moving to the *Daily Mail*, where he rose to become chief sub- editor. Pickering served in the Army during the Second World War and then returned to the *Daily*

Mail under Frank Owen as managing editor 1947-49 until joining the *Daily Express*.[12]

With Pickering earmarked to take over as editor, Charles Wintour, deputy editor of the *Evening Standard*, was told by Beaverbrook that he would become managing editor, and as he was to say:[13]

> It was a dreadful job for which I was quite unsuited but, naturally, I accepted. Everything seemed to go reasonably well on my first day. Next day, to my astonishment, Christiansen turned up in the office and took over the morning conference, kindly welcoming me to the staff .... No one had dared to tell him that he was no longer editor.

Wintour then told Max Aitken and co-chairman Tom Blackburn that if Christiansen were to be in charge he would rather go back to the *Evening Standard*: 'Meanwhile I returned to the editorial floor and there was Christiansen .... assuming that normal service would soon be resumed .... In the end Blackburn was deputed to offer Christiansen a lush panelled office in the *Standard* and some grandiloquent title such as editorial consultant'.

Beaverbrook wrote to him: 'When you emerge from your contact with the *Evening Standard* you will roll me over in commerce as you have always done in journalism.' But, failing to adjust to his new role, he resigned, and on 5 November 1959 the *Daily Express* announced that Arthur Christiansen, editor from 1933 to 1957, was leaving Beaverbrook Newspapers:

> His departure is marked by profound regret from the whole of the Beaverbrook Organisation. Mr Christiansen is 55. He joined the Beaverbrook Group in 1926, and seven years later, when he was twenty-nine, became Britain's youngest national newspaper editor. His years on the *Daily Express* were a brilliant era in both the writing and the presentation of the newspaper. The front page became the most imitated front page in British journalism. Mr Christiansen said in New York – he has been the guest of 800 bankers – that credit for that belongs to Lord Beaverbrook. 'What I can claim to have done on my own was to revolutionise the appearance of British newspapers.'

A little over a month later, on 13 December, Beaverbrook hosted a glittering black-tie dinner in honour of Christiansen at Claridge's. And among the many editors and famous columnists present were Hugh Cudlipp, Percy Cudlipp, Herbert Gunn, Francis Williams, Tom Driberg and Hannen Swaffer, who said of Christiansen: 'Under him the *Daily Express* became the most vital, imitated paper in Fleet Street.' And from Frank Owen: 'I do not know of a finer editor.'

The dinner opened on a note of much levity, Beaverbrook saying: 'Will all those who work on the *Daily Express* kindly leave the top table.' Then, with a twinkle in his eye: 'Will all those whom Christiansen has sacked please come to the top table!' No fewer than twenty-one of the guests had been fired by Christiansen. Yet they all went to the top table at the Beaver's bidding.

Beaverbrook, who had been worried about Christiansen's health, was to provide a handsome pension of £3000 a year and £35,000 in cash; and on 18 January 1960 he wrote from his home at Cherkley, near Leatherhead:[14]

Dear Chris,

'Thou hast scattered thine enemies with thy arm',
With congratulations,
Yours sincerely,
Beaverbrook

Christiansen was delighted – especially as the previous day he had been honoured by his peers at a dinner in the Press Club.

For the next few months, Christiansen was engaged in writing his memoirs, *Headlines All My Life*, which was to prove a bestseller. In the autumn he sent the manuscript to Beaverbrook, now on business in his native-Canada, and on 17 October he replied from the Beaverbrook Art Gallery, Frederickton:[15]

> My Dear Chris:
>
> I read your manuscript. It is a magnificent production and you are entitled to a very considerable sale. I have told the *Daily Express* they should buy the serial rights and I have asked that you should be given a good price for them.
>
> When your book comes out, the *Daily Express* should make a fuss about it, also the *Evening Standard* and the *Sunday Express*. Once more, I congratulate you on a brilliant piece of work,
>
> And with good regards,
> Yours ever,
> Beaverbrook

After leaving Fleet Street, Christiansen then appeared as editor of the *Daily Express* in an excellent film, *The Day the Earth Caught Fire*, but he was to devote most of his attention to television, writing: 'One medium of communication is new; the other is old. It will be fun to have straddled the twin giants in one life-time.' Unfortunately, his new career was of short duration: on 27 September 1963 he collapsed suddenly and died in a television studio at Norwich.

The Chronicle *Closes*

While Christiansen's autobiography was being well received in Fleet Street, from nearby Bouverie Street there was nothing but gloom – and on Monday 17 October 1960 it was announced that the *News Chronicle* had been merged with the *Daily Mail*, and its sister evening title, *The Star*, had been absorbed by the *Evening News*.

Very much involved in the sale was Walter Layton, who since the early 1930s had been chairman and in editorial charge of both titles. Once in command, he began to move the *Chronicle* to the left, a fact noticed by Lloyd George, when asked by Layton for assistance to start a Sunday paper with 'an advanced progressive policy'. Although Lloyd George was in agreement the title was not launched.

One of Layton's first moves was to dismiss Aylmer Vallance from the editorship of the *News Chronicle* in 1936, after a brief two years' tenure, for disagreeing with the proprietors on political and personal matters. He was succeeded by Gerald Barry, who had joined as features editor from the *New Statesman* two years earlier.

Although Barry and Layton were apparently friendly, differences were to emerge, notably the suppression by Layton of a leading article on the eve of Chamberlain's departure to Munich in 1938. Layton, a man of profound silences and hesitations, believed in 'responsible journalism', and this was very apparent on the day Chamberlain announced 'Peace for Our Time'.

With the appointment by Winston Churchill of Layton as Director-General of Programmes, Ministry of Supply in 1940, Barry had a new chairman in Laurence Cadbury, who was to be another person intent on editorial interference.

Barry's days were obviously numbered, but he was to remain editor until 1947, when disagreements with the returned Layton caused him to resign. Barry was to say that Layton wanted to decide everything that appeared in the paper – 'and I'm left as a kind of office boy'. One night when Barry returned from the Café Royal and found that once again Layton had been amending his leader, it proved too much: 'I'm the bloody editor. He's only the chairman.'[16] Barry restored the leader. On 10 March 1948, Barry was appointed director-general of the Festival of Britain, and its opening by George VI in 1951 heralded a great success. That same year he was knighted.

Throughout the early 1950s, the circulation of the *News Chronicle* continued to fall, leading Beaverbrook to write to Layton, suggesting that he would help to fund a management buy-out. (As part of the deal, Beaverbrook would put in Tom Blackburn, a senior manager, to run the paper.)

> I know nothing of the facts but if you want to buy those papers I would be glad to provide money for you. The basis of the arrangement I would suggest would be as follows. The policy of the paper and also the production of the newspapers would be entirely your responsibility. And I would not interfere. The business side would rest with me. You would deal with the situation openly and frankly leaving control in the keeping of yourself and your associates. We will make a community of interest between the *Express* and the *News Chronicle* which will be publicly declared.[17]

Although pleased with the offer, Layton declined gracefully, stating that the Cadbury family had no wish to sell and he, approaching seventy, considered that he was too old to embrace a new venture. There was also another reason: the papers were profitable; and in September 1955, when the price of the *News Chronicle* was raised from three-halfpence to twopence, it was noted that only once in the past twenty-four years had the paper been in the red; and as Layton could report:

> Today, at twopence, both papers are comfortably paying their way. This record shows that it is possible for a pair of associated papers which have received no subsidy from any outside source for many decades to hold their own simply on their merits. It is a terrific fight, but a very interesting one and well worth the effort.

Less than two months later, on 21 November 1955 – much to the surprise of Fleet Street – Lord Kemsley sold his Manchester-based *Daily Dispatch* (circulation 463,00) to the Cadbury family, and its absorption by the *News Chronicle* meant that overnight the paper had gained an extra 300,000 sales.

However, this was about to change: in 1957 the end of newsprint rationing meant that the more popular newspapers could immediately up-page, thereby carrying extra advertising and editorial – and the chief victim of this was to be the *News Chronicle*, which, even with sales of 1,162,000, 'by the standards of modern advertising is a very modest circulation indeed'. (In three years the *News Chronicle* had forfeited 257,000 readers and *The Star* more than 160,000.) Having suffered a loss of more than £100,000 in 1959, the paper was projected to suffer even further in 1960, with a deficit of £300,000.

For chairman Laurence Cadbury there now appeared to be only one way out; and on 5 October he wrote to Lord Rothermere:

> The fact that we should not be able, through economic reasons, to carry on our two newspapers distresses me greatly, but it must be faced .... We feel a considerable responsibility towards our readers and with this in mind I have discussed with you the prospect of the *News Chronicle* joining up with the *Daily Mail* .... We also feel that the *Evening News* is the natural home for *The Star* readers.

Replying, Rothermere said that he would 'do everything to help' and would place 'a large cash sum to enable you to safeguard your pensioners and give reasonable compensation to your staffs'.

On 20 October, three days after the demise of the *News Chronicle*, chairman Layton and fellow-director Geoffrey Crowther wrote to *The Times*, giving their reasons:[18]

> As the only members of the Daily News Trust who are not connected with the Cadbury family, we would like to place on record the fact that we entirely concurred in the decision to sell the *News Chronicle* and the *Star* to Associated Newspapers Ltd. To our infinite regret we could see no preferable alternative.
>
> First, the decision to sell the papers now was made in the interests of the staff. No doubt they could have struggled on for a long time yet. But that would have been justified only if there were a real hope of getting back fairly quickly to a profitable basis. We lost this hope some time ago ....
>
> The economics of the newspaper industry are very cruel to a popular paper with a relatively small circulation. It can sell less advertising space than its rivals, and therefore can give its readers less editorial matter to read. Inevitably it appears to offer less for the money. So its circulation ebbs away and advertisements are still harder to get.
>
> The second point follows the first. Why did we not accept any of the offers that were made to buy the papers and continue them? If the interests of the staff were to be protected, any prospective purchaser would have to establish that he had enough money not only to provide working capital and to meet the trading deficits but also, if and when he eventually failed, to provide the very large sum for the staff that is now available. No offer backed by any such sums was ever made.
>
> Thirdly, why all the secrecy and the suddeness? Why was there no prior consultations with the unions, other newspapers, the Liberal Party, and everybody else who is now claiming that he might have been able to think of something that might have helped? The reason for this is obvious. Associated Newspapers Ltd. (who have acted with great patience and understanding) were willing to pay a very substantial sum of money for the two papers – but only on the reasonable condition that they should have the maximum possible start over their competitors in the efforts to hold the circulation of the *News Chronicle* and the *Star*.

The decision was to bring heaps of opprobium upon the *Chronicle*'s management, and one of the first critics was to be James Cameron, himself a distinguished writer on the paper, who on 21 October wrote in his local *West London Press*:

> The death of the *News Chronicle* is the biggest journalistic tragedy for many years – I think it is the most meaningful collapse the newspaper business has seen in my generation .... Its greatest opportunities opened out before it, and it surrendered, because there was nothing at the top but timidity, conventionality and emptiness. In its closing days, the *News Chronicle* was a potential warhorse ridden by grocers. And thus it died, and a great number of the most gifted, loyal, frustrated, trained, perceptive and heartbroken men and women are now without a job, while the grocers survive.

Years later, Johnnie Johnson, a journalist on the paper, was to say that, with many of his colleagues, he went along to the nearby Press Club in Salisbury Square, where, amid the wake for the *Chronicle*, he was offered jobs on three Fleet Street titles.[19]

Cameron, though, was to follow his outburst in the *West London Press* with an article in *Reynolds' News*, a paper which was itself facing closure: 'Towards the end the *News Chronicle* may have been insecure, indefinite, compensating for vigour here by fatuity there, but it stood for something outside the Establishment .... Perhaps, after all, blood and tears would have been a better proposition than cocoa and water.'

There was to be an even more vituperative comment from Lady Violet Bonham Carter, who in a letter to Layton, one of her oldest friends, wrote:

> You must (of course) realise the pain and the utter bewilderment which the tragedy of the *News Chronicle* has brought to those who have given it their unswerving love and loyalty for countless years. Not only the fact of its death – but the manner of it – has shocked thousands who did not share its ideology and looked to it for light and leading and the expressions of their faith.

Continuing, she remarked upon the meetings that had been held – and attempted – during the previous months between leading Liberal figures, concerned at the finances and future of the paper, and the *Chronicle* management. At these meetings, the politicians had received no information.

> If Laurence Cadbury did not feel willing to continue to lose £100,000 a year at the paper no-one could force him to (though his TV station acquired by right of having a paper must have helped to cushion the loss). But surely you could, or should, have given its friends a chance of saving it – body and soul? Which they might well have done. The compensation money of £1.5 million would not have been necessary had it (the paper) continued in being. And it would have been a better paper.

Two years after the failure of the *News Chronicle* it was to feature strongly in the 1962 Royal Commission on the Press. Beaverbrook told the Commission:[20] 'It had no management. It passed from one weak management to another weak management with divided counsels. It had no will to survive. If they had placed it in the hands of any good man he would have been able to build it up.'

Another witness, Roy Thomson, told the Commission that he had been approached to buy the *News Chronicle* before its closure:

> I seriously considered it and discussed it, and I wanted to take it. We examined all the pros and cons, and we came up against the fact that if I could not make it go and I had to close it, in two years I would have faced a redundancy problem of two or three million pounds. That is what I had to face in the purchase of the *News Chronicle* and I would not do so. I would have taken it had there been no liability to face in connection with redundancy, and I would have run it. It would have been running today. I would have liked to have the *News Chronicle* and I think I could have saved it, but I was not sure and I could not afford to gamble two or three million pounds.

After receiving much written and oral evidence, the Commissioners considered that the *News Chronicle*'s main problem had been a lack of newspaper sales. 'When newsprint control was removed the full extent of the circulation struggle became apparent.' The Commission concluded:

> We are bound to say that the majority of witnesses who expressed their opinion on the matter blamed the management of the newspaper for the result. It is no part of our function to apportion responsibility in this matter, but we cannot escape the conclusion that the failure of the *News Chronicle* was not entirely the result of the inevitable law of newspaper economics; different and more consistent managerial and editorial policy may have saved this newspaper.

King is Dethroned

While the *News Chronicle* had suffered the harsh reality of being absorbed, life was very different for the *Daily Mirror*: the paper still had the highest daily circulation, and profits remained high – even though over-manning was rife in the production areas. As the Royal Commission on the Press 1961–62 was to report:[21]

> In national newspapers it would not be unreasonable to look for a reduction of about one third in the wages bill. The Daily Mirror Newspapers Ltd. examined its own staffing at our special request to see what could be saved if the staffing accorded with the management's assessment of what was reasonably required to publish the newspapers. It concluded that of the staffs in the machine rooms, publishing rooms and transport sections of the *Daily Mirror* and *Sunday Pictorial* – the departments employing the bulk of the wage-earners – nearly forty per cent could be dispensed with. The conclusion was strikingly confirmed by the independent report of Personnel Administration Ltd.

With such a profitable operation, there was no way that the *Mirror* would endeavour to reducing manning levels and suffer probable production stoppages – that would have to wait for another day and another owner . . . . Meanwhile, market share of the Mirror Group newspapers had increased dramatically over the past thirteen years, as the following tables show:

1948	%
Beaverbrook Newspapers	16
Associated Newspapers	14
Kemsley Newspapers	13
Top three	43

1961	%
Daily Mirror group	27
Associated Newspapers	19
Beaverbrook Newspapers	19
Top three	65

The continuing growth and profits of the *Daily Mirror*, under the forceful editorial direction of Hugh Cudlipp, meant that more and more the chairman – described by *Newsweek* as 'a tall massive man with cool, accusative eyes, a beaky nose, a heavy jaw, a bull neck and a charming smile' – was in the public limelight. Interviewed on television he was asked 'Why are you in journalism at all? What are you using your newspaper for?'[22] King replied: 'I think I have tried to serve the interests of my readers who are virtually the country – 43 per cent of all adults over the age of sixteen read the *Mirror* every day.' 'Are you trying to lead them?' King responded: 'It isn't the business of a newspaper to lead; it's the business of a politician to lead and a newspaper to comment. I think leadership should be supplied by the Prime Minister, and the newspaper should comment.' In the light of the happenings in May 1968, this was, indeed, a strange response.

Thanks to support from the *Daily Mirror*, Labour were successful in the 1964 election, and, in gratitude, Prime Minister Harold Wilson offered King a life peerage, and then the post of Minister of State at the Board of Trade. Neither was suitable for King, but the following year he did agree to become a director of the Bank of England. More and more King was becoming disenchanted with Wilson's premiership; and early in 1968 he told Frank Rogers, managing director of IPC, 'that he expected to be playing some part in the running of the country,' adding, 'Of course I shall be taking Hugh with me.'

On 19 February, *The Guardian* on its front page ran a story headed:[23]

> Making a new start with a Coalition Government.
> MR CECIL KING LEADING THE SOUNDINGS
> The leading figure in all this seems to be Mr King himself and the proposal is that if an embryonic coalition were found to exist a number of people and newspapers would, at a given signal, all announce simultaneously their separate convictions that the Wilson Government should be suspended by a radical coalition.

The following month, at an editorial dinner organized by Cudlipp, there was strong opposition to King's plans from Sydney Jacobson, now editorial director of the *Sun* and the *People*, and John Beavan, political editor of the *Daily* and *Sunday Mirror*.

Nevertheless, King was determined to proceed, and his appearance on BBC television was to lead to headlines in editor Donald Trelford's *Observer*: 'WILSON MUST GO, SAYS KING'.

On 8 May Cudlipp arranged a meeting between King and Lord Mountbatten at the latter's London home at which Sir Solly Zuckerman, the Government's chief scientific adviser, was also to be present; and as Bill Hagerty, the *Mirror*'s historian, was to write:

> Cudlipp . . . . recalled Cecil waiting for Zuckerman to arrive before giving his views on the parlous state of the nation and the need for urgent action. He envisaged 'bloodshed in the streets' and the involvement of the armed forces. In such circumstances would Mountbatten agree to be the titular head of an emergency administration, King inquired? Mountbatten then asked Zuckerman what he thought and Sir Solly, heading for the door

> . . . . paused long enough to say: 'This is rank treachery. All this talk of machine guns at street corners is appalling. I am a public servant and will have nothing to do with it. Nor should you, Dickie.' After Zuckerman had left, Mountbatten told King that his participation was 'simply not on'.

Two days later, on Friday 10 May 1968 – having resigned his directorship of the Bank of England – King in a signed article on the front page of the *Daily Mirror*, with massive headlines announcing ENOUGH IS ENOUGH and a side heading proclaiming DISASTER AT THE POLLS FOR LABOUR, wrote:

> The results of the local elections are fully confirming the verdicts of the opinion polls and of the Dudley by-election. Mr Wilson and his Government have lost all credibility; all authority.
>
> The Government which was voted into office with so much goodwill only three and a half years ago has revealed itself as lacking in foresight, in administrative ability, in political sensitivity. Mr Wilson is seen to be a brilliant Parliamentary tactician and nothing more.
>
> If these disastrous years only marked the decline of Mr Wilson and the Labour party, the damage to our political self-confidence would be serious enough, but the Labour Party came into power with such high hopes . . . .
>
> We are now threatened with the greatest financial crisis in our history. It is not to be removed by lies about our reserves, but only by a fresh start under a fresh leader. It is up to the Parliamentary Labour Party to give us that leader – and soon.

The article created a sensation with much condemnation from politicians; and as historian Ben Pimlott was to write: 'King's attack, one of the most blatant examples of a press chief seeking to exert power without responsibility since Stanley Baldwin's famous remark, saved the Prime Minister from more dangerous critics.'[24]

Asked by reporters what he thought of King's outburst, Wilson, in Bristol that day discussing regional problems, told a Press conference: 'I hope that newspaper proprietors will always be free to find as much space in their newspapers as other citizens.' There was immediate support from Richard Crossman – a former *Mirror* columnist, now Lord President of the Council: 'Mr King should take warning from the fate that attended his uncle Lord Rothermere's attempt to dictate Cabinet changes from the newspaper proprietor's office over thirty years ago.'

Randolph Churchill, always the outspoken critic, demanded: 'How fit is King to be Chairman of the International Publishing Corporation?' Within less than a fortnight he was to find out . . . . And Colin Valdar, a former editor of the *Sunday Pictorial*, now founder/editor of the *UK Press Gazette*, wrote: 'Close readers of "Enough is Enough" might sense the act of a man clearing up some unfinished business before emptying his desk drawers for his successor . . . . In pencil, perhaps, one might mark the file "Cecil King's Last Stand." '

Appalled at the reaction to the article, the directors of IPC, by a unanimous vote, now sought King's resignation; and early on the morning of 29 May the company secretary, John Chandler, delivered a letter, signed by every director, to King's Hampton Court home. Coming from the deputy chairman, Hugh Cudlipp, it said, in part:[25]

> The feeling is that your increasing preoccupation and intervention in national affairs in a personal sense rather than in the more objective publishing sense has created a situation between you and your colleagues which is detrimental to the present and future conduct of the business of IPC.
>
> It has been decided that the retirement age for Chairmen of IPC should be sixty-five, in keeping with the rule laid down by you for all other directors; that you should therefore retire immediately as Chairman. It has also been decided that I should succeed you as IPC Chairman . . . .
>
> Our view, again unanimous, is that the best course would be for you to announce your resignation tomorrow, Thursday.

Receiving no response, the following day, 30 May, Cudlipp, after once more having the unanimous backing of the directors, wrote, '. . . . the letter which was delivered to you this morning still stands. Accordingly, therefore, you have ceased to be the Chairman and a director of IPC.' Within minutes, King had phoned Independent Television News and this was followed with a call to the BBC. For the next twenty-four hours the dismissal of King was to be a major item on television news and in the newspapers.

The final word goes to Marmaduke Hussey, then managing director of Associated Newspapers:

> Cecil King ruled the newspaper world. He was chairman of the Newspaper Proprietors Association and confidant of prime ministers . . . . It fell to me to ring Esmond [Viscount Rothermere II, his chairman] and tell him. He was in tremendous form. 'There you are,' he shouted down the telephone, 'it's all arrogance. Cecil was arrogant, De Gaulle was arrogant, and they've fallen on the same day. Serves them right.'[26]

The Sun Rises

While the *Mirror* had been continuing on its profitable way, the group now had a major problem: the *Daily Herald*. In agreeing not to refer the Odhams takeover to the competition authorities in 1960, Labour leader Hugh Gaitskell – fearing that Cecil King wished to merge the paper with the *Daily Mirror*, thereby increasing the *Mirror*'s circulation by some one million – received an assurance that the *Herald* would continue as a separate title for seven years. And in the *Mirror*, King signed a short piece which Cudlipp had written:

1. The future of the *Herald* as a separate entity would be fought for with the utmost energy.
2. No amalgamation of the *Daily Herald* and *Daily Mirror* would ever take place during the period of the Mirror Group's control of Odhams.

George Brown, a future Foreign Secretary in a Labour government, was to write of the take-over: 'I was certain that the *Herald*, which the Labour Party badly needed, would be better off in the hands of Cudlipp and King. This put me rather at loggerheads with Gaitskell.'

However, with many of the *Herald*'s older readership dying and the market profile not popular with advertising agencies, the paper was losing more than £1 million a year. Research had shown that the paper's 59 per cent male readership was the highest of all morning titles, and, with the largest C2 DE profile, it was a state of affairs that could not continue. When Harold Wilson, following Gaitskell's sudden death at the age of 56, assumed leadership of the Labour Party, it was just the opportunity that King needed to renegotiate the deal. Pledging continuing Labour support from the *Mirror*, King was able to secure Wilson's agreement that the *Herald* should be relaunched as the *Sun*, a paper aimed at an entirely different market – a market directed at a younger, more affluent readership. Cudlipp, who had long considered that 'it was a bloated, listless boa constrictor suffering from a fatty degeneration of the heart', was in complete accord.

Prior to the launch, Cecil King had commissioned a survey by Dr Mark Abrahams, of Sussex University, entitled *The Newspaper Reading Public of Tomorrow*.[27] Pointing out that young people were better educated than their parents, and that commercial television was now their main entertainment medium, it added that leisure time for these pace-setters was of extreme importance. The report just confirmed the thoughts of King and Cudlipp who, with *Herald* editor Sydney Jacobson began planning the paper.

King having persuaded the Trades Union Council to sell IPC its 49 per cent shareholding and to agree that this new paper should be aimed at 'a middle-class couple, aged 28, with two children and living in Reading', who had Socialist sympathies, the way was now clear for a launch in September 1964. Established as 'The Paper Born of the Age We Live In', it proclaimed in its first issue:

> We welcome the age of automation, electronics, computers. We will campaign for the rapid modernisation of Britain . . . .
>
> Look how life has changed. Our children are better educated. The mental horizons of their parents has widened through travel, higher living standards and TV . . . .
>
> Steaks, cars, houses, refrigerators, washing-machines are no longer the prerogative of the 'upper crust', but the right of all. People believe, and the *Sun* believes with them, that the division of Britain into social classes is happily out of date.
>
> The New Woman: The present role of British women is the most significant and fruitful change in our social life. Women are no longer trapped between four walls. They are released from household drudgery by labour-saving devices, gadgets and intelligent house-planning. In 1938 only one married woman in ten went to work: the figure is now ONE in THREE and will soon increase . . . . Women are the pace-setters now.

After a spectacular first-day figure of 3,500,000 within less than a week sales had tumbled to 1,750,000; and 'unloved and under-financed it staggered on through the 1960s with its circulation sinking down towards the million'. Many years later, Jean Rook, the 'First Lady of Fleet Street', who had been engaged as fashion editor, was to write in her autobiography, *The Cowardly Lioness*:[28]

> The still-under-wraps, not-yet-published *Sun* had been the talk of Fleet Street, radio and TV for weeks. Its rising was to be a new, shining era in journalism. IPC's *Sun* was to be a

> brilliant morning broadsheet which would singe the eyes out of worshipping readers. And any journalist who joined it would be an overnight star. It didn't happen that way, of course .... On 15 September 1964, the *Sun* rose at dawn, in the biggest blaze of TV advertising in newspaper history. Even by 9 a.m the damned thing looked as if it was setting .... Its only glow was its red-blood politics, and they were decades out of date.

The new *Sun* failed; and Cudlipp was later to write: 'We couldn't play a new tune on the old *Herald* fiddle, not at least convincingly. Jacobson edited the new/old newspaper for its first year, followed by Dick Dinsdale when Sydney became Editorial Director of both the Odhams newspapers.' After eight years, sales of the *Herald* and *Sun* had fallen to 900,000 and the combined losses were more than £12,700,000.

With the seven-year pledge to the Labour Party and unions to continue producing the *Herald* and then *The Sun* about to pass, in the spring of 1969 Cudlipp as Chairman of IPC and Frank Rogers as managing director asked the Newspaper Division to come forward with a viable plan for the paper. At a board meeting of IPC held on 15 July the decision was taken that it would not be possible to produce the *Sun* after January 1970. Cudlipp was faced with four choices: he could shut down the paper with the loss of two thousand jobs and incur the wrath of the unions and probable industrial action on other IPC publications; he could merge the paper with the *Mirror* – again likely to cause industrial unrest; he could take the paper down market and go head-to-head with the *Mirror*; or he could sell the title.

In the event he decided to sell the paper. The last edition of the IPC *Sun* was published on Saturday 15 November 1969 – and two days later the Murdoch-owned *Sun* had risen .... [29]

18

Death of Beaverbrook

ON 25 MAY 1964, in honour of Lord Beaverbrook's 85th birthday, Lord Thomson hosted a great dinner at the Dorchester with six hundred guests. Beaverbrook, confined to a wheelchair, had been unwell for weeks and knew that he was dying of cancer. He feared that the great dinner would be too much of an ordeal. For days before the occasion he had scribbled fragments of his speech on scraps of paper. He had tried recording the speech but it was no good: his voice was too feeble. He was advised not to go – but Beaverbrook must have realised that this was to be his final public appearance.

He was driven to the Dorchester in the late afternoon and taken upstairs in a wheelchair. 'When the moment came he rose from his chair, balanced himself on Max Aitken's arm and walked sturdily to his place at the top table practically unaided.' It was a moment 'etched in the memory of everyone present'. As Hugh Cudlip was later to write:[1]

> There were six hundred of us, of all ages and most professions, happy or proud for one reason or another to be at the last gathering of the tribe, regarding the guest of honour either with awe or, with qualifications, affection. Nobody present, I reckon, has forgotten the nerve-tingling atmosphere of the occasion, as spellbinding as the last act of a Verdi opera without the scenery or the music or lighting effects. The compelling personality of the man, now physically frail and dying, was undiminished. Everybody knew, including Beaverbrook, that this was the last performance.

John Junor, editor of the *Sunday Express*, was to say: 'I wept for him. But at that dinner, after pedestrian speeches from Roy Thomson and Lord Rothermere, Max Lord Beaverbrook stood up and made a speech with such vigour, such wonder, that tears of pride came to my eyes.'[2]

In strong, clear tones, Beaverbrook declared that his theme was to be that of the 'Apprentice'. First an apprentice to finance in Canada: that was a life of daring adventure. Then London:

> And then I decided to become an apprentice in politics. After the war I became an apprentice in Fleet Street. And that was a real exciting experience. At last, I thought, I will be a Master. Fancy free. Instead, I became a slave of the Black Art. I did not know freedom for many a year.

He then spelled out his definition of a good journalist:

> First, he must be true to himself. The man who is not true to himself is no journalist. He must show courage, independence and initiative. He must also, I believe, be a man of optimism. He has no business to be a pedlar of gloom and despondency. He must be a respecter of persons, but able to deal with the highest and the lowest on the same basis, which is regard for the public interest and a determination to get at the facts. I take more pride in my experience as a journalist than any other experience I have had in my long and varied life.

The peroration was perfect:

> This is my final word. It is time for me to become an apprentice once more. I have not settled in which direction. But somewhere, sometime soon.

To uproarious applause and the strains of 'For He's a Jolly Good Fellow', he was escorted by Max Aitken into an anteroom. There he met his host, Lord Thomson, once more and Eric Cheadle, Thomson's right-hand man, who had organized the affair. Cheadle played back a recording of Beaverbrook's speech. With a twinkle in his eye, Beaverbrook then looked up at his son and said: 'There, Max, that's the way to do it!'

Beaverbrook returned to Cherkley that night, but, although mainly confined to a wheelchair, he was still actively involved in the *Daily Express*, and on 7 June, appalled at the previous year's editorial expenses, summoned Robert Edwards, the paper's editor, to Cherkley:[3]

> The sun was shining as usual as I was shown into the garden. He was sitting on a wickerwork seat outside the library with his feet on another. From chest to ankles he was covered in an old-fashioned car rug. He smiled at me genially. 'By God, Bob,' he said, after telling me the dreadful sum that had been spent, 'I'm going to sort out this racket if it's the last thing I do before I die. Will you support a reign of terror?' I said that most naturally I would, of course.

It was not to be – Beaverbrook died three days later on 10 June 1964.

'Young Max' In Charge

For the new proprietor, John William Maxwell Aitken, known for much of his life as 'Young Max', it had been a long wait. Aged fifty-four when he took over, he had been born in Montreal, Canada, and educated at Westminster School and Cambridge University. He was to served an extensive apprenticeship within the company, starting as a Linotype operator during vacations in the 1930s, and for this work the London Society of Compositors had even presented him with a membership card. His apprenticeship was broken for two years when he went to California as a pilot for Lockheed, and his return to England, Lord Beaverbrook said: 'Let's get on with the newspapers.'

Max Aitken's management roles had included spells of running the Glasgow operation, the *Evening Standard* and the *Daily Express* before becoming chairman of Beaverbrook Newspapers Ltd in 1955. His father, though, remained head of the Beaverbrook Foundation, which controlled the majority of the voting stock, while a long-serving executive, Tom Blackburn (later knighted), became executive chairman of the company.

Relationship between father and son had – despite the odd differences – been extremely close. Beaverbrook had even told an interviewer: 'Well I'm proud of my son. He's a fine fellow. He's a nicer man than I was. A much nicer man.' However, a few months before Beaverbrook's death, his almost-daily criticisms of the management of the papers had led a disillusioned Max Aitken to remonstrate for the first time:[4]

> I respect your judgement and along with all Fleet Street acknowledge your absolute leadership in journalism. For some thirty years I have gratefully accepted your criticism, usually I hope with good grace. But lately all we do or don't do is muddle and muddle. I agree some of our mistakes are silly but some of our successes are magnificent . . . . When you used to work at the office with your coat off, you drove everyone hard but you also made them laugh and feel that they were on the 'sunny side of the street'. This is still necessary and some of it must come from the master however far away he may be. Therefore I hope you will continue to hold us by the hand each and every day and beam an occasional smile our way.

Aitken, who had learnt to fly at Cambridge University, was already a member of the crack 601 Squadron when war was declared on 3 September 1939. He was among the bravest of the brave, in the midst of the fighting at the fall of France and in the Battle of Britain. During the remaining war years he commanded a Czech night fighter squadron before in 1943 leading a fighter group in the Middle East; and from 1944 he headed an anti-shipping strike wing based in Scotland. Refusing all promotion above group captain, so that he could continue flying, he ended the war in charge of the largest wing of Mosquitoes in Britain. A much decorated man with the DSO, DFC and Czech War Cross, having destroyed sixteen enemy aircraft, he was always proud to recall that he was in the air on the day war began and still in the air on the day it ended.

Sir Max Aitken – saying that there would be only one Lord Beaverbrook in his lifetime and having assumed the baronetcy – was about to inherit an organization which, during the previous decade, had seen dramatic changes in its leading personnel. E.J. Robertson, for more than thirty years the business head of the group, had suffered a stroke in 1955 and had lingered on for another five years; and Arthur Christiansen, the great editor of the *Daily Express*, had suffered a heart attack in July 1956 and left two years later for a career in television.

Christiansen's replacement was to be his deputy, Edward Pickering,[5] former managing editor of the *Daily Mail*, who was to be in charge at the *Express* from 1957 until 1961 and a director of Beaverbrook Newspapers, 1956–64. He then moved to Daily Mirror Newspapers as editorial director and four years later became chairman 1968–70. During those years he was also a director of the *Scottish Daily Record* and *Sunday Mail*. He had also been chairman of Mirror Group Newspapers, IPC Magazines and IPC Newspaper Division. He was knighted in 1977; and was to be be actively involved with the Press Council, the Commonwealth Press Union and the Stationers' Company. He became executive vice-chairman of Times Newspapers Ltd. in 1982; and he died on 8 August 2003.

His successsor as editor of the *Daily Express* was Bob Edwards, a former reporter on *The People* and then, for three years, editor of *Tribune*, transforming it from a *New Statesman/Spectator*-style weekly to a paper directed at Labour Party activists and political commentators, with a perceptible increase in sales. In 1955 he joined the *Evening Standard* as a leader writer, but 'wrote few leaders and many articles on social subjects'. Then he was persuaded to ghost articles for Beaverbrook under the pseudonym 'Richard Strong'. After declining to support the Suez War, he was appointed deputy editor of the *Sunday Express* in 1957, deputy editor of the *Daily Express in* 1959 and editor in 1961, and under his guidance sales reached a record figure of 4,328,525 – and he was fired nine months later.[6]

A Siberian period followed as editor of the Beaverbrook-owned Glasgow *Evening Citizen*, which he adored, but a year later he was restored as editor of the *Daily Express*. He survived this time for three years until, following Beaverbrook's death, he was fired by Sir Max Aitken. Hugh Cudlipp rescued him. He became editor of *The People* from 1966 until 1972, and of the *Sunday Mirror* for a record thirteen years.

Already cracks were beginning to appear in the Group. Beaverbrook believed that he ran his papers purely for the purpose of propaganda and with no other motive, and it was publish at any price, for which he was not averse to paying high wages. In January 1948 he had informed his managing director: 'I don't care whether we make money or not. All I want to see, Mr Robertson, is a great newspaper, strong in reserves and so completely and absolutely set up in finance that no other newspaper can ever challenge us. Even after you and I have laid down our task, Mr Robertson.'

Although a profitable formula for his own newspapers, it had a detrimental effect on less-successful groups, and as Cecil King was to write:

> For ten years I was chairman of the NPA and for many years before that had been a member of the Council representing my paper. The perennial problem before the London newspaper publishers was uneconomically high wages and massive over-manning. As the print unions always acted together, the only way the proprietors could hope to stand up to them was to stand together also. But whatever pledges were made or undertakings signed, when the crunch came the *Express* broke the united front. At an earlier stage in the history of the *Express* Beaverbrook calculated that he could afford to meet the extravagant demands of the unions while his rivals could not, but of course in the end the *Express* finances were as embarrassed as anyone else.

Thirty years ago, when newsprint was just £20 per ton compared with more than £300 in the 1970s, profits seemed endless. But, unlike other national newspaper groups, Beaverbrook was not structured to weather the lean years. Most groups had extensive interests outside the national newspapers, which acted as a buffer against the notorious fluctuations of Fleet Street. If Beaverbrook Newspapers had invested in commercial television, for instance, then its future might well have been different.

Coote Comes Aboard

In 1966, John Coote, a former submarine captain and close friend of Sir Max Aitken, was appointed managing director of the *Evening Standard*, and was later to write in *Altering Course: a Submariner in Fleet Street*:[7]

> The *Evening Standard* [was] in a run-down building on Shoe Lane near the Holborn Viaduct . . . . Beaverbrook was rightly proud of having started the Sunday newspaper from scratch in 1919 and built it up to become the hottest property in Fleet Street, but he was prouder still of the *Standard*'s place as required reading in the City, Westminster and Belgravia . . . . it was an alternative voice for promoting views and interests outside those governing the editorial policies of the two national newspapers in the group.

Coote was managing director for two years, and was to say: 'The nett sale steadied not far below 700,000 and, to general astonishment each week we started to contribute real profits to the group's exchequers.'

The same year as Coote's appointment, 1966, The Economist Intelligence unit had produced a study of the national newspaper industry which contained some harsh insights into Fleet Street and Beaverbrook Newspapers in particular. The report noted that of the potential savings of £4,875,000 obtainable through proper production levels more than £1 million could be achieved by Beaverbrook Newspapers: the *Daily Express*, £671,550; *Sunday Express*, £210,250; and *Evening Standard*, £264,470. Discussing Beaverbrook Newspapers it was noted that:

> There is a much greater concentration of editorial and non-executive representation on the board than would normally be considered ideal . . . . There may, therefore, have been a tendency to neglect the foundation of efficient and continuing management . . . . the general standard of middle and senior management with a few notable exceptions was not high . . . . communication within the company seemed to be poor, and at times senior management, even up to general manager level, did not always appear to be clear on the policy adopted by the Company.

Arising from this report, John Coote, now joint managing director of the Group, with Sir Max Aitken announced the formation of a Forward Planning Group. As the youngest member of the committee, acting as representative of the *Standard*, I can still recall its recommendations:[8]

> Integrate the *Evening Standard* into the *Express* building, possibly leading to the loss of 200 jobs; develop the *Standard* premises as lettable office space; develop a site beside the *Daily Express* building in Fleet Street (known as Racquet Court), and already owned by the company; this would house the combined *Express/Standard* operation and also provide space to let; replace old machinery with 71 new units, thereby reducing the number of presses from 185 to 157; develop property in Manchester and Glasgow, where the northern and Scottish editions of the *Daily* and *Sunday Express* were printed.

Even though the *Standard* was experimenting with an Intertype computer to provide TTS tape for servicing Monarch line-casting machines this was soon discontinued as uneconomical; and plans to be the first national newspaper to abandon 'hot metal' and enter the world of photocomposition, with a consequent reduction in manning levels, were to be thwarted by excessive demands from the unions.

For Sir Max Aitken, the decade following his father's death had not been easy; and a steady loss of circulation among the group's titles – especially the *Daily Express* – led to merger discussions in 1972 with Associated Newspapers, publishers of the *Daily Mail* and *Evening News*. The costs of national newspaper production were now becomng too high; and, for a number of months, senior executives had been secretly discussing setting up a joint publishing company, with one just one daily and one London evening. However, a meeting between owners Lord Rothermere II and Sir Max Aitken was not a success. Two years later, in March 1974, with further losses, production of the *Scottish Daily Express* and *Scottish Sunday Express* ceased in Glasgow and transferred to the Manchester office.

Leading the Associated Newspapers discussions had been Esmond Harmsworth, the second Viscount Rothermere, who, after serving in the Royal Marine Artillery during the First World War – in which both his elder brothers were killed – had acted as aide to Prime Minister Lloyd George at the 1919 Paris Peace Conference. Harmsworth entered Parliament that same year, having won a by-election in the Isle of Thanet as a Conservative, and was to remain in the House until 1929, when he left to concentrate on the family business. He became chairman of Associated Newspapers in 1932, helping to develop the successful provincial newspaper chain (Northcliffe Newspapers), which owned titles from Swansea in the west to Hull in the north.[9]

Two years later, in 1934, Esmond Harmsworth succeeded the recently-deceased Lord Riddell as chairman of the Newspaper Proprietors Association – an office he was to hold until 1961, and in which he was widely praised for his dealings with the print unions, government departments and newsprint manufacturers. In this last role he did much during the Second World War to ensure a fair distribution of newsprint between the various titles; and he was chairman of the Newsprint Supply Company from 1940 to 1959.

Esmond Harmsworth became Viscount Rothermere II in 1940; and for the next two decades he was to be locked in rivalry with Beaverbrook Newspapers. In 1952 Rothermere purchased the ailing tabloid *Daily Graphic* (formerly *Daily Sketch*) from Kemsley Newspapers, and within five years 'through its down-market working-class Tory stance' had watched its circulation rise to more than 1.3 million.

In 1960, much to the surprise of Fleet Street liberals, Rothermere, as noted, bought the *News Chronicle* and the *Star* from the Cadbury family: the *News Chronicle* was merged with the *Daily Mail* and the *Star* with the *Evening News*. That same year, his *Sunday Dispatch*, which had been known for its inclusion of racy fiction (*Forever Amber* had been a prime example) lost £600,000. Not content to carry that deficit, he closed down the paper and sold the title to Beaverbrook's *Sunday Express*, which now had the middle-market readership to itself.

As for Rothermere, having diversified his group into television, property, North Sea oil, taxis and pizza parlours – plus wide interests in the Canadian paper-making industry – he died in London on 12 July 1978. A dozen years earlier, he had written of his craft:[10] 'But whatever the physical material and mechanical changes in Fleet Street may be, it remains, and will remain, constant to one thing. That is its passionate love of liberty and its devotion to freedom of expression and the liberty of the individual. If these were ever lost Fleet Street would be no more.'

Enter Trafalgar House

Following the aborted talks of 1972, events had become even more serious, so that in the autumn of 1976 the Beaverbrook board decided once more to hold discussons with arch-rivals Associated Newspapers about the possibility of a merger. Michael Davie, writing in *The Observer*, was to note: 'For longer than anyone still in the newspaper business can remember, two dinosaurs, the *Mail* and the *Express* groups, have been slogging it out in the mud. Forests have been levelled, aeroplanes needlessly hired, expense accounts fudged and marriages smashed in pursuit of victory.'

With Sir Max Aitken in King's College Hospital recovering from a stroke, and his son, Maxwell, still only twenty-five, the weight of the negotiations was to fall on Jocelyn Stevens, deputy chairman and managing director of Beaverbrook Newspapers. The grandson of Sir Edward Hulton – one-time owner of the *Evening Standard* – Stevens had been educated at Eton and Cambridge, and, following National Service in the Rifle Brigade, had worked as a journalist at Hulton Press Ltd from 1955 to 1956. The next year, as a twenty-fifth birthday present to himself, he purchased *Queen*, and as editor, with the assistance of such personalities as Tony Armstrong-Jones and Mark Boxer, made it the magazine of its time.

Having rejected an offer to become editorial director of IPC's two hundred magazines, in 1968 Jocelyn Stevens sold *Queen* and joined Beaverbrook Newspapers as personal assistant to Sir Max Aitken. On 1 January 1969 he was appointed managing director of the *Evening Standard*. One of his earliest successes was to be the coverage of the Moon Landing: for the issue of Monday 21 July 1969 the bulk of the early editions, in full colour, were deliberately produced 24 hours before Armstrong stepped onto the moon! At the end of the day, the *Standard* had printed 1,2000,000 copies in eleven editions – 100 per cent more than normal. A champagne party in Charles Wintour's office was a fitting end to one of the greatest days in newspaper publishing.[11]

For the next three years, with Charles Wintour as editor, Stevens was to revolutionize the *Evening Standard*, with special coloured slip editions, promotions – and a great increase in classified advertising. As a result, he was appointed managing director of the *Daily Express* in 1972, and two years later became managing director of Beaverbrook Newspapers.

On 3 February 1977 the Beaverbrook team held a meeting with the third Viscount Rothermere, chairman of Associated Newspapers, and his managing director, Mick Shields, at the Master's Lodge of University College, Oxford. The son of the second Viscount Rothermere, Vere Harmsworth had been educated at Eton and Kent School in the United States. From 1948 until 1950 he had been with the Anglo-Canadian

Paper Mills, Quebec, and since 1952 with Associated Newspapers, becoming chairman in 1970, when his father resigned.

The following year, in January 1971, with David English as editor, he merged the *Daily Sketch* with the *Daily Mail*. In the May of the same year he relaunched the *Daily Mail*, and was to say: 'It was my decision to go tabloid. First of all I thought the size was a great advantage in every way .... with a tabloid, the whole page can be given a tremendous impact, and you get twice the number of pages for the same total of newsprint.' Success was not immediate, sales falling by almost 100,000, and circulation did not begin to rise for a further eighteen months, but from then on the growth was to be steady.

At the meeting between between Beaverbrook and Associated Newspapers – held under the aegis of Lord Goodman, Master of University College, Oxford, solicitor and former chairman of the NPA – the key point was a proposed merger between the *Evening News* and the *Evening Standard*. In the seven months up to January 1977, the *Standard* had lost £1.3 million. The *News*, though, was estimated to lose more than £4 million in 1977; and, although the *News* still outsold the *Standard* by 536,000 to 418,000, its market profile was lower and not so attractive to advertisers. After much discussion it was suggested that, through the establishment of a joint company, Associated would take a 50 per cent stake in Beaverbrook's new printing plant – Ampress machines capable of 70,000 copies per hour. Beaverbrook Newspapers would also get an infusion of much-needed capital in return for giving Associated control of the new evening paper.

However, as chairman and editor of the *Evening Standard* for more than twenty years, Charles Wintour would not let his beloved paper die without a fight.[12] Probably the most distinguished evening newspaper editor of the twentieth century, Charles Wintour had been educated at Peterhouse, Cambridge, and had served in the Army during the Second World War, being awarded the MBE (military), Croix de Guerre and American Bronze Star. Throughout his long career with Beaverbrook Newspapers he had worked in executive positions on the *Daily* and *Sunday Express*, including the role of managing director, but the *Evening Standard* was *his* paper.

During his tenure he recruited an exceptionally able group of people who enjoyed the paper and each other's company, including cartoonists Vicky and JAK. And among the staff he engaged were eight future Fleet Street editors: Peter Cole, *The Sunday Correspondent*; Trevor Grove, *The Sunday Telegraph*; [Sir] Max Hastings, *The Daily Telegraph* and *Evening Standard*; [Sir] Simon Jenkins, *Evening Standard* and *The Times*; Magnus Linklater, *London Daily News* and *The Scotsman*; Brian MacArthur, *Today*; Janet Street-Porter, *The Independent on Sunday*; and Roy Wright, *Daily Express*. Charles Wintour died on 4 November 1999, and in the words of one of his successors, Max Hastings: 'He made the *Standard* a legendary read, and a great campaigning force for London.'

Helping Wintour to defend the *Standard* had been a former editor of the paper, Michael Foot, Labour Leader of the Opposition, the current editor, Simon Jenkins, plus the paper's chapels, who took part in marches down Fleet Street[13] and lobbied at 'secret meetings'. For *The Daily Telegraph*, the thought that the *Evening Standard* was about to be subsumed brought forth a stinging leader on 29 April:

> While there can be no painless solutions to Fleet Street's dearth of profits, one that involved the disappearance of the *Evening Standard* would be hard to define. Here is a group that has one newspaper (*Daily Express*) which enjoys neither profitability nor particular prestige, one (*Sunday Express*) which enjoys profitability and one (*Evening Standard*) which enjoys prestige and the prospect of a return to profitability. . . . a main virture of the Press is the diversity. That virtue would be sadly diminished by the loss of one of London's two evening newspapers – and that, in the eyes of all persons seriously interested in public affairs and the arts, unquestionably the better of the two.

A newcomer had now entered the negotiations, Sir James Goldsmith; and in the midst of the discussions the *Standard* celebrated its 150th birthday on 26 May 1977 with its largest-ever issue, printed on pink newsprint, causing the Queen to send her felicitations: 'Whatever the future may hold, Her Majesty is happy to have had this opportunity of sending her congratulations on this notable anniversary.'

With Associated Newspapers still anxious to gain control, and Sir James Goldsmith submitting fresh proposals, there came forward two more candidates: Rupert Murdoch and Trafalgar House, the ultimate victor. On 30 June, Trafalgar House made their play and were to be successful with an improved offer of £13.69 million.

Accompanied by a BBC television team, Victor Matthews, chairman of Trafalgar House, immediately left for Fleet Street, telling his interviewer: 'I am just like any other chap that you see across the street who has got to the top.' For Sir Max Aitken, walking slowly to his car, it was a different story: 'I've given up because I got ill. No. I'm not disappointed. I think he [Beaverbrook] would have sold up long before.'[14]

Sir Max lived until 1985, and on his demise Prime Minister Margaret Thatcher said: 'Part of our heritage has gone tonight with his death, but the contribution that the Aitken family has made to British life will stay.' His obituarist in the *Daily Express* added: 'One of the Few, he was the bravest of the brave.'

The new chairman of Beaverbrook Newspapers – later to be renamed Express Newspapers – Victor Matthews, was born in London and during the Second World War served in the Royal Naval Volunteer Reserve. On demobilization, he became a trainee with Trollope and Colls and during the next thirty years was to play a prominent role in the firm's building and contract work, and with Nigel Broakes (later Sir Nigel) was to develop Trafalgar House into an international force, with interests in civil engineering, the Ritz Hotel and the Cunard shipping line, including the *QEII*.

A Star is Born

Victor Matthews was to remain as chairman of Express Newspapers until 1985, when United Newspapers purchased the group, and during those years was a leading influence in fighting the Fleet Street print unions: at one stage, this even involved closing down production and barricading the Express building – 121 Fleet Street (the Black Lubyanka) – with scaffolding and wire mesh. In 1978, he told *The Sunday*

Times: 'Fleet Street is not overmanned; it is underworked.' After dummies had been produced at Gerrards Cross in March 1978 of a down- market *Evening Star* for distribution in London and the plan abandoned, subsequently, in November that year, the *Daily Star* was launched from the group's Manchester office – the first new national newspaper for seventy-five years.

The *Star*'s first editor was Peter Grimsditch, a classicist from Oxford University, who had previously worked on the *Daily Express*, *Daily Mail* and *Sunday Mirror*. Editor-in-chief was veteran Derek Jameson, who had started as an office boy at Reuters in 1944, rising to become chief sub-editor. Later he joined the features staff of the *Daily Express* as picture editor, and in 1965 became assistant editor; from 1972 to 1976 he was northern editor of the *Daily Mirror* and the *Sunday Mirror*. He returned to Fleet Street in 1976 as managing editor of the *Daily Mirror*, but the following year was appointed editor of the *Daily Express*. 'It was in many ways the most coveted job of all in the world of newspapers.'[15]

As editor-in-chief, Jameson introduced bingo into the *Daily Star*, and with its aid the paper reached a circulation of 1.9 million, becoming a direct threat to *The Sun*. A bingo war then ensued with *The Sun* and the *Daily Mirror* joining in; and, as a counter-measure, to the *Star*'s £10,000 prize money, *The Sun* retaliated with an £85,000 jackpot. By the mid-1980s, first prizes of £1 million were being offered by both *The Sun* and its main opponent, the *Daily Mirror*, now owned by Robert Maxwell. As Derek Jameson was to say: 'Without doubt it was the biggest and best circulation builder in history, far outstripping anything a newspaper could do editorially.' Jameson left Express Newspapers in 1979 and two years later became editor of the *News of the World*, 1981–84, before launching a successful career on radio and television.

In 1980, Victor Matthews was created a life peer in the New Year Honours List, and later that year, following the closure of the *Evening News*, was elected chairman of the new *Evening Standard* company (50 per cent owned by Trafalgar House and 50 per cent owned by Associated Newspapers). On 5 March 1982, with Lord Matthews having played a prominent role, the de-merger of Trafalgar House's newspaper and magazine interests into a new company, Fleet Holdings, took place. This was to prove a brilliant move: 20p shares fell to 15p, but, at the purchase of the group by United Newspapers in October 1985, their price soared to £3.75 cash, more than twenty times the lowest figure.

Although, at the age of 58, he arrived late in Fleet Street, and was there for less than a decade, Victor Matthews made a tremendous impact. Charles Wintour was to write of him: 'His two really big achievements for the newspaper industry were the break-up of the Reuters Trust into a public company, and his employment of the law in securing a greater measure of industrial discipline.'[16]

After leaving Fleet Street, Lord Matthews moved to Jersey and died there on his birthday, aged 76, on 5 December 1995.

Trouble at The Times

While Express Newspapers had been successfully launching its *Daily Star* from Ancoats Street, Manchester, at Gray's Inn Road, London, there had been big problems with Times Newspapers and the unions. As far back as 1966, the Economist Intelligence Unit had declared that under the Astors '[*The Times*] was regarded as a national institution rather than a commercial business' – and it was a tradition that had been maintained by Lord Thomson and then his son, Kenneth (Lord Thomson II).

On 22 June 1974 *The Times* published its final issue from Printing House Square before moving to Gray's Inn Road, alongside *The Sunday Times* building. Until 1961, *The Sunday Times* had been printed under contract at *The Daily Telegraph* building in Fleet Street. However, within weeks of purchasing the paper, Lord Thomson was given six months'notice – subsequently extended to twelve – to find another printer. This gave the very minimum period to order and install new presses at Gray's Inn Road – plus engaging machine-room and publishing staff, many of whom worked for other titles during the week.

Most of the staff of *The Times* – known as the Companionship – were long-serving members, with a deep feeling for the paper, reflected in the fact that industrial stoppages there were the least of all Fleet Street titles. Nevertheless, the bringing together of two different work-forces meant that there was to be an exchange of views over wages and conditions, which was soon to be apparent in discussions with the management. 'There was tremendous jealousy and dislike on both sides. *The Sunday Times* production men were paid very highly for short weekend shifts, *The Times* men wanted parity or as near as they could get to it.' And as deputy editor Louis Heren was to say: 'The spirit of the old Companionship was not extinguished until the move to Gray's Inn Road where industrial indiscipline was endemic.'[17]

During the mid-1970s, the almost nightly battles with trade unions and the consequent loss of copies – plus envious glances at the provincial Press, which had so successfully converted to the new technology, replacing ancient 'hot metal' Linotypes with much faster, efficient and quieter photocomposition allied to web-offset printing – meant that more and more Fleet Street titles were looking to change their methods. Typical of these was *The Times,* which on 18 March 1976 published a leading article declaring that 'savings on the necessary scale can be obtained only by cutting production costs; and the development of new technology presents a last change for some papers and the opportunity of all of getting on to a more secure commercial foundation than for a great many years'.

Consequent to this, on 26 May 1976 *The Times* executives, led by managing director Marmaduke Hussey, made their presentation to the chapels. A former managing director of the *Daily Mail* and Vice-Chairman of the NPA, Hussey was to say: 'The new system was to be developed gradually, but from the beginning would be directly aimed at eliminating dual keyboarding; the build-up must be logical from the start, but our final requirements are to eliminate duplicate key-stroking and to speed-up and improve many ancillary operations.' The approach was to commence with *The*

Times Educational Supplement, *The Times Higher Education Supplement* and *The Times Literary Supplement*. After a settling-in period, the new technology would be introduced at *The Times* and finally *The Sunday Times*.

Some five months earlier, in the January issue of *Print*, John Bonfield, the General Secretary of the NGA, the union most likely to be affected by any change, had written:

> We go along with the introduction of the new technologies if only because the alternatives are worse. But we demand that the threat to our members' employment that this necessarily entails is dealt with in just and human social terms – which, first of all, means that there will be no compulsory redundancy . . . . and that those who may wish to leave the industry at this time have reasonable guarantees for their future living standards.

Within days of writing that article, Bonfield was dead and was succeeded by Joe Wade, who recognized that the NGA had no alternative to accepting the new technology. He thought that this would involve a reduction in the labour force, and thus lost membership, but that the reduction should be gradual, the financial terms generous, and the existing demarcation lines preserved. These points he forcibly stressed in April 1976, a few months after assuming the Secretaryship:[18]

> What frightens me is the way in which some national newspapers are rushing into new technology with all the verve and suicidal tendencies of a kamikaze pilot . . . . If unions and their members are to accept changes in technology – and I agree that they have no alternative – the employers must equally accept the social costs involved. Those people who see the new technology as an opportunity to sweep away at a stroke all the existing demarcation lines, they really are living in cloud-cuckoo land. The only realistic way in which new technology can get off the ground is to introduce it, at this stage, anyway, on the basis of existing demarcation lines so far as is practicable. Unless that is understood and accepted, the rest can be forgotten.

For almost two years, very little progress was made until in April 1978 *Times* management met secretly with the general secretaries of the unions in Birmingham at which they outlined their plans. Among the five clauses were: 'We negotiate with union representatives as a general wage restructuring. This will be based on the new technology and systems, and on efficient manning levels in all departments . . . . no compulsory redundancy will arise from the introduction of new technology systems. All negotiations shall be concluded by November 30, 1978.'

Editor William Rees-Mogg, in a signed article, wrote: 'In 1978 we have given our readers on *The Times* the least reliable service in the history of the paper; all the hard work of ninety per cent of the staff has repeatedly been destroyed by the unofficial and irresponsible action of small groups.'

During the next six months, progress in negotiations was agonizingly slow (at the time of the deadline only nineteen of the sixty-five chapels had signed agreements); and despite Government intervention, resulting in an extension to 13 December, the papers were to cease publication for almost twelve months.

From the commencement, the main stumbling block was to be the ceding of key-stroking by the NGA to journalists and advertising personnel. It was a condition on which neither management nor NGA would give way, even though, in time, a guarantee was given that NGA personnel would be kept on the payroll during the changeover to photocomposition. (In Britain, only one newspaper, the *Nottingham Evening Post*, was using direct entry, thus bypassing the NGA.)

The feelings of the NGA were to be summed up by Joe Wade:[19]

> It never fails to amaze me that some Fleet Street newspapers want to make the leap from Caxton to computer in one go without having any experience at all in the field of new technology. It is interesting to contrast that attitude with that which prevails in the provincial newspaper industry where a whole range of new techniques have already been introduced with the full co-operation of the unions.

Having assumed that the closure of the papers was likely to be of some months' duration – and as Eric Jacobs, a *Sunday Times* staff member and himself one of the union negotiators, was to write in his seminal account of the strike, *Stop Press*:

> Well before 30 November the unions had begun to prepare. They had organised levies from their members in Fleet Street and beyond, and, where they could, they had kept vacancies open in other publishing houses. In their search for alternative work the unions were soon helped out by the rivals of *The Times* and *The Sunday Times*. *The Guardian*, the *Financial Times*, *The Daily* and *Sunday Telegraph* and *The Observer* all began to print extra copies – especially *The Observer* – extra pages and even sections; and to cope with the additional work they put more machines into operation and took on extra union labour. Almost magically, an industry that was already notoriously over-manned absorbed the staff of *The Times* and *The Sunday Times* as it came off the company's payroll.

Much later, Sir Denis Hamilton, chairman and editor-in-chief, was to write:

> The shutdown bore out all my worst fears. It fuelled the ambitions of chapel leaders with eyes on union advancement . . . . Far from showing signs of collapse the chapels were rejoicing at their ability to find alternative employment for their locked-out troops. Far from helping the general secretaries to impose discipline over their chapels, we had merely exposed their impotence.[20]

In February 1979, in the midst of *The Times* stoppage, William Rees-Mogg addressed the Engineering Employers' Federation on the problems management were facing:

> Our position on *The Times* is like that of a man at the end of a wind-swept pier in some cold and out-of-season resort – perhaps Scarborough in late November. We are confronted with a set of seven rusty and ancient fruit machines. To reach agreement we have to line up three strawberries on each of the fruit machines at the same time. Somehow – heaven knows – we have managed to line up three of the strawberries on two machines, and we have a couple of strawberries registered on the third. On the others some reject the coin that is put in – however large – while one has a lemon and another has a raspberry rusted permanently in place on the centre of the dial.

By June, losses were running at £20 million plus ongoing monthly losses of £1.7 million, and, despite the efforts of management, there was always one union that could wreck at the last moment any possible agreement – and single keystroking continued to be a main stumbling block.

Determined to produce even one edition of *The Times* – as much as a morale booster as anything – the decision was now taken to print a 16-page paper near Frankfurt, hopefully to become a weekly event. Even though some were opposed to the idea, on a majority vote of the chapel the journalists decided to proceed. With printing about to start on the Saturday night, from early morning pickets had assembled outside the plant, becoming more aggressive during the day. Shortly before printing was due to begin, petrol-impregnated rags were found stuffed in the machinery; and as a result production was abandoned. Even though there was a much greater police presence the following day, so the pickets had increased. And, fearing a riot, it was announced that production would not take place, whereupon the crowd dispersed. However, following their departure, some 10,000 copies were printed – and sold in the United States and on the Continent. The venture itself was not repeated; and the copies – dateline 22 April 1979 – are now collectors' items.

When agreement was finally reached, *The Times* returned on 13 November and *The Sunday Times* on 18 November. Marmaduke Hussey was to write:[21]

> The benefits are very substantial and my main worry is that in getting new technology in at lower rates than is currently paid for the old technology we may still have wage differential problems. The whole secret lies in whether or not the continuous production is honoured. If it is, this will turn out to be an extremely good settlement.

The costs to management, though, had been heavy: £46 million in wages and lost advertising revenue, £3.5 million for the back-to-work settlement and £1 million for advertisements to herald the relaunch.

Much later, William Rees-Mogg was to tell Susan Goldenberg in her *The Thomson Empire*: 'The initial strategy was developed under Roy Thomson, who was highly aggressive and able to change situations to his own advantage. If he had been alive, he would have introduced the new machinery without perhaps a week's stoppage.'

Harold Evans, editor of *The Sunday Times*, was to write in his *Good Times, Bad Times*:

> The year's suspension solved nothing. I spent it trying to find a middle ground between management and unions; it proved a quicksand. The frustration and heartbreak began again the moment we resumed publication .... Petty disputes continued in key departments. Millions of pounds of revenue and millions of copies were lost on *The Sunday Times*.

And from editor-in-chief Sir Denis Hamilton: 'The closing of the papers would have broken Roy Thomson's heart. He did not view the new newspaper technology as leading to a reduction in employment but instead as creating opportunities for new magazines and newspapers.'

In August, within nine months of resuming production, there was to be further trouble, when, for the first time in its history, *Times* journalists went on strike. (They had been kept on full pay during the shutdown and upon resumption given large wage increases.) To quote Eric Jacobs again:[22]

> They had taken a pay claim to an arbitrator, who recommended a rise of 21 per cent. The company, however, insisted that it could not pay more than the 18 per cent it had already offered. Though the arbitration was not binding on either side according to the chapel's agreement with the company, the journalists held that it should be, in honour if nothing else.

For Hamilton it was too much:

> I had personally protected them and their families all through the shutdown; I could not but feel personally attacked and humiliated. Hussey's long battle had worn me out, mentally and physically; I simply did not see how I could explain to the proprietor why he should throw more good money after bad. Without the journalists' loyalty we had nothing left to fight for.

Within hours, Hamilton had telephoned Kenneth Thomson in Toronto and recommended that the papers should be put up for sale.

On 22 October 1980, the Board of Thomson British Holdings, under the chairmanship of Gordon Brunton, announced that it would be withdrawing from publishing *The Times*, *The Sunday Times* and its sister titles and that if no buyer were found by March 1981 the papers would be closed. It was then revealed that since the formation of Times Newspapers in 1967 more than £70 million had been provided by Thomson sources and that in the current year a pre-tax loss of £15 million was expected. (If no buyer were found, it was estimated that redundancy payments of more than £35 million would have to be paid.) That same day, Kenneth Thomson said:[23]

> My father and I have repeatedly made it clear that our continued support for Times Newspapers was conditional on the overall co-operation of the newspaper employees, and I have sadly concluded that this co-operation will not be forthcoming under our ownership. It grieves me greatly that in spite of the millons of pounds which have been provided to Times Newspapers over the years to enable these newspapers to survive, and in spite of the efforts of many loyal employees who have built up the papers to their present eminence, and to whom I express my deep gratitude, we have been unable to secure the co-operation of important sections of the workforce on a reliable and consistent basis. I believe that a change of ownership could provide Times Newspapers with the opportunity to create a new and constructive relationship with its staff.

Murdoch Buys The Times

With bids having to be submitted to merchant bank S.G. Warburg by 31 December, five major contenders were to express interest: Lord Rothermere, Associated Newspapers; Lord Matthews, Express Newspapers; Atlantic Richfield, already owners of *The Observer*; Robert Maxwell, of Pergamon Press, still anxious to secure a Fleet Street newspaper; and Rupert Murdoch, of News International. There were also two bids by the editors: one by Rees-Mogg heading a consortium Journalists of *The Times* (JOTT), keen to buy *The Times* and its supplements; and the other by Morgan Grenfell 'on behalf of Harold Evans, editor of the *Sunday Times* and chairman of the *Sunday Times* Executive Committee and his close associates on the Staff'.

The fact that Murdoch, who only the previous year had stated that 'to buy *The Times* would be a highly irresponsible thing to do for your shareholders', was a contender, and that immediately before the deadline he had put in an opening bid of £1 million 'just to get my foot in the door',[24] was a sure sign that he was interested.

For Evans, though, the withdrawal of *Guardian* support and the news from James Callaghan, the former Labour Prime Minister, that the unions would prefer to deal with Murdoch, meant that his bid would fail. Rees-Mogg, who had been supported by Sir Michael Swann(former chairman of the BBC), Lord Weinstock and Sir John Sainsbury, was also to be unsuccessful. By early January the contenders had been reduced to three: Lord Rothermere, Atlantic Richfield and Rupert Murdoch. More than ever, Murdoch wanted Times Newspapers, and already he had sounded out Gerald Long, managing director of Reuters, to see if he would become M.D. Long was to say 'yes'.

On the evening of 21 January 1981, at Stratford Place, the Thomson headquarters, Murdoch met the vetting committee of Sir Denis Hamilton, editor-in-chief of Times Newspapers; Lords Dacre, Green and Roll, the three national directors; plus editors William Rees-Mogg and Harold Evans. After midnight the deal was finally done, whereby Times Newspapers would be sold for £12 million. And 'that the number of national directors should be increased from four to six, that Times Newspapers should not be absorbed into News International but should retain its distinct existence, and that editorial authority and freedom should be respected .'

The next day, Murdoch and Hamilton announced the sale and this was followed by a news conference on 23 January, where Murdoch stated: 'I am not seeking to acquire these papers in order to change them into something entirely different.' And from Sir Denis Hamilton: 'I believe that Rupert Murdoch is one of the greatest newspaper executives in the world today. These newspapers, in the tough situation they are in, will be best in the hands of a fellow professional.' Joe Wade, for the NGA, was to comment: 'I know from personal experience that Mr Murdoch can be a tough and ruthless negotiator. But at the end of the day I know we can get a fair agreement with him.'[25]

Before Murdoch could complete his purchase, there was the threat of referral to the Monopolies Commission; and at a recent meeting with John Biffen, Secretary of State for Trade and Industry, and his Minister of State for Consumer Affairs, Sally Oppenheim, he had been told that this was likely to be the case. However, on 27 January, in an adjournment debate in the House of Commons opened by Labour's John Smith, Biffen announced that, subject to certain conditions, he had consented to the transfer. Here he was referring to Section 58(3) of the Act, whereby

> the Secretary of State was empowered to sanction a transfer of ownership without referral to the commission, if he was satisfied that the paper concerned was unprofitable, or that its survival was a matter of such urgency that the time required for consideration by the commission would make the difference between life and death.

Although there was some dissent from within his own Conservative Party – notably Jonathan Aitken and Peter Bottomley – there was support from a number of Labour members, including Ron Leighton, sponsored by NATSOPA, who said: 'The printing trade unions and, I understand, a very large number of journalists take the view that the best chance of keeping the publications in existence is Rupert Murdoch.' When the vote was taken, there was a majority of 42 in support of the transfer.

There now followed three weeks of intense negotiations with the unions, and when agreement was reached on 12 February, 'a voluntary redundancy scheme was accepted by some 563 full-time staff, representing a reduction of about 20 per cent of the workforce, and a move to electronic photocomposition was agreed by the NGA'. And it was also confirmed that the three supplements would in future be printed outside London.

For Lord Rothermere, who had been prepared to pay £20 million for both titles and £15 million for *The Sunday Times* alone, there was to be disappointment, but he was to say later: 'I didn't want *The Times*. I wanted *The Sunday Times*. What we wanted to do somehow was shunt off *The Times* where it would survive as a parish newspaper of the elite. So it would remain that way at a minimum loss situation because none of us could see how it could ever be made commercially viable.'[26]

Change of Editors

Upon Murdoch assuming control, Rees-Mogg informed him that he was standing down as editor of *The Times*, a position he had held since 1967, to run an antique bookshop in Pall Mall. Aside from his editorship, he has been much involved in public affairs, having been, among other things, vice-chairman of the Board of Governors of the BBC, 1981–86, and chairman, Arts Council of Great Britain, 1982–89. He was knighted in 1981 and created a life peer in 1988.

On his departure, he was succeeded by Harold Evans, editor of *The Sunday Times*. He was to be editor of *The Times* from March 1981, but it was not a happy relationship with his proprietor, and on Tuesday 15 March 1982 Evans resigned; he was later to recount the events in *Good Times, Bad Times* published the following year. Married to Tina Brown, he now lives in the United States and is a successful author and publisher. He was knighted in 2005.

The new editor of *The Sunday Times* was to be Frank Giles, who had served as deputy editor since 1967. A former ADC to the Governor of Bermuda, after a period in the Foreign Office he joined *The Times* in 1946, being a correspondent in Paris and Rome. From 1961 to 1977 he served as foreign editor of *The Sunday Times*, until being appointed deputy editor. Giles was to remain editor of *The Sunday Times* for two-and-a-half years, as related in his autobiography, *Sundry Times*, published in 1986.

With his editors in place, and agreements with the unions signed, Murdoch was hoping for a stress-free period. It was not to be . . . .

19

The road to Wapping

FOR FLEET STREET OBSERVERS, the greatest impact during the second half of the twentieth century had been the arrival from Adelaide of a young, forceful newspaper owner, Rupert Murdoch. The son of Sir Keith, the man who during the First World War had exposed the horrors of Gallipoli, and who later was a newspaper proprietor in South Australia, Rupert Murdoch was born in Melbourne and educated at Geelong Grammar School and Worcester College, Oxford; and he was still at Oxford when his father died in October 1952. Rupert Murdoch then spent six months – under the direction of Ted Pickering[1] – working as a sub- editor on the *Daily Express* in 1953: 'My biggest moment came when I was given the Korean story for page one . . . . I loved it; it was fabulous.'

He returned to Adelaide at the age of twenty-two and began his publishing career by taking control of News Limited, owners of the *News*, the number two newspaper in the city. After purchasing a small Sunday newspaper in Perth, he entered television in 1958 when he obtained a licence to run the Adelaide-based Channel 9 Station. Murdoch's next move was to buy the *Daily Mirror*, Sydney, from the Fairfax Group in May 1960; and, after further expansion through purchasing weeklies in Brisbane and Melbourne, plus magazines and more television involvement, in 1964 he launched *The Australian*, the country's first national newspaper.

Four years later, in the autumn of 1968, Robert Maxwell, Labour MP for Buckingham, made a bid to own the *News of the World*. His offer of £2.50 a share was to lead to the paper's editor, Stafford Somerfield, writing a front-page article on 20 October denouncing Maxwell's attempt to gain control:

> We are having a little local difficulty at the *News of the World*. It concerns the ownership of the paper. Mr Robert Maxwell, a Socialist MP, is trying to take it over. Personally, I don't think he will, and I, as Editor of your great paper for more than eight years and a member of the editorial staff for nearly a quarter of a century, hope his bid will fail . . . . this newspaper is as British as roast beef and Yorkshire pudding . . . . As far as my own position is concerned, I will not work with Mr Maxwell. I do not understand his views or his policy. I do not believe that he is the right man to control the greatest newspaper in the world.

Much later, Stafford Somerfield was to write: 'All hell broke out; particularly over the phrase: "The *News of the World* is as British as roast beef and Yorkshire pudding ." A good phrase I thought then, and still do.'[2]

Owned by the Carr family since 1895, the paper's major shareholder and chairman was Sir William Carr with 32 per cent, closely followed by his cousin, Professor Derek Jackson, a scientist, with 25 per cent. Now, with Jackson wishing to sell his shareholding, the company had 'come into play'; and – having had assurances from Fleet Street proprietors that they were not interested – the main contender was to be Robert Maxwell.

Although the leading Sunday paper in terms of circulation, the *News of the World* had since the Second World War seen its sales fall. In 1947 the Royal Commission on the Press revealed that with figures of 7.9 million the paper had 26.9 per cent of the Sunday market. Eight years later, *News of the World* sales were 8.1 million, dropping to 6.5 million in 1960 and 6.1 million in 1961. 'The paper then absorbed the *Empire News*, gaining 660,000 and, by dint of other efforts, was selling 6.2 million at the start of 1968.'

On the morning that Stafford Somerfield's outspoken leader appeared, Rupert Murdoch arrived hot-foot from Australia to bid for the paper. He had been contacted at the Caulfield Cup, Melbourne, one of Australia's most prestigious races, on the Friday afternoon. He immediately took a plane back to Sydney where he was met at the airport by his wife with a packed suitcase, passport and *News of the World* files before boarding a Lufthansa flight via Frankfurt to London. He was to say: 'I could *smell* the Establishment wouldn't let Maxwell have it, so I put my hand up.'

And some two months later, on 2 January 1969, at a crucial, crowded meeting held at the Connaught Rooms, London, Murdoch and afterwards Maxwell addressed the shareholders and Murdoch carried the day by 4,526,822 votes to 3,246,937. That evening, Murdoch gave a celebratory party at his flat on the Embankment and among the guests were Carr and Sir Max Aitken, of Beaverbrook Newspapers.

At eight o'clock the following morning, as managing director, the new 'boss' of the *News of the World* went to his office – to be greeted by SOGAT lady cleaners having a cup of tea on the chairman's desk. It was not long, though, before Murdoch began to make his presence felt.[3]

> Since a paper's success or failure depends on its editorial approach, why shouldn't I interfere when I see a way to strengthen its approach? What am I supposed to do, sit idly by and watch a paper go down the drain, simply because I'm not supposed to interfere? Rubbish! That's the reason the *News of the World* started to fade. There was no one there to trim the fat and wrench it out of its editorial complacency.

Owning The Sun

Later that year, the two rivals were again intent on buying the same newspaper: this time it was to be *The Sun*, a title owned by IPC. Launched in 1964, it had replaced the *Daily Herald*, but within three years, with circulation falling, *The Sun* had become a financial handicap (see chapter seventeen, p.339–340). Maxwell's plan was to turn the paper into an up-market left-wing tabloid to be printed at night on the *Evening Standard* presses in Shoe Lane; the author had been earmarked as production chief. But once more Maxwell was to lose out. On Monday 17 November 1969, with Larry

Lamb as editor, the Murdoch-owned 48-page tabloid *Sun* was launched as 'The paper that cares about people. About the kind of world we live in.' Inheriting a circulation of 850,000, sales would rise to a daily average of more than one million within a few weeks. Its mixture of bright, snappy stories, good sports coverage, plus exciting features and competitions made it compulsive reading.

Editor Larry Lamb had entered full-time journalism in 1953 on the *Brighouse News*, before joining the *Shields Gazette* and then the *Newcastle Journal*, one of the leading provincial mornings. His next move was to Fleet Street on the *Evening Standard*, followed by a spell as a sub-editor on the *Daily Mail* before joining the *Daily Mirror* in 1958, rising to become chief sub-editor. He then left to become northern editor of the *Daily Mail* and it was from there that he joined Rupert Murdoch.

To launch the new *Sun*, Lamb gathered around him such experienced individuals as Bernard Shrimsley (deputy editor), Peter Stephens, Arthur Brittenden, Dick Parrack and Vic Giles – plus an experienced women's team led by Joyce Hopkirk. Known as the 'Pacesetters', they included Patsy Chapman, Unity Hall, Claire Rayner, Bridget Rowe and Deidre McSharry. Vic Giles, art director, was later to say of those opening days: 'Rupert Murdoch was indeed somebody with a complete grasp of every aspect of the business. At conferences, no matter what the subject, he was the star turn, running rings around professional journalists, advertising people, accountants, circulation salesmen and printers.'[4]

Unusually, because of the change in ownership, there had been no time for dummy runs; and Larry Lamb could tell the *UK Press Gazette*: 'The staff have been marvellous. They are all hollow-eyed and working their guts out.' From Murdoch himself, at the end of the first week: 'It's bloody chaos – but we are getting a paper out.'[5] On the paper's first anniversary, *The Sun* printed its initial picture of a topless model with the caption 'We, like our readers, like pretty girls'. These 'Page Three Girls' were to bring a new phrase to the English language.

Sales of *The Sun* topped 2.5 million in 1971, and in 1978 the paper overtook the *Daily Mirror* with figures of more than four million, reaching a circulation in 1982 of 4.18 million per day. By owning the *News of the World* and *The Sun*, Murdoch now had the largest-selling Sunday and daily newspapers in the English-speaking world.

In 1972, Larry Lamb had become editorial director of both titles, having been succeeded as editor of *The Sun* by Bernard Shrimsley, who would later edit the *News of the World* and go on to be launch editor of *The Mail on Sunday* for Associated Newspapers. Lamb returned to edit *The Sun* two years later and in 1980 was knighted. He remained as editor until 1981 when he left. Between 1984 and 1986, Lamb edited the *Daily Express*, then became a consultant, advising provincial, national and international newspapers.

Succeeding Lamb was Kelvin MacKenzie, who was to be the most prominent tabloid editor of his time. The son of journalist parents, aged seventeen he became a district reporter for the *South-East London Mercury*; and after a spell with Ferrari's News Agency, Deptford, where a fellow reporter was Richard Stott, later to be editor of the *Daily Mirror*, he worked in Birmingham before joining the *Daily Express* as a sub-editor. In 1973 he moved to *The Sun*, but was soon selected by Murdoch to go to the United States as managing editor of the *New York Post*. MacKenzie returned to Fleet Street and *The Sun* as deputy night editor under Sir Larry Lamb, but in February 1981 moved to the *Daily Express* as night editor under Arthur Firth.

Almost immediately he was to be selected by Murdoch as the next editor of *The Sun*; and for MacKenzie there then followed a few whirlwind weeks of editing *The Sun* while at the same time acting as night editor for the *Daily Express* until he was released by Express Newspapers.[6] And for the next thirteen years – with such front-page headlines as GOTCHA, FREDDIE STARR ATE MY HAMSTER and IT'S THE SUN WOT WON IT! plus his 16-hour-a-day drive – MacKenzie was to make *The Sun* the most-talked-about newspaper in the land.

Rothermere's Sunday Title

While MacKenzie, in Bouverie Street, was getting to grips with his new editorship, a few hundred yards away Associated Newspapers, at Carmelite House, were busy planning their new title – and on 2 May 1982 *The Mail on Sunday* made its appearance.

It was not, however, the first Sunday title to have been launched by the family. On 9 April 1899 Alfred Harmsworth (later Lord Northcliffe) with his brother Harold (afterwards first Lord Rothermere) started the *Sunday Daily Mail*. It was launched to compete with Edward Lawson's *Sunday Daily Telegraph*, also making its debut on 9 April; and designed to fill the increasing demand for Sunday newspapers – and at the same time spread the press-room costs by printing on the seventh day.

One anonymous historian reported that the first number was 'a very mild production' and 'nothing likely to cause a ripple of sensation in Fleet Street or anywhere else, except in the most rigid Sabbatarian circles'. But among those leading the protests was the President of the Newspaper Society, Sir Hugh Gilzean Reid, of the *North Eastern Daily Gazette*; and he was supported by powerful articles in *The British Weekly* and *The Methodist*. With such vociferous opposition, Lawson decided not to continue, and closed down the title after just seven issues.[7]

Alfred Harmsworth's *Sunday Daily Mail* was to last for only six issues, ceasing on 17 May 1899. Here again, angry opposition from church leaders 'who fought stoutly for the puritan legacy of the English Sabbath with its millions lounging about in consecrated idleness' – plus disapproval from *Daily Mail* readers and the refusal of the London wholesalers to handle the paper – brought about its closure.

Within thirty-six hours, Harmsworth had received twenty thousand letters in support of the closure, and had even published one message from literary figure Edmund Gosse expressing why there was no need for seventh-day publication:

> Since you are good enough to urge me to express my views about Sunday newspapers, I must honestly tell you – that although I have no conscientious scruple about encouraging their circulation – I think them exhausting and unnecessary. I have never taken a Sunday newspaper and I am glad to have one day a week unlike the rest. The whole concept of a

> Sunday newspaper appears to me to accentuate the hurrying, wearying and trivial monotony of experience which is the curse of life nowadays.

Now, some eighty years later, for Alfred Harmsworth's great-nephew, Vere Harmsworth, to launch a Sunday newspaper had long been on his mind. He was, perhaps, fortunate that plans by Express Newspapers some five years earlier had not come to fruition. In 1977, a proposal by Jocelyn Stevens, deputy chairman; Charles Wintour, managing director; and the author, then production director; had aimed at producing a 64-page tabloid at Uxbridge, with further printing at Oxford and Bedford – all on presses then owned by Westminster Press. This printing on five Crabtree Crusader web-offset presses would have given a figure of more than one million copies; and added to this would have been a 48-page colour magazine produced by Woodrow Wyatt at Banbury. Unfortunately, due to probable opposition from Fleet Street chapels, the scheme did not proceed.

Ever since 1978, when his father had died and he had become chairman of Daily Mail and General Trust, Vere Harmsworth (Lord Rothermere III) had seen the need for a Sunday title; and in 1979 had bid for *The Times* and *The Sunday Times*, losing out to Rupert Murdoch. Much later he was to say: 'I was absolutely convinced there was a market. The *Sunday Express* had become so out of touch, nothing had changed there, an antique product. And to my mind there was an opportunity.'[8]

Rothermere's choice as editor for his new title, Bernard Shrimsley, was a widely experienced journalist, having been deputy editor, *Sunday Express*, Manchester; editor, *Daily Mirror*, Manchester; assistant editor, *Daily Mirror*, London; editor, *Daily Post*, Liverpool; before being appointed deputy editor of *The Sun*. In 1972 he became associate editor of the *News of the World* and later that year editor of *The Sun*. Three years later, he went back to the *News of the World* as editor. Shrimsley was also, from 1979 to 1980, a director of News Group Newspapers Ltd, when he moved to Associated Newspapers as editor designate and subsequently editor of *The Mail on Sunday*.

Launched as a 64-page tabloid without a colour supplement, it was the first new Sunday title in twenty-one years and the initial Fleet Street newspaper to be produced entirely using photocomposition. Bernard Shrimsley left later that year, moving to Express Newspapers as associate editor; and Sir David English, editor of the *Daily Mail*, then took on the additional responsibility of the *Mail on Sunday*. In autumn 1982, Stewart Steven, associate editor of the *Daily Mail*, was appointed editor, and with the aid of *YOU* (a colour magazine), an insert for comics and a cookery partwork the paper was relaunched. It was to meet with much success, overtaking the *Sunday Express* in 1989, and early in 1992 selling more than two million copies per issue.

Enter Robert Maxwell

Having lost out to Rupert Murdoch on two occasions – *News of the World* and *The Sun* – in 1984 Robert Maxwell made his entry into Fleet Street when he purchased

Mirror Group Newspapers (MGN) from Reed International for £113 million. At the time the combined sale of the *Daily Mirror* and the *Daily Record*, Scotland, was some four million copies daily; and the MGN Sunday titles – the *Sunday Mirror* and *The People* in England and the *Sunday Mail* in Scotland – sold about six million copies weekly. MGN also published the *Sporting Life*, Britain's oldest racing and sports daily.

His purchase, though, was not without controversy. With the Mirror Group – on a turnover of more than £200 million barely profitable – and anxious to move out of the newspaper industry the board of Reed had decided to float the group as a public company; and as a first step engaged Clive Thornton, the former chief executive of Abbey National Building Society, as the new chairman. Appalled at the restrictive practices of the production unions and the massive editorial expenses, Thornton immediately engaged in talks of worker participation, the non-replacement of staff, new titles and a large investment in up-to-date machinery.

In announcing their proposals, Reed declared that 'there should be a fifteen per cent limit on any individual owning shares in the new company' now downgraded to £48 million. Maxwell, eager to gain control, put in a bid of £80 million, pledging support for Labour, and Reed, in the interests of the shareholders, were obliged to listen. After a final offer of £113 million Maxwell was the new owner. The bid was announced on 5 July 1984, and Thornton, who had allowed a documentary crew to accompany him to a meeting of trade union representatives in Manchester, 'was actually filmed for TV being telephoned the shock, horror news.'[9]

For more than a decade, plans by the *Mirror* to move into new technology had been thwarted by the unions. However, Maxwell was to achieve those aims; and, within four years of taking over – having ordered twenty-one MAN-Roland presses at a cost of £68 million – the English titles, following the example of the Scottish papers, were being published in run-of-paper full colour. And on the union side, despite much disruption, he had succeeded in reducing the staffing by 1600 from a total of 6500.

The new owner of MGN, Robert Maxwell had been born Jan Ludwich Hoch in Czechoslovakia in 1923. One of seven children, he had grown up in deep poverty. Most of his family had perished at Auschwitz during the Holocaust, but as a teenager he escaped from Central Europe and made his way to France where he enlisted in the Czech Army. Following the defeat of France in 1940, he joined the British Army, and was commissioned in the field during the Battle of Normandy in 1944, receiving the Military Cross from Field Marshal Montgomery in 1945.

After the Second World War, Maxwell served for a brief period in the Foreign Office (German Section) as Head of the Military Government Press Section in Berlin; and following a meeting with Ferdinand Springer, the German scientific publisher, he set up the academic publishing company, Pergamon Press. In 1969 negotiations between Maxwell's Pergamon Press and the Leasco Data Processing Corporation broke down when the American company began to doubt the profit forecasts. An investigation by the Department of Trade and Industry led to a report which concluded that Robert Maxwell was 'not in our opinion a person who can be relied on to exercise proper stewardship of a publicly quoted company'.

In 1974 Maxwell became involved in the *Scottish Daily News*, launched as a workers' co-operative, following the closure of the Glasgow offices of the *Scottish Daily Express*. However, the *SDN* was not a success – and lasted just six months, graphically described by Ron McKay and Brian Barr in *The Story of the Scottish Daily News*. In its final report, *The Royal Commision on the Press*, July 1977, was to note: 'It is well known that both the consultants advised against the chances of success; even with reduced manning levels, they thought the paper unlikely to reach the circulation of 230,000 which was necessary for it to break even. In the event, the circulation averaged only 150,000.'

London Evenings Battle

Three years after his successful take-over of the *Daily Mirror* and its sister papers, Maxwell decided to take on the *Evening Standard* – now 100 per cent owned by Associated Newspapers – through launching the *London Daily News*. It made its debut on 24 February 1987 with Magnus Linklater as editor and Charles Wintour as editorial consultant plus a first-class editorial staff – dedicated to fight in the same ABC1 market place as the *Standard*. But as Charles Wintour was later to say:[10]

> The most serious mistake was to launch with the twenty-four hour concept. When Maxwell told a small executive group that this was what he wanted I said it would increase costs by at least sixty per cent. Maxwell simply shrugged his shoulders. I believe he thought he could get two newspapers for the price of one and a half .... Senior editorial executives never knew whether they were fighting the *Mail* or the *Standard*. There were other major weaknesses, particularly in production and distribution .... too much instant decision-making, too much over-optimism, too much waste.

For Associated Newspapers and its chairman the threat of a new evening challenging the *Standard* could not be entertained; and in a brilliant spoiling move Lord Rothermere, while visiting Tokyo, decided to revive the *Evening News* – a title the *Evening Standard* had absorbed in 1987. Meanwhile, Bert Hardy, the *Standard* managing director, put forward a masterly promotion, offering five free houses as prizes to readers, while at the same time tightening up the paper's distribution network, using the company's vans to carry both the *Standard* and the *Evening News*. Many years later, Hardy was to say: 'We launched it [Evening News] within three days of Vere making the decision. We won the battle because we confused the whole market.'[11]

Bert Hardy had been invited by the then chairman, Lord Matthews, to join the *Standard* on 9 October 1980. One of the most senior managerial figures in Fleet Street, his previous experience in advertising and general management had included the *Daily Mirror*, *Sunday Pictorial* and IPC-owned *Sun*. When Rupert Murdoch bought the *News of the World* in 1969 he appointed Hardy as advertisement director, and a few months later Hardy was also to be responsible for the relaunched tabloid *Sun*. Following a period with the new London Weekend Television, in which Murdoch had a stake, Hardy was subsequently promoted to the post of managing director.[12]

In October 1977 Murdoch announced he was giving up his role as News International chief executive, while continuing as chairman, and that Hardy would take over the title while also remaining as News Group Newspapers' managing director. Hardy remained with News Group until September 1979; and during his time there he was deeply involved in the building of the Wapping plant. He was later to tell the author: 'An extra plant with alternative machinery and new manning deals was the only way to provide a break with Fleet Street and its restrictive practices.'

Within eight months of becoming chief executive of the *New Standard* – the paper had changed its title in September 1980 – Hardy was to face a possible newcomer, when it was announced that Lonrho, owners of *The Observer*, were looking at launching a London evening. Joint managing director of *The Observer*, Brian Nicholson – and a former *Standard* senior executive – said in June 1981: 'We're going into this very carefully; it's not going to be an instant newspaper, if it happens.' Pointing out that 150,000 readers of the London evenings had been lost since the merger of the *News* and *Standard*, he remarked: 'Naturally, it would be worth finding out whether the new paper is not attracting those readers because they are dissatisfied. Why there's such a low level of advertising and why the *Standard* hasn't had the effect on the market that a monopoly paper should.'

Responding, Bert Hardy could say: 'Too much money, too much time and too much heartache have been spent to give way to a newcomer. There is going to be a very aggressive, very cut-throat war between ourselves and the new paper. We are not simply going to walk away. There will be a battle for every inch of copy, every centimetre of advertising.' In the event *The Observer* decided not to proceed, and it was to be a further seven years before a new evening was to enter the London market.

Now, under the guidance of John Leese, Lori Miles, fresh from editorial charge of *Chat*, was appointed editor of the *Evening News* – one of the first of the new band of women editors – and controlled a small team of 'some thirty-five *Standard* journalists and freelances detailed to get on with it'.

The scene was set for a three-way battle for the London evening market: 'The *Daily News*, like the *Standard*, was offered to the public at 20p a copy and the *Evening News* cut its price to 10p. When Maxwell was rash enough to match this, Leese halved its price again to a derisory 5p. It was the last set-piece battle of the Old Fleet Street, won by Leese with a poker-player's panache.' Caught between the *Standard* on the one hand and the more down-market *News* on the other, Maxwell's London *Daily News* folded on 24 July 1987, with heavy losses. The job done, the *Evening News*, selling 30,000 copies per issue, was closed down. Lori Miles left to make a great succes with *Take a Break*, later editing *TV Quick*.

Discussing his victory, Lord Rothermere told Raymond Snoddy of the *Financial Times* (and, later, the author):

> What gave me the greatest pleasure recently was the squashing of Bob Maxwell's *Daily News*. His product was aimed at the wrong market. It was badly thought out, poorly constructed and mechanically he didn't have the means of getting it to places he should have got it to. The whole thing was an ill-thought-out performance from beginning to end. It would have died anyway. The whole question was whether we could speed up its demise.

The Wapping Revolution

While Maxwell had been finalizing his plans for a new London daily, Rupert Murdoch – long disenchanted with the restrictions imposed by the print unions – had launched a revolution. Ever since he had assumed ownership of the *News of the World* and *The Sun*, followed in 1981 by *The Times* and *The Sunday Times* acquired from the second Lord Thomson, Murdoch had been beset by overmanning, restrictive practices and last-minute demands for higher pay, all of which had been contributing to print shortfalls, and a consequent loss of revenue.

Early in 1985 he met Bruce Matthews, his News International managing director, in up-state New York to discuss the possibility of a one-union print deal for the company's plant at Wapping – a plant designed to produce a new evening, the *London Post*, with Charles Wilson, former editor of *The Times*, as editorial director. The selected union would be the Electrical, Electronic, Telecommunications and Plumbing Union (EETPU).

A few weeks later, on Sunday 15 February , a key group of executives, having flown by Concorde, met Murdoch at his New York apartment. They included Matthews, Ken Taylor, technical director of News International, and Christopher Pole-Carew, former managing director of the *Nottingham Evening Post*, where he had introduced direct editorial inputting to Britain, now engaged as a consultant on computer technology.[13]

Realizing that a single-union print deal at Wapping, which excluded the NGA and SOGAT, could lead to strike action at his offices in Bouverie Street and Gray's Inn Road, Murdoch decided that the new plant would also have provision for a setting capacity: 'This was the first time we began to lay out a plan to have typesetting facilities there, and it was the first time we saw that we'd have to move the journalists there too.'

For its computer typesetting, News International decided on a well-proven operation. Murdoch selected Atex, a direct inputting system already in use at more than five hundred newspaper offices, saying: 'We want something off the shelf. We want simple processes because we are going to have half-trained manpower.' After setting, the columns would be pasted down on make-up sheets – there would be no electronic page make-up. Early in 1985, a $10 million order was placed with Atex; and, with the utmost secrecy, training and installation began under the direction of Pole-Carew – and on 1 May 1985 the test run was completed.[14]

With the print unions aware of News International's plans for printing at Wapping – but not for typesetting – Murdoch met with their executives at the end of September and said:

> I have strained myself and my senior colleagues physically, emotionally and financially to build this business and we have met with nothing but broken promises and total opposition. All national newspaper production departments are overmanned by from fifty to 300 per cent, with working practices that are a continuing disgrace to us all.

Throughout the summer, members of the EEPTU were being bussed to Wapping every day from Southampton, where they had been recruited. In October 1985, having seen copies of the *London Post*, smuggled from the plant, the SOGAT London Machine Branch Committee of *The Sun* recommended a strike – a recommendation turned down three to two by the membership.

Murdoch, now aiming to move all his titles to Wapping – and fully expecting circulation problems even if he were able to print the papers – arranged to set-up his own road distribution, while also ensuring that the plant was protected with razor wire and a 12ft-high spiked metal fence.[15]

On 19 January 1986 a *Sunday Times* advertisement supplement was printed at Wapping. The following week, at a meeting with News International executives, union leaders offered wide-ranging concessions on manning levels and working practices. It was too late. They were informed that their members would not be required at Wapping and that there would be heavy job losses at Bouverie Street and Gray's Inn Road,

Within 24 hours a strike had been called by the print unions on all four titles; and on Friday 24 January, more than 5000 print workers walked out. That same evening, editor Kelvin MacKenzie addressed *The Sun* journalists, resulting in their voting to go to Wapping 100 to 8. A few hours later *The Times* and the *News of the World* editorial chapels also voted in favour, and there was to be a similar approval by *The Sunday Times* journalists on the Monday. Following the first issues of *The Times* and *The Sun* being printed, Murdoch telephoned Bert Hardy, his former chief executive – and the man who had been responsible for the building of the Wapping plant – and said: 'Thank you Bert. You were right and I was wrong.'[16]

For more than a year, mass picketing by the print unions was to take place outside the News International plant at Wapping – including, on occasion, violent clashes with the police – but the papers always got through. The Wapping revolution showed that the old days of Fleet Street overmanning and restrictive practices had gone forever and that the National Press was about to enter a new era.

One person who had no doubt as to the result had been Charles Wintour, recently-retired editor of the *Evening Standard* and now editing the *Press Gazette*. In his leader of 20 January 1986 he had written: 'The two major print unions pinned themselves into a corner over Wapping. Now they are involved in a tragedy of their own making . . . . It is a dispute that now can have only one end. Fleet Street will never be the same again.'

Enter Eddy Shah

Just weeks after Rupert Murdoch had made his move to Wapping, on 4 March 1986, Eddy Shah, with Brian MacArthur[17] as editor, launched *Today*, Britain's first national colour seven-day newspaper, with state-of-the-art-technology, direct input by journalists and printed web-offset at satellite plants. It was a remarkable achievement for Shah who had previously run a group of free weeklies from Warrington. Following the first issue of *Today*, he proudly proclaimed: 'We said we'd go on March 4 two years ago and we were an hour and a half late. I think it's magic.'

After being educated at Gordonstoun, Eddy Shah had worked as a stage-hand, then as a floor manager with Granada Television before entering newspapers in 1974 as an advertisement salesman on the *Manchester Times*, a 220,000-circulation free newspaper (edited at the outset by the author). Following the closure of the *Manchester Times*, Shah launched the *Sale and Altrincham Messenger*, initially printed at West Midlands Press, Walsall.[18] In 1980, now owning four newspapers in the Manchester area, he decided to move the computer setting of his *Messenger* series from Carlisle to Stockport, but there he ran into trouble with the NGA, who demanded a closed shop. The culmination came on Tuesday, 29 November 1983 when four thousand pickets attempted to stop the *Messenger* being published at Warrington.

With the doors of his plant under attack from the pickets – inside there were just ten workers, six security guards and two dogs – Shah rang Andrew Neil, editor of *The Sunday Times*, and probably his biggest supporter. Neil immediately telephoned Leon Brittan, Home Secretary, but already the police – including the Manchester Tactical Aid Group in full riot gear – were in action; and shortly before five a.m. the road was cleared and the *Messenger* vans were able to depart. Charles Wintour was to write: 'The forecourt there was to witness the battle that decided the future of the newspaper industry.'[19]

The following morning, Andrew Neil wrote to Margaret Thatcher, the Prime Minister, outlining his grave concern:[20] 'We are no longer dealing with a challenge to the government's labour laws, but riotous assembly .... Mr Shah's resolve remains firm .... but he was clearly shaken by last night's events, which he told me were "touch and go".' In the next issue of *The Sunday Times*, 4 December, Neil devoted most of the news analysis pages to the 'Battle of Warrington', and in a strong leader attacked Fleet Street for its 'pusillanimous management, pig-headed unions and archaic technology'.

Shah was now a well-known figure, appearing in national newspapers and on television. He was later to say: 'I never approached Fleet Street, except when I appealed to *The Sunday Times* for help at the height of the Warrington crisis.' Shah met Neil, who, citing the example of *USA Today*, told him of the logic of using the new technology but with one union, and outlined the economics of starting a national newspaper on this basis. From this conversation was to emerge *Today*, and in February 1984, having raised £18 millions for the project – and with much advice from former senior Fleet Street executives – Eddy Shah was able to proceed.

For his editor, he chose Brian MacArthur,[21] in charge of the Northcliffe-owned *Western Morning News* since 1984. Prior to this, MacArthur had worked for the *Yorkshire Post*, *Daily Mail* and *The Guardian* before joining *The Times* in 1967, where he was, successively, education correspondent, deputy features editor, founder editor of *The Times Higher Education Supplement* (1971–76) and home news editor. From 1978 to 1979 he was deputy editor of the *Evening Standard*; and then he returned to Times Newspapers as chief assistant to Harold Evans, editor of *The Sunday Times*. He next worked as executive editor (news) under Evans on *The Times*, 1981–82, before returning to *The Sunday Times* as joint deputy editor.

Assisting Eddy Shah and Brian MacArthur was Jeremy Deedes, managing editor, who, after working as a reporter on the *Daily Sketch*, in 1969 joined the *Evening*

Standard, being the Diary editor, 1971–76. He then transferred to the *Daily Express* as deputy editor, 1976–79, when he returned to the *Standard* as managing editor, remaining there until 1985 before joining *Today*. Twenty years later he was to tell Bill Hagerty, editor, in *British Journalism Review*, no. 3, 2005;

> Eddy had made himself a household name through his exploits at Warrington, where he had effectively curbed the power of the trade unions. That in itself was the biggest problem for *Today*, because we had to deal with everyone outside the normal structure. We couldn't contract print because the printing works were all unionised and were not going to have anything to do with Eddy Shah. Similarly, all the distributors, both wholesale and retail, were unionised and were not going to touch *Today*. So we had to invent every single part of the chain, from putting the words on to a computer right through to delivering the paper through the letter-box.

Unfortunately, three months after its launch in March 1986, sales of *Today* had dropped to 400,000; and there was need for further investment. In June 1986, Lonrho, owners of *The Observer*, put up £10 million and bought out the original shareholders for a further £10 million. Shah remained as chairman and chief executive. However, Lonrho found the losses too severe. Robert Maxwell, with a bid for £10 million cash, plus taking more than £30 million in loan stock, looked set to be the new owner. He, in turn, informed Rupert Murdoch, in California, that *Today* would honour its contract to print copies of the *News of the World*.

Realizing that Maxwell had not yet purchased *Today*, Murdoch, with the aid of David Montgomery, editor of the *News of the World*, expressed an interest to Lonrho and secured the paper for £38 million, with Shah selling out his final 10 per cent holding. Montgomery was then appointed editor and managing director. Apart from *Today*, a sister paper, *Sunday Today*, was also launched, but this was closed down in 1987. Under Rupert Murdoch's ownership *Today* lasted until 16 November 1995 when it ceased publication.

Although Eddy Shah's *Today* had not been a financial success, it had been a catalyst for change. And to quote Charles Wintour:[22]

> He was the first to show that printing in inner London was no longer a necessity for a national newspaper . . . . He made every management in Fleet Street re-think its attitude to colour. He demonstrated that . . . . the industry was grossly over-manned. He became an important agent of reform and helped to ensure its (Fleet Street) continued and profitable survival.

In a leader, *The Times* wrote of Eddy Shah and his achievement with *Today*: 'Mr Shah had launched – and completed – a revolution.' Ten years later, Andrew Neil was to write:[23]

> But it is Eddy who deserves our gratitude. He had shown that the tyranny of the print unions could be overthrown if you have the guts to take them on – and a strategy for winning. The symbolism of his success should not be underestimated for the move to Wapping might never have happened without him: Shah shamed us into action

As for Eddy Shah, he returned to Warrington, and there, on 10 November 1988, with

Lloyd Turner, former *Daily Star* editor in charge, launched another daily, the *Post*, using desk-top publishing. Unfortunately, it was not a success, and closed after just thirty-three issues on 17 December, costing Shah £3.5 million. Shah later sold his Messenger group for £25 million and turned his attention to television production, afterwards becoming a successful novelist and being involved with country clubs.

Another of the new nationals to fail – launched as a result of 'the wind of change through Fleet Street' – was the *News on Sunday*, 'Britain's bravest and brightest', a paper partly financed by trade unions. Having raised £6.5 million, the 48-page tabloid monochrome paper was launched on 26 April 1987, with journalists inputting the copy and NGA compositors doing the paste-up. The initial print figure was 1,500,000 copies, but sales were just 518,000 and over the next few weeks circulation fell to 230,000.[24] 'It was estimated that each copy cost £5 to produce and was selling for 35p.' At the time of its closure in November 1986, sales had fallen to 130,000 and the paper was losing £85,000 a week.

The definitive story of the paper is contained in *Disaster! The Rise and Fall of News on Sunday: Anatomy of a business failure* by Peter Chippindale and Chris Horrie. On page 228, they write:

> *News on Sunday* wasn't all bad. The paper did counter the usual right-wing bias in the press, it did have some good stories, and although it was hopelessly gloomy, it was refreshing to have a tabloid without tits, cheescake and a lot of rubbish that fills its rivals. And with a longer run in its original form, it would undoubtedly have got better. The paper did pick up readers at the bottom end of the market who genuinely had given up newspapers in disgust and were cheered by its appearance. The desire for something 'decent for the masses' appealed to at least to a few of them.

A Successful Launch

However, there was one successful launch: *The Independent*, started by Andreas Whittam Smith, Matthew Symonds and Stephen Glover, all of *The Daily Telegraph*. As City editor, Whittam Smith knew where to seek professional advice and raise money; and he had little difficulty in recruiting journalists, including a number of people who did not want to work for News International or who disliked walking through the threatening picket lines at Fortress Wapping. The idea for a new upmarket broadsheet daily came to Whittam Smith following an announcement on 25 February 1985 that Eddy Shah was to start a national daily.

A month later Whittam Smith produced for his own use a memo outlining the plans for a new quality paper, including its aims, structure and how to secure the necessary cash. Realizing that most evening newspaper machine-rooms lay idle from late afternoon until the following day, he decided that there was no need to invest in presses for the new title, but, through the use of facsimile transmission, could use regional printing facilities. Then, obtaining the best possible advice from advertising agents, merchant bankers, stockbrokers and others, he was able to raise £18 million.

On 31 March 1985, Whittam Smith wrote:[25] 'I am now inclined to think that proclaiming an independent standpoint is actually making a definite position on the political spectrum'; and some eighteen months later, on 7 October 1986, *The Independent* was successfully launched, showing the result of a series of well-planned dummies, a fine staff of experienced journalists – a third of whom had joined from *The Times* or *The Sunday Times* – plus a first-class production operation, including the use of satellite printing. (This was the first occasion when a national newspaper had been launched using presses owned by regional newspaper groups.) Stephen Glover was later to write:[26] 'Our competence to launch a newspaper was never openly questioned by Saatchi's or any of our financial advisers. They simply took on trust that we could do it.'

Initially a success, sales fell to little more than 250,000 by January 1987, but by the year's end a circulation of 360,000 had been achieved; and during those months the paper had lived up to its title by not backing any political party in the general election of 1987. With its high-class foreign news coverage, strong features, in-depth sports and extra-large use of pictures, exceptionally well printed through the use of web-offset presses, *The Independent* was a paper born of the age – and it attracted a large readership from the young ABC1 types, an advertiser's dream market.

On 28 January 1990 *The Independent* launched a sister paper, the *Independent on Sunday*, edited by Stephen Glover, an up-market broadsheet with a tabloid business section. Four months earlier, on 17 September 1989, from Clerkenwell, London, the *Sunday Correspondent* – edited by Peter Cole with Nick Shott, ex-Express Newspapers, as chief executive – had made its debut. Less than twelve months later, on 20 August 1990, under the editorship of John Bryant, the *Correspondent* became the first quality Sunday tabloid, but unfortunately it ceased publication on 27 November of the same year.

In April 1992, *The Independent*'s circulation, 402,000, overtook that of *The Times*; and during the general election the paper had once again taken a non-partisan line, leading Andreas Whittam Smith to say: 'We've had a very good election campaign and sales are up around ten per cent. We've caught and overtaken *The Times*.'

Fleet Street Exodus

The dramatic move by News International to Wapping – leading to the weakening of trade unions, plus the large sums obtained by Fleet Street publishers through Reuters going public (see chapter twenty, p.383–384) – meant that all national newspaper groups were now looking at reducing their manning and introducing new technology: direct inputting by journalists and advertisement staffs. For the Newspaper Publishers Association, which for eighty years had looked after the interests of the employers, it was to be a changing world. No longer would there be the constant threat of nightly stoppages by local chapels demanding extra monies; and the need for national negotiations with trade unions belonged to the past. News International had laid down the marker – local agreements only. And this was to be followed by

Mirror Group Newspapers, *The Guardian* and the production operation of *The Daily Telegraph* (Westferry Road). Steve Oram, a future director of the NPA, was to write at the time:[27]

> These houses chose to withdraw from national negotations with the production unions in order to progress their own separate negotiations on matters to which a national agreement with the production unions would make little or no contribution. A decision was subsequently reached by the NPA Council to notify the unions that there would be no national negotiations for 1987 or for the forseeable future. This was followed by a further council decision to disband entirely the industrial relations department in 1987.

One person affected by the decision was Lord Marsh, Chairman of the NPA for the past eleven years, who in a farewell interview was to say:[28]

> I'm delighted to be going. The break-up of Fleet Street is the best thing that's happened in the history of national newspapers. It was inevitable – just like the arrival of new technology and the reduction in manning levels. The behaviour of the print unions caused it all to happen sooner than it otherwise would have happened. Fleet Street used to be a village and what everybody saw or heard, in terms of wages and conditions, was taken to be the norm. The unions would come in here and make the most outrageous demands. Now that they are spread out between the Isle of Dogs and Kensington they are having to do very different in-house deals. This couldn't have happened before because come lunchtime all the trade union negotiators were in the Fleet Street pubs comparing notes.

The Guardian *Converts*

A leader in the race to take advantage of this 'new dawn' was *The Guardian*, which in 1986 announced that printing of its title would move from Gray's Inn Road, where it was produced on *The Sunday Times* presses, to an enhanced web-offset plant in Docklands; and, at the same time, overall staffing would be reduced from 1000 to 800. The editorial office, though, would remain at Farringdon Road, north of Fleet Street. Managing director Harry Roche, pointing out the need to move away from the traditional Linotype setting to computer technology, said: 'We must go direct input and the all-electronic newsroom to be competitive.'

Although founded in pre-Victorian times by editor John Edward Taylor on 5 May 1821 as the *Manchester Guardian*, it was not until 1961 that the paper was published in London. It had for more than one hundred years been the most successful – and influential – of all provincial dailies. Taylor Snr. was succeeded by his son, John Edward, who in 1855 converted the title from a bi-weekly to a daily paper, and two years later reduced its price from twopence to one penny. In the late 1860s, a London office was established in the neighbourhood of the Houses of Parliament, and it was not until immediately prior to the First World War that this office was moved to Fleet Street.

Very much to the fore in provincial newspaper matters, in 1870 Taylor was the leader of those responsible for the formation of the Press Association. In February of the following year he engaged C.P. Scott, his 24-year-old cousin, for the paper and twelve months later Scott took over as editor. He was to *be* the *Manchester Guardian* for the next six decades; and was editor of the paper from 1872 until 1929, a record 57 years. Within a decade of assuming the editorship, he had, in 1880, made the *Manchester Guardian* the voice of Home Rule. 'Scott went on to make *The Guardian* into something unique in British journalism: a provincial paper which came to be accepted not only in Britain but in every part of the civilised world as the supreme expression of liberal spirit.'

From 1907 until 1913, Scott, apart from being editor, was also sole proprietor; until in 1914 he divided the bulk of his holding of ordinary shares between his two sons, Edward and John, and his son-in-law C.E. Montague. In 1921, the *Manchester Guardian* celebrated its centenary, giving Scott the opportunity, in a famous and much-quoted leader, to express his creed for the paper:[29] 'Its primary office is the gathering of news. At the peril of its soul it must see that the supply is not tainted. Neither in what it gives, nor in what it does not give, nor in the mode of presentation must the unclouded face of truth suffer wrong. Comment is free, but facts are sacred.'

Despite the acknowledgement that the *Manchester Guardian* under Scott deserved to be considered a great paper, it did not always make profits. Nevertheless, careful accumulation of reserves during prosperous years had made possible the purchase between 1923 and 1930 of the *Manchester Evening News*, which, with its profits in the years to come, was able to provide a cushion for *The Guardian*. When Scott retired he was succeeded by his son, Edward Taylor Scott, but his tenure as editor was all too brief, for on 22 April 1932 he was drowned in a boating accident on Lake Windermere.

The death of C.P. Scott on 1 January 1932, followed within weeks by the unexepected demise of his son Edward, meant that the company – now under the direction of C.P.'s other son, John – was facing strong demands from the Inland Revenue. Rather than leave his ordinary shares to his sons and nephews, John Scott now decided to form a trust; and on '10 June 1936 the Scott Trust was finally established, with all the ordinary shares being transferred to seven trustees – all of them closely connected with the paper'.[30]

Following Edward Taylor's death W.P. Crozier assumed the editorship, and he was succeeded by A.P. Wadsworth (1944–56). After Wadsworth came Alastair Hetherington (1956–75), who had joined the paper in 1950 as a leader writer and defence correspondent, rising to become foreign editor in 1953. He was to write:[31]

> Only one instruction is given to the editor of *The Guardian* on his appointment. It is to 'carry on the paper in the same spirit as before' – a gloriously liberal directive, leaving the editor great freedom. It was delivered to me by Laurence Scott, a grandson of C.P. and company chairman, as we walked round his garden at Alderley Edge in October 1956.

The paper's title changed to *The Guardian* in 1959, and since 1961 it has been produced in London. When Hetherington departed to become Controller of BBC Scotland in 1975, Peter Preston was appointed editor. Educated at St John's College, Oxford, he joined the Liverpool *Daily Post* in 1960, leaving three years later for *The Guardian*. During the Indo-Pakistan War, and in Bangladesh and Cyprus, he served as a war correspondent and foreign correspondent, and in 1972 was appointed production director. Preston was to remain editor until February 1995, when, in agreement with his fellow Trust members, he stepped down to become editor-in-chief, assuming more responsibility for the recently-acquired *Observer*.

His successor as editor was to be Alan Rusbridger, who, on leaving Magdalene College, Cambridge, was a reporter on the *Cambridge Evening News* in 1976. Three years later he moved to *The Guardian* in a similar role, later becoming diary editor, and remained there until 1986. He then joined *The Observer* as a critic before, in 1987, becoming Washington correspondent of the *London Daily News*. That same year he returned to England and *The Guardian*, this time as Weekend editor, and was subsequently features editor and deputy editor.

In 1987 a new print centre was opened on the Isle of Dogs, London; the following year the paper underwent a radical design, splitting into a two-section format, and an international edition of the paper began printing in Europe. A further new print centre was opened at Trafford Park, Manchester, in 1990 for the northern edition, but in 1996 the Isle of Dogs print works was put out of commission by an IRA bomb. Nevertheless, a full edition of the paper was produced and printed for distribution the following morning; and a new print site – Westferry Printers[32] – sharing with other nationals was found nearby. In 2002, The Newsroom, *The Guardian* and *Observer* archive and visitor centre, opened its doors.

Buying The Observer

Unlike the majority of national newspapers, whose editorial offices were now situated in Docklands, *The Observer* had moved from its base at Printing House Square, near Fleet Street, to Marco Polo House, Battersea, and there, as Britain's oldest Sunday newspaper, in 1991 celebrated its bicentenary. For the previous twelve months, sales of the paper had been hit by the launch of *The Independent on Sunday* and the brief life of the *Sunday Correspondent*, both of which were targeted at the same liberal readership.

In 1975, David Astor stood down as editor but remained on the board of trustees, charged with finding his successor. The board had been founded in February 1945 when Lord (Waldorf) Astor, David's father, had transferred ownership of the paper to the trustees: Waldorf himself; Tom Jones, an aide to Lloyd George in the First World War and deputy secretary of Cabinet 1916–30; and Arthur Mann, editor of the *Yorkshire Post*. Stephen Pritchard was to write:[33] 'Under the terms of the trust it was impossible for the paper to be bought and compulsory that its revenue be used for improving it, for promoting good journalism or for charitable purposes.'

Following war service, David Astor returned to the paper in 1945 as foreign editor, and three years later was appointed editor. As such he brought together a distinguished band of writers including George Orwell, Michael Davie, Vita Sackville-West, Kenneth Tynan, photographer Jane Bown, and a group of European émigré intellectuals led by Arthur Koestler.

For the next eight years, the circulation – and influence – of the paper was to grow steadily, but in November 1956 *The Observer*, unlike other titles, clashed with Prime Minister Anthony Eden over his handling of the Suez Invasion. In his leader, Astor was to declaim: 'We had not realised that our government was capable of such folly and such crookedness.' It was not, however, an opinion shared with thousands of the paper's readers who speedily withdrew their support – and several large corporations who ceased to advertise.

Although the doing away of newsprint rationing now meant the papers could up-page, for *The Observer*'s eight broadsheet pages weekly it presented a problem:

> Run on a shoestring, with no resources other than its income from advertising and circulation and whatever funds Astor could contribute, the paper could not compete for the big-name serials that were to become such a part of Sunday journalism. *The Sunday Telegraph* was launched in 1961, diverting advertisers away, and *The Sunday Times* fired back with the first colour supplement.

Reluctantly, Astor followed suit in 1964 with *The Observer Magazine*, which was to prove a success, and within three years circulation of the paper had reached a high of 905,248. During the next decade, though, the paper – like most other national titles – was to suffer a spate of industrial stoppages, causing endless discussion between unions and management, led by Arnold (later) Lord Goodman, chairman of the trustees, who was coincidentally chairman of the Newspaper Publishers Association. To save the paper, Goodman told the unions that unless massive savings were made the paper would die. This was to lead to a 20 per cent reduction in staff – something that had not been obtained by any other Fleet Street management.

After 27 years as editor, in December 1975 David Astor decided to step down; and in the search for his successor 'all the paper's journalists were canvassed and, of the five candidates, deputy editor Donald Trelford was their emphatic choice'.[34] Born in Coventry, after National Service as a pilot officer in the RAF he was an Open Exhibitioner at Selwyn College, Cambridge. He entered journalism as a reporter on the *Coventry Standard* in 1960 and the following year joined the *Sheffield Telegraph* as a reporter and sub-editor. From 1963 to 1966, he was editor of the *Times of Malawi*, and during this period was also correspondent in Africa for *The Times*, *The Observer* and the BBC. He returned to England as deputy news editor of *The Observer*, subsequently becoming assistant managing director, 1968; deputy editor, 1969; and editor 1975. In July 1992, Donald Trelford became chief executive/editor of *The Observer*.

Within weeks of assuming the editorship, Trelford was told by Astor and Goodman that, as the trustees could no longer fund the paper, it had been offered to Rupert Murdoch. Trelford immediately flew to New York and met Murdoch, who told him that he wanted to appoint Bruce Rothwell as editor-in-chief. With *The Observer* journalists bitterly opposed, Murdoch decided not to go ahead with any deal. For the next few months, there was to be deepening crisis, until later that year Kenneth Harris met Professor Douglass Cater at Rules Restaurant, London, and told him of the paper's plight. An interested Cater then telephoned Robert O. Anderson,

Texan head of Atlantic Richfield, a US oil company which funded the arts and the Aspen Institute for Humanistic Sciences.

Having talked with Lord Goodman, and having agreed to purchase the paper, Anderson was in London within days, and secured *The Observer* for a £1 note. Donald Trelford was to say:[35] 'I was the only person in the room with a £1 note, which I gave to Anderson.' Atlantic Richfield were to own *The Observer* from 1977 until 1981, when tiring of the millions that had been lost on the venture – and following a boardroom rebellion by Astor and Goodman, who had opposed a change in the management structure – they intended selling the paper to R.W. 'Tiny' Rowland.

Despite Trelford and his deputy, John Cole, forcing the takeover to be referred to the Monopolies and Mergers Commission, on 25 February 1981 Rowland was to be successful. Notwithstanding his opposition, 'Rowland kept Trelford on as editor and the paper grew in size, adding a separate Business section and expanding its arts and sports coverage'. Nevertheless, the next decade was not without its problems; and during this period there was speculation that Lonrho, its corporate owners, might be ready to sell the loss-making paper. The company's chief executive, 'Tiny' Rowland, had been criticized for exerting undue influence over the paper's business coverage of his long-standing feud with Mohamed Al Fayed over Harrods.

In 1993, *The Observer* was finally sold when it became part of the Guardian Media Group, who had outbid *The Independent*. At that point, Donald Trelford stood down as editor after eighteen years. Peter Preston was to write of Trelford's editorship:[36]

> He was fated, for many years, to be a defender as well as a crusader; a bruising role where he sometime felt himself beset on all sides. But Trelford was first and foremost a journalist and an editor: multi-talented, hands-on, a master of sport as well as news, shrewd and decisive. The paper, through his years, may often have been under attack, but it also won many awards and gathered together brilliant teams of writers who kept the flame of Astor alive. And Trelford, at the end, was there to pass *The Observer* on, unbroken and unbowed.

Trelford was succeeded by Jonathan Fenby, who had been deputy editor of *The Guardian*. As sales fell below the key average figure of 500,000 copies, Fenby was replaced by Andrew Jaspan in 1995, then by Will Hutton in 1996 and by Roger Alton in 1998. Following the sale of *The Observer* to the Guardian Media Group, the paper's editorial offices moved to *The Guardian* offices in Farringdon Road. It was noted that *The Observer* had appointed four editors in the space of five years, whereas the three previous editors – Donald Trelford, David Astor and J.L. Garvin – had served for 87 years of the twentieth century between them.

Trouble at the FT

Like most other groups the *Financial Times* had been beset with union difficulties. As far back as July 1975 the *FT* had announced that the paper would introduce computer typesetting with direct inputting by journalists, a decision which would lead to a reduction in staffing from 1400 to 900. However, despite the offer of handsome redundancy packages, retraining and no loss of earnings – plus the support of the

TUC Printing Industries Committee – the plan was abandoned because of union opposition.

Five years later, management were intent once more on introducing computerized typesetting, but again chapel negotiations were to become bogged down, leading Alan Hare, chairman of the *Financial Times*, to write in *The Times* on 12 December, 1982:

> A newspaper company loses irrevocable revenue in a dispute; most union members continue to be paid through stoppage or disruption .... In a world in which other media are proliferating and attracting advertisers and readers away from newspapers, the Fleet Street workforce is overpaid, overlarge and protected by restrictive practices .... Our outdated technology is the laughing stock of the rest of the world.

The following summer, though, it was not discussions over new technology that were to bring about a ten-week stoppage but a demarcation issue in the pressroom. The *FT* reappeared on 9 August 1983, and the cost to management for the ten-week stoppage was some £6 million in lost revenue. There was to be trouble the following year, when in a six-week period during the autumn of 1984 the *FT* lost 2.3 million copies, and throughout the year industrial unrest was to cost £3.2 million, leaving new chief executive Frank Barlow to deplore the 'nihilistic and destructive industrial action'.

There was to be one final confrontation after the *FT* had lost half its run. As David Kynaston was to write in his history of the *Financial Times*: 'Barlow warned members of the NGA machine chapel that the company would use the law if they were not prepared to honour agreements. The threat worked, for production went smoothly for the rest of the year and then throughout 1986 as well.' That same year the circulation passed 250,000 on the back of the 'No *FT* .... No Comment' campaign; and the printing processes moved from hot metal to cold set.

The editor was Geoffrey Owen, who had succeeded Fredy Fisher in 1980, and he was to remain in charge until the appointment of Richard Lambert in 1991. Two years earlier the *FT* London office had been relocated from Bracken House to One Southwark Bridge. Throughout the years, the global expansion of the *Financial Times* using satellite links has led to printing in London, Leeds, Dublin, Frankfurt, Brussels, Stockholm, Milan, Madrid, New York, Chicago, Los Angeles, San Francisco, Dallas, Atlanta, Orlando, Washington DC, Tokyo, Hong Kong, Singapore, Seoul, Dubai, Sydney, Johannesburg.

Associated Move West

Associated Newspapers, too, unveiled its plans when it announced that it would move its titles to Kensington High Street by 1988 at a cost of some £100 million. The first newspaper to proceed to the magnificent Northcliffe House was the *Evening Standard* in December 1988. The *Mail on Sunday* followed in July 1989, and the last to cross were the *Daily Mail* and its chairman, Lord Rothermere. Here again, an all-electronic newsroom, with direct inputting by journalists, was installed; and, like most of the other nationals, printing – after the pages had been electronically transmitted from the editorial offices – was now being undertaken at satellite plants, either company-owned or under contract.

Since moving to Kensington, the success story of Associated Newspapers had continued with greatly increased circulation on the *Daily Mail* and the *Mail on Sunday*. Appointed editor of the *Daily Mail* in July 1992, Paul Dacre had seen sales rise to 2,480,374. From 16 July 1998 he had also been editor-in-chief. Joining the *Daily Express* in 1971, he rose to become associate features editor; and from 1976 to 1979 was Washington and then New York correspondent. In 1980 he became bureau chief of the *Daily Mail* New York office, and in 1983 returned to Fleet Street as news editor. Three years later he was appointed assistant editor (news and features). He then became assistant editor (features) 1987, executive editor, 1988; and associate editor, 1989. Two years later he transferred to its sister paper the *Evening Standard* when he was appointed editor.

The decade, however, had not been without its sorrow, for in the space of less than three months the two men who had done so much to contribute to the success of Associated Newspapers were dead: on 10 June 1998, Sir David English; and on 3 September 1998, the third Viscount Rothermere.

David English had enjoyed a most distinguished career, working for the *Daily Mirror*, 1951–53; *Reynolds News*, 1954; *Daily Sketch*, *Sunday Dispatch*; and *Daily Express*, 1961–69. He was then appointed editor of the *Daily Sketch* and in 1971 became editor of the *Daily Mail*. And as the *Evening Standard* was to say: 'He applied his energy and vision to reverse declining circulation and, eventually, overtook the *Daily Express* [in 1988] which had for so long dominated the market . . . . He forged a unique personal relationship with Lord Rothermere (Vere Harmsworth), which persisted until the day he died.'

David English was also editor of the *Mail on Sunday*, 1981–82, and had been editor-in-chief of Associated Newspapers since 1981 and deputy chairman since 1988. He had been knighted in 1982; and in July 1991 after twenty-one years of editing the *Daily Mail* was appointed chairman of Associated Newspapers. His sudden death shocked the newspaper industry, and Lord Rothermere, in leading the tributes, was to say: 'He was simply the best of his generation and the most able and talented editor that I and Fleet Street have known.'

As chairman of the Daily Mail & General Trust, Lord Rothermere had believed entirely that his paper should be editorial-led, a policy that paid off with all his publications.[39] Among the many tributes paid to Lord Rothermere, the Prime Minister, Tony Blair, said: 'He was an extraordinary man and underneath that very bluff exterior was a sharp mind and a very kind personality. I grew to value his company and his conversation.' Former Prime Minister Baroness Thatcher commented: 'He was one of the great figures in the British newspaper industry.'

Desmond Takes Control

During this period, Express Newspapers – for so long Associated Newspapers' greatest rival – had also moved into the new age. Following staff cuts in the 1980s, the numbers employed fell from almost 7000 to 1700.[40] The famous black glass building – 121 Fleet Street – was sold to bankers Goldman Sachs, and on 17 November 1989 the *Daily Express* was printed there for the last time. Production then moved to Westferry Printers in London's Docklands – a joint venture with *The Daily Telegraph* – while editorial offices were sited across the Thames at Ludgate House, Blackfriars. Seven years later, in the spring of 1996, United News & Media (previously United Newspapers) merged with MAI and as a result, Lord Hollick, chairman of MAI, became chief executive of the new company, including the *Daily Express*, *Sunday Express* and *Daily Star*, with David Stevens, now Lord Stevens of Ludgate, remaining as chairman.

There had been one notable departure from Express Newspapers during this period, when in 1986 Sir John Junor (he had been knighted six years earlier) retired from the editorship of the *Sunday Express*, having held the post for thirty-two years, fully justifying Beaverbrook's comments: 'I will put a golden crown on your head.' For much of that time he wrote the hugely successful 'JJ' column, and in so doing brought fame to the Scottish village of Auchtermuchty. In the early days of his editorship, a leader on 16 December 1956, under the heading of 'Privilege', which attacked politicians' petrol allowances, was to lead to his being summoned to the Bar of the House of Common, the last editor in a line stretching back to the eighteenth century.

After leaving the *Sunday Express* in 1989, Junor joined Associated Newspapers, where he wrote a hugely popular column for *The Mail on Sunday*. He died in May 1997. Former Prime Minister John Major was to say: 'He was one of the great figures of Fleet Street – an innovative editor, a perceptive observer of the scene, a writer of style. He was a larger-than-life character who adorned Fleet Street in a way matched by few others.'

In November 2000, Richard Desmond – beating off the Barclay brothers and Associated Newspapers – became the new owner of Express Newspapers with a successful bid of £125 million, saying:[41]

> The Express newspapers represent a vital part of Britain's press heritage and we are proud to have their stewardship in the 21st century. We bring a commitment to investment and a wide experience in the management of media. N&S is committed to innovation and investing whatever it takes.

To prove this, on 15 September 2002 he launched *Daily Star Sunday*; and two years later, in October 2004, Express Newspapers plus *OK!* magazine and his other publications belonging to Northern & Shell Network moved into new offices – 10 Lower Thames Street – former headquarters of HSBC, one of the most dramatic riverside buildings in London, and purchased for less than £40 million. Desmond said at the time of the move: 'I think we rescued the *Express*. No doubt about that .... We are stable, and we are making money and we have got no debt.'[42]

Having launched a US edition of *OK!* in 2005, his next goal is to win the contract to distribute a free afternoon London newspaper on the Tube – in opposition to Associated Newspapers' free morning *Metro*. Discussing the future of newspapers, he said: 'I'm an optimist for any business that gives customers what they want.'

20

Towards the millennium

BY THE LAST DECADE of the century, the exodus from Fleet Street was complete. Four factors had contributed to this: legislation passed by the Conservative government leading to unions being penalized financially for secondary picketing and the sequestration of their funds (here the NGA was particularly affected); the opening-up of Docklands as a business region, with the attraction of long-term, low rentals; the realization of Fleet Street land values; and, importantly, the windfall from Reuters' shares. For the long-time denizens of the 'Street of Shame' – especially the journalists – the exodus was to be a culture shock.

To walk down Fleet Street now was to find a world of bankers, lawyers – and coffee bars. El Vino and the Cheshire Cheese, true, were still thriving, but the opportunity to meet fellow journalists in the many hostelries belonged to another age. Fleet Street today is far flung: from Kensington in the west to Canary Wharf in the east.

In the past, the Red Lion in Poppins Court – always called 'Poppins' – had been the 'home' of *Daily Express* journalists; the *Mirror* staff had frequented the White Hart in Fetter Lane, known as the 'Stab' because of the office politics that took place there; the King and Keys, conveniently adjacent to *The Daily Telegraph*, had been a haven for its journalists, while the Clachan was used by the *Guardian;* and *Daily Mail* staff drank at the White Swan, affectionately dubbed the 'Mucky Duck'. Simmonds the Booksellers, which at no. 16 Fleet Street had occupied the narrowest shop in the City, dating back to 1522, had departed. No longer was there this family business, run as an oasis of calm and friendly relaxation, where one would meet foreign correspondents returning to London.[1]

As for the newspaper offices, very little had changed in the previous fifty years: the editorial floor, almost always lino covered, was still chaotic mayhem. There was the smoke-filled atmosphere, the clattering of manual typewriters and the frequent shouts of 'boy' as messengers were called to take copy to the composing room or to seek cuttings from the library – or even to obtain cigarettes from the tobacconist next door. And on the floor below there was the regular noise from dozens of Linotypes setting the copy, whose operators, all on piece work, were the highest paid craftsmen in Fleet Street. Then came the page make-up in steel chases on the stone, ready for the stereo department, where a papier-mâché flong was taken before being sent to the foundry for the semi-cylindrical lead plates, each weighing more than fifty pounds, to be cast. All was now ready for the pressroom. Award-winning author and journalist Michael Frayn has left a splendid and evocative account of those days:[2]

> .... Great cylinders of newsprint went swinging above your head from the articulated lorries blocking every side-street. Through grimy pavement-level skylights here and there you could glimpse the web racing on the huge machines thundering in the basement .... And, wafting from every bay and ventilator and seedy lobby, that intoxicating smell [ink, hot metal, sweat ....]

True, only the black-glassed building of the *Daily Express* – 'in the entrance hall the gilding on the complicated bas-reliefs, packed with the symbols and heraldry of an Empire upon which it was anathema to suppose the sun would ever set'[3] – and the more traditional offices of *The Daily Telegraph* were actually in Fleet Street, but it *was* a village, with its dozens of minor roads and alleyways running off, many inhabited by other national newspapers and offices of regional publications; and from breakfast time, when the first editions of the *Evening News*, *Star* and *Evening Standard* hit the streets, until the early hours of the following morning, when the dailies had ceased their runs, the area seldom slept.

But for the journalists – most of the compositors having been made redundant – there was now to be a different world: direct inputting of copy and make-up of pages, thereby doing away with the Linotype operators, readers and stone hands; and, for everyone working in the newspaper industry, hot-metal methods belonged to the past. With printing sited far away from the editorial floor, no longer would journalists be able to savour the heady smells of ink and newsprint and hear the roar of the presses, or as Rudyard Kipling had written seventy-five years earlier when being taken around the *Daily Express* machine room by its editor, R.D. Blumenfeld:

> Who once had served to the sultry hour
> When roaring like a gale,
> The Harrild and the Hoe devour
> The league-long paper bale
> And has lit his pipe in the morning calm
> That follows the midnight stress;
> He has sold his heart to the old black art
> Men call the Daily Press

Much of the glamour had gone; and as Alan Watkins, the prize-winning columnist, was to write:[4]

> It was in Battersea that I realised the magnitude of the change that had overtaken journalism. People would spend hours, seven, eight or more, sitting in front of their computer screens, tapping energetically away, gazing lugubriously at them or, occasionally, making a telephone call. Some would create little shrines around them: photographs of nearest and dearest, potted plant flowers in jars, some mugs containing pencils and ball-point pens, others containing instant coffee.

And from Peter McKay, gossip columnist, on the *Daily Mail*: 'Fleet Street was a seething mass of printers, advertisers and journalists, drinking and punching each other every night, all night. People literally never went home .... Nowadays we sit in the far corners of London, like battery hens at computer terminals, pecking out our stuff, and never meeting one another.'[5] The last word, from Chris Moncrieff, former Press Association political editor: 'Every journalist wishes he was still there, because as you walked up and down Fleet Street there was always somebody you knew.'[6]

Reuters Goes Public

One of the reasons for the exodus from Fleet Street – and the introduction of modern technology plus state-of-the-art pressrooms – had been that with the flotation of Reuters all newspaper groups were now cash-rich. As noted in chapter fifteen (p.290–294), on 29 October 1941 it was announced that the Press Association and the Newspaper Proprietors Association, already owning some 25 per cent of the company through their regional newspapers, were now co-owners of Reuters.

To secure the independence of the agency, the Reuters Trust was now formed, which provided that Reuters should never pass into the hands of any one interest, group or faction, and that its integrity, independence and freedom should be preserved. Since 1941 the company had been owned by PA and the NPA, and in 1947 the Australian Associated Press (AAP) and the New Zealand Press Association (NZPA) joined the Trust. From 1944 to 1959, Christopher Chancellor was general manager of the company; and it was said that 'the newspaper owners of Reuters had aimed to do little more than balance the books – they expected to get their news cheap and pay the minimum annual contribution'.[7]

However, with the arrival of Gerald Long as chief executive, 1963 to 1981, there began a change in the character of the company, entering the market of computerized information in 1964 with Stockmaster, the desk-top market-quotation system. Nine years later, after the collapse of the Bretton Woods Agreement, which regulated rates of exchange, the company launched the Reuter Monitor Money Rates Service, followed in 1981 by the Reuter Monitor Dealing – and as a result profits were to increase dramatically: 1963, £53,000; 1973, £700,000; 1983, £55,000,000.

Realizing the immense potential, Lord Matthews, chairman of Fleet (Express Newspapers), began to urge for a public flotation, and at the annual general meeting of his company on 13 October 1982, in answer to a question on Reuters, declared: 'Their profits are rising fairly dramatically. For many years we've been helping to prop them up. Now suddenly there is a new look about them. In the end it will mean a market quotation.' As Charles Wintour was to write: 'The agreement of all the parties was needed but the pressure of ready money for the asking was growing.' Sir Denis Hamilton, chairman of Reuters, noted in his memoirs: 'To begin with, the Press Association was totally against a public flotation, but . . . . the momentum was hard to stop. It soon became obvious that a second gold rush had started.'[8]

On 11 April 1984 Reuters Holdings was registered as a public limited company. And from the flotation on the London Stock Exchange and on NASDAQ in the United States, with a market value of some £700 million, either through selling their shares or borrowing heavily on their holdings, all Fleet Street newspapers were to share in the bonanza. For example, within a year *The Daily Telegraph* had raised £110 million for two new printing works.

Sir Denis Hamilton said : 'The financial basis for Reuters' world-wide expansion was secured, without affecting the control and independence of the news agency. As my final contribution to the world of journalism, it was something to be proud of.' As for the Trust, the cause of much dissension in 1941, it was now much more secure; and as Donald Read was to write: 'Its authority was no longer founded simply upon a shareholders' agreement, which could be overturned. Moreover, in order further to protect the company they had introduced weighted "A" shares, even at the expense of reducing the market value of their own holdings.'[9]

Subsequent to its flotation, Reuters made a series of acquisitions including Visnews (1985 – renamed Reuters Television), Instinet (1986), TIBCO (formerly Teknekron) and Quotron (both in 1994). Reuters continued to grow rapidly, and product launches included Equities 2000 (1987), Dealing 2000-2 (1992), Business Briefing (1994), Reuters Television for the financial markets (1994), 3000 Series (1996) and the Reuters 3000 Xtra service in 1999. Four years later, Reuters established its 'Greenhouse Fund' to take minority investments in a range of start-up technology companies, initially in the United States. In October 2001, Reuters completed the largest acquisition in its history, buying most of the assets of Bridge Information Systems; and in March 2003 acquired Multex.com, Inc., a provider of global financial information.

Two years later, in the summer of 2005, Reuters began the move from its headquarters at 85 Fleet Street to a ten-storey building at South Colonnade, Canary Wharf; and as a result its 2500 staff previously scattered at six locations were now united. Having sold its former headquarters to the UBS bank for £32.3 million, it was envisaged that Reuters would make savings of £5 million a year in its new premises, which included a 340-seat newsroom, 200-seat auditorium plus a 100-metre ticker-type LED screen displaying real-time price information from the major exchanges around the world.

The move came as part of a three-year restructuring programme, launched in 2003, to improve profitability, with more than 2000 jobs being cut from the global workforce of 14,500 in 91 countries. Chief executive Tom Glocer said: 'Reuters' move to Canary Wharf is more than simply a change of address. We leave behind a beautiful Lutyens-designed building that has been synonymous with Reuters since 1939. We move to a modern, highly functional headquarters, close to our major financial services customers in which we can house more than just the senior executive staff.'[10]

Editorially, Reuters has a staff of 2300 working in 197 bureaux, making it the world's largest international news agency. It publishes more than eight million words a day in nineteen languages and produces 1000 pictures from its team of 600 photographers.

On Wednesday 15 June 2005 Tom Glocer told a crowded congregation at St Bride's Church – in a service to commemorate the departure of Reuters from the area – that Fleet Street had represented both the best and the worst of British journalism. Rupert

Murdoch, chairman and chief executive of the News Corporation, read from Ecclesiasticus: 'Let us now praise famous men.' And Canon David Meara, Rector of St Bride's, who led the service, said: 'This has widely been reported as the last rites of Fleet Street as a geographical home which is now just a deserted village full of ghosts and memories, but it remain the generic name for the press everywhere and St Bride's remains the spiritual home for the industry.'[11]

But even while the Press was commemorating Reuters at its special service elsewhere Dr Rowan Williams, the Archbishop of Canterbury, in a speech at Lambeth Palace, was attacking the media, believing that journalists were drawn from too narrow a class, educational and ethnic base. 'They were too London-based and had a strong tribal identity which may be pretty far removed from the specific local and civic loyalties that form the raw materials of serious discursive politics.' He considered that some aspects of current journalistic practice were 'lethally damaging' and contributed to the 'embarrassingly low level of trust' in the profession.[12]

Press Association

While Reuters had been providing a world service for more than 150 years, for much of that time the Press Association had been covering the British Isles. The only national news agency for Britain and Ireland, it was founded in 1868 and is owned by the regional Press. The PA has no views, carries no editorials, nor does it campaign. It simply distributes news, unspun and without thrills, for 24 hours a day, seven days a week. And from the date of its birth until now the three watch-words of the PA have been: speed, accuracy and impartiality. Those are the vital criteria of which all PA journalists must constantly remind themselves.[13]

The romantic story is that the PA was conceived in a hansom cab, befogged in London, in which four provincial newspaper chiefs pondered how best to produce a national news service, cheap and reliable, for newspapers throughout Britain. They were being served by private telegraph companies, whose charges were exorbitant, whose reports were untrustworthy and whose manner was cavalier. The nationalization of these companies in 1870 put the PA on the map.

Newspapers throughout the land subscribed to the burgeoning service and received a regular flow of stories at a relatively cheap rate. Then, newspapers relied on the PA to provide verbatim reports of speeches, both in Parliament and outside, of the leading politicians. 'The reporters all had impeccable shorthand and carried around sheaves of carbon paper on which to write their stories.' An army of messenger boys, all in uniform, for years trod well-worn paths from the PA's Fleet Street offices to the post offices, filing telegrams to newspapers, or racing back to headquarters with news stories handed to them by reporters on assignments.

One thing that has not changed since the earliest days of the PA's history: the broadest selection of news, sports features, photographs and graphics comes from the agency at a fraction of the price any editor would be faced with when acquiring it directly. Nor has the core ethos of the agency been diminished. Its reputation is still of the utmost importance. In 1952, Winston Churchill said: 'Without your help the public would be uninformed, and without your integrity they would be misled and defrauded.'

Over the years, the PA has occupied three different offices in Fleet Street, the most famous of which is 85 Fleet Street, which opened in 1939 and was vacated by PA in 1995 in a move to Vauxhall Bridge Road. There have been stunning scoops over the years including the death of Diana, Princess of Wales; the events leading to the abdication of Edward VIII; and the resignation of Margaret Thatcher. Until the 1960s, PA reporters rarely left the country. Overseas was regarded as Reuters territory. However, since then, royalty, top politicians and cricket and football teams are followed around the globe by PA journalists. In addition, the PA had men in the Falklands conflict, in the Gulf War and the Balkans.

The photographic department of the PA did not start until after the Second World War – first jointly with Reuters but now independent. There have been many memorable pictures, including the destruction of *HMS Antelope* in the Falklands and the poignant shot of three queens, the present Queen, Queen Elizabeth the Queen Mother and Queen Mary at the funeral of King George VI. The PA, in addition to issuing millions of words and hundreds of pictures each week, now dominates the field of racing, football and cricket data. Its four hundred journalists, strategically placed throughout the United Kingdom and beyond, are never, strictly, off duty. Beyond Britain, the PA has bureaux in Brussels and New York. But there have been moments of crisis. However, only rarely, and then only briefly, has the PA been stopped by industrial action. In the 1990s, the PA successfully fought off UK News.

In the United Kingdom – where its serves virtually all the morning and evening and evening newspapers and broadcasting organizations – the PA has spread its wings. Now key parts of the operation, including sport, the news library with its more than 13 million cuttings, and copy-takers have been moved to Leeds, Howden or Wetherby. 'The years ahead will be no less bumpy than the past – but no less exhilarating either.'

Press Complaints Commission

All national and daily regional newspapers subscribe to Reuters and the Press Association but they also have a third affiliation: the Press Complaints Commission. One of the few organizations still operating from the Fleet Street area – since March 2006 at 20–23, Holborn – for more than a decade the Press Complaints Commission (PCC), as an independent body, has been dealing with complaints from members of the public regarding editorial content in newspapers and magazines. Providing a free, quick and easy service, the central aim of its work is to resolve disputes between a newspaper or magazine and the person complaining.[14]

The creation of a voluntary Press Council in 1953 heralded the beginning of Press self-regulation. Its aim was to maintain high ethical standards of journalism and to promote Press freedom. However, during the 1980s a small number of publications failed in the view of many to observe the basic ethics of journalism. This in turn reinforced a belief among members of Parliament that the Press Council, which had lost the confidence of some in the Press, was not a sufficiently effective body. Some MPs believed that the public interest required the enactment of a law of privacy and a right of reply as a statutory Press Council wielding enforceable legal sanctions.

Given the serious implications of such a course of action, the Government appointed a Departmental Committee under David Calcutt QC to examine the entire matter. The terms of reference were: 'To consider what measures (whether legislative or otherwise) are needed to give further protection to individual privacy from the activities of the Press and improve recourse against the Press for the individual citizen, taking account of exising remedies, including the law on defamation and breach of confidence; and to make recommendations.'

The Report of the Calcutt Committee was published in June 1990, and it proposed the setting-up of a Press Complaints Committee in place of the Press Council. The new commission would have 18 months to demonstrate 'that non-statutory self-regulation can be made to work effectively. This is a stiff test for the Press. If it fails, we recommend that a statutory system for handling complaints should be introduced.' The Press responded with vigour to the report and acted with great speed and co-operation to set up an independent Press Complaints Commission at the beginning of 1991. A committee of national and regional editors then produced for the first time a Code of Practice for the new Press Complaints Commission to uphold.

All publishers and editors committed themselves to this and to ensuring secure and adequate funding of the PCC. A Press Standards Board of Finance (Pressbof), modelled on the self-regulatory system established by the advertising industry in 1974, was put in place and charged with raising a levy upon the newspaper and periodical industries to finance the Commission. This arrangement ensured financial support for the PCC, while its complete independence is at the same time guaranteed by a majority of lay members, and is a further sign of the industry's commitments to effective self-regulation. Comprising 16 members – lay (non-Press) persons are always in the majority whenever the Commission sits – the PCC is a self-regulating body which is independent of the newspaper industry and government and has no statutory functions.

To date the Commission has handled some 40,000 complaints; and in his Annual Review 2004, Sir Christopher Meyer, Chairman, noted that a total of 3618 complaints had been received, which was very similar to the figure for 2003 (3649). This represented a 40 per cent increase on 2002 levels. In all, the Commission had to make 900 rulings under the Code in 2004, which represented a drop of around 14 per cent from 2003. The complaints that raised a possible breach of the Code also fell by seven per cent. This meant that, despite complaints levels remaining the same, there was a noticeable drop in substantive concerns about the newspaper and magazine industry.

Against that background, however, the PCC was busier than ever. It conducted 10 per cent more investigations than in 2003, and achieved the highest number of resolved complaints in its 13-year-old history. In 98 per cent of cases raising a possible breach of the Code, the Commission was able to negotiate appropriate remedial action on behalf of the complainant; in only two per cent of possible breaches was no appropriate offer made. These complaints were all upheld. A breakdown revealed:

Privacy – rulings: national 34.6%; regional 51%; Scottish 4.9%; Northern Irish 2.9%; magazine 5.9%
Investigations: National 44%; regional 36.5%; Scottish 10.4; Northern Irish 2.4%; magazine 6.7%

Guy Black, a recent Director, Press Complaints Commission, says: 'Self-regulation continues to work well and efficiently. A tough Code of Practice ensures that standards of reporting are consistently raised, and the commitment of editors to the work of the PCC means that complaint can be dealt with speedily and efficiently.'

Death of Maxwell

On 13 July 1984, *Robert* Maxwell achieved a long-held ambition when he purchased the *Daily Mirror* and its sister papers; and that afternoon at a press conference announced:[15] '. . . . Under my management, editors in the group will be free to produce their newspapers without interference, with their journalistic skills and judgement.' Editor of the *Daily Mirror* was Mike Molloy, who had been appointed in 1975, remaining in that position until 1985, when he became editor-in-chief of Mirror Group Newspapers. He left in 1990. He was succeeded as editor by Richard Stott, 1985–89.

Despite his declaration of non-involvement, Maxwell was intent on interfering in every facet – plus publicizing himself and his companies almost daily. Roy Greenslade, editor of the *Daily Mirror*, 1990–91, was to write:[16] 'Certainly, from the start of my tenure, Maxwell attempted to play engine driver, signalman and stationmaster . . . . I noted that his compromise with the unions inhibited the freedom of journalists to do as they wished.'

Richard Stott believed that:[17] 'His effect on the Mirror Group, so long featherbedded in every department, was devastating.' (Stott holds a unique place in Fleet Street, having five times been editor of national newspapers. During his twelve years as an editor he was in charge of the *Daily Mirror* twice for a total of six years, the *People* twice and was the last editor of *Today*.) Following a dispute at the *Sporting Life*, which led to the *Mirror* titles being suspended in August 1985, and determined to take a lead over other Fleet Street companies, Maxwell introduced the *Mirror* 'Survival Plan'. This meant negotiations with 52 chapels, and, ultimately, the staff being reduced from 6000 to 4400.

Apart from the Mirror Group, Maxwell had, unsuccessfully, launched the *London Daily News* and the *European*; and among his expensive acquisitions had been the *New York Daily News*. Following the death of Maxwell at sea on 5 November 1991 off Tenerife, it was discovered that he had left mountainous debts. 'Soon it became clear that £426 million had gone, £350 million of which was money from the Mirror Group.'

With the company in administration and in crisis, David Montgomery – a former *Daily Mirror* journalist and editor of the *News of the World*, 1985–87, and managing director/editor *Today*, 1987–90 – was appointed chief executive. There then followed a period of unpopular cost-cutting. Roy Greenslade later wrote:[18]

> Montgomery's ruthless cost-cutting efficiency was matched by his determination to ensure that no *Mirror* employee would lose his or her pension. Maxwell had hired the former *Times* editor Charlie Wilson to run his popular racing daily, the *Sporting Life*, and he became editor-in-chief of all the *Mirror* titles. Wilson gave Monty support while he was preparing his coup and backed him at the crucial board vote when he arrived. Monty put him in charge of sorting out the pension mess, a task which he carried out with undeniable energy and eventual success.

Having been floated on the Stock Exchange in 1991, three years later the Mirror Group left Holborn Circus, near Fleet Street, for Canary Wharf. In October 1994 Kelvin MacKenzie, having resigned from *The Sun* editorship, and, after eight months as managing director of BskyB, joined the Mirror group in a senior position. His brief from Montgomery was to run Mirror Television, working closely with Janet Street-Porter to launch L!ve TV in June 1995. With his wide experience, McKenzie was soon involved in the editorial side, and in the summer of 1995 suggested to Montgomery that Piers Morgan, then editor of the *News of the World*, should succeed Colin Myler as editor of the *Daily Mirror*. This duly took place in the September, when Myler became managing director.

There had also been much activity within the group's Sunday titles: when Maxwell assumed control, Bob Edwards, editor of the *Sunday Mirror* for a record thirteen years, became deputy chairman, and retired in 1985. Peter Thompson was editor 1985–86, followed by Mike Molloy, 1986–88; and in May 1991 Eve Pollard, editor 1988–91, resigned as editor of the *Sunday Mirror* to take up a similar position on the *Sunday Express*. She was succeeded by Bridget Rowe, editor of *TV Times* who, on Montgomery taking control, transferred to *The People*.

Meanwhile, at *The People* there had been a succession of editors: Richard Stott, 1984–85; Ernest Burrington, 1985–88; John Blake, 1988–89; Wendy Henry, 1989; Richard Stott, 1989; Ernest Burrington, 1989–91; and Bill Hagerty, 1991–92. A journalist with wide experience, Hagerty had worked for the *Sunday Citizen* and *Daily Sketch*, 1960–67, before joining the *Daily Mirror* and rising to assistant editor. From 1981 to 1985, he was assistant editor on the *Sunday Mirror* and then *The People*, but left to become managing editor (features) on *Today*, and was then editor, *Sunday Today*, 1986–87. In 1988, he was appointed deputy editor of the *Sunday Mirror* and two years later took up a similar position with the *Daily Mirror*. He became editor of *The People* in 1991–92 and now edits the *British Journalism Review*.

On 17 May 1998 Hugh Cudlipp, the *Mirror*'s greatest journalist, died. Knighted upon his retirement in 1973 he had been made a life peer the following year. During his years at the paper, Cecil King had said: 'In the popular paper field in my time, Hugh Cudlipp has been the outstanding editor anywhere in the world.' Ellis Birk, a fellow director, was to agree: 'He was the greatest tabloid editor of all time. His particular skill was to articulate brilliantly extremely complicated events and to convert them into words that ordinary people could understand.' And from political editor

Geoffrey Goodman: 'Hugh Cudlipp was the greatest popular journalist produced by Fleet Street in the twentieth century.'

Twelve months earlier, in 1997 Mirror Group had acquired MIN, whose portfolio included the Birmingham Post & Mail Ltd. At the same time the company acquired a licence to publish the *Racing Post*. Two years later, following a takeover bid by regional newspaper group Trinity, Montgomery left the company; and in the September Trinity plc and Mirror Group plc merged to create the UK's biggest newspaper publisher, Trinity Mirror, and as a condition was required to sell the *Belfast Telegraph*. Tony O'Reilly's Independent News & Media was the buyer in 2000. Later that year Trinity Mirror bought Southnews, adding more than 80 titles to its regional portfolio.

Trinity came into being when the *Liverpool Post & Echo* was separated from its holding company in 1985; and in 1992 Scotland's largest group of paid-for and free newspapers, Scottish & Universal Newspapers, became the first of its many acquisitions. The next year it expanded into Yorkshire and Southern England with the *Huddersfield Daily Examiner* and Trinity Newspapers Southern, which included the Reading Newspaper Company and South London Press. In 1996, Trinity became the UK's largest regional publisher when it bought a group of daily and weekly newspapers from the Thomson Corporation. The following year it purchased the Dublin-based *Sunday Business Post*. Today, with more than 250 titles, Trinity Mirror remains the UK's largest newspaper publisher.

In 2003, Philip Graf, Trinity's chief executive, stepped down, and was succeeded by Sly Bailey who took office in the February. The former head of the consumer magazine group, IPC Media, she is one of only three female chief executives in the national Press – the others being Dame Marjorie Scardino, *Financial Times*; and Carolyn McCall, *theguardian*.

The current editor of the *Daily Mirror* is Richard Wallace, who succeeded the high-profile Piers Morgan, now a proprietor of *Press Gazette*, in June 2004.

The Independent *is Sold*

In July 1993, founder Andreas Whittam Smith stood down as chief executive of Newspaper Publishing, owners of *The Independent* and *Independent on Sunday*; two months later Rupert Murdoch launched a price war through *The Times* and one of the first to be affected was the *The Independent*. With a recent increase of 5p taking the price to 50p, the paper was now 20p more than its rival, which within six months was to lead to *The Independent* dropping circulation of some 60,000 copies, almost 20 per cent of its sales.

Following this fall-off in circulation and advertising revenue – plus key Spanish and Italian investors wishing to dispose of their 38 per cent holding – Newspaper Publishing 'came into play'. Two companies were now interested: the Mirror group, led by David Montgomery, and Tony O'Reilly's Independent Newspapers. 'Having lost out to Montgomery at the Mirror group, he was not keen to miss another chance to become a British press tycoon.'[19] In a dawn raid, O'Reilly secured 24.9 per cent of the stock for some £20 million, subsequently raising his stake to 29.9, the maximum before being forced to make a full bid. In 1994 Mirror Group and Independent Newspapers became joint owners of Newspaper Publishing; and four years later, in March 1998, Independent Newspapers bought out the remaining 50 per cent of the shares for £30 million.

The editor at the time was Rosie Boycott, who left for a similar role at the *Daily Express*. Andrew Marr, who had been appointed editor-in-chief, then joined the BBC as political editor. Looking back, he was to write: 'For me the *Independent* was a noble cause and a perpetual delight, not simply a newspaper. It gave me the best years of my working life, as well as some of my closest friends, when it was launched in 1986 and promised to change the face of broadsheet journalism.'

Having started at Old Street, in the City, *The Independent* and *Independent on Sunday* then moved to Canary Wharf. They are now based at 191 Marsh Wall.

The Daily Telegraph *Moves*

For *The Daily Telegraph* and its sister paper, *The Sunday Telegraph*, plans to move from Fleet Street and into new technology had first been discussed in 1984, when the paper's owners, the Berry family, had sought to raise money privately from banks and investors to cover the cost of new printing plants. In June 1985, *The Daily Telegraph* re-registered as an unquoted public company, The Daily Telegraph plc, with Canadian publisher Conrad Black, chairman of Hollinger Inc., buying a portion of the equity. In January the following year northern editions of *The Daily Telegraph* were printed on state-of-the-art presses in Manchester. And the next month Hollinger acquired a majority shareholding. At the same time, two new editors were appointed: Max Hastings, who was to succeed [Lord] Bill Deedes on *The Daily Telegraph* and Peregrine Worsthorne, who was to follow John Thompson on *The Sunday Telegraph*.

Now the doyen of Fleet Street, Bill Deedes has been a journalist for some 75 years and was honoured in April 2002 when he received a Lifetime Award from Prime Minister Tony Blair at the London Press Club's Awards Lunch.[20] Bill Deedes began his journalistic career on the *Morning Post* under H.A. Gwynne in 1931; six years later the paper was merged with *The Daily Telegraph*. During the Second World War, Deedes served in the Army, winning the Military Cross in 1944. On demobilization, he returned to *The Daily Telegraph* and remained there until 1954. Four years earlier, he had been elected Conservative MP for Ashford, Kent, 1950-74. He went back to *The Daily Telegraph* in 1957, and was appointed editor in December 1975, remaining in charge until April 1986. Since then he has contributed a weekly column and has travelled the world as a special correspondent.

The new editor of *The Daily Telegraph* – later to be editor-in-chief of The Daily Telegraph plc – Max Hastings had been a long-standing member of the *Evening Standard* staff. He had worked for BBC TV on the 'Great War' series before joining the *Standard* in 1965; and apart from three years back at the BBC, presenting more than one hundred film reports for 24 Hours, Midweek and Panorama, he was to remain with the paper from 1973 until 1985. For much of that time he served as a roving correspondent; and for his dispatches during the Falklands War, where he was the outstanding correspondent – including entering Port Stanley before the British troops – he was honoured as Journalist of the Year, 1982, and Granada TV Reporter of the Year.

Max Hastings was to remain with *The Daily Telegraph* until 1996 when he returned to the *Evening Standard* as editor, a position he was to hold until February 2002, resigning to write a major work on the Second World War. He was succeeded by Veronica Wadley, former deputy editor of the *Daily Mail* – and the first woman to be appointed editor of the *Evening Standard*. Max Hastings was knighted in 2003.

The new editor of *The Sunday Telegraph* in 1986, Peregrine Worsthorne, had entered journalism in 1946 as a sub-editor on the *Glasgow Herald*. Two years later he joined *The Times*, and after a few years at Printing House Square was appointed the paper's Washington correspondent. He left in 1953 for *The Daily Telegraph* as a leader writer, but also covered many of the fast-moving events in Africa; and remained with the paper until 1961, when he transferred to the newly-launched *Sunday Telegraph*. There, during the next three decades, he was successively, deputy editor, 1961–76; associate editor, 1976–86; and editor, 1986–89. He was knighted in 1991.

Worsthorne was succeeded as editor by Trevor Grove, who from 1978–80 had been assistant editor of *The Sunday Telegraph* before leaving for a similar role with *The Observer*. He was editor of *The Observer Magazine*, 1983–86, and was then assistant editor, *The Daily Telegraph*, 1986–89. Having been editor of *The Sunday Telegraph* for three years, in October 1992 he returned to *The Daily Telegraph*, as deputy editor, remaining there until 1994. He was succeeded as editor of *The Sunday Telegraph* by Charles Moore, a former editor of *The Spectator* and deputy editor of *The Daily Telegraph*.

Upon Max Hastings resigning on 29 September 1995 to take over the editorship of the *Evening Standard*, Conrad Black promoted Moore to become editor – a position he was to retain until he was succeeded by Martin Newland in October 2004.

The new editor of *The Sunday Telegraph* in 1995 had been Dominic Lawson, for the previous five years editor of *The Spectator*. Lawson remained in charge until the summer of 2005, when he was succeeded by Sarah Sands, former deputy editor of the *Evening Standard*, and, before her appointment, deputy editor of *The Daily Telegraph*. Charles Moore said: 'It's a great thing for a *Telegraph* title to have a female editor. I'm very glad that it's happened with her .... It's absolutely on merit, but there are things about her that will bring extra to what the *Telegraph* can offer and will add to the excitement.'

That same month, June 2005, it had been announced that the Barclay brothers – owners of *The Scotsman* – had purchased *The Daily Telegraph, The Sunday Telegraph* and *The Spectator* for £665 million, having outbid the Daily Mail and General Trust and German publisher Axel Springer. Chief executive Jeremy Deedes – having returned from a short-lived retirement to guide his former titles through their change of ownership – said that the purchase was the best possible outcome:

'Everything that the *Telegraph* stand for fits very squarely with the thinking of the Barclays and that must be a good thing.' Editorial director Kim Fletcher commented that over the next few weeks the new owners would be putting together a long-term strategy for the newspapers.[21]

Within days of the Barclays' purchase of The Telegraph Group, it was announced that Murdoch MacLennan, chief executive officer of Associated Newspapers, was joining the organization in a similar capacity. He had previously worked in senior managerial positions for Thomson Regional Newspapers, *Daily Mirror* and *Daily Express*; and one of his first appointments was that of Guy Black, former Director of the Press Complaints Council, as director of communications.

In December 2005, it was announced that the Telegraph Group was leaving Canary Wharf for premises at Victoria, aiming to be there in summer 2006.

Free newspapers

Although by the end of the century most weekly newspapers were free, it was not so with national newspaper groups. To look at the provinces: from a base of £3 million in 1971, revenue of free newspapers had leapt to a figure of £135 million in little more than a decade; and these were to increase their revenue by 31 per cent in 1982. Two years later, in October 1984, the first free daily newspaper in Europe, the *Daily News*, was launched in Birmingham by Chris Bullivant, who had already built up a successful chain of free weekly titles. However, the *Daily News*, which was distributed to 276,000 homes in and around Birmingham four mornings a week, would not have been possible without the support of Reed International's newspaper division, Reed Regional Newspapers. Initially a minority shareholder, Reed eventually bought out Chris Bullivant in 1987 and two years later merged the *Daily News* with their Worcester-based Berrows Group Newspapers.

A plan to start similar titles in up to twenty other provincial cities and towns in England was not pursued – due to the worst recession in the newspaper industry since the seventies – and in June 1991 the paper was converted into the weekly *Metronews*. Within months, Robert Maxwell – with the author's involvement – was intent on producing a nationwide free daily, but this was not followed up.

In July 1994, with the backing of Derek Clee, 'who had made a fortune as a tumble-drier manufacturer based in Halifax', *Tonight*, a free London evening to be given away during the week outside Tube stations, was launched. Edited by Peter Grimsditch, it was a 16-page tabloid, contractually printed web-offset, with a distribution of 100,000.[22] However, lack of advertising meant that by the year's end the paper was appearing weekly; and in January 1995 Grimsditch left for Beirut to edit the local *Daily Star*. *Tonight* itself closed a few months later. Although a failure, the thought of challenging the *Standard* with a free evening was to attract the attention of newspaper groups .... but it was to be another decade before the opportunity was likely to arise.

Nevertheless, the idea of a free tabloid daily newspaper – 48 to 56 pages in colour, stapled so that it would be easier to handle on the Tube or on a bus – emanating from

Fleet Street and printed in London and at regional centres was to remain an attractive proposition; and it was in the summer of 1997 that Vere Harmsworth read of the *Metro*, a newspaper being given away on the Stockholm underground that had in two years since its launch seen profit margins rise to more than 30 per cent. For Associated Newspapers, the possibility of a Swedish media group operating in London could not be ignored. The decision was taken, therefore, that Associated should launch its own free *Metro*.

Research had shown that the average Tube journey in London was just twenty minutes, so this new quality free newspaper, one which would not be overwhelmed by advertising, was designed for just that, but aimed primarily at the 18–35 market. It was later discovered that about 75 per cent of people on the Tube reading a paper were *Metro* readers and when they finished they left it for someone else. An initial move by News Corporation to be a partner was rejected as Associated were to insist on a major shareholding. Nevertheless, following agreement with London Transport on distribution, the *Metro*, edited by Ian MacGregor, was launched on 16 March 1999.

Within weeks, the decision was taken to expand the *Metro*'s circulation outside the London area, and – despite initial opposition from regional groups – the paper was to be established through Associated having franchise agreements with Trinity Mirror in Glasgow, Edinburgh, Birmingham and Newcastle; with Guardian Media in Manchester; and with Johnston Press in Leeds and Sheffield – giving a circulation, including London's 450,00, of 890,000 by January 2004. And that same month it was announced that through Associated's regional chain, Northcliffe Newspapers, the paper would be available in Bath, Bristol, Derby, Leicester and Nottingham, adding a further 90,000 copies. The benefits were to be two-fold: while Associated Newspapers supplied the national news copy and sold display advertising on a national basis the regional franchisees received a cut of the advertising sale and in return printed and distributed the paper plus selling local classifieds.[23]

The success was to continue, and in March 2004 chairman Jonathan Harmsworth (Lord Rothermere IV) was able to announce in the Daily Mail and General Trust's annual report that the *Metro* had gone into profit for the first time since its launch, with distribution up three per cent and display advertising up 28 per cent. By the spring of 2005, the *Metro* with a circulation of more than one million was the widest-read paper among the 18 to 45 urbanite audience it is aimed at. Media commentator Brian MacArthur wrote:[24]

> The *Metros* show that newspapers can reverse the trend of decline if they capture the zeitgeist, which in 2005 consists of being free, straight, apolitical and a quick ten to 20-minute news fix on the way to work. Forty-two daily *Metro* editions are now published in 17 countries in 16 languages. Their revenues last year were up by 48 per cent to $300 million (£168 million).

In October 2005, Associated Newspapers, in a joint venture with the *Irish Times* and Sweden-based Metro International, launched a Dublin edition. Printed on the presses of the *Irish Times*, 53,000 copies were distributed. However, there was to be strong opposition from Independent News and Media, which came out with a rival *Herald AM* from the offices of the *Evening Herald*.

Apart from its *Metro* edition, on Tuesday 14 December 2004 Associated Newspapers launched its free *Standard Lite* available during the lunchtime period – 11.30 a.m. until 2.30 p.m. – at limited locations in central London excluding the City. Forty years earlier, London could boast three evenings: *News*, *Star*, *Standard* with a combined circulation of more than 2.2 million. Now the *Standard*, the great survivor, having absorbed nine other evenings, was selling just 370,000 in a declining market; but, with the infusion of a 50,000 free, coloured *Standard Lite* advertisers were to be offered a 420,000 circulation package. Its welcoming editorial stated:

> The 48-page *Standard Lite* will be given away free by *Standard* vendors. A slimmed-down version of the full *Evening Standard* [it] will consist of short news reads, providing a quick digest of that day's events, plus an invaluable guide to that night's London life. In other words, *Standard Lite* will be an easy, accessible read – the perfect complement to your lunchtime coffee and sandwich. And, if you like the *Standard Lite*, our belief is that you will get even more enjoyment from the main edition of the *Evening Standard* with its brilliant features, incomparable commentary and analysis, up-to-the-minute news plus, of course, some of Britain's most admired columnists and critics.

Editor Veronica Wadley said: 'We are redefining evening newspapers. Evening sales all over the world are in decline and we've looked at the *Standard* which has a very strong sale and a very strong brand and looked at how we can produce a paper which complements what we do with the full West End final – and this is what we've come up with.' Research had shown that more than 1.2 million people work in central London, with some 600,000 leaving their offices at lunchtime – and it was these that the initial 50,000 circulation of *Standard Lite* was intended to reach.

Wadley did not believe that it would affect the paid-for edition of the *Standard*: 'You are reaching different readers. It's only available in a small area of central London. Our distribution goes right beyond the M25 all the way to the south coast, so that the paper won't be available to them. It also won't be available after 2.30 p.m. and our main sale, the West End final, is on the streets by 3 p.m.' Six months after its launch, the circulation of *Standard Lite* was 76,000 copies per day, with sales of the paid-for *Standard* dropping to 348,892. However, if the figures were combined it would have given a circulation increase of almost ten per cent year on.

There was to be further movement in the free newspaper world when on Monday 5 September 2005 *City A.M.*, the world's first free daily business newspaper, made its debut on the streets of London with an initial print of 60,000 – a figure expected to increase to more than 100,000 by the end of the year. Managing director Lawson Muncaster, formerly of *Metro International*, said: 'I believe [it] will appeal to those who currently don't buy a financial or business paper. There are 400,000 people in the City and Canary Wharf .' A 24-page all-colour tabloid, *City A.M.* describes itself as: 'A one-stop shop for all the latest business news, markets information and analyis of the financial world. As well as the most up-to-date news and stock market information, it also provides the latest in sport, motoring, style, leisure and what to do in your precious spare time.' Edited by former *Sunday Express* business editor David Parsley, the paper has a full-time editorial staff of twenty-five based at London Bridge with a further two dozen employed as freelances. Parsley told *Press Gazette*:[25] 'London has a clearly defined business and financial village. The Square Mile, Canary Wharf and other areas around Central London make up *City A.M.*'s parish .... our readers are the most affluent of any British newspaper, earning almost twice the national average .... This paper is interested in the people behind the deals, the names not usually seen in newspaper coverage.' In December 2005 *City A.M.* announced that it planned to launch in Bristol, Edinburgh, Leeds and Manchester during 2006.

Battle for Circulation

As the new century dawned, so there had been more and more an awareness of the steady drain of readership. With bingo prizes belonging to the past, newspapers now began to give away classic novels, CDs and DVDs in an effort to boost sales – it was almost as if the circulation war of the 1930s had been reinvented. But in almost every instance the extra sales gained – in many cases more than 250,000 – were short-lived, as canny readers just 'cherry-picked' the best offers. For *The Times*, the addition of a DVD had twice in the autumn of 2005 put the Saturday sale above the one million mark, while *The Daily Telegraph*, with its *Whistle Down The Wind*, increased its Saturday sale by 179,000; and the *Daily Mail*, with its *Rudolf the Red-Nosed Reindeer*, gained a massive 350,000. However, although these extra sales were welcome on the ABC figures, they came at a price, as it was estimated that each DVD cost on average 30p.

One proprietor not in favour of this new circulation ploy is Rupert Murdoch, who said: 'I personally hate this DVD craze .... The fact is, the sales go up for a day. And are right back to where they were the following day .... People grab the paper, tear off the DVD and throw away the paper. They've got to learn. That's got to stop.'[26]

The biggest factor, though, in the past decade had been the price war that had raged between *The Times* and *The Daily Telegraph* – a war that had also affected the circulations of *The Independent* and *The Guardian*. The dramatic decision by News International to lower the price of *The Times* from 45p to 30p in September 1993 was the most momentous development in modern British journalism and meant that within months its circulation was to double and at one point, after its cover price had been slashed to 20p, and 10p on Mondays, sales rose to some 880,000 copies per day. In July 1993, just two months prior to the start of the price war, *The Times*' circulation had been 359,822; *The Daily Telegraph* 1,017,483, *The Guardian* 402,157 and *The Independent* 334,993.

On Monday 5 September 2005, when *The Times* raised its price to 60p – the same as *The Daily Telegraph* and *The Guardian*, and only 5p less than *The Independent* – the war was over; but it was a war that was estimated to have cost News International £175 million. Now, in the period July-December 2005, circulation of *The Times* is 689,141; *The Daily Telegraph* 903,920; *theguardian* 382,291 and *The Independent* 259,178. Commenting on cover prices, Rupert Murdoch told Ian Reeves, editor, *Press Gazette*:[27]

> I think the daily papers are all over-priced. With Saturday and Sunday papers, people have a lot more time to read, and so I think they are a lot less price sensitive. But for the dailies, I think it's very important that the purchase of a newspaper should be insignificant as a price. I guess I'm just a bit out of date on this feeling, but 35p, 40p is a high price, it's sure a lot more than what it was 10 or 15 years ago. 'Could price be a battleground again in the near future?' I don't think any of the others could afford it, certainly not on a long-term basis. The reality is that we've seen the last of any serious price wars for a long time.

But it was not just a reduction in price that had dramatically changed *The Times*' circulation: during the decade there had been a gradual popularising of the paper, aiming for a younger readership. *The Times* was not alone in this. All up-market titles were seeking this elusive panacea. For some editors the way forward, with broadsheet titles whose sales were falling, was to relaunch as a tabloid. But what were to be the advantages?

As a tabloid is half the size of a broadsheet there would be twice as many pages, and the paper would 'bulk up' better – especially important with low pagination. There would be twice as many right-hand pages, much sought-after by advertisers; and, even though the type area of a tabloid is exactly the same as a half-page broadsheet, in the words of the late Lord Rothermere III: 'A page is a page is a page' – and an enhanced rate could be obtained over the broadsheet half-page. There would also be twice as many colour positions. And, finally, the tabloid would be easier to handle. The main disadvantage was that a tabloid page could carry only one main story, whereas on a broadsheet three 'tops' could be accommodated; and there was also slightly more waste upon start-up of the presses.

A term first used by Alfred Harmsworth (later Lord Northcliffe), Tabloid had been registered in 1884 by Messrs. Burroughs, Wellcome & Co. as a trademark reserved to chemical substances used in medicine and pharmacy. 'The name Tabloid "came to him" [Henry Wellcome] at half-past four one morning in 1884 by combining the word tablet and alkaloid, and he at once sent for his secretary to dictate, even at that early hour, a memorandum on the subject.' Anthony Delano was to write:

> So impressed was Joseph Pulitzer with the *Daily Mail* when it appeared that he invited Northcliffe to take over the New York *World* on 1 January 1901, the first day of the new century, to produce 'the newspaper of the future'. And released from the closet for one glorious outing, Northcliffe the secret tabloidist folded the plump broadsheet in two, cut the number of columns in half, wrote the headlines in sans serif type, warned the American reporters to write nothing longer than 250 words, coined the slogan All the News in Sixty Seconds for the page one 'ear' and borrowed a newly registered trade mark . . . . Tabloid.[28]

Now, one hundred years later, more than 90 per cent of evening and daily newspapers in the provincial Press are being produced in the tabloid format; and overseas, according to the World Association of Newspapers (WAN), 'in the past two years of format frenzy some 61 titles have downsized in the hope of stopping their circulation rot'. In October 2005 Jim Chisholm, WAN strategy adviser, said:[29] 'Smaller formats are a good idea but it's important to take time to consider the range of strategic options and operational issues that publishers must face when making such a move. Few newspapers were ever going to see significant or sustainable circulation gains from the smaller format.' He added: 'Many are now finding the issues relating to advertising are more complex than they expected. The smaller page presents a range of complexities regarding advertising layout.'

Of the national up-market titles, the short-lived *Sunday Correspondent* – launched as a broadsheet on 17 September 1989 – had converted to a tabloid on 20 August 1990 before closing on 27 November that same year; and the *Evening Standard* had for almost a century maintained that format – using a deeper cut-off in Shoe Lane until transferring to the *Daily Express* plant at 121 Fleet Street – but no quality daily had yet made the attempt to convert to tabloid or 'compact' as it was now to be called.

The Independent *Goes Compact*

It was to be more than a decade before the challenge was to be met when, under the editorship of Simon Kelner, on Monday 30 September 2003 *The Independent* began the conversion to compact size. Six years earlier, the then editor, Adrew Marr, later to achieve fame as a television personality, had also considered the merits of converting *The Independent*:[30]

> I decided to counter-attack by redesigning the paper entirely. My first plan was to go tabloid, or preferably 'qualoid' – the intermediate size favoured by the best-looking continental newspapers, which is for my money the ideal size for a newspaper. But continental-sized presses were not available. We could not remotely afford to tinker with someone else's presses or buy second-hand ones. As to a tabloid, this was quickly vetoed by management.

Editor Simon Kelner was a person of wide experience, having worked in executive positions on *The Independent*, *Sunday Correspondent*, *The Observer*, *Independent on Sunday* and the *Mail on Sunday*'s Night & Day magazine. The project was to be a success, for within twelve months the circulation, in a falling market, had risen from 217,417 to 262,588. Commenced originally in dual format – broadsheet or compact – within the M25 area, and then rolled out to the regions, it soon became apparent that readers preferred the latter; and by May 2004 the broadsheet was discontinued. A year after its successful launch, Simon Kelner said:[31]

> When we went compact the format change enabled us to draw in a new audience. Then you get locked into a virtuous circle where the paper is gaining circulation, people are saying nice things about it, people who work for the paper become more confident, the paper itself becomes more confident and more people start buying it as a result. People have said to me it was a very brave step you took. I don't think anyone ever saw it like that. It was very brave in terms of the investment it took from the company, but in pure marketing and journalistic terms the broadsheet was still there and what we produced was a different-size version of the broadsheet for people who wanted it. What we didn't foresee, of course, was that the compact paper would have a desirability way beyond those target areas – the commuter areas. It became clear very soon that even in areas

where there was no commuter traffic they liked the modernity and freshness of the compact.

On 14 October 2005 *The Independent*'s sister paper, *The Independent on Sunday* – sales at just over 200,000, and for the past three years named Best Designed Newspaper in the World – also converted to compact, with a main 104-page paper plus 24-page travel pull-out, business section, ABC arts magazine and Sunday Review. Discussing the new format, editor Tristan Davies commented:[32]

> I think the one thing that used to worry broadsheet papers about going compact was that you had to lower your tone. But that's not the case and *The Independent* has proved that. There will be absolutely no retreat from the serious journalism we do. The campaigning reporting, the long, analytical reads will all be there. What it does allow you to do is project a wider range of stories. Instead of 13 pages of news, we will have more than 40.

Davies believed that it was important that the *The Independent on Sunday* did not become a seventh-day *Independent*. 'We have a different staff, different approach. We do things our way and that will continue.' He said that dummies for a compact-sized paper had been put together some two years ago: 'It has been frustrating watching the daily newspaper getting to grips with a fantastic new format and making such a success of it. But you have to be patient. Our moment has come and we are going to make the most of it.'

The Times *Converts*

The 'sea-change' by *The Independent* in September 2003 when converting to compact – and its subsequent increase in sales – had not been missed by other groups, chief of which was News International; and seven weeks later on Wednesday 26 November 2003 *The Times*, likewise in a broadsheet and compact format, gradually followed suit. Editor Robert Thomson opined in his third leader:

> 'Change is the law of life.' Thus read our leading article on May 3, 1966, the day *The Times* apeared for the first time with news on the front page. 'The prime purpose of a newspaper is to give the news,' we explained. 'It should do so in the quickest and most convenient manner . . . . Today sees another landmark in our history. A compact edition is available for the first time, initially to readers in the Southeast . . . . In our very first edition the proprietor, John Walter I, outlined the philosophy of his new paper. He promised it would be a 'faithful recorder of every species of intelligence,' and added that 'like a well covered table it should contain something suited to every palate'. Now we can add 'and suited to the needs of every reader.'

Six months after the gradual change-over, circulation of *The Times* had increased by 40,000 copies to 661,330; and Thomson could say: 'We are learning how to use the tabloid format and I think it's fair to say that we struggled in the first few months to get the rhythm right. The rhythm of a broadsheet and a tabloid is very different. With each passing day the team is learning more tricks of the trade. If you look at the paper now, day after day it gets better. That's also showing in the sales figures.'

On Saturday 29 October 2004, almost one year after the first tentative steps into the compact format, *The Times*, in its final broadsheet shape, announced in its leader:

> TIMES CHANGE
>
> The quest for quality in a complicated modern age
>
> On this historic day, it is worth noting that we are not as innovative as we would like to believe. When *The Times* first appeared in 1785 (then called *The Daily Universal Register*) it was a sixpenny compact. It was 13 inches wide and 18 inches deep, not much larger than the new version of the compact, which is 11 inches wide and 14 inches deep. Dimensions aside, our belief is that, in a modest fashion, vibrant and interesting newspapers contribute to a vibrant and interesting society.

And from Monday 1 November 2005 *The Times* became a compact newspaper.

Ich Bin Ein Berliner

Meanwhile, at Farringdon Road, *Guardian* executives had been looking at other methods; and on Monday 12 September 2005, *theguardian* – as it is now called in its new-look masthead – made its debut as a Berliner-size newspaper. In a front-page statement, editor Alan Rusbridger announced:

> Welcome to the Berliner Guardian. No, we won't go on calling it that for long, and, yes, it's an inelegant name. We tried many alternatives, related either to size or to the European origins of the format. In the end 'the Berliner' stuck. But in a short time, we hope we can revert to being simple the Guardian. Starting with the most obvious, the page size is smaller. We believe the format combines the convenence of a tabloid with the sensibility of a broadsheet . . . . The next difference you may notice is colour. The paper is printed on state-of-the-art MAN Roland ColorMan presses, which give colour on every page – something that sets us apart from every other national newspaper.

The idea of a Berliner-style *Guardian* had struck Rusbridger when on holiday in August 2003, and, returning to the office, he showed fellow board members a copy of *La Repubblica*. Even though two tabloid dummies had been commissioned – and been received favourably in readership surveys – the idea of a 248-page paper was daunting. Thoughts, therefore, turned elsewhere. However, there was to be a major problem, for as the presses necessary to print a Berliner-style title were of a different cut-off to any currently used in Fleet Street it would be necessary to replant – at a cost of some £80 millions and with a probable three-year delay. Fortunately, through the extraordinary efforts of MAN Roland, the presses – each capable of 90,000 copies an hour – were installed at Trafford Park, Manchester, and Newsfax, East London, some eighteen months early.

For Rusbridger and his colleagues, the need for change was paramount: 'By the end of 2004 less than half the population was reading a national newspaper each day. In a time-compressed world, where people are bombarded with information, the press can easily be overlooked. It's not only about reinterpreting the paper for a particular age, but making the case for what we do and saying it has validity.'

From Carolyn McCall, chief executive officer of Guardian Newspapers Limited:[33] 'I'm very happy with the way the editorial and commercial side have been so collaborative. It was an editorially inspired concept that made commercial sense from a very early stage.' She added: 'This project is simultaneously about a building programme, advertising grids, retail display and distribution, as well as font sizes, colour palettes and the tone and quality of journalism.' With much of the extra revenue coming from increased colour advertisement positions, it is expected to recoup the £80 million costs within fifteen years. From Liz Forgan, chair of the Scott Trust: 'The business case was so well made and the arguments so overwhelming, the trust was absolutely all on side.' In his leader in the last issue of *The Guardian* as a broadsheet, Rusbridger reflected:

> Does size matter? A great many readers say yes. But – in all the conversation we have had with readers over the past couple of years – that 'yes' is a qualified one . . . . The great virtue of the British press is its diversity. It would be a dull world in which every paper ended up the same size. Some people will not be reading these words on paper at all, but on computer screens, mobile phones and Blackberries. They may be wondering what all the fuss is about, and in the long run they may even have a point. But, for the moment, let us celebrate a form of publication – ink on paper – which has survived in pretty rude health and which has always adapted to the demands of any given age. The broadsheet is dead. Long live the Berliner!

The Telegraph *Revamps*

Within weeks of the launch of *theguardian*'s Berliner, editor Martin Newland announced in *The Daily Telegraph*, on Monday 10 October 2005, a major investment, with extended news coverage, a separate business section and a 24-page sports tabloid:

> We have maintained, for the most part, our broadsheet format because we believe this to be the best environment to merge quality with impact. We believe in this format because more than two million discerning and influential *Telegraph* readers a day enjoy and value this newspaper's ability to be visually adventurous and editorially diverse. Investment in new print facilities means that our readers are being offered more colourful, more accessible packaging for a newspaper that has lost none of its gravitas, authority, breadth and fun.

In the new format, pagination will increase from 48 to 56 broadsheet pages, including twenty of these in colour; and, importantly, news – always the bedrock of the paper – will rise from a low of 12 pages to between 18 and 22. He said that his plan against the compact *Times* and *Independent* plus *theguardian* Berliner was: 'Stay quality and milk everything we can out of being the last broadsheet in the market.' Continuing, he said that given the type of *Telegraph* reader there were three things they were interested in: news, business and sport. 'You'll see a Monday to Friday product that says these things are important to us.' He added:[34]

> We sell this much and make this much money at the moment because we are a broadsheet and carry big ads – and we carry increasingly them in colour. We have an older influential readership profile, 300,000 of whom are subscribers, so they have bought a year ahead, and they like the broadsheet *Telegraph*. Our business model at the moment, which is far more successful than any other ones out there, lies in us staying the same.

Martin Newland resigned as editor of *The Daily Telegraph* in November 2005.

Meanwhile, under new editor Sarah Sands the re-vamped *Sunday Telegraph* – after considering converting some sections of the paper to tabloid – was also to remain broadsheet: 'We went through them all but we have to make a profit and advertisers want a broadsheet.' In March 2006, it was announced that Sarah Sands would be leaving and would be replaced by Patience Wheatcroft, business editor of *The Times*.

With all the activity in up-market titles converting in size and rejigging the sections, there had also been changes in the financial sector. In the spring of 2005 the *Financial Times* launched its free *FTpm*, a two-sided A4 designed to provide a brief update on the day's financial news. Having a distribution of more than 50,000, it is also a vehicle to promote the main paper. On 5 November 2005 Andrew Gowers resigned as editor of the *FT* and was succeeded by Lionel Barber, who had been with the paper for 20 years, most recently as US managing editor.

Three weeks earlier, on Monday, 16 October 2005, *The Wall Street Journal Europe*, circulation 86,156, switched to tabloid. (The main edition, selling some two million broadsheet copies, would remain unchanged.) Editor of *WSJ Europe*, Brussels-based Raju Naserati, commented: 'Our journalism doesn't change because the format has changed. There's a tendency to say that when you go tabloid you write some stories shorter and that's somehow shortchanging the readers. Writing shorter and writing tighter is much harder and some stories need to be shorter. Some readers don't need 40 inches to be told something they can understand in four inches.' He added: 'We're going through a real period of change. Nobody would have predicted the rebirth of the tabloid 10 years ago. And look now.' Dow Jones, the paper's parent company, believes that cost savings as a result of converting to tabloid could be some $17 million in 2006.

Colour Takes Off

Apart from the increased activity in up-market titles converting to tabloid or rejigging the paper's sections, all were now looking at the benefits of more and more full colour pagination. This was a far cry from the 1970s, when the nationals, still printed letterpress, were experimenting with spot colour – often out-of-register and poorly inked. True, Beaverbrook Newspapers had been in the vanguard with preprinted gravure colour on the *Evening Standard* and *Daily Express*, but this was not only costly, through not holding register on the presses, it was also extremely wasteful in paper. Strangely enough, the first 'coloured' newspaper, *Coloured News*, had been launched on 4 August 1855 – and collapsed seven weeks later on 29 September. And some seventeen years earlier, on 18 June 1838, *The Golden Sun* – no connection with the current *Sun* – was published to celebrate the coronation of Queen Victoria. (The gold ink used was really dusted bronze mixed with varnish.)

Now, in the early years of the twenty-first century, all newspapers – either with web-offset or flexography – were using full colour extensively. Eddy Shah, back in 1986 – had led the way when he launched *Today*, but it was really Robert Maxwell, through investing heavily in colour web-offset presses for the *Daily Mirror*, who had proved their full worth. 'Advertising director Roger Eastoe had met Maxwell at a conference in Athens the March before he bought the company, and for an hour they had talked about the editorial advantages and increased advertising potential colour printing could bring to a national.'[35]

In November 2004 Trinity Mirror – now the owners of the *Daily Mirror* – announced that it was to spend £45 million in colour printing at its Oldham operation and 'further investment at its Watford national printworks is expected this year'. That same month the *Daily Mail* had started printing on new machines costing £135 million – marking the end of a five-year project at its Harmsworth Quay plant, East London – and at satellite operations in Bristol, Derby and Stoke, with presses capable of producing a 128-page *Daily Mail* including 64 pages in full colour. Lord Rothermere (Jonathan Harmsworth) said: 'We can give readers and advertisers more pages and better printed newspapers than anyone else in the UK.'

Eight months later, in June 2005, the company went a stage further when it announced a £96 million investment, enabling the *Daily Mail*, up to 128 pages, and *The Mail on Sunday*, up to 160 pages, to be printed in full colour. To produce the enhanced titles – commencing in 2008 – Associated Newspapers is spending £80 million on a new press hall at Didcot, Oxfordshire; and £16 million on upgrading the existing Harmswoth Quay operation, East London. Lord Rothermere commented: 'This is further evidence of our commitment to the long-term future of our newspapers. At present on the presses at Harmsworth Quay in London we can produce half our pages in colour, but with the addition of the facilities at Didcot and enhancements to our existing press facilities, we will have the capacity to provide full, high-quality colour throughout the country.'

The other popular tabloids, too – *The Sun*, *Daily Express*, *Daily Mirror*, *The Star* – were also using more and more colour. And since its launch *theguardian* had been able to print full colour on every page. More colour was also now available on the *Telegraph* and *Independent* newspapers. However, the biggest move to all-colour newspapers was to come from News International in October 2004 when it announced that it intended to spend £600 million in moving its printing away from its Wapping site. A four-year programme would see new press halls built just off the M25 near Enfield, Middlesex; Knowsley, near Liverpool; and in Glasgow. And, because of the increase in efficiency with the 22 MAN-Roland presses, each capable of printing 120 full pages of colour at 86,000 copies an hour, it was envisaged that manning levels would fall from 1000 to 600.

The editorial and commercial floors of *The Times*, *The Sunday Times*, *The Sun* and *News of the World* would, however, remain at Wapping – and a plus factor was that later deadlines would now be possible and the regional content of different editions would be increased. Les Hinton, himself a former journalist, and now executive chairman of News International, said:

> The biggest change commercially over the past seven to eight years has been increasing demand for colour. Now with *The Sun* on Thursday, Friday and Saturday we have to buy contract printing all over the country to print a paper with enough colour to satisfy the advertisers. That's not efficient. We are the last national newspaper business whose journalists sit on top of the presses. Now already we print remotely in lots of sites. You

don't need to be on top of your presses any more and having a large manufacturing and distribution business in downtown London is a big logistical issue. Newspapers are big manufacturing and distribution organisations and like other manufacturing organisations we are taking advantage of new technology. Although there will be no jobs lost at all for at least two years, the remaining jobs will be spread over at least two to three years. Automation will mean fewer people.

Satellite Printing

Les Hinton had mentioned the need to 'print remotely in lots of sites', but News International were not alone in this. The need had been seen – and met – by other groups, especially the *Financial Times* (see chapter nineteen, p.378).

One of the first in the field had been Express Newspapers, and, following the successful facsimile transmission of the *Daily Star* from Manchester and its printing in Fleet Street during 1980, the author was involved in setting up printing of the *Daily Star* by satellite to the Sing Tao presses at New York and Toronto in January 1983, and the transmission of the *Sunday Express* to Singapore for printing at the *Straits Times* in January 1985.

For national newspapers, satellite printing in the UK really began with the launch of *Today* in the spring of 1986 followed six months later with *The Independent*. Now, Fleet Street titles are printed at dozens of regional plants, thereby making full use of the presses of the local evening newspapers. A similar position exists abroad; and as Donald Trelford has written:[36]

> In the past week, for example, the *Daily Mail* has been printed at satellite plants in Belgium, Marseilles, Valencia, Seville, Tenerife, Majorca, Athens and Orlando, Florida. Some of these plants are also used by their rivals, who share the distribution costs .... Other European cities targeted by British titles are Madrid, Istanbul and Charleroi. Some of these arrangements are all year round, others just for the summer months. *The Guardian* is printing in Marseilles from May to September, but in Frankfurt, Madrid and Roubix, France, all the time. *The Sun* is printing in Marseilles and Nantes from July to September as an experiment.

For the circulation directors it is paramount that their newspapers are available for readers when abroad. Nothing could be worse than the newspaper to be off sale – and a reader lost. While the production of UK national titles abroad through the use of satellite links and contract printing had been increasing during the past decade, for all newspapers there had been a growing awareness of the impact of the internet.

However, the next step on from 'traditional' satellite printing could well be the introduction of digital presses: a technology that would enable micro-edition production of national newspapers by providing shorter runs at a greater number of regional centres than is possible at present. This technology, which already exists in prototype form, would enable edition or page changes at full speed. And as Dr John Hill commented:[37]

This would also enable the interleaving of different newspapers so that the problems of sequential printing, that of having to wait for the printing of one publication to finish before starting the next, would no longer exist. These digital presses would be slower, and cheaper, than existing presses. However, where there are more printing centres the time constraints that exist within a centralised plant would no longer exist. If these presses were to be owned and operated by national newspaper groups it would also mean that local titles could be produced at the same centre.

21

The electronic future

TWENTY YEARS AGO, Professor Donald Trelford, then editor of *The Observer*, commented: 'Print has survived more than 20 years of TV. It will survive any kind of gadgetry. It will survive space invaders and news on Rubik Cubes.'[1] This point of view is shared by media columnist Stephen Glover, who in *The Independent* on Monday 14 November 2005, wrote:

> It would be useless to deny that something significant is going on, and yet I can't help feeling that the predictions of the death of newspapers are greatly overdone. I'll take a bet . . . . that in 20 years' time, national newspapers printed on newsprint will still collectively have a greater revenue than their online counterparts. Of course, they cannot compete with the internet in terms of up-to-the-minute information, but they still offer a portable form that many people will continue to find more convenient than a computer screen for reading long, more reflective (and less time-sensitive) pieces.

Another media columnist, Professor Roy Greenslade, former editor of the *Daily Mirror*, also believes in the future of the printed word, and does not agree with Philip Meyer, author of *The Vanishing Newspaper*, who considers that newspapers will die by 2040. To quote Greenslade: 'I'm not convinced because I believe that newspaper publishers are now beginning to respond to the challenge. Like many people, especially after the prick in the dotcom bubble, they have been surprised by the pace of technological development and thought websites would be little more than an add-on to papers.'[2]

Now, in the early years of the twenty-first century, all newspapers are mindful that to survive they must go forward and embrace the new online medium.

One person who had been aware of the threat was Rupert Murdoch, who, in an interview with Bill Hagerty in the *British Journalism Review*, vol. 10 no.4, 1999, declared:

> I don't know where the Internet begins and ends or whether it is just a matter of electronic communication, but there's a technological revolution happening, no question. With the Internet there is the ability to deliver all sorts of services to the public which we now deliver in print . . . . The Internet will be a great magnet for classified advertising. Will that be as a complement to newspapers or as an alternative? We don't know yet, but I think what we have to say is that the Internet can be a huge opportunity to start new businesses off the side of it.

Six years later, when addressing the American Society of Newspaper Editors at Washington in April 2005, he warned of the move away from newspapers by 18- to 34-year-olds, whose favourite vehicle for news was the internet. Research had shown that whereas only 19 per cent read a newspaper – and only nine per cent thought that they were trustworthy – more than 40 per cent were daily users of the web in the quest for news.

Murdoch, however, was confident in the future of newspapers, both in print and via electronic delivery platforms:[3] 'The data may show that young people aren't reading newspapers as much as their predecessors, but it doesn't show they don't want news. In fact, they want lots of news, just faster news of a different kind and delivered in a different way.' He continued:

> We have the experience, the brands, the resources, and the know-how to get it done. We have a unique content to differentiate ourselves in a world where news is becomingly increasingly commoditized. And most importantly we have a great new partner to help us reach this new consumer: the internet. [The viewers] want news on demand, continuously updated. They want a point of view about not just what happened, but why it happened. They want news that speaks to them personally, that affects their lives .... And they want the option to go out and get more information, or to seek a contrary point of view. And finally they want to be able to use the information in a larger community – to talk about, to debate, to question, and even to meet the people who think about the world in a similar or different way.

He believed that papers, instead of just reprinting the news on their websites, should be constantly updated and offer 'deep, deep local news; relevant national and international news; commentary and debate; gossip and humour'. Continuing, he said:

> What is required is a complete transformation of the way we think about our product. Unfortunately, however, I believe too many editors and reporters are out of touch with [their] readers. Too often the question we ask is: 'Do we have a story?' rather than 'Does anyone want the story? And the data support this unpleasant truth. Studies show we're in an odd position. We're more trusted by people who aren't reading us.

He concluded:

> By meeting the challenges I've raised, I'm confident we will not only improve our chances for success in the online world, but, as importantly, beget greater success in the printed medium. By streamlining our operations and becoming more nimble. By changing the way we write and edit stories. By listening more intently to our readers. I do not underestimate the tests before use. We may never become true digital natives, but we can and must begin to assimilate to their culture and way of thinking. It is a monumental, once-in-a-generation opportunity, but it is also an exciting one, because if we're successful, our industry has the potential to reshape itself, and to be healthier than ever before.

Two months later, media columnist Brian MacArthur wrote:[4]

> I recalled the speech last week as I travelled on a London bus to the City. It was packed with about 50 young men and women, but only three were reading newspapers (two of them were the free *Metro*). Many more were reading books or listening to music or radio.

> It was difficult to avoid the conclusion that newspapers did not matter to these 18 to 34-year-olds, the younger readers all newspapers are desperate to recruit.

Following up his ground-breaking address to the American Society of Newspaper Editors, Murdoch in July 2005, for $580 million, purchased the Los Angeles-based Intermix Media, which instantly doubled News Corp websites to 45 million unique monthly users. With the purchase of Intermix, owners of MySpace.com, there was now the entry to some 16 million monthly users, accessing 200,000 web pages created by music groups. As Edward Helmore was to write: 'They belong to the demographic the media crave, the honeypot of youth. About 24 per cent of MySpace viewers are aged 12 to 17, and 20 per cent are 18 to 24. With MySpace, Murdoch is jumping into a strategy others seek to follow.' And four months later, Les Hinton, Executive Chairman of News International, a key factor in the Murdoch empire, told staff members that the company aimed to become the 'leading online news, entertainment and sports provider in the UK'.

One person already much involved in the new wave is John McCall MacBain, founder of Trader Classified Media in 1987, whose publishing empire spans 20 countries and includes 56 websites and 575 print titles. He believes that classified advertising will increasingly migrate to the internet. He said that internet-based classified advertising businesses are driven by size and scale. People go to websites because other people do. A site with lots of local car advertisements[5] will attract far more buyers and sellers than one with few local car advertisements. 'If you can dominate a local market, these two factors, of locality and critical mass, create barriers to entry in classified advertising. These in turn allow profits, even in cyberspace where customers can migrate from one site to another with the click of a mouse.'

A Growing Awareness

In the UK – even though newspapers accounted for one third of the £44 billion advertising spend last year – there is certainly no complacency in the growth of online classifieds. In March 2005 Sly Bailey, chief executive, Trinity Mirror, which owns 250 local newspapers as well as the *Daily Mirror,* told shareholders:[6] 'What we want is simple: to win strong, profitable positions in key classified markets online.' More than half the jobs advertised in Trinity-Mirror's regional newspapers are now 'upsold' to the online, enabling two price rises within 18 months. 'In 2001, the company's turnover in the new medium was £900,000 with an operating loss of £23.5 million. By judicious cost-cutting and more sensible investment, the digital business generated a turnover of £6.3 million in 2003 and produced a profit of £700,000.' And it expected that this trend will continue.

For instance, early in 2005, for a sum of £80.6 million, Trinity Mirror purchased three advertising website firms: Financial Jobs Online, The Hotgroup and Smartnewhomes.com.; and in November bought Peldonsay, which owns recruitment site SecsintheCity.com. Meanwhile, DMGT, owners of the *Daily Mail*, have also been busy in the market, buying Jobsite.com in 2004 for £36 million and two small recruitment websites in August 2005 for £4.1 million, and in December 2005 purchasing property website Primelocation.com for £48 million.

Trinity Mirror with Guardian Media Group, Newsquest, Northcliffe Newspapers – owned by DMGT – plus three smaller companies is also a partner in Fish4, which represents some 650 regional newspapers – 60 per cent of the provincial Press – and with 1.3 million unique users a month is Britain's most visited recruitment site.

However, it is just not the online classified market that interests Trinity Mirror. In June the group started a digitized version of the Newcastle *Journal,* at a subscription cost of £9 a month, to test the market for full-price online newspapers. Humphrey Cobbold, director of strategy, said:[7] 'We are quite specific. This is a pilot to test a publishing model, to see how we will make it pay. There is no vanity publishing here.' If successful, digital editions of other titles could follow, including the *Birmingham Post* and the *South Wales Echo*. Editorial director Neil Benson declared: 'The *Journal* is one example of how we're looking to deepen our presence in our existing markets . . . . We believe the future for our newspaper businesses is to become true multi-platform local publishers, providing content across a range of media in whatever form our customers want.'

Another leading regional publisher, Johnston Press, is also keenly aware of the threat that the internet poses with regard to classified advertising. Last year, 72 per cent, or £281 million of its revenue, came from this sector. With classified advertising a main reason why many readers buy local newspapers, any drift away of this advertising to the internet could lead to a drop in circulation, and a fall-off in display advertising; hence the moves to develop a combined marketing strategy. EMAP, too, is aware of the drift of advertising to the internet.[8] 'Its *Nursing Times* publication is expecting a 30 per cent fall in revenue after the cash-strapped NHS decreed that all nursing jobs should be advertised solely on its own website.'

By the autumn of 2005 – with a growth of more than 60 per cent during the first half of the year – it was revealed that internet advertising now accounted for 5.8 per cent of the total UK spend, and, with a figure of £490.8 million in the first six months, was larger than radio and outdoor combined; and, according to the Internet Advertising Bureau, would be worth more than £1 billion by the end of the year. In the quality daily market the Advertising Association reported that classified advertisements had fallen by almost 11 per cent, while in the quality Sundays there had been a drop of 8.5 per cent during the nine-month period up to September 2005.[9]

Four months later, on 7 December 2005, it was announced that ITV had purchased Friends Reunited, which has 15 million members, for £175 million. Ranked no. 8 in the UK websites by users, this online business – with 40 per cent of its viewers in the 16-34 age group and 53 per cent in the ABC1 bracket – helps track long lost friends, trace a family tree or find a job. Charles Allen, chief executive of ITV, said: 'We see it as a new opportunity. Classified advertising is worth £2 billion a year in the UK. We see buying Friends Reunited as part of a strategy to access these revenues.' Media analyst Sarah Simon, of Morgan Stanley, commented:[10]

> There were several newspaper groups interested in this asset, which are major generators of classified advertising. If ITV has a strategy to get into the classified space and assuming Friends Reunited helps them do this then to allow a rival newspaper group to buy it would have made that strategy more difficult.

Meanwhile, across the complete national market, there had been a 44.8 per cent rise in online recruitment advertisements. The Recruitment and Employment Federation said that, despite a buoyant job market, recruitment in the National Press had fallen steadily in the past twelve months and was now half the level it was six years ago. 'ZenithOptimedia predicts that the internet's share of the total advertising market in the UK will rise to 6.9 per cent in 2007 compared with 1.2 per cent in 2001.'

The growth of the internet has not just been confined to advertising. Multiple stores were quick to see the advantage, and in November 2005 Interactive Media in Retail Group (IMRG), the industry body for internet retailers, announced that it 'expects some 24 million shoppers to spend £5 billion online this Christmas'. It is estimated that there are 26,000 online shops selling five million products. In October, the online spend was £1.8 billion, and, according to IMRG, online shopping is currently growing 130 times faster than sales in the high street. Although Ebay.co.uk dominates the market with 40 per cent, followed by Amazon.co.uk with 6.22 per cent, the next top eight companies – and all increasing their trade – are UK major retailers, showing how the link between conventional businesses and the internet is paying off.

For Fleet Street groups the above figures prove how wise it was for national newspapers to have been involved in online publishing for more than a decade. One of the first was Associated Newspapers, and in the summer of 1996 Martin Dunn, for the past four years editor-in-chief of the *New York Daily News*, was invited by Sir David English, Associated's chairman, to develop an interactive publishing division:[11] 'It was a big task, not least because of the need to identify which newspaper in the company's stable should be first to go online. The answer is, I believe, fundamental in understanding where internet publishing is going.' The title chosen was *This is London*, the *Evening Standard Online*. 'Literally within hours, we found our site accessed by internet users across the globe, and those figures have continued to grow.'

Now, ten years later, the advance of online publishing by national newspapers and other British media has been phenomenal. In the summer of 2005, BBC News announced that its website was viewed by 24.8 million unique visitors per month; and in December 2005, from data provided by com.Score, Guardian Unlimited has 2,732,000 unique users a month compared with 1,741,000 for The Sun Online, 1,537,000 for The Times Online, 1,350,000 for Telegraph.co.uk, 747,000 for Mirror.co.uk and 636,000 for Independent.co.uk. Discussing *The Guardian*'s online edition, Simon Waldman, director of digital publishing, explained why it appealed to a niche market:[12] 'It's people who have to get hold of previous copies of the paper or read the paper from overseas. It comes out of our own production systems so we are not paying significant sums to a third-party vendor and we are perfectly happy with it, but it's just a part of an overall digital publishing strategy.'

And for the 3.6 millions users and nearly 80,000 subscribers of the FT.com, the online version of the *Financial Times*, there is the facility for readers to tailor their consumption of news and analysis to suit their interests in specific sectors, regions or companies. For example, subscribers who sign up for News by e-mail services can have the content they need delivered straight to their desktops. Features such as the *FT* archive, markets coverage, analysis and an expanded Lex column with intra-day updates are available. FT.com also produces news-in-depth packages – from international corporate governance and accounting rules to the latest on Iraq – grouping all the news and analysis on the subject from specialist reporters and commentators.

But even with this rush into electronic publishing, for many 'Print journalism is more prestigious than online.'[13] A poll taken in the summer of 2005 of the two thousand registered members who use greatereporter.com site to syndicate and sell their journalism worldwide revealed that 66 per cent of respondents considered that print was superior. Richard Powell, managing director of greatereporter.com parent company Presswire Media, said: 'I feel the public holds print journalism in higher esteem than online, so therefore as a writer you get more credibility for getting published in print.' However, Emily Bell, Guardian Unlimited's editor-in-chief, felt that online journalism was the way forward: 'With audiences, ideas and journalistic formats developing more quickly online than off, journalists who really think print is more prestigious are going to find the next decade stressful and disappointing in equal measure.'

Her colleague, Simon Waldman, had said six months earlier: 'One of the things you should always do on the web is amplify your strengths. But the real issue is not about sitting here as newspapers and saying,[14] "What shall we do next?" You have to look at how the net is evolving as a medium.' One step taken by the paper in the spring of 2005 had been the launch of RSS (Really Simple Syndication). Waldman believed that RSS – the compilation of news and other reports from various internet sources without visiting and searching the sites – was a critical part of Guardian Newspapers, for, using a news reader progam, it is possible to select thematic stories from headlines. Other organizations involved include Telegraph.co.uk and BBC News, which in May reported 20 million 'click throughs' from headlines on RSS news readers. From a commercial viewpoint, there is now the opportunity to 'marry up' advertising with distinct thematic categories – total market penetration of a narrow sector.

American Online Publishing

Meanwhile, in the United States, according to the Audit Bureau of Circulation, during the summer of 2005 some 320 of the nation's 1422 newspapers were producing digital editions; and in September the Newspaper Association of America revealed that 32 per cent of all internet users had visited newspaper websites that month – more than 47 million people. Kim Dail, the US-based marketing director of Olive, an Israeli-firm specialising in producing internet newspapers, said:[15] 'Circulation of daily newspapers is generally falling during the weekdays, but we are seeing a trend where newspapers retain readers they would have otherwise lost to internet news by them subscribing to the electronic daily during the week and getting the weekend editions in print.'

One title that successfully embraced the digital world two years ago was *Investor's Business Daily*, which, with no printing or distribution costs, 47,000 subscribers, each paying $234 per annum – one fifth of the paper's circulation – has shown a 'significant boost to the company's profits'. Executive vice-president Karen Anderson revealed: 'It's very challenging getting the paper to all areas of the country, so the digital edition is ideal for people in remote areas. Our population is becoming more computer savvy and we have readers who prefer reading the digital edition.' On a smaller scale in Kansas the *Lawrence Journal-World*, circulation 20,000 in a township of 80,000 residents, has had a remarkable success with more than seven million 'hits' a month on its website.

In the spring of 2005 the *New York Times*, America's most influential newspaper, announced that readers of its daily online edition would be required to pay $49.95 a year from September. In April, the *New York Times* web site had 1.7 million daily visitors, while the paper's March circulation was 1,136,000. Launched in 1996, NYTimes.com had initially charged overseas readers before deciding that online advertisements would be its main source of income. In announcing the new move, the *New York Times* revealed that the paper was looking for extra revenues from subscriptions that would help smooth out future fluctuations.[16] 'Online advertising for us is growing at over 30 per cent a year. But at some point the rate of growth will decline,' a spokeswoman said.

Apart from traditional publishers using the internet, there has been a growing number of newcomers, one of which, craigslist.org, is the seventh most visited site in America and 'has diverted millions of dollars of advertising revenue from newspapers'. For instance, in the San Franciso region it is estimated that local newspapers lose $50 million a year in classified revenue to this internet newcomer. With a staff of just 18 people 'it posts 6.5 million classified ads each month at 190 local sites in 35 countries – most of them free'. Speaking in November at a seminar held at the Said Business School, Oxford, Craig Newmark, founder of craiglist. org, revealed that he expected 'to launch a project within the coming weeks to harness the "wisdom of the masses" that has fuelled his advertising site and apply it to daily journalism'. This new venture was likely to be interactive, 'so that users could decide which parts of the news really mattered to them and even report some of it themselves'. He told his audience:[17]

> Things need to change. The big issue in the US is that newspapers are afraid to talk truth to power. The White House press corps don't speak the truth to power – they are frightened to lose access they don't have anyway. Part of the problem lies with the newspapers themselves. The race for dollars has obscured the race for truth. They're being run as profit centres, and they're trying to get pretty high profit margins. As a result, investigative reporting has been seen as a problem.

Just days before Newmark's talk, on October 26 online search giant Google admitted that it was moving into classified advertising after unwittingly givers users a sneak preview of the new service. It would be a threat to newspapers, which have seen classified revenues squeezed by sites such as Craiglist. The service, Google Base, appeared briefly as a link to a website inviting people to list things such as cars for sale.

Operating in some ninety countries, and translated into almost one hundred languages, Google's index of web pages, more than three billion, is the largest in the world. Founded just seven years earlier, in September 2005 Google announced that profits for the previous three months were $381.2 million, more than seven times those of a year ago – and more than 90 per cent of its revenue came from online advertising. As the leader in Europe, Google is viewed by more than 120 million each month, searching some 26 billion pages. Jeff Levik, vertical markets director at Google, commented:[18]

> Google's mission statement is to organize the world's information and make it universally acceptable and useful. A large proportion of our funding is generated by advertising [estimated at £3.4 billion this year alone], which enables us to provide other services to our users for no fee, such as Google Earth, Froggle and Good Desktop. We are continuously exploring new ways to achieve our mission.

In December 2005 it emerged that Seattle-based Microsoft, not to be outdone, was developing an online classified service. And that same month, Stephen Uden, the corporation's head of citizenship, programmes and relationships, in unveiling Microsoft's blueprint for the next ten years, believed that the south-west of England had a 'golden opportunity to follow in the footsteps of the Seattle area – the home of the cutting edge careers in new technology combined with a fantastic life style'.

The Bloggers Awake

Launched in 1999, just a decade after the internet came into being, blogger.com is a personal online publishing tool that has raced ahead in the past few years. 'Its software, available free to anyone with an internet connection, allows them to publish their own news and commentary on any subject they like.' In 2000, OhmyNews, South Korea, encouraged members of the public to contribute stories and comment to a virtual newspaper – and the citizen reporter was born. The company now has almost 40,000 citizen reporters writing for its Korean and International editions. And in 2004, with bloggers for the first time receiving Press passes to cover the conventions during the US Presidential elections, the movement had been 'legitimized'.

In the UK, blogging – or citizen journalism – reached its peak following the bombings in London on 7 July 2005, when within hours the BBC had been assailed with '20,000 e-mails, 3000 text messages, 1000 pictures and at least 20 videos. Shocked members of the public found themselves with the technology – in the form of mobile camera phones – to provide instant, on-the-spot reports and photos'. As Vic Ray, Director of the BBC College of Journalism, was to write:[19]

> Organisations like the BBC are actively embracing the changes, using its audience to send in pictures and experiences as part of a closer relationship. BBC News online is aiming to

> offer its readers guidance on how to produce good videos and pictures. Of course, it needs responsible use of images and constant vigilance about the information submitted .... But this new phenomenon is here to stay. Journalism will still be the first draft of history. It's just that there are more people drafting it these days.

Within weeks of BBC News inviting its readers to get involved, on Monday 28 November *The Daily Telegraph* announced 'Snap & Send', a brilliant new way to be part of the paper.

> Have you ever found yourself in the midst of a major news event and wanted to share the experience with others? Now that so many people have mobile phones with cameras, the possibility exists for us all to contribute to the news agenda. Today, *The Daily Telegraph* launches a new service which enables our readers to do exactly that. All you have to do to take part is to take a picture with your mobile phone and send it to mypic@telegraph.co.uk. We will publish the best photographs in the newspaper and on our web site telegraph.co.uk, enabling others to see what you have experienced.'

In the autumn of 2005, in discussing the rise of the citizen reporter – now taken a stage further by *The Daily Telegraph* – Camilla Wright, founder and editor of Popbitch, the celebrity and pop culture site launched five years ago, had written:[20]

> As terrorist bombs first exploded across London, we saw a rerun of the 9/11 phenomenon. What occurred back in 2001 wasn't a one-off but the birth of a new trend showcasing new media's superiority over the lumbering old media behemoth in times of national and international crisis, when events unfold so fast that traditional methods of reporting just can't keep up .... In some ways, Popbitch has evolved to become an online version of an old Fleet Street pub back when newspapers were located cheek by jowl. It's the place where rumours, inside news and 'the stuff we can't print' can be shared in a rowdy, undisciplined atmosphere by newshounds and their friends.

The rise of blogging has been dramatic: from a low of four sites in 1999 there are now more than 20 million world-wide, with an estimate of 40,000 of these online journals being created daily – and some 300,000 in the UK; and according to a recent Guardian/IM survey 'a third of young people with internet access currently maintain a blog [short for weblog], or have done at some point'.[21] But what is a blog? 'The technical answer is that a blog is simply a few tweaks of a standard web page to make it easy to link to something elsewhere, comment upon it, quote from it, publish it on the web and thus enable others to do so further, in a continuous chain of conversation on whatever caught the originator's fancy.' It also affords the opportunity to challenge the traditional journalist. 'We bloggers are no longer passive consumers of whatever we are offered to read or watch; we are able to fact-check what we are offered; complain more about inaccuracies, correct them and in general complain with rather more effect than the traditional shouting at the TV or penning letters to the editor.'

Sir Simon Jenkins, former editor of *The Times* – although declaring that bloggers might not meet journalistic standards as far as fact-checking goes – is aware that, like himself, bloggers peddle opinion:[22] 'In truth, I, too, am a blogger, snatching at some item of passing news to argue a case and persuade. And I charge for it. The blogger does it for nothing. I am on my mettle as never before.'

For some observers, 'it is only a matter of time before the blog becomes a tool for advertisers. However, this presents another problem. Blogs may not necessarily be anti-business, but they are anti-commercialism.' Pioneering Max Blumberg commented:[23] 'Bloggers are the closest thing you'll get to the internet communist – they exist for the good of society rather than the good of any company. I once proposed a scheme that could help bloggers make money out of what they did and I was violently shouted down and told it was against the spirit of blogging.'

In the United States, according to commentator Jeff Jarvis:[24] 'People now own the printing press and the broadcast tower and the barrier to entry to the media has been blown away.' In July 2005 blog monitor Technorati.com, which tracks 14 million blogs, stated that the blogosphere is doubling in size every five months. Its founder David Sifry said: 'I would never have guessed . . . . that by putting simple personal publishing tools in the hands of anyone who wanted one would have so many ripple effects around the world.' And from Jonathan Miller, head of AOL in the US, came the comment that 'over 60 per cent of the time people spend on AOL is devoted to audience-generated content'.

The Way Forward

Very much aware of the effect of this electronic revolution is Bill Gates, the Microsoft chairman, and speaking in London in January 2005 he discussed Corbis, the world's second-largest image library – Getty is around three times its size – and said: 'The digital world would change the world of imaging. The recent purchase of German-based Zefa meant that it swings Corbis' advertising/editorial business split heavily in favour of ads, and gives the library far more European clout.' He commented:[25]

> Over time, more and more ads will be delivered in pure digital form . . . . that's the changing world of advertising – more digital, more targeted . . . . The internet is levelling the playing fields and connecting people. Of the six billion people on the planet, if you go back ten years, maybe 600 million were interacting with marketing and advertising. Over the next ten years it will be more like three billion.

On Friday 28 October 2005, Bill Gates said he was looking forward to 'a near-paperless world where we won't want magazines, students won't need textbooks, and paper forms will be redundant'. Tablet computers would contain all the information, which would be held like a clipboard with a flat screen on the front. He added:[26] 'There's a group of students that are going to college during this decade who, because they use the tablet in college, will, as they go into the workforce, think about the magazines they want to read and it will be obvious to them that digital is far superior.'

This is a point of view that had been put forward by Paul Carr, editor of the *London News Review*, the previous year:[27]

> But as soon as a compromise can be found – the moment someone invents a decent lightweight, ultra-thin electronic reader that looks and feels like a newspaper or a magazine but allows us to access electronic content on the move – there will be nothing to stop the total conversion of the two media. Suddenly there will be no need for us to use

> computer screens to read text-based web content any more and there'll certainly be no need for most of us to waste time or trees buying old-fashioned newspapers. We can simply grab our portable reader and access the online edition of our favourite publication or surf our favourite website from the comfort of the bus, train or bath.

Less than two years later, on 1 October 2005, Carr's hopes came true, when Fujitsu announced that it had created a workable technology – e-paper – that will turn a bulky newspaper into a single sheet of wafer-thin plastic film. Head of e-paper development at Fujitsu, Dr Takashi Uchiyama, said that his product 'will be everywhere, soon'. It is planned that its use will commence on Japanese commuter trains and in supermarkets during 2006. *The Times* reported:[28]

> E-paper's great strength is that, once a new image – files such as a newspaper page, a map or an advertisement – had been 'printed' on to its liquid crystal surface, the image will remain there without any additional power supply. In theory, a newspaper made of e-paper could be put into a bag, and it will be possible to flick through thousands of pages on the voltage of a watch battery. There are drawbacks: e-paper cannot be folded and the type is significantly less clear than the traditional printing page. The advantage is that it can renew its display, in full colour every three seconds, but at the moment it cannot show moving images. Fujitsu's e-paper is 0.8mm thick, about eight times thicker than paper, and an A4 sheet can be coiled into a cylinder with the diameter of a CD.

The Carnegie Corporation Report highlighted earlier in 2005:

> The future course of the news including the basic assumptions about how we consume news and information .... is being altered by technology-savvy young people no longer wedded to traditional news outlets or even accessing news in traditional ways. Through internet portal sites, handheld devices, blogs and instant messaging, we are accessing and processing information in ways that challenge the historic function of the news business and raise fundamental questions about the future.

For the journalists of the future a step forward was taken in September 2005 when regional publishers Johnston Press announced that with the University of Central Lancashire it 'was setting up the Institute of Digital Journalism to train a new generation of technologically proficient reporters and, just as importantly, to develop ways of distributing news through integrated print and web formats'.

One person aware of the urgency to embrace fully the electronic future is Andrew Gowers, recently editor of the *Financial Times*, who, writing in the *Evening Standard*, declared:[29]

> I am focused on what comes next. And I have already all but decided that, whatever it is, it will not be ink printed on dead trees .... working in print, pure and simple, is the early 21st century equivalent of running a record company specialising in vinyl. The future lies with the internet, and those newspapers that survive will be those that produce truly original content and learn fastest how to translate it into the all-encompassing, all-singing, all dancing new medium of the web.

Discussing the role of present-day management and its awareness of the future, he declared: 'The trouble is at least half of what used to be called Fleet Street is in denial about the scale and speed of the challenges to traditional newspapers. Many of those proprietors who are not in denial and now pay lip-service to the brave new world do not match their words consistently with deeds.'

The *Financial Times*, he said, had spotted the challenge ten years ago, and its site, FT.com, is now accessed by more people online 'than have ever read it in print; and online advertising revenues have long since passed the threshold of significance'. Gowers mentioned that he had met the head of one of America's largest technology companies recently, who said that he hardly ever glanced at a newspaper. He obtained his information from Yahoo Financial. Gowers concluded:[30]

> My broader point is the number of British newspaper outfits that have something unique to offer on the web in a global market place for news and comment can be counted on the fingers of one hand. Anyone who has seen the data on information consumption by 18- to 35-year-olds knows this is where the business is going. Many of them have never paid for a newspaper or read one in print. Soon, they will be the core target for everyone. How will they be reached?

The final word must go to Rupert Murdoch, the person with the greatest influence on the British Press during the past forty years. In an interview with Ian Reeves, editor of *Press Gazette*, he revealed that his internet strategy was not fully formed. 'It will never be fully formed. The internet is changing, very disruptive technology, and there are new inventions coming along every month. One has to stay awake and race to stay up with it, or if you get enough brilliant people around maybe you can get ahead of it.' Continuing, he said:[31]

> The point is the ease of entry. If someone has a good idea on the net the cost of entry is zero. We're going to have many, many more voices. We now have one billion people – not with broadband, but access to the net, and computer literate. In 20 years, 30 years, it's not going to be one billion, it'll be six billion. It's not going to be a huge force for good, but also a force for change in many ways that we can't forsee.

Regarding the recent purchase of community web site myspace.com and broadband provider Easynet signal, he remarked : 'It was a very careful strategy to go for the two biggest community sites for people under 30. If you take the number of page views in the US, we are the third biggest presence on the internet already. Now we're not the most profitable, or anything like it; we have a huge amount of work ahead to get that whole thing right. And we're working very hard to keep improving.' He said that 'with *The Times* online we're very sure where we're going. But with things like *The Sun*, and a lot of other papers out here, there are lots of plans, although I'd have to be honest and say some of them are experimental.'

And discussing the effect of the internet on classified advertising, once described as 'rivers of gold', he remarked that sometimes rivers dry up. 'This is a generational thing; we've been talking a 15- or 20-year slide on this. Certainly I don't know anybody under 30 who has ever looked at a classified advertisement in a newspaper. With broadband they do more and more transactions and job-seeking online.' Finally, he believed that with regard to editorial and the electronic media there would always be room for good journalists:

> Great journalism will always be needed but the product of their work may not always be on paper – it may ultimately just be electronically. But for many, many, many years to come it will be disseminated on both. There will always be room for good journalism and good reporting. And a need for it, to get the truth out.

Some four months later, in March 2006, in addressing an audience of industry figures at the Worshipful Company of Stationers and Newspaper Makers in London, Rupert Murdoch returned to the theme of the future of the media:

> I believe that traditional newspapers have many years of life left, but equally I think, in the future, newsprint and ink will be just one of many channels to our readers. Crucially, newspapers must give readers a choice of accessing their journalism on the pages of the paper or on websites such as Times Online or, and this is important, on any platform that appeals to them – mobile phones, hand-held devices, iPods, whatever.

He considered that never had the flow of information and ideas, of hard news and reasoned comment, been more important; and insisted that for the traditional media the key to survival was the ability to adapt:

> Journalism has a future in this technological age – great journalism will always attract readers.

Notes

1. Printing comes to Fleet Street

1. Morgan, (1973) p.55.
2. Westmancoat (1985) p.17.
3. Fox Bourne, H.R., *Progress of British Newspapers in the 19th Century Illustrated* (Simpkin, Marshall, Kent, 1901) p.164.
4. Louise Craven, 'The early newspaper press in England', in Griffiths (1992) p.2.
5. Boston, (1990) p.20.
6. Fox Bourne (1901) p.163.
7. Herd, (1952) p.14.
8. Boston (1990) p.23.
9. Williams, (1972) p.9.
10. Herd (1952) p.20.
11. Herd (1952) p.18.
12. Fox Bourne (1901) p.170.
13. Hudson (1945) p.12.
14. Mrs Herbert Richardson, *The Old English Newspaper* (London: The English Association, pamphlet no. 1933) p.13.
15. Herd (1952) p.25.
16. Griffiths (1992) p.369.
17. Fox Bourne (1901) p.171.
18. Williams (1971) pp. 14–17.
19. Boston (1990) p.28.
20. Child (1967) p.37.
21. Griffiths (1996) p.295.
22. Boston (1990) pp.32–3.
23. Griffiths (2002) p.10.
24. Griffiths (1996) p.4.
25. ibid. p.5.
26. Fox Bourne (1901) p.174.
27. Herd (1952) p.36.
28. Westmancoat (1985) p.23.
29. Dunton, *Sketches of the Printers, Stationers and Binders in the City of London 1689–1705*.
30. Morgan (1973) pp.121–125.
31. Gibbs (1952) pp.6–8.

2. The first daily newspaper

1. British Library Newspaper Library files, Colindale, London.
2. Siebert, (1952) p.279.
3. Dennis Griffiths, 'The first daily newspaper' in *Press2000* (London Press Club, 2001) p.8.

4. Gibbs (1952) p.8.
5. Griffiths (1992) p.196.
6. Herd (1952) p.50.
7. Black (1987) p.51.
8. Griffiths (1992) p.74.
9. Margaret Drabble, ed., *The Oxford Companion to English Literature* (Oxford: Oxford University Press, 1985) p.933.
10. John Guy, *The Present State of Wit*, p.11.
11. Drabble (1985) p.6.
12. Herd (1952) p.53.
13. Bound *Spectator* file, author's collection.
14. Herd (1952) p.54.
15. Herd (1958), 'The First Woman Editor', pp.27–45
16. ibid.
17. Charles Pebody, *English Journalism and the Men who have Made It* (Cassell, Peter, Galpin & Co., 1882) p.47.
18. Michael Harris, 'The Structure, Ownership and Control of the Press, 1620–1780' in *Newspaper History* (Constable, 1978) p. 84.
19. Griffiths (1992) p.433.
20. Melanie Parry, ed., *Chambers Biographical Dictionary* (Edinburgh: Chambers, 1997) p.993.
21. Siebert (1952) p.352.
22. Simon Winchester, *The Meaning of Everything: The Story of the Oxford English Dictionary* (Oxford: Oxford University Press, 2002) p.32.
23. Herd (1952) p.58.
24. Hudson (1945) p.22.
25. Boston (1990) p.23.
26. Siebert (1952) pp.356–63.
27. ibid.
28. Williams (1957) p.44.
29. Dibblee (1913) p.165.
30. *Junius Stat Nôminus Umbra* (Edinburgh: 1807) pp.151–68.
31. Herd (1952) p.75.

3. *Launching* The Times

1. Gibbs (1952) pp.149–50.
2. Morgan (1973) pp.198–200.
3. Aspinall (1949) p.6.
4. Hudson (1964) p.16.
5. Harris (1943) p.26.
6. *The St James's Chronicle* file, Guildhall Library, London.
7. Griffiths (1996) p.30.
8. Pebody (1882) p.73.
9. Harold Herd, *A Press Gallery* (London: Fleet Publications, 1958) pp. 64–73.
10. Griffiths (1992) p.340.
11. Anstey & Silverlight (1991) p.13.
12. Address by Rupert Murdoch, 11 March 2002, St Bride's Church, Fleet Street, to commemorate 300 Years of Fleet Street.
13. Morison, *The Times, 1785–1841*, vol.I (1935) p.32.
14. Elic Howe & Harold E. Waite, *The London Society of Compositors* (Cassell & Co., 1948) pp. 46.

15. Child (1967) p.51.
16. Woods & Bishop (1985) p.12
17. Griffiths (1996) p.34
18. Howe & Waite (1948) pp.41–5.
19. Griffiths (1992) p.461.
20. Boston (1990) p.48.
21. Escott (1911).
22. Pebody (1882) p.82.
23. *The St James's Chronicle* file, Guildhall Library, London.
24. *The Times* file, British Library Newspaper Library, Colindale, London.
25. Griffiths (1992) pp. 160–1.
26. *The St James Chronicle* file, Guildhall Library, London.

4. *Plant here* The Standard

1. Hudson (1943) p.1.
2. Woods & Bishop (1985) p.34.
3. Hudson (1943) pp.80–5.
4. Griffiths (1996) p.42.
5. Conversations with Earl of Halsbury, great-grandson of Dr Stanley Lees Giffard.
6. Margaret Forster, *William Makepeace Thackeray* (——, ——) p.59.
7. Herd (1955) pp.69–89.
8. *The Times* files, British Library Newspaper Library, Colindale.
9. Herd (1958) pp.11–26.
10. Griffiths (1996) p.73.
11. *The Standard* files, British Library Newspaper Library.
12. Griffiths (1992) p.144.
13. Harrison (1974) p.78.
14. Hindle (1937) p.155.
15. Hindle (1937) p.155.
16. Dasent (1908) pp.17–20.
17. Peel Papers, British Library.
18. *The Standard* files, British Library Newspaper Library.
19. *The Times* files, British Library Newspaper Library.
20. Hindle (1937) p.156.
21. *The Daily News* file, British Library Newspaper Library.
22. Dasent (1908) p.49.
23. Cook (1916) pp.59–93.
24. Harrison (1974) p.111.
25. *The Standard* files, British Library Newspaper Library.
26. *The Standard* files, British Library Newspaper Library.

5. *'Taxes on knowledge' repealed*

1. Wiener (1969) pp.261–3.
2. Williams (1957) p.97.
3. Herd (1952) pp. 147–55.
4. *The Times* files, British Library Newspaper Library, Colindale, London.
5. Interview with George Newkey-Burden, archivist, *The Daily Telegraph*, 16 June, 2003.
6. Newkey-Burden (2003).

7. London Press Club archives.
8. Newkey-Burden (2003).
9. Grant, (1871) p.317.
10. Griffiths (1996) p.97.
11. Author's collection.
12. Anstey & Silverlight (1991) p.17.
13. Hobson, Knightley, Russell, (1972) p.50.
14. ibid. p.51.
15. ibid. p.23.
16. Conversation with George Newkey-Burden, August 7, 2005.
17. Author's collection.
18. Author's collection.
19. Herd (1952) pp.197–200.
20. Griffiths (1992) pp. 376–7.
21. Virginia Berridge, *British Newspaper History from the 17th Century to the Present Day* (London: Constable, 1978) p.254.
22. ibid. p.254.
23. Simonis (1917) pp. 150–1.
24. Bainbridge & Stockdill (1993) pp. 24–5.
25. ibid. pp. 44–59.
26. Storey (1951) pp.9–12.
27. Donald Read, *The Power of the Press. The History of Reuters* (Oxford University Press, 1999) pp.23–4.
28. ibid. p.120.

6. *The New Journalism*

1. Laurel Brake, 'The Old Journalism and the New' in *Papers for the Million,* ed. Joel Weiner (New York: Greenwood Press, 1988) note 26, p.24. Matthew Arnold, 'Up to Easter', *Nineteenth Century XXI* (1887) p.629. See also Boston (1988) note 4, p.104.
2. Koss (1981) p.317.
3. Conversations with Professor Joseph O. Baylen, biographer, W.T. Stead.
4. ibid.
5. *Pall Mall Gazette* files, 6 July 1885, British Library Newspaper Library.
6. Clarke (2004) pp.258–62.
7. Herd (1952) pp.234–5.
8. Clarke (2004) p.263.
9. Griffiths (1992) pp.435–6
10. Koss (1981) p.278.
11. Pemberton, *Lord Northcliffe: a Memoir* (Hodder & Stoughton, 1922) p.24.
12. Giles (1962) pp.93–116.
13. Woods & Bishop (1985) pp.136–57
14. *Standard* archives.
15. Blumenfeld (1931) p.226.
16. *The Times* files, 20 October 1916, British Library Newspaper Library.
17. Williams (1957) pp.133–5.
18. Simonis (1917) p.3.
19. Taylor (1996) pp.14–22.
20. Wintour (1989) p.9.
21. Taylor (1996) pp.27–8.

22. Pemberton (1922) pp.58–9.
23. Jones (1920) p.131.
24. *Daily Mail files*, Northcliffe House.
25. Pound & Harmsworth (1959) p.204.
26. Pemberton (1922) pp.59–60.

7. *The greatest hustler*

1. *Daily Express* files, April 24, 1900 .
2. John Frost Newspapers, London.
3. Dark (1922) pp.28–37.
4. Blumenfeld (1930) pp.60–1.
5. Blumenfeld (1936) pp.32–3.
6. Blumenfeld (1930) p.91.
7. Blumenfeld (1930) p.112.
8. Blumenfeld (1930) p.95.
9. Blumenfeld (1933) p.193.
10. Dark (1922) p.123.
11. Dark (1922) p.104.
12. Hagerty (2003) p.10.
13. Hugh Cudlipp, *Publish and be Damned* (London: Andrew Dakers, 1953) p.10.
14. Pound & Harmsworth (1959) p.278.
15. Cudlipp (1953) p.17.
16. Paul Tritton, *John Montagu of Beaulieu, Motoring Pioneer and Prophet* (Golden Eagle, 1985), p.107.
17. Dark (1922) p.114.
18. *Daily Mail* files, Northcliffe House.
19. *Standard* files, British Library Newspaper Library.
20. Koss (1984) p.28.
21. Stephen Pritchard, *The Observer: a short history of the world's oldest Sunday newspaper* (The Observer Development Department, 2002) p.14.
22. Griffiths (2002) p.38.
23. Newspaper Publisher Association Archives, London.
24. ibid.
25. Morison, *The Times*, vol. III, 1884–1912 (1947) p.532.
26. Pound & Harmsworth (1959) p.311.
27. Dark (1922) p.127.

8. *Dalziel entrepreneur*

1. St Bride Printing Library, London.
2. Dark (1922) p.124.
3. R.P.T. Davenport-Hines, *Dictionary of Business Biography* (Butterworth) vol. 2, p.5.
4. Balfour Papers, British Library. See also Koss (1984) p.177.
5. Bonar Law Papers, House of Lords Library.
6. *Newspaper Editor* files, 1915, St Bride Printing Library.
7. Garvin (1948) p.55.
8. Ferris (1971) p.175.
9. Pound & Harmsworth (1959) p.415.
10. Gollin (1960) p.304.

11. *Guardian* Newsroom, Farringdon Road, London.
12. Wintour (1989) p.54.
13. Richards (1997) p.13.
14. ibid. p.14.
15. Williams (1959) p.189.
16. Richards (1997) p.22.
17. Victor Gray, *Essex Heritage: The Dunmow Progressives* (Oxford: Leopard's Head Press, 1992) p.285.
18. *Morning Post* files, British Library Newspaper Library.
19. Ted Morgan, *Churchill 1874–1915* (Jonathan Cape, 1982) p.366.
20. *Daily Express* archives.
21. Newspaper Proprietors archives, London.
22. Wilson (1988) p.36. (MS Gwynne 3)
23. Newspaper Proprietors archives.
24. Blumenfeld Papers, House of Lords Library.
25. Morgan (1982) pp.392–5.
26. *Morning Post* files, British Library Newspaper Library.
27. Wilson (1988) p.41. (MS Gwynne 3)
28. *The Observer* files, British Library Newspaper Library.

9. *Enter Max Aitken*

1. Dark (1922) p.139.
2. ibid. p.145.
3. *Evening Standard* files, 10 December 1921, British Library Newspaper Library.
4. *Daily Express* files, 10 December 1921, British Library Newspaper Library.
5. Taylor (1972) p.41.
6. Taylor (1972) p.52.
7. Blumenfeld (1931) p.206.
8. Chisholm & Michael Davie (1992) p.91.
9. Blumenfeld (1931) p.206.
10. Beaverbrook (1925) p.10.
11. Koss (1984) p.307.
12. General Sir Henry Wilson Papers, Imperial War Museum, London.
13. Clive Ponting, *Churchill* (Sinclair-Stevenson, 1994) p.177.
14. Wilson (1988) p.76.(HAG/35, 8, IWM)
15. Ponting (1994) p.183.
16. Clarke (1931) p.75.
17. ibid. p.78.
18. Frank Owen, *Tempestuous Journey. Lloyd George His Life* (Hutchinson, 1954) p.293.
19. Wilson (1988) p.92. (MS Gwynne 20)
20. Wood (1965) p.p.98.
21. Blumenfeld Papers, House of Lords Records Office.
22. Zwar (1980) p.25.
23. ibid. p.31.
24. Koss (1984) p.263.
25. Hansard (1935) p.169.
26. Michael Burn, *The Guardian*, 26 August 1985, p.6.
27. Falk (1933) p.24.
28. *Newspaper Editor* files, St Bride Printing Library.

29. Colley (1936) p.196.
30. Colley (1936) p.197.
31. *The Times* files, 17 March 1916, British Library Newspaper Library.
32. *Newspaper World* files, 1 April 1916, St Bride Printing Library.

10. Brothers from Wales

1. Hart-Davis (1990) p.18.
2. Hartwell (1992) p.34.
3. Hobson, Knightley, Russell (1972) p.70.
4. Hartwell (1992) p.87.
5. Andrews & Taylor (1970) p.38.
6. John McEwen (ed.) *The Riddell Diaries 1908–1923* (Athlone Press, 1986) pp.226–7.
7. ibid. p.229.
8. Andrews & Taylor (1970) p.41.
9. Kynaston (1988) p.84.
10. Thompson (2000) p.269.
11. Greenwall (1957) p.150.
12. Clarke (1950) p.145.
13. Koss (1986) p.307.
14. *Sunday Express* archives.
15. Beaverbrook (1925) p.10.
16. ibid. p.34.
17. Newspaper Publishers Association archives, London.
18. Pound & Harmsworth (1959) p.836.
19. Ferris (1971) p.255.
20. Pound & Harmsworth (1959) pp.855–6.
21. *The Times* files, 15 August 1922, British Library Newspaper Library.
22. Griffiths (1996) p.220.
23. Falk (1933) p.29.
24. Conversations with Sir Jocelyn Stevens, managing director, *Evening Standard*, and grandson of Sir Edward Hulton.
25. Hartwell (1992) p.116.
26. Taylor (1972) p.215.

11. The General Strike

1. Renshaw (1975) p.4.
2. *Evening Standard* files, 1 May 1926, Northcliffe House, London.
3. Griffiths (1996) p.228.
4. Taylor (1972) p.23.
5. *Daily Express* archives, London.
6. Williams (1970).
7. Newspaper Publishers Association archives, London.
8. Wilson (1990) pp.261–2. (MS Gwynne 32)
9. *Daily Express* archives, London.
10. Woods & Bishop (1985) pp.256–64.
11. Wilson (1993) p.231.
12. Sinclair (1983) pp.318–19.
13. John Frost Newspapers, London.

14. *Strike Nights* (1926) p.29.
15. *The Times* files, 12 May 1926, British Library Newspaper Library.
16. Young (1966) p.84.
17. ibid. p.85.
18. Author's collection.
19. *Daily Express* file, 6 May 1926.
20. Christiansen (1961) pp.45–6.
21. Burnham (1955) p.133.
22. Wilson (1990) p.226.
23. Ponting (1994) p.309–10.
24. Author's collection.
25. *Strike Nights* (1926) p.29.
26. ibid. p.40.
27. Newspaper Publishers Association archives.
28. Taylor (1972) p.232.

12. *Burnham sells* the Telegraph

1. Camrose (1947) pp.28–9.
2. Camrose (1947) pp.30–1.
3. Wintour (1989) p.37.
4. Burnham (1955) p.117.
5. *Morning Post* files, *Daily Telegraph* Library.
6. Koss (1984) p.562.
7. *The Times* files, 2 June 1930, British Library Newspaper Library.
8. Griffiths (1992) p.138.
9. Glenton & Pattinson (1963) p.25.
10. Wintour (1989) p.69.
11. Hubback (1985) p.131.
12. Griffiths (1992) pp.219–20.
13. *The Economist*, 16 January 1937, p.103, British Library Newspaper Library.
14. *Report on The British Press* (London: Political and Economic Planning, 1938) p.88.
15. Newspaper Publishers files, London.
16. Conversations with author.
17. Hagerty (2003) p.39.
18. Baxter (1935) pp.99–104.
19. Tom Clarke, *Newspaper World*, 3 September 1938, St Bride Printing Library.
20. Christiansen, (1961) pp.68–72.
21. ibid. p.106.
22. Cyril Aynsley, *Press2000* (London: London Press Club, summer 1999) pp.8–9.

13. *Prerogative of the harlot*

1. Hugh Cudlipp (1980) p.260.
2. Driberg (1956) p.195.
3. Taylor (1972) ch.12.
4. Bourne (1990) p.108.
5. Wood (1965) p.190.
6. Ferris (1971) p.293.
7. *Evening Standard* files, 17 March 1931, British Library Newspaper Library.

8. Driberg (1956) pp.213–14.
9. Cooper (1953) p.177.
10. Nicolson (1952) p.531.
11. Conversation with author; see also William Deedes, *1936, As Recorded by The Spectator* (ed. by Charles Moore & Christopher Hawtree) (1986) p.358.
12. Nicolson (1966) p.276.
13. Windsor (1953) p.291.
14. Michael Bloch, *The Reign & Abdication of Edward VIII* (London: Bantam Press, 1990) p.81.
15. Channon (1967) p.105.
16. *History of The Times, 1921–1948*, part II (1952) p.1036.
17. Channon (1967) p.118.
18. Wrench (1955) p.355.
19. *Evening Standard* files, 13 March, 1936, British Library Newspaper Library.
20. The Earl of Avon, *The Eden Memoirs: Facing the Dictators* (Cassell, 1962) pp.590–602.
21. Cox (1988) p.33–4.
22. Cockett (1989) p.75.
23. Conversation with Iverach McDonald, *The Times* correspondent in Vienna and Prague; later Deputy Editor.
24. *History of The Times*, vol. IV (1989) pp. 929–34.
25. Conversations with Michael Foot, Editor, *Evening Standard.*
26. *Daily Sketch* files, John Frost Newspapers, London.
27. Williams (1970) p.147.
28. Gannon (1971) p.280.

14. *Fleet Street at war*

1. E.J. Robertson files, *Daily Express* archives.
2. Griffiths (1996) p.292.
3. Conversations with Michael Foot.
4. E.J. Robertson files, *Daily Express* archives.
5. *Daily Mail* files, British Library Newspaper Library.
6. Bourne (1990) p.112.
7. Cudlipp (1980) p.161.
8. Taylor (1996) p.301.
9. ibid. p.311.
10. A.J.P. Taylor (1972) p.422.
11. Somerfield (1979) p.85.
12. Conversations with George Griffiths, author's father.
13. Ayerst (1985) p.207.
14. E.J. Robertson files, *Daily Express* archives.
15. ibid.
16. *Daily Worker* files, 1 January 1930, British Library Newspaper Library.
17. Rust (1949) p.80.
18. ibid. p.82.
19. Camrose (1948) p.76.
20. King (1970) p.94.
21. Rust (1949) p.95.
22. Cudlipp (1953) pp.175–82.
23. King, (1970) p.165.
24. Hagerty (2003) p.53.

25. Conversations with Roy Oliver, Deputy Chief Engineer, *Evening Standard*.
26. Wrench (1955) p.431.
27. Robbins (1944) p.16.
28. Morgan (1973) p.226.
29. Rust (1949) p.88.
30. Ziegler (1995) p.161.

15. *Shortage of newsprint*

1. Newspaper Publishers Archives, London.
2. ibid.
3. ibid.
4. Hart-Davis (1990) p.105.
5. Newspaper Publishers Archives, London.
6. Nevett (1982) pp.170–1.
7. Turner (1952) p.226.
8. Griffiths (1992): Justine Taylor, 'Reuters', p.679.
9. Jones (1951) p.250.
10. Read (1999) p.173.
11. ibid. p.211.
12. Newspaper Publishers Archives, London.
13. Moncrieff (2001) p.118.
14. Newspaper Publishers Archives, London.
15. Cudlipp (1976) p.149.
16. ibid. p.153.
17. Williams (1993) pp. 108–9.
18. ibid. pp.83-8.
19. Michael Anglo, *Service Newspapers in the Second World War* (Jupiter Books, 1977) p.14.
20. Conversations with author.
21. ibid.
22. Newspaper Publishers Archives, London.
23. Hudson & Stanier (1997) p.62.
24. *The Daily Telegraph*, Tuesday 1 March 2005, p.10.
25. Cockett (1990) p.47.
26. Griffiths (1992) pp.124–5.
27. Nicolson (1967) p.174.
28. Knightley (1975) p.242.
29. Collier (1989) p.8.
30. Lysaght (1979) p.245.

16. *Press Council proposed*

1. Bundock (1957) p.185.
2. Camrose (1947) p.2.
3. *World Press News*, 31 October 1946, p.8 (St Bride Printing Library).
4. E.J. Robertson Archives, *Daily Express*.
5. Hamilton (1989) p.68.
6. *Royal Commission* (1949) p.180.
7. King (1969) p.128.
8. Newspaper Publishers Archives, London.

9. Conversations with author (see also Griffiths (1992), pp.56–7).
10. *World Press News*, 9 May 1946, p.4 (St Bride Printing Library).
11. ibid.
12. *World Press News*, 24 October 1946, p.1.
13. *Times* files, 22 March 1954, British Library Newspaper Library.
14. Camrose (1947) p.8.
15. Kynaston (1988) pp.19–20.
16. Hartwell (1992) p.319.
17. Cockett (1990) pp.205–6.
18. Camrose (1947) p.69.
19. Hamilton (1989) p.53.
20. Goldenberg (1985) pp.21–2.
21. Thomson (1975) p.43.
22. Personal knowledge.
23. Conversations with Iverach McDonald, Deputy Editor, *The Times*.
24. ibid.
25. Thomson (1975) pp.166–7.
26. ibid p.173.
27. Hamilton (1981) p.141.
28. Personal knowledge.

17. *The* Mirror *triumphant*

1. Hugh Cudlipp, 'The Godfather of the British Tabloids', *British Journalism Review*, vol. 8, no.2, p.38.
2. ibid p.36.
3. Cudlipp (1976) p.183.
4. King (1969) p.123.
5. Geoffrey Goodman speaking at Hugh Cudlipp Memorial Lecture, London Press Club, October 2003.
6 Horrie (2003) p.76.
7. Conversations with George Griffiths, author's father.
8. Conversations with author (see also *Newspaper Year Book 1997*).
9. *Daily Express* archives.
10. Conversations with Sheila Black.
11. Hagerty (2003).
12. Conversation with Sir Edward Pickering.
13. Conversations with author see also Wintour (1989) p.96.
14. Christiansen Archives, London Press Club.
15. ibid.
16. Griffiths (1992) p.364.
17. Hubback (1985) p.232.
18. *The Times* files, October 20 1960, British Library Newspaper Library.
19. Conversations with author.
20. Hubback (1985) p.249.
21. *Royal Commission* (1962) pp. 31–2.
22. Edelman (1966) p.156.
23. Edwards (2003) p.361.
24. Ben Pimlott, *Harold Wilson* (HarperCollins, 1992) p.506.
25. Cudlipp (1976) p.351.

26. Hussey (2001) p.90.
27. Horrie (2003) p.115.
28. Rook (1989) pp. 49–50.
29. Personal knowledge.

18. Death of Beaverbrook

1. Cudlipp (1980) pp.296–7.
2. Junor (1990) pp.139–40.
3. Conversations with Robert Edwards.
4. Taylor (1972) pp.661–2.
5. Interview with Sir Edward Pickering.
6. Conversations with Robert Edwards.
7. Coote (1992) p.51.
8. Personal knowledge.
9. Griffiths (1992) p.293.
10. London Press Club, *Fleet Street* (1966) p.22.
11. Personal knowledge.
12. Conversations with Charles Wintour.
13. Personal knowledge.
14. Chester & Fenby (1979) p.239.
15. Conversations with Derek Jameson.
16. Wintour (1989) p.169.
17. Conversation with Louis Heren.
18. *Print*, April 1976, p.4.
19. Conversations with Joe Wade.
20. Jacobs (1980) p.72.
21. Hussey (2001) p.171.
22. Jacobs (1980) p.156.
23. Woods & Bishop (1985) p.374.
24. Shawcross (1992) p.227.
25. Tuccille (1989) pp.81–2.
26. Taylor (2002) p.180, plus conversation with Lord Rothermere.

19. The road to Wapping

1. Interview with Sir Edward Pickering.
2. Somerfield (1979) p.160.
3. Shawcross (1992) p.144.
4. Conversations with author.
5. Grose (1989) p.15.
6. Personal knowledge.
7. George Newkey-Burden, *The Daily Telegraph* archives.
8. Taylor (2002) p.181.
9. Edwards (1988) p.222; also interview with author.
10. Conversations with author; see also Wintour (1989) p.212.
11. Conversations with author; see also Roy Greenslade interview, *Media Guardian*, 26 September 2005.
12. Also interview with author.
13. Conversations with author.

14. ibid.
15. ibid.
16. Conversations with Bert Hardy.
17. Conversations with Brian McArthur.
18. Conversation with Eddy Shah.
19. Wintour (1989) p.254.
20. Neil (1996) p.73.
21. Conversations with Brian McArthur.
22. Conversations with Charles Wintour; see also Wintour (1989) p.258.
23. Neil (1996) p.80.
24. Greenslade (2003) p.495.
25. Crozier (1988) p.11.
26. Glover (1993) p.32.
27. Steve Oram: conversations with author.
28. Lord Marsh, *UK Press Gazette*, 4 January 1988.
29. Richard Scott, *The Guardian Past & Present Newsroom,* (London, 2002) p.38.
30. Ayerst (1971) p.00.
31. Hetherington (1981) p.ix, foreword.
32. Personal knowledge.
33. Stephen Pritchard, *The Observer* (2002) p.28.
34. Conversations with Donald Trelford.
35. ibid.
36. ibid.
37. Personal knowledge.
38. Conversation with author.
39. Conversation with author.
40. Personal knowledge.
41. *Press Gazette*, 4 November 2005, p.24: Backissues: Jon Slattery.
42. *The Independent*, 25 October 2004, p.5: interview with Raymond Snoddy.
43. *The Sunday Times*, 24 July 2005, p.8: interview with William Lewis.

20. *Towards the millennium*

1. Conversations with David Simmonds.
2. Frayn (1967) p.vii.
3. Osbert Lancaster, *With an Eye to the Future* (John Murray, 1967) p.150.
4. Watkins (2000) p.202.
5. *The Independent*, 15 June 2005, 'Farewell to Fleet Street', p.13.
6. Interview with Philippa Kennedy, *Out of Print* radio programme, quoted in *Press Gazette*, 30 January 2004.
7. Griffiths (1992): Justine Taylor, 'Reuters', p.680.
8. Hamilton (1981) p.190.
9. Read (1999) p.436.
10. *Press Gazette*, 5 May 2005.
11. ibid.
12. *The Guardian*, 16 June 2005.
13. Griffiths (2002) pp. 64–5.
14. Information from Guy Black, Director Press Complaints Commission 2002.
15. Bower (1991) p.382.
16. Greenslade (2003) p.512.

17. Stott (2002) p.233.
18. Greenslade (2003) pp.569–70.
19. ibid p.579.
20. personal knowledge.
21. *Press Gazette*, 5 August 2005.
22. personal knowledge.
23. *Press Gazette*, 5 February 2005.
24. *The Times*, 18 February 2005.
25. *Press Gazette*, 2 September 2005.
26. *Press Gazette*, 11 November 2005.
27. ibid.
28. Anthony Delano, *The invention and re-invention of the tabloid newspaper*, September 1999, (unpublished manuscript).
29. *The Guardian*, 19 September 2005.
30. Marr (2004) p.201.
31. *Press Gazette*, 1 October 2004.
32. *Press Gazette*, 14 October 2004.
33. *The Observer*, 11 September 2005.
34. *Press Gazette*, 7 October 2005.
35. Hagerty (2003) p.172.
36. *The Independent*, August 1, 2005.
37. Conversations with author.

21. *The electronic future*

1. Conversation with author.
2. Conversation with author; see also *The Daily Telegraph*, 22 October, 2005.
3. *The Times*, 15 April 2005; *The Independent*, 18 April 2005; *The Guardian* 18 April 2005; *Press Gazette*, 22 April 2005.
4. *The Times*, 17 June 2005.
5. *The Observer*, 24 July 2005.
6. *The Sunday Telegraph*, 5 June 2005.
7. *The Observer*, 13 November 2005.
8. *The Guardian*, 18 April 2005.
9. *The Observer*, 13 November 2005.
10. *The Sunday Times*, 27 November 2005.
11. Conversation with author.
12. *Press Gazette*, 3 June 2005.
13. *Press Gazette*, 29 July 2005.
14. ibid.
15. *The Sunday Times*, 22 May 2005; *Evening Standard*, 25 May 2005.
16. *The Independent*, 23 November 2005.
17. *Evening Standard*, 26 October 2005.
18. *theguardian*, 27 November 2005.
19. *Radio Times*, 26 November–2 December 2005.
20. *The Observer*, 31 July 2005.
21. *The Times*, 19 November 2005.
22. *The Sunday Times*, 29 May 2005.
23. *The Sunday Telegraph*, 4 September 2005.
24. *The Observer*, 31 July 2005.

25. *campaign*, 28 January 2005.
26. *The Times*, 29 October 2005.
27. *The Guardian*, 9 February 2004.
28. *The Times*, 1 October, 2005.
29. *Evening Standard*, 9 November 2005.
30. ibid.
31. *Press Gazette*, 25 November 2005.

Bibliography

Books were first published in London unless otherwise stated.

Aitken, Kidd, Janet, 1987. *The Beaverbrook Girl* (Collins).
Allen, Robert & Frost, John, 1981. *Daily Mirror* (Cambridge: Patrick Stephens).
Allen, R. & Frost, John, 1983. *Voice of Britain: the Inside Story of the Daily Express* (Cambridge: Patrick Stephens).
Andrews, Alexander, 1859. *History of British Journalism*, 2 vols (Richard Bentley).
Andrews, Linton & Taylor, H.A., 1970. *Lords and Laborers of the Press* (Carbondale & Edwardsville: Southern Illinois University Press).
Anglo, Michael, 1977. *Service Newspapers in the Second World War* (Jupiter Books).
Anon., 1900. *Progress of British Newspapers in the Nineteenth Century* (Simpkin, Marshall, Hamilton & Kent).
Anon., 1936. *The Newspaper Society 1836–1936* (The Newspaper Society).
Anstey, Joanna & Silverlight, John, 1991. *The Observer Observed* (Barrie & Jenkins).
Aspinall, A., 1949. *Politics and the Press c.1789–1850* (Home & Van Thal).
Associated Newspapers Ltd, 1946. *News In Our Time: 1896–1946* (Daily Mail).
Austin, Alfred, 1909. *Autobiography*.
Ayerst, David, 1971. *Guardian. Biography of a Newspaper* (Collins).
Ayerst, David, 1973. *The Guardian Omnibus 1821–1971* (Collins).
Ayerst, David, 1985. *Garvin of the Observer* (Croom Helm).

Bagnall, Nicholas, 2002. *A Little Overmatter* (Lewes, Sussex: Southover).
Bainbridge, Cyril & Stockdill, Roy 1993. *The News of the World Story* (HarperCollins).
Baistow, Tom, 1985. *Fourth Rate Estate: Anatomy of Fleet Street* (Comedia).
Barker, Felix et al., 1982. *100 Years of Fleet Street* (London Press Club).
Barson, Susie & Saint, Andrew, 1988. *A Farewell to Fleet Street* (English Heritage).
Batty, Peter, 2000. *The Life and Times of the Guvnor of Fleet Street* (Headline).
Baxter, Beverley, 1935. *Strange Street* (Hutchinson).
Beaverbrook, Lord, 1925. *Politicians and the Press* (Hutchinson).
Beaverbrook, Lord, 1955. *Don't Trust to Luck* (Daily Express Publications).
Beaverbrook, Lord, 1956. *Men and Power 1917-1918* (Hutchinson).
Beaverbrook, Lord, 1963. *The Decline and Fall of Lloyd George* (Collins).
Belfield, Richard; Hird, Christopher; Kelly, Sharon, 1991. *Murdoch. The Decline of an Empire* (Macdonald).
Belfield, Richard; Hird, Christopher; Kelly, Sharon,1994. *Murdoch. The Great Escape* (Warner Books).
Berrey, R. Power, *c.* 1930. *The Romance of a Great Newspaper* (News of the World).
Berridge, Virginia, 1978. *British Newspaper History from the 17th Century to the Present Day* (London: Constable).

Black, Jeremy, 1987. *The English Press in the Eighteenth Century* (Beckenham, Kent: Croom Helm).
Black, Jeremy, 2001. *The English Press 1621–1821* (Sutton).
Blumenfeld, R.D., 1930. *R.D.B.'s Diary* (William Heinemann).
Blumenfeld, R.D., 1931. *All in a Lifetime* (Benn).
Blumenfeld, R.D., 1933. *The Press In My Time* (Rich & Cowan).
Blumenfeld, R.D. et al, 1934. *Anywhere For A News Story* (The Bodley Head).
Blumenfeld, R.D., 1935. *R.D.B.'s Procession* (Ivor Nicholson & Watson).
Blumenfeld, R.D., 1944. *Home Town* (Hutchinson).
Boorman, H.R. Pratt (compiler), 1961. *Newspaper Society. 125 Years of Progress* (Maidstone: Kent Messenger).
Boston, Ray, 1990. *The Essential Fleet Street: its History and Influence* (Blandford).
Bourne, Richard, 1990 *Lords of Fleet Street. The Harmsworth Dynasty* (Unwin Hyman).
Bower, Tom, 1991 *Maxwell The Outsider* (Heinemann).
Bower, Tom, 1993. *Tiny Rowland. A Rebel Tycoon* (Heinemann).
Bower, Tom, 1995. *The Final Verdict* (HarperCollins).
Boyle, Thomas, 1989. *Black Swine in the Sewers of Hampstead* (Viking).
Boyce, George et al, 1978. *Newspaper History from the 17th Century to the Present Day* (Constable).
Braddon, Russell, 1965. *Roy Thomson of Fleet Street* (Collins).
Brake, Laurel, 1988. 'The Old Journalism and the New' in *Papers for the Million*, ed. Joel Weiner (New York: Greenwood Press).
Brake, Laurel et al, 1990. *Investigating Victorian Journalism* (Macmillan).
Brendon, Piers, 1982. *The Life and Death of the Press Barons* (Secker & Warburg).
Bright-Holmes, John (ed.), 1981. *Like It Was. The Diaries of Malcolm Muggeridge* (Collins).
Broackes, Nigel, 1979. *A Growing Concern* (Weidenfeld & Nicolson).
Brown, Lucy, 1985 *Victorian News and Newspapers* (Oxford, Clarendon Press).
Browne, Christopher, 1996 *The Prying Game* (Robson Books).
Bryant, Mark (ed.), 1991 *The Complete Colonel Blimp* (Bellew Publishing).
Bryant, Mark & Heneage, Simon, 1994. *Dictionary of British Cartoonists and Caricaturists 1730–1980* (Aldershot: Scolar Press).
Bryant, Mark, 2001. *Private Lives* (Cassell).
Bundock, Clement J., 1957. *The National Union of Journalists* (Oxford University Press).
Burnham, Lord, 1955. *Peterborough Court: The Story of The Daily Telegraph* (Cassell).

Cameron, James, 1968. *Point of Departure. An Autobiography* (Arthur Barker).
Camrose, Viscount, 1947. *British Newspapers and their Controllers* (Cassell).
Carey, John (ed.), 1987. *The Faber Book of Reportage* (Faber & Faber).
Catling, Thos. (ed.), 1909. *The Press Album* (John Murray,).
Channon, Sir Henry (ed. Robert Rhodes James), 1967. *Chips. The Diaries of Sir Henry Channon* (Weidenfeld & Nicolson).
Chapman, Caroline, 1984. *Russell of The Times* (Bell & Hyman).
Chapman-Huston, Desmond, 1936. *The Lost Historian. A Memoir of Sir Sidney Low* (John Murray).
Chester, Lewis & Fenby, Jonathan, 1979. *The Fall of the House of Beaverbrook* (Andre Deutsch).
Child, John, 1967. *Industrial Relations in the British Printing Industry* (Allen & Unwin)
Chippindale, Peter & Horrie, Chris, 1988. *Disaster! The Rise and Fall of News on Sunday* (Sphere Books).
Chippindale, Peter & Horrie, Chris, 1990. *Stick It Up Your Punter!* (Heinemann).
Chisholm, Anne & Davie, Michael, 1992. *Beaverbrook. A Life* (Hutchinson).
Christiansen, Arthur, 1961. *Headlines All My Life* (Heinemann).
Churchill, Randolph, 1957. *What I Said About the Press* (Weidenfeld & Nicolson).
Churchill, Winston, 1996. *His Father's Son. The Life of Randolph Churchill* (Weidenfeld & Nicolson).

Clarke, Bob, 2004. *From Grub Street to Fleet Street* (Aldershot: Ashgate).
Clarke, Tom, 1931. *My Northcliffe Diary* (Gollancz).
Clarke, Tom, 1950. *Northcliffe in History: an intimate story of press power* (Hutchinson).
Cleverley, Graham, 1976. *The Fleet Street Disaster* (Constable).
Cockett, Richard, 1989. *Twilight of Truth* (Weidenfeld & Nicolson).
Cockett, Richard (ed.), 1990. *My Dear Max: the Correspondence of Brendan Bracken and Lord Beaverbrook, 1928–1958* (Historians' Press).
Cockett, Richard, 1991. *David Astor and The Observer* (Deutsch).
Cohen, Stanley and Young, Jock, 1981. *The Manufacture of News* (Constable).
Coleridge, Nicholas, 1993. *Paper Tigers* (Heinemann).
Colley, William, 1936. *News Hunter* (Hutchinson).
Collier, Richard, 1989. *The Warcos. The War Correspondents of World War II* (Weidenfeld & Nicolson).
Collins, Henry M., 1925. *From Pigeon Post to Wireless* (Hodder & Stoughton).
Colville, John, 1976. *Footprints in Time* (Collins).
Colville, John, 1985. *The Fringes of Power* (Hodder & Stoughton).
Connor, Robert, 1969. *Cassandra. Reflections in a Mirror* (Cassell).
Cook, R. Edward, 1916. *Delane of The Times* (Constable).
Cooper, Duff, 1953. *Old Men Forget* (Hart-Davis).
Coote, Colin, 1965. *Editorial* (Eyre & Spottiswoode).
Coote, John, 1992. *Altering Course. A Submariner in Fleet Street* (Leo Cooper).
Cox, Geoffrey, 1988. *Countdown to War: a Personal Memoir of Europe, 1938–40* (William Kimber).
Cranfield, G.A., 1962. *The Development of the Provincial Newspaper 1700–1760* (Oxford University Press).
Crewe, Quentin, 1991. *Well, I Forget the Rest* (Hutchinson).
Crozier, Michael, 1988. *The Making of The Independent* (Gordon Fraser).
Cudlipp, Hugh, 1953. *Publish and be Damned* (Andrew Dakers).
Cudlipp, Hugh, 1962. *At Your Peril* (Weidenfeld & Nicolson).
Cudlipp, Hugh, 1976. *Walking on the Water* (The Bodley Head).
Cudlipp, Hugh, 1980. *The Prerogative of the Harlot: Press Barons and Power* (The Bodley Head).
Curran, James, 1978. *The British Press: a Manifesto* (Macmillan).
Curran, James and Seaton, Jean, 1988. *Power Without Responsibility* (Routledge).
Curtis, Michael, 1951. *The Press* (News Chronicle).

Dark, Sidney, 1922. *The Life of Sir Arthur Pearson* (Hodder & Stoughton).
Dark, Sidney, 1925. *Mainly About People* (Hodder & Stoughton).
Dasent, A.L., 1908. *John Delane 1817–1879*, 2 vols (John Murray).
Davidson, John, 1896. *Fleet Street Eclogues* (Bodley Head,).
Davie, Michael (ed.), 1976. *The Diaries of Evelyn Waugh* (Little, Brown).
Davies, Russell & Ottaway, Liz, 1987. *Vicky* (Secker & Warburg).
Deakin, Phyllis A., 1984. *Press On* (Worthing).
Deedes, William, *1936, As Recorded by The Spectator* (ed. by Charles Moore & Christopher Hawtree) (1986).
Deedes, W.F., 1997. *Dear Bill. W.F. Deedes Reports* (Macmillan).
Deedes, W.F., 2003. *At War With Waugh. The Real Story of Scoop* (Macmillan).
Deedes, W.F., 2004. *Brief Lives* (Macmillan).
Dibblee, G. Binney, 1913. *The Newspaper* (Williams & Norgate).
Douglas, James, 1930. *Down Shoe Lane* (Herbert Joseph).
Drabble, Margaret, 1976. *Arnold Bennett. A Biography* (Weidenfeld & Nicolson).
Driberg, Tom, 1956. *Beaverbrook. A Study in Power and Frustration* (Weidenfeld & Nicolson).

Driberg, Tom, 1974. *'Swaff'. The Life and Times of Hannen Swaffer* (Macdonald).
Driberg, Tom, 1988. *Ruling Passions* (Jonathan Cape).

Edelman, M., 1966. *The Mirror – A Political History* (Hamish Hamilton).
Edgar, Donald, 1981. *Express '58* (John Clare).
Edinburgh, HRH the Duke of (foreword), 1966. *Fleet Street. The Inside Story of Journalism* (Macdonald).
Edwards, Robert, 1988. *Goodbye Fleet Street* (Jonathan Cape).
Edwards, Ruth Dudley, 2003. *Newspapermen* (Secker & Warburg).
Elton, Oliver, 1929. *C.E. Montague: A Memoir* (Chatto & Windus).
Engel, Matthew, 1996. *Tickle the Public* (Victor Gollancz).
Escott, T.H.S., 1895. *Platform, Press, Politics and Play* (J.W. Arrowsmith).
Escott, T.H.S., 1911. *Masters of English Journalism* (T. Fisher Unwin).
Evans, Harold, 1973. *Editing and Design* (Heinemann).
Evans, Harold, 1979. *News Headlines* (Heinemann).
Evans, Harold, 1983. *Good Times, Bad Times* (Weidenfeld & Nicolson).
Evans, Harold, 1984. *Front Page History* (Quiller Press).
Evans, R.J., 1948. *The Victorian Age, 1815–1914* (Edward Arnold).

Falk, Bernard, 1933. *He Laughed in Fleet Street* (Hutchinson).
Falk, Bernard, 1937. *Five Years Dead* (Hutchinson).
Fallon, Ivan, 1994. *The Player. The Life of Tony O'Reilly* (Hodder & Stoughton).
Farrer, David, 1942. *A Difficult Fellow* (Lane Publications).
Ferris, Paul, 1971. *The House of Northcliffe: The Harmsworths of Fleet Street* (Weidenfeld & Nicolson).
Fleming, Alice, 1970. *Reporters at War* (New York: Cowles Book Co.).
Foot, Michael, 1980. *Debts of Honour* (Davis-Poynter).
Fox Bourne, Henry Richard, 1887. *English Newspapers*, 2 vols (Chatto & Windus).
Fox Bourne, H.R., 1901. *Progress of British Newspapers in the 19th Century Illustrated* (Simpkin, Marshall, Kent).
Frank, Joseph, 1961. *The Beginnings of the English Newspaper 1620–60* (Cambridge, Mass.).
Frayn, Michael, 1967. *Towards the End of the Morning* (Collins).
French, Philip and Rossell, Deac, 1981. *The Press. Observed and Projected* (NFT).
Furneaux, Rupert, 1964. *News of the War* (Max Parrish).

Gannon, Franklin Reid, 1971. *The British Press and Germany 1936–39* (Oxford Clarendon Press).
Garland, Nicholas, 1990. *Not Many Dead. Journal of a Year in Fleet Street* (Hutchinson).
Garvin, J.L. (foreword), 1921. *The Observer 1791–1921* (Observer House).
Garvin, Katharine, 1948. *J.L. Garvin. A Memoir* (Heinemann).
Gellhorn, Martha, 1978. *Travels with Myself and Another* (Allen Lane).
Gennard, John, 1990. *A History of the National Graphical Association* (Unwin Hyman).
Gibbs, Phillip, 1946. *The Pageant of Years* (Heinemann).
Gibbs, Phillip, 1952. *The Journalists' London* (Alan Wingate).
Gilbert, Martin, 1966–88. *Winston Churchill*, vols. I-IV (Heinemann).
Giles, Frank, 1962. *A Prince of Journalists* (Faber & Faber).
Giles, Frank, 1986. *Sundry Times. Autobiography* (John Murray).
Giles, Vic & Hodgson, F.W., 1990. *Creative Newspaper Design* (Heinemann).
Glendenning, Victoria, 1983. *Vita. The Life of V. Sackville-West* (Weidenfeld & Nicolson).
Glenton, George & Pattinson, William, 1963. *The Last Chronicle of Bouverie Street* (George Allen & Unwin).
Glover, Stephen, 1993. *Paper Dreams* (Jonathan Cape).

Glover, Stephen, 1999. *Secrets of the Press* (Allen Lane, the Penguin Press).
Goldenberg, Susan, 1985. *The Thomson Empire* (Sidgwick & Jackson).
Gollin, A.M., 1960. *The Observer and J.L. Garvin* (Oxford University Press).
Goodhart, David & Wintour, Patrick, 1986. *Eddie Shah and the Newspaper Revolution* (Coronet).
Goodman, Arnold, 1993. *Tell Them I'm On My Way* (Chapmans).
Goodman, Geoffrey, 2003. *From Bevan to Blair* (Pluto Press).
Gordon, Anne Wolridge, 1969. *Peter Howard Life & Letters* (Hodder & Stoughton).
Gourlay, Logan (ed.), 1984. *The Beaverbrook I Knew* (Quartet Books).
Grant, James, 1872. *The Newspaper Press: Its Origins, Progress and Present Position*, 3 vols. (Tinsley Brothers, 1871; Routledge).
Gray, Tony, 1990. *Fleet Street Remembered* (Heinemann).
Greenslade, Roy, 1992. *Maxwell's Fall* (Simon & Schuster).
Greenslade, Roy, 2003. *Press Gang* (Macmillan).
Greenwall, H.J., 1957. *Northcliffe. The Napoleon of Fleet Street* (Alan Wingate).
Griffiths, Dennis (ed.), 1992. *Encyclopedia of the British Press* (Macmillan).
Griffiths, Dennis,1996. *Plant Here The Standard* (Macmillan).
Griffiths, Dennis, 'The first daily newspaper' in *Press2000* (London Press Club, 2001).
Griffiths, Dennis, 2002. *300 Years of Fleet Street* (London Press Club).
Griffiths, Dennis, 2006. *A History of the NPA 1906–2006* (Newspaper Publishers Association).
Grose, Roslyn, 1989. *The Sun-sation* (Angus & Robertson).
Grundy, Bill, 1976. *The Press Inside Out* (W.H. Allen).

Hagerty, Bill, 2003. *Read All About It! 100 Sensational Years of the Daily Mirror* (Lydney, Glos.: First Stone).
Haines, Joe, 1988. *Maxwell* (Macdonald).
Hamilton, Denis, 1989. *Editor-in-Chief. Fleet Street Memoirs* (Hamish Hamilton).
Hammerton, J.A., 1932. *With Northcliffe in Fleet Street* (Hutchinson).
Hammond, J.L., 1934. *C.P. Scott* (G. Bell & Sons).
Hansard, B.M., 1935. *In and Out of Fleet Street* (Gosport, Hants: Hansard).
Harris, Michael, 1988. *London Newspapers in the Age of Walpole* (Cranbury, N.J./ London: Associated University Presses).
Harris, W., 1943. *The Daily Press* (Cambridge University Press).
Harrison, Stanley, 1974. *Poor Men's Guardians* (Lawrence & Wishart).
Hart-Davis, Duff, 1990. *The House the Berrys Built* (Hodder & Stoughton).
Hartwell, Lord, 1992. *William Camrose. Giant of Fleet Street* (Weidenfeld & Nicolson).
Hastings, Max, 2000. *Going to the Wars* (Macmillan).
Hastings, Max, 2002. *Editor: an Inside Story of Newspapers* (Macmillan).
Hastings, Max & Jenkins, Simon, 1983. *The Battle for the Falklands* (Michael Joseph).
Hatton, Joseph, 1970. *Journalistic London* (Sampson, Low).
Hedley, Peter & Aynsley, Cyril, 1967. *The D-Notice Affair* (Michael Joseph).
Heighway, Arthur, 1948. *Inky Way Annual* (World's Press News).
Henry, H., 1978. *Behind The Headlines – The Business of the British Press* (Associated Business Press).
Herd, Harold, 1952. *The March of Journalism* (Allen & Unwin).
Herd, Harold, 1955. *Seven Editors* (Allen & Unwin).
Herd, Harold, 1958. *A Press Gallery* (Fleet Publications).
Heren, Louis, 1985. *The Power of the Press* (Orbis).
Heren, Louis, 1988. *Memories of Times Past* (Hamish Hamilton).
Hetherington, Alistair, 1981. *Guardian Years* (Chatto & Windus).
Hetherington, Alistair, 1989. *News in the Regions* (Macmillan).
Hindle, Wilfred, 1937. *The Morning Post, 1772–1937* (Routledge).

Hirsch, F. & Garden, D., 1975. *Newspaper Money* (Hutchinson).
Hobson, Harold; Knightley, Phillip; Russell, Leonard, 1972. *The Pearl of Days. An Intimate Memoir of The Sunday Times 1822–1972* (Hamish Hamilton).
Hodgson, F.W., 1989. *Modern Newspaper Practice* (Heinemann).
Hogben, John, 1899. *Richard Holt Hutton of The Spectator* (Oliver & Boyd).
Hoggart, Simon & Leigh, David, 1981. *Michael Foot. A Portrait* (Hodder & Stoughton).
Hohenberg, John, 1964. *Foreign Correspondence. The Great Reporters and Their Times* (New York Columbia University Press).
Holden, Anthony (ed.), 1990. *The Last Paragraph* (Heinemann).
Holden, Anthony, 2004. *The Wit in the Dungeon. A Life of Leigh Hunt* (Little, Brown).
Hollingworth, Clare, 1990. *Front Line* (Jonathan Cape).
Hollis, P., 1976. *The Pauper Press* (Oxford University Press).
Horrie, Chris, 2003. *Tabloid Nation* (Deutsch).
Howard, Peter, 1964. *Beaverbrook. A Study of Max the Unknown* (Hutchinson).
Howard, Philip, 1985. *We Thundered Out* (Times Books).
Howe, E. & Waite, Harold, 1948. *The London Society of Compositors* (Cassell).
Hubback, David, 1985. *No Ordinary Press Baron a Life of Walter Layton* (Weidenfeld & Nicolson).
Hudson, Derek, 1943. *Thomas Barnes of The Times* (Cambridge University Press).
Hudson, Derek, 1945. *British Journalists and Newspapers* (Collins).
Hudson, Miles & Stanier, John, 1997. *War and the Media* (Stroud, Glos: Sutton Publishing).
Hussey, Marmaduke, 2001. *A Memoir. Chance Governs All* (Macmillan).
Hutt, Alan, 1973. *The Changing Newspaper* (Gordon Fraser).
Hutt, Alan & James, Bob, 1989. *Newspaper Design Today* (Lund Humphries).

Ingrams, Richard, 2005. *The Life and Adventures of William Cobbett* (HarperCollins).

Jacobs, Eric, 1980. *Stop Press. The Inside Story of The Times Dispute* (Deutsch).
Jaffa, Sam, 1992. *Maxwell Stories* (Robson Books).
Jameson, Derek, 1988. *Touched By Angels* (Ebury Press).
Jameson, Derek, 1990. *Last of the Hot Metal Men* (Ebury Press).
Jeffries, J.M.N., 1935. *Front Everywhere* (Hutchinson).
Jenkins, Simon, 1979. *Newspapers: the Power and the Money* (Faber & Faber).
Jenkins, Simon, 1986. *The Market for Glory. Fleet Street Ownership in the 20th Century* (Faber & Faber).
Jones, Kennedy, 1920. *Fleet Street and Downing Street* (Hutchinson).
Jones, Mervyn, 1994. *Michael Foot* (Victor Gollancz).
Jones, Michael Wynn, 1974. *A Newspaper History of the World* (David & Charles).
Jones, Roderick, 1951. *A Life in Reuters* (Hodder and Stoughton).
Junor, John, 1990. *Memoirs. Listening for a Midnight Tram* (Chapmans).
Junor, Penny, 1979. *Newspaper* (Macdonald Educational).
Junor, Penny, 2002. *Home Truths. Life Around My Father* (HarperCollins).

Kee, Robert, 1984. *The World We Left Behind: 1939* (Hamish Hamilton).
Kee, Robert, 1985. *The World We Fought For: 1945* (Hamish Hamilton).
Kemsley, Viscount (intro.), 1952. *The Kemsley Manual of Journalism* (Cassell).
Kenin, Richard, 1979. *Return to Albion* (New York Holt, Rinehart & Winston).
Kersh, Cyril, 1990. *A Few Gross Words* (Simon & Schuster).
King, Cecil, 1969. *Strictly Personal* (Weidenfeld & Nicolson).
King, Cecil, 1970. *With Malice Toward None* (Sidgwick & Jackson).
Kitchen, George, 1970. *Sir Roger L'Estrange: Contribution to the History of the Press in the Seventeenth Century* (Augustus M. Kelleyx).

Kleinman, Philip, 1977 *Advertising Inside Out* (W.H. Allen).
Knightley, Phillip, 1975. *The First Casualty* (New York: Harcourt Brace).
Knightley, Phillip, 1997. *A Hack's Progress* (Jonathan Cape).
Koss, Stephen, 1973. *Fleet Street Radical* (Allen Lane).
Koss, Stephen, 1981, 1984. *The Rise and Fall of the Political Press in Britain*, vol. I, *The Nineteenth Century;* vol. II, *The Twentieth Century* (Hamish Hamilton).
Kynaston, David, 1988. *The Financial Times. A Centenary History* (Viking).

Lake, Brian, 1984 *British Newspapers* (Sheppard Press).
Lamb, Larry, 1989. *Sunrise* (Macmillan).
Lane, Margaret, 1939. *Edgar Wallace: a Biography* (The Book Club).
Lansbury, George, 1925. *The Miracle of Fleet Street* (Victoria House).
Lawrenson, John & Barber, Lionel, 1985. *The Price of Truth: the Story of the Reuters Millions* (Edinburgh: Mainstream).
Leapman, Michael, 1992. *Dangerous Estate. The Press after Fleet Street* (Hodder & Stoughton).
Lee, Alan J., 1976. *The Origins of the Popular Press in England 1855–1914* (Croom Helm).
Leslie, Anita, 1982. *Cousin Randolph. The Life of Randolph Churchill* (Hutchinson).
Liebling, A.J., 1961. *Press* (Ballantine Books).
Linton, David & Boston, Ray, 1987. *The Newspaper Press in Britain. An Annotated Bibliography* (Mansell).
Linton, David (introduction Ray Boston), 1994. *The Twentieth Century Newspaper Press in Britain. An Annotated Bibliography* (Mansell).
Lockhart, Bruce, 1945. *Guns and Butter* (Putnam).
London Press Club, 1966. *Fleet Street* (Macdonald).
Low, David, 1956. *Low's Autobiography* (Michael Joseph).
Low, Robert (ed.), 1991. *The Observer Book of Profiles* (W.H. Allen).
Lowe, Charles, 1892. *The Tale of a Times Correspondent Berlin 1878–1891* (Hutchinson).
Lucas, Reginald, 1910. *Lord Glenesk and the Morning Post* (Alston Rivers).
Lysaght, Charles Edward, 1979. *Brendan Bracken* (Allen Lane).

MacArthur, Brian, 1988. *Eddy Shah. Today and the Newspaper Revolution* (David & Charles).
MacArthur, Brian, 1991. *Deadline Sunday* (Hodder & Stoughton).
McKay, Peter (foreword), 1997. *John Junor Remembered* (Solo Books).
McKay, Ron & Barr, Brian, 1976. *The Story of the Scottish Daily News* (Canongate).
Mackenzie, A., 1931. *Lord Beaverbrook* (Jarrolds).
McLachlan, Donald, 1971. *In the Chair. Barrington Ward of The Times 1927–1948* (Weidenfeld & Nicolson).
McNish, Jacquie & Stewart, Sinclair, 2004. *The Fall of Conrad Black* (Allen Lane, the Penguin Press)
Marr, Andrew, 2004. *My Trade* (Macmillan).
Martell, Edward & Butler, Ewan, 1960. *The Murder of the News Chronicle and the Star* (Christopher Johnson).
Martin, Roderick, 1981. *New Technology and Industrial Relations in Fleet Street* (Oxford University Press).
Massingham, Henry William, 1892. *The London Daily Press* (Religious Tract Society).
Melvern, Linda, 1986. *The End of the Street* (Methuen).
Middleton, Edgar, 1934. *Beaverbrook. The Statesman and the Man* (Stanley Paul).
Moncrieff, Chris, 2001. *Living On a Deadline. A History of the Press Association* (Virgin).
Moore, Charles & Hawtree, Christopher, 1986. *1936 As Recorded By The Spectator* (Michael Joseph).
Moran, James, 1971. *Stanley Morison* (Lund Humphries).
Morgan, Dewi, 1973. *Phoenix of Fleet Street: 2000 Years of St Bride's* (Charles Knight).
Morgan, Piers, 2005. *The Insider* (Ebury Press).

Morison, Stanley, 1932. *The English Newspaper: some account of the physical development of journals printed in London between 1622 and the present day* (Cambridge University Press).
Morris, Claud, 1963. *I Bought a Newspaper* (Arthur Baker).
Moseley, Sydney A., 1935. *The Truth About a Journalist* (Sir Isaac Pitman & Sons).
Muggeridge, Malcolm, 1972, 1973. *Chronicles of Wasted Time*, 2 vols (Collins).
Munster, George, 1985. *Rupert Murdoch. A Paper Prince* (Viking).
Musson, A.E., 1954 *The Typographical Association* (Oxford University Press).
Mylett, Andrew (ed.), 1974. *Arnold Bennett. The Evening Standard Years* (Chatto & Windus).

Needham, L.W. 'Bill', 1974. *Fifty Years of Fleet Street* (Michael Joseph).
Neil, Andrew, 1996. *Full Disclosure* (Macmillan).
Nelson, C. & Seccombe, M., 1987. *British Newspapers and Periodicals 1641–1700. A short title catalogue* (New York: MLA).
Nevett, T.R., 1982. *Advertising in Britain* (Heinemann).
Nevinson, Henry et al, 1934. *Anywhere for a News Story* (The Bodley Head).
Nicolson, Harold, 1952. *George V* (Constable).
Nicolson, Nigel (ed.), 1966. *Harold Nicolson Diaries and Letters, vol. I, 1930–1939* (Collins).
Nicolson, Nigel (ed.), 1967. *Harold Nicolson Diaries and Letters, vol. II, 1939–1945* (Collins).

Oram, Hugh, 1983. *The Newspaper Book. A History of Newspapers in Ireland* (Dublin: MO Books).
Owen, Louise, 1931. *Northcliffe. The Facts* (Privately printed).

Page, Bruce, 2003. *The Murdoch Archipelago* (Simon & Schuster).
Palmer, A.W., 1962. *A Dictionary of Modern History* (Penguin).
Pebody, Charles, 1882. *English Journalism and the Men who have Made It* (Cassell, Peter, Galpin & Co.)
Pemberton, 1922. *Lord Northcliffe: a Memoir* (Hodder & Stoughton).
Pocock, Tom, 1990. *Alan Moorehead* (Bodley Head).
Pound, Reginald & Harmsworth, Geoffrey, 1959. *Northcliffe* (Cassell).
Powell, Enoch, 1977. *Joseph Chamberlain* (Thames & Hudson).
Priestley, Mary, 1929. *The Female Spectator* (John Lane, The Bodley Head).
Pritchard, Stephen, 2002. *The Observer: a short history of the world's oldest Sunday newspaper* (The Observer Development Department).

Randall, Mike, 1988. *The Funny Side of The Street* (Bloomsbury).
Read, Donald, 1961. *Press and People 1790–1850* (Edwin Arnold).
Read, Donald, 1992. *The Power of News. The History of Reuters* (Oxford University Press).
Rehe, Rolf F., 1985. *Typography and Design for Newspapers* (IFRA).
Renshaw, Patrick, 1975. *Nine Days in May. The General Strike* (Eyre Methuen).
Richards, Huw, 1997. *The Bloody Circus. The Daily Herald and the Left* (Pluto Press).
Richardson, Mrs Herbert, *The Old English Newspaper* (London: The English Association, pamphlet no. 1933).
Robbins, Gordon, 1944. *Fleet Street Blitzkrieg Diary* (Ernest Benn).
Roe, Nicholas, 2004. *Fiery Heart: The First Life of Leigh Hunt* (Pimlico).
Rook, Jean, 1989. *The Cowardly Lioness* (Sidgwick & Jackson).
Rosebery, Earl (foreword), 1909. *A Parliament of the Press. The First Imperial Press Conference 1909* (Horace Marshall & Son).
Rosenberg, R., 1965. *English Rights and Liberties, Richard and Anne Baldwin, Whig Patriot Publishers* (New Haven & London: Yale University Press).
Rust, William, 1949. *The Story of the Daily Worker* (People's Press Printing Society).
Ryan, A.P., 1953. *Lord Northcliffe* (Collins).

Sala, George Augustus, 1896. *The Life and Adventures of George Augustus Sala* (Cassell).
Schaaber, M.A., 1965. *Some Forerunners of the Newspaper in England 1476–1776* (Urbana: University of Illinois Press).
Schofield, Guy, 1974. *The Men that Carry the News* (Cranford Press).
Scott, George, 1968. *Reporter Anonymous. The Story of the Press Association* (Hutchinson).
Scott, J.M., 1972. *Extel 100* (Ernest Benn).
Scott, J.W. Robertson, 1947. *Faith and Works in Fleet Street* (Hodder & Stoughton).
Scott, J.W. Robertson, 1952. *The Life and Death of a Newspaper* (Methuen).
Scott, R., 2002. *The Guardian Past & Present Newsroom,* (London).
Sebba, Anne, 1994. *Battling for News. The Rise of the Woman Reporter* (John Curtis, Hodder & Stoughton).
Seymour, David & Seymour, Emily (eds), 2003. *A Century of News* (Contender Books).
Shattock, Joanne & Wolff, Michael, 1982. *The Victorian Periodical Press* (Leicester University Press).
Shawcross, William, 1992. *Murdoch* (Chatto & Windus).
Shulman, Milton, 1998. *Marilyn, Hitler and Me* (Deutsch).
Siebert, Frederick, 1952. *Freedom of the Press in England 1476–1776* (Urbana: University of Illinois Press).
Siklos, Richard, 1995. *Shades of Black* (Heinemann).
Simonis, H., 1917. *The Street of Ink* (Cassell).
Sinclair, David, 1983. *Dynasty: the Astors and Their Times* (Dent).
Sisson, Keith, 1975. *Industrial Relations in Fleet Street* (Oxford, Basil Blackwell).
Smith, A.C.H., 1975. *Paper Voices* (Chatto & Windus).
Smith, Anthony, 1979. *The Newspaper. An International History* (Thames & Hudson).
Smith, Anthony, 1980. *Goodbye Gutenberg* (Oxford University Press).
Smith, Wareham, 1932. *Spilt Ink* (Ernest Benn).
Snoddy, Raymond, 1992. *The Good, the Bad and the Unacceptable* (Faber & Faber).
Somerfield, Stafford, 1979. *Banner Headlines* (Shoreham by Sea, Sussex: Scan Books).
Standage, Tom, 1998. *The Victorian Internet* (Weidenfeld & Nicolson).
Stannard, Russell, 1934. *With The Dictators in Fleet Street* (Hutchinson).
Stead, W.T. (ed.), 1892. *Review of Reviews* (Mowbray House).
Storey, Graham, 1951. *Reuters' Century* (Max Parrish).
Stott, Richard, 2002. *Dogs and Lampposts* (Metro).
Straus, Ralph, 1942. *Sala. The Portrait of an Eminent Victorian* (Constable).
Sutherland, James, 1985. *The Restoration Newspaper and its Development* (Cambridge University Press).
Symon, J.D., 1914. *The Press and Its Story* (Seeley, Service).
Symons, Julian, 1955. *Horatio Bottomley* (Cresset Press).

Taylor, A.J.P., 1972. *Beaverbrook* (Hamish Hamilton).
Taylor, Geoffrey, 1993. *Changing Faces. A History of The Guardian 1956–88.* (Fourth Estate).
Taylor, S.J., 1991. *Shock!! Horror! The Tabloids in Action* (Bantam Press).
Taylor, S.J., 1996. *The Great Outsiders* (Weidenfeld & Nicolson).
Taylor, S.J., 1998. *The Reluctant Press Lord* (Weidenfeld & Nicolson).
Taylor, S.J., 2002. An Unlikely Hero (Weidenfeld & Nicolson).
Thayer, F., 1954. *Newspaper Business Management* (Bailey Bros & Winfer).
The Times, History of, vols. I–VI, 1935, 1939, 1947, 1952, 1982, 1993, 2005. (The Times Publishing Co.).
Strike Nights in Printing House Square: an Episode in the History of The Times, 1926. (Privately printed).
The Times. Past and Present, 1932. (At the office of The Times).

A Newspaper History 1785–1935, 1935. (The Times Publishing Co.).
Thompson, J. Lee, 2000. *Northcliffe. Press Baron in Politics 1865–1922* (John Murray).
Thomson, George Malcolm, 1973. *Lord Castlerosse* (Weidenfeld & Nicolson).
Thomson, Lord, 1975. *After I Was Sixty* (Hamish Hamilton).
Tuccille, Jerome, 1989. *Rupert Murdoch* (New York: Donald I. Fine Inc.).
Tunstall, Jeremy, 1966. *Newspaper Power* (Oxford University Press).
Turner, E.S., 1952. *The Shocking History of Advertising* (Michael Joseph).
Turner, E.S., 1998. *Unholy Pursuits. The Wayward Parsons of Grub Street* (The Book Guild).

Vines, C.M., 1968. *A Little Nut-Brown Man. My Three Years with Lord Beaverbrook* (Frewin).

Walker, Martin, 1982. *Powers of the Press. The World's Greatest Newspapers* (Quartet).
Watkins, Alan, 2000. *A Short Walk Down Fleet Street* (Duckworth).
Waterhouse, Robert, 2004. *The Other Fleet Street* (Altrincham, Cheshire: First Edition).
Werkmeister, L., 1963. *The London Daily Press, 1772–1792* (Lincoln: University of Nebraska Press).
Westmancoat, John, *Newspapers* (The British Library, 1985).
Whitcomb, Noel, 1990. *A Particular Kind of Fool* (Anthony Blond).
Wickwar, W.H., 1928. *The Struggle for the Freedom of the Press 1819–1832* (Allen & Unwin).
Wiener, Joel, 1969. *The War of the Unstamped* (Ithaca, N.Y.Cornell University Press).
Wiener, Joel (ed.), 1988. *Papers for the Millions: The New Journalism in Britain 1850 to 1914* (Greenwood Press).
Wiles, R.M., 1965. *Freshest Advices: Early Provincial Newspapers in England* (Columbus:Ohio State University Press).
Wilkes, Roger, 2002. *Scandals. A Scurrilous History of Gossip* (Atlantic Books).
Wilkinson-Latham, Robert, 1979. *From Our Special Correspondent* (Hodder & Stoughton).
Wilson, Charles, 1985. *First With the News* (Jonathan Cape).
Wilson, Derek, 1993. *The Astors: the Life and Times of the Astor Dynasty 1763–1992* (Weidenfeld & Nicolson).
Williams, Francis, 1957. *Dangerous Estate* (Longmans).
Williams, Francis, 1970. *Nothing So Strange* (Cassell).
Williams, Gron, 1993. *Firebrand. The Frank Owen Story* (Hereford: Square One Publications).
Williams, Keith, 1977. *The English Newspaper: an Illustrated History to 1900* (Springwood Books).
Williams, Roger, 1998. *Time Traveller. Best of the News from 150 Years* (Cover Publishing).
Wilson, J. MacNair, 1927. *Lord Northcliffe* (Ernest Benn).
Wilson, Keith, ed., 1988. *The Rasp of War* (Sidgwick & Jackson).
Wilson, Keith, 1990. *A Study in the History and Politics of the Morning Post 1905–1926* (Lewiston/Queenston/Lampeter: The Edwin Mellor Press).
Winchester, Simon, 2003. *The Meaning of Everything* (Oxford University Press).
Windsor, HRH The Duke of, 1953. *A King's Story* (Cassell).
Wintour, Charles, 1972. *Pressures on The Press. An Editor Looks at Fleet Street* (Andre Deutsch).
Wintour, Charles, 1989. *The Rise and Fall of Fleet Street* (Hutchinson).
Wood, Alan, 1965. *The True History of Lord Beaverbrook* (Heinemann).
Woods, Alan, 1963. *Modern Newspaper Production* (New York: Harper & Row).
Woods, Oliver & Bishop, James, 1985. *The Story of The Times. Bicentenary Edition 1785–1985* (Michael Joseph).
Worsthorne, Peregrine, 1993. *Tricks of Memory* (Weidenfeld & Nicolson).
Wrench, John Evelyn, 1955. *Geoffrey Dawson and Our Times* (Hutchinson).

Young, Kenneth, 1966. *Churchill and Beaverbrook* (Eyre & Spottiswoode).
Young, Kenneth (ed.), 1973. *The Diaries of Sir Bruce Lockhart* (Macmillan).

Ziegler, Philip, 1981. *Lady Diana Cooper* (Collins).
Ziegler, Philip, 1995. *London at War 1939–45* (Sinclair-Stevenson).
Zwar, Desmond, 1980. *In Search of Keith Murdoch* (Melbourne: Macmillan).

Manuscript collections

Austin, Alfred	The Library, University of Bristol
Baldwin, Henry	Study Centre, Exeter
Baldwin, Richard	High Wycombe Reference Library
Bathurst, Countess	The Library, Leeds University
Beaverbrook, Lord	House of Lords Records Office
Blackburn, Sir Thomas	Daily Express Archives
Blumenfeld, R.D.	House of Lords Records Office
Bracken, Viscount	Churchill College, Cambridge
Bruce Lockhart, Sir Robert	House of Lords Records Office
Chamberlain, Joseph	The Library, Birmingham University
Christiansen, Arthur	London Press Club Archives
Cudlipp, Lord	University of Wales, Cardiff
Disraeli, Benjamin	Boldeian Library, Oxford
Donald, Sir Robert	House of Lords Records Office
Escott, T.H.S.	British Library
Giffard, Stanley Lees	Earl of Halsbury
Gladstone, W.E.	British Library
Goodman, Lord	Newspaper Publishers Association, London
Gwynne, H.A.	Bodleian Library, Oxford
Hamber, Thomas	Oriel College, Oxford
Jones, Sir Roderick	Reuters, London
Low, Sir David	Centre for Cartoons and Caricature, University of Kent
Nicolson, Sir Harold	Balliol College, Oxford
Northcliffe, Lord	British Library
Owen, Frank	House of Lords Records Office
Peel, Sir Robert	British Library
Riddell, Lord	Newspaper Publishers Association, London
Robertson, E.J.	Daily Express Archives
Wellington, Duke of	The Library, Southampton University
Wilson, General Sir Henry	Imperial War Museum

Index

Index

Index

Index